This is the first full-scale study of the drawings and paintings of the Brontë sisters and their brother Branwell, including the first catalogue of all known Brontë illustrations, published and unpublished. *The Art of the Brontës* comprises almost four hundred illustrated entries, recording such details as medium, dating, provenance, sources, style, and arguments for attribution; and documenting many previously unknown drawings and paintings. In addition, a sequence of narrative chapters provides new material on each of the four Brontë siblings and their relationships to the visual arts, suggesting ways in which their experience of drawing influenced their writing. An annotated and illustrated catalogue which is also a work of scholarly criticism, this publication is a landmark in Brontë studies and in the fields of nineteenth-century literature and painting generally.

Christine Alexander was educated at the Universities of Canterbury (New Zealand) and Cambridge. She is an Associate Professor in English Literature at the University of New South Wales and currently holds an Australian Senior Research Fellowship. She has written and edited a number of books on the Brontës, including a multi-volume critical edition of Charlotte Brontë's early writings and the British Academy award-winning book, *The Early Writings of Charlotte Brontë* (1983).

Jane Sellars is the Director of the Brontë Parsonage Museum in Haworth, West Yorkshire, and was formerly Education Officer at the Walker Art Gallery, Liverpool, where she pioneered the study of women's art and curated the exhibition *Women's Works*. She now writes, lectures, and broadcasts widely on women, art and the Brontës.

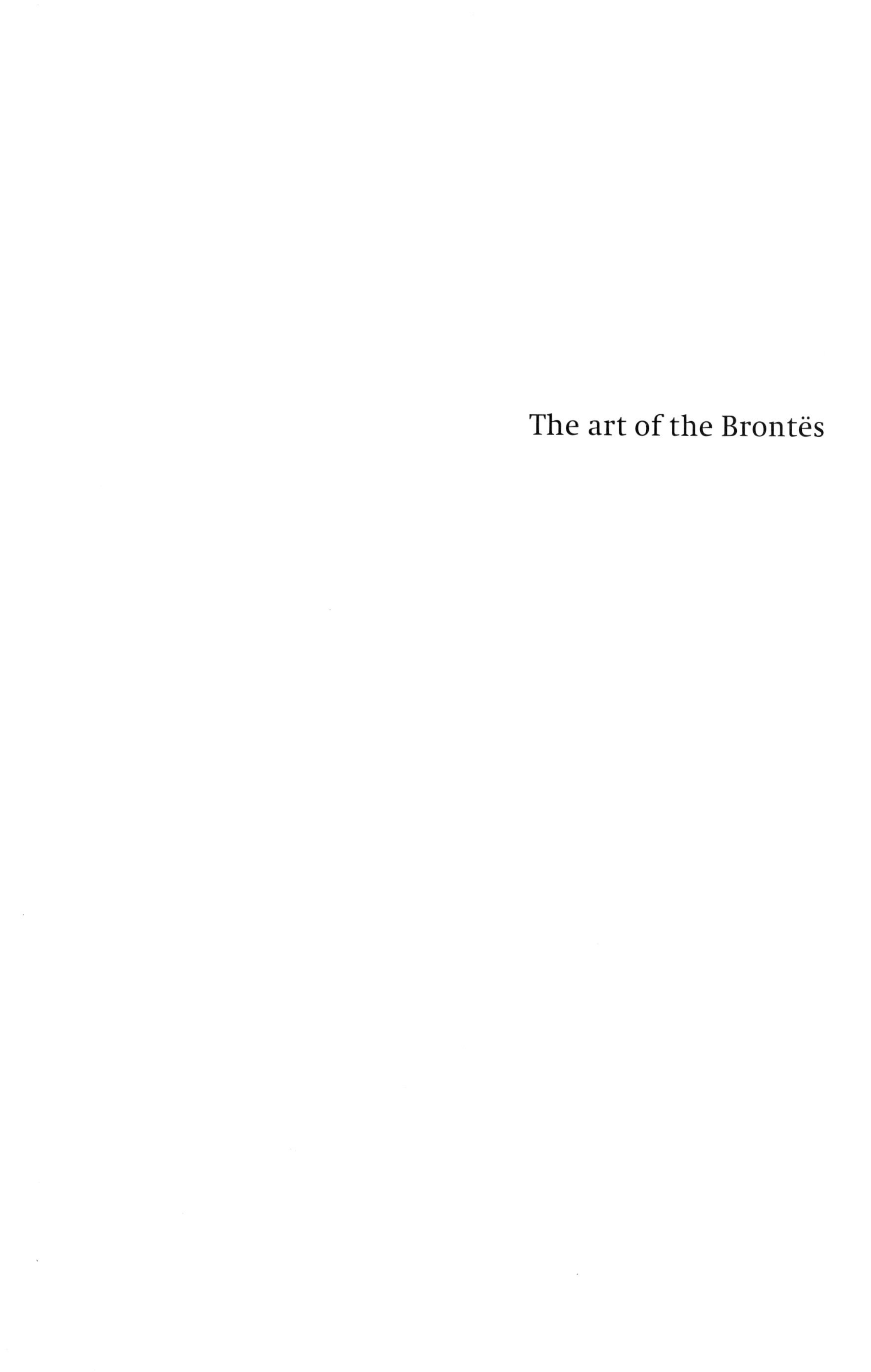

# The art of the Brontës

# The art of the Brontës

CHRISTINE ALEXANDER

AND JANE SELLARS

Published by the Press Syndicate of the University of Cambridge
The Pitt Building, Trumpington Street, Cambridge CB2 1RP
40 West 20th Street, New York, NY 10011–4211, USA
10 Stamford Road, Oakleigh, Melbourne 3166, Australia



First Published 1995

Printed in Great Britain at the University Press, Cambridge

*A catalogue record for this book is available from the British Library*

*Library of Congress cataloguing in publication data*

Alexander, Christine.
The art of the Brontës / Christine Alexander and Jane Sellars.
p. cm.
'The book has been planned to accompany the First International Exhibition of Brontë Art'– CIP p. xii.
Includes bibliographical references and index.
ISBN 0 521 43248 0 (hardback). ISBN 0 521 43841 1 (paperback).
1. Brontë family– Exhibitions. 2. Authors as artists–England– Exhibitions.
I. Sellars, Jane.
N6797. B758A4 1995
759.2–dc20 94–4251 CIP

ISBN 0 521 43248 0 hardback
ISBN 0 521 43841 1 paperback

TAG

*To Rebecca, Roland and Simon*

# Contents


*List of illustrations* page x
*Foreword by Lord Briggs* xv
*Acknowledgements* xvi
*Select chronology* xx

Introduction 1

The influence of the visual arts on the Brontës 9
*Christine Alexander*

Charlotte Brontë: the earnest amateur 36
*Christine Alexander*

The art of Branwell Brontë 65
*Jane Sellars*

The art of Emily Brontë 100
*Christine Alexander*

The art of Anne Brontë 134
*Jane Sellars*

Catalogue of Brontë drawings and paintings
CHARLOTTE BRONTË 153
BRANWELL BRONTË 283
EMILY BRONTË 369
ANNE BRONTË 395

Appendix A: List of books owned by the Brontës, with sketches and scribbles 422

Appendix B: Note on the provenance of Brontë art works 432

*Bibliography* 445
*Acknowledgement of sources* 458
*Index of drawings and paintings* 460
*Index of names and subjects* 467

# *Illustrations*

PLATES IN THE ESSAYS


PLATE 1 'The Disconsolate' (**40**), a watercolour by Charlotte Brontë, copied from an engraving in the *Forget Me Not* Annual of 1831 — Page 15

PLATE 2 'Alexander Soult' (**102**), pencil drawing of Byron by Charlotte Brontë after the engraving 'Childe Harold and Ianthe', in *The Literary Souvenir*, 1830 — 19

PLATE 3 'Childe Harold and Ianthe', engraving by E. Portbury, from a drawing by R. Westall, for *The Literary Souvenir*, 1830 — 19

PLATE 4 John Martin, 'The Temptation', hand-coloured lithograph from *The Sacred Annual*, by Robert Montgomery, 1834 — 21

PLATE 5 John Bradley (1787–1844), founder-member of the Keighley Mechanics' Institute and art teacher to the young Brontës — 23

PLATE 6 'A night-eruption of Vesuvius', by Olivio d'Anno, 1794; a painting seen by Charlotte Brontë at The Red House, Gomersal, the home of her friend Mary Taylor — 25

PLATE 7 'Roe Head', Mirfield; pencil drawing by the art teacher, Susan Carter, of the school attended by the Brontës — 42

PLATE 8 Handcrafted 'lady-like accomplishments' produced by the Brontës, including Charlotte Brontë's painting of 'Stylized flowers and bird on silk' (**73**), a collar made from one of her designs, her needle-case (bottom centre) decorated with tiny pencil drawings (**75**), and her paintbox — 48

PLATE 9 'Kirkstall Abbey' (**117**), pencil drawing by Charlotte Brontë, exhibited at the summer exhibition of the Royal Northern Society for the Encouragement of the Fine Arts, Leeds, 1834 52

PLATE 10 'Jacob's Dream', engraving by E. Goodall, from a painting by W. Allston, for *The Literary Souvenir*, 1830; copied by Branwell Brontë (**235**) 81

PLATE 11 Branwell Brontë, 'Self-portrait' (**267**), drawn c. 1840 88

PLATE 12 Branwell Brontë, 'A Parody' (**304**), drawn c. 1848 95

PLATE 13 Pen-and-ink sketch of Emily Brontë and her animals (**331**), drawn by Emily at the foot of her diary paper for 1845 104

PLATE 14 'The North Wind' (**325**), watercolour by Emily Brontë, copied from William Finden's engraving of Richard Westall's 'Ianthe', first published as the frontispiece to volume 2 of Thomas Moore's *Life of Byron*, 1839 114

PLATE 15 'Study of a fir tree' (**326**), pencil drawing from nature, made by Emily Brontë in Brussels, 1842 116

PLATE 16 'Landscape with trees' (**368**), pencil drawing by Anne Brontë, 1843 139

PLATE 17 'Woodland with deer' (**352**), by Anne Brontë, c. 1839 141

## *Plate section* (between pages 151 and 152)

### COLOUR PLATES

I Charlotte Brontë, 'The Mountain Sparrow', 1830 (**26**)

II Branwell Brontë, 'Gos Hawk', 1833 (**218**)

III Emily Brontë, 'Keeper – from life', 1838 (**319**)

IV Emily Brontë, Flossy, c. 1843 (**327**)

V Emily Brontë, 'Grasper – from life', 1834 (**313**)

VI Emily Brontë, Nero, 1841 (**324**)

VII Charlotte Brontë, Copy of a portrait of Mrs Brontë, 1830 (**36**)

VIII Charlotte Brontë, Portrait of Anne Brontë, c. 1833 (**92**)

IX Charlotte Brontë, 'Bessy Bell and Mary Gray', 1830 (**39**)

X Branwell Brontë, 'Terror', 1830 (**202**)

XI Branwell Brontë, 'Hermit', 1830 (**200**)

XII Branwell Brontë, 'Queen Esther', 1830 (**207**)

XIII Charlotte Brontë, The Atheist viewing the dead body of his Wife, c. 1835–1836 (**136**)

XIV Charlotte Brontë, 'Wild Roses From Nature', 1830 (**28**)

XV Charlotte Brontë, Study of a primrose, c. 1830 (**33**)

XVI Charlotte Brontë, 'Lycidas', 1835 (**129**)

XVII Charlotte Brontë, Study of a heartsease, 1832 (**84**)

XVIII Charlotte Brontë, Pink begonia, 1832 (**86**)

XIX Charlotte Brontë, Blue convolvulus, 1832 (**87**)

XX Anne Brontë, Portrait of a little girl with a posy, 1843 (**366**)

XXI Charlotte Brontë, 'Portrait of A French Brunette', c. 1833 (**93**)

XXII Charlotte Brontë, The Maid of Saragoza, c. 1834 (**127**)

XXIII Branwell Brontë, Emily Jane Brontë, c. 1833–1834 (**224**)

XXIV Branwell Brontë, The Brontë sisters, c. 1834 (**225**)

XXV Charlotte Brontë, Woman in leopard fur, 1839 (**147**)

XXVI Charlotte Brontë, Lake and castle, 1833 (**94**)

XXVII Charlotte Brontë, Portrait of a child with hat and basket, 1830 (**35**)

XXVIII Charlotte Brontë, 'King of Angria, Duke of Zamorna', c. 1834 (**113**)

XXIX Branwell Brontë, John Brown (1804–1855), c. 1835–1839 (**243**)

XXX Branwell Brontë, Miss Margaret Hartley, c. 1838–1839 (**254**)

XXXI Branwell Brontë, Isaac Kirby, 1838–1839 (**257**)

XXXII Branwell Brontë, Mrs Isaac Kirby, 1838–1839 (**258**)

## BLACK AND WHITE PLATES

XXXIII Anne Brontë, Church surrounded by trees, 1828 (**332**)

XXXIV Branwell Brontë, Ruined tower, 1828 (**184**)

XXXV Charlotte Brontë, Ruined tower, 1828 (**9**)

XXXVI Charlotte Brontë, Thatched cottage, 1828 (**10**)

XXXVII Charlotte Brontë, 'Zenobia Marchioness Ellrington', 1833 (**100**)

XXXVIII Charlotte Brontë, 'Arthur Adrian Marquis of Douro' 2, 1833 (**101**)

XXXIX Charlotte Brontë, Portrait of a young lady, 1834 (**111**)

XL Charlotte Brontë, Study of noses, c. 1831 (**44**)

XLI Charlotte Brontë, Study of eyes, 1831 (**42**)

XLII Charlotte Brontë, Study of two profiles, c. 1831 (**49**)

XLIII Charlotte Brontë, Roman head, 1835 (**131**)

XLIV Charlotte Brontë, Classical head, c. 1835 (**132**)

XLV Charlotte Brontë, Madonna and child, c. 1835 (**133**)

XLVI Charlotte Brontë, Kirkstall Abbey amongst trees, 1832 (**82**)

XLVII Charlotte Brontë, 'Cockermouth', c. 1833 (**90**)

XLVIII Charlotte Brontë, Study of a tree and cottage, 1842 (**155**)

XLIX Charlotte Brontë, William Weightman, 1840 (**149**)

L Anne Brontë, Woman gazing at a sunrise over a seascape, 1839 (**350**)

LI Anne Brontë, 'What you please', 1840 (**353**)

LII Anne Brontë, Man with a dog before a villa, 1836 (**345**)

LIII Emily Brontë, Woman's head with tiara, 1841 (**323**)

LIV Emily Brontë, Diary paper, 1837 (**316**)

LV Emily Brontë, 'Forget me not', c. 1830 (**309**)

LVI Emily Brontë, Guwald Tower, Haddington, 1832 (**311**)

LVII Branwell Brontë, Portrait of a man holding aloft a wineglass, c. 1840–1842 (**273**)

LVIII Charlotte Brontë, Two male portraits and buildings, c. 1833–1834 (**98**)

LIX Branwell Brontë, Jacob's dream, c. 1834–1838 (**235**)

LX Branwell Brontë, The Old Hall, Thorp Green, 1844 (**282**)

LXI Branwell Brontë, 'Zamorna. 35.', 1835 (**239**)

LXII Branwell Brontë, The pirate, c. 1835 (**241**)

## PLATES IN APPENDIX A


PLATE 18 Pine marten, in *The Gardens and Menagerie of the Zoological Society Delineated* 422

PLATE 19 Emaciated cattle, in William Darton, *A Description of London* 424

PLATE 20 Branwell Brontë, Battle scene, in William De la Motte, *Characters of Trees* 425

PLATE 21 Sketches in Goldsmith's *Grammar of General Geography* 427

PLATE 22 Frowning man in John Hornsey, *The Pronouncing Expositor* 427

PLATE 23 Charlotte Brontë, Woman with veil, in *Russell's General Atlas; of Modern Geography* 429

# *Foreword*

by Lord Briggs

As President of the Brontë Society I am delighted to write a brief foreword to this fascinating and important book. The Society, which is committed to the encouragement of research on the Brontë family, has from the start been interested in this project, one of whose authors is Director of the Brontë Parsonage Museum, and its Council has given it all the support in its power. The fact that the other author of the book is affiliated in Australia and has done a good deal of her work on the book there, with frequent research trips to the UK, is testimony in itself to the international appeal of the Brontës. The Brontë Society has many overseas members, and Brontë research flourishes as much outside Britain as in it. Like all the best work, the research that has gone into the compilation of this first full book on the Brontës' art has been long and detailed and equally rewarding.

The well-informed authors are concerned both with what the Brontës achieved through visual expression and to what they aspired. The relationship between verbal and visual expression and communication is of increasing scholarly interest not least in relation to the study of nineteenth-century history, and it is as an historian as well as President of the Brontë Society that I introduce a volume the merits of which speak for themselves.

Lewes, Sussex.

# Acknowledgements

The very generous support of two institutions has made this study possible: the Brontë Society and the Australian Research Council. Both have provided the authors with substantial material and research assistance.

The majority of Brontë paintings and drawings are located at the Brontë Parsonage Museum (BPM), Haworth. Without the generous and unstinted access the authors have had to this treasure-trove of paintings, manuscripts and books originally belonging to the Brontë family, this study would have been severely hampered. The book has been planned to accompany the first International Exhibition of Brontë Art, and to this end the Brontë Society Council has provided the authors with material support, in particular their generous assistance with the photography. In her capacity as Director of the Brontë Parsonage Museum and as a private art historian, Jane Sellars has been supported by a loyal and willing staff. Without the encouragement of the Brontë Society Council this project would have been impossible. The authors are especially grateful to the members of the Council for allowing their art works to be reassessed and their records to be scrutinized for details of provenance and for allowing knowledge of the Brontës' art works to reach a world-wide audience.

A generous grant from the Australian Research Council allowed the authors, working on different sides of the globe, to meet and discuss the project with the original paintings and drawings in front of them. It supported Christine Alexander's travel and research in libraries and private collections throughout Britain and the USA, and funded the research assistance and time necessary to pursue this project.

Christine Alexander would also like to express her gratitude to the Master and Fellows of Pembroke College, Cambridge, who elected her as Visiting Scholar for the academic year 1990–1. She benefited greatly from being able to pursue her research in an atmosphere of friendly academic inquiry and from the generous support of college facilities and staff.

We would like to record our thanks to the staff of the following libraries and museums, both for their willingness to answer queries and for their permission to use photographs of their Brontë holdings: The British Library (Department of Manuscripts: Sally Brown), The Harry Ransom Humanities Research Center (Elizabeth Neubauer and Cathy Henderson), The Houghton Library (Leslie A. Morris and Jennie Rathbun), The King's School, Canterbury (Hugh Walpole Collection: David S. Goodes), Leeds University Library (The Brotherton Collection: C. D. W. Sheppard and P. Morrish), The New York Public Library (The Berg Collection: Francis O. Mattson, Stephen Crook, Wayne Furman and Philip Milito), The Pierpont Morgan Library (Robert E. Parks and Christine Nelson), and the Princeton University Libraries (The Robert H. Taylor Collection: Mark R. Farrell; and William L. Joyce). Other libraries and museums that have provided photos and assistance include The Baillieu Library of the University of Melbourne, The Bayle Museum Trust (John S. Walker), Bradford Central Reference Library (Bob Duckett), The British Museum (Department of Prints and Drawings: Dr Kim Sloan), Cambridge University Library (Colin T. Clarkson), Cartwright Hall Art Gallery (Christine Hopper), Cherryburn (Thomas Bewick's Birthplace: Stewart Thirkell), Harold B. Lee Young Library at Brigham Young University (Dr L. L. Baker), Hastings Central Library (Brion Purdey), The John Rylands Library, Sheffield University Library, Keighley Reference Library, Kirklees Cultural Services (Red House Museum: Helga Hughes and Catherine Hall), Leeds City Art Gallery (Alex Robertson, Corinne Miller and Nigel Walsh), Leeds City Reference Library, Museum of London (Andrea Milburn), The National

Portrait Gallery Archives, London, The Portico Library, the Social Sciences and Humanities Library of the University of New South Wales (Pam O'Brien and Ruth Arenz), The University of Queensland Central Library (Alison Stewart), The Victoria and Albert Museum (Marian Keyes and Lionel Lambourne), and The Library, Windsor Castle (Oliver Everett).

The Brontë Parsonage Museum had already begun much of the basic cataloguing of the Brontë art work under Dr Juliet Barker when she was curator/librarian; from this, and from the work of former Brontë Museum librarians, we have benefited. We owe our thanks, too, to the present librarians, Kathryn White and her assistant Ann Dinsdale; and in particular to Tracey Messenger, who was employed specifically for work on the art project. Her substantial contribution to this book is reflected in Appendix B.

Many private collectors, both those who have chosen to remain anonymous and those who are named in the following pages, have given generously of their time and knowledge to this project. We would like to express our sincere thanks to all these owners of Brontë items and to the family members who have provided information on provenance, in particular Professor Alan H. Adamson, Sir James Graham, Joyce Harriette Hart, Mary Eleanore Lang, Angelina Light, A. F. I. Parmeter, Tonia B. Simpson, Jennifer Spanton-Flexton, Ian Stevenson and Don Thomas. Others, including Professor Ann Bermingham, Roger Davey (East Sussex County Archivist), Ian Dewhirst, Sarah Fermi, Audrey G. Hall, Graham Harris, John Mason, the late John Nussey, Derek Roper, Anthony Rota, Humphrey Smith, Barbara Whitehead and Gladys Young (Battle and District Historical Society), have also assisted in various ways, especially in the location of sources.

We have gained greatly from discussion with other Brontë scholars, in particular Dr Juliet Barker, Professor Victor Neufeldt and Margaret Smith. Margaret Smith's knowledge of Brontë letters, chronology and handwriting and Edward Chitham's work on Anne Brontë have been of immense help to the authors. Christine Alexander would particularly like to thank William St Clair, who generously made available his Byron collection and greatly helped her in the search for the sources of Brontë paintings. Michael Campbell also assisted with his expert knowledge on the engravings of John Martin; and Margaret Thomas and Emma Pearce (Technical Adviser at Windsor & Newton) provided valuable assistance in dating Charlotte Brontë's paintbox. Many other people have offered help and encouragement over the course of this project and among these we would like to thank Professor Ian Jack and Professor Herbert Rosengarten.

The catalogue section of this book owes much to the technical guidance and expertise of Rowland Hilder, who patiently initiated Christine Alexander into the mysteries of a complicated computer database program, and who was always ready to offer help. Without this and the valuable assistance of Vanessa Benson in typing much of the catalogue, searching for secondary material and checking entries, the authors would never have met their tight publishing deadline. We are grateful, too, for the photographic expertise of Simon Warner, Sue Doust and Belinda Allen; for Kate Sumner's assistance in helping Christine Alexander prepare the final manuscript; for the superb editorial skills of Ann Mason; and for the support of Cambridge University Press.

Above all, our thanks go to our families, without whose constant support and tolerance this detailed project would not have been completed. In particular Christine owes a special debt to her husband Peter, whose unfailing encouragement and unselfish parenting have made it possible for her to spend time on this book. The authors have dedicated the work to Christine's children Rebecca and Roland, and to Jane's son Simon.

# *Select chronology*

| | |
|---|---|
| 1777 | Patrick Brontë born at Emdale, County Down. |
| 1783 | Maria Branwell born at Penzance, Cornwall. |
| 1802 | Patrick Brontë enters St John's College, Cambridge. |
| 1811 | Patrick Brontë begins duties as minister of Hartshead, near Dewsbury. |
| 29 December 1812 | Marriage of Patrick Brontë and Maria Branwell, Guiseley Church, near Leeds. |
| 23 April 1814 | Maria, their first child, christened. |
| 8 February 1815 | Elizabeth born. |
| 19 May 1815 | Patrick Brontë moves to St James's Church, Thornton. |
| 26 August 1815 | Elizabeth christened. |
| 21 April 1816 | Charlotte born. |
| 26 June 1817 | Patrick Branwell born. |
| 30 July 1818 | Emily Jane born. |
| 17 January 1820 | Anne born. |
| 25 February 1820 | Patrick Brontë licensed to the Perpetual Curacy of Haworth. |
| April 1820 | The Brontë family move to the parsonage, Haworth. |
| May 1821 | Elizabeth Branwell ('Aunt Branwell') arrives in Haworth. |
| 15 September 1821 | Mrs Maria Brontë dies, aged 38. |
| 21 July 1824 | Maria and Elizabeth go to Cowan Bridge School, near Kirby Lonsdale. |
| 10 August 1824 | Charlotte enters Cowan Bridge School. |

| | |
|---|---|
| 25 November 1824 | Emily enters Cowan Bridge School. |
| 1824 | Tabitha Aykroyd ('Tabby') engaged as servant. |
| 1825 | Mechanics' Institute, Keighley, founded. |
| 6 May 1825 | Maria dies of consumption, having been sent home from school ill on 14 February. |
| 1 June 1825 | Charlotte and Emily come home. |
| 15 June 1825 | Elizabeth dies, having left school 'in decline', 31 May. |
| 5 June 1826 | Patrick Brontë returns from a clerical conference in Leeds with a box of toy soldiers for Branwell. The Young Men's Play begins, leading to the Brontë children's imaginary sagas of Glass Town, Gondal and Angria. |
| 12 March 1827 | Branwell's earliest extant manuscript, 'Battell Book', illustrated with pencil and watercolour. |
| January 1828 | Branwell's earliest extant drawing, 'A sleeping cat'. |
| 1828 | Charlotte's earliest extant manuscript, 'There was once a little girl and her name was Ane', illustrated with tiny watercolours. |
| 29 August 1828 | Anne's earliest extant drawing, 'Church surrounded by trees'. |
| 2 September 1828 | Charlotte's earliest extant drawing, 'Ruined tower'. |
| 1829–1830 | The Brontës receive art lessons from John Bradley of Keighley. |
| 19 January 1829 | Emily's earliest extant drawing, 'Mullioned window'. |
| 23 September 1829 | The Brontë children stay with their Uncle Fennell, Parsonage House, Crosstone; Charlotte's earliest surviving letter with the first written reference to drawing. |
| 17 January 1831 | Charlotte goes to Margaret Wooler's school at Roe Head, Mirfield, near Dewsbury. |
| May 1832 | Charlotte leaves Roe Head. |
| 1833 | Patrick Brontë joins Keighley Mechanics' Institute, with access to the library, reading room and lectures. |
| September 1833 | The Brontës visit Bolton Abbey with the Nusseys. |
| March 1834 | Installation service of the new organ at Haworth Parish Church. |
| June 1834 | The Brontës visit the summer exhibition of the Royal Northern |

| | |
|---|---|
| | Society for the Encouragement of the Fine Arts, in Leeds. Charlotte exhibits two pencil drawings, 'Bolton Abbey' and 'Kirkstall Abbey'. William Robinson also exhibits and is later engaged as art teacher for Branwell. |
| 24 November 1834 | Emily and Anne write their first extant diary paper, including earliest mention of Gondal. |
| 30 May 1835 | Branwell visits Liverpool, purchases Byron's *Childe Harold's Pilgrimage.* |
| June–July 1835 | Branwell drafts a letter to the Royal Academy of Arts asking where and when to present his drawings. |
| 2 July 1835 | Charlotte tells her friend Ellen Nussey of plans for Branwell to go to the Royal Academy, Charlotte to go to Roe Head as a teacher, and Emily to accompany her as a pupil. |
| 29 July 1835 | Charlotte and Emily leave Haworth for Roe Head. |
| mid-September 1835 | Branwell's course of art lessons with William Robinson, in Leeds, completed. |
| late October 1835 | Anne replaces Emily at Roe Head. |
| 25 April 1836 | Branwell installed as full member of Freemasons' Lodge of the Three Graces, Haworth, by this date; acts as secretary at subsequent Masonic meetings. |
| March 1837 | Robert Southey advises Charlotte not to embark on a literary career. |
| December 1837 | Charlotte disagrees with Margaret Wooler over Anne's illness and both return home abruptly from Roe Head; Charlotte returns after the holidays. |
| May 1838 | Branwell sets up as a portrait painter in Bradford, lodging with Mr and Mrs Kirkby until May 1839. |
| 23 May 1838 | Charlotte leaves Margaret Wooler's school (now at Heald's House, Dewsbury Moor) suffering from nervous depression; returns in June. |
| end September 1838 | Emily takes a teaching post at Miss Patchett's school at Law Hill, near Halifax. |
| December 1838 | Charlotte leaves Margaret Wooler's school. |
| March 1839 | Emily returns to Haworth from Law Hill. |
| 8 April 1839 | Anne goes as governess to the Inghams, Blake Hall, Mirfield. |

| | |
|---|---|
| mid-May 1839 | Branwell gives up his unsuccessful studio in Bradford, returning to Haworth. |
| May 1839 | Charlotte goes as governess to the Sidgwicks at Stonegappe, near Skipton. |
| 19 July 1839 | Charlotte leaves Stonegappe and returns to Haworth. |
| July 1839 | Branwell visits Liverpool. |
| August 1839 | William Weightman comes as curate to Haworth. |
| September 1839 | Charlotte goes with Ellen Nussey to stay three weeks at Easton, and one week at the sea nearby, at Bridlington (then called Burlington). |
| (late) 1839 | Charlotte writes her 'Farewell to Angria'. |
| December 1839 | Anne leaves her position with the Inghams. |
| 1 January 1840 | Branwell installed as tutor to the Postlethwaites at Broughton-in-Furness. |
| ?1 May 1840 | Branwell visits Hartley Coleridge at Rydal Water, near Ambleside. |
| ?8 May 1840 | Anne goes as governess to the Robinsons at Thorp Green Hall, Little Ouseburn, near York. |
| June 1840 | Branwell dismissed by the Postlethwaites; returns to Haworth. |
| 31 August 1840 | Branwell engaged as Assistant Clerk in Charge at Sowerby Bridge Railway Station. |
| 1840 | Martha Brown comes to live at the parsonage, gradually replacing Tabby as servant. |
| March 1841 | Charlotte goes as governess to the Whites of Upperwood House, Rawdon, near Bradford. |
| 1 April 1841 | Branwell moves to Luddenden Foot as Clerk in Charge of the station. |
| 5 June 1841 | Branwell publishes some poems in the *Halifax Guardian*, making him the first of the Brontë siblings to become a published author. |
| July 1841 | Charlotte, Emily and Anne plan to start a school of their own. |
| 29 September 1841 | Charlotte asks Elizabeth Branwell for financial help for her and Emily to perfect their languages in Brussels, in preparation for opening a school. |
| October 1841 | Charlotte declines an offer to take over Margaret Wooler's school. |
| December 1841 | Charlotte leaves her post with the Whites. |

| | |
|---|---|
| 15 February 1842 | Patrick Brontë, Charlotte and Emily arrive at the Pensionnat Heger, Brussels, staying in London en route. |
| 26 March 1842 | Charlotte visits her old school-friend Mary Taylor and her sister Martha, also at school in Brussels. |
| 31 March 1842 | Branwell dismissed by the railways as a result of a discrepancy in the accounts for which he is held responsible. |
| 6 September 1842 | William Weightman dies of cholera, aged 28. |
| 12 October 1842 | Martha Taylor dies of cholera, aged 23, in Brussels. |
| 29 October 1842 | Elizabeth Branwell dies, leaving a legacy of £350 for each of her nieces. |
| | Anne returns to Haworth for the funeral, 3 November. |
| 8 November 1842 | Charlotte and Emily return to Haworth. |
| 29 November 1842 | Anne returns to Thorp Green Hall. |
| January 1843 | Branwell joins Anne at Thorp Green, where he is to be tutor to Edmund Robinson. |
| 27 January 1843 | Charlotte leaves Haworth to return to Brussels as both teacher and pupil. |
| 1 January 1844 | Charlotte leaves Brussels to return to Haworth. |
| February 1844 | Emily begins to transcribe her poems into two notebooks, one titled 'Gondal Poems', the other untitled. |
| November 1844 | Charlotte gives up hope of starting a school, after unsuccessful advertising. |
| May 1845 | Arthur Bell Nicholls appointed curate at Haworth. |
| 11 June 1845 | Branwell receives his final salary as tutor at Thorp Green. |
| June 1845 | Anne and Branwell return to Haworth, Anne having terminated her employment with the Robinsons. |
| 30 June 1845 | Anne and Emily make their 'first long journey' together to York. |
| ?17 July 1845 | Branwell, having returned briefly to Thorp Green, is dismissed from his post as tutor (an event reported to Charlotte by Branwell, although he may have received his dismissal as early as 11 June). |
| 29 July 1845 | Branwell sent to Wales with John Brown to look after him, until 3 August. |
| September 1845 | Charlotte discovers one of Emily's notebooks of poetry. |

| | |
|---|---|
| 6 February 1846 | Charlotte sends manuscript of poems to the publishers Aylott & Jones the work of three relatives, the Bell brothers. |
| April 1846 | Branwell goes to Halifax for three days 'on business'. |
| end May 1846 | *Poems* by Currer, Ellis and Acton Bell published. |
| 27 June 1846 | Date at the end of Charlotte's manuscript of *The Professor*. |
| 19 August 1846 | Charlotte goes with her father to Manchester for an operation on the cataract of his left eye; they remain there until 24/25 September. |
| 16 March 1847 | Aire Valley railway from Leeds extended to Keighley. |
| July 1847 | Emily's *Wuthering Heights* and Anne's *Agnes Grey* accepted for publication by Thomas Newby, but not Charlotte's *The Professor*. |
| 19 October 1847 | *Jane Eyre* published by Smith, Elder & Co. |
| December 1847 | *Wuthering Heights* and *Agnes Grey* published. |
| June 1848 | *The Tenant of Wildfell Hall* published by Thomas Newby. |
| 7 July 1848 | Charlotte and Anne travel to London to prove there is more than one author named 'Bell'. They go to the opera with George Smith and his sisters, visit the Great Exhibition, the Royal Academy Exhibition and the National Gallery. |
| 24 September 1848 | Branwell dies, aged 31. |
| November 1848 | Emily very ill, refuses to see a doctor; scarcely allows her condition to be referred to. |
| 19 December 1848 | Emily dies of consumption, aged 30. |
| January 1849 | The doctor reports that Anne is unlikely to live. |
| 8 May 1849 | Anne decides to use the £200 legacy left her by her godmother, Miss Outhwaite, to go to Scarborough. |
| 24 May 1849 | Charlotte, Anne and Ellen Nussey leave for Scarborough, via York. |
| 28 May 1849 | Anne dies, aged 29, and is buried in St Mary's Churchyard, Scarborough. |
| 7 June 1849 | Charlotte and Ellen Nussey go down the east coast to Filey and Bridlington, before returning to Haworth. |
| 26 October 1849 | *Shirley* published by Smith, Elder & Co. |
| 29 November 1849 | Charlotte goes to London, staying with the Smiths until 15 December; meets Thackeray, visits a Turner exhibition at the National Gallery, sees Macready in *Othello* and *Macbeth*. |

| | |
|---|---|
| 30 May 1850 | Charlotte visits London, again staying with the Smiths, until 25 June; visits the Royal Academy, sees the Duke of Wellington and has her portrait drawn by George Richmond. |
| 3 July 1850 | Charlotte goes to Edinburgh, meeting George Smith there. |
| 19 August 1850 | Charlotte goes to stay with Sir James Kay Shuttleworth in Windermere, where she meets Elizabeth Gaskell. |
| 10 December 1850 | Charlotte's 'edited' edition of *Wuthering Heights* and *Agnes Grey*, with 'Notice' about her sisters, is published. |
| 28 May 1851 | Charlotte goes to London, until 27 June; attends Thackeray's lecture, sees the Great Exhibition three times, sees Rachel act twice, and visits Dr Brown, a phrenologist, where she and George Smith (as Mr and Miss Fraser) have their characters read. |
| 28 January 1853 | *Villette* published by Smith, Elder & Co. |
| 22 April 1853 | Charlotte goes to stay with Elizabeth Gaskell at Manchester. |
| 19 September 1853 | Elizabeth Gaskell visits Charlotte at Haworth. |
| late September 1853 | Charlotte visits Ellen Nussey, then goes to stay with Margaret Wooler at Hornsea. |
| 29 June 1854 | Charlotte marries the Reverend Arthur Bell Nicholls, and leaves for a honeymoon in Ireland, where she meets Nicholls's uncle and aunt who raised him. |
| 1 August 1854 | Charlotte and Nicholls return to Haworth, to live at the parsonage and look after Patrick Brontë. |
| 31 March 1855 | Charlotte dies, aged 38. |
| 25 March 1857 | Elizabeth Gaskell's *Life of Charlotte Brontë* published in two volumes. |
| 6 June 1857 | *The Professor* published by Smith, Elder & Co., with a preface by Nicholls. |
| 7 June 1861 | Patrick Brontë dies, aged 85. |
| | Nicholls returns to Ireland; marries his cousin, Mary Anne Bell, on 25 August 1864. |

# Introduction

*Christine Alexander and Jane Sellars*

The Brontës are well known as writers, but, apart from one or two works by Branwell, they are seldom associated with the visual arts. The aim of this book is to present for the first time an accurate record of their productions and aspirations as artists. Few of the works in the following pages could be considered as masterpieces in themselves, and yet the training and habit of drawing and painting had significance for the nascent authors that reached far beyond their tangible productions. The following essays attempt to explain this: to chart the early childhood influences, the efforts of the adolescent siblings to gain expertise in drawing and painting, the struggles of Charlotte and Branwell to carve out careers as artists, and the various ways in which the Brontës' practice of the visual arts contributed to their writings and to their tragically brief adult lives.

There are a significant number of new discoveries in the following pages, not only of new drawings but of new biographical evidence, such as the surprising news that Charlotte Brontë was an exhibited artist in her own lifetime. There is new information about the Brontës' education in art, about Charlotte's school-friends and pupils, about the books read by the Brontës and contemporary engravings that stimulated their imaginations. A chronological study of the drawings helps to date school holidays and corroborates our knowledge both of periods of fatigue and stress (when few paintings were executed) and of periods of intense preoccupation with the imaginative worlds of Glass Town, Gondal and Angria (when drawing and painting dovetails with the frenetic writing of manuscripts). The evidence of Branwell's artistic industry and output should help to burnish his tarnished reputation and to bring critical opinion closer to John Drinkwater's qualified acknowledgement of his talents.[1]

The book includes 180 known illustrations by Charlotte, 131 by Branwell, 29 by Emily, 37 by Anne, and 22 which are of dubious attribution. They range from large oil paintings to cameo watercolour portraits and tiny pencil sketches.

Every extant illustration by the Brontës is reproduced in the following pages, except for a few crude sketches by Branwell that appear on the verso of other works and within the text and margins of his manuscripts, and except for some rough sketches and scribbles by various hands found in printed books owned by the Brontës. The latter are represented by selected illustrations only, in Appendix A as described below. Where possible, paintings which are no longer extant are illustrated by surviving photographs.

All extant drawings, paintings and sketches, no matter how small (and including those few not illustrated), are described in the catalogue entries. Illustrations on the recto and verso of a single sheet of paper have usually been given two separate entries. Illustrations by the Brontës that appear in their early manuscripts and letters have also been given individual entries. Illustrations by the Brontës on the leaves of printed books, once in Haworth Parsonage, are listed separately in Appendix A, since it is impossible to distinguish exactly which Brontë 'doodled' on which page, a habit that was, surprisingly, tolerated by the Reverend Patrick Brontë. There is an amusing example in the Brontë juvenilia of punishment for such a crime (which may have had some precedent in reality), when Charles Wellesley is forced to learn a page of recipes from *The Cook's Guide* for having 'drawn a scrawk' across an engraving of Lady Julia Sydney.[2]

The catalogue is arranged according to individual Brontë family members, each of whose works are arranged chronologically and numbered for easy reference. The catalogue numbers are printed in bold type and are used throughout (instead of titles) for cross-referencing. Works titled by the Brontës themselves are given in inverted commas, in many cases correctly transcribed for the first time ('Santa Maura' (**96**), for example, was previously known as 'Santa Maria'). Untitled works have been given simple descriptive names by the authors. As with their early manuscripts, the Brontës were unusually diligent in ascribing dates to their drawings and paintings. Nevertheless, twenty-three per cent of their works remain undated and have been assigned an approximate date (denoted by 'c.' before the date) by the authors, according to internal evidence (watermark, type of paper, size, medium, style, handwriting, subject) and external evidence such as provenance and biographical details gleaned from letters and memoirs. Even the shape of the paper can provide vital clues as to which paintings were executed at the same time (see **31** and **32**).

Nor is the attribution of works to individual members of the Brontë family always straightforward. It is easier to say that a work is not by a Brontë than it is to distinguish between the work of Charlotte, Emily and Anne. Branwell's style is distinctive and he painted almost exclusively in oils, the distinguishing mark of his masculinity. (He was not in the habit of signing his oil paintings, a fact not generally known and one which has caused some Brontë enthusiasts to mistake certain pictures by a late nineteenth-century landscape painter named B. Bronte for Branwell's work.) The productions of the sisters, however, reflect their common middle-class training in art as an accomplishment, a preparation for a future life as wife or governess. This is less true in Emily's case where an independence of spirit, nurtured away from the schooling and governess posts of Charlotte's and Anne's experience, shows itself in the style of her endearing studies of animals and birds.

Some works have been reattributed, according to the evidence of style, medium, watermark, etc. Where this might cause confusion, they have been cross-referenced under their former attribution (for example, **327** 'Flossy' has long been thought to be by Charlotte and often published as such: its reattribution is noted at the end of Charlotte's section and the main entry is under Emily.) In such cases, the evidence for reattribution is clearly laid before the reader. Several works have been removed from the Brontë canon; others have been illustrated but classified as dubious, as in the case of the well-known 'Mr Brocklehurst', where there is simply no evidence to show that it is by Charlotte or any of the Brontës. Where the attribution of a work is at all uncertain, as in the case of Charlotte's and Emily's copies of the same engraving from the *Forget Me Not* Annual of 1831 (**40** and **309**), the work has been entered under the most likely author and the various options and evidence are clearly stated for the reader.

Each entry in the catalogue follows a similar pattern, recording the number and title of the work in bold print, the date, medium, dimensions (height × width), inscriptions and other relevant details such as watermark and verso markings, provenance, location, description (for archival identification) and relevant notes. A discussion of the various media used by the Brontës can be found on pp.44–9, in the essay on 'Charlotte Brontë: the earnest amateur'. Although the authors have been fortunate enough to examine first-hand almost all Brontë drawings and paintings (in eight cases only they have had to work from colour photographs and this has been noted in the relevant entries), some of the locations are listed as 'Private owner', not to baffle the curious reader but to preserve the requested anonymity of the owner, for whose co-operation the authors are especially grateful.

The Brontës used a bewildering variety of handwritings and forms of signature over a number of years, and often within the same year. A careful study has been made of each individual hand in order to identify the author of dates, inscriptions, and even signatures which are occasionally added by subsequent owners. Often an early recipient of a drawing (pupil, friend or servant of Charlotte or her father) inscribed the work (for example, 'By C B') or made a distinguishing note on the verso. Ellen Nussey, in particular, followed this practice, and the authors have made every effort to identify both Brontë inscriptions and those of others. Such notes help to trace the provenance of the Brontë art works, which – like that of the manuscripts – is a fascinating history, a story constructed as much by 'the reader' and collector as by the works themselves and one that has yet to be fully told. A brief survey of the provenance of the Brontë art works can be found in Appendix B, and further details on individual drawings and paintings are listed in the catalogue.[3]

The following sources have been scrutinized for records of drawings and paintings: early sale catalogues; records of museum and library holdings in Britain and the United States; the reminiscences of people who visited Patrick Brontë after his children's deaths, who collected mementoes from Charlotte's widower, the Reverend Arthur Bell Nicholls, and his second wife in Ireland, and who bought illustrations and manuscripts from the Brontës' former friends and servants; early articles on the Brontës in newspapers and journals, including *Brontë Society Transactions* which is an especially valuable source; and the recollections of early visitors to the first Brontë Museum established by the fledgling Brontë Society in 1895 above the Yorkshire Penny Bank, where the Haworth Tourist Information Centre is now housed.

This search has elicited not only material on provenance but knowledge of a number of illustrations that the authors have been unable to locate. These include seven named illustrations by Charlotte (**83**, **110**, **118**, **134**, **137a**, **138** and **145**); and several items listed as 'Framed pencil drawing', by Charlotte, and 'Pencil portrait' and 'Three framed oil paintings' by Branwell, all recorded as having been lent to the Brontë Society for display in 1896 (see F. C. Galloway, *A Descriptive Catalogue of Objects in the Museum of the Brontë Society at Haworth* (Bradford, 1896). Records of a further twelve illustrations by Branwell have emerged but their locations have not been found (**190**, **191**, **192**, **199**, **233**, **252**, **255**, **259**, **261**, **284**, **286**, **287**). The Bill of Sale on the death of Patrick Brontë lists two oil paintings in frames, namely 'Bolton Abbey' and 'Kirkstall Abbey', which may have been by Branwell since the acquisition of such oil paintings would have been beyond the reach of a parish clergyman without independent means. Emily's watercolour of 'Keeper, Flossy and Tiger' (**329**) remains a tantalizing mystery, with one writer recording that he saw it on the wall in the Haworth Parsonage in 1858 when he visited Patrick Brontë; it has been traced from the Irish home of Charlotte's widower to the sale rooms of Bernard Quaritch Ltd, London, who purchased it from Sotheby's sale of the library of Clement K. Shorter, on 17 March 1937, but its present location is unknown. There are a further five known but unlocated illustrations by Emily listed in the following pages (**310**, **322**, **325**, **331**, **331a**).

Sale catalogues provide more conundrums. It is impossible to tell if any Brontë items were included in lot 186, 'Album of choice Sketches', at the sale of the effects of Ellen Nussey on 18 and 19 May 1898. Items sold from the Law Collection at the Hodgson & Co. sale of 31 March 1933 included, as part of lot 450, a cardboard box with two water-colour drawings that remain unidentified and unlocated, although the following pages suggest answers to this problem (see **8** and **120**). And in 1948, a local Yorkshire artist identified one of Charlotte's drawings as a copy of Hayter's portrait of Leigh Hunt (see Charlotte: Dubious section), but there is no record at all of the original.

The catalogue entries are not intended simply for the archivist and librarian; they have been written to tell a story – of the history of the paintings, and the way they reflect the interests and skills of the Brontës. Responsibility for catalogue entries has been divided between the authors, the sections on Charlotte and Emily being compiled by Christine Alexander, and those on Branwell and Anne being compiled by Jane Sellars. Although the authors have received assistance from innumerable sources, in particular from Tracey Messenger who wrote Appendix B, they accept full responsibility for any errors.

Although every effort has been made to include all extant material, the authors are well aware that this book is incomplete. Previous owners record having thrown away Brontë drawings and paintings (see p. 131, n.25); but other illustrations, such as those described above, may yet be located. As the book went to press, nine new illustrations came to light from various sources; this necessitated some hasty rearrangement to include them in chronological order and several 'a' numbers had to be inserted, for example **41a**. The authors look forward to hearing of further discoveries of artistic works by the Brontës and welcome correspondence from private collectors whom they have been unable to trace.

The authors have made no judgement as to what they consider to be 'art'. The correspondence between visual and written text, no matter how insignificant the sketches may appear, can be a vital part of the creative process. For this reason, all significant doodles and sketches related to text have been recorded, as in the case of Emily's 'Winged serpent sketches' (**321**). Every effort has been made to present the best available record of the crucial role that the practice of painting and drawing played in the lives of the Brontës.

# *Notes*

1 *The Miscellaneous and Unpublished Writings of Charlotte and Patrick Branwell Brontë*, ed. Thomas James Wise and John Alexander Symington, 2 vols. (Oxford: Basil Blackwell for the Shakespeare Head Press, 1936–8), vol. 2, p. 429.

2 'A Peep Into A Picture Book', *An Edition of the Early Writings of Charlotte Brontë*, ed. Christine Alexander, 2 vols. (Oxford: Basil Blackwell for the Shakespeare Head Press, 1987; 1991), vol. 2, part 2, p. 95.

3 See also Christine Alexander, *A Bibliography of the Manuscripts of Charlotte Brontë* (Haworth and New York: The Brontë Society in association with Meckler Publishing, 1982) for a brief survey of the colourful provenance of Charlotte Brontë's manuscripts, which also traces much of the story of the Brontë art works.

# The influence of the visual arts on the Brontës

*Christine Alexander*

> Walls without pictures are like houses without windows; for pictures are loopholes of escape to the mind, leading it to other scenes and spheres, as it were through the frame of an exquisite picture, where the fancy for the moment may revel, refreshed and delighted. Pictures are consolers of loneliness; they are a sweet flattery to the imagination; they are a relief to the jaded mind; they are windows to the imprisoned thought; they are Books; they are Histories and Sermons. They make up for the want of many other enjoyments to those whose life is passed amidst the smoke and din, the bustle and noise of an over-crowded city.
>
> W. S. Gilbert, *Catalogue of Engravings* [1]

The visual image sustained and nurtured the early lives of the Brontës. In a variety of ways, suggested by this nineteenth-century quotation from a *Catalogue of Engravings*, pictures enabled the four surviving Brontë children, Charlotte, Branwell, Emily and Anne, to visualize other worlds, to escape the sorrow of their mother's and two older sisters' deaths, and to combat both the boredom of life in an isolated moorland village and the later loneliness of the life of a governess. Published prints enabled the Brontës to acquire their own skills in drawing and painting; but, more importantly, they enabled the young writers to transpose the subjects and language of pictures into their literary work. Even in the case of Branwell, who was a professional artist for a short time, contemporary engravings provided the basis of his artistic training and inspired several of his later oil paintings. His surviving early manuscripts, like those of his sister Charlotte, are studded with quotation from nineteenth-century prints. For all the Brontës, a knowledge of the visual arts, the habit of reading pictures, and the practice of drawing and painting, were crucial to their development as writers.

The earliest record we have of the four Brontë children drawing is found in a letter written by Charlotte to her father, the Reverend Patrick Brontë, on 23 September 1829, when she was thirteen. The children were staying at Parsonage House, Crosstone, twelve miles from Haworth, and Charlotte reports that they have spent their time 'very pleasantly, between reading, working, and learning our lessons, which Uncle Fennell has been so kind as to teach us every day. Branwell has taken two sketches from nature, and Emily, Anne, and myself have likewise each of us drawn a piece from some views of the lakes which Mr Fennell brought with him from Westmoreland. The whole of these he intends keeping.'[2]

Already the eleven-year-old Branwell is distinguished from his sisters in his early practice of sketching 'from nature'. Although the girls were eventually to follow suit – in particular Emily whose love of nature was manifested as much in her painting as in her later writing – their early notion of art was articulated by Mrs Ellis, whose books on the character and education of women went through many editions in the nineteenth century. In *The Daughters of England, Their Position In Society, Character and Responsibilities*, she notes that an artist's life is full of difficulties; these, however, did not apply to women, for it was not 'an object of desirable attainment that they should study the art of painting to this extent'.[3] Art should simply be an accomplishment, acquired gracefully by copying suitable engravings of flowers, landscapes and heads. It is significant that all the heroines of the Brontë juvenilia convey this attitude to their artistic accomplishments, despite the prestigious position professional male artists hold in the world of Glass Town and Angria. In her 'Last Will and Testament', Marian Hume leaves to the young Ellen Grenville 'my botanical books and apparatus, my paintings of fruit and flowers, my pencil sketches and all my drawing materials',[4] symbols of her status as an amateur female artist.

The following pages prove that the Brontë sisters acquired this 'accomplishment art', but their letters, early writings and novels, and the sheer number of their surviving illustrations, indicate that their ambitions exceeded Mrs Ellis's refined and lady-like parameters. At least until the age of twenty,[5] Charlotte aspired to some kind of career in art, possibly that of a miniaturist, which would have answered the problem of her extreme short-sightedness; and Anne saw drawing as a necessary qualification for her career as a teacher. Emily was the exception: her art confirms her private vision of life; but initially she too acquired her skill as an artist through the method of copying prints. Even Branwell joined his sisters in believing that 'the art-faculty consisted of little more than mechanical dexterity, and could be obtained by long study and practice in manipulation', a habit described by Lucy Snowe in *Villette*.[6] Charlotte's school friend, Mary Taylor, recalled that 'Whenever an opportunity offered of examining a picture or cut of any kind, she went over it piecemeal, with her eyes close to the paper, looking so long that we used to ask her "what she saw in it." She could always see plenty, and explained it very well.'[7]

The Brontës were not exceptional in being fascinated by engravings before the days of television or the wide availability of pictures generally. The following experience of Sir Samuel Romilly must have been that of many contemporary children:

> [My father] was an admirer of the fine arts but pictures being too costly for his purchase, he limited himself to prints. . . I found a great deal of amusement in turning over the prints he was possessed of, became a great admirer of pictures, never omitted an opportunity of seeing a good collection, knew the peculiar style of almost every master. . . . I love to transport myself in idea into our little parlour, with its green paper, and the beautiful prints of Vivares, Bartolozzi, or Strange, from the pictures of Claude, Caracci, Raphael, and Corregio [*sic*] with which its walls were elegantly adorned.[8]

The Brontës, too, knew the names of famous artists, not only from engravings but also from the pages of their father's magazines. At thirteen, Charlotte compiled a 'List of painters whose works I wish to see', including Guido Reni, Giulio Romano, Titian, Raphael,

Michelangelo, Correggio, Annibale Carracci, Leonardo da Vinci, Fra Bartolommeo, Carlo Cignani, van Dyck, Rubens, Bartolommeo Ramenghi.[9] Engravings by these artists became especially popular in the eighteenth century and provided images for the many drawing manuals that developed in the second half of the century and became fashionable in the Brontës' day.

Innovations in technology also increased the availability of prints. The introduction in 1820 of steel mezzotints (rather than the softer copper already in use) meant that more copies could be printed from a single plate and the price reduced, enabling people on limited incomes (like Patrick Brontë) to own their favourite pictures. At least three large mezzotints by John Martin, which retailed from £2.12s.6d (proofs were dearer at £5–£6), hung on the parsonage walls soon after they appeared on the market between 1826 and 1832;[10] and Branwell is said to have had an engraving of Benjamin West's 'Death of General Wolfe' in his bedroom when he was a boy.[11]

The earliest indication of an awareness of the value of engravings in the Brontë household appears in the first of Charlotte's tiny hand-sewn volumes of 'Blackwood's Young Men's Magazine', August 1829. Here we find among the advertisements, modelled on the pages of their father's *Blackwood's Edinburgh Magazine*, 'A copyright of a book containing 5 splendid engravings, crown octavo, to be sold. Apply to Sergeant Gloveinhand, Brandy Lane, Glass Town. NB/ The engravings are in mezotinto style; nothing but the most absolute necessity has induced the advertiser to part with them.'[12] The bibliographical jargon of the young writers and their attitude to such precious commodities both satirizes and endorses the values of the original. In 'The Monthly Intelligencer' (27 March 1833), Branwell describes – in his extravagant style and minuscule writing – the preoccupation of Glass Town society with engravings:

> I steered immediately toward the principle table where were standing divers groups o[f] visitors admiring the various and costly works of art under which it groaned. before one party lay spread the magnificent nay glorious work, Dr Lisle's 'Verdopolita delineata' a vast Elephant-Folio of perhaps the most splendid engraving of the

> most splendid Architecture which ever existed. Others were examining the 5 quartos of Dundee's Scenery of the Glass town countrys others a profusion of the most richly bound richly engraven and costly works which could be conceived.[13]

It is obvious Branwell had read about, even if he had not seen, the magnificent *Vitruvius Britannicus* (1745), which recorded the finest classical-style buildings in England. His passion for architecture, in particular the work of Palladio, can be traced partly to such works and to articles in *Blackwood's*. His own humble version of these volumes, *A Description of London*, which he acquired when he was ten, is 'embellished' with engravings 'of all the most celebrated Public Buildings'. The pages are also decorated with his own juvenile designs and sketches (see Appendix A).

The maps and battle scenes in the following catalogue illustrate Branwell's other early passions for exploration and warfare (see, for example, **174** and **209**). These owe as much to contemporary engravings as they do to 'Remarks on Captain Parry's Expedition' or descriptions of 'Campaigns of the British Army at Washington' in the pages of *Blackwood's*.[14] He led the way in map drawing, adapting the maps in *Blackwood's* and various geography books to the adventures of Glass Town and Angria. When, as Captain Henry Hastings, the nineteen-year-old Branwell describes the Angrian Battle of Danceton Bridge, he recalls the many prints of battle scenes, such as the death of Wolfe, that impressed him as a child and that fill the pages of his unpublished manuscripts:

> Images treasured up from childhood when beneath the portraits of Great Commanders I had seen the cannon balls and standards piled one at [?another] in the Background a Gun rolling its smoke over the dying with a flag topping the Cloud of Battle sublime enlargements of a long lost little print where a heap of Dead lay underneath just such a shady sky. Still father back scenes of the Battle of Issus or Arbela coloured to suit the taste of a six year old.[15]

Such engravings satisfied a social as much as an artistic need. They provided the only visual commentary on contemporary events, reinforcing contemporary taste and attitudes, which the Brontës readily absorbed: pictures of domestic pets, women's fashions, seaside resorts, picturesque lakeland views, country churchyards, military heroism and public transport. Book- and print-sellers like Ackermann & Co. in the Strand in London would advertise widely throughout the British Empire, offering, for example, *Twelve Coloured Views of the Liverpool and Manchester Railway*, *Finden's Portraits of the Female Aristocracy*, *J. S. Prout's Castles and Abbeys in Monmouthshire*, *Reading the Scriptures*, and *Wellington At Waterloo*.[16] Because they so often copied such prints, the art of the Brontës is a reflection of the manners and morals of the times, unambiguously announced in the titles of these engravings.

It is salutary to read the opinion of Thackeray, Charlotte's later hero, on such taste and values. In *Paris Sketch Book* (1840), he deplores the English passion for engraving which he sees as reflecting commercial enterprise and materialism rather than an educated taste for art:

> Take the standard 'Album' for instance – that unfortunate collection of deformed Zuleikas and Medoras (from the Byron Beauties, the Flowers, Gems, Souvenirs, Casquets of Loveliness, Beauty, as they may be called); glaring caricatures of flowers, singly, in groups, in flower-pots, or with hideous deformed little Cupids sporting among them; of what are called 'mezzotinto' pencil drawings, 'poonah-paintings,' and what not. 'The Album' is to be found invariably upon the round, rosewood, brass-inlaid drawing-room table of the middle classes, and with a couple of 'Annuals' besides, which flank it on the same table, represents the art of the house.[17]

The fashionable Annuals were generously illustrated little books designed chiefly for women as Christmas, New Year or birthday gifts. They were a direct result of the revolution in engraving, which allowed for reasonably priced books with steel engravings to reach a large middle-class market. There were still the expensive, limited editions of aquatinted books, like Robert Montgomery's *The Sacred Annual*, from which Charlotte copied one of the hand-coloured plates (**136**, and colour plate XIII); and at the other end of the market there were still the cheap books, illustrated by woodcuts or wood engravings, which Thomas Bewick, in his turn, gradually revolutionized. But the majority of the books owned by the Brontës, and from which they copied, had steel-engraved plates.

The young Brontës would have found it hard to agree with Thackeray's judgement on the Annuals. To them the little books were prized possessions, valued chiefly for their pictures. It seems likely that they owned at least three copies: *Friendship's Offering* for 1829, *The Literary Souvenir* for 1830, and the *Forget Me Not* of 1831, since ten engravings were painstakingly copied by Charlotte, Branwell and Emily Brontë from these volumes.[18] One of these is 'The Disconsolate' (**40**, plate 1), a picturesque scene that is suggestive of forsaken love; certainly 'L. E. L.' (Letitia Elizabeth Landon) thought this when she wrote the sentimental poem that accompanies it. Interestingly, Landon refers to the treachery of De Lisle, a name the Brontës use for one of their celebrated Glass Town artists. Emily's copy of this engraving (**309**, and plate LV) has been preserved in the Berg Collection of the New York Public Library for some years, but Charlotte's version of the same picture has only recently come to light in private hands. Although the margins of the original have been damaged, the colours – which Charlotte herself added to the black and white original – still maintain their freshness and delicacy. The Brontës' reversal of this engraving to its original status as a colour painting is an interesting example of the dissemination of art.

'late 1 'The Disconsolate' (**40**), a watercolour by Charlotte Brontë, opied from an engraving in the *orget Me Not* Annual of 1831

The Brontës were not undiscriminating, however, in their attitude to the texts of the Annuals. Although they absorbed their Byronic mood and gothic overtones, they were often critical of the forced association between text and picture, occasioned by the poetry or prose being commissioned to accompany an already completed engraving. Thackeray would have approved of Charlotte's critiques of three of the engravings in *Friendship's Offering*, modelled on the art reviews she had read in the pages of *Blackwood's*.[19] In her discussion of the plate 'Castle Campbell', she directs the reader to its picturesque conventions and draws attention to the importance of perspective. Her own copies, such as 'Bessy Bell and Mary Gray' (**39**, colour plate IX), indicate that the Annuals were one of the major factors influencing her preference for the picturesque in her later writing.[20] This was reinforced by the popular topographical works and drawing manuals that the children copied.

In *Shirley*, for example, Caroline Helstone and Shirley Keeldar describe their surroundings on Nunnely Common in terms which recall both Gilpin's theory of picturesque landscape, illustrated so assiduously in the pages of the Annuals, and Charlotte Brontë's own drawing of 'The Cross of Rivaulx' (**137**). Shirley points out 'a dell; a deep, hollow cup, lined with turf as green and short as the sod of this Common; the very oldest of the trees, gnarled mighty oaks, crowd about the brink of this dell: in the bottom lie the ruins of a nunnery'.[21] They agree to take their pencils and sketchbooks there, since Caroline knows 'groups of trees that ravish the eye with their perfect, picture-like effects: rude oak, delicate birch, glossy beech, clustered in contrast; and ash trees stately as Saul, standing isolated, and superannuated wood-giants clad in bright shrouds of ivy'. Anne Brontë's love of picturesque trees is evident here (see **337**, **338** and **367**), and lends further support to the theory that Caroline is, in part, a portrait of Anne.

Apart from the illustrated Annuals, the books the Brontës were most familiar with and which echo throughout their writing were also those most likely to be illustrated in the early nineteenth century: the works of popular romantic poets such as Scott, Burns, Byron, Campbell and Moore; and editions of Shakespeare, Milton and Bunyan. Some texts had specially designed engravings, but in most cases they appeared in soft covers with only a frontispiece, and the illustrations were sold separately with directions for where to place them when the owner bound the edition, usually in leather. This is why it is impossible to say conclusively which edition of Byron the Brontës owned. No single edition of his works before 1839[22] contained all six of the plates they copied, nor were they to be found in Thomas Moore's *Letters and Journals of Lord Byron*; yet we know that Patrick Brontë owned Byron's works well before this. Besides, Charlotte's copies of 'Santa Maura' (**96**), 'Geneva' (**125**), and 'Countess of Jersey' (which she renamed 'English Lady', **128**), are all clearly dated 1833–4. It is most likely that the Brontës never owned an illustrated edition of

Byron, but that they either bought or had access (at school at Roe Head or elsewhere) to a series of engravings advertised as a *Byron Gallery*, 'embellishments to illustrate the poetical works of Lord Byron . . . adapted by their size and excellence to bind up with and embellish every edition'.[23] It was also possible to hire these engravings separately from art-dealers or libraries. Sometimes plates would remain in albums separate from the text they were intended to illustrate, since they came 'in a new and elegant binding, forming a splendid ornament for the Drawing-Room table'.

Engravings illustrating the poetry and life of Byron were the greatest single influence on the subject and style of the Brontës' drawings, and this was reinforced by the Annuals with their fashionable beauties and sublime landscapes. The many sketches of Byronic-style heads (see **97** for example), and Byron's obvious influence in their poetry and prose during the years 1833 to 1835, show clearly that the Brontës' reading was concentrated on Byron at this time. Claire Clairmont's pursuit of Byron echoes and re-echoes throughout the juvenilia. Both Charlotte and Branwell quote Byron on numerous occasions, as epigraphs to their stories and in the speech of their central characters, who – almost invariably – have Byronic originals. A number of Gondal poems show a close resemblance to Byron's early poetry. The names of Emily's heroine Augusta and her lover Lord of Elbë have Byronic associations (Augusta was Byron's half-sister and 'Albë' was Shelley's name for Byron). His influence was profound and its sway over the later Brontë novels is well documented.

'A Peep Into A Picture Book', written by Charlotte in June 1834,[24] suggests that she has at least seen one of the sumptuous editions of *Finden's Royal Gallery of British Art* or *Finden's Byron Beauties*, possibly at the home of Mary Taylor or another of her school-friends. The narrator, Lord Charles Wellesley, browses through three large volumes of picture books, with 'green watered-silk quarto covers and gilt backs', describing their contents. He says: 'The second volume is nearest to my hand, and I will raise first from the shadow of gossamer paper, waving as I turn it like a web of woven air, the spirit whosoever it be, male or female, crowned or coronetted, that animates its frontispiece.'

The book is 'Tree's Portrait Gallery of the Aristocracy of Africa', engraved by Edward Finden from paintings by Frederick De Lisle, the Reynolds of Glass Town. Lord Charles's response is ecstatic as he 'reads' the faces of these 'pictured representations': 'Reader, before me I behold the earthly tabernacle of Northangerland's unsounded soul! There he stands! What a vessel to be moulded from the coarse clay of mortality! What a plant to spring from the rank soil of human existence! . . . I have looked at you till words seem to issue from your lips.' One imagines that the Brontës' own early response to engravings of Byron's works had something of this excitement and awe.

Edward and William Finden's engravings of scenes in Byron's poetry and of his travels – the Greek isles ('Santa Maura' **96**), the Swiss and Italian landscape ('Geneva' **125**, and 'Bridge of Egripo' **123**) – are reproduced by Charlotte in pencil and paint, and translated into her early writings. Branwell's re-creations are more imaginative. 'The pirate', in both his illustration (**241**, and plate LXII) and his juvenile story of the same name, is in imitation of Byron's *Lara* and *The Corsair*. His portraits of Zamorna (**239**, and plate LXI) and Alexander Percy, Duke of Northangerland (**298**), are two versions of the Byronic hero, the proud, defiant womanizer of *Childe Harold* and the unredeemed Faustian figure of *Cain*. Both images obsessed Charlotte and Branwell as they wove the intricate relationships of their Angrian heroes.

Illustrations of the women related to Byron become Angrian heroines. A miniature portrait of Lady Blessington, copied in pencil by Charlotte in October 1833, is renamed by her 'Zenobia Marchioness Ellrington' (**100**, and plate XXXVII), who (like Lady Blessington) is an accomplished author, known not only for her scholarship but for her relationship with two men. A youthful image of Arthur Wellesley, the historical Duke of Wellington, becomes 'Arthur Adrian Marquis of Douro' (**101**, and plate XXXVIII) in the hands of the young artist. And, most intriguing of all, a picture of Byron himself is copied by Charlotte and renamed 'Alexander Soult' (**102**, and plate 2), a Glass Town poet (and early pseudonym for Branwell) who later appropriates Byron's aristocratic heritage and exotic associations as Marquis of Marseilles, Duke of Dalmatia, confidant of the King and Angrian Ambassador to Verdopolis.

Plate 2 'Alexander Soult' (**102**), pencil drawing of Byron by Charlotte Brontë after the engraving 'Childe Harold and Ianthe,' in *The Literary Souvenir*, 1830

Plate 3 'Childe Harold and Ianthe', engraving by E. Portbury, from a drawing by R. Westall, for *The Literary Souvenir*, 1830

This tiny half-length portrait of a fine-featured young man resembles several well-known studies of Byron, such as the miniature by James Holmes reproduced in *The Connoisseur*, 1911, the engraving of a drawing by George Henry Harlow that was widely reproduced, or even Richard Westall's famous painting of Byron in the National Portrait Gallery. The most likely original for Charlotte's copy, however, is an engraving by E. Portbury, based on a drawing by Westall entitled 'Childe Harold and Ianthe' (see plate 3). This appeared in *The Literary Souvenir* for 1830, one of the Annuals which the Brontës probably owned since they copied two other plates from this source (**110** and **235**).

It is interesting, too, to compare the face of Ianthe in this engraving with Charlotte's many portraits of delicate-featured young women, such as 'Young woman with "Fairy Legend"' (**103**) and 'Portrait of a young woman' (**107**). 'Ianthe' also appealed to Emily, who made her own copy from William Finden's engraving of Westall's 'Ianthe', published as the frontispiece to the second volume of Moore's *Letters and Journals of Lord Byron: With Notices of His Life* (commonly known as his *Life of Byron*), and in later editions of Byron's poems. Emily's version (**325**, plate 14), which she apparently named 'The North Wind', has all the features of the first Catherine in *Wuthering Heights*, though it could equally well have suggested one of the heroines of the Gondal saga. The poem 'To Ianthe' formed the dedication to Byron's *Childe Harold*. It was addressed to Lady Charlotte Mary Harley, who was only eleven years old at the time. Shelley, too, evoked Ianthe: in his poem 'Queen Mab', she is the maiden to whom the fairy grants a vision of the world. The young Brontës might well have seen themselves as Ianthe, since for many years Byron's *Childe Harold* was their vision of the world. In the Brontë Parsonage Museum, we can still see Branwell's well-used, cheap, pirated pocket-version of the poem that accompanied him continually, if not in reality then always in spirit. It took Charlotte a long struggle to dispel the enchantment of Byron; Branwell's last vivid pen-and-ink sketches show that the image of the unredeemed wanderer haunted him until his death.

The other two great visual influences on the Brontës were the works of John Martin and Thomas Bewick. Unlike the Finden engravings, however, Martin's grandiose productions had relatively little influence on their drawing; and their copies of Bewick's engravings are confined to their earliest lessons in art. This is perhaps surprising, given the powerful influence these two artists had on the Brontë juvenilia and the later novels. Only the twelve-year-old Branwell chose to reproduce Martin's extravagant style in his painting of Finden's engraving of 'Queen Esther' (**207**, and colour plate XII), from the *Forget Me Not* Annual of 1831. His success is impressive for one so young, not least in his imaginative attempt to reintroduce his own idea of the gaudy colours of the original which he read about in a review in *Fraser's Magazine* for July of the same year, written while the painting was being exhibited in the Suffolk Street Galleries.

One would have expected Brontë copies of Martin's many mezzotint plates for *Paradise Lost*, which appeared in 1827, or of his widely publicized *Illustrations Of The Bible* (1831–5), two engravings of which were framed by Patrick Brontë. We have always known about three large mezzotints by Martin on the walls of the parsonage,[25] but the newspaper Bill of Sale on the death of Patrick Brontë announces further framed engravings belonging to the Brontës, one of which was most certainly Martin's print of 'St Paul Preaching at Athens' and another was probably a pirated version of Martin's 'Passage of the Red Sea'.[26] We should not forget that many Brontë drawings have been lost over the years, and our judgements on their art must necessarily be based on the surviving works as representative of their output. We know from 'Queen Esther' and from Branwell's painting of 'Jacob's dream' (**235**, and plate LIX) that he was interested in copying Biblical scenes. It is unlikely that he would not also have attempted to copy these five Martin engravings so readily at hand on the walls of the parsonage.

Martin's early landscapes were also available in the pages of the Annuals and we know that the Brontës saw and translated into their descriptions of the Glass Town landscape not only his vast apocalyptic designs but also his images of the Garden of Eden. The monumental architecture, the River Niger flowing into the great bay, the fertile valley, hanging groves and gardens, cornfields, 'mountains whose azure tint almost melted into the serene horizon' and the 'mellowing veil of mist'[27] are recreated throughout the Brontës' early writings. So close was Charlotte's description to Martin's hand-coloured lithograph of 'The Temptation' (plate 4), frontispiece to *The Sacred Annual* (another of whose plates she copied),[28] that for many years Martin's plate has been mistakenly published as her painting of the Bay of Glass Town. It is part of the Bonnell Collection in the Brontë Parsonage, most of which was originally owned by Charlotte's widower, the Reverend Arthur Bell Nicholls,[29] suggesting that this version of Martin's 'The Temptation', and certainly 'The Atheist viewing the dead body of his Wife' (see **136**), had been owned by the Brontës. *The Sacred Annual* itself is a luxury volume, bound in embossed purple velvet with gilt edges and a metal clasp, not the kind of item one would expect in the Brontë

Plate 4 John Martin, 'The Temptation', hand-coloured lithograph from *The Sacred Annual*, by Robert Montgomery, 1834

Parsonage and an extremely rare book today (only four copies are known to be in existence).

The two volumes of Bewick's 1816 edition of *A History of British Birds* are not so scarce and can be examined in most library collections of rare books. This was the version that provided the first copybook for all four of the Brontë children. From 1828 until 1833, Charlotte, Branwell, Emily and Anne made six copies of Bewick's miniature wood engravings from volume 1, *Containing the History and Description of Land Birds*; and again the four Brontës made five more copies from volume 2, *of Water Birds*.[30] Several other drawings exist, of ruins, castles and animals, that also indicate the influence of Bewick during these formative years. On the fly-leaf of another of his natural history books, *The Gardens and Menagerie of the Zoological Society Delineated*, purchased in 1831, Patrick Brontë proclaims: 'The wooden cuts, in this Book, are excellent – Being done by the first of living engravers, on Wood.'[31] Although Bewick's name is not mentioned on the title page, he is known to have assisted in many of the engravings in this volume, among them the 'Palm squirrel' (**74**), which Charlotte chose to copy. It was their father's interests, manifested in his books and opinions, that directed the imaginations of his children. Bewick's name seldom appears in the juvenilia. His black and white representations of birds and his whimsical vignettes of the realities of rural life are hardly the stuff of Byronic dreams; yet the often crude and sordid sketches of the Glass Town taverns must owe something to his realistic depiction of life. Branwell's later pen-and-ink drawings indicate the debt he owed to Bewick (see **281**), and the opening pages of *Jane Eyre* are surely the finest tribute ever made to Bewick's ability to seize the imagination. Even as early as 1832, Charlotte spoke of his 'enchanted page' with its 'pictured thoughts that breathe and speak and burn'.[32]

Bewick's line engravings are excellent exercises in outline and it is possible that some of these copies were set as lessons by the children's art teacher, John Bradley (plate 5). He was not a professional teacher (though he had exhibited in local exhibitions)[33] and would no doubt have been glad to find the book on the parsonage shelves, since he seems to have given the children art lessons as a favour to Patrick

Plate 5 John Bradley (1787–1844), founder-member of the Keighley Mechanics' Institute and art teacher to the young Brontës

Brontë, a fellow member of the Keighley Mechanics' Institute Library from where the Brontës borrowed their books each week.[34] Bradley (1784–1844) was one of the four founder–members of the Keighley Institute in 1825, its first secretary and elected vice-president in 1831, and later described as the architect of its new building.[35] Yet according to Baines's Directory of 1823, he was actually a house- and sign-painter, whose hobby was oil-painting. Little is known of Bradley's relationship with the Brontë family. He is said to be the painter of one of the few surviving portraits of Patrick Brontë[36] and may well have encouraged Branwell in his early use of oils and enthusiasm for architecture. An unauthenticated memorandum compiled in 1894 records that Charlotte, Emily and Branwell visited him in New Bridge Street, Keighley, to receive their lessons,[37] but Bradley probably visited the parsonage as well. On the back of Charlotte's watercolour copy of Bewick's 'The Mountain Sparrow' (**26**, and colour plate 1), executed on 11 March 1830, probably under Bradley's supervision, is the inscription: 'Thomas Bradley's Picture/ given to him by C. Brontë', followed by a scribbled note indicating an order for oil paints from a local art-dealer: '2 bladders White/ 2 Do Naples yellow/ R Inchbold/ Leeds'. Bradley had a son named John Thomas and this little painting, probably executed on paper provided by Bradley and bought by him with paints from Leeds, became a present for his son.[38] An early 'Study of a primula' (**34**), made by Charlotte about the same time, is recorded as having had a similar inscription. These inscriptions indicate just one of the many ways in which a study of the drawings adds to our biographical evidence on the Brontës, since apart from these notes, there is little to substantiate William Dearden's statement in the *Bradford Observer* (27 June 1861) that Bradley taught the Brontës art. The Brontës' early illustrations suggest that Bradley's lessons took place during 1829 and 1830. Charlotte had left for Roe Head by January 1831, and Bradley himself emigrated to the United States in 1831.[39]

Although so many of their illustrations were spontaneous responses to an attractive picture or the wish to preserve a likeness in paint, the Brontës' paintings and drawings clearly reflect the educational attitudes of those who taught them. The 1828 sketches of ruined towers and buildings by Charlotte and Branwell indicate the possibility of some early lessons by Thomas Plummer of Keighley in the copying of picturesque models.[40] Bradley seems to have continued the tradition of copying and introduced the use of a drawing manual and flower painting 'from nature' (see p. 40). The many later classical heads, flowers and landscapes of Charlotte and Anne reflect the conventional female art education they received at Roe Head (see pp. 42–4). Emily's paintings are distinguished by their absence of convention and the more liberal attitude towards art that she encountered at school in Brussels (see p. 115). For Branwell, the role model of William Robinson, successful local portrait painter and one-time student at the Royal Academy, was decisive in his choice of a career.

One must remember that until they went to London, the Brontës' experience of great art had been second-hand. Knowledge of 'the vigorous sternness of Michael Angelo, the grace and beauty of Raphael and the glorious colouring of Titian, together with the exquisite finish of Leonardo da Vinci, the living portraits of Vandyke and the sacred sublimity of Fra Bartolommeo'[41] had all been gleaned from books and engravings. The Brontës knew of the leading artists of the day – Lawrence, Turner, Landseer, Fuseli, Martin, Etty and others – but had

Plate 6 'A night-eruption of Vesuvius' by Olivio d'Anno, 1794: a painting seen by Charlotte Brontë at The Red House, Gomersal, the home of her friend Mary Taylor

never actually seen their works. Charlotte had been lucky enough to encounter some original paintings at The Red House, Gomersal, the home of her school-friend Mary Taylor, whose father (the model for Hiram Yorke in *Shirley*) was a cloth-manufacturer who, on his business travels to the Continent, collected paintings, art-albums and books. These made a lasting impression on the adolescent Charlotte, in particular 'A night-eruption of Vesuvius' (plate 6), by an eighteenth-century Italian painter, which still hangs in the Taylors' old home, and which she recalled in *Shirley*.[42] It has all the fiery colour and chiaroscuro she would have imagined in her own family's black and white engravings of Martin's cataclysmic landscapes.

It was their visit to the summer exhibition of the Royal Northern Society for the Encouragement of the Fine Arts in Leeds in 1834 and their subsequent introduction to William Robinson that gave them their first taste of professional painting. This was an annual event which the Brontës had known of since their first lessons with John Bradley, who had regularly exhibited during the 1820s; yet there is no evidence that they had attended the exhibition before this date. Exhibitions were a luxury and this was an important event. Names like Richard Westall, William Turner, William Mulready and Sir Thomas Lawrence had appeared in the catalogues of previous years. It must have been with some trepidation that Charlotte herself, in 1834, submitted two of her detailed pencil copies of engravings for exhibition, 'Bolton Abbey' (**116**) and 'Kirkstall Abbey' (**117**, and plate 9), famous views of two local landmarks. One can only imagine her pride and anticipation. The excitement for the Brontës of attending such an exhibition should not be underestimated, not only because Charlotte's drawings were exhibited amongst the works of professional artists, although this would have been cause enough for rejoicing. They saw landscapes by Copley Fielding, Alexander Nasmyth, John Linnel, Robert Macreth and others, in watercolour and oil; historical paintings by H. Fradelle; seascapes by Carmichael; animal paintings by Schwanfelder; portraits by William Bewick and William Robinson; and sculpture by Joseph Bentley Leyland.[43] Fired with enthusiasm, Branwell seems to have persuaded his father to engage the services of William Robinson, whose career was already associated with such illustrious names as Sir Thomas Lawrence and Henry Fuseli.[44]

Robinson seems to have given only a few lessons at the parsonage, possibly soon after the exhibition, at a cost of two guineas for each visit; but the following year it was arranged that Branwell should receive a 'course of lessons'[45] at Robinson's studio in Leeds. Francis Leyland tells how Branwell stayed at an inn in Briggate for this purpose but occasionally took his master's pictures home to Haworth to copy.[46] The lessons terminated in mid-September 1835, soon after Patrick Brontë wrote to thank Robinson for his 'great kindness towards my son'. Branwell's dreams of emulating Robinson, his aborted plans to enter the Royal Academy in London as a student, his early admission to Freemasonry because he intended 'going abroad . . . for the purpose of acquiring information or instruction',[47] and his experience as a professional portrait painter in Bradford provide the sequel to this story (see pp. 76–9). It appears, however, that Robinson had little influence on the art work of the Brontë women. There is no evidence to suggest that they attended any of his art lessons at Haworth, and Branwell's lessons in Leeds took place while Charlotte and Emily were at Roe Head.

They were well aware, however, of the content of those lessons and had for some time followed Branwell's enthusiasm for oil painting and his acquisition of canvases and mechanical devices with interest and some amusement. Charlotte's stories from 1834 onwards feature the Angrian artist 'Sir William Etty, R. A.', based on the successful Yorkshire painter of this name, whose works they knew from such books as *The Sacred Annual*.[48] The paraphernalia of the fictional Etty's studio owes much to Charlotte's experience of her brother's preparations for *her* chosen career:

> Numerous pictures, some in heavy gilt frames, others as yet unfinished, leant against the walls; several busts, plaster casts, etc., stood on stands or on the table amidst a miscellaneous heap of loose sketches, engravings, crayons, coulour boxes, gilt and morocco-bound tomes, etc., etc. In one corner a lay figure spread its arms abroad. In another stood a large camera lucida. The artist himself stood at his easel busily engaged on a large picture which, though yet incomplete, seemed from the freshness and vivid truth of its coulouring absolutely to start from the inanimate canvas on which it was pourtrayed.[49]

All the professional artists in the Brontë juvenilia are male and they seldom have a bad press, unlike the poetasters and squabbling writers of the early Glass Town. The only misfit is Patrick Benjamin Wiggins, a satirical portrait of Branwell with his wild enthusiasms for writing, music and art. Charlotte wrote that, as an apprentice artist, he 'wasn't satisfied with being a sign-painter at Howard'; he must become a painter to whom even Claude Lorrain must yield.[50] Branwell himself was keenly aware of his own personality and the distance between his ideal image of Byronic adventurer and romantic artist, and the diminutive, excitable and slightly absurd figure he presented to the world. Wiggins is found first in his manuscripts, as a 'colour-grinder' in the great Sir Edward de Lisle's studio: 'a Lad of perhaps 17 years of age . . . meagre freckled visage and large Roman nose thatched by a thick matt of red hair . . . spectacles . . . stammering . . .'.[51] It is interesting to compare this verbal self-portrait with his image in ink, executed about six years later (**267**, and plate 11).

The study of personality and art had much in common in the early nineteenth century. The Brontës shared their contemporaries' interest in the pseudo-sciences of physiognomy and phrenology, both based on the belief that certain features of the face and head (in phrenology the skull was of particular significance) reflect the moral disposition of the owner. The many studies of heads and parts of the face in fashionable drawing manuals often derived from the pages of Lavater's *Physiognomische Fragmente* illustrated by Fuseli and translated in numerous editions, with often as many as four hundred profiles.[52] Le Brun's studies of the passions – laughter, bodily pain, rapture, anger with scorn, despair – were special favourites, repeatedly used throughout the eighteenth and nineteenth centuries. They usually followed exercises in eyes, ears, noses, profiles and children's heads.[53] Branwell's 'Terror' (**202**, and colour plate x) and Charlotte's studies of 'Laughing child' (**53**) and 'Crying child' (**54**) are derived from this genre. The drawings of Anne and Charlotte, executed while they were at Roe Head, illustrate the correspondence between artistic training (in which one learns to observe a variety of facial features) and the 'reading' of character. John Varley, the noted watercolourist, who produced many painting manuals for the amateur artist, also wrote *A Treatise on Zodiacal Physiognomy; Illustrated by Engravings of Heads and Features*.[54] Others saw the similarity between animal heads and those of humans as indicating character traits, a belief that accompanied the Victorian passion for pets and the increase in illustrations of animals.

Beneath a sketch of a tiny figure (**17**), made as early as 1829, Charlotte has inscribed the name 'Baron de Cuvier', and we find his name frequently cited in the Brontës' copy of *The Gardens and Menagerie of the Zoological Society Delineated*.[55] Cuvier was a French zoologist who established the sciences of comparative anatomy and paleontology, and whose work was of interest to the phrenologists (see notes for **17**). Such references indicate just how early the Brontës became aware of contemporary debates in natural history and proto-psychology, and just how closely they were related to their interest in drawing. All Charlotte's heroines are distinguished by their ability to observe and to 'read' a face, and all are amateur painters; her own experience in art lies at the basis of this analysis of character. Anne's studies of heads also account for similar references in her novels, such as Arthur Huntingdon's amusing defence of his inattention in church because he had not been given 'a proper organ of veneration'.[56] Only two heads by Emily (**323**, **325**) survive to suggest a possible connection between her drawing and the numerous physiognomical portraits that punctuate the narration of Nelly Dean in *Wuthering Heights*.[57]

It is clear that the Brontës' practice of drawing and painting provided them with a language and experience that could be used in their writing. The conventions of the picturesque and the theories of physiognomy so evident in the engravings they copied were recalled long after the pencil and brush had been laid aside. But the legacy of their early practice in art – the hundreds of portraits, landscapes, flowers, animals, juvenile scribbles and comical sketches that are the subject of this book – is a fascinating documentary of early Victorian art education and a reminder of the commonplace material that is transmuted in the hands of literary genius.

# Notes

1 W. S. Gilbert, *Catalogue of Engravings* (London: Frost & Reed). The original edition of this catalogue has no date; the quotation appears throughout the many editions of the catalogue, even after it changes its name to *The 'Homelovers' Book of Etchings, Engravings and Colour Prints*, 23rd edn (Bristol and London: Frost & Reed, [1938]). Gilbert's talent as an illustrator is less known than his fame as a dramatist.

2 *The Brontës: Their Lives, Friendships and Correspondence*, ed. Thomas James Wise and John Alexander Symington, 4 vols. (Oxford: Basil Blackwell for the Shakespeare Head Press, 1932), vol. 1, p. 82.

3 Mrs Ellis, *The Daughters of England, Their Position In Society, Character and Responsibilities* (London: Fisher, 1845), p. 112.

4 *An Edition of the Early Writings of Charlotte Brontë*, ed. Christine Alexander, 2 vols. (Oxford: Basil Blackwell for the Shakespeare Head Press, 1987; 1991), vol. 2, part 1, p. 318.

5 Some time in 1836 or 1837, Charlotte Brontë told Robert Southey that she had formed the ambition 'to be for ever known' as a poetess (Margaret Smith, 'The Letters of Charlotte Brontë: some new insights into her life and writing', *Conference Papers*, The Brontë Society and The Gaskell Society Joint Conference, 1990, p. 63).

6 Quoted on p. 39. The quotation here is from Francis A. Leyland, *The Brontë Family With Special Reference to Patrick Branwell Brontë*, 2 vols. (London: Hurst & Blackett, 1886), vol. 1, pp. 124, 139.

7 E. C. Gaskell, *The Life of Charlotte Brontë*, 2 vols. (London: Smith, Elder & Co., 1857), vol. 1, p. 109.

8 Quoted in Elizabeth Wheeler Manwaring, *Italian Landscape in Eighteenth Century England* (London and New York: Oxford University Press, 1925), p. 86.

9 Gaskell, *The Life of Charlotte Brontë*, vol. 1, p. 91; the manuscript list of painters (without title page), dated 1829, is in the BPM: B80(13).

10 'Belshazzar's Feast', 1826 and 1832; 'Joshua Commanding the Sun to stand still', 1827; and 'The Deluge', 1828. For contemporary prices see Advertisements in the *Forget Me Not, a Christmas and New Year's Present* (London: R. Ackermann & Co., 1839).

11 Winifred Gérin, *Branwell Brontë: A Biography* (London: Hutchinson, 1961), p. 78.

12 *An Edition of the Early Writings of Charlotte Brontë*, ed. Alexander, vol. 1, p. 61.

13 Transcribed from the manuscript (BPM: No. 6); original spelling and punctuation preserved.

14 *Blackwood's Edinburgh Magazine*, November 1820, p. 225; and May 1821, p. 180.

15 Transcript of facsimile manuscript fragment (January 1836), *The Miscellaneous and Unpublished Writings of Charlotte and Patrick Branwell Brontë*, ed. Thomas James Wise and John Alexander Symington, 2 vols. (Oxford: Basil Blackwell for the Shakespeare Head Press, 1936–8), vol. 2, p. 119.

16 Quoted from the Advertisements in the final pages of the *Forget Me Not*, 1839.

17 'Caricatures and Lithography in Paris', *The Paris Sketch Book and Art Criticisms*, ed. George Saintsbury (London, New York and Toronto: Oxford University Press [1908]), p. 170.

18 See catalogue entries **35**, **38**, **39**, **40**, **41**, **102** (part only), **110**, **207**, **235** and **309**.

19 See Christine Alexander, 'Art and Artists in Charlotte Brontë's Juvenilia', *Brontë Society Transactions* (1991), vol. 20, part 4, pp. 186–9.

20 See Christine Alexander, '"That Kingdom of Gloom": Charlotte Brontë, the Annuals, and the Gothic', *Nineteenth-Century Literature*, vol. 47, no. 4, March 1993, 409–36.

21 Charlotte Brontë, *Shirley*, ed. Herbert Rosengarten and Margaret Smith (Oxford and New York: Clarendon Press, 1979), p. 238.

22 Lord George Gordan Byron, *The Poetical Works of Lord Byron*, 8 vols. (London: John Murray, 1839), has the six engravings copied by the Brontës.

23 Prospectus at the back of *Friendship's Offering, A Literary Album* (London: Lupton Relfe, 1844), announcing a *Byron Gallery* from Smith, Elder & Co., for 21 shillings.

24 *An Edition of the Early Writings of Charlotte Brontë*, ed. Alexander, vol. 2, part 2, pp. 84–96.

25 See n. 10 above.

26 Martin never made independent engravings of either of these paintings: Patrick Brontë's copy of 'St Paul Preaching at Athens' was probably a separate small plate from Richard Westall and John Martin's *Illustrations Of The New Testament* (London: Edward Churton, 1836); and his 'Passage of the Red Sea' was either from *Illustrations Of The Bible* (London: Edward Churton, 1835) or from a larger version of 'The Destruction of Pharaoh's Host' in Martin's *Illustrations Of The Bible* (London: published by John Martin, 1831–5), made by S. Lucas, undated and probably a piracy: see Thomas Balston, *John Martin 1789–1854: His Life and Works* (London: Duckworth, 1947), pp. 285–91. It is also possible that Patrick Brontë's copy of the latter was not by Martin at all, since G. H. Phillips's engraving of Francis Danby's 'The Passage of the Red Sea' was also widely available at the same time (see contemporary advertisements in the Annuals). I have been unable to identify a third engraving recorded in the Bill of Sale, namely 'The Resurrection announced to the Apostles'.

27 An *Edition of the Early Writings of Charlotte Brontë*, ed. Alexander, vol. 2, part 1, p. 51; see also Branwell's 'Letters from an Englishman', *The Miscellaneous and Unpublished Writings of Charlotte and Patrick Branwell Brontë*, ed. Wise and Symington, vol. 1, p. 126–7.

28 A. B. Clayton's hand-coloured lithograph of 'The Atheist viewing the dead body of his Wife', from the fourth edition of Robert Montgomery's *The Sacred Annual: Being the Messiah, A Poem, In Six Books* (London: John Turrill, 1834), p. 40; a source first identified by Michael Campbell (*The Times*, 11 August 1984). Michael Campbell was also responsible for the correct identification of the Brontë Parsonage Museum's copy of 'The Temptation'.

29 Henry Houston Bonnell acquired most of his collection, subsequently bequeathed to the Brontë Parsonage Museum and the Pierpont Morgan Library, New York, at the 1907 Sotheby's sale of the effects of the Reverend Arthur Bell Nicholls, and at Sotheby's sale of the effects of Nicholls's second wife Mary Anne Nicholls, in 1914.

30 See following catalogue entries **14**, **24**, **26**, **181**, **192**, **218**, **306**, **307**, **308**, **333**, **334**.

31 [E. T. Bennet], *The Gardens and Menagerie of the Zoological Society Delineated* (London: John Sharpe, 1830); in BPM: bb69; see also Appendix A.

32 'Lines on the Celebrated Bewick', 27 November 1832; *The Poems of Charlotte Brontë: A New Text and Commentary*, ed. Victor A. Neufeldt (New York and London: Garland Publishing, Inc., 1985), p. 101.

33 Catalogues for *The Works Of British Artists, In The Gallery of The Royal Northern Society, for the Encouragement of the Fine Arts* indicate that John Bradley exhibited during the 1820s. In 1823, for example, he exhibited 'North East View of Bolton Abbey, Evening' and 'View of Kirby Malham Dale' and sold both works for three guineas each.

34 See Clifford Whone, 'Where the Brontës Borrowed Books', *Brontë Society Transactions* (1950), vol. 11, part 60, pp. 344–58. This list of the library's holdings shows a predominance of scientific, travel and philosophical books; but there were three volumes of 'Reynolds's (Sir Joshua) Works', 'Byron's Works, 6 vols.', 'Milton's Paradise Lost', and 'Shakespeare's Works, 10 vols.', all of which may have had engravings.

35 Ian Dewhirst, 'Almost forgotten artist whose self-portrait is seen by many people', *Keighley News*, 27 February 1965. See also a letter from William Dearden to the *Bradford Observer*, 27 June 1861.

36 John Lock and W. T. Dixon, *A Man of Sorrow: The Life, Letters and Times of the Rev. Patrick Brontë 1777–1861* (London: Thomas Nelson & Sons Ltd, 1965), p. 274. The painting referred to is in the BPM (Bonnell 64). The *Catalogue of the Bonnell Collection in the Brontë Parsonage Museum*, compiled by C. W. Hatfield (Haworth, 1932; rpt. London: Wm. Dawson & Sons Ltd, 1968), records that this attribution was originally made by Joseph Wright of Keighley, who said that Bradley painted cheap portraits before the days of photography (p. 23).

37 See Ian Dewhirst, 'Drawing Master to the Brontës', *Yorkshire Ridings Magazine*, June 1968, 26.

38 A Trade Directory of 1861 lists Thomas Wiseman Bradley as a painter of Keighley, under both trades and as an individual; this may be the same John Thomas, who like his father became a house- and sign-painter with more artistic ambitions.

39 Ian Dewhirst (see n. 37 above) records Bradley's sudden mysterious departure, the miserable experience of his family in Philadelphia, and his return to Keighley in 1833.

40 *The Bradford Observer*, 17 February 1894, claims that a Thomas Plummer of Keighley gave Branwell art lessons, but no further evidence of this has been found. However, Ian Dewhirst (former Keighley Reference Librarian) recalls, in a recent letter to the present author, that he once saw a written statement by a Keighley woman, who died at the age of ninety in the 1920s, to the effect that her mother had told her that she often used to see Branwell Brontë in Keighley when he came to visit an artist called Plummer. According to the 1851 Census, Thomas Plummer, a 'Portrait Painter' aged 40, lived in Chapel Lane, Keighley, with his widowed mother and two brothers. His father (also Thomas Plummer) had been master of the Keighley Free Grammar School from 1804 to 1840.

41 'The Swiss Artist', *An Edition of the Early Writings of Charlotte Brontë*, ed. Alexander, vol. 1, p. 116.

42 *Shirley*, p. 164. Although Charlotte may have had John Martin's 'Destruction of Herculaneum and Pompeii' (1822) in mind here, as the editors suggest (p. 759), the original is more likely to have been the Taylors' own painting by Olivio d'Anno, inscribed 'Eruzione del Vesuvio accaduta la notte de' 15 Giugno dell' anno 1794', which Joshua Taylor brought back from Italy in 1802.

43 Leyland, *The Brontë Family With Special Reference to Patrick Branwell Brontë*, vol. 1, p. 130.

44 See p. 74.

45 Patrick Brontë to William Robinson, letter of 7 September 1835, in *The Brontës: Their Lives, Friendships and Correspondence*, ed. Wise and Symington, vol. 1, p. 132.

46 Leyland, *The Brontë Family With Special Reference to Patrick Branwell Brontë*, vol. 1, p. 174. This is confirmed by Patrick Brontë's letter cited above.

47 Letter from John Brown and Joseph Redman (Lodge of the Three Graces, Haworth) to Robert Carr (Provincial Lodge of Free Masons, Wakefield), 11 February 1836. I am grateful to Juliet Barker for this new information which will appear in her forthcoming biography of the Brontë family.

48 A hand-coloured lithograph of William Etty's painting 'Christ appearing to Mary at the Tomb' appears as plate 11 in Robert Montgomery, *The Sacred Annual* (see note 28 above).

49 'A Leaf from an Unopened Volume', *An Edition of the Early Writings of Charlotte Brontë*, ed. Alexander, vol. 2, part 1, p. 327.

50 *An Edition of the Early Writings of Charlotte Brontë*, ed. Alexander, vol. 2, part 2, p. 250.

51 'The Wool Is Rising' (26 June 1834), transcribed from facsimile of original manuscript in *The Miscellaneous and Unpublished Writings of Charlotte and Patrick Branwell Brontë*, ed. Wise and Symington, vol. 1, p. 424.

52 Ian Jack, 'Physiognomy, Phrenology and Characterisation in the Novels of Charlotte Brontë', *Brontë Society Transactions* (1970), vol. 15, part 80, p. 381.

53 See, for example, [G. Smith], *The School of Art; or Most Compleat Drawing Book Extant: Consisting of an Extensive Series of well chosen Examples, selected from the Designs of those eminent masters Watteau, Boucher, Bouchardon, Le Brun, Eisen, etc. Etc.* (London: John Bowles; Robert Sayer; Carrington Bowles, 1765).

54 John Varley, *A Treatise on Zodiacal Physiognomy; Illustrated by Engravings of Heads and Features; And accompanied by Tables of the Time of Rising of the Twelve Signs of the Zodiac; and Containing also New and Astrological Explanations of some remarkable portions of Ancient Mythological History* (London: Published by the Author and sold by Longman & Co., 1828).

55 See Appendix A.

56 Anne Brontë, *The Tenant of Wildfell Hall*, ed. Herbert Rosengarten (Oxford: Clarendon Press, 1992), p. 206.

57 For example, Nelly Dean discovers promise in Hareton's face: 'Still, I thought I could detect in his physiognomy a mind owning better qualities than his father ever possessed'; Emily Brontë, *Wuthering Heights*, ed. Hilda Marsden and Ian Jack (Oxford: Clarendon Press, 1976), p. 241.

# Charlotte Brontë: the earnest amateur

*Christine Alexander*

Charlotte Brontë's publisher recognized her skill not only with her pen but also with her paint brush when, in 1848, he asked her to illustrate the second edition of *Jane Eyre* herself. She had, after all, exhibited two drawings in the summer exhibition of the Royal Northern Society for the Encouragement of the Fine Arts in Leeds, in 1834,[1] and her novel and letters would have indicated to her publishers her knowledge and discernment in the visual arts. Her reply to W. S. Williams, the reader at Smith, Elder & Co., was modest but it also indicates that she was aware of the conventional nature of her artistic education:

> It is not enough to have the artist's eye, one must also have the artist's hand to turn the first gift to practical account. I have, in my day, wasted a certain quantity of Bristol board and drawing-paper, crayons and cakes of colour, but when I examine the contents of my portfolio now, it seems as if during the years it has been lying closed some fairy has changed what I once thought sterling coin into dry leaves, and I feel much inclined to consign the whole collection of drawings to the fire.[2]

Charlotte Brontë's verdict is not that of social art historians, literary experts or Brontë lovers today. It is fortunate for us that she did *not* consign her 'whole collection of drawings to the fire', for they have a value irrespective of their artistic merit. Their importance – as is the case of all the Brontës' art works – lies not solely in their artistic merit, but in their position within the Brontë œuvre. They are artefacts that not only tell their own tale but modify our view of the Brontës and of early nineteenth-century amateur art in general.

It is not too strong to say that Charlotte Brontë had a fetish for pictures. Just as she 'picked up every scrap of information concerning painting, sculpture, poetry, music, etc., as if it were gold'[3] in order to improve her mind, so, too, she ferreted out pictures and copied every illustration that appealed to her in her bid to become an artist and escape the dreaded prospect of governess. 'So strong was this intention [to become a painter], that she could scarcely be convinced that it was not her true vocation', recorded Branwell's friend and biographer, Francis Leyland.[4] Only later in life did she realize that she lacked the skill she discerned in others. Until then, she applied herself to the task of acquiring an artistic training as best she could and with remarkable determination.

The earliest extant illustrations by Charlotte are the tiny watercolours found in the first Brontë manuscript: a hand-sewn booklet measuring only 36 × 56 mm, in which Charlotte has written a story for her youngest sister Anne, beginning 'There was once a little girl and her name was Ane.'[5] The six little paintings, each no bigger than a postage stamp, illustrate this typical bedtime tale centred on its first reader. Like all the Brontë juvenilia it is a fascinating amalgam of fantasy and fact, telling how little 'Ane', an only child but 'not too much indulged', was born in the village of Thornton of rich parents. They took her to visit a castle in London and cruise on a sailing ship, wishful thinking for the young motherless Brontës, marooned by distance and financial circumstances on the Yorkshire moors. Anne was probably suffering from asthma at the time, and brother and sisters had conspired to cheer her with their attention and gifts. Four juvenile copies of picturesque cottages and ruins (**9**, **10**, **184**, **188**, and plates XXXIV–XXXVI), executed by Charlotte and Branwell, also survive to tell of their concern for their sister.

These little pencil sketches and watercolour illustrations are significant in themselves as the first surviving records of Charlotte's art work. But there is a further value to all the Brontë illustrations. We can see in the following pages, for the first time, the chronological progression of the paintings and drawings. This allows us not only to date many paintings for the first time, but also to modify other biographical information. A comparison of these first little watercolours with Charlotte's works in subsequent years quickly shows us that they were made earlier than 1829. Her earliest manuscript has always been dated between 1824 and 1829; a more recent dating of 1828[6] can now be confirmed by a study of these little watercolours, together with the dated drawings 'For Anne' (September 1828), made when Charlotte was twelve years old. The little watercolours also tell us that Charlotte had access to paints by 1828; and her surviving paintbox (plate 8), still to be seen in the Brontë Parsonage Museum, supports an early dating.[7]

The drawings 'For Anne' tell us still more: we learn that from the beginning of their education, the children's notion of 'correct' art was one of copying. A third of Charlotte's surviving sketches, drawings and paintings are copies from contemporary engravings, and the earliest written record we have of her drawing is of her as copyist (see p. 10). When we consider the brilliant colours and sweep of line found in children's paintings today, the contrast with Charlotte's early works is dramatic. Despite a predilection for the educational philosophy of Wordsworth in the Brontë household and the enjoyment of nature, there was no such encouragement in creative artistic development. Apart from the first tiny watercolours already referred to and the rough sketches on the backs of finished works, there are no boldly imaginative drawings by Charlotte, despite a fertile imagination and a shortage of engravings to copy. And there are relatively few works 'from nature'. What imaginative flourishes there are, are found in the margins of manuscripts or on the pages of printed books. They are chiefly rough sketches of heads or animals (all recorded in the following pages); all are a far cry from Jane Eyre's portfolio of surreal images that arouse the interest of Mr Rochester.

Charlotte Brontë's letter to W. S. Williams makes it clear that by 1848 she was well aware of the limitations of her artistic talent and of the way she had practised painting. Jane Eyre's experience also documents Charlotte's gradual growth in perception. Jane's response to Bewick's pictures, her picturesque copies at Lowood school, her prescient images examined at Thornfield, and her final 'views from nature, taken in the Vale of Morton',[8] all chart Jane Eyre's state of mind at crucial stages of her life. Her early 'ideal drawings' are rejected by both her and Rochester, but the book does not deny the value of what she learnt in producing them. Her education, rigid and inadequate as it was, provided her with the resilience and ability to express herself in times of crisis and emotional starvation. This art education which was so restricting and which seemed so misguided, even to enlightened contemporary art theoreticians such as Sir Henry Cole,[9] was also Charlotte Brontë's experience of art.

In 1882, F. Edward Hulme, the author of *Art Instruction In England*, railed against the system of art education practised in Charlotte Brontë's day:

> Our fathers and mothers, but chiefly our mothers (for drawing was a mere accomplishment, and the boys were rarely troubled with anything so unpractical) had their weekly lessons in drawing, and very unsatisfactory these lessons were. The system is now almost exploded, but its reform was attended by great difficulties. . . . These difficulties are still to some degree felt, and the old system yet lingers in some ladies' schools. The system is simply this, the blind copying of drawings, often themselves faulty, but in any case as mechanical and senseless an operation as can well be imagined, and of as much value in the acquirement of real art power as the careful copying by one of these ladies of a page of Greek would advance her in the study of that language.[10]

Charlotte Brontë's drawings, so earnestly executed with a view to becoming a professional artist, document the shortcomings of the system described above. Her own criticism, predating the authorities by thirty years, is articulated in *Villette* by Lucy Snowe:

> I sat bent over my desk, drawing – that is, copying an elaborate line engraving, tediously working up my copy to the finish of the original, for that was my practical notion of art; and, strange to say, I took extreme pleasure in the labour, and could even produce curiously finical Chinese fac-similes of steel or mezzotint plates – things about as valuable as so many achievements in worsted-work, but I thought pretty well of them in those days.[11]

Hulme quotes an Inspector of Schools, who reported that 'Drawing from finished copies of heads in pencil, sepia, and watercolour is encouraged or allowed to the exclusion of the less attractive but more necessary subjects of geometrical drawing and perspective.' Only one geometrical drawing (**317**) survives from the hands of one of the Brontës, Emily, to suggest that they had a cursory introduction to the subject. More typical are the heads, flowers and landscapes in pencil, sepia and watercolour.

It is interesting to speculate on their early guidance in this direction. One drawing at least survives from this early period to prove that Charlotte was initiated into the conventional system of art education before she went to school at Roe Head. This is a watercolour wash entitled 'Dulwich' (**13**), a copy of a painting by Sutherland made in 1809 and included as a plate in many early nineteenth-century art manuals. It was clearly dated '1829' by Charlotte, yet it is a surprisingly mature work compared to her other drawings at this stage, suggesting that the work may have been 'touched up' by a teacher, a common practice at the time. This was probably the year in which John Bradley gave some lessons at the parsonage;[12] and the son of Patrick Brontë's tailor also recalled a Thomas Plummer of Keighley as the Brontë children's art teacher.[13]

Whether Charlotte copied 'Dulwich' under the guidance of a teacher or whether her father purchased a drawing manual featuring the engraving is debatable. Certainly the manuals, written by professional artists and teachers to supplement their income, were usually intended to be self-explanatory. There were basically two types of art manual, those with written text and those without. The latter were simply a series of plates, arranged in order of difficulty and designed to be copied progressively. 'Dulwich' belongs to the former type, manuals with commentary on the engravings included. The author of the commentary in *Ackermann's New Drawing Book of Light and Shadow, in Imitation of Indian Ink*, in which 'Dulwich' appears, for example, suggests that this work would be more successful in colour since 'the lights upon certain parts are too sudden'.[14] He continues with the recommendation that those who wish to improve themselves in 'the art of drawing in water colours' should 'observe with attention the works of the most approved masters, particularly those whose works are annually exhibited by the two societies of artists, who paint in water colours. Their labours might be studied by the amateur, as the professors study nature.' The final comment here is significant: Charlotte's drawings show that she had little encouragement to work 'from life', which was usually the prerogative of the professional or the male amateur. When she did attempt to paint 'from life', as in her earliest flower paintings or portraiture, the effect is an obvious lack of understanding of the formal aspects of art (see for example **37**).

It was not unknown, however, for women to draw 'from nature'. Sketching in the countryside was a pastime recommended to many young women of the time. Mrs Loudon in *The Lady's Country Companion* strongly recommends it as 'a very delightful country amusement'.[15] There is evidence that Anne Brontë made several landscapes 'en plein air'. Charlotte and Emily also enjoyed this pursuit during their schooling in Brussels (**154**, **155**, **156**, **326**); but before she had accepted the prospect of governess, Charlotte was in earnest. Art education was not simply a delightful amusement; she intended to make it a career.

With this aim in mind, Charlotte Brontë set out for Roe Head on 17 January 1831. Roe Head (plate 7) was a small private school situated at Mirfield, near Dewsbury, twenty miles from Haworth, and run by Margaret Wooler and her three sisters. There were only about ten pupils at the school, chiefly the daughters of the new wealthy manufacturing families who figure so prominently in Charlotte's later novel *Shirley*. They had come, unlike the Brontës, to acquire the 'lady-like' accomplishments associated with their new status, literacy and the rudiments of language, history, geography, arithmetic, and, in particular, the 'extra' accomplishment arts of French, music and drawing. Ellen Nussey recalls how Charlotte stood apart from her fellow pupils by her serious attitude to life:

> She did not play or amuse herself when others did. When her companions were merry round the fire, or otherwise enjoying themselves during the twilight, which was always a precious time of relaxation, she would be kneeling close to the window busy with her studies, and this would last so long that she was accused of seeing in the dark.[16]

Plate 7 'Roe Head', Mirfield; pencil drawing by the art teacher, Susan Carter, of the school attended by the Brontës

It was clear that Charlotte had had previous art instruction: 'She used to draw much better, and more quickly, than anything we had seen before', Mary Taylor told Elizabeth Gaskell;[17] yet comparison between Charlotte's Roe Head drawings and those of her contemporaries shows little evidence of superior talent.

At Roe Head, Charlotte received the 'old system' of art instruction that rigorously followed a series of prescribed steps. The generally accepted view was that a carefully graded series of copies should be made before a student was experienced enough to translate nature. This was the chief function of the drawing manuals, many of which are identical, with simply the same plates rearranged and reissued under different titles with different commentaries. The teacher might supplement the lessons in copying with her own collection of engravings or with illustrations she had made herself, as Westall did in his art lessons for the young Princess Victoria.[18] Charlotte Brontë's drawings at Roe Head can be read as if from the pages of a typical manual and they provide clear documentary evidence of the system of art education received by middle-class young women of the period.

Almost as soon as she arrived at the school, Charlotte was set to work copying pictures of eyes, ears, noses and mouths into a single drawing book, which has since been broken up.[19] Her first exercise was a study of the eye (**42**, and plate XLI), drawn from various angles ten times on the same page and dated 29 January 1831. The unfinished eye in the top left corner of the sheet clearly shows the way she was taught to draw, by the use of carefully measured squares to make sure the proportions were correct. This is the same exercise that can be found in such manuals as *Bowles's New Preceptor in Drawing*, 'Designed chiefly for young Beginners, and now published from the author's Originals, very necessary and useful for all Drawing, Boarding Schools, etc.' as the title page declares. By March Charlotte was already drawing the complete head, studies of women's and children's heads in various positions, occasionally altering them to resemble a schoolmate like Amelia Walker, the daughter of a local woollen manufacturer, Joseph Walker of Lascelles Hall, Huddersfield (see **51**). By June she had progressed to copying engravings of landscapes (**57**) and by December a detailed pencil copy of 'Annual Lavatera' (**61**), entitled in copperplate writing, indicates that although she was still working in pencil, Charlotte had also begun copying the popular engravings of flowers.

Prints were also available separately, to be bought or hired. Contemporary Annuals and magazines advertise long lists of 'Drawing Books and Rudiments' and 'Drawings Let Out to Copy'. In the *Forget Me Not* for 1839, for example, Ackermann & Co. advertise their 'Circulating Portfolios', which included drawings and prints of figures, landscapes, flowers and fruit, at varying rates of subscription. It is quite probable that at a small private school like Roe Head, the headmistress, Miss Wooler, would take out a yearly subscription for four guineas and then have the freedom to exchange the prints whenever necessary. She may even have owned a small stock of engravings herself. Certainly the girls all copied the same prints, since there are surviving copies of the same picture made by different pupils. Both Charlotte and Emily made a copy of 'Guwald Tower' at different times (**57**, **311**, and plate LVI); and a recently discovered album, originally belonging to a mysterious 'F. R.' (a pupil or teacher at Roe Head), has the same drawing of 'Ludlow Castle' as the one made by Charlotte at school (**64**).[20] When Charlotte left Roe Head in May 1832, she also 'signed' this album with a painstakingly detailed pencil drawing, neatly titled 'St Martin's Parsonage, Birmingham' (**77**).

The remaining pages of this album are filled with the productions of her fellow pupils, providing us with valuable new knowledge of the girls at Roe Head: a landscape of Caernarvon Castle, a watercolour copy of Raphael's 'Madonna della Sedia' and of a ruined church by Mary and Martha Taylor; decorative flowers by J. Brooke; a detailed illustration of a music book by A. M. Kitson; a primrose similar to one by Charlotte, a sketch of the St Gothard Pass and others that are tantalizingly signed only with initials. The pages of this album show that although none of Charlotte's watercolours of flowers is dated 1831–2, she was clearly able to use paints at school. At least five of her undated fruit and flower paintings were probably done at school in her second year, after she had mastered the basic requirements in pencil and wash. They also appear to be copied from the same unrealistic decorative arrangements of flowers as those of her school-friends.

It is interesting that although the majority of the artistic contributions in this album are in watercolour, Charlotte has chosen to use pencil to represent her new achievement in art. It is certainly the medium she found easiest to work with and in which she achieved her best results. Many years later when she made an accomplished portrait of William Weightman (**149**, and plate XLIX), she again chose pencil as her medium. Black lead pencils, paper and an India rubber are the three items that head the list in most drawing manuals of the period. 'It is necessary to be provided with a drawing board, a T square, Indian rubber, and good black lead pencils; such as are free from grittiness, may be easily cut to a point without breaking, and give clear markings, when drawn on the paper',[21] proclaims David Cox, the watercolourist, who published the same basic lessons in at least four manuals with different titles from 1811 to 1823.

The T-square was chiefly for lining up the frame of the picture with the edge of the paper or Bristol board (stiff card consisting of sheets of stout paper pressed together), which Charlotte often used. 'Black lead' or graphite pencils were not widely used until the late eighteenth century and only became really popular in the early 1800s when it was increasingly difficult to obtain good natural black chalks, the favoured drawing medium before this. There are no chalk drawings by any of the Brontës. To obtain a more solid effect, Charlotte was encouraged to use the 'drawing stick' known as Conté crayon, a relatively new medium invented (by Nicolas Jacques Conté) during the Napoleonic Wars when graphite was in short supply. This was a mixture of refined graphite and clay, which allowed for less graphite in pencils and varying degrees of hardness. The resulting versatility of Conté's invention increased the popularity of pencils, as the overwhelming number of pencil drawings by the Brontës attest. The varying grades of pencil can be clearly seen in the sketch of Roe Head by Susan Carter (plate 7), the visiting art mistress at the school and sister of the principal. Charlotte's drawing of the same scene (**62**) is less skilful in its range of tone, and Anne, who made the same drawing several years later (**339**), used 'black lead' almost exclusively. In January 1834, Charlotte made a large 'Portrait of a young lady' (**111**, and plate XXXIX) entirely in Conté crayon, which she came to prefer to ordinary pencil. But for her finely detailed copies of copper and steel engravings, such as 'Hartlepool Harbour' (**89**) and 'Cockermouth' (**90**, and plate XLVII), both taken from Allom's picturesque views of the northern counties of England, she continued to use black lead, as she did for her sensitive – but also tentative – portrait of her sister Anne (**91**).

In his drawing books, Cox consistently recommends a 'Series of Progressive lessons . . . in Pencil, Indian Ink, Sepia, and Colours'. The chronological arrangement of Charlotte's work at school shows that she followed this strict pattern, not even indulging in sepia (a pigment extracted from the ink bag of the cuttlefish) until she left school (**82**, dated October 1832). There are no examples of her use of indian ink; 'Dulwich', which appears to be in ink, is actually in watercolour, used in imitation of ink, as recommended in *Ackermann's New Drawing Book*. Although Charlotte had used watercolour before coming to school, she seems to have concentrated on following the correct system. She took seriously the view expressed in Alston's *Hints to Young Practitioners in the study of Landscape Painting. Illustrated by Ten Engravings, Intended to show the Different Stages of the Neutral Tint* (1804), that 'There can be nothing more preposterous than teachers giving their scholars high-finished coloured drawings to copy, before they are capable of drawing the simple outline.'

Charlotte seldom showed confidence in outline. There are very few sketches that show evidence of this basic training. The very early 'Boy and Dog' (**16**) and 'A Fancy Piece' (**19**), both made in May 1829, are typical of the plates in manuals for beginners, that encourage concentration on line only; but even these show a considerable amount of the light and dark shading that became so fashionable in early nineteenth-century amateur drawing. The popular aim was to achieve a 'pretty' effect as soon as possible. Hulme states: 'We have seen young pupils, girls of ten and eleven years of age, drawing heads at a private school, the original example and the copy each squared all over, and the work filled in much as a piece of Berlin woolwork would be.'[22] The problem of copying the outline was overcome by this simple method of transferring (with the use of the T-square, and scaling either up or down as necessary) the original to the blank sheet of paper. The character and tone of the piece is then expressed by adding light and shadow, produced by 'etching or hatching, washing, chiaro oscuro, painting, modelling, sculpture, etc.'.[23]

Charlotte Brontë's method can be clearly seen in a number of her unfinished illustrations. 'Unfinished portrait of a boy' (**151**) shows only the faint outline, with the first touches of the initial wash around the face which she intended to complete first. 'Alexander Percy' (**105**) is a watercolour portrait several stages on from this: the head has been completed and Charlotte was completing the torso when she abandoned the portrait. The pencil outline beneath the first wash of colour can be clearly seen on half of the coat and the remainder shows the careful building up of a solid dark blue. 'Study of flowers 3' (**72**), a rejected work, also shows the pencil outline through the first wash of watercolour, used as bodycolour. Charlotte's few painted landscapes are done chiefly in the transparent watercolour: see, for example,

'Lake and castle' (**94**, and colour plate XXVI), and her unfinished 'Landscape with bridge and cross' (**126**), although she may have intended to use an opaque bodycolour in the foreground of the latter. In 1834 Windsor & Newton introduced Chinese White (zinc oxide), which was marketed as a substitute bodycolour for lead white. Charlotte made good use of these white blocks of paint, which can still be found in her paintbox. The use of bodycolour reached its greatest popularity in England at the time she was painting. Watercolourists, such as Turner, exploited it to the full, by combining the opacity of the lights with the transparency of the washes of colour. Charlotte made skilful use of it chiefly in her portraits, such as 'Portrait of A French Brunette' (**93**, and colour plate XXI), where she uses it exclusively.

Generally, however, Charlotte Brontë's 'watercolours' are a combination of transparent pigments and opaque ones, as can be seen in 'The Disconsolate' (**40**, plate 1), with watercolour used exclusively for the background and trees, and bodycolour (often a mixture of watercolour with the white) used for the figure and archway which require more solidity and contrasting tones. In wash drawings, such as 'Landscape of tower and river' (**81**) and 'Kirkstall Abbey amongst trees' (**82**), Charlotte uses a combination of both bodycolour (applied to the surface) and scraping out (see **81**), to achieve heightening effects. Many of her paintings are completed with a wash of gum arabic, a natural secretion of the acacia tree, still used in the manufacture of watercolours to increase the adherence of the paint to paper. But in the Victorian period it became fashionable to apply a transparent film of gum over one's work, to add depth and richness of tone to the colour. We can clearly see Charlotte's imitation of this fashion in 'The Atheist viewing the dead body of his Wife' (**136**, and colour plate XIII) and 'Woman in leopard fur' (**147**, and colour plate XXV), which show the tell-tale superficial cracking of the gum.

A paintbox was a necessary possession for a young Victorian woman. Charlotte's husband, the Reverend Arthur Bell Nicholls, carefully preserved her paintbox, which unfolds a history of its own and gives us a glimpse into the manufacturing of art materials in the

Plate 8 Handcrafted 'lady-like accomplishments' produced by the Brontës, including Charlotte Brontë's painting of 'Stylized flowers and bird on silk' (**73**), a collar made from one of her designs, her needlecase (bottom centre) decorated with tiny pencil drawings (**75**), and her paint box

period. Plate 8 clearly shows its contents: twenty-three cakes of paint in varying states of wear, the porcelain mixing wells and palettes, tiny lead pencil, steel-nib pen and two hog-hair paint brushes, one made from a quill. Inside the paintbox lid at the top is the Artist Colourman's trade card: 'G. Blackman, Superfine Colour Preparer, London'. Below this is an endorsement of his expertise and status, namely a copy of a letter from the Society for the Encouragement of Arts Manufactures and Commerce (now the Royal Society of Arts), voting him their Great Silver Pallet Award for 'Improvement in Superfine Colours in Cakes'.[24]

The range of colours used by Charlotte is listed on the edge of the compartments and includes exotic names like Prussian Blue, Crome Yellow, Lake, Vermilion, Sap Green, Yellow Ochre and Van Brown. A colour chart of daubs of paint can be seen along the edge of 'Study of a primrose' (**33**; see colour plate XV), so providing us with a unique record of her experiments in combining colours and the effect of overlaying one colour on another. The unused cakes in her paintbox clearly show the embossed heraldic device of Prince of Wales feathers and a crown, the trademark of both George Blackman and his pupil John Newman. Charlotte would have replenished her supplies as needed from one of the art-dealers in Leeds or Bradford. Supplies of wove-paper and Bristol board she could purchase from the local stationer in Haworth and nearby Keighley. Much of the paper Charlotte used bears the watermark 'J WHATMAN' and the dates 1827 to 1833, indicating that she used the finest white paper of her day.[25]

Charlotte Brontë's most successful use of watercolour can be seen in her portraits, in 'The Maid of Saragoza' (**127**, and colour plate XXII), for example; in her two studies of Anne (**92**, and colour plate VIII; **119**); and in the five flower studies she made at the end of 1832 (**84–88**, and colour plates XVII–XIX), after she had left school and was free to concentrate on her drawing and writing. The flowers are highly stylized and have been taken from one of the numerous flower-painting guides available, such as Patrick Syme's *Practical Directions for Learning Flower Drawing* (1810), which was 'intended to illustrate the art of Drawing and painting Flowers, by progressive delineations, consisting of Eighteen Drawings, accurately copied from Nature'. Charlotte's earlier 'Wild Roses' (**28**) also bears the title 'From Nature'; but they are hardly natural. The spate of flower-painting manuals in the first quarter of the nineteenth century displayed nature methodized. They were aimed specifically at women, who were thought to have that 'fine and delicate feeling which some art critics believed flower-painting needed'.[26] In 1834, a Miss Young recommends such pursuits to her young friends 'to beguile the tediousness of a lingering indisposition', and some years later, Mary Russell Mitford calls it 'a most quiet, unpretending womanly employment'. A review in the *Literary Gazette*, 1842, on *The Sentiment of Flowers; or Language of Flora*, written by Robert Tyas and containing 170 coloured plates by James Andrews, pronounced that 'it is precisely the thing for a fair lady's boudoir'.[27] It is hard to judge how far Charlotte Brontë was aware at this stage that, rather than training herself for an artistic career, she was the victim of social mores. Although Helen Huntingdon, heroine of Anne Brontë's *The Tenant of Wildfell Hall*, supplements her income by her flower-painting, women had not yet dislodged men from their dominance of even this minor artistic niche. The many Victorian flower-painters and authors of flower-painting manuals were still chiefly male.

Several fan-shaped drawings (**58**, **59**, **95**) demonstrate the practical nature of some of Charlotte Brontë's art. The elaborate shapes of the cards on which they are drawn indicate that they were intended to be made into needle-cases as gifts for friends or family. A much-faded but completed needle-case made by Charlotte still survives (seen in plate 8). It is lined and bound with pink silk, and 'decorated' with two tiny pencil drawings of a bird's nest and bounding spaniel (**75**, **76**), resembling Anne Brontë's dog Flossy. The tiny watercolour vignette, 'Palm squirrel' (**74**), copied by Charlotte from an engraving in her father's 1831 edition of *The Gardens and Menagerie of the Zoological Society Delineated*,[28] is also sewn into a silk binding, ready to be made into another needle-case or decorative gift; and a 'Miniature of a lady' (**146**), said to be a likeness by Charlotte of her school-friend Ellen Nussey, has two needle-holes at the top of the head where it has been sewn into a small leather case containing a silver watch, chain and some needles. The skilful decoration of such objects was a requisite sign of the accomplished Victorian lady. The various items illustrated here indicate that Charlotte had overcome the slur of her early report at Cowan Bridge School, that she 'works neatly', but 'knows nothing' of accomplishments, which would have included drawing.[29]

Painting was seen as assisting in needlework, since a knowledge of composition and colour was considered necessary for embroidery. For the Brontës, sewing was as much a practical necessity as a lady-like pursuit, but a number of designs for embroidered cuffs and collars were found in Charlotte's desk after her death, as well as a pattern for a coin purse and several sample designs for wallpaper which may have been painted by her (see **164–173**). Such items suggest that there was some practical application for the art taught to girls at home and in schools at the time, although art as an accomplishment was the prime motivation. More typical was the popular pursuit of painting on velvet, a fashion Charlotte never indulged in, possibly because of the cost involved; but while she was staying with her other close friend, Mary Taylor, she did try her hand at the accomplishment art of painting on silk (see plate 8).[30]

Hannah More described the 'frenzy of accomplishments' amongst Charlotte Brontë's contemporaries in her *Strictures on the Modern System of Female Education*:

> the middle orders have caught the contagion, and it rages downward with increasing violence, from the elegantly dressed but slenderly portioned curate's daughter, to the equally fashionable daughter of the little tradesman, and of the more opulent but not more judicious farmer. And is it not obvious, that as far as this epidemical mania has spread, this very valuable part of society is declining in usefulness, as it rises in its unlucky pretensions to elegance?[31]

There is no doubt that the art manuals pandered to this fashion, which included 'the use of the pencil, [and] the performance of exquisite but unnecessary works'. In the preface to *The Artist Or, Young Ladies' Instructor in Ornamental Painting, Drawing, etc.*, B. F. Gandee writes: 'The object of this Work is to furnish young persons with varied and innocent amusement, and to aid them in the useful employment of hours not devoted to more important occupations',[32] a view that would have offended the conscientious Charlotte Brontë, who saw drawing as a means to an end. Gandee's lessons consist of 'Grecian and Japan painting, oriental tinting' (with flower illustrations very like those of Charlotte), mezzotinting, transferring, inlaying and 'manufacturing Ornamented articles for Fancy Fairs'. This is just the sort of drawing manual that would have appealed to the fashionable Miss Rattle in Hannah More's novel, *Coelebs In Search of a Wife*. Every winter she was taken to London and taught 'to paint flowers and shells, and to draw ruins and buildings, and to take views',[33] as well as varnishing, gilding, japanning, modelling, etching and engraving in mezzotinto and aquatinta. Like Miss Murray in Anne Brontë's *Agnes Grey*, Miss Rattle was only interested in 'such drawing as might produce the greatest show with the smallest labour',[34] and expected her teacher to finish the composition.

Only gradually did Charlotte realize that the system of art education she was taught was directed more towards fitting middle-class girls for society and prospective husbands, than towards acquiring the skills necessary for entering a profession in art. It was adequate for the needs of a governess, but she had hoped for more than this for herself. On her return from Roe Head in May 1832, she put her newly acquired skills into practice, with a view to becoming a professional artist. All evidence points to the fact that this was the period in which her hopes

Plate 9 'Kirkstall Abbey' (**117**), pencil drawing by Charlotte Brontë, exhibited at the summer exhibition of the Royal Northern Society for the Encouragement of the Fine Arts, Leeds, 1834

of earning a living by painting were seriously considered. It seems likely that she thought of becoming a miniaturist, painting tiny portraits, scenes and flowers for ornamental use. Her extreme short-sightedness and her concentration on pencil and watercolour portraits during this period certainly suggest this possibility. Above all, her submission of work to the Leeds exhibition in 1834 confirms her artistic ambitions. Her two drawings, 'Bolton Abbey' (**116**) and 'Kirkstall Abbey' (**117**, plate 9), were entered as items 430 and 437 (both marked for sale) amongst 464 sculptures, paintings and drawings exhibited. To see her name in *A Catalogue of The Works Of British Artists, In The Gallery of The Royal Northern Society, for the Encouragement of the Fine Arts*, only eight items down from that of William Turner, whose works she had copied,[35] must have provided the elation and encouragement to persevere with her painstaking apprenticeship. It is clear from her juvenilia and from the family's plans for Branwell that she was well aware of the training required for a professional artist, yet she never attempted painting in oils. Nor was there any possibility that Patrick Brontë could afford to pay for two children to have private art lessons, enter the Academy schools or be provided with a studio in Bradford. Charlotte had clearly resigned herself to drawing in miniature with pencil and watercolour.

In the three uninterrupted years at home from May 1832 to June 1835, she produced an extraordinary number of paintings and drawings. The number of works surviving from this period is especially impressive when one considers the household duties required of the females in the family (see for example the descriptions in Emily's diary papers, discussed on p. 103) and in particular the number of juvenile manuscripts, both poetry and prose, written by Charlotte during these years. Twenty-six prose works alone, including substantial novelettes such as 'High Life In Verdopolis' and 'The Spell', survive from the years 1833 and 1834.

For the first six months after her return, however, the sixteen-year-old Charlotte wrote very few stories. Much of her time was occupied in imparting her new knowledge to her sisters, a duty she readily acknowledged and performed with enthusiasm. On 21 July 1832, she wrote to Ellen Nussey describing her new regime:

> You ask me to give you a description of the manner in which I have passed every day since I left School: this is soon done, as an account of one day is an account of all. In the morning from nine o'clock till half-past twelve, I instruct my Sisters and draw, then we walk till dinner, after dinner I sew till tea time, and after tea I either read, write, do a little fancy work or draw, as I please. Thus in one delightful, though somewhat monotonous course my life is passed.[36]

She concentrated on fulfilling her usual New Year's resolution for self-improvement. She tried to initiate a regular French correspondence with Ellen Nussey and embarked on a reading programme that included, in particular, the works of Scott and Byron. To this period we can also ascribe the reading of books recommended by Charlotte for Ellen's perusal: the plays of Shakespeare; history by Hume and Rollin; the poetry of 'Milton, Shakespeare, Thomson, Goldsmith, Pope (if you will though I don't admire him) Scott, Byron, Campbell, Wordsworth and Southey'; biographies such as Boswell's *Life of Johnson*, Southey's *Life of Nelson*, Lockhart's *Life of Burns*, Moore's *Life of Byron*, and natural history by Bewick, Audubon, Goldsmith and White.[37] The sources for many of Charlotte's drawings can be found in the pages of these books (noted under the relevant entries in the following catalogue). She complained to Mary Taylor 'that her supply of books was very small in proportion to her wants'[38] at this time. Books with engravings might be borrowed from the Keighley Mechanics' Institute Library and engravings hired at a price, but Charlotte's chief source for illustration appears to have been the many Annuals now on the market. *Friendship's Offering*, *The Literary Souvenir*, and the *Forget Me Not*, in particular, provided models for her drawing and writing (see pp. 14–20). They joined forces with the works of Gilpin, Radcliffe, Scott, Wordsworth and Byron to provide her with a way of 'reading' the landscape, that was reinforced by contemporary theories of art discussed in the pages of *Blackwood's Edinburgh Magazine* and *Fraser's Magazine*.

Her analysis and copying of popular picturesque scenes and her familiarity with the conventional artistic attitudes of contemporary Annuals and periodicals taught her a particular way of representing reality that was translated into her writing. The 'classic scenery' surrounding Percy Hall in Charlotte's early novelette, 'High Life In Verdopolis', recalls the picturesque scenes she so often copied during these halcyon years at home: 'The picture of the splendid and venerable pile of buildings that constitute the hall, the slopes of sunny verdure that surround it, the noble trees, principally elms of the grandest dimensions, that cover those slopes with trembling gloom, interlaced by continual bursts of light'. All the paraphernalia of the picturesque is evoked here, with the elm trees casting 'their mighty morning shadows', 'their trunks and roots' surrounded by wild flowers, the 'many gables all grey and time honoured', the 'picturesque stacks of chimneys', 'an horizon of blue, misty hills and a nearer prospect of many groups of deer [that] completed the magnificent panorama now presented to my eyes'.[39]

Later in the same story, a set piece recalls her copies of 'The Italian Scene' (**41**), 'Conway Castle' (**65**), 'Derwentwater' (**83**), 'Santa Maura' (**96**) and 'Geneva' (**125**). This view of 'the distant prospect', described in the language and shape of a picturesque painting, can be found throughout her early writing:

> Warner was tempted to stop in order to reconnoitre the scenery by which he was surrounded. The low acclivity that formed his station sloped into a small hollow, a sequestered and solitary spot which formerly had been entirely shut from sight by the intervening boughs of a tall chestnut. It was now hewn down and its trunk, branches and withering leaves lay prostrate: a stately ruin on the hill they had once shadowed. The gleam of a little lake was visible at the bottom of the hollow, its tiny billows glittering in the moonlight and its banks overhung by a single tree whose boughs, strangely contorted by the wind, seemed as they waved and writhed above the water almost instinct with life. At its foot lay a broken seat, green with moss and weather stains. Beyond this glen and the hillocks that bounded it, a wide plain stretched, of that pastoral character which is so frequent in Wellington's Land. There was a proud castellated mansion, seemingly the seat of some dominant aristocrat, embosomed in its hereditary woods, parks and lawns. Fields, orchards, cottages and a small village, distinguishable in the extreme background by its many twinkling lights, filled up the picture. All was softened and obscured by the shower of silvery dimness which the union of mist and moonlight diffused over all visible objects.

The conventional art lessons at Roe Head were crucial in instilling in Charlotte Brontë a 'learnt' way of seeing and the many prints copied from books like Allom's *Picturesque Rambles in Westmorland, Cumberland, Durham and Northumberland* and *Finden's Illustrations of the Life and Works of Lord Byron* reinforced this tendency to see natural objects and surroundings in terms of pictures.

A comparison between the drawings and early writings reveals that, for Charlotte, the composition of word and visual image went hand in hand. Again, the engravings of the Findens were significant. Although in most cases Charlotte had already formed her initial conception of her heroines, her careful copies of Finden's plates of Byronic heroines allowed her to modify her literary pictures to conform more closely with the originals. Her exquisite copy of William Finden's 'Countess of Jersey', which Charlotte renamed 'English Lady' on 15 October 1834 (**128**; and front cover illustration), closely resembles her descriptions of her heroine Marian Hume, with her 'small delicate features', brilliantly clear eyes, 'beautiful nutty curls and frail-looking form'.[40] It is interesting to note that the description of Marian that is usually associated with the engraving, recording the long chain that hangs below her waist and the small crescent of pearls,[41] actually appears two years earlier than Charlotte's copy (August 1832), suggesting either that she saw and wrote about the engraving soon after it was published or that she chose to copy it because it confirmed her earlier image of Marian Hume. Charlotte's copy of Finden's 'The Maid of Saragoza' (**127**; see colour plate XXII), however, was probably made at the same time as her appearance as Zamorna's mistress in 'High Life In Verdopolis'. As in the original, she has 'a profusion of dark hair and a complexion of the richest brunette, which her dress of black satin with gold chain, cross and earings served well to set off'.[42] Charlotte, however, has modified both these images in her drawing, exchanging fashionable side ringlets for the ear-rings and adding features more reminiscent of the socialites in *Heath's Book of Beauty* than of Byron's Italian peasant girl.

This association between the pictorial image and the written text in the juvenilia is translated into Charlotte's mature writing in a variety of ways. Critics remark especially on her close observation of detail in character and scene, her sensitivity to colour revealed in description and imagery, her fondness for the vignette, her method of analysing a scene as if it were a painting, and her tendency to structure a novel as if it were a portfolio of paintings ('Three – nay four pictures line the four-walled cell where are stored for me the Records of the Past', says William Crimsworth as he embarks on an analysis of his life).[43] George Lewes praised *Jane Eyre* for its word-painting: 'The pictures stand out distinctly before you: they are pictures, and not mere bits of "fine writing". The writer is evidently painting by words a picture that she has in her mind, not "making up" from vague remembrances, and with the consecrated phrases of "poetical prose".'[44]

When she returned to Roe Head as a teacher in July 1835, Charlotte was forced to paint only in her imagination. The long hours of teaching and supervision, and the emotional strain of having to live at close quarters with others for so long (she had to sleep in a dormitory with the girls), left her exhausted and with little time for leisure. When her mind finally relaxed after twelve weary hours of duty, fragmentary pictures would flood into view. She records: 'The toil of the day, succeeded by this moment of divine leisure, had acted on me like opium and was coiling about me a disturbed but fascinating spell, such as I never felt before. What I imagined grew morbidly vivid. I remember I quite seemed to see, with my bodily eyes, a lady standing in the hall of a gentleman's house, as if waiting for someone.'[45] But she had no time to pursue such visions, let alone record them in pencil or paint.

She drew little during the school term. All her drawings during these teaching years are dated near or during the holidays; and they decrease in number. Two highly accomplished Roman heads (**131**, **132**, and plates XLIII and XLIV), one dated just before her first December vacation, and a large copy of Raphael's 'Madonna of the Fish' (**133**, and plate XLV) remind us that at Roe Head she was again exposed to the conventions of the drawing manual. It is probable that she herself gave lessons in drawing, reiterating the principles she had been taught. A small copy of an engraving, lovingly preserved by a former pupil, still survives in the Brontë Parsonage Museum (**139**), suggesting that 'Miss Brontë' replaced Susan Carter as the art mistress, among other duties. Not until she reached Brussels, where she went in February 1842 to improve her qualifications as a governess, did she participate in a more imaginative education in art. There is solid evidence that both she and Emily had lessons there in sketching 'after nature' (see p. 118). And when she returned to Brussels on her own in 1843, to continue her lessons and teach, in an effort to prolong her relationship with her beloved 'master', Constantin Heger, her ability to draw must have provided some consolation during a period of bitter frustration and loneliness (see **159** and **161**). In so many ways, the experiences at the Pensionnat Heger provided a turning point in her life, not least, it seems, in her attitude to her accomplishments in art.

There are few extant drawings by Charlotte after her return from Brussels (January 1844), only a couple of picturesque scenes (**162**, **163**) and possibly several sketches of cottages (see Dubious attributions, dated c. 30 April 1844), just as there are no more juvenile manuscripts after that date. Her early drawing and writing were part of the ideals and aspirations of childhood and adolescence. There were no such beautiful women in real life, no scenes constructed like Claude Lorrain's paintings unless one chose to see them this way. Despite her diligence, she realized that she had not acquired sufficient skill – and probably lacked the talent – to become a professional miniaturist. Charlotte would now turn to the business of life, to the task of becoming an author, determined to suppress all 'ornamented and redundant' composition.[46] In her first (though last published) novel, *The Professor*, William Crimsworth exclaims, 'Let the idealists – the dreamers about earthly angels and human flowers, just look here, while I open my portfolio and shew them a sketch or two, pencilled after nature.'[47] He produces real people, warts and all. The highly coloured beautiful Byronic heroines have gone, the delicately chiselled sketches of Angrian young men and the minute copies of picturesque engravings are a thing of the past. Crimsworth has no 'gentle virgin head, circled with a halo, some sweet personification of Innocence, clasping the dove of peace to her bosom' in his portfolio.

Charlotte recalls the illusory delight of her early artistic productions, when, in her misery at Lowood, Jane Eyre feasts on 'the spectacle of ideal drawings . . . freely pencilled houses and trees, picturesque rocks and ruins, Cuyp-like groups of cattle, sweet paintings of butterflies hovering over unblown roses, or birds picking at ripe cherries, of wrens' nests enclosing pearl-like eggs, wreathed about with young ivy sprays';[48] yet both she and Lucy Snowe learn to reject the social conceptions of the beautiful and the picturesque. Lucy, for example, dismisses a Rubenesque painting of Cleopatra as 'an enormous piece of claptrap'. 'It seemed to me that an original and good picture was just as scarce as an original and good book; nor did I, in the end, tremble to say to myself, standing before certain *chef d'œuvres* bearing great names, "These are not a whit like nature. Nature's daylight never had that colour; never was made so turbid, either by storm or cloud, as it is laid out there, under a sky of indigo: and that indigo is not ether; and those dark weeds plastered upon it are not trees".'[49]

Charlotte Brontë's rigid artistic training had left her with no skill in representing life 'from nature', let alone imagination. There was no place in accomplishment art for studies from the nude and, in any case, life classes were for men only;[50] the copying of heads, hands and feet was the closest most elementary manuals got to figure drawing. The following illustrations make it clear that Charlotte seldom made a sketch of an actual scene, though she did record the features of those dear to her, a desirable attainment for every young Victorian female.[51] Yet her heroes and heroines – William Crimsworth, Jane Eyre, Shirley Keeldar and Lucy Snowe – all demand that the painter should work 'after nature', that the novelist should 'cherish the plain truth', should look 'life in its iron face', or endeavour to bring the thoughts and feelings of the heart 'into the safe fold of common sense'.[52]

It was now clear to Charlotte that, like Jane Eyre, she was 'powerless to realize' this 'truth' in paint.[53] In a manner not admitted, though surely understood by Charlotte, 'some fairy' had changed what she 'once thought sterling coin', not into 'dry leaves' but into the text of her writing. The transformation involved in this creative process has only been hinted at in this essay; but the results are triumphantly proclaimed in the pages of her novels. Her drawings and paintings remain as evidence, limited and stereotyped as it is, of the training of her visual imagination.

# Notes

1 'Bolton Abbey' (**116**) and 'Kirkstall Abbey' (**117**): see pp. 25–6.

2 Charlotte Brontë (writing as 'C. Bell') to W. S. Williams, 11 March 1848: *The Brontës: Their Lives, Friendships and Correspondence*, ed. Thomas James Wise and John Alexander Symington, 4 vols. (Oxford: Basil Blackwell for the Shakespeare Head Press, 1932), vol. 2, p. 197.

3 *The Brontës: Their Lives, Friendships and Correspondence*, ed. Wise and Symington, vol. 1, p. 92.

4 Francis A. Leyland, *The Brontë Family With Special Reference to Patrick Branwell Brontë*, 2 vols. (London: Hurst & Blackett, 1886), vol. 1, p. 127.

5 See *An Edition of the Early Writings of Charlotte Brontë*, ed. Christine Alexander, 2 vols. (Oxford: Basil Blackwell for the Shakespeare Head Press, 1987; 1991), vol. 1, p. 3.

6 Christine Alexander, *The Early Writings of Charlotte Brontë* (Oxford: Basil Blackwell, 1983), pp. 258–9, n. 1. Branwell's earliest manuscript is dated a year earlier than this (see **174–179**) and one of his two drawings 'For Anne' (**188**) was made slightly later than those of Charlotte, but this does not alter the argument made, here and in *Early Writings*, for dating Charlotte's first manuscript in 1828.

7 Charlotte Brontë's paintbox was made by George Blackman, whose premises were in Oxford Street, London, from 1790 to 1814 (the last date Blackman's business is mentioned in trade directories). A paintbox in the Margaret Thomas Collection of Antique Watercolour Boxes (private collection, Highgate, London) suggests that he may still have been in practice at mid century: see *The Artists' Colourmen's Story*

(London: Windsor & Newton, 1984); although Margaret Thomas herself, an expert on early paintboxes, dates the Brontë paintbox about 1800. The colourcakes in the Brontë paintbox, frequently not part of the original equipment of boxes, are of varying makes and were added later. See p. 48.

8 *Jane Eyre*, ed. Jane Jack and Margaret Smith (London: Clarendon Press, 1969), p. 471.

9 Sir Henry Cole (1808–82), artist, editor and driving force of the London Exhibitions of 1851 and 1862, was virtually the founder of the Victoria and Albert Museum. In even his earliest publications, he stressed the importance of understanding nature rather than mechanical copying in art: 'The desire to aid increasing numbers, to enrich themselves with the powers of seeing and appreciating the beauties which nature displays to the eye, rather than of teaching the rules or practice of art, is the object of this little work', Introduction to *First Exercises for Children in Light, Shade, and Colour, with numerous illustrations. Being a supplement to 'Drawing for Young Children'* (London: Charles Knight & Co., 1840).

10 F. Edward Hulme, *Art Instruction In England* (London: Longmans, Green & Co., 1882), p. 3.

11 *Villette*, ed. Herbert Rosengarten and Margaret Smith (Oxford and New York: Clarendon Press, 1984), p. 577. As the editors point out (p. 745), the distinction here is slightly unclear, since mezzotint engravings may be produced on either steel or copper plates.

12 See p. 22–4.

13 See p. 34, n. 40.

14 *Ackermann's New Drawing Book of Light and Shadow, in Imitation of Indian Ink* (London: Printed For R. Ackermann, Repository of Arts, 1812), plate 12.

15 Mrs [Jane] Loudon, *The Lady's Country Companion, Or How to Enjoy A Country Life Rationally* (London: Longman, Brown, Green & Longmans, 1845), pp. 370–1.

16 Ellen Nussey, 'Reminiscences of Charlotte Brontë', *Scribner's Monthly* (New York: Scribner & Co.), May 1871, 20.

17 E. C. Gaskell, *The Life of Charlotte Brontë*, 2 vols. (London: Smith, Elder & Co., 1857), vol. 1, p. 109.

18 Marina Warner, *Queen Victoria's Sketchbook* (London: Macmillan, 1979), pp. 18–19.

19 A notice in the *Leeds Mercury*, 29 January 1886, describing the sale of Brontë relics belonging to Benjamin Binns of Saltaire (husband of the sister of Martha Brown, the Brontës' servant), records 'a drawing-book full of physiognomical studies in pencil, which was sold for 32s 6d'.

20 Album dated 'Dewsbury, Feb$^{y}$ 26$^{th}$ 1831'; owned by Jane Hickson (née Cazenove), who inherited it through her mother's family who were related to the Rev. Thomas Allbutt and his wife Marianne Wooler, who taught at her sister's school at Roe Head. I am especially grateful to Mrs Hickson for her kindness in lending the album for examination.

21 [David Cox], *A Series of Progressive Lessons Intended to Elucidate the Art of Painting in Water Colours* (London: T. Clay, 1811).

22 *Art Instruction in England*, p. 5.

23 *Bowles's Complete Drawing-Book, Containing an Extensive Collection of Examples, on a Great Variety of Subjects, For the Improvement of Youth, In the Pleasant and Useful Art of Drawing*, 9th edn (London: for the proprietors, Bowles & Carver, n.d.), p. 2.

24 This award was actually won in 1781 by William and Thomas Reeves for the invention of the moist paint-cake and George Blackman did not set up his own business until 1790 (see n. 7 above); but he was entitled to use the endorsement since he had previously been a partner of William Reeves, his father-in-law.

25 John Krill (*English Artists Paper Renaissance to Regency* (London: Trefoil, 1987), p. 104) records that by 1794, James Whatman II had sold his paper-making business to Hollingworth & Balston who continued to use his name and watermarks until 1806, when they broke up. The Hollingworth brothers kept the watermark 'J Whatman Turkey Mill', which appears on several of Charlotte Brontë's illustrations, and William Balston kept the watermark 'J Whatman', which can be found on a large number of Brontë drawings.

26 Anne Scott-James, Ray Desmond and Frances Wood, *The British Museum Book of Flowers* (London: British Museum Publications, 1989); the following two quotations are also from this source.

27 Cited in 'Notices to the First Edition', London: R. Tyas, 1842.

28 [Bennett, E. T.], *The Gardens and Menagerie of the Zoological Society Delineated* (London: John Sharpe, 1830), vol. 1: *Quadrupeds*, p. 50; purchased by Patrick Brontë in 1831 (BPM: bb69).

29 Cowan Bridge School records, in Ernest Raymond, *In the Steps of the Brontës* (London: Rich & Cowan, 1948); Charlotte left this school in 1825, aged nine years.

30 'A very fine piece of needlework by Charlotte of a pastoral scene', in which the faces of the figures are painted in watercolour, is frequently cited in catalogues and newspaper articles describing the collection of Alfred Gledhill of Keighley, subsequently sold to Robinson and Francis Brown, booksellers of Haworth and Keighley (see, for example, the *Bradford Observer*, 5 January 1889); it is most unlikely, however, that this was by one of the Brontës, as W. W. Yates points out in 'Some Relics of the Brontës', *The New Review*, no. 59 (April 1894), 485–6. Furthermore, Gledhill probably acquired this item from the Binns sale, Saltaire, 1886 (see Appendix B), where there were several items with no obvious Brontë connection listed in the catalogue under 'Art Needle-work' as 'rustic' scenes with shepherds and shepherdesses.

31 Originally published 1799; Hannah More, *Strictures on the Modern System of Female Education, with a View of the Principles and Conduct Prevalent Among Women of Rank and Fortune* (New York: Evert Duyckinck, 1813), p. 30.

32 B. F. Gandee, *The Artist Or, Young Ladies' Instructor in Ornamental Painting, Drawing, etc.* (London: Chapman & Hall, 1835), Preface.

33 Hannah More, *Coelebs In Search of a Wife* (London: T. Cadell & W. Davies, 1808), vol. 1, p. 333.

34 *Agnes Grey*, ed. Hilda Marsden and Robert Inglesfield (Oxford: Clarendon Press, 1988), p. 67.

35 *A Catalogue of The Works Of British Artists, In The Gallery of The Royal Northern Society, for the Encouragement of the Fine Arts*, 1834 (Leeds: printed by R. Perring, Intelligencer Office, Commercial Street, 1834), p. 24 (copy in the Leeds Public Library).

36 *The Brontës: Their Lives, Friendships and Correspondence*, ed. Wise and Symington, vol. 1, p. 103.

37 Ibid., p. 122.

38 E. C. Gaskell, *The Life of Charlotte Brontë*, 3rd edn, 'revised and corrected' (London: Smith, Elder & Co., 1857), vol. 1, p. 135.

39 'High Life In Verdopolis', *An Edition of the Early Writings of Charlotte Brontë*, ed. Alexander, vol. 2, part 2, p. 36.

40 'A Peep Into A Picture Book', ibid., p. 91.

41 'The Bridal', ibid., vol. 1, p. 339.

42 'High Life In Verdopolis', ibid., vol. 2, part 2, p. 53.

43 *The Professor*, ed. Margaret Smith and Herbert Rosengarten (Oxford and New York: Clarendon Press, 1987), p. 55.

44 From an unsigned review by George Lewes in *Fraser's Magazine* (December 1847), in *Charlotte Brontë: 'Jane Eyre' and 'Villette': a casebook*, ed. Miriam Allott (London and Basingstoke: Macmillan, 1973), p. 55.

45 'All this day I have been in a dream', *Jane Eyre*, ed. Richard J. Dunn, 2nd edn (New York: W. W. Norton & Co., 1987), p. 415.

46 Preface to *The Professor*, p. 3.

47 Ibid., p. 97.

48 *Jane Eyre*, p. 87.

49 *Villette*, p. 284.

50 No woman was allowed to draw from the nude at the Royal Academy's school until after 1893, when the partially draped figure was introduced into female life classes.

51 See Mrs Ellis, *The Daughters of England, Their Position In Society, Character and Responsibilities* (London: Fisher, 1845), p. 118.

52 *The Professor*, p. 97; Jane Eyre, p. 200.

53 *Jane Eyre*, p. 154.

# The art of Branwell Brontë

*Jane Sellars*

Charlotte's biographer Elizabeth Gaskell described Branwell Brontë's best-known painting (**225**, and colour plate XXIV) as a 'rough, common-looking' thing.[1] Charlotte pretended to her publisher that there were no known likenesses of her sisters[2] whilst all the time two family portraits by Branwell were closeted away in Haworth Parsonage. After the deaths of all the Brontës, Branwell's brother-in-law Arthur Bell Nicholls destroyed one of these works, except for the fragment showing Emily (**224**, and colour plate XXIII), hiding this and the other portrait on top of a wardrobe.[3] All the Brontë biographers since have more or less dismissed his paintings and drawings as the worthless daubs and scribbles of a hopeless drug addict and alcoholic whose main claim to fame is that he made the lives of his famous literary sisters even more miserable than they already were by his selfish and decadent behaviour. Charlotte tried to conceal the unhappiness of his last years, but died before the first unexpurgated edition of Elizabeth Gaskell's *Life* brought it all to light. The speculation about Branwell's affair with Mrs Robinson of Thorp Green Hall has tended to overshadow the rest of his history which in some parts remains obscure. Like 'dear, gentle Anne', the other 'minor' Brontë, Branwell has suffered from a form of biographical pigeon-holing which, glossing over the more active parts of his life, has produced a one-dimensional image – in his case, that of a wastrel. He has been assigned his role in the Brontë story, like a character in one of his own sisters' novels, and his not inconsiderable volume of art work has been largely ignored. No claims are made here for the re-evaluation of Branwell Brontë as a great artist, but he is certainly a neglected and interesting one whose work deserves considered scrutiny. This is repaid by some surprising new insights into the much-discussed history of the Brontës.

Great expectations gilded the early life of Patrick Branwell Brontë. As the only boy in a motherless family of girls he held a special place within the hearts and minds of all the members of the extraordinary Brontë family: a privileged status which, apparently, he progressively abused throughout his brief life of thirty-one years. Clearly, his intellectual father the Reverend Patrick Brontë at first expected the same of his son as he had of himself: a relentless pursuit of knowledge and self-improvement through education. Patrick Brontë had grasped every opportunity to steer himself away from his lowly Irish origins into Cambridge University and on to teaching and the Church, and in his view Branwell, as the son of a cleric, had a head start in life. But it seems that, from the beginning, both father and sisters believed that Branwell had not only intellectual ability but also a great artistic talent. Talent was, perhaps, to be Branwell's downfall. Certainly, he possessed it in both his writing and his drawing, but he was afflicted by an unfortunate arrogance and a consequent lack of application in learning the craft of art. These inherent weaknesses of character and temperament, combined with unsympathetic circumstances throughout his life, eventually caused him to fall prey to the infamous drug and alcohol addiction which led to his early death.

Visual art had a place in the lives of all the Brontës: for Charlotte (who would herself have liked an artistic career), the appreciation and practice of art provided a key to her richly descriptive writing; for Emily it was a more peripheral feature, a means of enjoying the natural world – through close study of her beloved pet animals, for example; and for pragmatic Anne the ability to draw was, perhaps, a prerequisite for employment as a governess. But for Branwell, art was his chosen profession. To what extent the Brontë family were aware of what the proper pursuit of this career might entail, and the reasons for Branwell's manifest lack of success, will emerge in this essay. But there is more to tell of the art of Branwell Brontë than a short, sorry tale of failure as a provincial portraitist. After all, he was the creator, at about the age of seventeen, of one of the best-known and most loved literary portraits in the world: the group of 'The Brontë sisters' (**225**) now in the National Portrait Gallery in London, and the executor of the delicate tones in the fragment portrait of Emily (**224**) – all that remains of the so-called 'Gun Group' portrait, also in the National Portrait Gallery. There is a substantial amount of surviving work by Branwell, and many of the numerous and less well-known drawings, watercolours and marginal sketches in manuscripts display an intriguing complexity which invites exploration and analysis.

Brontë biographers, according to a tradition established by Elizabeth Gaskell[4] – 'he was very clever, no doubt; perhaps, to begin with, the greatest genius in this rare family' – have, on the whole, continued to condemn Branwell as one whose decline was all the more reprehensible because he not only squandered his genius, but in doing so caused great pain to his noble sisters. As early as 1923 John Drinkwater, in his Introduction to Branwell's translation of *The Odes of Quintus Horatius Flaccus*, Book I, made some attempt to retrieve Brontë's poor reputation:

> Branwell made a mess of his life, and he was a cause of great suffering to three brave and devoted women. When drink and opium made an end . . . natural affection can but have been conscious of a deep anxiety gone. But, while bad remains bad, there are aspects of the badness in this case that have, perhaps, been overlooked by Branwell's detractors.[5]

But on the whole his artistic life has only recently emerged from the shadow of the great fame and accomplishment of Charlotte, Emily and Anne, to begin to be studied. Not until Tom Winnifrith produced his edition of *The Poems of Patrick Branwell Brontë* (1983) and Victor A. Neufeldt published *The Poems of Patrick Branwell Brontë: A New Text and Commentary* (1990) did we have a more accurate and, as far as possible, complete volume by which to judge Branwell's achievements as a poet.

The purpose here, therefore, is to provide as complete and as precise a critical study of the art of Branwell Brontë as the body of existing drawings and paintings will allow. It remains the prerogative of the reader to decide whether or not the artist's inglorious reputation is wholly deserved.

The earliest example of Branwell's art is to be found in one of his little books, his 'Battell Book' (see **174–179**) produced in March 1827. The previous June Patrick Brontë had brought home from Leeds the gift of wooden toy soldiers which was to spark off the Brontës' literary imaginations. Already avid readers of *Blackwood's Magazine*, the young Brontës christened the toy soldiers after contemporary heroes and had them act out the battles they had read about, and explore the countries they knew from the household copy of Goldsmith's *Grammar of General Geography* (see Appendix A). These imaginative exploits materialized into progressively more elaborate miniature facsimiles of books, magazines and newspapers, thus providing the children with a thorough literary apprenticeship.

In his 'History Of The Young Men' (1830) Branwell describes the soldiers' apparel in detail:

> It consisted of a high black cap with several hieroglyphical figures on it, the meaning of which is unknown, their coat or rather jacket was shaped after the manner of sailors and was in colour a light scarlet. They also wore light pantaloons of the same colour, but their shoes were the most curious part of their apparel. This shoe, for each man only had one! was like a round flat cake with two holes in the middle into which his feet were inserted as in stocks.[6]

The minute illustrations in his 'Battell Book' are based simultaneously on Branwell's close observation of the toy figures and his reading in the issue of *Blackwood's Magazine* for March 1827 of an account of the Battle of Washington. At less than ten years old he demonstrates the ability to combine both visual and literary information with decorative flair in his portrayal of the action of the battle.

Branwell was from a tender age capable of producing drawings from his imagination and of drawing from life. Indeed, the majority of his drawings and paintings in existence are original productions. On 23 September 1829, Charlotte noted that 'Branwell has taken two sketches from nature' whereas she, Emily and Anne were copying engravings.[7] This suggests that the Brontës may have had some early art lessons from Thomas Plummer, a Keighley artist.[8] Branwell's pencil drawing of 'A sleeping cat' (**180**), made in January 1828 when he was ten years old, exhibits highly competent powers of observation at work, in the rendering of the cat's languid pose, its stripy fur and somnolent expression. As we know from Emily's famous diary papers, household pets at Haworth Parsonage were doted on, and one can easily visualize the young boy lying prone on the stone-flagged kitchen floor to make his careful study of the sleeping cat.

This enviable ability to draw from life notwithstanding, Branwell shared with his sisters the delights of Thomas Bewick's illustrations in *A History of British Birds*, and in particular the quirky, sometimes gruesome, vignettes or 'tail-pieces' with which Bewick decorated his text. Three of Branwell's copies from Bewick are known: 'Farmyard scene with dog and chickens' (**181**), 'Rural scene with two figures, cottage and castle' (**192**) and 'Gos Hawk' (**218**, and colour plate II). His watercolour painting of the goshawk demonstrates Branwell's facility for translating the original black and white wood-engraved image into colour by means of careful reading of Bewick's written description of the bird:

> the bill blue, tipped with black; cere green; eyes yellow; a whitish line passes over each eye: the head and all the upper parts are of a deep brown; each side of the neck is irregularly marked with white: the breast and belly are white, with a number of wavy lines or bars of black; the tail long, of an ash colour, and crossed with four or five dusky bars; legs yellow; claws black; the wings are much shorter than the tail.[9]

The young artist meticulously follows every detail in making his paintings. Other comments in Bewick's entry on the bird may also have appealed to Branwell's romantic imagination; the graphic description of how the goshawk 'eagerly devours raw flesh' and his tales of how it was used by the Emperor of China on his sporting excursions, the custom of carrying a hawk being traditionally confined to men of high distinction and 'Even the ladies in those times were partakers of this gallant sport, and have been represented in sculpture with Hawks on their hands.'[10]

Branwell, the only Brontë to pursue a professional career as an artist, was the only one of the family to paint in oils. Otherwise he explored the possibilities of the limited media available to all of them. We can, of course, refer only to the works which are known to us, but it would appear that Branwell worked in pencil, pen and ink, ink wash, watercolour and oils. There is in the Brontë Parsonage Museum a group of four early watercolours by Branwell all of which were painted in 1830: 'Hermit' (**200**), 'Study' (**201**), 'Terror' (**202**) and 'Queen Esther', after John Martin (**207**; see colour plates X and XII). 'Queen Esther' is copied from a print in the *Forget Me Not* Annual for 1831. It is most likely that the other three prints, despite the inscribed claims that they are 'Original', were also copied from a similar source. 'Hermit', 'Study' and 'Terror' are all signed and dated by the artist to 30 April, 6 May and 11 May 1830 and were therefore executed within less than two weeks of each other.[11] They are clearly intended to be viewed as a group because each is inscribed in a similar way, with the title written in decorative capital letters with the word 'Original' below. 'Study' and 'Terror' share especially similar features: both have a single half-length male figure as the main subject and the composition is in portrait formula. The pictures could be read as allegories, representing the opposites of the peace of study and the disorder of war. As we have already established, Branwell had a great interest in both reading and writing about battles. His heroes are invariably military ones who command tremendous battle campaigns and survive through remarkable acts of daring or die heroic deaths. Indeed, one of the images Branwell most admired in his childhood was William Woollett's engraving of Benjamin West's painting of 1771, 'The Death of General Wolfe', a copy of which was said to hang in his bedroom at Haworth Parsonage.[12] Fighting armed figures populate the margins of his texts and are drawn freely on the backs of other drawings, both his own and his sisters'. Branwell even used the backs of a set of prints of De la Motte's *Characters of Trees* (1822), more soberly used by his sisters for the legitimate purpose of copying, to draw ambitious scenes of war (see Appendix A, plate 20).

'Hermit' is similar to 'Study' in that it depicts a figure engrossed in his books. The details in the painting, of the book and scroll and the red drapery of the cardinal's robes and hat, suggest that this picture is based on a representation of St Jerome. Jerome was one of the Four Doctors of the Western Church and is thought to have been the translator of the Vulgate. As a child he was a voracious reader of classical literature, which he renounced on his calling to Christianity, going to live as a hermit in the Holy Land where he spent long hours in devout study in order to serve the Church – surely a subject of special appeal to the young Brontës for its literary associations.

Branwell is extraordinary for his drawing in pen and ink, a medium in which he produced some of his most powerful work. Overall, his drawings display a confidence in his materials, a certain bravura, which is nowhere to be found in the careful studies of his sisters. It is likely that he drew in pen and ink because it was the instrument with which he wrote and therefore the one most often to hand. His ink drawings of his heroes, Alexander Percy in his role of 'The pirate' (**241**) and 'Zamorna. 35.' (**239**), have a strength and immediacy which come straight from his imagination, fired by his writings about their exciting exploits. The majority of Branwell's working manuscripts, and even some of his best copies, are peppered with tiny sketches of faces, figures, buildings, landscapes and fantastic-looking machinery, all described in detail in the following catalogue. Sometimes the drawings expand to take over all available space at the foot of the page. It would appear that his visual imagination worked hand in hand with his literary imaginings in an imperative manner that is quite different from Charlotte's detailed translation of the visual into the written word.

There is a spontaneity in these youthful ink drawings, a sense of the rapid search for the desired effect, seen in the furiously hatched and strongly drawn lines, that at an early stage seems to point to Branwell's unsuitability for the rigours of a professional art education. He was clearly an artist of the immediate response, temperamentally unsuited to the demands of the long classical training he would have had to undergo in order to become a successful professional artist in the mid-nineteenth century; had he lived just over one hundred years later Branwell would have flourished in a British art college of the 1960s, when the classical curriculum was abandoned in favour of the free expression of the individual. The fact that Branwell was never subjected to the disciplines of school must have contributed to his inability to conform to the conventions of employment in later life. It is not certain why Patrick Brontë did not send his son to school as well as his daughters, although there are a number of theories. The Rector was well able to tutor his son himself, and he did so, to a higher standard of education than most schools of the day. However, Patrick Brontë had to run his Parish, so Branwell was inevitably left to his own devices for a great deal of the time. It has also been suggested that the father kept his highly strung and possibly epileptic son at home in order to protect him from the rigours of the outside world.[13]

Whatever the reason for his lack of a school education, in his teens Branwell was able to enjoy an unusual amount of freedom. While Charlotte, armed with her Roe Head education, taught his sisters at home, he pursued his own interests, studied Greek and Latin with his father and continued to draw and paint. He would have had the liberty to wander at will around the neighbourhood, no doubt often taking his sketchpad with him. Two drawings of local buildings made in July 1833 when Branwell was sixteen years old (**219**, **220**) would testify to this. The drawing made on 1 July looks intriguingly like a view of the south elevation of Haworth Parsonage as it may have looked in the 1830s, with its isolated location, the lie of the land on which it stands, the one-storey outbuildings and the wicket fence. The parsonage, with its elegant Georgian design, is unusually tall compared with other houses in the area, as is the building in this drawing. The wicket fence appears in an early ambrotype of the parsonage[14] and also in what could be a childhood thumbnail sketch of the parsonage (**197**) by one of the Brontës which is among the drawings to be found on the verso of Charlotte's drawing of 'A Fancy Piece' (**19**). This is speculation, of course, but the family home would seem to be an obvious choice of subject for the young artist. The main building in the drawing of 21 July shows a typical moorland farmhouse, low in height and huddled into a protective hillside with a solitary skeletal tree looming over it.

It could be almost any farm in the immediate environs of Haworth. Indeed, it is not dissimilar to the now ruined Top Withens near Stanbury which is generally regarded as the site Emily Brontë had in her mind for the farmhouse of *Wuthering Heights.*

Another obvious choice for Branwell's artistic eye was his own family. There were surely other portraits in pencil and watercolour, but only one complete oil painting survives, 'The Brontë sisters' portrait in the National Portrait Gallery, London (**225**), as mentioned earlier, and a fragment image of Emily Brontë, also in the National Portrait Gallery (**224**). This came from a work commonly called the 'Gun Group' which is now known only from a recently discovered photograph of poor quality, the engraving of a drawing which was produced from this photograph as an illustration for J. Horsfall Turner's book (*Haworth – Past and Present: A History of Haworth, Stanbury and Oxenhope*, 1879), and a set of three tracings made of the figures of Charlotte, Emily and Anne by John Greenwood, the Haworth stationer, before the original painting was destroyed. Both of these portraits have a convoluted history and there has been much speculation as to why Branwell apparently erased his own image from 'The Brontë sisters' portrait, and in what circumstances the 'Gun Group' painting was destroyed.[15]

The date of 'The Brontë sisters' has been established to be c. 1834, according to the apparent ages of the girls as determined by Elizabeth Gaskell when she first saw the portrait. 'One day, Miss Brontë brought down a rough, common-looking oil-painting, done by her brother, of herself, – a little rather prim-looking girl of eighteen, – and the two other sisters, girls of 16 and 14, with cropped hair, and sad, dreamy-looking eyes.'[16] In June 1834 the momentous decision had been made that Branwell was to be a painter and Patrick Brontë had already engaged the services of the Leeds artist William Robinson as his son's teacher.

The Brontës first saw Robinson's work at the 1834 summer exhibition of the Royal Northern Society for the Encouragement of the Fine Arts in Leeds. Robinson had been a student at the Royal Academy of Arts in London and a pupil of the greatest English portrait painter of the early nineteenth century, Sir Thomas Lawrence. As Susan Foister has pointed out, Branwell enjoyed a direct link with Lawrence through the instruction of his master which left out the mundanity of provincial art and connected him to the traditions of high art with which the Brontës were already familiar through their reading of contemporary journals.[17] From Robinson, Branwell would have learnt the importance of good draughtsmanship, and the technique of making a pencil underdrawing directly onto his canvas when preparing a portrait, a practice which is clearly visible in 'The Brontë sisters'.

'The Brontë sisters' portrait has some remarkable qualities, but these qualities are not entirely attributable to the talents of the artist. What is sometimes forgotten in discussions of this portrait is that it is a painting of Branwell's immaturity. Indeed, it must have been one of his first attempts at a work in oils. Technically, it is a poor construction and in the composition of the subject Branwell presented himself with the spatial problem of creating a harmonious group of four large-scale figures within a vertical frame, an exercise which has taxed greater artists than he. The work's greatest qualities, its fragile beauty and haunting mystery, derive from its extraordinary subject, the three Brontë sisters themselves. Branwell's achievement is to convey so much of their individual characters in his painting of the faces. Each girl gazes in a different direction, Anne to the right beyond the viewer, displaying a rather engaging slight squint in her upraised eyes. Charlotte looks determinedly, and less dreamily than her sisters, into the middle-distance. Only the enigmatic Emily seems to look at the spectator, but with such an abstracted stare that we can feel her absorption in her own inner world. There are no domestic props in the picture to give us any further documentary information about the young women's lives so that we are tempted to regard them as a timeless, perhaps classical group such as the 'Three Graces'. The rarity of images of the Brontës adds to the significance of this work. What is more, the poor physical condition of the picture tells of its tortured history, scarred by the effects of over fifty years spent bundled up on top of a wardrobe in an Irish farmhouse before it was rediscovered by

Nicholls's widow and passed into the National Portrait Gallery's collection.[18] The work was certainly regarded with disdain by Charlotte Brontë and her husband, so it is extraordinary that it has survived at all.

The versos of a couple of the Brontë drawings in the Brontë Parsonage Museum reveal a number of pencil studies which may be related to this oil painting. On the verso of a strange drawing of a group of Fuseli-like figures huddled around the entrance to a cave (**222**) there are two pencil drawings of arrangements of groups of three and four figures as if Branwell were experimenting with the composition of the group. Also, beneath his pencil portrait of 'Grimshaw, H.' (**271**), not the legendary William Grimshaw (Patrick Brontë's predecessor in the curacy of Haworth) but probably one of his Halifax cronies, there is a faint line drawing of the head of Emily Brontë. The head is tilted at a slightly different angle from that in the oil but the facial features are clearly Emily's, as described in the group portrait.

The physical fragility of the portrait fragment bearing the image of Emily Brontë, together with its tortured history, its pleasant muted tones and the enigmatic nature of Emily herself, combine to create an image of curious and intriguing beauty. In 1858 John Elliot Cairnes, an Irish professor who had recently visited the parsonage, wrote in a letter a description of a painting he saw there which must have been the 'Gun Group' from which the fragment came, although he mistakes it for the 'pillar portrait' ('The Brontë sisters') Elizabeth Gaskell wrote of in the *Life*:

> The oil-painting Mrs G. speaks of by Bramwell [*sic*] of the three sisters is on the first landing on the way upstairs – It is a shocking daub, not up to the rudest sign board style. The artist stands himself in the middle with bright red hair divided from the centre, and a straight line along the nose to mark its highest point.[19]

From what we can tell from the existing poor reproductions (see **224**) of Branwell's 'Gun Group' portrait, so-called because the self-portrait holds a gun in the crook of his arm, the composition of the group of himself and his three sisters is altogether more successful than 'The Brontë sisters', given that he was not compelled to erase any of the figures. The horizontal format he has chosen provides a simpler solution to the problems of composing a group of four. The inclusion of the group of objects on the table in front of the group – the brace of game, the books and papers – conforms to the centuries-old artistic tradition of introducing objects into a portrait to convey information about the status and interests of the sitters. In the presentation of himself as the sportsman holding the gun with his booty displayed in front of him, Branwell puts a specific emphasis on his own masculinity, contrasting with the perceived femininity of his sisters' literary pursuits, symbolized by the books and papers. His figure towers a whole head above the girls and he is the only member of the group to meet the viewer's gaze; the women look inwards towards each other. His overall intention seems to be to present the Brontës as members of the aristocracy whose lives are devoted to the upper-class leisure pursuits of sport and art. Technically, irrespective of the poor quality of the surviving reproductions, this painting was evidently not a triumph. Indeed, the whole convoluted saga of its disappearance hinges on the fact that Arthur Nicholls considered it to be such a poor portrait of all the Brontës except Emily, that he saw fit to destroy all but the image of her.

In September 1835, Branwell is supposed to have made his ill-fated trip to London to apply for a place at the Royal Academy of Arts. The evidence of intention for his plan is to be found in an undated draft letter in his handwriting which reads:

> Sir, — Having an earnest desire to enter as probationary student in the Royal Academy, but not being possessed of information as to the means of obtaining my desire, I presume to request from you, as Secretary to the Institution, an answer to the questions –
>
> Where am I to present my drawings?
> At what time?
> and especially,
> Can I do it in August or September?[20]

In July 1835, Charlotte wrote to Ellen Nussey with the news that Branwell was off to London.[21] In September, Patrick Brontë wrote to

Mr Robinson, expressing his admiration for Robinson's portrait of a little girl which Branwell had brought home to copy and referring to Branwell's last lesson with him: 'Branwell hopes to be with you on Friday next, in order to finish his course of lessons.'[22] Tuition was free at the Drawing Schools as the annual exhibitions paid for them, so he would only have needed to find his living expenses. All students were accepted on merit and he would have been expected to show a portfolio of ten works of his own choice with drawings 'from Life' included. The standard was high, as Robinson knew, and surely he would have prepared his pupil for this.

No one knows exactly what happened to Branwell in London or, indeed, whether he actually went at all. But if he did go, the general theory is that he lost his confidence when faced with the realities of the great metropolis for which he had yearned for so long, and, having squandered his money in public houses, came home. In May 1836 Branwell wrote about Charles Wentworth's visit to Verdopolis, in a piece of writing which is accepted by some as a true account of Branwell's disastrous trip to London. The image he presents of Wentworth/himself is of a lost soul: 'of a sudden, the tears came starting into his eyes, and a feeling like a wind seemed to pass across his spirits, because now he felt that not even the flashes of glory which these streets and buildings had struck from his soul, not even these feelings which he had reckoned on as something to supply years of dulness, could preserve his thoughts from aimless depression.'[23]

When he was as young as ten years old Branwell had proprietorially written his name in the Brontës' copy of *A Description of London* by William Darton (see Appendix A) and had written his opinion of the architecture of all the major city buildings beneath the coloured plates in the book, his judgements ranging from 'capital' to 'execrable'. Perhaps, like Wentworth, he found the reality of such sights altogether overwhelming. Perhaps he never made the journey at all, realizing his own inadequacies with a jolt, when Robinson actually explained the procedure for admission. He may well have received a prompt reply to his own letter to the Royal Academy Schools, although no original exists in their archives.[24]

The truth was that Branwell did have sufficient talent to have made a success of the study of art, and a humble background had been no handicap to other artists who had gone to London with great hopes; what he lacked was perseverance. Compare the example of Joseph Bentley Leyland the sculptor, Branwell's friend in later years, who had gone to London in December 1833 and had obtained a letter from the artist Stothard to introduce himself to Ottley, curator of the Elgin marbles at the British Museum. Leyland went on to meet other artists of the calibre of Chantry, Westmacott, Nasmyth, Varley and Haydon, some of them the very artists whose pictures the young Branwell had pored over in the illustrated Annuals. Did Branwell, or did he not, make any attempt to achieve his goal? Near the end of his life he wrote a letter to Leyland which refers to this time: it suggests that Branwell had in fact never even set foot in the British Museum:

> I used to think that if I could have for a week the free range of the British Museum – the Library included – I could feel as though I were placed for seven days in Paradise, but now, really, dear sir, my eyes would roam over the Elgin marbles, the Egyptian saloon and the most treasured volumes like the eyes of a dead cod fish.[25]

The failure of the London expedition, whether or not it got beyond the planning stage, was Branwell's first major disappointment, both for himself and for his family. For most of the following two years, 1836 and 1837, he stayed at home in Haworth, not hiding away in the parsonage as Emily did but joining in with village life. Despite his depressive tendencies, Branwell was a sociable creature who was generally liked in Haworth. Surprisingly, he taught in the Sunday School and, ironically, became secretary of the Temperance Society in the same period when he seems to have taken up drinking in earnest. He became a member of the Haworth Freemasons' Lodge, 'The Three Graces', which was attended by professional men and tradesmen – good contacts for his next venture as a portrait painter in nearby Bradford. The lessons with Robinson were resumed in order to prepare him for his return to art, and it is thought that Branwell went again to his teacher's studio in Leeds.[26] Branwell may at this time have produced some of his portraits of Haworth people as practice pieces.

In order to understand Branwell's situation as a prospective provincial artist it is necessary to understand the role of the professional artist in the provinces in the early nineteenth century. Such artists – in Birmingham, Manchester, Liverpool, Leeds, Bradford and Bristol – tended to be flexible, specializing according to demand, as portraitists, miniaturists, painters of animal portraits, landscapes, seascapes or still-lifes, sculptors, carvers, engravers, lithographers, heraldic or sign painters, theatrical scene painters, house painters and decorators or industrial artists. The Leeds artist Schwanfelder, for example, had a career which included house-painting, animal portraiture and decorating snuff-box lids.[27] They could also offer related services: teaching drawing, art dealing, picture restoration, copying and selling prints and artists' materials.

Portraiture itself served a broad market, ranging from the humble silhouette, affordable for most people, to the full-length portrait in oils. Branwell may eventually have been able to charge around three guineas, the average for a commissioned portrait, although to begin with he may have charged less than a guinea. He would not have found it difficult to supplement his income by teaching, had he wished it, for there was a huge market. Drawing-teachers supplied their pupils with their own drawings and canvases from which to copy and there were also numerous drawing manuals: during the period 1800–30, 149 of these drawing books were published.[28] The most successful nineteenth-century artists made fortunes from selling licences to produce prints of their paintings. The portraitist's greatest hope of success was that he might manage to raise enough subscribers to produce a portrait print of a painting of a local celebrity. Branwell never got this far but his fellow Bradford artist W. O. Geller did with one of Branwell's own subjects, Henry Heap, Vicar of Bradford.[29]

Branwell was to some extent disadvantaged in his chosen career, despite the support and encouragement of his family. At best, provincial artists could hope to achieve only basic training at home. Some, like the celebrated neo-classical sculptor John Gibson of Liverpool, were fortunate in finding wealthy and enlightened patrons who gave them access to private collections of Old Masters and even to foreign galleries. The vast majority, like Branwell's friend Joseph Leyland, had to make do with executing dull memorial plaques. Collections of casts from the antique were important resources for the trainee artist in some larger towns; Bradford, however, had no such riches to offer. An alternative option for training was apprenticeship to a master, which could be the best way of learning, although conditions and advantages varied and an apprentice could end up doing all the menial studio tasks.

The prevailing method of instruction in the early nineteenth century was to encourage the student to learn not from nature, but from the master's own working methods and productions. Branwell would watch his teacher at work and then attempt to imitate his actions. He would have learnt Robinson's techniques, his short-cut methods and the idiosyncrasies of his personal style. Indeed, the purpose of this kind of teaching was that the pupil should adopt the master's own style. Certainly, when one looks at Robinson's own painting, for example his self-portrait in Leeds City Art Gallery, and then at Branwell's Bradford portraits there is a strong similarity in manner. There is no material evidence from his time with Robinson of Branwell having undergone rigorous study of the human anatomy through drawing from the model or from the antique, which was the cornerstone of high art and a prerequisite for entry to the Royal Academy Schools. The only tiny piece of anatomical drawing is to be found by scouring the margins of one of the annotated books once owned by the Brontës: William Darton's *A Description of London* (see Appendix A). Poignantly, at the end of his life Branwell displayed some knowledge of figure drawing in the portraits of himself as corpse in his letters to Joseph Bentley Leyland (see for example **302**).

A number of crude and clumsy oil paintings of landscapes, biblical scenes and a copy from a sporting print in the Brontë Parsonage Museum collection would suggest that Robinson set his pupil to painting oil copies as a means of learning. Indeed, in the American Charles Hale's account of a visit to Haworth in 1861 we find some evidence of this (see **235**).[30]

Plate 10 'Jacob's dream', engraving by E. Goodall, from a painting by W. Allston, for *The Literary Souvenir*, 1830; copied by Branwell Brontë (**235**)

A closer look at the oil painting 'Jacob's dream' (**235**, and plate LIX), which Branwell made by copying from a black and white engraving (see plate 10), shows the limitations of this method of study. The tiny engraving from which he copied is in the Brontë Parsonage Museum collection and one can see that his painting conscientiously differs very little in composition from his model, except in the spacing of the foreground figures. However, the use of oil colour presented him with problems. It is apparent from his use of colour that Branwell translated the image tonally rather than attempting to achieve any painterly richness and warmth of hue. The choice of particular colours, mainly sombre purplish greys, mauve, green and a few splashes of dull crimson, is obviously random. The whole is dulled by his choice of a brownish beige ground rather than the red or white ground which a properly trained painter would have used to brighten up the colour.

There are only a handful of non-portrait subjects in oils by Branwell in the Brontë Parsonage Museum, all of them unsigned and most of them in a very poor condition as a result of the artist's lack of technical knowledge, so presumably they were all produced when he was attempting to learn his craft. The provenance of most of these is obscure but in one case, that of 'The Lonely Shepherd' (**265**), an interesting early connection has been unearthed. This picture was presented to the Brontë Society in 1901 by Miss Anna Harris, the daughter of Alfred Harris, a banker and member of a wealthy Bradford Quaker family, who was a patron and collector of art. According to the donor, Harris bought the picture from Branwell in the 1840s. It would be unusual for Branwell to sell a painting other than a commissioned portrait to a buyer outside the family circle and the circumstances remain unclear. The Harrises, however, were a family not dissimilar to the Brontës, being both Conservative and artistic, but far above the Brontës' social station. It is possible that there was some connection between Patrick Brontë and Alfred Harris as both were interested in elementary working-class education. Alternatively, Harris could have belonged to, or had connections with, the local Freemasons, a potential sphere of clients which Branwell is known to have exploited (see **260**).

The picture's title, 'The Lonely Shepherd', is derived from a note on an old catalogue card in the Brontë Parsonage Museum. The subject of the shepherd's loneliness is one that would have appealed to Branwell's sense of the romantic, and he could have made a connection in his mind with 'The Old Shepherd's Chief Mourner' painted by Edwin Landseer in 1837 and made famous by prints which appeared as early as 1838.[31] Landseer's work prompted Branwell to write his sonnet 'On Landseer's painting – "The Shepherd's Chief Mourner" A dog keeping watch at twilight over its master's grave', written 28 April 1842.[32]

From May 1838 until May 1839, Branwell worked as a portrait painter in Bradford. The Reverend William Morgan found him lodgings and a studio in his own respectable street, with the family of Isaac Kirby, an ale and porter merchant. Bradford was a prosperous if philistine city and Branwell's neighbourhood abounded with the kind of professional people and tradesmen who were self-important enough to wish to have a flattering yet recognizable 'likeness' taken. William Morgan sat for one of Branwell's first commissions (**259**), and persuaded his friend the Reverend Henry Heap to do likewise (**255**).[33] (Neither picture is now traceable.) All seemed set fair for a rather plodding career in the provinces, but Branwell was on the lookout for more exciting diversions, which he was soon to find in Bradford's Bohemian circles.

This year must have been a high point in Branwell's life, giving him access to the kind of lively, artistic male society which he most relished. Here he made the acquaintance of the whole host of Bradford painters and engravers: Joseph Clayton Bentley, William Overend Geller, James Gelder, Joseph, John and Charles Cousen, John Wilson Anderson and John Hunter Thompson. Most of these artists had studied in London and, unlike Branwell, had persevered with their ambitions. J. H. Thompson, Branwell's particular friend whom he met as a fellow pupil of William Robinson in Leeds, was the only one of these to specialize in portrait painting. The others in the main accepted the fact that portraiture was in decline with the invention of the daguerreotype and moved into the more lucrative field of engraving. Geller was a successful engraver and an imitator of the Brontës' hero John Martin; John Cousen engraved plates of Turner's landscape paintings and J. C. Bentley made plates for Allom's Lake District albums.[34]

Professionally, however, the Bradford venture was a failure. It would appear that Branwell set his sights too high from the beginning, imagining, perhaps, that it was just one simple step to the heights reached by famous artists such as John Martin and William Etty. He must have disdained the idea of a humble apprenticeship and regarded engraving as a secondary art, when in fact his drawing skills would have given him a natural facility for such work. Branwell would have been well advised to follow his more successful friend Thompson in taking anatomy lessons from a Bradford doctor: his disproportionate figure painting betrays his lack of knowledge in this area. Francis A. Leyland provides us with an astute analysis of why Branwell's abilities failed him as a portrait painter:

> Being gifted with a keen and distinct observation, combined with the faculty of retaining impressions once formed, and being an

> excellent draughtsman, he could with ease produce admirable representations of the persons he portrayed on canvas. But it is quite clear that he had never been instructed either in the right mode of mixing his pigments, or how to use them when properly prepared, or, perhaps, he had not been an apt scholar. He was, therefore, unable to obtain the necessary flesh tints, which require so much delicacy in handling, or the gradations of light and shade so requisite in the painting of a good portrait or picture. Had Branwell possessed this knowledge, the portraits he painted would have been valuable works from his hand; but the colours he used have all but vanished, and scarcely any tint, beyond that of the boiled oil with which they appear to have been mixed, remains.[35]

A few good paintings came out of the Bradford year, however: the best of these, the portraits of the Kirby family with whom he lodged, are the only known commissioned works in which he comes near to conveying something of the personalities of his sitters. Isaac Kirby (**257**, and colour plate XXXI), a long-faced, swarthily good-looking man, stares rather woefully out at us, and small wonder if Branwell's image of the tight-lipped Mrs Kirby (**258**, and colour plate XXXII), miserable in an incongruous frilly bonnet, is a truthful one. The Kirbys' young niece Margaret Hartley (**254**, and colour plate XXX), on the other hand, conveys a character of sweet-faced shyness and one senses a sympathetic relationship between artist and sitter, one that is substantiated in Margaret's later account of her memories of Branwell: 'He was a very steady young gentleman, his conduct was exemplary, and we liked him very much.'[36] The portrait of Margaret Hartley is not only sensitive to the sitter's character but it contains some rare passages of good painting, found in his rendering of her dark, glossy ringlets of hair, the gleam on her pearl drop ear-rings and the use of enlivening dark red and maroon shadows beneath her chin. The folds of her dark green satin dress are described by carefully placed turquoise highlights. Nonetheless, the picture has its customary faults which betray Branwell's lack of training, particularly in the proportions of the figure with its peculiarly elongated arms.

Branwell's career as a portrait painter was short, like all his other career ventures. The lure of the social scene in the Bradford inns, principally the George Hotel in Market Street and the Queen Hotel in Bridge Street, must have overtaken him. Here artists and writers got together to declaim their poetry, to sing, to talk and to drink. Branwell's closest comrade in this world was probably J. H. Thompson, also the son of an Ulsterman, and like Branwell, a sociable type and a noted raconteur. Whilst his fellow artists on the whole managed to combine work and pleasure, Branwell did not, and the effort of pressing for clients did not come easily to him. He was not well prepared for the sheer hard work of the trade of painting and he must also have suffered a great sense of disillusionment about such a career. Naïvely, Branwell must have believed that his natural talent would prevail to lift him from drawing in the dining room at the parsonage to membership of the Royal Academy of Arts. The truth was that he could not even sustain a humble career as a local artist. Finally, he gave up his studio and once again returned to Haworth. He was not, however, to be away from the West Yorkshire public houses for very long.

One drawing (**266**) survives from Branwell's next brief period of employment from January to June 1840, as a tutor to the sons of Mr Postlethwaite of Broughton-in-Furness in Cumbria. Broughton is a small town perched up on a hill, not dissimilar to Haworth except that instead of dismal blackened stone buildings it has a cluster of soft grey stone houses roofed in slate. The Parish Church of St Mary Magdalene is situated on an ancient site on the valley floor immediately below the main street with a magnificent view from the churchyard of distant Black Comb, about which Branwell wrote a sonnet, inspired by Wordsworth's poem 'View from the top of Black Comb'. Branwell proved to be an unsatisfactory tutor. From an unspecified source, Winifred Gérin gives an account of how his employer interviewed his boys about their teacher's behaviour and 'found that lately he had taught them very little, spending most of their lesson time in sketching and making up stories in connection with his pictures'.[37] We know that in 1840 Branwell was working hard on the second draft of his translation of the Odes of Horace. He also visited Hartley Coleridge at Nab Cottage, Rydal Water, and received positive encouragement in his writing.

Branwell must have agreed to go to the post in Cumbria because of his artist's interest in the romantic landscape of the domain of the Lakeland poets. Indeed, he had himself written a famously conceited, and unanswered, letter to William Wordsworth on 19 January 1837.[38] There must have been many other drawings produced during this six-month period, if Branwell really did neglect his charges and roam the picturesque hills and valleys with sketchbook in hand. It is unlikely that he produced any oil paintings whilst he was there, although there is a suggestion from Mrs Ellis H. Chadwick that he did so: 'Broughton-in-Furness is a beautiful district on the northern shores of Morecambe Bay, and Branwell seems to have been impressed by the charm of the place, for some of his crude oil paintings are of the district around the Black Comb.'[39] Mrs Chadwick was writing in the early days of twentieth-century Brontë biography, in 1914, and it is uncertain to which paintings she refers and in whose hands they were at the time. The only possible known candidates for such a description, 'Landscape with figures' (**264**) and 'Landscape with cottage, river and bridge' (**238**), both of which contain views of distant mountains similar in shape to Black Comb, seem to pre-date 1840. Indeed, it is possible that after the failure of his portrait studio in 1839 Branwell never painted in oils again. Disillusioned, he seems to have returned to writing as his main creative activity and his drawing became a sideline.

Art would not appear to have much relevance to Branwell's next career: as Assistant Clerk in Charge at Sowerby Bridge, Halifax, on the new Leeds–Manchester railway. Charlotte ridiculed Branwell's new post in a letter to Ellen Nussey of 29 September 1840:

> A distant relation of mine, one Patrick Boanerges, has set off to seek his fortune in the wild, wandering, adventurous, romantic, knight-errant-like capacity of clerk on the Leeds and Manchester Railroad. Leeds and Manchester, where are they? Cities in a wilderness – like Tadmor, alias Palmyra – are they not?[40]

In fact the birth of the railway age did provide exciting prospects for young men in the 1840s but Branwell swiftly relegated his job to a secondary position in his life while he concentrated on re-creating in

Halifax the sort of public-house-based social life he had enjoyed so much in Bradford.

The presence of his friend Joseph Leyland and family must have been a deciding factor in Branwell's going to Halifax, and through Leyland he found an entrée into the local circle of writers and artists which included William Dearden, George Hogarth and John Nicholson. Leyland had a sculpture studio in the town and his family owned a publishing house: through this connection Branwell succeeded in becoming a published author before his sisters, when six of his poems were published in the *Halifax Guardian* between June 1841 and July 1842. Friends from the Bradford days gravitated towards Halifax, including John Wilson Anderson, landscape painter, who had also failed in his career in Bradford and returned to his home town to become keeper of the public baths. New friends were made, including Francis Henry Grundy, an engineer on the railway and later a somewhat unreliable biographer of Branwell who was responsible for the idea that Branwell's time in Halifax was wholly miserable. He wrote:

> Had a position been chosen for this strange creature for the express purpose of driving him several steps to the bad, this must have been it. Alone, in the wilds of Yorkshire, with few books, little to do, no prospects and wretched pay, with no society congenial to his better tastes, but plenty of wild, rollicking, hard-headed half-educated manufacturers, who would welcome him to their houses, and drink with him as often as he chose to come, what was this morbid man who couldn't bear to be alone to do?[41]

The established public-house circuit for artists in the 1840s included Bradford, Halifax, Haworth and Hebden Bridge, and also Luddenden Foot, where Branwell moved to become Clerk in Charge on the railway in April 1841.[42] The group met together at these locations to read and criticize each other's work, to talk and to drink. Here Branwell would have mixed with a combination of both cultured and uneducated men, the kind of unpredictable society in which he thrived. Away from the refining influence of his quiet sisters he must have revelled in the sheer maleness of the way of life he followed during these eighteen months on the railway.

Some of the few drawings to survive from this period are to be found in a little maroon leather-bound notebook which Branwell kept whilst at Luddenden Foot, an intriguing document where scribbled notes on coal tonnage are found cheek by jowl with drafts of poems and pencil portraits of his drinking cronies. The notebook would seem to mirror the long tedious hours spent sitting in the clerk's office awaiting the arrival of the next train and the lively nights spent in the ale-houses where Branwell must have been prevailed upon to display his skills at achieving a likeness in a hurried pencil portrait, such as the drawing of John Murgatroyd, owner of the local mill, lolling back comfortably in his high-backed chair (**279**). A thumbnail sketch of sparring boxers (**276**), possibly copied from a sporting print of the type made popular by Thomas Rowlandson, is found in the corner of one of its pages, reminding us of Branwell's interest in boxing, a sport which he later uses as a pictorial metaphor for the ghastly struggles of his last years in his confessional letters to Joseph Leyland. On another page we find one of Branwell's self-portrait drawings, here presented as a relentless caricature of his long-nosed profile (**278**), a cruder version of his earlier self-portrait (**267**, and plate 11).

Plate 11 Branwell Brontë, 'Self-portrait' (**267**), c. 1840

A group of more finished pencil portraits from this period shows Branwell making slightly better use of his talents. All the same, it is unlikely that these were executed for anything other than the entertainment of his friends, and to while away hours of boredom. Judging by their working clothes, and the possible identification of 'Duncan' (**269**) as George Duncan, the Clerk in Charge at Sowerby Bridge station during Branwell's time there, two of the portraits seem to be of railwaymen, the other being Henry Scott (**272**). Both sitters have broad features, unkempt hair and mild, blank expressions. By contrast, 'Grimshaw, H.' (**271**) is smartly dressed with carefully curled hair and a self-consciously serious look in his face. The elaborate form of the title, written in a decorative script, would also suggest that this was one of Branwell's more sophisticated friends. The portrait titled 'Alexander Percy Esq$^{re}$ M.P. Ætat 21' (**270**) is drawn with such attention to the details of costume, face and hair that it is more likely a study from life which Branwell decided to rechristen in the mode of one of his lifelong imaginary heroes, demonstrating an attachment to the world of fantasy in the midst of his ordinary working life. The most powerful of the drawings is the unfinished and therefore untitled pencil portrait of a drunken man with debauched features, holding aloft a wineglass (**273**, and plate LVII). This study was perhaps derived from life but has been worked up into a caricature of a drunkard, with his coarse features, leering expression and unkempt clothes and hair.

Branwell's pursuit of social pleasures caused him to neglect his duties at Luddenden Foot station, allowing an employee in his charge to embezzle the accounts, and the inevitable occurred. On 31 March 1842 he was dismissed and returned home, this time a failed railway clerk with a string of bad debts. He found himself at home with only his aunt and father for company as Charlotte and Emily were in Brussels and Anne at Thorp Green. On 22 May he wrote to Grundy, asking him for help in finding another post, but writing at greater length of his misery and depression. Reflecting melodramatically on the railway days, he wrote: 'I would rather give my hand than undergo again the grovelling carelessness, the malignant yet cold debauchery, the determination to find how far mind could carry body without both being chucked into hell, which too often marked my conduct when there, lost as I was to all I really liked, and seeking relief in the indulgence of feelings which form the black spot on my character.'[43] The rest of the year was totally unproductive of any significant art works. Indeed, Branwell devoted more time to securing a mundane commission for Joseph Leyland to design a memorial tablet to the Haworth surgeon than to any work of his own. The death of Aunt Branwell, in whom the girls lost an important financial patron, and all of them a fond relative, brought the rest of the family home in October 1842, and a few months later, in January 1843, Branwell set off with Anne to Thorp Green where he was to be tutor to the young Edmund Robinson.

By now, with art pushed to the peripheries of Branwell's existence, the rest of the family must have abandoned all expectations of fame and fortune for the only Brontë son. A teaching post with the respectable Robinson family was the best they could hope for him, despite his failure in a similar post. All that exists from Branwell's time at Thorp Green is an ink drawing he made of the 'Old Hall', his name for Monk's House where he lodged, inscribed with a line about its history (**282**, and plate LX). It shows that he had some time to devote to his own leisure, and that in his new, elegant country house surroundings he had more picturesque subjects to hand than his Halifax drinking cronies. However, there is on the verso of the drawing a tiny pencil sketch which is more evocative of debauchery than any known product of the time in Halifax, depicting a group of men smoking pipes and masturbating (**283**). It is quite likely that Branwell was in the habit of making drawings with explicit sexual references and this one has survived by default. It may have been drawn at Thorp Green or possibly later at Haworth as his obsession with past disappointments distorted under the influence of drink and opium.

It was at Thorp Green that Branwell's sexual passions were awakened by the handsome form of his employer's wife, Lydia Robinson; he was dismissed from the house in June or July 1845. Every effort was made by the Brontës and the Robinsons to suppress the truth about Branwell's intrigue with Mrs Robinson and the facts remain obscure. However, Branwell's later letters say enough to persuade us that there was a love affair, from his point of view at least. Everard Flintoff has discovered from his retrieval of lost poems, now known only in the manuscript fragments and from old photographs of manuscripts, that Branwell wrote quite a few poems at Thorp Green.[44] In one of them, 'I saw a picture yesterday', he refers to a painting of a Crucifixion which he has seen, and also a self-portrait drawing made by a woman who is the object of his love, presumably Lydia.[45] Flintoff speculates that Branwell may also have been Lydia Robinson's art teacher as well as Edmund's tutor, although there is no other evidence than the poem to suggest this. Certainly, if he was Lydia's art teacher he would have had legitimate access to her company. Flintoff goes on to imagine a serene and happy life for Branwell at Thorp Green, with ample opportunity for walking in the beautiful countryside of the Vale of York and for making drawings, his enjoyment increased by his sexual attraction to Lydia Robinson. He wrote a number of landscape poems, and just as it is certain that he made landscape drawings there too, he must also have made portrait studies of Lydia, all now lost.

Branwell was dismissed from Thorp Green in the summer of 1845 when, it is generally supposed, either Mr Robinson got wind of the affair, or Mrs Robinson tired of the attentions of the intense young tutor and contrived to be rid of him. From that point onwards he became totally dependent on the drugs and alcohol in which he had indulged throughout his adult life. Inevitably this addiction, in an already weak constitution now further disturbed by failure in love, led to a physical decline, and ultimately to his death at the age of thirty-one in September 1848. In these last years Branwell's childhood habit of drawing in the margins was transformed and enlarged into an exercise of emotional exorcism. He used ink drawings in his letters and alongside his poetry manuscripts as a way of purging his feelings and reinforcing the emotions expressed in his writing.

It has been suggested that Branwell was influenced by his reading of Thomas De Quincey's *Confessions of an English Opium Eater*, first published in 1822, and, encouraged by his artist friend Thompson in Bradford, that he took opium as an aid to literary inspiration and possibly for protection from consumption.[46] However, it is far more likely that he initially took opium in the form of laudanum as a medicine, as was the common practice in the early nineteenth century, and that his addiction was gradual up to 1845. At that time opium was not regarded as a dangerous addictive drug and it was sold freely in village chemists' shops, including Haworth. It was used as an analgesic, a tranquillizer, a remedy for hangovers, a treatment for alcoholism and a soothing cordial for babies. Laudanum was the commonest form of opium available, made into a reddish-brown liquid with alcohol, and cheaper to buy than gin or beer. Much research has been carried out to determine the particular personality types most disposed towards drug addiction and it is clear that Branwell Brontë fell into these categories. Those with a restless mental curiosity, an imaginative and sensitive intellectual temperament, are vulnerable to addiction. So, too, are those who long for freedom from anxiety and are unable to face up to painful situations and therefore find their escape in narcotics.

Another type is the person who delights in secret rites and hidden fellowships and finds comfort in the arcane world of drug addicts.[47]

Opium addiction alone cannot cause death; it is a condition that can be controlled so that the addict may lead a more or less normal life. But Branwell was not in control of his life and already dependent on alcohol. The combination would have made him unable to eat and therefore prone to the kind of infections that were rife in the unhealthy climate of Haworth in the 1840s. Although there were more coherent periods during the last three years of his life when he was able to write some good poetry, the effects of his addictions show, especially in the illustration to letters which he sent to his friend Joseph Bentley Leyland (**285–289**, **291–295**, **302–304**). Branwell must have passed quickly beyond the first pleasurable stage of taking opium into the second stage of true addiction, when to stop is to risk the agony of withdrawal. At this stage he would have suffered feelings of gloom and apathy, an indifference to the anguish he was causing his family and a sense of isolation driving him to seek solitude. Unable by then to sustain any act of imaginative creation, his memory would become useless in dealing with everyday life although distant memories of childhood would be strongly evoked. In a colourless, joyless world of his own he would find it difficult to sleep, being afflicted by terrible nightmares from which he would wake screaming. All his cunning would go into procuring more supplies of opium at the expense of his art.

This state of self-obsession is chronicled in a number of self-portrait drawings which tell of his personal deterioration. The first of these appear in some entries he made in Mary Pearson's 'Common-place Book' when staying with her father at Ovenden Cross in the autumn of 1846. Beneath the lines of the sonnet which opens:

> Why hold young eyes the fullest fount of tears,
> And why do happiest hearts most sadly sigh
> When fancied friends forsake, or lovers die
> Or other's heart-strings crack, oerstrained by cares?

Branwell drew a head-and-shoulders portrait entitled 'The results of Sorrow' (**296**). The high forehead and prominent nose and chin are his own and the whole head bears the ravages of the pain of lost love, with sunken eyes, lined flesh and drooping mouth. A further page bears a stark image of death, a lopsided gravestone with the inscription 'I implore for rest' and in the background the tower of Haworth church (**297**). Alexander Percy resurfaces on another page in a vigorous portrait of an optimistic young man, juxtaposed with a rough outline drawing of a male corpse lying on a funeral bier (**298**). The two drawings complement the lines from Lord Byron which Branwell has inscribed between them:

> No more – no more – oh never more on me
> The freshness of the heart shall fall like dew,
> Which, out of all the lovely things we see
> Extracts emotions beautiful and new!

The implication is that the lively portrait of Percy and the lifeless body represent the artist's former and present self. A fourth page is designed in a similar manner with a haggard-looking self-portrait at the head of the page, some lines of verse on despair in the centre and at the foot of the page a symbolic drawing of a weeping male figure stranded on a rock in the sea with a sinking shipwreck in the background (**299**). Overleaf, Mary Pearson provides a lengthy and pious commentary on Branwell's addiction, written for the benefit of her own son. Of this last drawing she wrote: '. . . the other little sketch is highly descriptive of the morbid state of mind under which he then laboured, the result as I was subsequently told of A disappointment in love, At the time we speak of he was an inveterate drunkard his whole energies and talents were shipwrecked.'

In these last years Branwell leaned heavily on the support, both financial and spiritual, of his friend Joseph Leyland. Letters he wrote to Leyland (now preserved in the Brotherton Collection at Leeds University Library) date from 1847 until July 1848, just a couple of months before Branwell died (see especially **301–304**). A number of drawings, either enclosed with the letters or interspersed within the text, provide us with a pictorial history of the writer's decline. The main theme of these drawings is Branwell's obsession with his own death. Recurrent references are made to the art of sculpture, to pugilism and to the male environs of public houses (see for example **303**), the only world Branwell then knew outside of Haworth Parsonage.

Boxing had always been an interest of Branwell's. He is reputed to have boxed himself in Haworth and he is known to have been an avid reader of the sporting papers where he could have found an account of a match in which William Thompson or 'Bendigo' beat Benjamin Caunt on 9 September 1845. The following day he wrote to Leyland and adorned his letter with a half-page sketch in ink of the two boxers facing each other on their knees, with Bendigo 'taking a sight' (**285**). Caunt is represented with chains on his wrists symbolizing his defeat. It is tempting to interpret this slumped figure as a reference to Branwell himself, defeated by life. This letter, written only months after his departure from Thorp Green, contained a further drawing, now lost, which makes an overt reference to Branwell's relationship to Lydia Robinson. Entitled 'A Cast – cast down but not castaway' (**286**), the drawing depicts Lydia in the role of sculptress, tools in her hand, looking down on the shattered cast of a head of Branwell. The references to sculpture would strike a chord with Leyland the sculptor. In a letter of 28 April 1846 Branwell went further and enclosed 'an ill-drawn daub', as he described it, representing a marble statue of a drooping woman entitled 'Our Lady of greif [*sic*]' (**288**), intended as a portrait of Lydia. In this reference to a marble sculpture Branwell is implying that the lady's feelings are as cold and intractable as the material itself. There is, too, the association throughout with the funereal nature of marble sculpture.

In his letters to Leyland Branwell does not flinch from portraying himself confronting death. In June 1846 he sent a crude line drawing of himself as a martyr, tied to a stake with the flames licking around his body (**289**), in January 1847 as a tomb sculpture (**302**) and in January 1848 about to be hanged with a rope noose around his neck (**303**). Between these dates the tone is sometimes lighter, as in a letter of October 1846 where Branwell seems to be mocking his own situation. He opens with an amusing sketch of his friend John Brown, the stone mason, joyously drunk in a vignette labelled 'Paradise' and despondent at his work in the churchyard above the heading 'Purgatory' (**291**).

Plate 12 Branwell Brontë, 'A Parody' (**304**), drawn c. 1848

Further on he interjects a tiny drawing of Leyland's plaster relief of Branwell, jokingly entitled 'Augustus Caesar' (**292**), followed by himself falling into an abyss (**293**). Then there is a droll image of 'an old Maid's squeamish Cat' (**294**) grimacing as 'dry toast soaked six hours in a glass of cold water' is thrust at its face, which must be Branwell's comment on his family's attempts to get him to eat. The letter ends with a tail-piece of John Brown grinning at the gallows (**295**), very much in the manner of Thomas Bewick, a conceit which is a poignant reminder of more innocent and carefree days.

Branwell's last known drawing was probably sent with a letter to Leyland around 22 July 1848, only two months before his death. 'A Parody' (**304**, and plate 12), drawn in the style of a cartoon, brings together the recurrent themes of all Branwell's last drawings. He uses a boxing metaphor, titling the drawing 'Jack Shaw, the Guardsman, and Jack Painter of Norfolk' after two pugilists of the day. His self-portrait lies half-naked, huddled in bed, resisting the challenge to fight a hugely tall skeleton representing death. In the background he has drawn the familiar outline of Haworth Church tower, a recurring image and apparently a symbol of his misery rather than of hope. Morbid, slight and crudely made as these last introspective drawings are, they remain as evidence that Branwell saw with an artist's eye to the bitter end. He had a natural, fluid talent for drawing which none of the other Brontës possessed. Had he thought less in terms of 'Paradise' and 'Purgatory' and more about taking up the challenge to fight the humdrum world, he might have achieved a reasonable career as an artist.

# *Notes*

1 *The Letters of Mrs Gaskell*, ed. J. A. V. Chapple and Arthur Pollard (Manchester: Manchester University Press, 1966), p. 249.

2 Charlotte Brontë to W. S. Williams, 29 September 1850: *The Brontës: Their Lives, Friendships and Correspondence*, ed. Thomas James Wise and John Alexander Symington, 4 vols. (Oxford: Basil Blackwell for the Shakespeare Head Press, 1932), vol. 3, p. 165.

3 See **224** and **225** for the history of 'The Brontë sisters' portrait and the 'Gun Group' portrait.

4 E. C. Gaskell, *The Life of Charlotte Brontë*, 2 vols. (London: Smith, Elder & Co., 1857), vol. 1, p. 153.

5 *The Odes of Quintus Horatius Flaccus*, Book I, trans. Patrick Branwell Brontë, ed. John Drinkwater (London: privately published, 1923), p. xi.

6 *The Miscellaneous and Unpublished Writings of Charlotte and Patrick Branwell Brontë*, ed. Thomas James Wise and John Alexander Symington, 2 vols. (Oxford: Basil Blackwell for the Shakespeare Head Press, 1936–8), vol. 1, p. 85.

7 *The Brontës: Their Lives, Friendships and Correspondence*, ed. Wise and Symington, vol. 1, p. 82.

8 See p. 34, n. 40.

9 Thomas Bewick, *A History of British Birds*, 2 vols. (Newcastle: T. Bewick; London: Longman & Co. , 1816), vol. 1, p. 65.

10 Ibid.

11 'May 11' could have been written in Roman numerals, in which case it would have been produced on 2 May 1830.

12 Winifred Gérin, *Branwell Brontë: A Biography* (London: Hutchinson, 1961), p. 25.

13 Ibid., p. 19.

14 BPM: Ph117, ambrotype of a view of Haworth Parsonage taken from the tower of the church of St Michael and All Angels (c. 1850–70). Presented by Jill Kendrick, 1990, also the donor of a watercolour portrait of John Barraclough of Haworth, said to have been painted by Branwell (**232**).

15 I am indebted to Richard Ormond (*National Portrait Gallery: Early Victorian Portraits*, 2 vols. (London: Her Majesty's Stationery Office, 1973), vol. 1, pp. 57–63) for the information contained in his catalogue entries on the portraits of the Brontës. More recent research by Susan Foister ('The Brontë Portraits', *Brontë Society Transactions* (1985), vol. 18, part 95, p. 339) and Juliet Barker ('The Brontë Portraits: A Mystery Solved', *Brontë Society Transactions* (1990), vol. 20, part 1, p. 3) has brought this information up to date.

16 *The Letters of Mrs Gaskell*, ed. Chapple and Pollard, p. 249.

17 Foister, 'The Brontë Portraits', p. 343.

18 Ormond, *National Portrait Gallery: Early Victorian Portraits*, vol. 1, p. 58.

19 T. P. Foley, 'John Elliot Cairnes' visit to Haworth Parsonage', *Brontë Society Transactions* (1984), vol. 18, part 94, p. 293.

20 BPM: Bonnell 147: 1–4v in fragments; published in *The Brontës: Their Lives, Friendships and Correspondence*, ed. Wise and Symington, vol. 1, p.128.

21 Charlotte Brontë to Ellen Nussey, 2 July 1835: *The Brontës: Their Lives, Friendships and Correspondence*, ed. Wise and Symington, vol. 1, p. 129.

22 Patrick Brontë to William Robinson, 7 September 1835: ibid., p. 132.

23 The relevant portion of the manuscript, which is in the Brotherton Collection, Leeds University Library, is reproduced in facsimile in *The Miscellaneous and Unpublished Writings of Charlotte and Patrick Branwell Brontë*, ed. Wise and Symington, vol. 2, pp. 180–1.

24 Gérin, *Branwell Brontë: A Biography*, p. 97.

25 Letter from Branwell to Joseph Bentley Leyland, 24 January 1847, beginning: 'My Dear Sir, I am going to write a scrawl; for the querulous egotism of which I must intreat your mercy. . .' (*Patrick Branwell Brontë: A Complete Transcript of the Leyland Manuscripts*, ed. J. Alex. Symington and C. W. Hatfield (Leeds: privately printed, 1925), pp. 39–42).

26 Francis A. Leyland, *The Brontë Family With Special Reference to Patrick Branwell Brontë*, 2 vols. (London: Hurst & Blackett, 1886), vol. 1, p. 174.

27 Trevor Fawcett, *The Rise of English Provincial Art: Artist, Patrons, and Institutions outside London, 1800–1830* (Oxford: Clarendon Press, 1974), pp. 19–20.

28 Ibid., p. 33.

29 Butler Wood, 'Some Old Bradford Artists', *The Bradford Antiquary*, 1895, pp. 198–209.

30 Charles Hale, 'An American Visitor at Haworth, 1861', *Brontë Society Transactions* (1967), vol. 15, part 77, p. 131.

31 Hilary Beck, *Victorian Engravings* (London: Victoria and Albert Museum, 1973), pp. 57–8.

32 BPM: BS 132; published in *The Poems of Patrick Branwell Brontë: A New Text and Commentary*, ed Victor A. Neufeldt (New York and London: Garland Publishing, 1990), pp. 456–7.

33 Leyland, *The Brontë Family With Special Reference to Patrick Branwell Brontë*, vol. 1, p. 175.

34 Wood, 'Some Old Bradford Artists', pp. 198–209.

35 Leyland, *The Brontë Family With Special Reference to Patrick Branwell Brontë*, vol. 1, p. 135.

36 W. W. Yates, 'The Bronte Family: A Suggestion. Two Years in the Life of Branwell Bronte', *Dewsbury Reporter*, 25 November 1893.

37 Gérin, *Branwell Brontë: A Biography*, p. 175.

38 Branwell Brontë to William Wordsworth, 19 January 1837: *The Brontës: Their Lives, Friendships and Correspondence*, ed. Wise and Symington, vol. 1, p. 151.

39 Mrs Ellis H. Chadwick, *In the Footsteps of the Brontës* (London: Sir Isaac Pitman & Sons Ltd, 1914), p. 161.

40 Charlotte Brontë to Ellen Nussey, 29 September 1840: *The Brontës: Their Lives, Friendships and Correspondence*, ed. Wise and Symington, vol. 1, p. 216.

41 F. H. Grundy, *Pictures of the Past: Memories of Men I have met and Places I have seen* (London: Griffith & Farran, 1879), p. 75.

42 John Longbottom, 'Bradford Literary Circle', *Yorkshire Notes and Queries*, vol. 1, no. 4, July 1904, p. 129.

43 Branwell Brontë to Francis H. Grundy, 22 May 1842: *The Brontës: Their Lives, Friendships and Correspondence*, ed. Wise and Symington, vol. 1, p. 264.

44 Everard Flintoff, 'Some Unpublished Poems of Branwell Brontë', *Durham University Journal*, vol. 81, June 1989.

45 'I saw a picture yesterday. . .', published in *The Poems of Patrick Branwell Brontë: A New Text and Commentary*, ed. Neufeldt, p. 262.

46 Rebecca Fraser, *Charlotte Brontë* (London: Methuen, 1988), pp. 116–7.

47 Alethea Hayter, *Opium and the Romantic Imagination: Addiction and Creativity in De Quincey, Coleridge, Baudelaire and Others* (Wellingborough: Crucible, 1988), pp. 39–41.

# The art of Emily Brontë

*Christine Alexander*

Emily Brontë was quite unlike her sisters. She was eccentric, anti-social, painfully shy, and probably meant what she said when she expressed a preference for dogs over people.[1] One would expect therefore that her paintings would show a personal character absent in those of her sisters. One would anticipate more individuality and originality; and to a large extent this is the case. When we look at her illustrations for the first time, we are immediately struck by their special sensitivity to the natural world. The delicate watercolours of the family pets Keeper, Nero and Flossy, and the confident pencil strokes of the drawings of Grasper and a blighted fir tree, are evidence enough of an original talent that was never brought to fruition in painting. Of her twenty-nine surviving paintings and drawings, only nine are not connected to the natural environment. Three of these nine illustrations are hasty pen-and-ink sketches illustrating diary papers (one of which again includes the family pets), four are copies of engravings (altogether she made eight copies of engravings, and possibly two more now missing), one is a geometry exercise and one is a vigorous pen-and-ink sketch illustrating a drama fragment. It is evident that Emily was less interested in mechanical copying than her sisters – though she was quite capable of doing so with excellent results – and that she was less interested in people than in the world around and within her.

Unlike Charlotte and Branwell, Emily left few drafts, few exercises, to tell the story of her apprenticeship in painting. Her drawings and rough sketches are as fragmentary, and as elusive of interpretation, as her surviving poetry. They are inclined to raise more questions than answers. Judging by surviving examples, Emily made fewer copies of engravings than her siblings. Did she follow the same training as her sisters, the painstaking copying that stunted Charlotte's imaginative development in painting? Apart from the hasty sketches of Anne and herself in the diary papers, there are no portraits 'from life' by Emily, yet there are numerous lovingly executed illustrations of her pets. Did she, like her siblings, ever attempt formal portraits of her family and friends? Or did she deliberately choose to reproduce the creatures with whom she felt she had most rapport? If we are to make any sense of the body of surviving work, we must read the gaps in the story as much as the material products illustrated in the following pages. Facts about her experience of the visual arts are not readily available, but those paintings that do survive provide vital evidence of her special genius.

Her finished pictures are among the most proficient of the Brontë sisters' accomplishments in painting, despite the fact that – or possibly because – she had so little formal tuition. Her periods of institutional schooling were brief and the external events of her life are soon told. At three years old Emily Brontë lost her mother. At the age of six, she joined her three elder sisters at the Clergy Daughters' School at Cowan Bridge, only to be removed six months later. She watched her two eldest sisters, Maria and Elizabeth, die in close succession as a result of consumption and the harsh regime at school. Not until her seventeenth birthday was there any attempt to send her to school again. On 29 July 1835 she joined Charlotte, now a teacher, at Roe Head, but stayed there only three months. Her sister later explained that the change for Emily 'from her own very noiseless, very secluded, but unrestricted and inartificial mode of life, to one of disciplined routine (though under the kindliest auspices), was what she failed in enduring'.[2] Yet, eager to earn her own living, Emily went in September 1838 as a teacher to Miss Patchett's school at Law Hill, near Halifax, for six months, and in 1842 she accompanied Charlotte to the Pensionnat Heger, in Brussels. She was recalled home in November by her aunt's death and from then on she remained at Haworth as housekeeper for Patrick Brontë and Branwell, drawing consolation from her writing, her imagination and the surrounding moors. She died on 19 December 1848, aged thirty and a victim of consumption, having caught a cold at Branwell's funeral just three months before.

The trials and desolation of this brief life are not evident in the illustrations. They are relatively public performances, monitored by teachers and admired by family. The corners of several illustrations (**308**, **313**, **317** and **319**) have been carefully rounded with scissors to make them more attractive for display. Certainly Patrick Brontë, after the deaths of his children, and later Arthur Bell Nicholls (Charlotte's widower), had at least one of Emily's works (**329**) framed on the walls of their homes; and it seems likely that Emily's pictures of the favourite family pets, which she made on her return from Brussels, were also displayed in the parsonage during her lifetime.

Yet Emily herself does not appear to have valued her paintings in the way that her sisters valued theirs. Charlotte, as we have seen, carefully preserved her own portfolio of paintings as an example of her skill for a future career as an artist, and later, with Anne, as a record of her proficiency to teach art as a governess. There was no such necessity for Emily, though she may have presented several paintings with her application for employment at Law Hill. Consequently her work cannot be traced to a particular sketchbook or group of illustrations preserved together in a single collection. It is not surprising, then, that many of her illustrations were lost or destroyed, possibly by Emily herself or by Charlotte acting on her sister's orders after her death, as she is thought to have done with some of Emily's manuscripts. We are fortunate, however, that the few illustrations that do survive are varied enough to allow us to chart her development as a visual artist and to suggest ways in which her experience of art contributed to her literary career and expressed her evolving philosophy of life.

Although she may have exerted more independence than her sisters in her choice of subject, her illustrations – those, at least, that have survived – appear to make the same social statements. They record her tuition in art and her personal interests. Only in three rough sketches do we find hints of that intensely private world of her poetry. The first is a scene of sadistic brutality, 'Images of cruelty' (**320**), which accompanies a fragment of drama discussing actions of justice and law, the only surviving prose manuscript (apart from the diary papers and a fragment from the *Aeneid* [3]) in Emily's hand. Here, in the image of a man abusing a child while another man stands complacently by, we receive a graphic foretaste of the cruelty encountered in *Wuthering Heights* and of the violent action that was so much a part of Emily's Gondal saga. The close correspondence between visual and written text here also suggests that there might once have been similar illustrations amongst her early prose manuscripts. The other two sketches are 'doodles', embellishing the margins of poetry manuscripts: 'Dancing stick figure' (**320a**) and 'Winged serpent sketches' (**321**), both suggestive of a mind receptive to a life force in nature. These two sketches, however, like the illustrations associated with her diary papers, have a quaintness and cosiness about them more in keeping with the stories of Emily's domesticity than those of her eccentric passionate personality.

The six diary papers were written jointly by Emily and Anne in 1834 and 1837, and separately by them in 1841 and 1845, with a view to recording events in their lives and reviewing them four years later. The terse statements of everyday chores, such as peeling potatoes or apples for the midday meal, having to practise B major scale on the piano, or reading *Blackwood's Magazine*, give a graphic picture of parsonage life. And the cryptic references to the Gondal characters suggest the prolific nature of Emily and Anne's early prose writing and the extent to which their imaginative life impinged on their reality. The vivid pen-and-ink sketches made by Emily on three of her papers, as hasty and untidy in appearance as the writing itself, are an integral part of the text and indicate how closely she associated visual and written media.

The first, 'Diary paper sketch of Anne and Emily' (**316**, and plate LIV), illustrates the two sisters composing their joint paper of 26 June 1837. Emily, with her back to us, is writing; Anne is bent forward over the table, her head resting on her hands and elbows on the table, in a thoughtful pose. Books and 'papers' lie scattered on the table beside 'The Tin Box', in which the carefully folded diary papers were preserved

Plate 13 Pen-and-ink sketch of Emily Brontë and her animals (**331**), drawn by Emily at the foot of her diary paper for 1845

and which still survives in the Brontë Parsonage Museum today. Two tiny thumb-nail sketches occupy Emily's diary paper of 30 July 1841 (**322**). Written by her alone, while Anne was at Scarborough, occupied as governess to the Robinsons of Thorp Green, and both Charlotte and Branwell were also away from home, Emily depicts herself as a tiny solitary figure. In the first sketch she is working hard at her desk, but in the second the table and chair lie deserted and Emily stands at the window, surveying the 'bleak look-out' described in the text. In the final 'Diary paper sketch of Emily with her animals' (**331**, and plate 13), 30 [31] July 1845, Emily is seen working in her small bedroom, with the dog Keeper at her feet and Flossy and a cat on her bed. She is seated on her little wooden foot-stool with her portable rosewood writing desk on her knees, two objects that constantly accompanied her during leisure hours at home and that can still be seen in Haworth today. Tabitha Ratcliffe, sister of the Brontë servant Martha Brown, once owned both these treasured relics and insisted that they should always go together: for 'Miss Emily always carried the stool into the garden or put it before the kitchen fire and then put the desk on her knee when she was about writing'.[4] All the sketches are in outline;

there is no attempt to depict facial features or incidental detail. Their preoccupation is with the moment of composition, a hasty record of the creative act. The faceless persona and the essentially outward records of Emily's situations in the sketches, which is to a large extent the nature of visual art itself, provide few clues to the imaginative life hinted at in the written text.

It is to her writing and not to her painting that we must turn for further insight into her private world. Her writing was the result of an intense inner life, formed in childhood and nurtured with increasing commitment until her death. There are records throughout Charlotte's and Branwell's early manuscripts of Emily's active participation in the collaborative creative life of the young Brontës, but later records suggest that she became secretive about her views on life and the imaginative world that sustained her, withholding information even from Anne, the closest of her siblings and her early literary partner.[5]

In June 1826, Emily shared her siblings' excitement over Branwell's new toy soldiers. She chose as her special character 'a grave-looking fellow', whose initial name 'Gravey' was soon changed to 'Parry', after the explorer Captain Parry. He became her hero in the early Glass Town saga, the series of stories and poems written by the four Brontë children. She participated, too, in other early 'plays', such as the 'Islanders' Play'. Here she took a major role, one of the adventures being 'played out' by her and Charlotte alone, and the 'School Rebellion' being instigated by Emily's characters, suggesting that this might have been the genesis of her own island saga of Gondal.[6] All the plays were acted out, written down and often illustrated.[7] From the start, Emily appears to have been a strong-minded partner, insisting on the realistic Yorkshire character of Parry's Land in contrast to the brilliant fantasy of Charlotte's and Branwell's Great Glass Town. Her imagination would always work best in its familiar moorland surroundings. Just as Emily preferred to paint natural subjects, so she felt no need to glamorize her fictional world. Charlotte's aristocratic Lord Charles is scornful of the heavy northern dialect, the uncouth manners and basic diet of roast beef, Yorkshire pudding and mashed potatoes he experiences in Parry's palace.[8] It is little wonder that we find so few of the fashionable beauties copied by Charlotte from the popular Annuals among Emily's paintings and drawings.

In 1831 she further asserted her independence, and, leading her younger sister Anne, she created a new world more to her liking. This was the Gondal saga about which we know very little, since no prose manuscripts have survived. The earliest dated reference to Gondal is in the diary paper of 24 November 1834, which includes the sketch of 'A bit of Lady Julet's [*sic*] hair done by Anne' (**336**).[9] Here we learn that the inhabitants of Gondal, an island in the North Pacific, have recently discovered and colonized Gaaldine, another island in the South Pacific. The ensuing saga appears to have been one of exploration, rebellion and betrayal in love, a self-generating epic that was also related to 'real' time and history.[10] For example, the diary paper associated with the sketch of Emily and Anne composing their diary notes on 26 June 1837 (**316**) mentions preparations for a coronation in Gondal which coincides with the coronation of Queen Victoria.

Emily's surviving poetry dating from 1832[11] tells us a little more. It explores moments of emotional intensity or crisis in the epic, assuming the 'plot' which was embodied in the lost prose and in the minds of its creators. We learn especially of the violent love and hate of the heroine Augusta Geraldine Almeda, a strong-minded woman whose features are suggested in Emily's portrait, 'Woman's head with tiara' (**323**, and plate LIII). Apart from superficial similarities, there is nothing to indicate that this drawing has any Gondal associations, yet it is not unreasonable to assume that if Charlotte's copies of engravings suggested Glass Town and Angrian characters, then some of Emily's drawings might also be related to Gondal. But without the prose manuscripts and without the Angrian titles Charlotte and Branwell affixed to their drawings, we can only glimpse and guess the nature of the kingdom Emily created, acted out,[12] chronicled and possibly painted.

In 1844, Emily began to transcribe her poems into two note-books, separating her Gondal poems from those she considered to be more personal utterances. By this date all her paintings had been completed, apart from the single diary paper sketch made the following year, which again shows her working at her desk (**331**). Until this time her extant illustrations are spread more or less evenly throughout the years, yet curiously none survive from the years in which she was writing her single novel, *Wuthering Heights*, published in 1847. Are we to assume that the artistic energies of visual observation and formal composition employed in her painting were subsumed into this magnificent work?

There is no doubt that *Wuthering Heights*, like *Jane Eyre* and other Brontë novels, exhibits a visual awareness that is the result of Emily Brontë's experience of art. Characters draw pictures in books, on window panes, and in words.[13] They watch and read each others' faces, study paintings of each other and steal them in an effort to possess the original. Nelly Dean, housekeeper and narrator, for example, watches Linton 'to catch his impressions in his countenance'; the narrator Lockwood examines Edgar Linton's portrait; and Heathcliff removes Catherine Earnshaw's portrait to the Heights, just after he has opened her coffin, 'Not because I need it, but–'.[14] 'Certain old pictures' have the power to initiate reconciliation through their ability to stimulate imagination: they act as a go-between for Catherine Linton and Hareton, giving the illustrated book a power superior to human intervention.[15] Much of Nelly Dean's story is told as a series of vignettes, in which even the climactic scene between Catherine Earnshaw and Heathcliff 'made a strange and fearful picture'.[16] And the author herself, like Hareton, appears to be 'studying the familiar landscape with a stranger's and an artist's interest'.[17]

Emily Brontë's drawings and paintings, then, should be seen as belonging to her formative period as an artist. They are evidence of her training in detailed observation, especially of the natural world, of her growing sense of composition and colour, and of the sources she read and copied in the process of developing her own distinctive style as painter and writer. The chronological progression of subject and increasing maturity of style that we see in the paintings, from the early copies of Thomas Bewick's engravings to the accomplished animal watercolours, echoes the gradual development of her individual lyric voice.

Furthermore, the early habit of copying, as part of the process of creating an individual expression out of the works of others – seen so clearly already in the case of Charlotte – is entirely compatible with Emily's apprenticeship in writing. Like Charlotte and Branwell, whose early prose writings reveal a myriad of literary and artistic sources, Emily had early copied and imitated writers she had been exposed to in childhood. Shakespeare, Milton, Scott, Wordsworth, Coleridge, Shelley, Byron and Hogg, among others, are echoed throughout her poetry and novel. Echoes from the pages of *Blackwood's* and *Fraser's*, which discussed the latest philosophical, psychological or artistic debates, or from the Annuals, with their fashionable plates and gothic tales, can be found in the pages of *Wuthering Heights*.

Contrary to what might be suggested by the better-known naturalistic studies of her pet animals, Emily Brontë's early artistic career also followed the same imitation of models as that of her siblings. Like them she participated in the drawing lessons arranged by her father at home. During 1829 and 1830, John Bradley, and possibly Thomas Plummer before him,[18] taught the eleven-year-old Emily the rudiments of art as they were laid down in the drawing manuals of the day.[19] Her earliest surviving drawing, 'Mullioned window' (**305**), and three drawings copied from Thomas Bewick's *History of British Birds* (**306**, **307**, **308**) date from this period.

'Mullioned window' is typical of the plates included in contemporary drawing manuals devoted to 'landscape embellishments'. Once a pupil had mastered the prescribed early lessons of drawing various parts of the face, such as the examples of eyes, noses, mouths surviving in Charlotte's portfolio, it was customary to progress to the elements of landscape. David Cox's many 'Progressive Lessons', for example, are typical of such works, which illustrate elements of landscape that progress in complication. His *Young Artist's Companion; Or, Drawing-Book of Studies and Landscape Embellishments*[20] includes bridges, stiles, rocks, chimneys, lintels, windows, cottages, gnarled trees, ruined towers, country churches, cornfields, and complete picturesque scenes. Judging from the Brontës' earliest surviving drawings – the ruined towers by Charlotte and Branwell, the thatched cottage by

Charlotte, the church by Anne and the mullioned window by Emily – their first copy-book was rather like this one, devoted to elements of landscape. It appears that their teacher skipped the early lessons on parts of the face and body, which were later taught at Roe Head, and used what materials he had on hand, a landscape manual and the Brontës' own books.

Yet even in this first exercise, Emily's peculiar talent stands apart from the more pedestrian products of her brother and sisters. As close as it is to the prescribed lessons of the manuals, its execution is individual enough (in the inaccuracies in lighting and perspective) to suggest that it may have been copied from life. Such stone mullions and lattice panes are still common throughout Yorkshire and beyond; and the broken pane would not be uncommon in a district of neglected farmhouses, dotted along the heights of the rolling moorland and deserted by their inhabitants for work in the factories in the valleys below. These are the same lattices found at the Heights in Emily's novel. They are the same lattices, easily broken by a terrified Lockwood as Catherine Earnshaw's ghastly little hand reaches in for refuge. There are other examples of the Brontë children learning to draw from life before they have completed the prescribed exercises: Branwell's 'Sleeping cat' (**180**) and Charlotte's paintings of flowers,[21] for example; yet, as with 'Mullioned window', the received image from the pattern books seems to dictate the conception of the work. Thus we may never know the exact source of this picture. Like her enigmatic poems, which often defy definition of time or place, 'Mullioned window' warns us from the start that it is impossible to be dogmatic about any of Emily Brontë's art works: all interpretation must be to a large extent suggestive.

It is clear, however, that illustrated books played as vital a role in the development of her artistic talent as they did in nurturing her literary imagination. In *Wuthering Heights*, the young Catherine Linton is not only reconciled to her cousin Hareton through the medium of engraved books; they also allow her to reclaim him for humanity. Their prints, like the plates of the Annuals that the Brontës themselves pored over for hours on end, entrance the illiterate Hareton and inspire in him an urgent desire to read, to fathom further the meaning of the illustrated page. Nelly Dean reports that 'The work they studied was full of costly pictures; and those, and their position, had charm enough to keep them unmoved, till Joseph came home.'[22] Their shared pleasure in the illustrated page repeats the similar shared activity of the first Catherine and Heathcliff (when Heathcliff is deprived of an education by Hindley and Catherine Earnshaw teaches him everything she learns), reinforcing symbolically similarities between the couples and emphasizing the natural rightness of each partner for the other.

There is no doubt that Emily, like her brother and sisters, learnt to draw by copying manuals and popular prints of the day. We have the evidence of Charlotte's letter to her father on 23 September 1829, that Emily joined her sisters in reproducing some views of Westmorland that their uncle had purchased on a recent trip to the Lake District.[23] The drawings of Charlotte, Branwell and Emily all show the influence of Thomas Bewick on their imaginations. His *History of British Birds*[24] consisted of a series of illustrated descriptions, with substantial woodcuts at the beginning of each entry and much smaller vignettes or 'tail-pieces' at the end. Emily made two detailed pencil copies of local moorland birds, 'The Whinchat' (**306**) and the 'Ring ouzel' (**308**), both from the first volume, which concentrates on land birds; and 'The farmer's wife' (**307**), a copy of a lively little tail-piece from volume 2, which describes water birds. The tail-pieces, often unrelated to the text, are usually matter-of-fact comments on everyday life. They tell their own story, and the tiny illustration Emily chose to copy depicts a farmer's wife being attacked by a goose as she attempts to collect the eggs. The realistic, often grim, sense of humour evident in Bewick's tail-pieces would have appealed to the creator of the initial scenes of *Wuthering Heights*, with the black humour of Lockwood's gauche response to the inhospitable inmates of the Heights. It would not be surprising if more copies by Emily of Bewick's illustrations came to light.

We know of at least six of Emily's drawings that are now lost,[25] but there must have been a substantial early output, possibly three times the number that now exist. It seems likely that most of these missing illustrations were made between 1829 and 1834 when all four children were busy at home with their pens and pencils. Some were given away as gifts, some discarded[26] and others used in barter as the only currency the young Brontës had. William Wood, the village carpenter who claimed to be the most familiar with the Brontës of all the local Haworth population, showed Charles Hale, an American visitor to Haworth in 1861, an early pencil sketch of a girl and dog (**331a**), now lost but apparently signed by Emily Brontë 'in juvenile letters'.[27] This was probably an early drawing exercise in outline, a copy of a 'fancy piece' rather like Charlotte's 'Boy and Dog' (**16**). According to his sons, William Wood once had many of these little Brontë drawings and some of their paintings stuffed into a drawer in his house at the bottom of Main Street. Only later, when the Brontës became famous, did he realize their value but by this time most of his little pictures had disappeared. But he never tired of telling how he obtained them, 'how the Vicar's children were in the habit of coming to his workshop to obtain frames for their drawings; they were too proud to accept them as presents, and they were accustomed to give him a drawing in exchange for a frame, which he usually made from the odds and ends of his larger picture frames'.[28]

His wife, Sarah Wood, who occasionally helped out at Haworth Parsonage where her cousin Martha Brown was servant, had her own memories of the Brontës, especially Emily: 'She were always scribblin' and writin', were Miss Emily . . . Many is the time I've seen her in t' kitchen, waitin' for t' kettle t' boil, or t' bread t' bake, scribblin' away on bits o' paper.'[29] Sarah Wood proudly preserved an old japanned coffee-pot that was 'embellished' with initials, dates, rough profiles and odd sketches, and 'signed' with scratch marks on the bottom, 'E. Brontë, Haworth Parsonage'.

All the young Brontës would scribble notes and sketches on anything they could find, just like the two Catherines in *Wuthering Heights*. Lockwood records that 'scarcely one chapter [of Catherine Earnshaw's book] had escaped a pen-and-ink commentary – at least, the appearance of one – covering every morsel of blank that the printer had left'.

Appendix A, which records the Brontës' sketches in printed books, shows that it is impossible to exclude Emily from what we might now consider an exceptionally liberal way of encouraging creativity in children. Our conventional attitude is echoed by Lockwood as he describes Catherine's use of her books 'not altogether for a legitimate purpose':

> Some were detached sentences; other parts took the form of a regular diary, scrawled in an unformed, childish hand. At the top of an extra page, quite a treasure probably when first lighted on, I was greatly amused to behold an excellent caricature of my friend Joseph, rudely yet powerfully sketched.
>
> An immediate interest kindled within me for the unknown Catherine, and I began, forthwith, to decipher her faded hieroglyphics.[30]

It is this satirical sketch, like so many that Emily herself probably made in bold outline like that of 'Images of cruelty' (**320**), that sparks both Lockwood's and the reader's interest in the unknown Catherine. The author is well aware that the visual has an immediate appeal and power (as we've seen it had for Hareton) that the printed page can never rival. Yet in *Wuthering Heights* the two art forms are intertwined: the sketch of Joseph encourages Lockwood to decipher Catherine's scrawl, and the rich engravings of the second Catherine's books help to inspire Hareton to read.

In late 1830, the twelve-year-old Emily joined her older brother and sister in copying the engraved plates of the *Forget Me Not* Annual of 1831, which had appeared several months earlier in time for the Christmas market.[31] Both she and Charlotte made a copy of 'The Disconsolate', a typically picturesque piece by H. Corbould, engraved by C. Rolls (**40** and **309**). This is the first of Emily's extant paintings (see plate LV), crude in its delineation of the human form and drapery, but showing considerable skill in chiaroscuro, in depicting the landscape and in the use of colour, which she has added to the black and white original. The scene records a moment of revelation, expressing the grief of a young woman deserted by her childhood sweetheart, which is retold in the accompanying poem by Letitia Elizabeth Landon. The cloistered setting, the gnarled tree, the sympathetic dog and even the dramatic situation of the heroine in distress, would have appealed to the gothic-loving author of Gondal, with its poems of broken pledges, jealousies and forsaken love. There has been some dispute about the attribution of this painting in the absence of other early watercolour copies by Emily,[32] but it is not easy to explain away the title and signature in her hand above and below the illustration, which is now catalogued under her name in the Berg Collection of the New York Public Library.

Charlotte's return in 1832 from her eighteen months at Roe Head initiated even more intense activity in drawing and painting, as she taught her sisters all she had learnt at school. Emily was a ready learner and again she followed her sister's lead in copying. Her duplication of 'Guwald Tower, Haddington' (**311**, and plate LVI) is as expert as Charlotte's original, which was copied in turn from a plate or drawing manual at school. Emily's missing pencil study entitled 'Roe Head' (**310**) may be another copy of one of Charlotte's sketches (**62**), since it is also dated December 1832, when Emily was busy learning all her sister had to offer.

The following year, 4 March 1833, Emily copied an engraving of the ascetic 'St. Simeon Stylites, Hermit of the Pillar', an illustration from *The Every-Day Book; Or, Everlasting Calendar of Popular Amusements*, which might have been borrowed from the local Keighley Mechanics' Institute Library (**312**). The accompanying text describes in horrific detail the various mortifications of the flesh practised by the fifth-century St Simeon Stylites of Syria, culminating in thirty years crouched on the top of a high pillar. The eccentric taste suggested here in the choice of topic by a fifteen-year-old girl contrasts dramatically with the fashionable beauties Charlotte chose to copy at this time. The next surviving drawing, Emily's sensitive study of her father's dog Grasper (**313**, and colour plate V), also reinforces our sense of her preference for the non-material things of life, for the real rather than the reproduced.

Yet we should beware of reading a preconceived image of Emily as an original genius into her paintings and drawings. A third of her

Plate 14 'The North Wind' (**325**), watercolour by Emily Brontë, copied from William Finden's engraving of Richard Westall's 'Ianthe', first published as the frontispiece to volume 2 of Thomas Moore's *Life of Byron*, 1839

works are copies of engravings, and even as late as 1842 she was still making occasional copies from favourite books, such as Moore's *Life of Byron* (see **325**, and plate 14). This does not deny, of course, that the remainder of her art works show an original talent above that of her sisters. Furthermore, imitation of models was an accepted method of education;[33] it need not deteriorate into mechanical reproduction, as it threatened to do for Charlotte and for so many of her contemporaries eager to acquire the lady-like accomplishment of drawing. Without the same worldly ambition, Emily felt no compulsion to adhere rigidly to conventional artistic practices. She could pick and choose from the available methodology, rather than follow the dictates of those 'stern mistresses', Duty and Necessity, that Charlotte felt obliged to obey.[34] Thus the majority of Emily's surviving art works show genuine personal choice of subject, despite their relatively public performance and her early training in copying.

For almost three months at Roe Head, Emily herself would have benefited from the same exposure as her sisters to the rudiments of drawing, and although no illustrations of eyes, noses, ears or hands survive under her signature, an introduction to such practice helps to account for the proficiency of her two later heads (**323**, **325**). Only two slight sketches of cows (**314**, **315**), made by Emily on 23 October 1835, remain from her time at Roe Head. They are not unlike the studies of cattle and horses in contemporary drawing manuals, to be copied after the human faces, hands and feet have been perfected; but the schematic pencil strokes suggest that they have been drawn from nature. There is a realistic quality in these outlines that again reminds us of Emily's preference for drawing natural objects. It seems likely that on one of her walks she carried a notebook, since the sketches have been drawn on paper torn from the same type of notebook she often used for her poetry. The countryside surrounding Roe Head is benign compared with that of Haworth and an abundance of farm animals would have been a novelty for Emily. Open fields extend from the front of the school towards the park of neighbouring Kirklees Hall and down the Calder Valley, providing fine views and plenty of opportunity for the observation of nature. It is possible that she may have made more sketches here of the landscape, although the absence of similar local views among the work of fellow pupils indicates the priority given to the imitation of models in the context of the classroom.

Once home again, for the next six years, she was free to write and draw as she chose. Two diary sketches (**316**, **322**), her paintings of Keeper and Nero (**319**, **324**, and plates III and VI), her 'Woman's head with tiara' (**323**), 'Geometric figures' and 'Sketches of buildings' (**317**, **318**) survive from this period, together with numerous poems including her early Gondal poem of 12 July 1836 ('Will the day be bright or cloudy?', BPM). Only her six months teaching at Miss Patchett's school at Law Hill interrupted the intense activity of Gondal writing in poetry and prose. There she tried to subdue her longing for home and the freedom it offered, but the rigid regime and long hours of supervision expected of her overcame her resistance. A second failure to remain away from home, as her sisters had done, must have rankled with her strong sense of personal will. When a third chance to overcome this weakness offered itself in 1842, she appears to have accepted it with stoicism.

In her diary paper of 1841, Emily had spoken with enthusiasm of 'A Scheme . . . at present in agitation for setting us up in A School of our own as yet nothing is determined but I hope and trust it may go on and prosper and answer our highest expectations' (see **322**); and when Charlotte determined that the sisters should improve their chances of attracting pupils by gaining language qualifications and contacts on the Continent, Emily agreed to accompany her to the Pensionnat Heger in Brussels, in February 1842. Charlotte records that through 'mere force of resolution', Emily – now twenty-three – conquered her ailing spirit and persevered with her studies there for almost a year.[35]

The more liberal approach to education in composition and art practised at the Pensionnat Heger would have appealed to Emily and assisted her struggle. She made rapid progress with her studies. But, older than the other pupils and increasingly reclusive and anti-social, Emily made little effort to develop socially, despite Constantin Heger's admiration for her strong intellect and the school's

Plate 15 'Study of a fir tree' (**326**), pencil drawing from nature, made by Emily Brontë in Brussels, 1842.

approbation of her musical ability. Her inexperience with French proved a handicap to begin with: in May Charlotte reported that 'Emily works like a horse, and she has had great difficulties to contend with';[36] but by July, she was 'making rapid progress in French, German, Music and Drawing–Monsieur and Madam Heger begin to recognize the valuable points of her character under her singularities'. Her progress in drawing is evident in the two surviving works made while she was in Brussels: 'The North Wind' (**325**; plate 14) and 'Study of a fir tree' (**326**; plate 15); both survive because they were given as presents to her teacher and a fellow pupil, and both reveal a marked improvement in style and a strong continuing interest in romantic imagery.

'The North Wind' is Emily Brontë's version of William Finden's engraving of 'Ianthe' (see p. 19), painted by Richard Westall and published as the frontispiece to Thomas Moore's *Life of Byron* (London: John Murray, 1839), vol. 2. Her portrait of the young woman fleeing has a more mature, challenging expression compared to the wide-eyed innocence of Westall's original. Beauty though she is, her piercing gaze, translucent skin, and flowing dark hair are reminiscent of the first Catherine in *Wuthering Heights*.

Like all the Brontës, Emily had already been profoundly influenced by the writing of Byron, in particular by the super-human struggle of the individual will against the forces of nature that she had encountered in *Childe Harold* and *Manfred*. Given that both Byron and Shelley evoked 'Ianthe' (see discussion of this topic on p. 20), Emily's choice is hardly surprising; and her title, 'The North Wind', reminds us of her many Shelley-like evocations of the wind:

> Yes, I could swear that glorious wind
> Has swept the world aside,
> Has dashed its memory from thy mind
> Like foam-bells from the tide –[37]

In Emily Brontë's personal mythology, it is usually the west wind that sweeps aside the imprisoning world and allows the soul to escape from 'gloom, and desolate despair'.[38] The Gondal heroine A. G.

Rochelle describes the recurring visionary experience that comes 'with western winds':

> A messenger of Hope, comes every night to me,
> And offers for short life, eternal liberty.
> He comes with western winds, with evening's wandering airs,
> With that clear dusk of heaven that brings the thickest stars.
> Winds take a pensive tone, and stars a tender fire,
> And visions rise, and change, that kill me with desire.

Did Emily Brontë also picture the liberating wind as an embodied form, as 'The North Wind' suggests? Gondal was still uppermost in her mind in Brussels and the Byronic engraving she copied has an energy and other-worldliness quite unlike the Finden brothers' other 'Byron Beauties'.[39] The heroine is in full flight, perhaps from the world.

Whatever one's view on 'The North Wind', it is clear that Emily's predilection for romantic imagery was reinforced during her stay in Brussels. Heger's enthusiasm for romantic writers brought her closer to the German romantics she had been introduced to in *Blackwood's* and *Fraser's*. He taught French composition and adopted the use of models in his teaching. But he did not expect slavish imitation. He would read the texts of a number of celebrated authors in the hope that his pupils might distinguish and reproduce the variety of styles. Emily's reaction was probably typical of her attitude to all copying, including her copying of engravings. She apparently 'saw no good to be derived from it; and that, by adopting it, they should lose all originality of thought and expression'.[40] Elizabeth Gaskell reports that Emily would have entered into an argument on the subject but Heger had no time for this. As with her drawing, however, she realized the value of imitation as an educational strategy. She acquiesced in the system, constantly mindful of her need to preserve her individuality of thought and expression. Beside copying from engravings, the pupils at the Pensionnat Heger were encouraged to sketch from nature views which were then completed in the classroom, as in the case of Charlotte's 'River scene with trees' (**154**), dated 4 August 1842. Two other illustrations by Charlotte (**155** and **156**) and Emily's 'Study of a fir tree' suggest that the Brontës spent a considerable time sketching 'en plein air', either in the August school holidays or as part of their drawing lessons. The Pensionnat Heger closed for the holidays on 15 August 1842, but Charlotte and Emily (together with the other English pupils, the Wheelwright sisters) were obliged to remain at school. During this time it was possible for them to make drawing expeditions into the surrounding countryside, just as they were free on occasional holidays to visit the Château de Koekelberg on the outskirts of Brussels, where their old friends Martha and Mary Taylor were now at school.

On one of these occasions, Emily made her 'Study of a fir tree', a large pencil drawing that is amongst her most discerning works. An examination of Charlotte's 'Landscape with fallen trees' (**156**) reveals that the two sisters sketched the same bedraggled fir tree from opposite sides. The fallen, decaying tree trunks of other firs lying nearby are in front of the fir tree in Charlotte's drawing, whereas they lie behind Emily's tree. The trees in both drawings have the same broken top, the same straggling branches and are near the same large rocks; and the sudden rise of the surrounding hills can be seen in the background of both. Each work shows clearly the tell-tale signs of sketching from nature, such as the rubbed surface of the picture where the artist has leant across the paper as she worked with a board on her lap. Charlotte's work returned with her to Haworth, where it was later endorsed by a proud and grieving father, and given to the servant Martha Brown after Charlotte's death. Emily's 'Study of a fir tree' remained in Brussels until the Brontë Parsonage Museum acquired it in 1929 from the nephew of Louise de Bassompierre, to whom Emily had given it seventy-seven years before. The sixteen-year-old Louise de Bassompierre had been a receptive pupil and a friend of Emily, whom she found 'less brilliant' but nicer ('*plus sympathique*') than Charlotte,[41] an unusual response by the only recorded friend Emily ever had, apart from Charlotte's friend Ellen Nussey and the Taylor family. Louise de Bassompierre noted that Emily 'wished to perfect her study of art, and had acquired a real talent there. She gave me a pretty landscape, signed with her name, which I treasured.' But it is Charlotte's rather than Emily's drawing that is 'a pretty landscape'.

The remarkable thing about these two drawings is their difference in conception; Charlotte's conventional picturesque interpretation of the whole scene and Emily's dramatic foregrounding of the decayed tree itself clearly articulate their different attitudes to nature and art. Even when sketching from nature, Charlotte's view is seen to be dictated by a learnt way of 'seeing': she has reproduced a 'pretty' scene as if from a nineteenth-century Annual, preserving a foreground of stream, rocks and fallen tree trunks, placing the fir in the middle-distance, and depicting the hazy outline of a town high on a hill beyond. The light pencil strokes and soft shading speak of familiarity and containment. The vegetation surrounding the fallen logs is soft and delicate, reminiscent of the effect produced by copperplate engraving. Nature is framed, balanced and benign. In contrast, Emily's view of the scene is strikingly different. The tree predominates in all its decayed glory. Whereas the foliage of Charlotte's fir tree hangs down, uniform, stiff and lifeless, Emily's contrasting shading and impressionistic technique renders the foliage active and life-like. The gnarled trunk, spare limbs and even the decayed debris at its base are boldly delineated in solid outline and shading so that they appear to have a life of their own. The trunk literally flows into the surrounding rocks and vegetation, so that all natural objects take on the life of the tree. There is fluidity and movement in the whole scene, with the suggested swirl of the rocks in the foreground, the stark vertical tree trunk rising through the centre of the picture balanced by the horizontal fallen trunks behind, and the branches that reach diagonally across the page, stretching their limbs 'as if craving alms of the sun'.[42]

Is it simply coincidence that it is 'merely the branch of a fir-tree' beating against the lattice window that rouses the ghost of Catherine in *Wuthering Heights*? The blasted tree was a common romantic motif, used by painters and poets alike, and it is probably fanciful to speculate further. For all its seeming originality, compared with Charlotte's drawing, Emily's fir tree can also be seen as part of conventional romantic iconography. William Gilpin, the late eighteenth-century landscape theorist whose picturesque precepts the Brontës clearly understood, described the decayed tree as a particularly effective adjunct in landscape painting and design. In *Remarks on Forest Scenery*, he recommended to the artist exactly the type of tree Emily has drawn:

> What is more beautiful, for instance, on a rugged foreground, than an old tree with a *hollow trunk*? or with a *dead arm*, a *drooping bough*, or a *dying branch*? all which phrases, I apprehend are nearly synonymous.
>
> From the *withered top* also great use, and beauty may result in the composition of landscape; when we wish to break the regularity of some continued line; which we would not intirely hide.[43]

Gilpin cites the works of Salvator Rosa, who often used 'the ruins of a noble tree' to preserve 'the dignity of his subject'. Emily was familiar with the 'gothic' pictures of Salvator Rosa and, judging from her own illustration, clearly understood the romanticism Gilpin found in Rosa's use of decayed nature:

> These splendid remnants of decaying grandeur speak to the imagination in a stile of eloquence, which the stripling cannot reach: they record the history of some storm, some blast of lightening, or other great event, which transfers it's [*sic*] grand ideas to the landscape; and in the representation of elevated subjects assists the sublime.

Yet trees seem to have had special significance for the Brontës,[44] as can be seen not only in their writing but in Anne's specific studies of trees.[45] It is to the symbolism of a tree that Charlotte turns when she wants to describe her sister Emily's intellect in the Preface to the second edition of *Wuthering Heights*: 'Had she lived, her mind would of itself have grown like a strong tree, loftier, straighter, wider-spreading, and its matured fruits would have attained a mellower ripeness and sunnier bloom.' In the novel itself, the savagery of nature is measured by the tenuous life of trees in an inhospitable environment: 'On one side of the road rose a high, rough bank, where hazels and stunted oaks, with their roots half exposed, held uncertain tenure: the soil was too loose for the latter; and strong winds had blown some nearly horizontal.'[46]

There is an energy in Emily's 'Study of a fir tree' that suggests an elemental quality, the kind of single-mindedness and spiritual insight we have come to associate with the romantic landscapes of Caspar David Friedrich, whose originality in paint bears a strong resemblance to Emily Brontë's genius with words. She would never have heard of this reclusive German painter, yet his philosophy and methodology suggest her own: 'Close your bodily eye, so that you may see your picture first with your spiritual eye', he wrote, 'then bring to the light of day that which you have seen in the darkness so that it may react on others from the outside inwards.'[47] Friedrich's haunting spiritual landscapes were initially misunderstood by contemporaries, but, as in the case of *Wuthering Heights*, his greatness began to be recognized towards the end of the nineteenth century. Something of this same genius can be seen in 'Study of a fir tree', which suggests that although Emily Brontë never chose to pursue her artistic talent, she was able to match in visual terms the imaginative qualities so powerfully displayed both in her poetry and in *Wuthering Heights*.

Her independent spirit, which threatened to destroy her elsewhere, could find succour and nourishment in the natural landscape at home. There she might record again in paint the creatures that meant so much to her. It is surely not coincidence that two of the best-known Brontë animal portraits, 'Flossy' (**327**) and 'Keeper, Flossy and Tiger' (**329**), were executed soon after her return to Haworth. They should be grouped with the earlier 'Grasper–from life' (**313**), 'Keeper–from life' (**319**), and 'Nero' (**324**), three illustrations that have defined Emily Brontë's character as a visual artist since her death, and that continue to be seen as the most successful and best loved of her works (see colour plates III and VI). This book reinstates 'Flossy' amongst Emily's œuvre: originally described by Benjamin Binns (brother-in-law to Martha Brown), as a 'spirited watercolour. . . by Emily, of Flossy, Anne's dog, a brown and white spaniel, chasing a bird over the moor',[48] it was mistakenly described in the sale catalogue for the auction of his effects in 1886, and has been mis-attributed to Charlotte Brontë ever since.[49]

Because these animal portraits are among Emily Brontë's few finished illustrations, they are excellent examples of her skill with watercolour and pencil. The strong outline and confident use of the soft lead pencil for shading demonstrate her assurance in this medium, which can clearly be seen in 'Grasper–from life'. Her handling of watercolour is entirely different. Light pencil sketches (as seen in her 'Unfinished sketches of Flossy' (**328**)) are covered first with a ground of colour and then gradually built up with painstakingly delicate brush strokes, so that the individual hairs or feathers are discernible. The tiny lines of paint representing the silky short fur of 'Keeper–from life', for example, indicate Emily's deep affection for her subject and belie the reputation for ferocity that this huge labrador/mastiff cross-breed had in the village of Haworth. Here she has caught the independent life of a creature that was most familiar and most dear.

The quality of these animal illustrations underscores Emily Brontë's affinity with the natural world. So far as her intensely personal beliefs can be defined, she was a pantheist, seeing all life as One – the visible and the invisible, imbued with the same spiritual force. Is it too imaginative to see in these pictures the intense communion she felt with these creatures? Was her statement of preference for the dog rather than the pupils at Law Hill simply black humour? Or was she expressing a genuine kinship and choice? Her anti-social behaviour is well documented and the special relationship suggested in her animal portraits reinforces stories told by Haworth residents of her rapport with animals. Elizabeth Gaskell recognized that it was often the fierce, wild, intractability of an animal that recommended it to Emily, characteristics Emily associated with her own sense of personal freedom. One local person told Elizabeth Gaskell that Emily 'never showed regard to any human creature; all her love was reserved for animals'.[50] Exaggerated as this report no doubt was, it shows the extent to which Emily was associated with animals during her lifetime. The stories of Emily's offer of water to a mad dog and the subsequent bite which she cauterized herself with a hot iron, telling no one until the wound was healed, and of her separation of the fighting Keeper and another powerful dog, 'two savage brutes each holding the other by the throat, in deadly grip',[51] while several village men stood by, were recalled by

Charlotte in her novel *Shirley* and have been retold by every biographer since Elizabeth Gaskell. Charlotte's verbal portrait of Shirley's habitual pose in the evenings, absorbed with book and dog, is generally seen as an image of Emily's intense relationship with Keeper:

> After tea Shirley reads, and she is just about as tenacious of her book as she is lax of her needle. . . . The tawny and lion-like bulk of Tartar is ever stretched beside her; his negro muzzle laid on his fore paws, straight, strong, and shapely as the limbs of an Alpine wolf. One hand of the mistress generally reposes on the loving serf's rude head, because if she takes it away he groans and is discontented. Shirley's mind is given to her book; she lifts not her eyes; she neither stirs nor speaks.[52]

Emily Brontë's animals were important to her sense of independence and to her cosmic vision of man in his natural setting.

The treatment of animals in her paintings parallels the fundamental role they played in forming her philosophy on life and anticipates their role in *Wuthering Heights*. Emily's special emphasis in the titles, '–from nature', suggests her wish to underline the genuineness of both her portrayal and the nature of her subject. She saw the antisocial behaviour of her dogs as sincerity, compared with the hypocrisy of human civilities. Her attitude to cats was rather different. The succession of cats at Haworth left her in no doubt as to why they ingratiate themselves with humans. Kipling had the same tale to tell in 'The Cat that Walks by Himself'. In 'Le Chat', an essay written for Constantin Heger, Emily associates the insinuating nature of cats with human hypocrisy, which we perversely call 'politeness'. Evoking the misanthropic spirit of Timon, from Shakespeare's play, she adds that 'those who didn't use it to disguize their true feelings would soon be hounded from society'.[53] We display the same animal instincts masked in different terminology. Fox-hunting, Emily points out, is little different from the way cats play with their victims before killing them: humans are no less cruel, she suggests, than cats. Indeed, humans have much to learn from animals, which make no attempt to disguise the methods they employ.

The same attitude lies behind the author's judgements on 'civilized' nineteenth-century attitudes in *Wuthering Heights*, and again animals are used to introduce the subject. The dogs at the Heights immediately reject Lockwood's hypocritical attempts at friendship, providing a touchstone for the savage relationships in the novel. When he returns the next day, Lockwood 'politely' admires the dog that had bitten him the day before:

> 'A beautiful animal!' I commenced again. 'Do you intend parting with the little ones, madam?'
>
> 'They are not mine,' said the amiable hostess more repellingly than Heathcliff himself could have replied.
>
> 'Ah, your favourites are among these!' I continued, turning to an obscure cushion full of something like cats.
>
> 'A strange choice of favourites,' she observed scornfully.
>
> Unluckily, it was a heap of dead rabbits–[54]

There is a grim humour in Lockwood's inappropriate chatter. It is inept and unsuccessful, emphasizing the distance civilized man has travelled from the savage reality of nature.

Yet the animal in man remains below the hypocritical surface – not attractive but an essential part of our being. Lockwood himself reverts to instinctive cruelty in his dream, when in terror he rubs the wrist of the child Catherine Earnshaw to and fro on the broken window pane, 'till the blood ran down and soaked the bed-clothes'.[55] Throughout the novel, characters are defined in terms of animals: we see Heathcliff as the wolf, Isabella as both canary and tigress, and Edgar as leveret. Yet there is no condemnation of the animal in their natures:

> Do I despise the timid deer,
> Because his limbs are fleet with fear?
> Or, would I mock the wolf's death-howl,
> Because his form is gaunt and foul?
> Or, hear with joy the leveret's cry,
> Because it cannot bravely die?[56]

It is to the beast and not to the man in Heathcliff that Emily Brontë extends her sympathy, and she has no more illusions about nature than Catherine had about Heathcliff. Catherine's 'picture' of him is of 'a fierce, pitiless, wolfish man. . . . and I'm his friend', she tells Isabella Linton.[57]

It would seem that Emily, like Charlotte, not only copied the illustrations of Bewick's *History of British Birds* in childhood, but also absorbed much of the text. The introductions to the two volumes, written by the Reverend Mr Cotes of Bedlington, contain the germ of her later belief about the natural world. They stress the amazing variety and interdependence of nature, and describe an eternal cycle of destruction and regeneration operating under the auspices of a powerful Providence. In particular, the survival of the fittest is emphasized, well before Charles Darwin popularized the view in *The Origin of Species* (1859):

> It is a melancholy reflection, that, from man, downwards, to the smallest living creature, all are found to prey upon and devour each other. The philosophic mind, however, sees this waste of animal life again and again repaired by fresh stores, ever ready to supply the void, and the great work of generation and destruction perpetually going on, and to this dispensation of an all-wise Providence, so interesting to humanity, bows in awful silence.[58]

This is the same lesson that Emily apparently gave the young Ellen Nussey, as she philosophized about the tadpoles in the stream. At the age of fifteen, Emily, 'half reclining on a slab of stone, played like a young child with the tadpoles in the water, making them swim about, and then fell to moralizing on the strong and the weak, the brave and the cowardly, as she chased them with her hand'.[59]

Nature for Emily Brontë was a mysterious and powerful force, dominating life with unremitting will. In 'Le Papillon', another essay written in Brussels, Emily again articulates these ideas: 'Nature is an inexplicable problem, based on a principle of destruction; everything must necessarily be the unfailing instrument of death to others, or else die itself.'[60] Her attempt at the end of the essay to evoke the goodness of God, manifested in the beauty of a butterfly, is unconvincing beside her earlier vision of the universe as 'a vast machine constructed simply to produce evil'.

Man is no exception in this universal struggle, as we saw in Emily's harsh judgement of humanity in 'Le Chat'. In *Wuthering Heights*, a 'civilized' guard dog bites the young Catherine Earnshaw and forces her to take refuge inside Thrushcross Grange, leaving her kindred spirit Heathcliff to retrace his steps home across the moor. There she too is 'civilized', her hair curled, her body dressed in fine clothes. She becomes like the Lintons' unnaturally pampered dog, refined and socialized. When she returns to the Heights, her new values lead her to reject her natural self, embodied in Heathcliff, and to choose to marry the cultivated Edgar Linton, a decision which ultimately causes her illness and death. Catherine suffered in the struggle of life because she was not true to herself. The housekeeper Nelly Dean echoes Emily Brontë's sentiments in 'Le Papillon': 'Well, we *must* be for ourselves in the long run; the mild and generous are only more justly selfish than the domineering.'[61] Emily's vision is a pantheistic one, in which man is part of a great natural cycle, where the strong simply survive a little longer than the weak. We all have freedom to choose, yet it is on the choice of liberty to be oneself that our survival depends in a world that exists on 'a principle of destruction'.

Thus it is that nature will always be in conflict with civilized values and only through an understanding of the animal world can man remain in tune with his essential self. If reconciliation is to be achieved in the drama between nature and civilization that had been working itself out in various ways throughout the Brontës' early writings, then civilization must take place within a natural cycle of birth and death. Spring follows winter, and the balance of nature reasserts itself at the end of *Wuthering Heights*. Nelly recognizes the potential for good in the savage young Hareton, reading his face as an artist might observe a subject:

> Still, I thought I could detect in his physiognomy a mind owning better qualities than his father ever possessed. Good things lost

> amid a wilderness of weeds, to be sure, whose rankness far overtopped their neglected growth; yet, notwithstanding, evidence of a wealthy soil that might yield luxuriant crops under other and favourable circumstances.[62]

Nature is powerful and destructive, but there is a place for civilization and its accoutrements. As in *King Lear*, the natural order reasserts itself, and Hareton thrives in an atmosphere of natural sincerity, tempered by the civilizing power of books.

In her devoir, 'Le Palais de la Mort', Emily coupled her condemnation of civilization with intemperance. These were two themes that had constantly fascinated the young Brontës as they chronicled the decline and fall of their imaginary empires. Here the study of the natural world joins forces with the lessons Emily absorbed from the classics. Her choice of name for her pet hawk Nero was not coincidental. Her painting (**324**) shows her rapport with the bird, yet its name suggests that she has no illusions about its nature. Through Emily and Anne's Gondal saga runs the theme of decline and fall of empire, dictated by the powerful passions and natural savagery of individual rulers. This is paralleled in the Angrian legends of Charlotte and Branwell. Charlotte's hero Zamorna becomes increasingly like a despotic Roman emperor, the Emperor Adrian Augustus, his imperial kingdom destined to fall as a result of the onslaught of barbarian tribes and his own corrupting pride. Branwell's prose manuscripts chronicle a succession of conquests and insurrections which occur with bewildering rapidity; no regime is stable for long. The struggles in Angria and Gondal reflect the same principle of cyclical destruction that Emily found in the natural world, a scenario that is played out with the predetermination of a Greek tragedy.

It is against this background that we must place the best of Emily Brontë's paintings and drawings, since they can clearly be seen as contributing to her later artistic development. Her animal portraits might be seen as the visual equivalent of her nature poetry and the 'Study of a fir tree' as an early analogue for *Wuthering Heights*. In these art works we see the same powerful identification with her subject that we encounter in her writing and the same ability to express with paint and pencil a freedom immanent in the world around us. We see in the subjects she chose to illustrate an independence of choice and fluency of style absent from her sisters' works. We see a self-contained woman, uninhibited by conventional artistic practice, drawing sustenance and inspiration from two primary sources, books and nature.

The drawings and paintings provide us with further evidence of the books she chose to read and the engravings she chose to copy, the subjects she preferred and the individual stance she adopted towards animals and natural objects. Above all, they provide us with a visual analogue for a life that became increasingly introspective. From the little Bewick sketches copied in the family circle, through duplications of Charlotte's work as part of her education, to the romanticism of her fir tree and the powerful sensitivity of her animal portraits, we can see something of the personality that grew to shun the material values of the civilized world, and that finally took refuge in a pantheistic communion.

# Notes

1 While a teacher at Law Hill, Emily Brontë apparently told her pupils that the school dog was dearer to her than they were (Mrs Ellis H. Chadwick, *In the Footsteps of the Brontës* (London: Sir Isaac Pitman & Sons Ltd, 1914), p. 124).

2 'Extract from the Prefatory Note to "Selections from Poems by Ellis Bell"', in *Wuthering Heights*, ed. Hilda Marsden and Ian Jack (Oxford: Clarendon Press, 1976), Appendix I, p. 446.

3 An unpublished fragmentary manuscript by Emily Brontë of an English translation from Book 1 of Virgil's *Aeneid* (The King's School, Canterbury), which indicates that she had more than a cursory knowledge of the classics. This manuscript is located with 'Images of cruelty': see **320**.

4 Helen H. Arnold, 'The Reminiscences of Emma Huidekoper Cortazzo: A Friend of Ellen Nussey', *Brontë Society Transactions* (1958), vol. 13, part 68, p. 225.

5 In her diary paper written at home on 30 [31] July 1845, Anne Brontë says: 'Emily is engaged in writing the Emperor Julius's life. She has read some of it, and I want very much to hear the rest. She is writing some poetry, too. I wonder what it is about?' (*Gondal's Queen: A Novel in Verse by Emily Jane Brontë*, ed. Fannie E. Ratchford (Austin: University of Texas Press, 1955), Appendix 2, p. 194).

6 See Christine Alexander, *The Early Writings of Charlotte Brontë* (Oxford: Basil Blackwell, 1983), p. 47.

7 The following catalogue entries, for example, illustrate drawings and paintings associated with the Glass Town and Angrian sagas:

**7, 8, 21, 23, 25, 41a, 97 102, 105, 113, 114, 127, 128, 136, 174–178, 187, 209, 239–241, 270, 298.**

8 'A Day at Parry's Palace' in 'Young Men's Magazine', *An Edition of the Early Writings of Charlotte Brontë*, ed. Christine Alexander, 2 vols. (Oxford: Basil Blackwell for the Shakespeare Head Press, 1987; 1991), vol. 1, p. 232.

9 Anne Brontë's list of Gondal names pencilled on a scrap of paper (printed in *Gondal's Queen*, ed. Ratchford, p. 195) and the place names written in her hand in Goldsmith's *Grammar of General Geography* are possibly earlier but undated (see Appendix A).

10 See Inga-stina Ewbank, 'Appendix IV: "Wuthering Heights" and Gondal', in *Wuthering Heights*, ed. Marsden and Jack, which is one of the best summaries of the evidence of the Gondal saga.

11 'What winter floods what showers of spring', 27 March 1832; the date has been questioned because it is four years earlier than that of any other surviving poem: see *Emily Jane Brontë: The Complete Poems*, ed. Janet Gezari (London: Penguin, 1992), p. 282.

12 In 1845, when Emily was 26 and Anne 25, they still 'played at' being Gondal characters, escaping from the Republican Palace of Instruction to join their fellow Royalists, while they were on a visit to York: see **331** and *Gondal's Queen*, ed. Ratchford, p. 192.

13 See for example, *Wuthering Heights*, ed. Marsden and Jack, pp. 24, 378, and 348 respectively.

14 Ibid., pp. 253, 82 and 348.

15 Ibid., p. 359.

16 Ibid., p. 195.

17 Ibid., p. 267.

18 See pp. 23–4.

19 See discussion on pp. 40–1.

20 David Cox, *Young Artist's Companion; Or, Drawing-Book of Studies and Landscape Embellishments: Comprising A Great Variety of the Most Picturesque Objects Required in the Various Compositions of Landscape Scenery, Arranged as Progressive Lessons* (London: S. & J. Fuller, 1825).

21 See pp. 41 and 69.

22 *Wuthering Heights*, ed. Marsden and Jack, p. 382.

23 *The Brontës: Their Lives, Friendships and Correspondence*, ed. Thomas James Wise and John Alexander Symington, 4 vols. (Oxford: Basil Blackwell for the Shakespeare Head Press, 1932), vol. 1, p. 82.

24 The Brontës owned the 1816 edition of Thomas Bewick, *A History of British Birds*, 2 vols. (Newcastle: T. Bewick; London: Longman & Co., 1816).

25 See **310**, **322**, **325**, **329**, **331** and **331a**. The sale catalogue of the contents of Moor Lane House, May 1898 (BPM), following Ellen Nussey's death, lists under 'Books' (lot 192) 'E. Brontë's drawing of a cockatoo', purchased by Mrs Richard Needham. Audrey G. Hall, who inherited much of Mrs Needham's Nussey material, has told the author that she believes she inadvertently destroyed this drawing of a cockatoo some years ago, not knowing that it was by Emily Brontë.

26 There are several stories of servants and visitors rescuing Brontë illustrations from the fire or rubbish bin: see, for example, **30**. Emily Brontë gave **325** and **326** as gifts.

27 Charles Hale, 'An American Visitor at Haworth, 1861', *Brontë Society Transactions* (1967), vol. 15, part 77, p. 137.

28 Chadwick, *In the Footsteps of the Brontës*, p. 102.

29 Arnold, 'The Reminiscences of Emma Huidekoper Cortazzo', p. 226.

30 *Wuthering Heights*, ed. Marsden and Jack, p. 24.

31 See p. 15.

32 See **309**.

33 It might even be seen as radically liberal, as in the case of Heger's unusual method of teaching French to Charlotte and Emily (discussed below).

34 'I am sad, very sad at the thoughts of leaving home but Duty–Necessity–these are stern mistresses who will not be disobeyed', Charlotte Brontë to Ellen Nussey, 2 July 1835: *The Brontës: Their Lives, Friendships and Correspondence*, ed. Wise and Symington, vol. 1, p. 129.

35 'Extract from the Prefatory Note to "Selections from Poems by Ellis Bell"', *Wuthering Heights*, ed. Marsden and Jack, p. 446.

36 Charlotte Brontë to Ellen Nussey, May 1842: *The Brontës: Their Lives, Friendships and Correspondence*, ed. Wise and Symington, vol. 1, p. 261.

37 'Aye there it is! It wakes tonight', dated 6 July 1841, in *Emily Jane Brontë: The Complete Poems*, ed. Gezari, p. 131. Winifred Gérin (*Emily Brontë: A Biography* (Oxford: Clarendon Press, 1971), p. 154) was the first to cite Shelley in relation to this poem.

38 'The Prisoner' (A Fragment), *Emily Jane Brontë: The Complete Poems*, ed. Gezari, p. 15.

39 William and Edward Finden, *Finden's Byron Beauties: Or, The Principal Female Characters in Lord Byron's Poems. Engraved from Original Paintings under the superintendence of W. and E. Finden* (London: Charles Tilt, 1836). Compare, for example, Charlotte Brontë's **128**.

40 E. C. Gaskell, *The Life of Charlotte Brontë*, 2 vols. (London: Smith, Elder & Co., 1857), vol. 1, p. 255.

41 Louise de Bassompierre, whose name was used for one of the characters in *Villette*, was still alive in 1913, when her picture and letter in French describing her acquisition of the drawing were published by Butler Wood in 'Two Brussels Schoolfellows of Charlotte Brontë', *Brontë Society Transactions* (1913), vol. 5, part 23, pp. 25–7.

42 *Wuthering Heights*, ed. Marsden and Jack, p. 5.

43 William Gilpin, *Remarks on Forest Scenery, and other Woodland Views, (Relative Chiefly to Picturesque Beauty)*, 2nd edn, 2 vols. (London: R. Blamire, 1794), vol. 1, p. 4.

44 Edward Chitham discusses at length the possible associations between Anne Brontë's poem about two trees that 'at the root were one', Emily Brontë's drawing of the fir tree, her poem 'There let thy bleeding branch atone', and the story of a fruit tree broken by Emily in childhood (Edward Chitham, *A Life of Emily Brontë* (Oxford and New York: Basil Blackwell, 1987), pp. 150–2).

45 The most obvious use of tree symbolism is the blasted chestnut in *Jane Eyre*, but trees are also an object of interest to the heroines of

*Shirley*, where they are associated with sketching (see p. 16). See also the following essay for a discussion of Anne Brontë's drawings of trees.

46 *Wuthering Heights*, ed. Marsden and Jack, p. 280.

47 *Caspar David Friedrich: Line and Transparency*, ed. Jacqueline and Maurice Guillaud (Paris: Centre Culturel du Marais, 1984), p. 12.

48 Arnold, 'The Reminiscences of Emma Huidekoper Cortazzo', pp. 226–7.

49 See **327** for further provenance and justification of reattribution to Emily Brontë.

50 Gaskell, *The Life of Charlotte Brontë*, vol. 1, p. 308. Gaskell also tells the amazing story of Emily fiercely pummelling Keeper's eyes with her fists as punishment, and then lovingly caring for his swelled head herself (p. 310).

51 Recorded in the 'diary' of John Greenwood, Haworth stationer, and quoted by Gérin, *Emily Brontë*, p. 146.

52 Charlotte Brontë, *Shirley*, ed. Herbert Rosengarten and Margaret Smith (Oxford and New York: Clarendon Press, 1979), p. 436.

53 Gérin, *Emily Brontë*, Appendix A: 'Emily Brontë's French Devoirs', p. 267 (French text only). Emily Brontë's source for Timon here would be Shakespeare's play *Timon of Athens*, though she may also have known the references to him in Lucian's *Dialogues* and in Alexander Pope's *Moral Essays, Epistle IV*.

54 *Wuthering Heights*, ed. Marsden and Jack, p. 13.

55 Ibid., p. 31.

56 'Stanzas to –', *Emily Jane Brontë: The Complete Poems*, ed. Gezari, p. 26.

57 *Wuthering Heights*, ed. Marsden and Jack, pp. 126–7.

58 Bewick, *A History of British Birds*, vol. 2, p. XVIII.

59 Ellen Nussey, 'Reminiscences of Charlotte Brontë', *Scribner's Monthly*, May 1871, p. 27.

60 Gérin, *Emily Brontë*, p. 272.

61 *Wuthering Heights*, ed. Marsden and Jack, p. 114.

62 Ibid., p. 241.

# The art of Anne Brontë

*Jane Sellars*

Art was important enough in Anne Brontë's life for her to create an artist as heroine in her novel *The Tenant of Wildfell Hall*, published in 1848. It is apparent from the novel that Anne was familiar with artists' methods, the business of making and selling paintings and the language of pictures themselves. In *Agnes Grey*, published with *Wuthering Heights* in 1847, there are many mentions of the art practices of the governess which were taken directly from Anne's own experience. We have no documentation of the writer's personal views on art but we can attempt to interpret them by reading her novels and by scrutinizing the small number of her own drawings still in existence. Anne did not, as far as we know, ever cherish an ambition to be a professional artist herself, as Charlotte once did. But she did have a similar talent for drawing and an observant eye for nature, both skills which she used to great effect in her writing.

More than half of the thirty-seven known drawings by Anne Brontë were treasured after her death by her sister Charlotte. They were later preserved by Arthur Bell Nicholls, Charlotte's widower, and were then offered at the sale of Nicholls's effects at Sotheby's in London in 1907. Most of them were purchased by the American collector of Brontëana Henry Houston Bonnell and twenty years later were bequeathed, with the bulk of his large collection of manuscripts, drawings, books and memorabilia, to the newly opened Brontë Parsonage Museum at Haworth. Others were acquired via the family of the Brontë servant, Martha Brown, through descendants of Miss

Wooler of Roe Head, or the descendants of a former pupil at the school; two works derive from sources related to Thorp Green Hall where Anne spent five years as governess to the Robinson children. A batch of ten drawings, formerly owned by John Greenwood, the Haworth stationer in the Brontës' time who sold them their writing paper, remains in private hands.

Only five of these works are in watercolour; the rest are in pencil. They include six tiny juvenile sketches; thirteen drawings, mostly landscapes and studies of heads executed at Roe Head where Anne was a pupil from late 1835 until December 1837; one picture made during the time Anne was a governess to the Ingham family at Blake Hall, Mirfield, April to December, 1839; an unfinished drawing made some time between 1839 and 1843; and a group of approximately sixteen works produced during the time Anne was a governess at Thorp Green Hall, from May 1840 until June 1845. Most of Anne's drawings were copied from prints from the same sources exploited by her brother and sisters, but there is at least one drawn largely from her imagination (**350**, and plate L), and the existence of a sketch block designed specifically for use in the open air, owned by Anne in 1843, provides us with some evidence that she did study directly from nature.

From the beginnings of Brontë biography, with Elizabeth Gaskell's *Life of Charlotte Brontë*, Anne has suffered from a relegation to the sidelines of the Brontë history which has affected the general appreciation of her novels. *The Tenant of Wildfell Hall*, her masterpiece, has yet to win the recognition it deserves as a milestone feminist novel. This down-grading of the youngest Brontë has much to do with Charlotte's suppression of the republication of this novel after Anne's death and her censorious views on it which she expressed in her Biographical Notice included in the 1850 edition of *Wuthering Heights*:

> The choice of subject was an entire mistake. Nothing less congruous with the writer's nature could be conceived. The motives which dictated this choice were pure, but, I think, slightly morbid. She had, in the course of her life, been called on to contemplate, near at hand and for a long time, the terrible effects of talents misused and faculties abused; hers was naturally a sensitive, reserved,

> and dejected nature; what she saw sank very deeply into her mind; it did her harm.[1]

But it also owes something to Anne's position as the youngest child.

Mrs Maria Brontë had a child every year from 1814 until July 1818 when Emily was born. It is quite likely that she suffered a miscarriage in 1819 and then Anne was born in January 1820. The Brontës were therefore very close together in age but Anne was nearly eighteen months younger than Emily, her closest sibling. Anne lost her mother when she was less than two years old and her two eldest sisters died when she was five. She had a very close relationship with her aunt Elizabeth Branwell, whom she must have accepted as a mother figure far more readily than the rest of the children. No doubt Anne's babyhood was a cosseted one, unnaturally extended by her position as youngest child, and in her infancy she was probably left out of her siblings' activities. Anne cannot have failed to be affected by the excitement generated by her older brother and sisters as they wrote about and drew the invented worlds of their childhood, and in 1828, when she was eight years old, she had obviously been admitted into that world herself, as a number of drawings exist from this year and the following one. Anne's earliest known art efforts are tiny little hesitant sketches of a church (**332**, and plate XXXIII), a cottage (**333**), a magpie (**334**), and broken fences and clumps of rock (**335**), all derived from engravings in Thomas Bewick's *History of British Birds*. These belong to a group of similar drawings by all the young Brontës, some of which are dedicated to Anne by Branwell and Charlotte (**9**, **10**, **184**, **188**; see plates XXXIV–XXXVI).

Very little is known about Anne's life between the ages of eleven and seventeen years, and there is a dearth of drawings from the period 1830–5. We know that in 1830 Anne was being taught to sew by her aunt – there is a sampler by her dated 23 January[2] – and Charlotte was teaching her to write.[3] In January 1831 Charlotte went to school at Roe Head for eighteen months and Anne and Emily became each other's confidante, inventing their shared imaginary world of Gondal. In 1834 they produced together their 24 November 'Diary Paper', Anne's contribution being a rough drawing of a tress of hair titled 'A bit of Lady

Julet's [*sic*] hair done by Anne', whilst Emily scrawled a wonderfully misspelt account of everyday life in the parsonage (**336**). Although there are no surviving drawings by Anne from the early 1830s there are several pictures of her, produced by both Charlotte and Branwell. Charlotte made four drawings of Anne in both pencil and watercolour (**91**, **92**, **119**, **134**), so perhaps she was a compliant and willing model, anxious to please her sister, whereas Emily and Branwell probably refused to be sitters. Also, in 1833–4 Anne was twice painted by her art student brother in his family group portraits (**224**, **225**, and colour plate XXIV) so we have a better idea of what she looked like when a young girl than we do of Emily and Charlotte. These portraits complement Ellen Nussey's well-known written description of her:

> Anne–dear, gentle Anne–was quite different in appearance from the others. She was her aunt's favourite. Her hair was a very pretty light brown, and fell on her neck in graceful curls. She had lovely violet-blue eyes, fine penciled eyebrows, and clear, almost transparent complexion.[4]

In July 1835 Emily went to Roe Head as a pupil with Charlotte promoted to a teaching position, but Emily could not bear to be away from home and Anne stoically took her place, probably in October that year. More than a third of Anne's existing drawings were made whilst she was at school. The fact that they have survived shows that she must have felt a well-deserved pride in her work and kept them in her portfolio for the rest of her life. It is possible, too, that she hung on to them should she need to present them as evidence of her artistic skills when applying for a job as a governess. We do not have a great deal of information about the regime at Roe Head, or about its pupils, but we know that it was a small girls' school based in a large house and set in a typical semi-rural industrial West Riding area with large gardens, fields within view and mills and coal-miners' cottages as next-door neighbours. Just as her sister Charlotte had done before her (**62**), Anne made a drawing of a view of Roe Head (**339**) which is practically identical in its details. The Brontës were distinguished from the other pupils by their relative poverty, as their fellow students were typically the daughters of local mill-owners and landowners, such as

Charlotte's friends Ellen Nussey and Mary Taylor. The curriculum would have been worthy but dull and the teaching of art would depend almost solely on the art of imitation.

The classroom at Roe Head must have held a practically unchanging stock of prints for copying as there is at least one certain example in Anne's 'Head and shoulders of a young woman' (**340**) of her copying in 1835–7 from the same print that Charlotte copied from in 1831 (**52**). There was a huge market in prints from the early days of the nineteenth century, expanding progressively as print technology improved, and there were many sources from which the amateur artist might copy, which is one of the reasons why it has proved so difficult to identify precisely the plates from which the Brontës copied both at home and at school. It is worthwhile looking at the list of 'Works of Art' available from Ackermann & Co., 'Book and Printsellers and Superfine Water-colour Manufacturers to Their Majesties' in 1835.[5] The most expensive items were portfolios containing as many as fifty facsimile sketches, such as Samuel Prout's views made in Flanders and Germany, on sale for £6.6s. on India paper or £5.5s. on 'tinted grey touched with white'. Individual prints of popular paintings of the day such as Landseer's 'High Life' and 'Low Life', anthropomorphic studies of dogs which were probably admired by Emily Brontë, were available for 9s. Also on Ackermann's list were genre subjects, portraits, historical subjects and a long list of sporting and animal prints. The kind of items which may have been accessible to Anne at Roe Head include *New Drawing-Books* by W. Eldridge: 'Landscape, three numbers. Each containing four subjects. Price 1s.6d. per number.' The most humble items advertised were large collections of unspecified drawings and prints for 'Scrap Books and Albums'. Ackermann's also offered 'Drawings Let Out to Copy' of figures, landscapes, flowers, fruit and so on for a yearly subscription of four guineas, and such aids to drawing accurately from nature as 'The Graphic Mirror', for which the claim was made that 'The difficulties known to exist in the Camera Lucida are obviated in this instrument.'

The earliest surviving drawings produced by Anne at Roe Head are two meticulous studies of trees, the 'Oak Tree' (**337**) and 'An Elm Tree'

(**338**), made during her first weeks there in October and November respectively. Anne's love of trees was shown also in her poetry, for example in 'Lines composed in a wood on a windy day', written in 1846 in memory of a walk in the Long Plantation at Thorp Green:

> The long withered grass in the sunshine is glancing,
> The bare trees are tossing their branches on high;
> The dead leaves beneath them are merrily dancing,
> The white clouds are scudding across the blue sky.[6]

The drawings of the oak and the elm and a later drawing of an ash or lime tree made on 19 October 1843 when Anne was at Thorp Green (**367**) are all similar to each other, depicting a single tree with minute attention to the details of its characteristic features. These would all seem to be copied from the kind of plates mentioned above in Eldridge's drawing books. In *The Tenant of Wildfell Hall*, however, we find Helen Graham working directly from nature, 'studying the distinctive characters of the different varieties of trees in their winter nakedness, and copying, with a spirited, though delicate touch, their various ramifications'.[7]

On 16 December 1843 Anne made an ambitious pencil drawing of a 'Landscape with trees' (**368**, and plate 16) which is intriguingly marked on the surface as if by splashes of rain, suggesting that Anne may have drawn the scene from life at Thorp Green. Certainly, the landscape of the Vale of York around the Robinsons' home is soft, verdant and wooded as in the drawing, but the precise attention to detail is more suggestive of a copy from a print. It is irresistible, however, to make a connection with the drawing and the poem above. Furthermore, Anne provides us with an exposition of her emotional sensitivity to such a landscape in *The Tenant of Wildfell Hall*, where we find Helen unable to enjoy the beauty of nature because of Arthur Huntingdon's absence:

ate 16 'Landscape with trees' (**368**), encil drawing by Anne Brontë, 1834

> and when I wander in the ancient woods, and meet the little wild-flowers smiling in my path, or sit in the shadow of our noble ash-trees by the waterside, with their branches gently swaying in the light summer breeze that murmurs through their feathery

> foliage – my ears full of that low music mingled with the dreamy hum of insects, my eyes abstractedly gazing on the glassy surface of the little lake before me, with the trees that crowd about its bank, some gracefully bending to kiss its waters, some rearing their stately heads high above, but stretching their wide arms over its margin, all faithfully mirrored far, far down in its glassy depth – though sometimes the images are partly broken by the sport of aquatic insects, and sometimes, for a moment, the whole is showered into trembling fragments by a transient breeze that swept the surface too roughly – still I have no pleasure . . .[8]

In another part of the book Helen talks to Gilbert Markham about the beauty of the light shining through the leaves in the trees and the author uses Gilbert's thoughts to describe in more technical terms the effect of light as seen by the artist's eye:

> where at intervals the level rays of the sun, penetrating the thickness of the trees and shrubs on the opposite side of the path before us, relieved their dusky verdure by displaying patches of semi-transparent leaves of resplendent golden green.[9]

Anne obviously learnt a great deal from her studious copying from prints and did not regard it merely as the mechanical process it probably was for most of her schoolfellows. Close study of good art is an effective way of learning and training the powers of observation, even though it does not encourage individual expression, but in the early nineteenth century individuality was an alien concept for all amateur artists and most professionals. There are five meticulously drawn landscapes which were probably produced at Roe Head in 1836: 'A ruined church' (**342**), 'Landscape with castles' (**343**), 'Landscape with castle, bridge and female figure' (**344**), 'Man with a dog before a villa' (**345**, and plate LII) and 'Landscape with cattle and haycart' (**346**). Looking at these in chronological order it is possible to see how Anne's skills improve from one drawing to the next. The earliest work, the church drawn in February 1836, depends more on line than on tone to construct the image, whereas in her May drawing of an Italian scene (**345**) she works within a far wider tonal range to create a sense of depth which is absent from the earlier drawing. An unfinished landscape drawing of woodland with deer exists to tell us something of Anne's working methods (**352**, and plate 17). We can see how she first of all mapped out her subject in line only and then, working from the centre outwards so as not to smudge her finished work, she began to model the forms. In this central portion she establishes the range of tones for the drawing, extending from the black of the central tree trunk to the cream of the card support itself. Valuable information on Anne's drawings in their very early stages can be found in the fascinating group of unfinished sketches preserved in a sketch block dating from 1843 (**360–365**).

Plate 17 'Woodland with deer' (**352**), by Anne Brontë, c. 1839

There is one tiny landscape drawing which is out of kilter with the rest of Anne's work and therefore worth a mention. The style of her 'Landscape with trees and lake' (**341**) is quite different from the 1836 drawings, drawn with soft pencil in a sketchy manner which omits any attention to detail. It is tempting to regard it as a drawing from life but the lakeside scene is too much like the kind of views to be found in the landscape books copied at Roe Head, from where it is believed to originate, to be considered typical of the environs of Mirfield.

Anne was less successful in representing the human face and figure than she was in drawing landscapes. This is a failing of most women's art for almost all of the nineteenth century because it was considered improper for women to study directly from the human figure, whether draped or undraped. Even though Anne's figure drawings are nearly all copies from prints she was unable to bring to these works any real understanding of human anatomy. Indeed, her drawings of children's heads (**347**, **348**, **349**) and a portrait of a woman (**340**) produced at Roe Head were copied from prints which were a substitute for the real thing. On 13 November 1839, at Mirfield, during her first post of governess, Anne made a symbolic drawing in which she included a full-length female figure, 'Woman gazing at a sunrise over a seascape' (**350**). The image of the solitary girl seen with her back to the viewer, gazing out towards a far horizon, is one that is often found in nineteenth-century northern European romantic art, notably in the melancholy *Rückenfiguren* in the work of the German landscape painter Caspar David Friedrich (1774–1840). It is uncertain whether or not Anne Brontë could have seen reproductions of Friedrich's art but the figure of the young woman here expresses the emotion of yearning for contact with a larger world than her own in the manner of romantic art, the symbolism of which would have been understood by her. As Edward Chitham has pointed out, in *The Tenant of Wildfell Hall* Anne more than once uses the device of a painting to express the true feelings of Helen Huntingdon, and he goes further to suggest that the figure in this drawing is a self-portrait at the point in Anne's life when she was becoming aware of feelings of affection for William Weightman, her father's new young curate, who was to die so tragically of cholera just three years later.[10]

The picture is outstanding within Anne's œuvre not only because of its apparent symbolic content but also because certain aspects of its handling suggest that it is drawn partly from the artist's imagination, rather than being the usual straightforward copy from a print. There is a softness and slight uncertainty about the description of the figure and the handling of the shading which is quite different from the assured, crisp lines of her copying work. The figure of the girl is badly constructed in both pose and proportions; the left arm is far too long and the head sits uneasily on the shoulders. The rock formation which runs up the left side of the picture is especially curious, possibly deriving from a print but with added imaginative touches which create a more fantastic form than can be seen anywhere else in Anne's drawings. Nonetheless, it is refreshing to look at a drawing by Anne in which she has invested some of her own feelings.

In July 1840, only two months after taking up her new job at Thorp Green, Anne produced a second picture of a female figure in a landscape which she enigmatically titled 'What you please' (**353**, and plate LI). Chitham has meticulously dated the production of this drawing to a time when Anne was staying with her employers at Scarborough, a fashionable seaside resort in North Yorkshire, when she presumably had more leisure for her own pursuits.[11] In it we see a pretty young girl standing nervously at the edge of a wood, surrounded by the beauties of nature. This must have been a period of great excitement as a new world opened before her. She had only briefly had the chance to become acquainted with the opulence of Thorp Green, and now here she was enjoying the delights of being close to the sea. Chitham has suggested that this is a further self-portrait representing Anne poised on the edge of her new life.[12] Anne probably did identify with the young woman in her drawing who appears to be in harmony with nature, something which pleased her and which may explain the title. The manner of its execution, however, suggests that the subject was probably derived from a print rather than from the imagination. In nineteenth-century British art images of a young girl poised on the edge of womanhood are numerous, very often set in a spring landscape such as this one, to symbolize female youth and virginity. Indeed, in *The Tenant of Wildfell Hall* Helen is found at work on a painting of this precise subject:

> The scene represented was an open glade in a wood. A group of dark Scotch firs was introduced in the middle distance to relieve the prevailing freshness of the rest: but in the foreground were part of the gnarled trunk and of the spreading boughs of a large forest tree, whose foliage was a brilliant golden green.

At this point we are reminded strongly of Anne's drawing of a 'Landscape with trees' (**368**) which pictures a glade in a leafy wood with a stunted fir in the middle and a large spreading tree to the side. In Helen's painting a pair of amorous doves sit in the bough of this tree whilst beneath it:

> a young girl was kneeling on a daisy-spangled turf, with head thrown back and masses of fair hair falling on her shoulders, her hands clasped, lips parted, and eyes intently gazing upward in pleased, yet earnest contemplation of these feathered lovers.

When Arthur Huntingdon finds Helen at work on her masterpiece he reads the picture for himself, identifying it as a pictorial metaphor for her own situation. He calls it 'a very fitting study for a young lady – Spring just opening into summer – morning just approaching noon – girlhood-just ripening into womanhood – and hope just verging into fruition'.[13]

In 1841 life at Thorp Green began to pall for Anne. On 15 March that year the Robinsons' baby daughter Georgina Jane died, a sad event which must have affected the compassionate young governess. In July that year she wrote in the now lost diary paper: 'I dislike the situation and wish to change it for another.'[14] No drawings survive from that year but there is a 'Portrait of a young woman' from 1842 (**359**). It was drawn at Haworth when Anne was at home on holiday for her customary fortnight in June. She was obviously unhappy with her handiwork and has written on the back of the paper: 'A very bad picture drawn June 24th 1842'. Chitham has suggested that this may be a portrait of one of the Robinson girls, and that 'bad' means a poor likeness.[15] Various features of the work suggest that it was in fact drawn from life and that it is a possible self-portrait. The girl would seem to look at the viewer, as if Anne were regarding herself in a mirror. The disproportionately large arm may be the result of Anne's exact description of her own arm as she saw it, enlarged in the mirror's reflection. One arm is not in sight as the hand is busy drawing. The drapery she holds around her shoulders is reminiscent of that which she wore when she posed for Charlotte nine years earlier (**91**), perhaps in imitation of a classical goddess. If it is a self-portrait it is an idealized one as Anne gives herself a full, plump face, although the ringleted hair, the large eyes and the pencilled eyebrows are her own.

There is a similar 'Portrait of a young woman in blue' (**357**) worked in watercolour and bodycolour which was attributed to Charlotte when it was acquired by the Brontë Parsonage Museum in 1950, even though it came via a Thorp Green connection, presented to a neighbour by the Robinson girls. It depicts a similarly full-faced young woman with thick dark hair, Anne's characteristically over-large eyes and blue drapery around her shoulders. Anne taught drawing and painting to the Misses Robinson in the way that she had studied it herself, through copying from prints, and again this work reminds us, for example, of Heath's 'Beauties'. There is a passage in *Agnes Grey*, from which we learn a great deal about Anne's teaching methods, where she describes circumstances in which this particular drawing may have been produced:

> Miss Murray was gone forth to enjoy a quiet ramble with a new fashionable novel for her companion, leaving me in the school-room, hard at work upon a water-colour I had promised to do for her, and which she insisted upon my finishing that day.[16]

In January 1843, Anne's responsibilities at Thorp Green were reduced because Bessie Robinson had reached the age of seventeen and no longer required a governess's attention. Anne's time would have largely been taken up with Mary, then aged fourteen, but she would have had more opportunity for her own leisure pursuits in music, art and studying the German language. In June 1843 she inscribed her new music manuscript book, in September she bought two German grammars, and in August she made a purchase which must have given her great pleasure: a French-style sketching block designed specifically for drawing in the open air. This is an ingenious piece of equipment for the amateur artist, the advantages of which are described at length on the label pasted inside the front cover (see **360**), with its smooth tablet of paper, and the handy envelope sleeve in which to tuck one's finished drawings to save them from blowing away.

A number of unfinished sketches survive with the block on which they were made (cherished by a private owner of Brontë relics), and from them we can learn something more of Anne's working methods, and speculate on her choice of subject matter. The sketch block – inscribed with Anne's name and the date 29 August 1843 inside the front cover – is in itself evidence of her interest in sketching out of doors. It is possible to imagine Anne freely exploring the countryside around Thorp Green with sketch block in hand, studying from nature in just the way she described her own artist heroine, Helen Huntingdon. Plantations of fir trees, for instance, were to be seen in the Vale of York; one such is sketched lightly onto a page of the sketch block, with a curving river and a charming group of deer (**360**). Buildings, too, were carefully scrutinized in other unfinished studies which were sketched on sheets of paper from the same block (**361**, **362**, **363**).

Another work which has a Thorp Green provenance has only recently come to light in the ownership of a descendant of Ann Marshall who was Mrs Robinson's confidential maid, to whom it is believed Anne made a present of the picture. According to Winifred Gérin, Ann Marshall had a role in the Brontë story as she was believed by Branwell to be his confidante too and letters were exchanged between them after his departure from Thorp Green, but evidence of money gifts to her found in Mr Robinson's account books may suggest that she was playing a three-cornered game with her employers and the infatuated tutor. However, this has not been proven. Poor Ann Marshall died of consumption in 1847 when she was only thirty-eight.[17] The picture in question is a charming watercolour of a little girl clutching a posy of flowers, painted in September 1843 (**366**, and colour plate XX). Flowers were often included in pictures of children to symbolize their transient innocence and beauty. It is again a copy from a print of a type which was especially popular throughout the nineteenth century. The prettiness and innocence of girl children was much exploited as a subject across the whole gamut of British art, from the illustrated Annuals to the oil paintings hung on the walls of the Royal Academy of Arts. Women artists in particular specialized in paintings of sweet-looking children. Indeed, in *The Tenant of Wildfell Hall* Markham comes across one of Helen's paintings in her studio which could be a melancholy counterpart to this sunny image:

> a simple but striking little picture of a child brooding with looks of silent, but deep and sorrowful regret, over a handful of withered flowers, with glimpses of dark low hills and autumnal fields behind it, and a dull beclouded sky above.[18]

In addition to Anne's finished portraits of young women there is an unfinished one of a girl petting a dog (**354**). The girl in the work is very like the maiden who stands on the edge of the wood in 'What you please' (**353**), with her hair in ringlets and wearing a white dress. The spaniel resembles Flossy, the dog given to Anne by the Robinsons in 1843 which was also painted by Emily in her now lost watercolour of an animal group (**329**) and depicted chasing a bird across a moorland landscape in a painting formerly attributed to Charlotte and now reassigned to Emily (**327**). In the background of 'Portrait of a girl with a dog' (**354**) there is a view of a Palladian-style mansion set in large grounds which, although it looks like Kirby Hall, the neighbouring house to Thorp Green, is a typical feature of prints of picturesque landscape views. The depiction of the spaniel is very close to that in two unfinished watercolours of a dog sitting in a window sill previously attributed to Charlotte, but also more likely to be the work of Anne (**355**, **356**). All three works were probably begun by Anne at Thorp Green and never completed. Maybe the unhappiness of her last days there, caused by Branwell's unacceptable behaviour in his intrigue with Mrs Lydia Robinson, disheartened her from finishing the drawing and paintings.

The only other surviving work by Anne Brontë is a pencil drawing of 'Little Ouseburn Church' (**358**), unsigned and undated, which she drew from life from a vantage point in a field opposite what was then a lake on the east side of the church. This is the church that she attended on Sundays, within easy walking distance of the site of Thorp Green Hall, which is now rebuilt as Thorp Underwood Hall and home to a girls' school. The church stands beside the Monk's House, the house where Branwell lodged, depicted by him in one of his ink drawings (**282**, and plate LX). The artificial lake in front of the church in Anne's time has now reverted to a narrow beck. The landscape around Thorp Underwood is the lush and gentle Vale of York, which must have seemed like a foreign land to Anne after the dark, bleak hills of Haworth, and she must surely have enjoyed the softness of the countryside and the much gentler climate. The little church would have looked as picturesque as any to be found in the plates of the illustrated Annuals from which she used to copy. The view of it today remains unchanged from the one seen by Anne's eyes. Behind the church there is the Mausoleum, which was there in the 1840s but Anne would only have had a view of its roof from her standpoint and has chosen to omit it. The drawing is worked with a softer, impressionistic touch than in her copies. Although she has struggled a little with the perspective of the building, the leafy trees are drawn with her usual sensitivity, and she achieves the effect of the church seen mirrored in the lake.

In *The Tenant of Wildfell Hall*, the artist heroine reflects on what her art means to her:

> 'I almost wished I were not a painter,' observed my companion.
>
> 'Why so? One would think at such a time you would almost exult in your privilege of being able to imitate the various brilliant and delightful touches of nature.'
>
> 'No; for instead of delivering myself up to the full enjoyment of them as others do, I am always troubling my head about how I could produce the same effect on canvas; and that can never be done, it is mere vanity and vexation of the spirit.'
>
> 'Perhaps you cannot do it to satisfy yourself, but you may and do succeed in delighting others with the result of your endeavours.'
>
> 'Well, after all I should not complain: perhaps few people gain their livelihood with so much pleasure in their toil as I do.'[19]

We have very slender evidence from which to judge the significance of art in Anne Brontë's own life, but the very fact that she created a woman artist as a major character in fiction would seem to tell us that her art was more to her than a mere tool of the governess's trade. The passages in *The Tenant of Wildfell Hall* which describe the beauties of nature as seen through the artist's eye also indicate an innate sensitivity to the visual world. At her best, Anne Brontë drew with an assured eye and a highly competent hand. It is possible to track her increasing confidence in her materials, to sense her enjoyment in describing in finely pencilled detail the luxuriant foliage of a summertime tree. Although Anne has been characterized in Brontë biography as a gentle, fragile being, it would appear that she was in fact far more pragmatic than her sisters. This, perhaps, was the key to her attitude towards her art: it helped her to earn her living as a teacher and it gave her pleasure in her leisure hours.

# *Notes*

1 *Wuthering Heights*, ed. Hilda Marsden and Ian Jack (Oxford: Clarendon Press, 1976), Appendix 1, p. 439.

2 Brontë Parsonage Museum: S12: 'Sampler/ 23 January 1830/ wool and cotton mix/ 324 x 206 mm/ Anne Brontë'. Gift of the late Clement K. Shorter, 1928; formerly owned by Arthur Bell Nicholls who gave it to Shorter.

3 Fragment of Anne Brontë's childhood copywriting; seven copy-book lines signed 'Anne Bronte' on reverse of a prose fragment by Charlotte of 220 words dated 14 July 1829, beginning 'Sir it is well known that the Geni . . .' (BPM: Bonnell 79).

4 Ellen Nussey, 'Reminiscences of Charlotte Brontë', *Scribner's Monthly*, May 1871, p. 27.

5 *Forget Me Not, a Christmas and New Year's Present* (London: Ackermann & Co., 1835), unnumbered back pages of advertisements.

6 Edward Chitham, *The Poems of Anne Brontë: A New Text and Commentary* (London and Basingstoke: Macmillan, 1979), p. 88.

7 *The Tenant of Wildfell Hall*, ed. Herbert Rosengarten (Oxford: Clarendon Press, 1992), vol. 1, p. 50.

8 Ibid., vol. 2, pp. 224–5.

9 Ibid., vol. 1, p. 83.

10 Edward Chitham, *A Life of Anne Brontë* (Oxford and Cambridge, Massachusetts: Basil Blackwell, 1991), pp. 65–6.

11 Ibid., p. 79.

12 Ibid.

13 *The Tenant of Wildfell Hall*, ed. Rosengarten, vol. 1, p. 156.

14 Clement K. Shorter, *Charlotte Brontë and Her Circle* (London: Hodder & Stoughton, 1896), pp. 148–9.

15 Chitham, *A Life of Anne Brontë*, pp. 93–4.

16 *Agnes Grey*, ed. Hilda Marsden and Robert Inglesfield (Oxford: Clarendon Press, 1988), p. 118.

17 Winifred Gérin, *Branwell Brontë: A Biography* (London: Hutchinson, 1961), pp. 236–8.

18 *The Tenant of Wildfell Hall*, ed. Rosengarten, vol. 1, p. 43.

19 Ibid., vol. 1, p. 83.

# Plate section

I Charlotte Brontë, 'The Mountain Sparrow', 1830 (**26**)

II Branwell Brontë, 'Gos Hawk', 1833 (**218**)

Keeper - from life - April 24th 1838 - Emily Jane Brontë -


III Emily Brontë, 'Keeper – from life', 1838 (**319**)

IV Emily Brontë, Flossy, c. 1843 (**327**)

V Emily Brontë, 'Grasper – from life', 1834 (**313**)

VI Emily Brontë, Nero, 1841 (**324**)

VII Charlotte Brontë, Copy of a portrait of Mrs Brontë, 1830 (**36**)

VIII Charlotte Brontë, Portrait of Anne Brontë, c. 1833 (**92**)

IX Charlotte Brontë, 'Bessy Bell and Mary Gray', 1830 (**39**)

X Branwell Brontë, 'Terror', 1830 (**202**)

XI Branwell Brontë, 'Hermit', 1830 (**200**)

XII Branwell Brontë, 'Queen Esther', 1830 (**207**)

XIII Charlotte Brontë, 'The Atheist viewing the dead body of his Wife', c. 1835–1836 (**136**)

XIV Charlotte Brontë, 'Wild Roses From Nature', 1830 (**28**)

XV Charlotte Brontë, Study of a primrose, c. 1830 (**33**)

XVI Charlotte Brontë, 'Lycidas', 1835 (**129**)

XVII Charlotte Brontë, Study of a heartsease, 1832 (**84**)

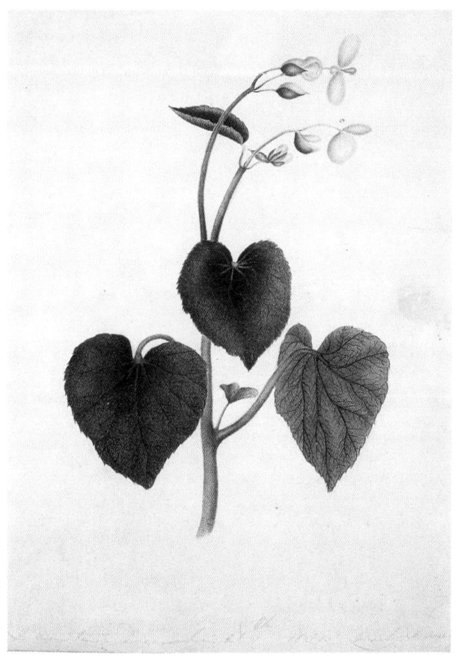

XVIII Charlotte Brontë, Pink begonia, 1832 (**86**)

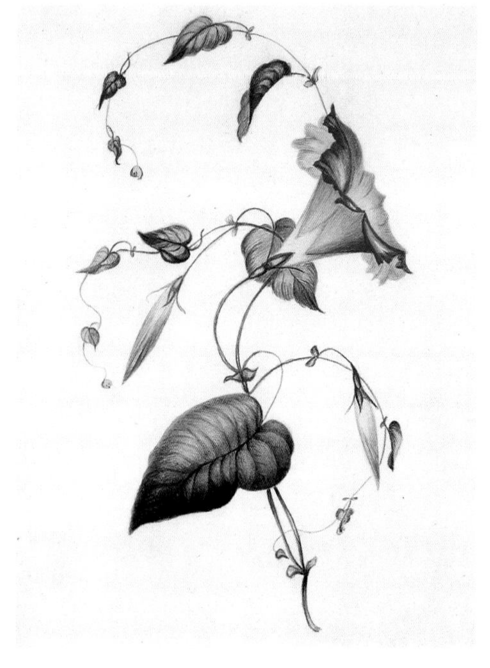

XIX Charlotte Brontë, Blue convolvulus, 1832 (**87**)

xx Anne Brontë, Portrait of a little girl with a posy, 1843 (**366**)

XXI Charlotte Brontë, 'Portrait of A French Brunette', c. 1833 (**93**)

XXII Charlotte Brontë, The Maid of Saragoza, c. 1834 (**127**)

XXIII Branwell Brontë, Emily Jane Brontë, c. 1833–1834 (**224**)

XXIV Branwell Brontë, The Brontë sisters, c. 1834 (**225**)

XXV Charlotte Brontë, Woman in leopard fur, 1839 (**147**)

XXVI Charlotte Brontë, Lake and castle, 1833 (**94**)

XXVII Charlotte Brontë, Portrait of a child with hat and basket, 1830 (**35**)

XXVIII Charlotte Brontë, 'King of Angria, Duke of Zamorna', c. 1834 (**113**)

XXIX Branwell Brontë, John Brown (1804–1855), c. 1835–1839 (**243**)

XXX Branwell Brontë, Miss Margaret Hartley, c. 1838–1839 (**254**)

XXXI Branwell Brontë, Isaac Kirby, 1838–1839 (**257**)

XXXII Branwell Brontë, Mrs Isaac Kirby, 1838–1839 (**258**)

XXXIII Anne Brontë, Church surrounded by trees, 1828 (**332**)

XXXIV Branwell Brontë, Ruined tower, 1828 (**184**)

XXXV Charlotte Brontë, Ruined tower, 1828 (**9**)

XXXVI Charlotte Brontë, Thatched cottage, 1828 (**10**)

XXXVII Charlotte Brontë, 'Zenobia Marchioness Ellrington', 1833 (**100**)

XXXVIII Charlotte Brontë, 'Arthur Adrian Marquis of Douro' 2, 1833 (**101**)

XXXIX Charlotte Brontë, Portrait of a young lady, 1834 (**111**)

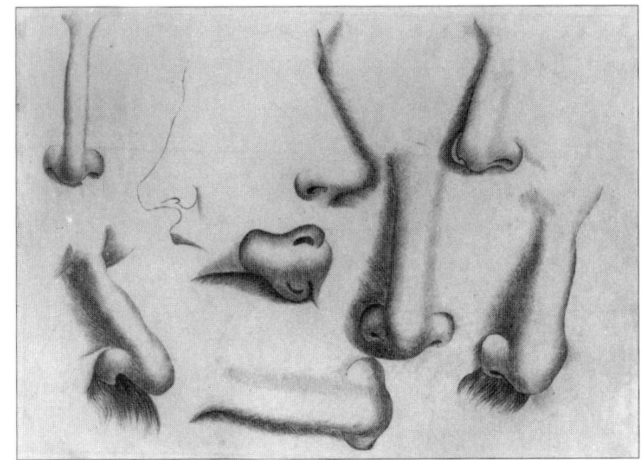

XL Charlotte Brontë, Study of noses, c. 1831 (**44**)

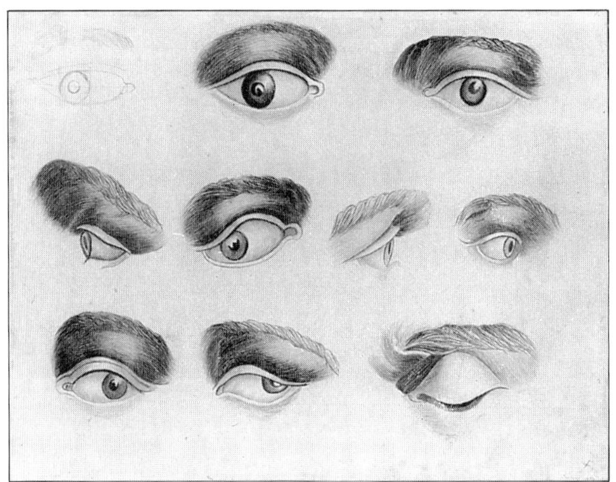

XLI Charlotte Brontë, Study of eyes, 1831 (**42**)

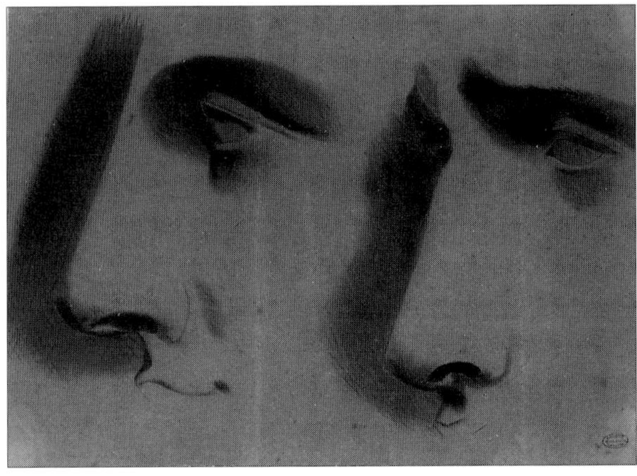

XLII Charlotte Brontë, Study of two profiles, c. 1831 (**49**)

XLIII Charlotte Brontë, Roman head, 1835 (**131**)

XLIV Charlotte Brontë, Classical head, c. 1835 (**132**)

XLV Charlotte Brontë, Madonna and child, c. 1835 (**133**)

XLVI Charlotte Brontë, Kirkstall Abbey amongst trees, 1832 (**82**)

XLVII Charlotte Brontë, 'Cockermouth', c. 1833 (**90**)

XLVIII Charlotte Brontë, Study of a tree and cottage, 1842 (**155**)

XLIX Charlotte Brontë, William Weightman, 1840 (**149**)

l Anne Brontë, Woman gazing at a sunrise over a seascape, 1839 (**350**)

LI Anne Brontë, 'What you please', 1840 (**353**)

LII Anne Brontë, Man with a dog before a villa, 1836 (**345**)

LIII Emily Brontë, Woman's head with tiara, 1841 (**323**)

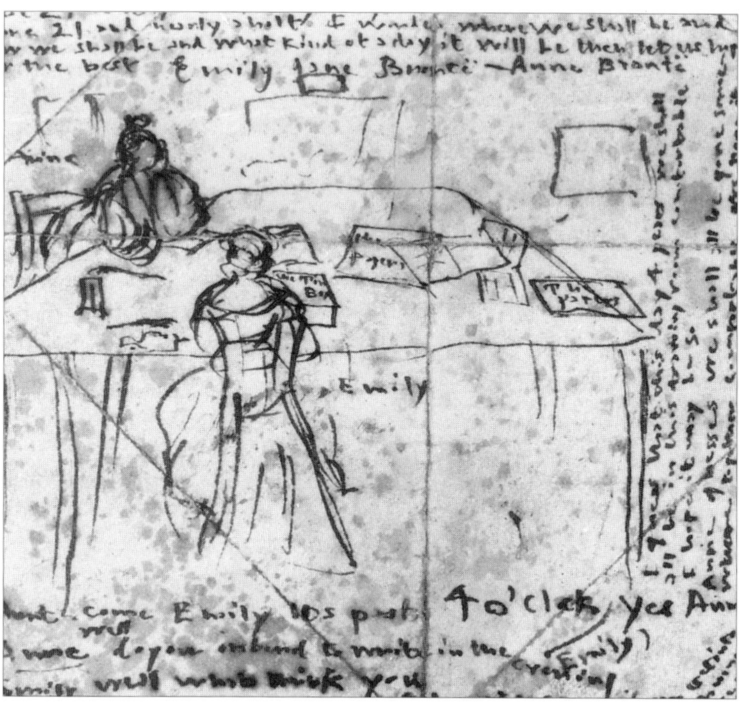


LIV Emily Brontë, Diary paper, 1837 (**316**)

LV Emily Brontë, 'Forget me not', c. 1830 (**309**)

LVI Emily Brontë, Guwald Tower, Haddington, 1832 (**311**)

LVII Branwell Brontë, Portrait of a man holding aloft a wineglass, c. 1840–1842 (**273**)

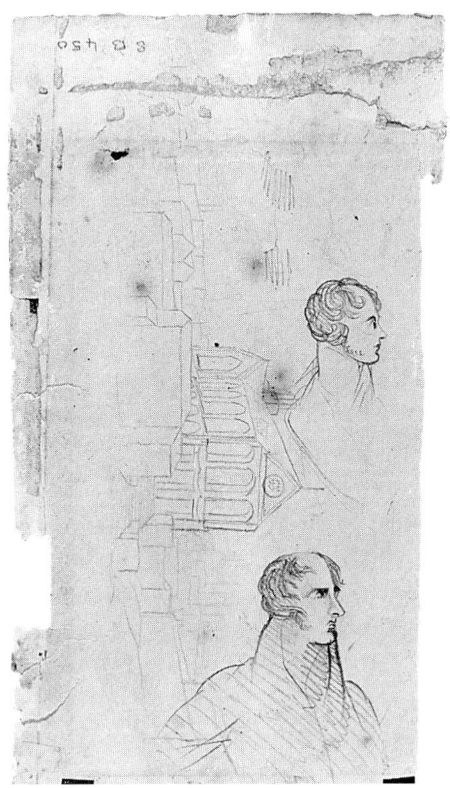

LVIII Charlotte Brontë, Two male portraits and buildings, c. 1833–1834 (**98**)

LIX Branwell Brontë, Jacob's dream, c. 1834–1838 (**235**)

LX Branwell Brontë, The Old Hall, Thorp Green, 1844 (**282**)

LXI Branwell Brontë, 'Zamorna. 35.', 1835 (**239**)

LXII Branwell Brontë, The pirate, c. 1835 (**241**)

# Charlotte Brontë

1

## Juvenile painting of a house

1828
Watercolour on paper
28 × 36 mm

The illustration occupies half of p. 1 (56 × 36 mm) of Charlotte Brontë's earliest extant manuscript. The remainder of the page is occupied by the beginning of her first juvenile story: 'There was once a little girl and her name was Ane'. The page is the first of a 16-page hand-sewn booklet, enclosed in a cover of grey and blue spotted wallpaper.

Bequest of Henry Houston Bonnell, 1927, who acquired the manuscript at Sotheby's sale of the effects of Mary Anne Nicholls, cousin and second wife of Arthur Bell Nicholls, 19 June 1914, lot 191.

*Brontë Parsonage Museum: Bonnell 78*

Tiny landscape with a grey-roofed house in the centre, a fence extending on either side to the edge of the drawing and trees behind; two sides of the house are visible, a yellow path leading from the red front door, four windows, a chimney.

One of six watercolours illustrating this story about Anne, possibly composed about the same date as Charlotte's and Branwell's early drawings 'For Anne', dated late 1828: see p. 38 and **9**, **10**, **184** and **188**.

2

## Juvenile painting of a castle

1828
Watercolour on paper
28 × 36 mm

The illustration occupies the top half of a manuscript page (56 × 36 mm); a second illustration occupies the remainder of the page: see **3**. Both are part of Charlotte's earliest juvenile manuscript: 'There was once a little girl and her name was Ane', a 16-page hand-sewn booklet, enclosed in a cover of grey and blue spotted wallpaper.

Bequest of Henry Houston Bonnell, 1927, who acquired the manuscript at Sotheby's sale of the effects of Mary Anne Nicholls, 19 June 1914, lot 191.

*Brontë Parsonage Museum: Bonnell 78*

Tiny watercolour of a brown castle with a red flag flying from the top on a yellow mast, two doors (yellow and red), four blue windows, a woman and child in foreground and a tree behind on right. See **1** for further information.

3

## Juvenile painting of a rowing boat

1828
Watercolour on paper
28 × 36 mm

The illustration occupies the second half of a manuscript page (56 × 36 mm); another illustration occupies the remainder of the page: see **2**. Both are part of Charlotte's earliest juvenile manuscript: 'There was once a little girl and her name was Ane', a 16-page hand-sewn booklet, enclosed in a cover of grey and blue spotted wallpaper.

Bequest of Henry Houston Bonnell, 1927, who acquired the manuscript at Sotheby's sale of the effects of Mary Anne Nicholls, 19 June 1914, lot 191.

*Brontë Parsonage Museum: Bonnell 78*

Scene of a rowing boat on lake with two people, rocky background, trees, overcast sky. See **1** for further information.

4

## Juvenile painting of a sailing ship

1828

Watercolour on paper

22 × 36 mm

The illustration occupies almost half of a manuscript page (56 × 36 mm). The remainder of the page consists of three lines of text and another illustration: see **5**. Part of Charlotte's earliest extant manuscript: 'There was once a little girl and her name was Ane', a 16-page hand-sewn booklet, enclosed in a cover of grey and blue spotted wallpaper.

Bequest of Henry Houston Bonnell, 1927, who acquired the manuscript at Sotheby's sale of the effects of Mary Anne Nicholls, 19 June 1914, lot 191.

*Brontë Parsonage Museum: Bonnell 78*

Seascape depicting a sailing ship between two cliffs; blue cloud, water and sail, red flag on ship, seagulls; pencil outline of cliffs clearly visible beneath brown wash. See **1** for further information.

5

## Juvenile painting of a lady walking

1828

Watercolour on paper

28 × 36 mm

The illustration occupies half of a manuscript page (56 × 36 mm). The remainder of the page consists of three lines of text and another illustration: see **4**. Part of Charlotte's earliest extant manuscript: 'There was once a little girl and her name was Ane', a 16-page hand-sewn booklet, enclosed in a cover of grey and blue spotted wallpaper.

Bequest of Henry Houston Bonnell, 1927, who acquired the manuscript at Sotheby's sale of the effects of Mary Anne Nicholls, 19 June 1914, lot 191.

*Brontë Parsonage Museum: Bonnell 78*

Tiny scene depicting a lady dressed in red with some flowers in her hand, walking towards a tree on the right; faint blue sky, brown ground. See **1** for further information.

## 6

## Juvenile painting of a sick-room

1828
Watercolour on paper
28 × 36 mm

The illustration occupies the top half of a manuscript page (56 × 36 mm). The remainder of the page consists of five lines of text, part of Charlotte's earliest extant manuscript: 'There was once a little girl and her name was Ane', a 16-page hand-sewn booklet, enclosed in a cover of grey and blue spotted wallpaper.

Bequest of Henry Houston Bonnell, 1927, who acquired the manuscript at Sotheby's sale of the effects of Mary Anne Nicholls, 19 June 1914, lot 191.
*Brontë Parsonage Museum: Bonnell 78*

Sick-room showing a bed with canopy on right, table and chair in centre, two windows behind and a door on far left, patterned floor-covering. A person is clearly visible lying in the bed and a child sits at the foot of the bed (this latter image unclear). See **1** for further information.

## 7

## Earliest map of Glass Town

1828
Watercolour on paper
36 × 56 mm

Painted on p. 9 of Charlotte's earliest extant manuscript: 'There was once a little girl and her name was Ane', a 16-page hand-sewn booklet, enclosed in a cover of grey and blue spotted wallpaper.

Bequest of Henry Houston Bonnell, 1927, who acquired the manuscript at Sotheby's sale of the effects of Mary Anne Nicholls, 19 June 1914, lot 191.
*Brontë Parsonage Museum: Bonnell 78*

Small map of four countries with boundaries marked in different colours, the sea forming a right-hand border to the land and two long rivers flowing across the map with tiny circles representing towns marked along them. The countries are labelled 'Taley', 'Brany', 'Vittoria' and 'Wa[i]ting', names associated with each of the four Brontë children in their early stories about the toy soldiers. For further information about the significance of this map see Christine Alexander, *The Early Writings of Charlotte Brontë* (Oxford: Basil Blackwell, 1983), p. 32.

## 8

### Glass Town peasant woman

c. 1828
Watercolour on paper
191 × 111 mm

Formerly in the Law Collection at Honresfeld (see **15**); possibly part of lot 450, sold at Hodgson & Co. sale, London, 31 March 1933, to Maggs Bros. for 70 guineas (see catalogue of sale in BPM). Item 4 of lot 450 describes 'a cardboard Box in five sections, with two Water-Colour Drawings and silk edgings'; the other watercolour may be **120**, 'Profile of a woman, possibly Elizabeth Branwell'.
*Private owner*

Juvenile painting of a woman in peasant dress, with short dark hair, white cap, black ribbon around the throat, blouse and apron, black laced bodice, and red skirt. The figure has a fat face with a startled look, obviously an early production by a child. The watercolour is thick and pasty in appearance, and has obviously been mixed badly with the white bodycolour.

This appears to be a painting of a typical peasant character from the Glass Town saga, probably a 'wamon' from Mons and Wamon's Island or Stumps's Island. The early inhabitants of Glass Town (derived originally from the Young Men's Play) retreated to several islands off the coast of the Great Bay of Glass Town. These included Stumps's Island, Monkey's Island and Mons and Wamon's Island, whose inhabitants are described by Charlotte in 'The Foundling' as 'odd little specimens of humanity' with 'one great round wooden shoe' (recalling Branwell's original toy soldiers), peasant costume and speaking in the 'old young men tongue' (an early attempt at regional dialect). For further information on these characters see Christine Alexander, *The Early Writings of Charlotte Brontë* (Oxford: Basil Blackwell, 1983), pp. 95–6; and **187**, Branwell's early illustration of 'Mon and Wamon'.

## 9

### Ruined tower

2 September 1828
Pencil on paper
59 × 90 mm

Signed and dated bottom left: 'C.B September the 2 1828/ for Anne A Copy'.
For verso see **11**.
Gift of Margaret Illingworth (Mrs Alfred Illingworth in early records), 1910, together with **10**, **11**, **12**, **19**, **80**, **81**, **155**, **184**, **185**, **188**, **189**, **197** and **334**. 'Ruined tower' and five of these items were framed together, and may be the drawings referred to in an autograph note by Patrick Brontë, sold at Sotheby's as part of the Robinson and Francis Brown collection, 2 July 1898 (lot 24): 'Certain drawings by my/ Children–that were/ given to my Daughter Anne,/ and left in her box,/ I have given to my/ Servant Martha Brown,/ as fond mementos–/ leaving to myself, any/ of these which I might / claim, for any particular/ purposes. If I should/ not claim them, they/ will be entirley [*sic*] at/ her disposal./ P. Bronte, A. B./ Incumbent of/ Haworth,/ Yorkshire.' (BPM: BS179). See **29** for information on the Brown collection.
*Brontë Parsonage Museum: C2*

Round tower with gothic-arched doorway, and arrow-slits; top ruinated with overhanging moss; shrub on left and grassy, shaded area in foreground, as in 'Thatched cottage' (**10**). Both drawings were made 'for Anne', within two days of each other: see **1**.

It is possible that they were either done under the supervision of a drawing-master or copied from a drawing manual, since they are typical of the early exercises taught to beginners in art at the time. Progressive lessons with plates of elements of landscape, such as ruins, bridges, walls, trees, gnarled trunks and finally whole scenes can be found in books such as Joshua Bryant's *Progressive Lessons, In Landscape* (London, n.d.).

**10**

## Thatched cottage

4 September 1828
Pencil on paper
79 × 119 mm

Signed and dated along the bottom: 'C B September the 4. 1828 A Copy for Anne Brontë'. For verso see **12**. Gift of Margaret Illingworth, 1910, together with **9**, **11**, **12**, **19**, **80**, **81**, **155**, **184**, **185**, **188**, **189**, **197** and **334**. There are no records of Margaret Illingworth's acquisition, though she may have obtained these items from one of Martha Brown's relatives: see **9**.

*Brontë Parsonage Museum: C1*

Stone cottage with thatched roof, latticed window on left side facing viewer, chimney at far right end, central door and two windows at front facing right; shaded grassy slope with small shrubs surrounding cottage.

Copied two days later than 'Ruined tower' (**9**), possibly from a drawing manual: see **1** and **9**.

**11**

## Rough sketches of heads, dogs and Roman

c. 1828
Pencil on paper
59 × 90 mm

On verso of **9**.

Gift of Margaret Illingworth, 1910: for provenance see **9**.

*Brontë Parsonage Museum: C2v*

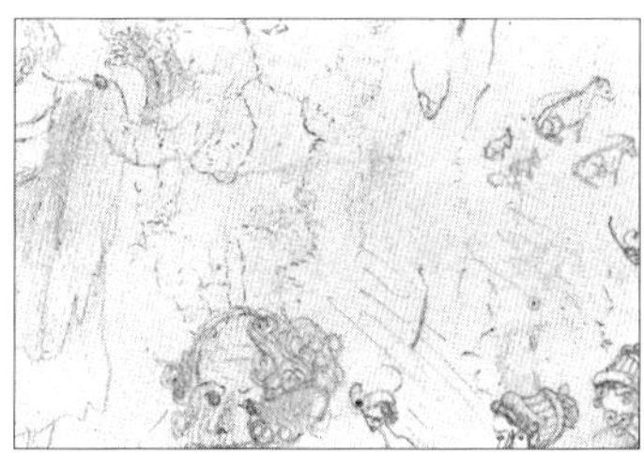

Four women's heads with Roman (?) hair-styles, four small profiles of a dog, half of a male figure in Roman dress; most of the sketches partly obscured by the edge of the page being cut for drawing on the reverse: see **12** for possible explanation.

## 12

## Sketches of woman in long gown

c. 1828
Pencil on paper
79 × 119 mm

On verso of **10**.

Gift of Margaret Illingworth, 1910: for provenance see **9**.

*Brontë Parsonage Museum: C1v*

Four rough sketches of woman in profile, one kneeling; other crude heads on top left.

These rough sketches are on the verso of **10**, a copy of a thatched cottage made for Anne. It is clear that they predate **10** since the heads of two of the figures have been cut in half and removed. Paper was in short supply in the parsonage and both sides were regularly used. **9**, drawn for Anne within a few days of **10**, also has rough sketches on the verso. It appears that Charlotte (and possibly Branwell) cut a previously used large sheet of paper up and used the reverse for their careful drawings for Anne.

## 13

## 'Dulwich'

5 January 1829
Watercolour on paper; edges torn
182 × 232 mm

Signed, titled and dated along bottom border, on left in longhand: 'C Brontë'; centre: 'DULWICH'; on right in longhand: 'January 5 1829'.

Purchased from Rose Emma Longbottom, 1906; together with **74**, **129**, **200**, **201**, **202** and **207**. Rose Longbottom (listed as a worsted weaver in the Bingley census for 1891) was the great-granddaughter of Rose Bower, married sister of Tabitha Aykroyd, the Brontë servant. Rose married John Bower (1757–1827), a shoemaker and farmer of Cockcroft Fold, Harden, and several Brontë items were passed down through their descendants (see, for example, **40**). The name Aykroyd was spelt variously by different members of the family, viz. Aykroyd, Akroyd, and Ackroyd. We have chosen to use 'Aykroyd', the form found on Tabitha's gravestone and in the burials register, Haworth Church, which was signed by Arthur Bell Nicholls.

*Brontë Parsonage Museum: C3*

Rear of stone cottage with large chimney, two wooden doors and two windows, slate roof; woman carrying a bucket standing at a water pump, in front of a fence, bottom left corner; rocky hilly ground in front of and behind cottage on left; trees in distance and on right of cottage.

This illustration is a copy of a painting by Sutherland, 1809, which was included in a number of contemporary drawing manuals, such as *Ackermann's New Drawing Book of Light and Shadow, in Imitation of Indian Ink* (London: For R. Ackermann, Repository of Arts, 101 Strand, 1812). This particular drawing manual has two plates entitled 'Dulwich': Plate X, which includes a cottage and a small girl fishing in foreground, and Plate XII, which is identical to Charlotte Brontë's copy illustrated above. Both plates are accompanied by commentary, stressing the importance of attention to light and shadow rather than mere outline. Plate XII has the following text, which Charlotte Brontë most probably read:

> The gable end of the cottage which forms the principal feature of the annexed plate, holds a mass of light, which as described in the preceding subject, is thinly diffused to the figure, on one side, and the stile upon the other, the whole of the sky is under shadow. It would be an advantage to the work before us, were some of the plates coloured, as the lights upon certain parts are too sudden, which a thin wash of colour would subdue, without injuring the sunny appearance.
>
> It might be recommended to those who wish to improve themselves in the art of drawing in water colours, to observe with attention the works of the most approved masters, particularly those whose works are annually exhibited by the two societies of artists, who paint in water colours. Their labours might be studied by the amateur, as the professors study nature. The great Reynolds used to say, 'It was of the first importance to a painter to endeavour to learn to read nature'; this observation perhaps may appear unintelligible to many; but his meaning pointed to the necessity of learning to reason upon the causes of relief, and the contrasts of light and shadow. The artists alluded to can give reason upon principle for every part of their pictures, as to form, composition, light, shadow, and colour. For want of attention to these general principles, many amateurs of considerable taste proceed in continued error, who, would they contemplate this necessary part of study, might soon be enabled to produce very pleasing pictures.

## 14

## Cormorant on rocky coast

24 January 1829
Pencil on paper
122 × 176 mm

Signed and dated bottom left: 'CB Jan 24 1829'. On verso untitled sketches of soldiers by Branwell: see **198**.

Gift of M. Barbara Smith (née Killick), West Sussex, 1981; acquired with **67**, **82** and **198**. An accompanying letter by Abraham Holroyd (Bradford bookseller, author and publisher, who met Charlotte Brontë in 1853) describes the early provenance: 'In the year 1856, I saw at the house of Mr Ben Ratcliffe's there some pencil drawings done by Charlotte Brontë, and Branwell Brontë; and Mrs B. Ratcliffe very kindly made me a present of two of those by Charlotte Brontë. One of them "an Old Man standing under a tree in a shower of rain", I gave to Mr Geo. Ackroyd Banker of Bradford; and the other "a Sea bird perched on a rocky coast", I gave to Mr John Emanuel Preston, Artist, of Gilstead. Both of these drawings are evidently copied from Bewick. Signed by me, August 1877 Abraham Holroyd'. The drawing therefore passed in succession from Ben Ratcliffe to Abraham Holroyd, and then to John Emanuel Preston (an artist of Gilstead, Bingley). Subsequent succession is recorded in correspondence as follows: from Preston to Robert Power (c. 1880), D. Whitell (1882), George Aykroyd (1882, the Geo. Ackroyd listed above, of Manningham, Bradford), and Henry Fison Killick (1915), grandfather of the donor. There is an ambrotype of this drawing in the BPM (Ph68), given, together with another of 'Fisherman sheltering against a tree', by Mrs C. Hartley of Harrogate, in 1975.

*Brontë Parsonage Museum: C3.5*

Seascape with rocky coast and birds on left, rough sea on right and swirling around rocks in left foreground; on a prominent rock stands a cormorant facing right.

Copied from Thomas Bewick, *A History of British Birds*, vol. 2: *Containing the History and Description of Water Birds* (Newcastle: T. Bewick; London: Longman & Co., 1816), p. 216. This particular engraving is attributed to Luke Clennell, chiefly on grounds of style (see Reynolds Stone, *Wood Engravings of Thomas Bewick* (London: Rupert Hart-Davis, 1953), p. 51).

It is interesting to compare this early picture of a cormorant with the first of Jane Eyre's three visionary pictures, which depicts 'a cormorant, dark and large, with wings flecked with foam; its beak held a gold bracelet set with gems, that I had touched with as brilliant tints as my palette could yield and as glittering distinctness as my pencil could impart' (*Jane Eyre*, ed. Jane Jack and Margaret Smith (London: Clarendon Press, 1969), p. 153). The bird is perched on a half-submerged floating mast and sinking below him is a drowned corpse. It is likely that the thirteen-year-old Charlotte who copied the Bewick engraving was already aware of the Miltonic associations of temptation and death evoked in her imaginary picture in *Jane Eyre*. In *Paradise Lost*, Book IV, Satan enters the Garden of Eden in disguise:

> on the Tree of Life,
> The middle Tree and highest there that grew,
> Sat like a Cormorant; yet not true Life
> Thereby regaind, but sat devising Death
> To them who liv'd.
>
> (II. 194–8)

15

## Diminutive sketches

28 April 1829
Pen and ink on paper
c. 200 × 120 mm

The tiny sketches are on pages (measurement above) at either end of Charlotte's manuscript volume 'Two Romantic Tales', dated 28 April 1829. The manuscript includes two stories: 'A Romantic Tale', dated 15 April 1829; and 'An Adventure in Ireland', dated 28 April 1829. (The manuscript is not available for exact transcription, but it is described in Davidson Cook, 'Brontë Manuscripts in The Law Collection', *The Bookman*, vol. 69, no. 410, November 1925, p. 101, as '11 small octavo pages'.)

Sold at Hodgson & Co. sale, London, 31 March 1933, lot 437; listed as 'The Property of a Collector', but formerly in the collection of Sir Alfred J. Law, Honresfeld. Sir Alfred J. Law, MP for Rochdale, had inherited his substantial collection of Brontëana from his uncle William Law, flannel and leather manufacturer of the firm A. & J. Law, who had begun collecting Brontë relics in the early 1890s (see **38**). Davidson Cook (p. 102) noted that there were in the collection 'fourteen original pencil and water-colour drawings executed by Charlotte and Emily Brontë' and, 'in a small cardboard box', a further 'two of Charlotte's ventures with the brush–water colours precious beyond their artistic merit to those who glory in the glamour of the Brontës'. There were 15 paintings and drawings in lots 446–9 at the Hodgson & Co. sale, plus the two watercolours by Charlotte referred to by Cook, in lot 450 (see **8** and **120**).
*Private owner*

The only evidence available for these tiny sketches is the description in *A Catalogue of Fine and Rare Books*, p. 32, for the Hodgson sale recorded above. Charlotte's manuscript 'Two Romantic Tales' is listed under lot 437, which describes 'leaves of scribbling at either end, one bearing a microscopic signature, "C. Bronte's Book, 1829, Ano," with the initials of the three sisters and their brother (and small outlines of their chins) on verso, and another having a diminutive pen-and-ink sketch'.

## 16

## 'Boy and Dog'

18 May 1829
Pencil on paper
211 × 269 mm

Signed, titled and dated in pencil, bottom left: 'May the ~~23~~ 18 1829'; bottom centre: 'Boy and Dog'; bottom right: 'C Bronte'. On verso, untitled pencil sketch of a boy's head, together with numerous other small sketches, all cancelled: see **17**.

Gift of Richard Henry Rudd, 1905, a well-known Bradford manufacturer, who was on the Brontë Society Council for several years.
*Brontë Parsonage Museum: C5*

Small boy riding a large black and white St Bernard dog: boy in girl's dress (as typical for male child of nineteenth century), black boots, sash of dress waving behind, plumed hat lying on ground in front; dog has mouth open, eyes and tail raised, right paw raised and pushing a wooden gate in a brick wall behind; faint tree in far right distance. The boy's face, with marked eyebrows and curly hair, is the finished version of a false start on verso: see **17**.

This is a typical 'fancy piece' or 'fancy picture', an ornamental genre scene, that was commonly included in children's drawing manuals of the late eighteenth and early nineteenth centuries. Simple versions of these illustrations, such as the one here, were intended to teach young pupils skill in outline. See also **19**, **108** and **138**.

## 17

## Sketches of boy's head, towers, figures and faces

c. 18 May 1829
Pencil on paper
211 × 269 mm

Beneath a tiny figure is inscribed: 'Baron de Cuvier'. Signed and dated on verso: see **16**.

Gift of Richard Henry Rudd, 1905.
*Brontë Parsonage Museum: C5v*

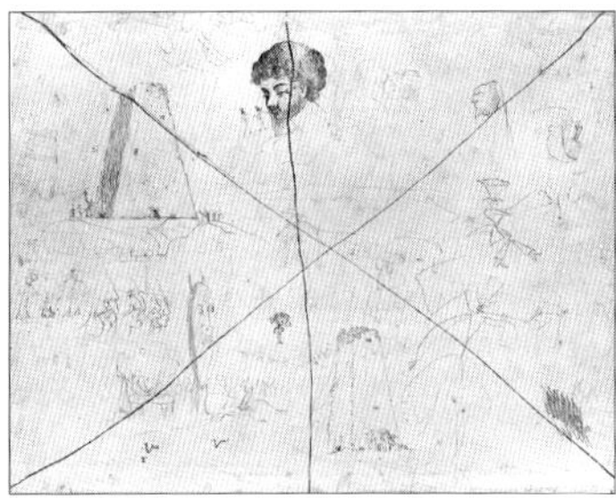

Pencil sketch of a boy's head, the same as the finished drawing on the recto, suggesting a false start on this side of the sheet of paper. A beard and lines on the forehead have been added later to the head (possibly in another hand–Branwell?), together with numerous small sketches of grotesque heads, towers, soldiers and tiny figures with top hats and coat-tails. One sketch shows figures worshipping an image with a burning sacrifice nearby. The whole is crossed through from top to bottom and diagonally.

The name of Baron Georges Cuvier (1769–1832) is intriguing here. Cuvier was a French zoologist and statesman who established the sciences of comparative anatomy and paleontology. His work was of interest to and often cited by the phrenologists. This may have been the channel by which his name reached the young Brontës, since it occurs frequently in books like the 1815 London edition of *Outlines of the Physiognomical System of Drs. Gall and Spurzheim*, where his work is disputed by Spurzheim. Cuvier, like Lavater, composed tables to indicate the facial angles of men and different animals, as a possible means of measuring the intellectual faculties.

Branwell was probably responsible for the later additions to Charlotte's draft sketch here, in particular the tiny figure of 'Baron de Cuvier', since the name 'Cuvier' also occurs at the end of volume I of Branwell's miniature booklet entitled 'A Collection of Poems by Young Soult the Ryhmer [*sic*]', dated 30 September 1829 and therefore completed four months later than this drawing by Charlotte. He refers to another 'edition' of Young Soult's poems: 'the Octavo one of his Ryhmes—by Cuvier which is not compleat having no notes which it very much needed [*sic*]'. This reference, together with the tiny sketch of 'Cuvier', suggests that by 1829 the historical figure had been transposed into Branwell's Glass Town scene. Cuvier would have fitted easily into Branwell's 'Frenchy Land', which centred on characters like Napoleon, Murat and Chateaubriand.

## 18

## 'The ruins of [?Caractacus] Palace'

20 May 1829
Pencil on paper
55 × 91 mm

Signed and dated in pencil, bottom left: 'C B May 20'; bottom right: '1829'. Title beneath in centre: 'The ruins of [?Caractacus]/ Palace'. The bottom left corner of the page has been cut away. The drawing is on the same sheet of paper as Charlotte's manuscript 'The Keep of the Bridge', 13 July 1829; the sheet has been folded in half to form four pages. The first page is occupied by her drawing illustrating the story (see **21**), p. 2 by the story itself, p. 3 by 'The ruins of [?Caractacus] Palace', and p. 4 is blank.

Acquired in 1941; part of the library of W. T. H. Howe. An inscription on auction sale slip records: 'Bought sale library Wm. Mathews Walpole Gallery 11/17/1916'. Previously sold at Sotheby's sale of the effects of Mary Anne Nicholls, 19 June 1914, lot 200.
*New York Public Library: Berg Collection*

Landscape sketch of one tall column with vegetation growing from its broken capital, a shrub and plinth surmounted by an urn on left, two ruined stumps of columns on right. The tiny figure of a man carrying a long staff stands on a rock pointing with his right arm to what looks like a falling urn; the man is still too large in relation to the ruins. A fallen column lies in the grass, left foreground; hills faintly sketched in distance.

Probably a copy of an engraving. If the reading of the title is correct, this drawing may be related to Branwell Brontë's unpublished miniature hand-sewn booklet entitled 'Caractacus. A Dramatic Poem', 26–28 June 1830 (the Brotherton Collection, Leeds University Library). Caractacus, however, was a British king during the Roman occupation and was unlikely to have had a Roman-style palace.

## 19

### 'A Fancy Piece'

22 May 1829
Pencil on paper
137 × 212 mm

Signed and dated in pencil, in longhand, below drawing: 'A Fancy Piece by Chr$^{e}$ Br$^{e}$ May 22$^{nd}$ 1829–'. On verso untitled pencil sketches of figures and buildings, mostly by Branwell: see **197**.

Gift of Margaret Illingworth, 1910, together with **9**, **10**, **11**, **12**, **80**, **81**, **155**, **184**, **185**, **188**, **189**, **197** and **334**. There are no records of Margaret Illingworth's acquisition, though she may have obtained these items from one of Martha Brown's relatives: see **9**.

*Brontë Parsonage Museum: C6*

Genre scene of three girls with a baby, gathering flowers and fruit: one seated holding out a bunch of flowers to the second girl who stands holding the baby with one arm and holding out her apron with the other arm to receive the flowers; the third girl is climbing a tree on right to pick fruit or nuts. Flowers and plants in foreground, water-pump with small stream on left behind stone wall, paling fence behind figures with opening on right leading to cottage in distance; two trees behind fence, one with the girl on right, the other behind the fence and water-pump on left.

See **16** for a note on the genre of this illustration.

## 20

### 'Revenante Castle'

26 May 1829
Pencil on paper
54 × 93 mm

Signed, titled and dated, in pencil, in printed script larger than Charlotte's usual minuscule size, bottom left: 'C Bronte'; bottom centre: 'Revenante Castle/1829'; bottom right, in longhand: 'May 26'. The BPM number '30' is inscribed in pencil, top right corner of drawing. The tiny sketch occupies one of two pages, formed by folding a single sheet (107 × 93 mm) in half. On the verso there is another early sketch drawn two months later: see **22**.

Bequest of Henry Houston Bonnell, 1927; acquired by him from Violet M. Bolster, née Bell, niece and executrix of Arthur Bell Nicholls.

*Brontë Parsonage Museum: Bonnell 30*

Early simple landscape sketch of a building on the right and trees on the left, hills faintly shaded in the distance and open grass in the foreground. The castle shows little sense of perspective; it consists of the front only (a central tower with steep pointed roof, flanked by two identical wings), although viewed slightly from the right side.

## 21

# 'The Keep of the Bridge'

13 July 1829
Pencil on paper
53 × 90 mm

Signed, dated and titled in ink, bottom left: 'C B 1829'; bottom centre: 'The Keep of the Bridge'. The drawing is on the first of four pages formed by folding a single sheet in half; p. 2 has a story of the same name written in minuscule script and signed and dated at the end: 'C B July 13 1829'; p. 3 is occupied by another pencil sketch (see **18**) and p. 4 is blank.

Acquired in 1941; part of the library of W. T. H. Howe. An inscription on auction sale slip records: 'Bought sale library Wm. Mathews Walpole Gallery 11/17/1916'. Previously sold at Sotheby's sale of the effects of Mary Anne Nicholls, 19 June 1914, lot 200.
*New York Public Library: Berg Collection*

Sketch of a stone bridge with a round Norman keep behind it on the right side. Probably copied by Charlotte from an engraving to accompany her manuscript of the same name.

For the story, 'The Keep of the Bridge', see *An Edition of The Early Writings of Charlotte Brontë*, ed. Christine Alexander, vol. 1 (Oxford: Basil Blackwell for the Shakespeare Head Press, 1987), pp. 36–8.

## 22

# 'The Temple of Shamrocks'

28 July 1829
Pencil on paper
54 × 93 mm

Signed, titled and dated, in pencil, in large printed script on three sides of the drawing; along left side: 'C Bronte taken from'; along the top: 'the Temple of Shamrocks'; down right side: 'July 28. 1829 nature'. The BPM number '29' is written in ink, top left corner of drawing, and again in pencil on right. Stamped: 'BRONTË/ MUSEUM / HAWORTH', encircled. The drawing occupies one of two pages, formed by folding a single sheet (107 × 93 mm) in half. On the verso there is another early sketch drawn two months before: see **20**.

Bequest of Henry Houston Bonnell, 1927; acquired by him from Violet M. Bolster, née Bell, niece and executrix of Arthur Bell Nicholls.
*Brontë Parsonage Museum: Bonnell 29*

Early simple sketch 'from nature' of a stone wall with a tree in leaf growing behind and one branch leaning over the wall on the right. The top of the tree separates the words 'Temple' and 'of' in the inscription. The wall consists of three tiers of stone, with a brick construction on the top left and three rails of a balustrade spaced along the rest of the top, all overlaid with flat stone on top.

The sketch was probably copied from an elementary drawing manual, many of which illustrate rustic fences, gates and walls as early exercises in drawing landscape (see p. 108).

## 22a

### Branch of a tree

1829
Pencil on paper
74 × 54 mm

The sketch is on the verso of **41a** 'Wellington monument', which forms one of the pages of Charlotte Brontë's manuscript 'Anecdotes of the Duke of Wellington', signed throughout by Charlotte Brontë and dated from 2 October 1829. The sketch was clearly made before the tiny pages were cut to form this manuscript booklet, as the branch was obviously part of a larger drawing of a tree. See **41a** for provenance.
*Private owner*

This is a crude early pencil sketch which was clearly part of a larger drawing of a tree, possibly made under the supervision of John Bradley, as a drawing exercise. It represents a branch reaching diagonally across the picture from the right fork of a trunk in the bottom left corner. Crude pencil markings suggest the bark and a variety of strokes represent foliage behind the branch and in the top right corner.

The versos of several early drawings by Charlotte (see **11** and **12**) indicate the Brontës' reuse of paper. In this case, the large tree appears to have been part of a discarded drawing lesson. Where the paper was blank on both sides, it has been cut to form one of the typical early miniature booklets made by Charlotte, and the drawing associated with the manuscript has been made on the verso of a sheet with part of the original drawing.

## 23

### Sketches of Glass Town characters

9 October 1829
Pen and ink on paper
70 × 60 mm

The sketches occupy a quarter of a manuscript page 124 × 105 mm. The two poems in minuscule script, which occupy the remainder of the page, are both titled, signed and dated: 'Sunset', 'C B Octber 8. 1829'; 'SUNRISE', 'Charlotte Brontë Octber 9 1829'. The sketches are labelled as described below.

Bequest of Henry Houston Bonnell, 1927; acquired by him 'from Williamson collection' (see Bonnell's own catalogue compiled 1922, in BPM).
*Brontë Parsonage Museum: Bonnell 80 (2 and 3)*

Sketches arranged in three rows. Along the top: five small head-and-shoulders portraits of rather bedraggled female-looking characters, labelled from left to right: 'Y Murat' (below); 'M [?Louis]' (above), ~~Y Soult~~' (below); 'Y Lucian' (below); 'Y Nap' (below); 'Eugene' (below); and at the far right, a tiny sketch of a book, labelled above 'The book of/Nature'. Along the second row: a small head-and-shoulders sketch of 'Young Soult' (labelled below); and a desert scene with the sun rising or setting behind a hill, and five palm trees in the foreground, grouped two on both the left and right and each group labelled below, 'Us Two'; the central tall palm tree extends above the first row of sketches and is labelled below, 'Me'. The bottom row of sketches includes an unfinished outline of a head and a larger head-and-shoulders portrait of a woman with curly hair and long ear-rings.

The tiny sketches are all fairly crude, the products of a childish hand. They depict various French characters in the early Glass Town saga, rogues from Branwell's Frenchy Land. Young Soult becomes a respectable poet (one of Branwell's early pseudonyms) and both he and Murat become favourites of the Duke of Zamorna. All the characters are based on historical figures.

Several early poems in 'Blackwood's Young Men's Magazine' are signed 'UT', which represents 'Us Two', either collaborative efforts by Charlotte and Branwell or by the Marquis of Douro and Lord Charles Wellesley, Charlotte's two pseudonyms: see Christine Alexander, *The Early Writings of Charlotte Brontë* (Oxford: Basil Blackwell, 1983), p. 38.

## 24

## Fisherman sheltering against a tree

23 October 1829
Pencil on paper
122 × 175 mm

Signed in pencil in minuscule script, bottom left corner: 'Charlotte Brontë'; and dated bottom right corner: 'October 23 1829'.

Belonged to the present owner's mother who originally came from Bradford, Yorkshire, before emigrating to Canada. There is also an ambrotype of this drawing in the BPM (Ph67), given (together with another of 'Cormorant on rocky coast') by Mrs C. Hartley of Harrogate, in 1975. This suggests that the two items had a similar early provenance since they were 'photographed' together; and this is confirmed by a note accompanying **14** which records the successive early ownership of 'Fisherman sheltering against a tree' by Ben Ratcliffe, Abraham Holroyd, and George Aykroyd, before it was taken to Canada.

*Private owner: Jennifer Spanton-Flexton*

Fisherman with hat and long-tailed coat, huddled beneath a windswept tree fishing in a wide river visible to left of tree; three rods bending over the river amongst windswept reeds on riverbank and bivouac on right of tree in foreground; ruined castle on mount on far bank in distance and driving rain running diagonally across the whole drawing.

Copied from Thomas Bewick, *A History of British Birds*, vol. 2: *Containing the History and Description of Water Birds* (Newcastle: T. Bewick; London: Longman & Co., 1816), p. 47.

## 25

## 'Lady Jephia Bud'

6 December 1829
Wash over pencil on paper
97 × 64 mm

Signed and titled in ink, in longhand, along the bottom: 'Lady Jephia Bud--C B'. Dated in Charlotte's hand, at top left: 'Dec 6'; top right: '1829'. Inscribed, probably by Charlotte, on right above left shoulder of figure: '50 yrs'. Inscribed on verso at bottom: 'Mrs Bud comonly [*sic*] called M$^{rs}$ Binn'.

Part of the Henry Houston Bonnell Brontë Collection, given by Helen Safford Bonnell in 1963, in memory of her husband, who died in 1926. Acquired by Bonnell from Violet M. Bolster, née Bell, niece and executrix of Arthur Bell Nicholls. According to a list made by Bonnell in 1922, this drawing was enclosed in an envelope when he received it, inscribed: '~~Three~~ one pencil sketches/ by Charlotte Brontë, Signed./ &/ 1 sketch of Mr Nicholls,/ when he first went to Haworth'. The first sketch refers to 'Lady Jephia Bud', the second to 'Sketch of Mr Nicholls': see Dubious list at the end of Charlotte Brontë entries.
*Pierpont Morgan Library: Bonnell Collection MA 2696*

Three-quarter-length front portrait of a woman with head turned towards the left: short thick curly hair dressed with a feather spray and two flowers; small pointed features, long neck, arms disproportionately large and wrongly placed; ear-ring visible on left ear, two-strand necklace, lace or muslim scarf around neck-line of dress fastened in centre above bust by a jewelled clasp, jewel-studded belt and cuffs of short puffed sleeves. The dress appears to be made of a chiffon or voile material. A brown-grey wash has been brushed over the pencil drawing.

Captain John Bud, Glass Town historian, political writer and antiquarian, plays a large part in the early writings of Charlotte and Branwell Brontë. His son, Sergeant Bud, a rascally lawyer, also appears in the early stories but the only reference to any females in the Bud family is the title to this drawing.

The reference on the verso to Mrs Bud commonly being called 'Mrs Binn' is curious. It raises the possibility that some of the more colourful Glass Town characters may have been based on local Haworth residents, since 'Binns' is a common name in the area. The Brontë servant, Martha Brown's sister Ann, for example, married Benjamin Binns in 1845. Charlotte's inscription may refer to one of his relatives.

## 26

## 'The Mountain Sparrow'

11 March 1830
Watercolour on thin card; gum arabic glaze
139 × 160 mm

Titled, signed and dated beneath the illustration: 'The Mountain Sparrow = By Charlotte Brontë March 11$^{th}$ 1830–'. Stamped 'BRONTË / MUSEUM / HAWORTH', encircled. Inscribed on verso in pencil, top right: 'Thomas Bradley'; in ink below: 'Thomas Bradley's Picture/ given to him by C. Bronte', followed by a series of scribbles; and in pencil (non-Brontë): '2 bladders White/ 2 Do Naples yellow/ R. Inchbold/ Leeds' (see below). Purchased in 1907 (together with **34**), from T. A. Smith of Keighley, who had previously lent this

item to the Brontë Society: see F. C. Galloway's *A Descriptive Catalogue of Objects in the Museum of the Brontë Society at Haworth* (Bradford, 1896), p. 21.
*Brontë Parsonage Museum: C9*

Illustration depicts a mountain sparrow standing on a tree stump on bare ground, with green foliage in foreground and snowy mountains in distance.

Copied from Thomas Bewick, *A History of British Birds*, vol. 1: *Containing the History and Description of Land Birds* (Newcastle: T. Bewick; London: Longman & Co., 1816), p. 178. Bewick notes that 'this species is frequent in Yorkshire, Lancashire, and also in Lincolnshire, but has not been seen further north than those counties: it differs from the House Sparrow in making its nest in trees and not in buildings.... It is a lively, active little bird, and, when it alights, has a variety of motions, whirling about and jerking its tail upwards and downwards, like a Wagtail.'

The inscription is particularly significant: it is the best evidence we have that John Bradley gave the Brontë children art lessons at this time. Bradley apparently had a son named John Thomas and this little painting, probably executed under the watchful eye of Bradley, became a present for his son. It indicates, too, where Bradley obtained his art supplies, namely from R. Inchbold, in Leeds.

The words '2 bladders White/ 2 Do Naples yellow' are also interesting. Pigments for oil painting (as distinct from cakes of watercolour paint made for ladies' paintboxes) were stored and sold in pigs' bladders, before the invention of the collapsible tube. A list of paints sold at Middleton's shop in St Martin's Lane, London, appeared in the *Repository of Arts* (an illustrated magazine published by the printseller Ackermann in 1809) as follows:

> Fine white, red, light and dark yellow-lake, brown, Prussian blue, verdigris, and Naples yellow are 6d. a bladder; burnt terra di Sienna, 4d; Nottingham white or common white, raw and burnt umber, light and brown ochre, ivory black, blue black, terra verte and Indian red, 3d a bladder. Some colours are bought in powders and mixed up when wanted. Such are vermillion 1s 8d. an ounce .... Carmine will not mix well with oil. The price is one guinea and upwards, and very good near £2 an ounce. Like ultramarine, its high price greatly confines its use.

Charlotte Brontë's use of the transparent gum arabic as a glaze for 'The Mountain Sparrow' was a common practice amongst Victorian watercolourists. This natural secretion of the acacia tree, which is still used in the manufacture of watercolours today, was applied on its own, on top of areas of watercolour, to give a richer tone to the paint. The glossy finish and tiny cracks on the surface of the painting often betray this practice: see for example **136** and **148**. Occasionally the gum arabic was also mixed with the darker watercolours, as in **147**.

## 27

## Two tiny sketches of heads

31 May 1830
Ink on paper
10 × 30 mm

The sketches occupy a space of 10 × 30 mm at the bottom of p. 1 (184 × 112 mm) of a twelve-page manuscript volume entitled 'Miscellaneous Poems By C Brontë May 31 1830'. Pages 1 and 2 are occupied by 'The Churchyard A Poemn', written in Charlotte Brontë's longhand script and signed and dated at the end: 'Charlotte Brontë December 24 1829', indicating the date of original composition.

Part of the Henry Houston Bonnell Brontë Collection, given by Helen Safford Bonnell in 1963, in memory of her husband, who died in 1926.

*Pierpont Morgan Library: Bonnell Collection MA 2538*

Two tiny head-and-shoulders sketches of women.

The sketches would have been made at the date the hand-sewn manuscript volume was compiled, viz. 31 May 1830, and not in December 1829 when the poem on the same page was originally written. The latest date of the eight poems in the manuscript volume is 29 May 1830, so these tiny sketches were drawn between then and 31 May.

## 28

## 'Wild Roses From Nature'

13 July 1830
Watercolour on paper
130 × 115 mm

Signed and dated in pencil, bottom left edge: 'Charlotte Brontë'; centre: 'From Nature'; bottom right edge: 'July 13 1830'; and at the base of stems 'Wild Roses'. Watermark partly visible: 'WH[ATMAN]/18[?]'.

Gift of Mrs E. J. Barrans, 1921; probably inadvertently, since this watercolour had become attached to another (**39**, also given by Mrs E. J. Barrans), and was discovered only when it was removed from its frame for cleaning in 1984. The freshness of the colours of 'Wild Roses' suggests that the two paintings had been stuck together for a considerable time, possibly since Charlotte's lifetime. 'Wild Roses From Nature' was not mentioned (and presumably not noticed) in 1896 when **39** was lent by F. C. Barrans, Manningham, Bradford, to the Brontë Society for display: see F. C. Galloway's *A Descriptive Catalogue of Objects in the Museum of the Brontë Society at Haworth* (Bradford, 1896), p. 10.

*Brontë Parsonage Museum: C9.5*

Three stems of pink dog roses, one fully open, one half-open and one in bud; rose leaves behind; stems fastened together with green band.

Despite the inscription 'From Nature', this painting resembles the many stylized illustrations of roses found in flower drawing and painting manuals of the early nineteenth century: see for example the plates in Patrick Syme, *Practical Directions for Learning Flower-Drawing* (Edinburgh: for the Author, 1810) and Edward Pretty, *A Practical Essay on Flower Painting in Water Colours* (London: S. & J. Fuller, 1810). Judging from the following flower studies (**29–34**), Charlotte's early lessons in flower painting consisted of a combination of copying from nature and from a drawing manual.

## 29

## Study of a white rose

1830
Watercolour on paper
145 × 118 mm

Signed and dated, lower right corner: 'C Brontë 1830'.

Purchased from the Brown collection of Brontë relics,

sold by Sotheby's, 2 July 1898 (possibly lot 16, 'Water-colour Drawing of Flowers, by C. Brontë'). Previously acquired by Robinson and Francis Brown (nephews of John Brown, Haworth sexton and stonemason, and cousins of Martha Brown, Brontë servant) either through their Brown connections; or through their acquisitions from the dealer Alfred Gledhill of Keighley and the book-seller James Miles of Leeds, and the Bradford author William Scruton; or through Charlotte's friend Ellen Nussey. See **42** for further information on the Brown collection.

*Brontë Parsonage Museum: C12*

The single open white flower with yellow stamens appears to be an old-fashioned rose; it is attached to a single stem with two buds, four leaves and another drooping bud and leaf to the right of the open flower. The colour has faded badly and the original white bodycolour now shows through the leaves, exposing the blue paint of the veins underlying the later green paint. The leaves resemble those of a quince, but the flower is closer to a wild rose and may even have been pink originally.

Although this early painting is dated simply 1830, it is likely that it was executed in July, at the same time as Charlotte's 'Wild Roses From Nature' (**28**). The style and use of paint is similar, except that the watercolour of the latter has not faded as this one has (see **28** for its unintentional 'preservation'). This comparison also allows us to assume that the above 'white rose' was another study 'From Nature'.

30

## Pink roses

c. 1830

Watercolour on paper, gum arabic glaze

105 × 142 mm

Purchased in 1898 from Jane Helen (also 'Ellen') Widdop of Haworth, daughter of John Greenwood and wife of John Widdop, son of Martha Redman and William Widdop (see **112**). Jane Widdop says in an accompanying letter (dictated to W. T. Field, Brontë Society official, and signed by Jane Widdop, 28 March 1898): 'My father, Mr John Greenwood, was the Book-seller in Haworth from whom the Rev. Patrick Brontë purchased books. One day my father went up to the Vicarage on business and just as he was entering the sitting room, Charlotte was in the act of burning a small water-colour which she had painted, when father asked if he might have it. Charlotte readily consented and he took it away with him. The Drawing has been in my possession ever since father's death' (letter in BPM Stock Book no. 1). It was still in the possession of John Greenwood (bookseller, stationer and relieving officer at Haworth) when Charles Hale saw it in 1861 ('An American Visitor at Haworth, 1861', *Brontë Society Transactions* (1967), vol. 15, part 77, p. 137).

*Brontë Parsonage Museum: C45*

Unfinished study of two pink wild roses: one above fully open with yellow stamens, the other drooping below and viewed from the side; two rose leaves on either side. The unfinished stem is sketched in pencil, bottom right. See **26** for note on gum arabic.

This unfinished flower study, with a drooping bud, has the appearance of being made from nature. It has little of the decorative quality of the plates in contemporary manuals on flower painting, and was probably executed in 1830, when Charlotte first tried her hand at watercolour representations 'From Nature' (see **28**).

## 31

## Tiger lilies

c. July 1830
Watercolour and pencil on paper
360 × 261 mm

Signed in pencil, in minuscule longhand, bottom right corner of the painting: 'C. Brontë'.

Purchased from the Brown collection of Brontë relics, sold by Sotheby's, 2 July 1898 (possibly lot 17, 'Water-colour Drawing of Flowers, by C. Brontë'): see provenance of **29** for sources of the Brown collection.
*Brontë Parsonage Museum: C14*

Single stem of three orange tiger lilies, enclosed in a painted frame consisting of two oval lines. The veins of the olive-coloured leaves, speckled petals and stamens of the flowers are carefully defined, but the study is clearly an early production compared to Charlotte's later highly finished and detailed flower paintings.

The painting is on a sheet of paper originally torn from a sketchbook. The bottom left corner has been irregularly cut out and fits exactly the small sheet that contains Charlotte's illustration 'Pale pink flowers' (**32**). Both studies were probably executed in July 1830, when Charlotte first tried her hand at watercolour representations 'From Nature' (see **28**).

## 32

## Pale pink flowers

c. July 1830
Watercolour and pencil on paper
129 × 76 mm

Inscribed in minuscule longhand, above bottom left leaf: 'C. Brontë'. The paper is irregular and appears to have been cut out from the bottom left corner of **31**.

Purchased from the Brown collection of Brontë relics, sold by Sotheby's, 2 July 1898 (lot 7, 'Water-colour, Flowers, by C. Brontë'): see provenance of **29** for sources of the Brown collection.
*Brontë Parsonage Museum: C42*

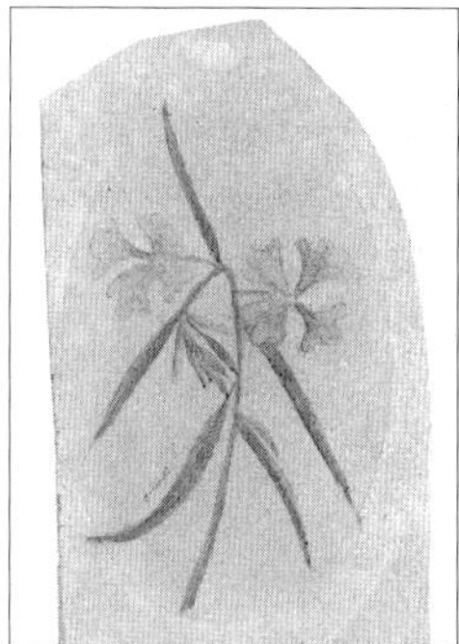

Single stem with five thin leaves, two open pink flowers at the top and a group of buds hanging from the top of the stem which is bent towards the left. An oval-shaped impression has been left by a previous mount and the edges of the leaves extend beyond this 'line'.

This fairly crude flower study appears to have been done soon after 'Tiger lilies' (**31**), since it is painted on paper cut from the latter. Both were probably executed in July 1830, when Charlotte first tried her hand at watercolour studies of flowers from nature (see **28**).

## 33

## Study of a primrose

c. 1830
Watercolour on paper
279 × 197 mm

Gift of Eleanor Burgess, East Sheen, 1950. Acquired with cartes de visite of Martha Brown and of Charlotte, and a piece of a dress worn by Charlotte (BPM: D135), the latter accompanied by an envelope on which is written: 'Piece of a dress worn by Charlotte / Brontë given by her to Martha Brown / who left it to her niece Ellen Binns / Given to Fanny by Florence / given from Fanny to me / S. M.' (BPM: SB1552d). The Florence referred to here may be Florence Armitage, of Victoria Road, Saltaire, a neighbour of the Binns family (see **58**). See also 'Recent Gifts and Other Additions to the Museum and Library', *Brontë Society Transactions* (1951), vol. 12, part 61, p. 54, which mentions 'two water-colour drawings' from this source, the second being misattributed to Charlotte (recorded as 'Dubious 2', BPM).
*Brontë Parsonage Museum: C91*

Unfinished study of two primrose flowers, four buds (two partially open) and three leaves (two completed and one simply blocked in); the finished leaves have red central veins and white is used on the green to give the effect of a thick glossy texture. The flowers are blocked in in pale yellow, with occasional daubs of bright yellow, and fine pale mauve brush strokes to suggest shadows on the petals.

A colour chart of daubs of paint along the far left side provides us with a unique record of Charlotte's experiments with watercolour, the combination of colours and the effect of overlaying one colour on another. This study appears to have been made before Charlotte had formal training in art at Roe Head. The picture indicates that she either had some early lessons in painting flowers or was carefully following one of the many contemporary art manuals on the subject. A combination of these practices seems most likely (see **28**), although early nineteenth-century art manuals did not encourage flower painting before the rudiments of drawing had been acquired.

## 34

## Study of a primula

c. 1830
Watercolour on paper
181 × 136 mm

Signed with a fine brush, in the same red paint used for the flowers, bottom left corner: 'C Brontë' (the 'C B' is painted in dots). Stamped: 'BRONTË/ MUSEUM/ HAWORTH', encircled. The Brontë scholar Dr Mildred Christian, who compiled a card index at the BPM in 1956, noted that this item was inscribed on the verso: 'Miss Bronte/ Given to T. W. Bradley'; this may have been on an original mount, no longer extant. Purchased in 1907 (together with **26**) from T. A. Smith of Keighley, who had previously lent this item to the Brontë Society: see F. C. Galloway's *A Descriptive Catalogue of Objects in the Museum of the Brontë Society at Haworth* (Bradford, 1896), p. 21. If the inscription on the original mount (mentioned above) is correct, then this item was originally given by Charlotte Brontë to T. W. Bradley, possibly a relative of John Bradley of Keighley, the

Brontë children's art teacher (see pp. 23–4 and **26** for similar evidence).

*Brontë Parsonage Museum: C41*

Study of a *Primula auricula*: single stem with two leaves at the base and a cluster of burgundy-red flowers at the top: two open showing yellow centre with brown stamens, one half-open and four buds.

The style and technique of this watercolour are similar to Charlotte's other flower studies of late 1830, when she was possibly having drawing lessons and being encouraged to paint from nature: see **28** and **33**.

35

## Portrait of a child with hat and basket

15 July 1830
Watercolour on paper, gum arabic glaze
57 × 94 mm

Signed in printed script beneath picture, on left: 'C Brontë'; and dated on right: 'July 15 1830'.
Gift of Mrs Haughton, 1944.
*Brontë Parsonage Museum: C10*

Child in blue dress, plaid three-quarter socks, large straw hat, seated beside a basket of flowers and facing right towards a spindly flowering shrub. Charlotte has copied the figure (a boy in the original but looking more like a girl in her painting) from an engraving by J. A. White of a painting entitled 'Hours of Innocence' by E. Landseer, printed in *Friendship's Offering, a Literary Album*, 1829. She has added colour and handled the difficult posture well for her age but her painting is static, with the flowering shrub replacing the dog of the original engraving, which is emerging from a river with a toy boat in its mouth and presenting it to the seated boy. For Charlotte's use of gum arabic, see **26**.

36

## Copy of a portrait of Mrs Brontë

October 1830
Watercolour, pencil and ink on paper, cut into an oval shape
77 × 63 mm

Inscribed in ink on verso, in longhand by Patrick Brontë: 'A portrait/ of M[rs] Brontė,–/ Drawn by her/ Daughter Charlotte/ Brontė, & presented/ to her dear Aunt–/ in Oct[r] 1830./ [line ruled beneath]/'.

Purchased from H. L. Smart, Kent, 1964; previously owned by Smart's father. The donor records in a letter that his father was an artist who spent some years in Devon and Cornwall and may have met some of Charlotte Brontë's relations there (letter in BPM to former curator Joanna Hutton, 15 July 1964, BPM Stock Book no. 1935). H. L. Smart also claimed to have owned miniatures of Patrick Brontë and Maria Brontë which he had preserved for '50 odd years' but was unable to find in 1964 (letter to Geoffrey Beard, former curator of the BPM, 12 July 1964, BPM Stock Book no. 1935).
*Brontë Parsonage Museum: C10.5*

Half-length profile of a young woman in a pale pink lace cap and Regency-style dress, facing left: the cap is trimmed in front with bows of blue ribbon and the same blue ribbon denotes the end of the small puff sleeve and the high waistline; elaborate lace collar with brooch in front; a chain draped around the neck, over the shoulder and fastened under the bust; prominent nose, small mouth, brown eye, long bare neck; brown curls protruding from the front of the cap.

The original of this portrait of Maria Brontë (née Branwell) survives in the BPM, painter unknown. There was apparently a companion portrait of Patrick Brontë, which had disappeared by 1964.

## 37

## Portrait of a lady

c. 1830–1833
Pencil on paper
210 × 158 mm

Original backing inscribed by unknown hand: 'Drawn by Charlotte Brontë'; removed during conservation in 1983, no longer extant.

Purchased from James Hartley, husband of Martha Brown's sister Hannah, in 1896.

*Brontë Parsonage Museum: C50*

Three-quarter-length profile portrait of young woman facing left and holding a book with the left hand. Both hands are too small, being out of proportion with the rest of the figure. The drawing appears to have been made to display the fashionable hair-style and dress with tight bodice and lace collar and cuffs. The back half of the hair is gathered tightly into a bun held by a lace net, while the front is brushed down at the sides into a ringlet, a fashion common in the 1830s. The left ear is clearly visible with a drop ear-ring. Some pencil rubbing is obvious.

Having tried her hand at flowers, this appears to be an early attempt by Charlotte to draw 'from life'. The style is not especially similar to other Brontë works, although other items from this source are authentic and there is the same lack of hard outline typical of Charlotte's drawings.

## 38

## Woman with lyre

26 November 1830
Watercolour on paper
190 × 122 mm

Signed in pencil, bottom right: 'C Brontë'; dated in pencil, bottom left: 'Nov$^{br}$ 26 1830'. Below the signature there is another darker date in Charlotte's writing: 'Nov 26 1830'. Inscribed on verso: 'Wm Wood' (in ink); 'Drawing by Charlotte Brontë' (in pencil).

Acquired in 1941; part of the library of W. T. H. Howe. Previously purchased by Maggs Bros. at Hodgson & Co. sale, London, 31 March 1933, part of lot 446. It was formerly part of the collection of Sir Alfred J. Law (see **15**), acquired by his uncle William Law from the Haworth joiner, William Wood, whose name appears on the verso. The painting was in Wood's hands when Charles Hale saw it in 1861, and described it as 'a sketch, colored by Charlotte Brontë of a goddess with diadem and harp–Minerva (quaere.)' ('An American Visitor at Haworth, 1861', *Brontë Society Transactions* (1967), vol. 15, part 77, p. 137).

*New York Public Library: Berg Collection*

Woman in Greco-Roman dress, leaning against a small pillar with a lyre resting on top. The figure is facing forward, right arm stretched out from the body and hand holding a pick; left arm behind the lyre and hand holding it; weight resting on right leg beneath drapery, right toes just visible; left leg crossed over and foot with sandal showing beneath skirt; outer gown gathered at waist and tied at shoulders; arms, chest and neck bare; head faces to the left in profile, straight forehead and nose, small features, ringlets around side of face and hanging from back of head beneath a lattice ribbon head-dress.

Charlotte's drawing is a copy of the engraving on the title page of the *Forget Me Not*, 1831, a vignette engraved by W. Chevalier from a drawing by F. Burney: see also **39**, **40** and **41**. Her only deviation from the original is that her figure and pillar stand on a small patch of brown earth, rather than on a cloud as in the original. Her date of 'November 1830' suggests that she copied the engraving soon after the Annual appeared at the end of the year, in time for the Christmas market or for a New Year's gift, as its subtitle declares. It seems likely that the Brontë family owned this edition of the *Forget Me Not*, since three other copies by Charlotte (**39**, **40**, **41**), one by Branwell (**207**), and one by Emily (**309**) were made from engravings in this volume.

## 39

## 'Bessy Bell and Mary Gray'

15 December 1830
Watercolour on paper; gum arabic glaze
116 × 131 mm

Dated and titled in pencil immediately beneath the painting, on left: 'Dec^br^ 15'; centre: 'BESSY BELL, AND–/ MARY GRAY'; on right: '1830'. Signed in ink along lower edge: 'Copied by Charlotte Brontë, Dec^r^ 15^th^ 1830–'. Stamped: 'BRONTË/ MUSEUM/ HAWORTH', encircled. Each corner inked across in black suggesting photo hinges: cf. **129**.

Gift of Mrs E. J. Barrans, 1921, following the death of her husband, F. C. Barrans, formerly of Manningham, Bradford, who had lent the painting to the Brontë Society (see F. C. Galloway's *A Descriptive Catalogue of Objects in the Museum of the Brontë Society at Haworth* (Bradford, 1896), p. 10). Barrans may have acquired the painting from Rose Emma Longbottom (great-niece of the Brontë servant, Tabitha Aykroyd: see **13**), since the BPM card index compiled by Dr Mildred Christian (see **34**) records: 'Attached to cardboard. Pasted on back of cardboard is a card with a.s.n. R. E. Longbottom (great nephew [*sic*] of Tabitha Ackroyd).' Neither the cardboard nor the autograph signed note (a.s.n.) now exist. During cleaning in 1984, another painting, 'Wild Roses From Nature' (**28**), was found attached to the back; this may have been the 'cardboard' mentioned above.

*Brontë Parsonage Museum: C11*

Charlotte has copied this illustration from an engraving by W. Finden after a painting by J. R. West, which accompanied the tale of 'Bessy Bell and Mary Gray: A Scottish Legend of 1666' by Delta (David Macbeth Moir), featured in the *Forget Me Not*, 1831: see also **38**, **40** and **41**.

The scene illustrates Bessy Bell and Mary Gray (centre) in rural seclusion, standing beside a gnarled split oak covered with ivy (left) and listening to their friend Bruce of Powfoulis Priory, who is lying on a grassy bank playing a shepherd's pipe (bottom right corner). Their bower of turf and moss beside the right bank of the Brauchie-burn (the figures are on the left) graces the right middle-distance of this typically picturesque production, and beyond is the Almond River and its surrounding hills – all described in the accompanying story.

In Charlotte's version the colours, too, are translated from the story since they are absent from the original engraving: Bruce is dressed in blue with a red sash and bare feet; Bessy Bell (with light brown hair and pink dress) stands behind Mary Gray (with black hair and white and blue dress) and leans her right arm on Mary Gray's left shoulder. Charlotte has also introduced four pink roses into the foliage to the left of the girls, and the girls themselves are less buxom than their originals.

The effect of Charlotte's painting is to soften the original engraving, which by its nature can produce fine hard lines. Her foliage here is less detailed and further from the original than in her pencil copies of similar engravings. Gum arabic has been used on the blue of the dress only, to give a deeper tone to the colour.

## 40

## The Disconsolate

c. December 1830

Watercolour on paper

178 × 127 mm

Titled in very faint pencil above the painting: 'F[?orget] me not'. Possibly pencil inscription below but partly obliterated by missing section of paper from the blank surrounding border. Other sections of paper missing from the blank border on both sides, plus part of the painting on the left side and top left corner. An old fold line running horizontally across the centre of painting.

Attributed to Emily Brontë by previous owners and known as 'The Disconsolate Maid'. Ian D. Stevenson, Dorset, inherited the painting from his mother, Maria Stevenson (née Bower), who was a descendant of Rose Aykroyd (see **13**). The painting passed from her sister Tabitha Aykroyd to either Rose or her son Jonas Bower (1791–1863), then to his son Thomas (1838–1923), father of Maria Stevenson.

*Ian D. Stevenson, Dorset*

Woman seated in an arched cloister, leaning her right arm and head against the side of the arch in a pose of distress; a dog (whippet?) sits at her feet, bottom right corner, and a letter has fallen to the ground beside her right foot, bottom left. The arch frames the top and left side of the picture. The woman has brown hair fastened behind in a bun, curls around her face, left ear and drop ear-ring clearly visible, long white neck, chest and shoulders; double-string gold necklace; off-the-shoulder long white gown, long sleeves and white cloak draped behind and over the right raised arm; red ribbon belt and red slippers. Through the arch in the distance can be seen, in receding order, a fence and tall tree, a fir tree and castle amongst more trees.

Charlotte's painting is a copy of 'The Disconsolate', by H. Corbould, engraved by C. Rolls, for the *Forget Me Not* Annual of 1831; also copied by Emily Brontë (see **309**). Charlotte appears to have made her copies from this little Annual as soon as it appeared late in 1830, in time for the Christmas market as a year book for 1831 (see also **38**, **39** and **41**). This copy was probably executed late in December 1830, just before Charlotte left for Roe Head the following January.

The illustration is accompanied by a poem of the same name, by 'L. E. L.' (Letitia Elizabeth Landon), expressing the grief of a young woman deserted by her childhood sweetheart. The 68-line poem begins:

> Down from her hand it fell, the scroll
> She could no longer trace;
> The grief of love is in her soul,
> Its shame upon her face.
>
> Her head has dropp'd against her arm,
> The faintness of despair;
> Her lip has lost its red rose charm,
> For all but death is there.
>
> (p. 215)

This watercolour copy is not as accurate as Charlotte's copies in pencil (see **41** for example), where she is able to achieve a more delicate result. The background is rather hasty and impressionistic. Charlotte has omitted the lake in the middle-distance, part of the castle and much of the thick vegetation of the background, where she has emphasized a fir tree more than in the original. Her figure is also distorted compared to the original, and the necklace, belt and angle of the feet differ in Charlotte's version.

As described above, the painting was previously attributed to Emily Brontë, who painted another version of this picture, entitled 'Forget Me Not' (**309**). Not only is it unlikely that Emily would have made two copies of the same picture in such different styles, but the handling of the paint in 'The Disconsolate' is closest to Charlotte's technique, especially in the execution of the drapery and leaves. The leaves, for example, are laboriously painted using tiny, delicate touches of paint similar to her other watercolours such as 'Landscape with bridge and cross' (**126**). Moreover, the other watercolour copy from this source, 'Bessy Bell and Mary Gray' (**39**), is also by Charlotte and clearly shows a similar technique.

## 41

## 'The Italian Scene'

c. December 1830
Pencil on card
131 × 168 mm

Signed in pencil, in longhand, under picture: 'The Italian / [?Scene]'. Inscribed by Ellen Nussey in longhand, in ink, bottom left margin: 'C. B.' Stamped: 'BRONTË / MUSEUM / HAWORTH', encircled. Inscribed on verso, probably by Samuel Edgerley, a Brontë Society official: 'S. E.'

Purchased in 1899, from H. E. Gorfin, an agent of Thomas James Wise (see **89**). The inscription indicates probable early ownership by Ellen Nussey.

*Brontë Parsonage Museum: C67*

Picturesque scene of Roman ruins in lush countryside, typical of the many Claudian-style landscapes of the late eighteenth and early nineteenth centuries. Roman temple amongst dense foliage and scattered capitals in left foreground, three couchant goats with long horns in centre and three female figures under tall trees in the right foreground; two more goats in the central middle-distance, in front of a lake, and a colonnaded palace on the far side of the lake; more buildings and high hills in the distance.

This is a faithful copy (except that Charlotte's goats look more like deer!) of an engraving by Freebairn, after a painting by Barrett, entitled 'An Italian Scene', which appeared in the *Forget Me Not* for 1831. Charlotte appears to have made her copies from this little Annual as soon as it appeared late in 1830, in time for the Christmas market as a year book for 1831 (see **38**, **39** and **40**). This copy was probably executed late in December 1830, or just before Charlotte left for Roe Head the following January.

On the page facing the original engraving (p. 60) is the story of 'An Adventure in Italy', by W. H. Harrison, written not so much to evoke the Claudian atmosphere of the engraving as to exploit the wild Italian scenery and banditti of Salvator Rosa. It is a mock-gothic production, which would have appealed to the creator of Lord Charles Wellesley and his anti-gothic tales: see Christine Alexander, '"That Kingdom of Gloom": Charlotte Brontë, the Annuals, and the Gothic', *Nineteenth-Century Literature*, vol. 47, no. 4, March 1993, pp. 409–36.

## 41a

## Wellington monument

January 1831
Ink on paper
54 × 74 mm

The drawing is on a separate tiny sheet which forms one of the pages of Charlotte Brontë's manuscript 'Anecdotes of the Duke of Wellington'. The first two pages of the manuscript are in the BPM (B81) and include anecdotes that are signed and dated 1829: see *An Edition of the Early Writings of Charlotte Brontë*, ed. Christine Alexander, vol. 1 (Oxford: Basil Blackwell for the Shakespeare Head Press, 1987), pp. 88–90. The dates on the continuing three pages (which accompany the drawing) range from 4 November 1829 to 4 January 1831. The drawing has been dated according to the last of these dates, although it may have been executed slightly earlier: 'London Paper/ January 4/ 1831 Charlotte/ Brontë'.

Originally owned by Arthur Bell Nicholls, the drawing passed to his cousin and second wife, Mary Anne Nicholls; then to her nephew, Alan Joseph Adamson, who had emigrated to Canada in 1873 and whose wife, Julia Turriff Adamson, gave the manuscript and drawings to her daughter Harriet Bell Adamson, who then gave them to her niece. See **61**, 'Annual Lavatera', which came from the same source, for further details on the relationship between the Adamson and Bell families.

*Private owner*

Tiny ink drawing depicting a tall monument, surmounted by an urn and set in a picturesque landscape. The monument occupies the centre of the picture and stands on a grassy knoll in the foreground. A river meanders from the right foreground, behind the monument and disappears in the distance. The foliage of tall trees is obvious on the left behind the monument and the fairly crude ink strokes in the remainder of the picture suggest further scattered trees and vegetation.

Because this forms part of the little booklet recording anecdotes of the Duke of Wellington, Charlotte Brontë's childhood hero, it seems likely that this monument is dedicated to Wellington.

42

## Study of eyes

29 January 1831
Pencil on paper
205 × 268 mm

Signed and dated in pencil in minuscule script, bottom right corner: 'January the 29th 1831 CB'. Inscribed in pencil top right corner: '7'.

Purchased from Gladys Jane Brown of Ramsgill, 1950; previously withdrawn (lot 9) with a number of other drawings (**43–48**, **50–52**, **55–56**, **68–69**, **104** and **107**) from Sotheby's 1898 sale of Brown collection of Brontë relics, owned by Robinson and Francis Brown. These drawings were originally given to Martha Brown (Brontë servant) by Patrick Brontë or Arthur Bell Nicholls, then passed to Benjamin and Ann Binns (sister of Martha Brown). Acquired by Alfred Gledhill of Keighley at the Binns sale, Saltaire, 27 January 1886; then by Francis Brown, cousin of Martha Brown and father of Gladys Brown. See also **29** for further sources of the Brown collection.
*Brontë Parsonage Museum: C58*

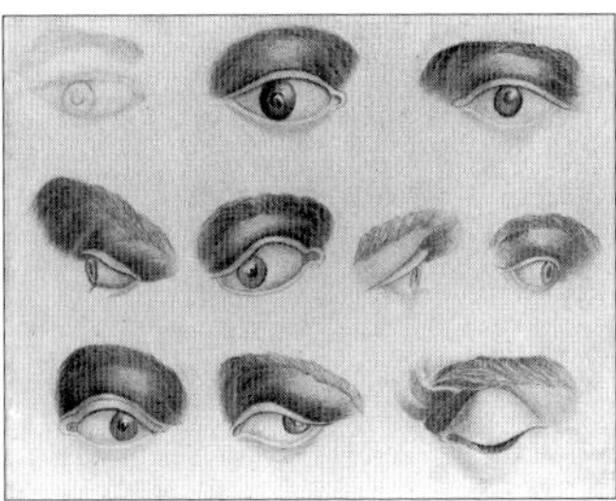

Studies of ten eyes and eyebrows observed from different angles and arranged in three rows: three across the top (the first eye unfinished), four across centre, three along bottom (the last with the eyelid closed).

This is an exercise, drawn on a leaf cut from a sketchbook used by Charlotte as a pupil at Roe Head. An unfinished eye in the top left corner of this sheet clearly shows the way she was taught to draw, by the use of carefully measured squares to make sure the proportions were correct.

This particular drawing is included at the front of a large number of late eighteenth- and early nineteenth-century drawing manuals. It can be found, for example, in *The elements of drawing, in its various branches, for the Use of Students, By George Hamilton, Drawing-master* (London: Richard Phillips, 1812). It is illustrated by 51 engravings, 'containing several hundred examples, from the works of the greatest masters.... And to be had by all Booksellers, with the full allowance to masters and schools'.

A number of illustrations, purchased in 1950 from Gladys Brown, were all cut from the same sketchbook, which was still intact when it was sold at the Binns sale in 1886. A report in the *Leeds Mercury*, 29 January 1886, describes the sale of 'a drawing-book full of physiognomical studies in pencil, which sold for 32s 6d'. The original book included the following twelve drawings: **42**, **43**, **44**, **45**, **46**, **47**, **48**, **50**, **51**, **52**, **55** and **56**. Judging from the size and type of paper, it is likely that other drawings were also part of this sketchbook, viz. **53**, **54**, **68**, **69** and possibly **49**. A reconstruction of the book and its contents throws light on the art education of the Brontës and other young girls of the period: see p. 43.

43

## Study of ears

9 February 1831
Pencil on paper
205 × 270 mm

Signed and dated in pencil, in miniature script, bottom right corner: 'Charlotte Bronte February 9 1831'. Watermark: 'J WHATMAN / 1829'. Inscribed in pencil on verso: '4' encircled.

Purchased from Gladys Jane Brown of Ramsgill, 1950, having been withdrawn from Sotheby's 1898 sale of Brown collection of Brontë relics (lot 5): see **42** for further provenance.

*Brontë Parsonage Museum: C52*

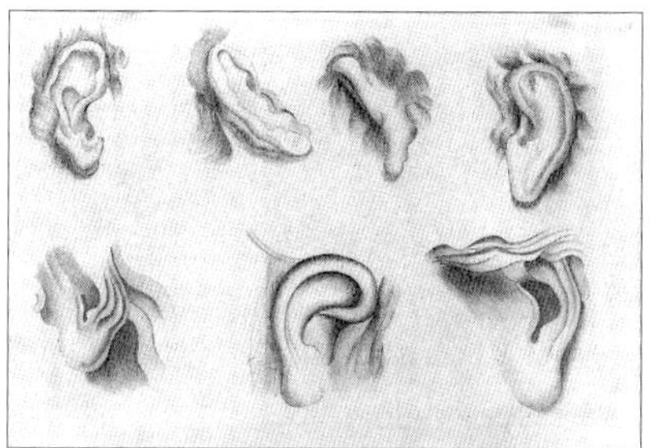

Study of four small ears surrounded by curly hair along the top of the paper; three larger ears with wavy hair looped around them along the bottom.

An exercise, copied from a drawing manual and drawn on a leaf cut from a sketchbook used by Charlotte Brontë at Roe Head: see **42** for a discussion of the sketchbook and source for this copy.

## 44

## Study of noses

c. February 1831
Pencil on paper
205 × 276 mm

Inscribed in pencil, top right corner: '2'; on verso in pencil, bottom centre: '1' encircled. Watermark: 'J WHATMAN/ 1829'.

Purchased from Gladys Jane Brown of Ramsgill, 1950, having been withdrawn from Sotheby's 1898 sale of Brown collection of Brontë relics (lot 32): see **42** for further provenance.

*Brontë Parsonage Museum: C56*

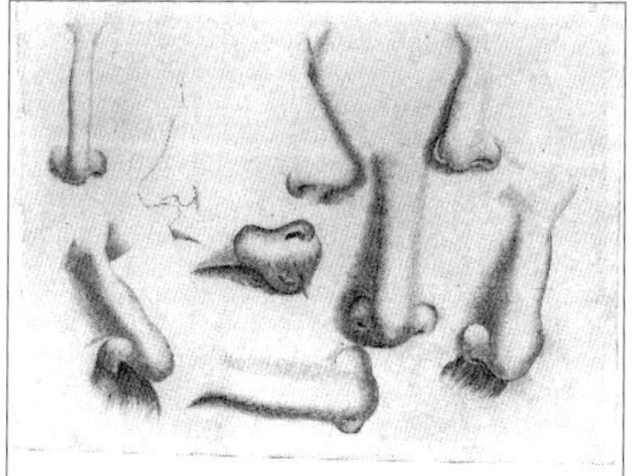

Study of nine noses, drawn from various angles and two with moustaches.

An exercise, copied from a drawing manual and drawn on a leaf cut from a sketchbook used by Charlotte Brontë at Roe Head: see **42**. The lines marking squares and proportions for several noses are clearly visible, especially around the nose in the top left corner.

## 45

## Study of lower face

12 February 1831
Pencil on paper
205 × 273 mm

Signed and dated in pencil in minuscule script, bottom right: 'Charlotte Brontë February 12 1831'. Watermark: 'J WHATMAN/ 1829'. Inscribed in pencil on verso: '5' encircled.

Purchased from Gladys Jane Brown of Ramsgill, 1950, having been withdrawn from Sotheby's 1898 sale of Brown collection of Brontë relics (lot 10): see **42** for further provenance.

*Brontë Parsonage Museum: C55*

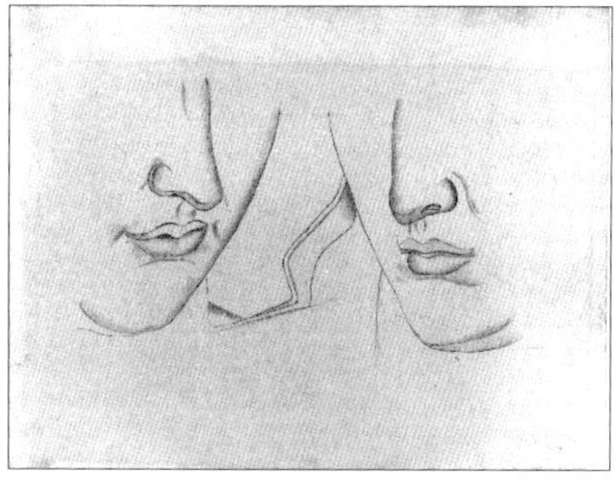

Two studies of the lower face (nose, mouth, chin and cheek), on right and left of the paper, facing towards the centre. The two drawings are connected by a strange waving form, slightly shaded.

An exercise, copied from a drawing manual and drawn on a leaf cut from a sketchbook used by Charlotte Brontë at Roe Head: see **42**.

## 46

## Study of mouths

c. February 1831
Pencil on paper
205 × 272 mm

Inscribed in pencil, top right corner: '8'; on verso in pencil, bottom right: '11' encircled.

Purchased from Gladys Jane Brown of Ramsgill, 1950, having been withdrawn from Sotheby's 1898 sale of Brown collection of Brontë relics (lot 29, 30, 31 or 40): see **42** for further provenance.

*Brontë Parsonage Museum: C57*

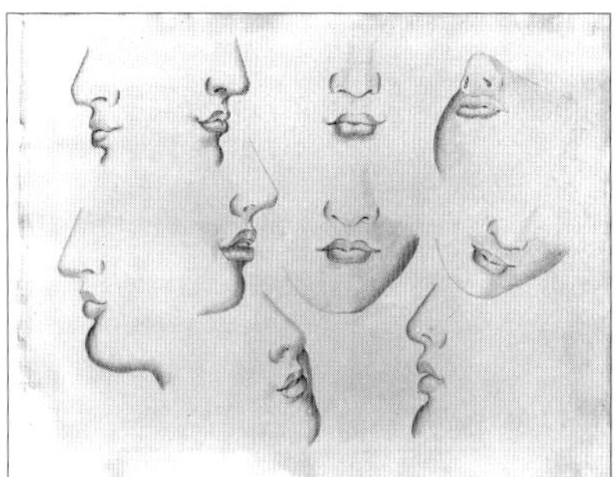

Ten studies of nose and mouth viewed from various angles. An exercise, copied from a drawing manual and drawn on a leaf cut from a sketchbook used by Charlotte Brontë at Roe Head: see **42**.

## 47

## Study of mouth and nose

c. February 1831
Pencil on paper
205 × 272 mm

Inscribed in pencil, top right corner: '7'; on verso in pencil, bottom: '12' encircled.

Purchased from Gladys Jane Brown of Ramsgill, 1950, having been withdrawn from Sotheby's 1898 sale of Brown collection of Brontë relics (lot 29, 30, 31 or 40): see **42** for further provenance.

*Brontë Parsonage Musuem: C53*

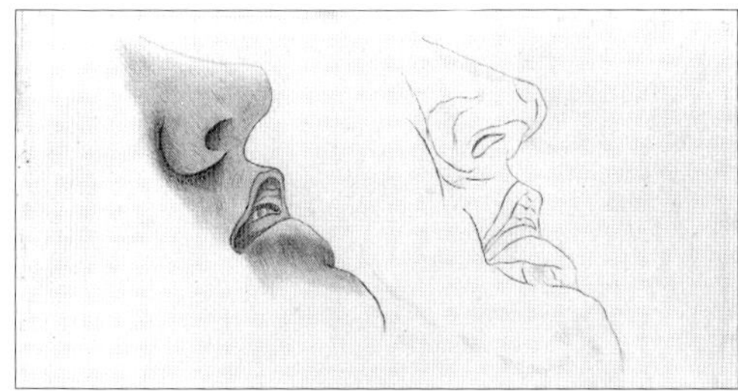

Two profiles of nose and mouth, tilted upwards and facing top right corner of sheet: mouth open and chin dropped down. The right profile is an unfinished outline; the left is carefully shaded.

An exercise, copied from a drawing manual and drawn on a leaf cut from a sketchbook used by Charlotte Brontë at Roe Head: see **42**.

## 48

## Profile of face and nose

c. February 1831
Pencil on paper
205 × 273 mm

Inscribed in pencil, top right corner: '5'. Watemark: 'J WHATMAN/ 1829'.

Purchased from Gladys Jane Brown of Ramsgill, 1950, having been withdrawn from Sotheby's 1898 sale of Brown collection of Brontë relics (lot 29, 30, 31 or 40): see **42** for further provenance.

*Brontë Parsonage Museum: C63*

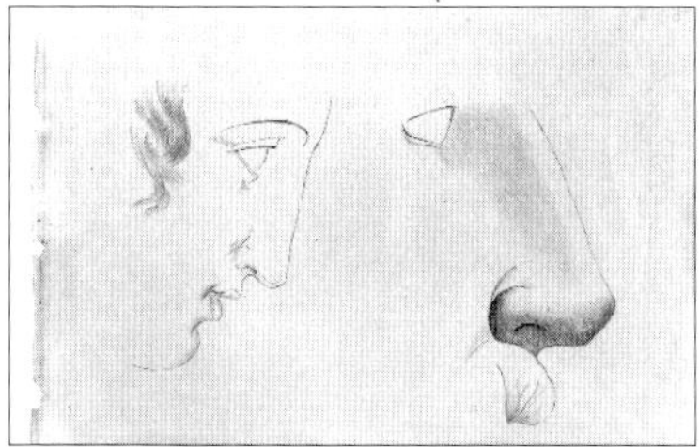

Profile study of a young woman's face, on left, and of a nose, with eye and top lip in outline, on right; both studies are facing towards the right, the face looking slightly down.

An exercise, copied from a drawing manual and drawn on a leaf cut from a sketchbook used by Charlotte Brontë at Roe Head: see **42**.

## 49

### Study of two profiles

c. February 1831
Conté crayon on paper
159 × 222 mm

Inscribed in charcoal on verso: 'Charlotte Bronte'; and in another hand in pencil: 'Bronte Relics Sale at Saltaire/ 1886/ A Riley'. Stamped: 'BRONTË/ MUSEUM/ HAWORTH', encircled.

Purchased from J. H. Turton, Pudsey, 1904. An envelope pasted to the cardboard back contains a note from J. H. Turton, Pudsey, 4 January 1904, to W. T. Field (secretary of the Brontë Society 1897–1920), which reads: 'the drawing was acquired at the sale at Saltaire by Mr Riley along with many other Brontë relics'. Abraham Riley was an auctioneer and valuer of Bramley, Leeds, with an antique shop in Ilkley. He bought the painting at the Binns sale, Saltaire, 27 January 1886. Benjamin and Ann Binns had acquired it from Ann's sister, Martha Brown, the Brontës' servant. For Riley's association with spurious Brontë items, see Dubious list at end of Branwell Brontë entries.

*Brontë Parsonage Museum: C51*

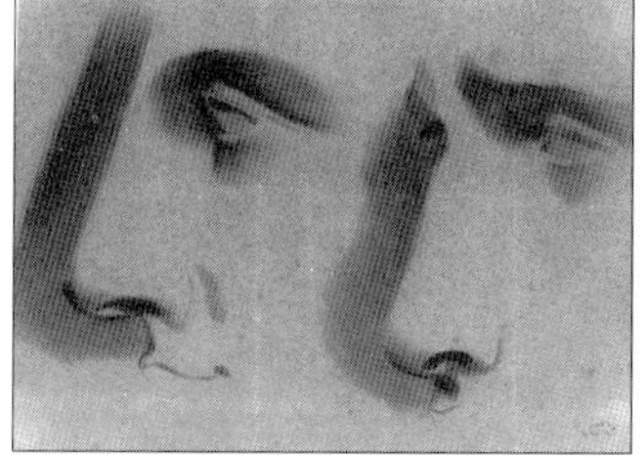

A study of the same face in two slightly different left profiles, concentrating on the nose and eye; extensive cross-hatching behind nose and beneath eyebrow.

An exercise, copied from a drawing manual.

## 50

### Study of bearded profiles

c. February 1831
Pencil on paper
205 × 272 mm

Inscribed in pencil, top right corner: '6'; on verso in pencil, bottom right corner: '12' encircled.

Purchased from Gladys Jane Brown of Ramsgill, 1950, having been withdrawn from Sotheby's 1898 sale of Brown collection of Brontë relics (lot 29 or 30): see **42** for further provenance.

*Brontë Parsonage Museum: C54*

Two bearded right profiles, each showing half the face only: the left, a profile of nose, mouth (slightly open revealing tip of tongue) and bearded chin; the right, forehead, eye and nose with moustache only.

An exercise, copied from a drawing manual and drawn on a leaf cut from a sketchbook used by Charlotte Brontë at Roe Head: see **42**. This same exercise can been seen in a number of contemporary drawing books which recycled the same engravings, such as *The Principles of Design. A Compleat Drawing book for the Improvement of Youth* [n.d.], which has this same plate of bearded profiles as in the classic eighteenth-century manuals of Bernard Lens, drawing-master to Christ's Hospital: see **317** for further information on Lens and his manuals.

## 51

# 'Amelia Walker'

17 March 1831
Pencil on paper
266 × 205 mm

Titled, signed and dated in pencil, minuscule script, bottom right: 'Amelia Walker : : : : : March 17th. Charlotte Brontë 183 [?1]'; the word 'Miss' has been erased before 'Amelia'. Inscribed in a later hand in pencil, bottom right: '12'.

Purchased from Gladys Jane Brown of Ramsgill, 1950; withdrawn from Sotheby's 1898 sale of Brown collection of Brontë relics (lot 4). This item was originally given to Martha Brown (Brontë servant) by Patrick Brontë or Arthur Bell Nicholls, then passed to Benjamin and Ann Binns (sister of Martha Brown). It was acquired by either James Miles, bookseller of Leeds, or Alfred Gledhill, dealer of Keighley, at the Binns sale, Saltaire, 27 January 1886; then by Francis Brown, cousin of Martha Brown and father of Gladys Brown.
*Brontë Parsonage Museum: C62*

Head-and-shoulders portrait of young woman with head turned slightly down and towards the right: short wavy hair, parted in centre and piled loosely on top, side swept behind ear; large wide-open eyes, straight nose and slightly pursed lips all giving the effect of a wistful appearance. Cut from a sketchbook used at Roe Head: see **42**.

Although this is titled 'Amelia Walker' by Charlotte, it appears to have been a drawing exercise executed while she and Amelia Walker were at Roe Head together, since the eye, ear, nose and mouth are similar to Charlotte's studies of parts of the face (see **42**, **43** and **46**) and her similar studies of other heads (see **52**, **55** and **56**), all originally part of the same sketchbook. None of Charlotte's other classical-style heads are positively identified but it appears that the pupils were encouraged to take the opportunity during drawing classes to practise portraiture 'from life', in this case using a younger pupil as model. Despite the model, however, this portrait appears slavishly close to an ideal type, typical of those illustrated in the drawing manuals of the day.

Amelia Walker, the younger daughter of Joseph Walker of Lascelles Hall, Huddersfield, and of Broadlands, Torquay, was a contemporary of Charlotte's at Roe Head (1831–2), although she was about five years younger than Charlotte. It appears that Amelia Walker was still at the school when Charlotte returned there in July 1835, since she left Roe Head with a memento from her drawing-teacher, Charlotte Brontë: see **139**.

## 52

# Head and shoulders of a young woman

6 April 1831
Pencil on paper
268 × 205 mm

Dated in pencil in Charlotte's minuscule hand, bottom right corner: 'April 6th 1831'.

Purchased from Gladys Jane Brown of Ramsgill, 1950; withdrawn from Sotheby's 1898 sale of Brown collection of Brontë relics (lot 2 or 3). Francis Brown (father of Gladys Brown) probably acquired this item from either Alfred Gledhill of Keighley or James Miles of Leeds, dealer and bookseller respectively, who both bought a number of pencil sketches described variously as 'Head', 'Head of Lady' or 'Pencil Study of a Head' at the Binns sale, Saltaire, 27 January 1886. Originally owned by Martha Brown and inherited by her sister Ann Binns.

*Brontë Parsonage Museum: C59*

Head-and-shoulders three-quarter portrait of a young woman: hair parted in centre and tied back over a head-band, fine wisps of wavy hair just in front of the left ear and down the neck at the neck at the back, secured with a band of cloth; small features, tight mouth, intent serious eyes looking towards the left, thick neck, unnaturally oval face and poorly drawn ear.

Drawn on a sheet cut from a sketchbook. A number of illustrations, purchased in 1950 from Gladys Brown, were cut from the same sketchbook: see **42**.

This portrait is identical to a drawing by Anne (**340**), which suggests that it was probably an art exercise at Roe Head. It confirms that the pupils at Miss Wooler's school used the same subjects and copied the same illustrations from a single source, as part of their drawing lessons. In this particular case, Charlotte may have modified the original to make it look more like a fellow pupil, who served as a model for practice in incorporating the various exercises in drawing ears, eyes, noses, etc.; this would account for the variations with Anne's copy of the same original.

Charlotte's portrait is noticeably less rigid in its portrayal of classical features than the solid, sculptured look of Anne's young woman, with her prominent, staring eyes, flared nostril and dimpled chin, details absent from Charlotte's version. Her handling of the left ear is markedly less accomplished than that of Anne whose copy, made some four years later, is closer to an engraved original.

The subject of Charlotte's portrait has been thought to be Amelia Walker, who was a pupil at Roe Head when Charlotte was there in 1831–2. Without corroborating illustrations of Amelia Walker, however, it is difficult to say for certain that she is the subject, although this portrait by Charlotte has the same slightly languid look expressed in her drawing entitled 'Amelia Walker' (**51**), also executed at Roe Head.

## 53

## Laughing child

c. 1831
Pencil on paper
267 × 205 mm

Inscribed in pencil, bottom right corner: '15'.

Purchased from the Brown collection of Brontë relics, sold by Sotheby's, 2 July 1898 (lot 35, 'Pencil Drawing, "The Laughing Child," by C. Brontë'). Originally given to Martha Brown (Brontë servant) by Patrick Brontë or Arthur Bell Nicholls, then passed to Benjamin and Ann Binns. Acquired by Alfred Gledhill of Keighley at the Binns sale, Saltaire, 27 January 1886; and then by Francis Brown. While in the possession of Gledhill it was exhibited at the 'Keighley Conversaziones', held by the Keighley Mechanics' Institute, in January 1889 (*The Yorkshire Post*, 8 January 1889).

*Brontë Parsonage Museum: C48*

Head-and-shoulders portrait of laughing, chubby child: three-quarter view with left ear clearly visible, short curly fair hair, eyes half-closed and mouth open.

A school exercise, copied from a drawing manual and cut from a sketchbook: see **42** and **54**. Children's heads appear, together with faces expressing the passions, in a number of contemporary drawing books: see for example [G. Smith], *The School of Art; or Most Compleat Drawing Book Extant: Consisting of an Extensive Series of well chosen Examples, selected from the Designs of those eminent masters Watteau, Boucher, Bouchardon, Le Brun, Eisen, etc. Etc.* (London: John Bowles; Robert Sayer; Carrington Bowles, 1765).

## 54

## Crying child

c. 1831
Pencil on paper, irregularly cut oval shape
250 x 205 mm

Watermark down length of paper: 'J WHATMAN / 1829'.
Purchased from the Brown collection of Brontë relics, sold by Sotheby's, 2 July 1898 (lot 34, 'Pencil Drawing, "The Crying Child," by C. Brontë').

Originally given to Martha Brown (Brontë servant) by Patrick Brontë or Arthur Bell Nicholls, then passed to Benjamin and Ann Binns (sister of Martha Brown). Acquired by Alfred Gledhill of Keighley at the Binns sale, Saltaire, 27 January 1886; and then by Francis Brown. While in the possession of Gledhill it was exhibited at the 'Keighley Conversaziones', held by the Keighley Mechanics' Institute, in January 1889 (*The Yorkshire Post*, 8 January 1889).

*Brontë Parsonage Museum: C49*

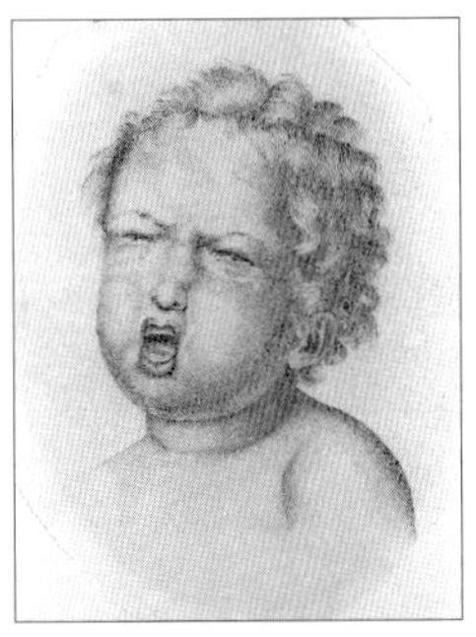

Three-quarter head-and-shoulders study of a chubby, crying child: short curly fair hair; face contorted with eyes half-closed, nose wrinkled, mouth wide open; left ear clearly visible but set rather too low on the head.

Companion exercise to **53**; copied from a drawing manual and cut from a sketchbook used by Charlotte Brontë at Roe Head: see **42**.

## 55

## Portrait of a classical head

c. 1831
Pencil on paper
268 × 205 mm

Inscribed in pencil on verso, bottom: '9 Cu[?l] A[?ul] $9^1/_2$% $7^1/_2$'.

Purchased from Gladys Jane Brown of Ramsgill, 1950; withdrawn from Sotheby's 1898 sale of Brown collection of Brontë relics (lot 1), where it was described as 'Annie Brontë by C. Brontë'. Francis Brown (father of Gladys Brown) probably acquired this item from either Alfred Gledhill of Keighley or James Miles of Leeds, dealer and bookseller respectively, who both bought a number of pencil sketches described variously as 'Head' or 'Head of Lady', at the Binns sale, Saltaire, 27 January 1886. It may be 'the pencil drawing of the head and bust of her sister Anne' exhibited by Alfred Gledhill of Keighley at the 'Keighley Conversaziones', held by the Keighley Mechanics' Institute, in January 1889 (*The Yorkshire Post*, 8 January 1889), although this could also refer to **134**. Originally owned by Martha Brown and inherited by her sister Ann Binns.

*Brontë Parsonage Museum: C60*

Head-and-shoulder right profile portrait of epicene figure: long wavy shoulder-length hair, down-cast eye, straight classical nose and brow, full lips; V-shaped neckline of unidentified attire.

An exercise: copy of a Raphael-style face or an extension of Charlotte's studies of parts of the face (see **42**, **43** and **46** for example). Originally part of a sketchbook used at Roe Head: see **42**.

## 56

### Study of a head

c. 1831
Pencil on paper
268 × 205 mm

Inscribed in pencil, bottom right corner. '13'; on verso, encircled in pencil: '2'.

Purchased from Gladys Jane Brown of Ramsgill, 1950; withdrawn from Sotheby's 1898 sale of Brown collection of Brontë Relics (lot 2 or 3). Francis Brown (father of Gladys Brown) probably acquired this item from either Alfred Gledhill of Keighley or James Miles of Leeds, dealer and bookseller respectively, who both bought a number of pencil sketches described variously as 'Head' or 'Head of Lady' at the Binns sale, Saltaire, 27 January 1886. Originally owned by Martha Brown and inherited by her sister Ann Binns.

*Brontë Parsonage Museum: C61*

Classical-style head-and-shoulders portrait of a figure looking and leaning towards the left: short curly tousled fair hair, swept back from the ear; straight nose, closed full lips, thick neck and long line of right, bare shoulder extends towards bottom left corner.

An exercise: the ear, eye, nose and mouth are similar to Charlotte's other studies of the face and head (see **52** and **55**). Originally part of a sketchbook used at Roe Head: see **42**.

## 57

### 'Guwald Tower Haddington'

June 1831
Pencil on paper
190 × 150 mm

Inscribed below in longhand by Charlotte: 'G[?u]wald Tower Haddington'; and signed along right edge: 'Charlotte Brontë / June 1831'. Marked in another hand in pencil, bottom right corner: '348'. Inscribed in ink on verso 'given to baby/ on her first Birthday/ Martha Brown/ August 23th 1871'. The BPM card index compiled by Dr Mildred Christian (see **34**) records an autograph note by 'Charlotte Brontë Nicholl [*sic*] of Bath', identifying this sketch (and **109**) as 'Two pencil drawings of / Charlotte Brontë's, which she put into these frames herself'; the drawings are no longer in the original frames.

Gift (together with **109**) of Charlotte Brontë Nicholl, daughter of Arthur Bell Nicholls's brother Alan, 1930; she acquired the drawing from her aunt, second wife of Nicholls. See also **116** and **117**, given earlier by Charlotte Brontë Nicholl with Charlotte Brontë's inlaid workbox (H88).

*Brontë Parsonage Museum: C16*

Picturesque landscape divided by a river flowing from the bottom left to centre, then obscured; trees on left and tall ruined tower in centre, both on left bank; two cottages and a mound in foreground on right. The tower, smoking chimney of the left-hand cottage and two saplings on the mound constitute the central features.

Copy of an engraving: an art exercise at Roe Head. This drawing is identical (except for very minor stylistic differences) to one by Emily Brontë, signed along the right side: 'E J Brontë', and inscribed 'Roe Head': see **311**.

## 58

## Mermaid fountain and urn

12 June 1831
Pencil on card
93 × 142 mm, irregular scalloped shape

Dated in Charlotte's minuscule script along base of picture, on left: 'June 12'; on right: '1831'. Inscribed in pencil along bottom right corner, in non-Brontë hand: 'By C Brontë'. The BPM card catalogue records a note on the back of the original frame (no longer extant): 'June, 1835/ By Miss C. Brontë' (date incorrect). The note continues: 'Copy made by M. E. Gaskell 7 February 1889/ "Mr Cornish, Dealer Feb. 5th 1889. 14 Victoria Road, Saltaire. All the articles that I have let you have of the Brontë relics are authentic and quite genuine in every respect and will give my guarantee". Mrs Binns (signed by) "This is the signature of Mrs Binns, sister to Martha Brown, that servant of the Brontës, who lived with them from been a child Yours I [?J]. Armitage."'

Gift of Elizabeth Maud Gordon, Northants, 1986, as part of the Seton-Gordon bequest; Elizabeth Gordon was the granddaughter of George Smith, Charlotte Brontë's publisher. Originally owned by Martha Brown and left in her will to her sister Ann Binns. A report in the *Leeds Mercury* on the Binns sale at Saltaire, 27 January 1886, describes 'a small and finely executed pencil drawing – apparently copied from one of those artificial garden scenes, with an urn, a statue, a fountain, and a grove, which were such favourite vignette pieces for title pages 80 or 100 years ago–50s.'. The drawing, however, appears to have remained in the hands of Mrs Binns until February 1889 when she sold it to 'Mr Cornish, Dealer' (see above), with an affidavit witnessed by her neighbour Joseph Armitage. (Armitage and his wife Florence also owned several Brontë items purchased by the Brontë Society in 1902: see F. C. Galloway, *A Descriptive Catalogue of Objects in the Museum of the Brontë Society at Haworth* (Bradford, 1896).) Mr Cornish then sold the drawing to Margaret Emily ('Meta') Gaskell (see above), daughter of Charlotte's friend and biographer, Elizabeth Gaskell. It was sold as part of Meta Gaskell's effects at 84 Plymouth Grove, Manchester, 13 February 1914, lot 1663, described as 'Small Sketch by Charlotte Brontë (Signed)' (sale catalogue, Manchester Central Library).

The drawing was published (together with **138**) while in the possession of Meta Gaskell and her sister Julia, at Plymouth Grove, Manchester. It appeared in Marion Leslie, 'Mrs Gaskell's House and Its Memories', *The Woman at Home*, no. 45, June 1897; a record of Gaskell manuscripts and relics. It was still owned by Meta Gaskell in November 1909, when she wrote to the Brontë Society declining an invitation to attend their AGM but offering to send two pencil drawings of Charlotte's for inspection (Correspondence in the Harold B. Lee Library, Brigham Young University, Utah).

The BPM also possesses an early photo of the drawing (Ph64), given by Miss Judson, 21 Parkfield Road, Warrington, in August 1935; and previously owned by Joseph Binns, a retired tailor of Manningham, Bradford, who lent the photo (together with photos of **110** and **138**) to the Brontë Society in 1896 (F. C. Galloway, *A Descriptive Catalogue of Objects in the Museum of the Brontë Society at Haworth*, p. 10). Binns had lived in Haworth as a young man, but it is not known whether he was connected to the Binns family of Saltaire.

*Brontë Parsonage Museum: C103*

View of an ornamental garden: fountain with mermaid on pedestal in the centre of a pond; grass slopes rising behind with trees on top; urn on pedestal, left foreground, with bushes at its base and a weeping willow tree behind leaning over the pond; small ornamental tree on grass mound, right foreground.

The elaborate fan-shape of the paper, with scalloped edges, suggests that the drawing may be a copy from or an illustration for a needle-case: cf. **59** and **95**. It is not surprising to see Charlotte illustrating and making such objects, as this is the kind of accomplishment art that was encouraged in all girls' boarding schools in the early nineteenth century.

## 59

## Castle on a hill

c. 1831–1832
Pencil on fan-shaped card
Upper edge 159 mm; lower edge 85 mm; sides 49 mm (irregular shape).

Inscribed in ink, top left corner: '1013'. Stamped: 'BRONTË/ MUSEUM/ HAWORTH', encircled.

Purchased at Hodgson & Co. sale, London, 31 March 1933, lot 449; formerly in the collection of Sir Alfred J. Law, Honresfeld (see **15**).

*Brontë Parsonage Museum: C76*

Tiny landscape drawing with a turreted castle (or fortified dwelling) on a mound; high rocky mountains rising behind; bushes and low vegetation in the foreground with two soldiers standing on the left.

The elaborate fan-shape of the paper suggests that the drawing may be an illustration for a needle-case. Several examples of Charlotte's expertise in this accomplishment art have survived: see p. 50.

## 60

## 'Muccross Abbey, Lake of Kilarney'

15 December 1831
Pencil on paper
250 x 356 mm

Signed right corner: 'Miss Brontë Roe Head/ Dec$^{br}$ 15$^{th}$ 1831./ [rule beneath date]'. Inscribed by Charlotte in longhand, bottom centre: 'Muccross Abbey, Lake of Kilarney'. Water stain over right half of drawing, less visible since conservation.

Purchased from James Hartley, 1896; previously owned by his wife Hannah, a sister of the Brontë servant Martha Brown. By the terms of Martha's will, her property was divided equally amongst her five sisters: see Appendix B.

*Brontë Parsonage Museum: C17*

Picturesque landscape of moss-covered ruined abbey with square tower, framed by trees in left foreground and on right; three deer in centre in front of abbey. Probably a copy of an engraving.

## 61

## 'Annual Lavatera'

15 December 1831
Pencil on card
259 × 172 mm

Titled by Charlotte, in pencil, in copperplate writing down left side of length of stem: 'Annual Lavatera.' Signed in pencil by the same hand, bottom right corner: 'Miss Brontë./ Roe Head./ Dec$^{br}$ 15$^{th}$ 1831'. Inscribed on verso, in pencil, in non-Brontë hand: '81/ 18/ Mrs Adamson/ 161 Mayfair/ 6 7/8/ × 10 1/4 / [?before] you show/ [?sig]hting at folt[?]'; part of final word cut away. Julia Turriff Adamson was the wife of Alan Joseph Adamson (see below), and the address identifies their Winnipeg home from the early 1900s to 1925.

Loan from Lilias Adamson, Winnipeg, Canada, 1976. The drawing originally belonged to Arthur Bell Nicholls and was inherited by his second wife, his cousin, Mary Anne Bell, in 1906. Some time between then and her death in 1915, Mary Anne Nicholls gave the drawing to her nephew, Alan Joseph Adamson (1857–1928), who had emigrated to Western Canada in 1873. It seems likely that he would have been given the painting on a return visit to Banagher, since he made at least two such trips to Britain before 1915. He gave the drawing to his wife, Julia Turriff Adamson (d. 1925), and it then passed to their fourth son, Alan Bell Adamson (d. 1965), and his first wife Ethel Mason (d. 1955). It is at present owned by Alan Bell Adamson's second wife, Lilias Adamson, née Mason.

Arthur Bell Nicholls frequently mentioned in his letters that a Colonel Adamson and his daughter had stayed at the Hill House, Banagher, as for example in his letter to Martha Brown, 8 January 1863 (BPM: BS251). Nicholls's aunt and later mother-in-law, Mrs Bell, was born Harriette Lucinda Adamson (see Frances E. Bell, *A Hundred Years of Life*, Bath: privately printed, n.d.); the above Colonel was her brother (Major P. E. Adamson, 'The Adamson Saga 1536–1936', Edmonton Robarts Limited). See also H. K. Bell, 'Charlotte Brontë's Husband: his later life and surroundings', *The Cornhill Magazine*, January 1927.

The Adamsons were a well-known Dublin family of Anglo-Irish descent. They intermarried three times with the Bells, who were from Ulster, and originally from Scotland. See also **41a**.

*Brontë Parsonage Museum: C101 LOAN*

Study of an old-fashioned flower, *Lavatera trimestris* or 'Rose Mallow': a single stem with two small branches; central full-blown flower showing stamens and petal markings; large triangular leaf bottom left, smaller leaf drooping down on right, other small leaves to the left and above central flower with three buds, one on the top right half-open.

The name written down the side of the stem indicates that the drawing was probably copied from an engraving or coloured plate, as are all Charlotte's flower drawings executed while she was at Roe Head.

62

## Roe Head

c. 1831–1832

Conté crayon on paper, mounted on card

94 × 130 mm

The drawing glued onto card (165 × 218 mm) and the card inscribed in ink, below drawing: 'By my D^r Daughter Charlotte P Bronté/ Min^r of Haworth.' Drawing stamped: 'BRONTË/ MUSEUM/ HAWORTH', encircled. Card inscribed in ink with BPM number top right: '32'. Inscribed in pencil on verso of card: 'Purchased by me from M^rs Hartley/ Martha Brown's Sister/ S. B.'; and at right angles to this: 'M^rs Hartley'.

Bequest of Henry Houston Bonnell, 1927; acquired by him from Maggs Bros. sale, London, n.d. (lot 669), at the same time as **139**, **308** and **324**. Previously owned by Sidney Biddell, Bolton Gardens, London, who is the author of the inscription above; he purchased the drawing in 1881, from Hannah Hartley, who inherited it from her sister Martha Brown, former Brontë servant.

There is a further authenticating inscription attached to the verso: 'Charlotte Brontës "Roe Head."/ Purchased by me of M^rs Hartley, 3 [?Ingleby] Place,/ Legram's Lane, Bradford–Martha Brown's Sister –/ Feb^y. 4^th 1881.–/ In the division of Martha Brown's effects,/ M^rs Hartley received this drawing and/ also, inter alia, Emily Brontës "Starling"/ both which I purchased in Feb^y. 1881./ Sidney Biddell/ 32 The Grove – Bolton, S.W./ December 8^th 1884.–' Emily Brontë's 'Starling' here refers to her 'Ring ouzel': see **308**.

*Brontë Parsonage Museum: Bonnell 32*

View from the front gate of Miss Wooler's school, Roe Head, named after the hamlet of the same name on the northern edge of Mirfield, overlooking Dewsbury and the Calder valley, twenty miles away from Haworth.

The drawing is an exercise, done while Charlotte Brontë was a pupil at Roe Head. It shows the large double-fronted house with its tall chimneys; the double bow-front of the left side, with large bay windows that look out across the park of neighbouring Kirklees Hall and down the valley; and the right front with entrance door and kitchen extensions on the far right at the back. (These have since been extensively added to, to form accommodation first for the Verona Fathers who owned the house for some years and, more recently, for Hollybank School for pupils and students with special needs.) The windows of the three floors can be clearly seen in the drawing: the uninhabited top floor, the first-floor sleeping quarters, and the dining room, school room and sitting room on the ground floor.

The girls apparently had lessons in one of the large front rooms on the left with the wide view of the landscape and within earshot on a summer day of Huddersfield Parish Church. Charlotte later recalls in her Roe Head Journal, 'a sound of inexpressible sweetness' which relieved the tedious school routine:

> I looked in that direction. Huddersfield and the hills beyond it were all veiled in blue mist; the woods of Hopton and Heaton Lodge were clouding the water's edge; and the Calder, silent but bright, was shooting among them like a silver arrow. I listened. The sound sailed full and liquid down the descent. It was the bells of Huddersfield parish church. I shut the window and went back to my seat. ('All this day I have been in a dream', 14 October 1836; *Jane Eyre*, ed. Richard J. Dunn, 2nd edn (New York: W. W. Norton & Co., 1987), p. 413.)

The drawing shows the large grounds of the school, the tall trees on the left, the long sweeping drive from the right to the house in the centre, and the steps and shrubbery of the more intimate formal garden area on the right, which still exists today. Some ornamental bushes and foliage have been added to the foreground of the drawing to place the house in perspective; and a tall tree in the right foreground helps to frame the picture.

The school at Roe Head was run by Margaret Wooler and her three sisters, who had connections in the district with the new wealthy manufacturers, whose daughters they could call upon as pupils. The school was opened in 1830 and there were only ten pupils when Charlotte arrived to board in January 1831, staying until May 1832. She returned in July 1835 as a teacher, remaining until December 1838.

During her time as a pupil, drawing lessons were taught by Susan Carter, a fifth Wooler sister married to the Rev. Edward Nicholl Carter, curate of nearby Mirfield Parish Church, where Charlotte was confirmed. Susan Carter was the visiting teacher for drawing until the birth of her first child in December 1832.

One of Susan Carter's exercises for new pupils was to draw this view of the school: two other versions of this view of Roe Head exist, viz. one by Anne Brontë (**339**), made at a later date when the foliage of the tall tree on the right obscured the formal garden behind, and another by Susan Carter herself (see plate 7), probably drawn at the same time as Charlotte's since the format and cloud formations are similar. The drawings are all made from the same position at Roe Head; it was obviously a favourite spot for sketching the building 'from life' (the schematic lines of the windows and minor differences compared to Anne's later version suggest this), although the work was probably completed in the classroom where the stylized foreground was added. A fourth version of 'Roe Head' (**310**) may have been made by Emily, copied from Charlotte's illustration after her return home, when she was teaching her sisters everything she had learnt at school.

## 63

## Greta Bridge

c. 1831–1832
Conté crayon on paper
91 × 133 mm

The drawing has been glued onto a larger sheet of paper (165 × 212 mm), which is inscribed below the drawing: 'By my D[r] Daughter Charlotte/ P. Brontë M[r] of Haworth.'

Gift of Sir James Roberts, 1934; acquired by him at Hodgson & Co. sale, London, 6 July 1933, lot 207.
*Brontë Parsonage Museum: C26*

Landscape with broad river, rocks and foliage in foreground; stone embankment, trees and cottages on left, river disappearing under double-arched bridge with three silhouetted figures crossing and four cottages (one chimney smoking) in centre middle-distance, dense trees on right and behind cottages; hills and mountains behind.

The subject resembles the many engraved plates of Greta Bridge, County Durham, found in the popular nineteenth-century books of views of lake and mountain scenery, such as Thomas Allom's *The British Switzerland, Or, Picturesque Rambles in the English Lake District: Comprising a Series of Views of the Lake and Mountain Scenery in Westmorland, Cumberland, Lancashire, Durham, and Northumberland* (London and New York: The London Printing & Publishing Co., n.d.).

Although this is a copy, the medium, size and technique are similar to her earliest efforts in landscape drawing which she executed as a pupil at Roe Head (compare, for example, **62**). At Roe Head, too, Charlotte was experimenting with Conté crayon for the first time. This was a mixture of refined graphite and clay used in pencils, which allowed for varying degrees of hardness and a wider range of tone in pencil drawings.

## 64

## 'Ludlow Castle Shropshire'

c. 1831–1832
Pencil on card, with raised, embossed border
221 × 265 mm

Signed in pencil in minuscule hand, bottom left corner beneath a rock: 'C Brontë'. Titled in faint pencil, probably by Charlotte, bottom right in river: 'Ludlow Castle Shropshire'; and on bottom border in pencil, in unknown hand: 'LUDLOW'. Inscription on verso in an unknown hand: 'By Miss Charlotte Brontë Currer Bell'.

Several labels at one time attached to the back of the original frame are inscribed as follows: (1) 'Pencil Drawing by/ Charlotte Brontë'; and in another hand: 'G. C. M. S./ (Heirloom)/ 30 Aug. 1897'; (2) 'Pencil Drawing by/ Charlotte Brontë./ The Curator,/ Brontë Museum,/ Haworth,/ York.' A third person has written beside the first two lines of the first inscription: 'Hand of Ellen Nussey' (although there is no Nussey connection with this item); beside the second inscription: 'This note is in the hand of Miss Katherine Cortazzo.' Dr Mildred Christian (see **34**) suggested that these initials might stand for Gomersal Church Missionary Society, but they seem more likely to be George Charles Moore Smith (see below).

Gift of Miss E. J. Moore Smith, Sheffield, 1941; originally given by Charlotte to Elizabeth Franks of Kipping House, Thornton, family friend of the Brontës and grandmother of Professor George Charles Moore Smith who published an article entitled 'The Brontës at Thornton' in *The Bookman*, vol. 27, no. 157, October 1904. This article describes a pencil drawing in his keeping 'executed on a card with an embossed frame, in the fine or finicky manner of the period, and represents a castle, with moat, bridge, trees, and two very badly drawn figures. It is inscribed in a flowing hand on the right of the foreground, "Ludlow Castle, Shropshire" ...' Since Elizabeth Franks (née Firth) died on 11 September 1837, Charlotte must have given her the drawing before this date, possibly when she and Anne visited the Franks for a week during the school holidays in June 1836.
*Brontë Parsonage Museum: C29*

View of castle from right foreground receding to centre middle-distance; river on right foreground in front of castle, two figures in centre crossing a stone bridge to the castle; trees and rocks on left, hills in distance.

Copy of an engraving, executed at school and given soon after to Elizabeth Franks, as described above.

Another copy of the same engraving survives in an album belonging to Mrs Jane Hickson, a descendant of the Rev. Thomas Allbutt, who married one of the Wooler sisters who taught Charlotte at Roe Head (see pp. 43–4 and **77**). This second copy, also titled 'Ludlow Castle Shropshire', is smaller (135 × 160 mm) but closer to the viewer, with the pencil lines more distinct and detailed than Charlotte's version (where a softer pencil and rubbing technique are used). The figures are also larger and more realistic. The initials 'S. C./ V. M.', signed in bottom right corner of the page, suggest that this second copy may have been made by Susan Carter, sister of Margaret Wooler. Another drawing by Susan Carter, made while she was a teacher at Roe Head, survives in the BPM (see plate 7).

It is possible that the two views of Ludlow Castle were copied at the same time, while Charlotte was a pupil at Roe Head (1831–2), but it seems more likely that the same set of engravings were used by different students over the years, as exercises in copying.

## 65

## Conway Castle

c. 1831–1832
Pencil on paper
163 × 212 mm

Inscribed in pencil, possibly in Brontë hand, along right edge: 'Currer Bell / [double rule beneath]'. Stamped embossed circular watermark: impossible to identify. Watermark: 'J WHATMAN / 1829' (part only).

Purchased from executors of Emma Wright of Bradford, 1932; together with an album, originally owned by her mother, Sarah Thomas, containing autograph stanzas 'Death of a Christian' by Charlotte and six stanzas by Patrick Brontë.

*Brontë Parsonage Museum: C75*

Picturesque landscape of Conway Castle, North Wales, beside the river in centre middle-distance; a swing bridge and mountains in the hazy distance to the right of the castle; tall trees in the left foreground and smaller trees on a bank on the right, frame the picture; two men on horses in the centre left foreground, one waving to a man with a rowing boat further away at the water's edge; a small sailing boat on the water in front of the castle.

Copy of an engraving, suggestive of the many views of Conway Castle in circulation at the time and in such drawing manuals as John Varley, *Precepts for Designs in Landscape* (n.d.). Charlotte's view is especially close to W. H. Bartlett's drawing, engraved by J. C. Armytage and published in vol. 2 of W. Beatie, *The Ports, Harbours, Watering Places and Coast Scenery of Great Britain* (London: G. Virtue, 1842). With its spectacular towers, Conway Castle was a popular subject for amateur artists. Charlotte's close friend, Mary Taylor, painted a vigorous watercolour copy of a similar view in a school-friend's album (see p. 44 for a discussion of this album, 1831–2).

## 66

## River scene with church and bridge

c. 1831–1832
Pencil on thin card
165 × 211 mm

Inscribed below: 'By my Daughter Charlottë [*sic*], P. Brontë Min[r]'. Watermark: 'J WHATMAN / 1829'.

Purchased from Frances E. Bell of Dublin, 1918, together with **150** and **350**, Charlotte's pocket book (BS22), a photo of Martha Brown (Ph71) and Harriet Martineau's visiting card; formerly given by Arthur Bell Nicholls to his second wife, Mary Anne Nicholls (née Bell), aunt of Frances Bell. In subsequent years other items were acquired by the BPM from Frances Bell, viz. **130** and Charlotte's workbasket (H176) in 1919; Nicholls's watch (J1) and chain and seal (J2) in 1941; and Charlotte's

cameo brooch (J60) in 1947. The Brontë Society refused the offer of 'A book containing ferns gathered and pressed by Charlotte Bronte during her stay at Killarney' (letter from Frances Bell, 3 March 1919, BPM).
*Brontë Parsonage Museum: C27*

Landscape of broad river, flowing from left foreground and disappearing centre middle-distance under three-arched bridge; saplings left foreground and a man carrying a boat; footpath along right embankment leads to square-towered church and cottages in middle-distance to the right of bridge; man in boat on river and two trees on front right; trees, house and hills in the distance.

Charlotte has drawn a pencil frame around the illustration, 2 mm from the edge of the drawing, which she possibly executed as a pupil at Roe Head (1831–2), since the style of her copy is looser and the pencil less heavily worked over than her later pencil copies of engravings.

## 67

## Red grouse

c. 1831–1832
Pencil and watercolour on card
145 × 186 mm

Signed and dated bottom left, 'CB 1829' (erroneous: see below). The BPM Stock Book entry records an inscription on the original backing, no longer extant: 'Bought many years ago from T. K. Stubbins at Bradford. No proof of who was the painter apart from "C. B. 1828 [*sic*]" in the left hand corner. Not likely to be spurious and probably copied from Bewick. Miss B was born 26 April [*sic*] 1816'.

Gift of M. Barbara Smith, West Sussex, 1981; acquired with **14** and **82**. Previously owned by Henry Fison Killick (Ellen Nussey's solicitor and grandfather of the donor), who was probably the author of the above note and bought the drawing from T. K. Stubbins.
*Brontë Parsonage Museum: C4.5*

Two red-brown adult grouse and three chicks in centre foreground, small shrub on right in pencil; large rotted tree trunk behind bird on left and dense bush and trees in distance; sloping hill and cornfield in right distance.

This drawing, with only its birds in watercolour, is surprisingly mature compared to Charlotte's other works of 1829. The signature and date may have been inscribed by another hand, attributing the drawing to an incorrect date: the 'B' of 'CB' in the signature is suspiciously unlike Charlotte's capital 'B' on other drawings of the same period (cf. **14**), although the remainder of the inscription looks authentic. The style is more in keeping with her work of 1831–2 or later; perhaps this was a school exercise, since it is similar to the illustrations in the Hickson album (see **64** and p. 44).

68

## Study of fruit 1

c. 1831–1832
Pencil and watercolour on paper; gum arabic glaze
165 × 216 mm

Unsigned and undated. Watermark: 'crown' (i.e. illustration of crown).

Purchased from Gladys Jane Brown of Ramsgill, 1950; previously withdrawn from Sotheby's 1898 sale of Brown collection of Brontë relics (lot 14 or 15): see **42** for early provenance.
*Brontë Parsonage Museum: C39*

Study of two central peaches surrounded by cherries, grapes, greengages and leaves: in centre, two peach leaves below the peaches, on right a bunch of grapes with green / brown leaf, loose grapes and sprigs of cherries arranged behind the peaches.

Similar fruits are used again in **69**; both are typical compositions for illustrations of fruit, found in plates in drawing manuals of the period. It is exactly the type of exercise Charlotte and her fellow pupils would have been set at Roe Head, probably late 1831 or early 1832, after she had mastered the drawing exercises on the human form. The use of gum arabic also suggests her introduction, in a classroom situation, to this common Victorian practice, although Charlotte appears to have used it earlier under the tutelage of John Bradley: see **26**.

69

## Study of fruit 2

c. 1831–1832
Watercolour on paper; gum arabic glaze
164 × 216 mm

Unsigned and undated. Watermark: 'Fellows'.

Purchased from Gladys Jane Brown of Ramsgill, 1950; previously withdrawn from Sotheby's 1898 sale of Brown collection of Brontë relics (lot 14 or 15): see **42** for earlier provenance.
*Brontë Parsonage Museum: C40*

Study of two peaches surrounded by leaves, grapes clustered behind and below, two cherries on sprig on right, two grey/red cherries on sprig top left.

Although this appears to be a school exercise in still life 'from nature', since most of the fruits in **68** have been used again and rearranged, the watercolour is more likely to be a copy of a print from one of the many contemporary manuals on flower painting.

See **26** for note on the use of gum arabic.

## 70

### Study of flowers 1

c. 1831–1832
Watercolour on card; gum arabic glaze
115 × 148 mm

Unsigned and undated.

Purchased from the Brown collection of Brontë relics, sold by Sotheby's, 2 July 1898 (possibly lot 16, 'Watercolour Drawing of Flowers, by C. Brontë'): see provenance of **29** for sources of the Brown collection.
*Brontë Parsonage Museum: C43*

Flowers arranged on decorative flat surface: central white cistus or rock-rose with four large petals, brilliant blue convolvulus on right (morning glory), three pale pink star-shaped flowers below, two yellow and blue pansies on left and five pink fuchsia-like flowers above the central white flower, together with surrounding leaves from the various flowers.

Probably a school exercise, made in the brief period of Charlotte's schooling at Roe Head, from one of the many contemporary manuals on flower and fruit painting: see **26** and **68** for notes on gum arabic.

## 71

### Study of flowers 2

c. 1831–1832
Watercolour on card
112 × 155 mm

Unsigned and undated.

Purchased from the Brown collection of Brontë relics, sold by Sotheby's, 2 July 1898 (possibly lot 17, 'Watercolour Drawing of Flowers, by C. Brontë', see provenance of **29** for sources of the Brown collection.
*Brontë Parsonage Museum: C44*

Decorative flower study with large pink rose on right, two yellow and blue pansies below with two buds; on left, large blue flower with yellow centre and eight petals (probably a clematis); and large pink bud with two blue sweet pea buds below, leaves and tendrils on far left.

Probably a school exercise, made in the brief period of Charlotte's schooling at Roe Head, from one of the many contemporary manuals on flower and fruit painting: see **26** and **68** for notes on gum arabic.

## 72

## Study of flowers 3

c. 1831–1832
Watercolour on paper
112 × 155 mm

Inadvertently purchased from the Brown sale, 2 July 1898: found on back of 'Study of flowers 2' (**71**) when it was being cleaned, 1987.
*Brontë Parsonage Museum: C44v*

Decorative flower study of large crimson rose or camellia on left and blue flower with gold, red and white patterned centre and fourteen petals (probably an anemone) on right; leaves and three yellow flowers with red centres above, one gold trumpet-shaped flower and leaf below, two blue sweet peas with tendrils and buds on either side; swirls of a brown wash along bottom edge and sides, suggesting that this was a rejected early draft.

Probably an unfinished school exercise, made in the brief period of Charlotte's schooling at Roe Head, from one of the many contemporary manuals on flower and fruit painting: see **26** and **68** for notes on gum arabic.

## 73

## Stylized flowers and bird on silk

c. 1831–1832
Painting on silk
245 x 285 mm

Painting mounted and framed; measurements record area visible through mount only. Inscribed on the back of the frame, top left: 'THIS SILK WAS PAINTED/ BY CHARLOTTE BRONTË/ AT THE RED HOUSE/ GOMERSAL. NR. LEEDS'; repeated at top of frame: 'THIS SILK WAS PAINTED BY/ CHARLOTTE BRONTË. AND/ AT THE RED HOUSE –/ –GOMERSAL. NR. LEEDS'.

Provenance unknown.
*Brontë Parsonage Museum: C98*

Six stylized flowers and attached green leaves arranged in one group of four (two yellow below and two plum colour above), in centre at the bottom, and one plum flower on each side of the painting. Arising from these flowers and connecting them are four different, long swirling tendrils of stylized leaves and two long bows of thin dark green ribbon in the right and left corners. An ornamental grey bird (with red comb, beak and eye; red legs and claws; red and black tail feathers; white wings with grey markings) perches on one of the left tendrils.

Painting on silk was a common practice for the nineteenth-century amateur woman artist. This is the only evidence we have that the Brontës may have practised this lady-like accomplishment. It is significant that Charlotte made this work while staying with her friend Mary Taylor's family, at the Red House, Gomersal; silk was expensive and it is not the kind of decorative, feminine art she was keen to indulge in.

## 74

## Palm squirrel

c. 1831
Watercolour on card; gum arabic glaze
75 mm diameter; circular shape

The card is sewn into a silk binding, possibly intended as a needle-case cover: see **75**.

Purchased from Rose Emma Longbottom, 1906 (together with **13**, **129**, **200**, **201**, **202** and **207**). Rose Longbottom was the great-granddaughter of Rose Bower, married sister of Tabitha Aykroyd: see **13**.
*Brontë Parsonage Museum: C70*

Squirrel-like animal crouched and alert, facing left with green/ brown bushes to the left and behind; beige legs, underbody and bushy tail curling high over the back of the animal; dark brown and beige striped back, round ears, pointed face, whiskers, large round left eye.

Copied from an engraving in [E. T. Bennet], *The Gardens and Menagerie of the Zoological Society Delineated*, vol. 1: *Quadrupeds* (London: John Sharpe, 1830), p. 50; purchased by Patrick Brontë in 1831 (bb69) and probably copied by Charlotte about this date, during her school holidays. The drawings in this volume are by William Harvey, engraved by Branston and Wright, 'the first of living engravers, on Wood', a judgement proclaimed in the inscription on the fly-leaf of this book by Patrick Brontë (see Appendix A). Some of the drawings, including the Palm Squirrel, are based on engravings by Thomas Bewick, former teacher of William Harvey.

The text of the above book, written by E. T. Bennett, describes in detail two palm squirrels that were in the Society's Menagerie and notes that they were both 'remarkably tame, and similar in their manners to the genuine Squirrels'. However, it appears that Charlotte was attracted to this engraving, not because of its zoological curiosity, but because the composition of the picture lent itself to a circular design, suitable for a needle-case or other decorative art work. The fact that it was associated with Bewick would have added to its appeal for someone always ready to improve her technique by copying the best available masters.

An entry on the palm squirrel also appears, without illustration, in Thomas Bewick's *A General History of Quadrupeds* (London: Longman, Hurst, Rees, Orme, & Brown, 1811), p. 391. It follows his reference to the Barbary squirrel and Bewick notes that 'Both these Squirrels inhabit Barbary and other hot countries. They live chiefly in palm trees, from whence the latter has its name'. Bewick's woodcut of the Barbary squirrel is thought to be the model for the palm squirrel in *The Gardens and Menagerie of the Zoological Society Delineated*.

## 75

## Bird's nest

c. 1829–1832
Pencil on card
45 × 63 mm

The drawing is on the front cover of a hand-sewn needle-case, lined and bound with pink silk. The pink silk is sewn round the edge of the illustration, which is inscribed in pencil, top right corner: '1143'. A second illustration on verso: see **76**. Unsigned but attributed by the original owners to Charlotte Brontë.

Donated by Sybil Kay, Sun Street, Haworth, May 1935; originally owned by Martha Brown and given by her to Linda Kay, a relative of the donor and friend of Martha Brown's nieces, the Misses Ratcliffe.
*Brontë Parsonage Museum: C69*

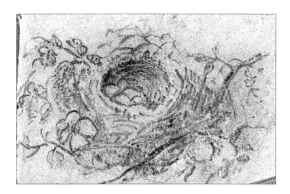

The tiny pencil drawing of a bird's nest and five eggs, surrounded by branches of flowers and leaves, has been drawn on one half of a single small sheet of cardboard (90 × 63 mm) folded down the centre to form the two covers of a needle-case. The back cover has a tiny pencil drawing of a bounding dog, rather like a spaniel. The cardboard has been lined inside with pink silk and overlapped on the outside to form a binding with tiny stitches around the illustrated covers. Inside are two pink felt leaves edged with pink satin, for the storage of needles and pins. These are sewn into the central fold of the cardboard and covered with a pink velvet ribbon tied on the outside around the 'spine' of the needle-case. The pink satin and ribbon are badly faded and the needle-case appears to have been well used, probably by Charlotte herself.

## 76

## Tiny dog

c. 1829–1832
Pencil on card
45 × 63 mm

The drawing is on the back cover of a hand-sewn needle-case: see **75**.

Donated by Sybil Kay, Sun Street, Haworth, May 1935; see **75** for early provenance.

*Brontë Parsonage Museum: C69*

This tiny pencil drawing of a bounding dog, rather like a spaniel, is drawn on one half of a single small sheet of cardboard (90 × 63 mm) folded down the centre to form the two covers of a needle-case (see **75**).

## 77

## 'St Martin's Parsonage, Birmingham'

May 1832
Pencil on paper
200 × 250 mm

Signed in pencil immediately below the drawing, bottom left corner: 'C. Brontë'; dated in pencil on an upward slope around the bottom right corner of drawing: 'Roehead May 1832'; titled in pencil, bottom centre just beneath drawing: 'St Martin's Parsonage, Birmingham'. Inscribed on verso, in unknown hand: 'Charlotte Brontë / May 1832'.

The drawing is in an album which was inherited by Jane Hickson from her mother, a descendant of Dr George Allbutt of Batley, who married Anna Maria Brooke of Dewsbury. His brother was the Rev. Thomas Allbutt who married Marianne Wooler, one of the teachers at Roe Head while Charlotte was there.

*Private owner*

Scene of St Martin's Parsonage, a large rambling half-timbered and gabled house, surrounded by trees and long grass and flowers. The right of the house is partly obscured by five birch trees in the foreground all bending to the right, two on the centre and right, three on the left. The house appears to have been added to at various times; it has six windows visible, a tiled roof with two chimneys, a conservatory door on the right opening onto the garden, a portico on the left beneath which a man stands with arms outstretched towards another man approaching the house with a basket; a dog bounds towards the second man to greet him. To the left of the house, behind the figures, there is a tall wall with an arched gateway leading into the churchyard behind; more trees and the church steeple rise faintly in the background.

Charlotte Brontë never visited Birmingham. This was probably copied from an engraving, drawn for pleasure as a gift for a teacher or friend, since it is part of an album still intact: see p. 44 for a discussion of this album and its contents.

78

## Woman with a veil

June 1832
Pencil on paper
323 × 250 mm (area visible inside mount)

Inscribed in pencil, in longhand, in centre below the portrait: 'Drawn By Charlotte Brontë = June 1832–/ [long line ruled here]'. The drawing is glued to a backing board, inscribed on verso: '129/4', a number repeated on the frame.

Acquired by present owner on 20 November 1974, at auction held by Messrs Hepper, Watson & Sons, Leeds (lot 339), who said that the picture had come from a family in the north-east. A label on the back confirms that it was framed by Mawson, Swan & Morgan of Grainger Street, Newcastle-upon-Tyne, and bears the ink inscription '129/25.1.66', presumably the date of framing. The provenance appears to be connected with Martha Brown's sister Mary, who married John Jopling, a schoolmaster of Leadgate, County Durham: Martha left her property to be divided equally between her sisters. Betty Crosland, a granddaughter of Mary and John Jopling, has recently identified the picture as one originally in her family home in Newcastle, sold by her mother 'early in the 1960s along with most of my father's possessions' (BPM letter March 1993); she recalls the intriguing fact that there was an envelope stuck to the back of the drawing which her mother would not allow anyone to open.

*Private owner.*

Head-and-shoulders portrait of a young woman with a veil draped over the right side of her head and falling over her right shoulder. She wears a simple Grecian-style dress of soft flowing material arranged over the right shoulder only, left shoulder and arm bare. She has an unusually (distorted?) long neck; her head is turned to the left while her body faces the right; she has a wistful, simpering expression, with her large eyes turned slightly up; long straight nose, small mouth. Her hair is parted in the centre and plaited in a coronet behind; she wears a circlet of flowers on her head, partly obscured by the veil. She wears a pearl drop necklace and matching drop ear-rings. The drawing has a soft, delicate appearance, portraying expert skill in the handling of pencil.

## 79

## Portrait of a lady with wreath

24 July 1832
Pencil on paper
146 × 103 mm

Signed and dated in pencil, along bottom edge, on left: 'C Brontë'; right: 'July 24th 32'. Stamped 'BRONTË/ MUSEUM/ HAWORTH', encircled. A card in the BPM written by Dr Mildred Christian (see **34**) records an inscription on the verso of original backing, no longer extant: 'Drawing by Charlotte Bronte/ given me/ by Mrs Nicholls/ July 1914'; inscription signed 'C W', said to be 'C. White of Switzerland'.

Gift of Miss C. White, 1938; acquired with **346**, together with a photograph of Arthur Bell Nicholls in Banagher 1890, a photograph of his home in Ireland and various correspondence with Rosse Butterfield, Honorary Curator of the BPM 1930–5. The items probably belonged to Nicholls's second wife, as suggested above; and it seems that Miss White may also have lived at Banagher, since Mrs Chadwick acknowledges the assistance of 'Miss White of Banagher', in her preface to *In the Footsteps of the Brontës* (London: Sir Isaac Pitman & Sons Ltd, 1914).
*Brontë Parsonage Museum: C7*

Three-quarter front view of young woman wearing a wreath of flowers, long ringlets, bare neck and chest, dress tied with a ribbon below the bust.

## 80

## Head of Scottish soldier

c. 1832
Pencil on paper
35 × 50 mm

This sketch predates illustration on the other side, which is signed and endorsed by Patrick Brontë: see **81**.

Gift of Margaret Illingworth, 1910: see **9**.
*Brontë Parsonage Museum: C68v*

This piece of paper (135 × 182 mm) has clearly been cut out of a larger sheet, as the figure of a Scottish soldier in the bottom left corner has been cropped at the edge of the paper. His nationality is identified by the tam o'shanter decorated with a tall feather. A cloak, possibly plaid or fur, draped across his left shoulder can just be seen. The man's face has small delicate features, with large dark eyes, a beard and moustache. Although Branwell made drawings of Scottish soldiers (see Appendix A), the style of this drawing suggests it was made by Charlotte.

An additional sketch of the head of an old man (also illustrated above), at the bottom centre of the paper, may have been made by Branwell. The face is long and thin with pronounced cheekbones and nose, deeply set eyes and strong frown lines between the eyes. The head has skimpy hair hanging forward and an open collar has been sketched in around the man's neck.

## 81

## Landscape of tower and river

c. October 1832
Ink wash on paper
135 × 182 mm

Signed in longhand, in very faint pencil, below picture on right: 'CB'. Inscribed in ink, below centre of picture: 'By my Daughter,/ Charlotte. P. Brontë Min$^{r}$'. Rough sketches on verso, one possibly by Branwell: see **80**.

Gift of Margaret Illingworth, 1910, together with **9**, **10**, **11**, **12**, **19**, **80**, **155**, **184**, **185**, **188**, **189**, **197** and **334**. There are no records of Margaret Illingworth's acquisition, though she may have obtained these items from one of Martha Brown's relatives: see **9**.

*Brontë Parsonage Museum: C68*

Dramatically lit scene, possibly by moonlight although no moon visible; drawn in the shape of a vignette. Low land in foreground with bushes, and grass, several trees near the river bank on right; steps on far left lead up a cliff to more trees and a tower with several low buildings to the right of it, all standing high above the river on the left bank; a dark shadowy cliff looms behind the tower on the far left; the river winds from right foreground around the right bank in middle-distance and disappears amongst high cliffs in the distance; billowy clouds fill the sky.

The figures of three men in pencil outline can be discerned in the central foreground, evidence of a change in intention. This is a good example of Charlotte's accomplishment in monochrome wash drawing, the use of a fine brush with ink mixed with water. The white areas of the illustration are produced in several ways: by applying bodycolour (lead white) on top, by leaving the surface unpainted, and by scraping out (the removal of paint or ink with a sharp instrument, immediately after it has been applied).

## 82

## Kirkstall Abbey amongst trees

10 October 1832
Ink and watercolour wash on paper
146 × 206 mm

Signed and dated in watercolour wash, bottom left: 'Oct$^{br}$ 10$^{th}$ 1832'; bottom right: 'C Brontë'.

Gift of M. Barbara Smith, West Sussex, 1981 (together with **14**, **67** and **198**); originally passed from Arthur Bell Nicholls to Martha Brown, then to Eliza Popplewell (née Brown). Rev. C. Hatton, Vicar of Calverley and maternal grandfather of Mrs Smith, then purchased the drawing on behalf of Henry Fison Killick, Ellen Nussey's solicitor and paternal grandfather of Mrs Smith.

*Brontë Parsonage Museum: C29.5*

Landscape of ruined abbey overgrown by trees and foliage; rolling grassland, river and three cows on a mound in foreground. This is another good example of Charlotte's proficiency in monochrome wash drawing and her use of bodycolour and scraping-out techniques: see **81**.

Kirkstall Abbey, situated on the outskirts of Leeds, West Yorkshire, had a special significance for the Brontë family, since this was where the Rev. Patrick Brontë had proposed to Maria Branwell. Charlotte's parents had visited the abbey many times during their courtship and her father recorded his enthusiasm for the place in his poem 'Kirkstall Abbey, A Fragment Of A Romantic Tale', published by him in *The Rural Minstrel: A Miscellany of Descriptive Poems* (Halifax: privately printed for the author, 1813):

Hail ruined tower! that like a learned sage,
With lofty brow, looks thoughtful on the night;
The sable ebony, and silver white
Thy ragged sides from age to age,
With charming art inlays,
When Luna's lovely rays,
Fall trembling on the night,
And round the smiling landscape throw,
And on the ruined walls below,
Their mild uncertain light.
How heavenly fair, the arches ivy-crowned,
Look forth on all around!
Enchant the heart, and charm the sight,
And give the soul serene delight!

(ll. 72–85)

Although Charlotte would probably have visited the abbey herself, this illustration appears to be a copy of an engraving. See **117** and **118** for further versions of Kirkstall Abbey by Charlotte.

## 83

## Derwentwater

October 1832
Pencil on paper

Signed: 'Charlotte Brontë, October, 1832'.

Owned by J. Horsfall Turner in 1896 and lent by him to the Brontë Society: see F. C. Galloway, *A Descriptive Catalogue of Objects in the Museum of the Brontë Society at Haworth* (Bradford, 1896), p. 21.
*Location unknown*

The drawing is apparently a copy of an engraving of one of Thomas Allom's drawings of Cumberland, which appear in a number of his publications with text by Thomas Rose, including *Picturesque Rambles in Westmorland, Cumberland, Durham and Northumberland: Illustrated From Drawings on the Spot by Thomas Allom* (London: Peter Jackson, Late Fisher, Son & Co., 1837); *Westmorland, Cumberland, Durham and Northumberland. Illustrated From Original Drawings by Thomas Allom* (London: Fisher, 1832); and *The British Switzerland, Or, Picturesque Rambles in the English Lake District: Comprising a Series of Views of the Lake and Mountain Scenery in Westmorland, Cumberland, Lancashire, Durham, and Northumberland* (London and New York: The London Printing & Publishing Co., n.d.). Charlotte made several copies of drawings by Allom at about the same time (see also **89** and **90**), suggesting a common source in one of these publications.

It is difficult to say which view of Derwentwater Charlotte may have copied here, since all these publications include a number of such views. The title 'Derwent Water' usually appears in combination with another name, such as the view of 'Derwent Water, & Lowdore, Cumberland'. Judging from the type of scene Charlotte was in the habit of copying, however, it is possible to suggest that she copied either 'Derwent Water, from Applethwaite' or 'Derwent Water, from the Castle Head, Cumberland', possibly the latter (illustrated below) since it is the most famous view.

## 84

## Study of a heartsease

3 November 1832
Watercolour on card
150 × 158 mm

Signed in pencil, in longhand, along bottom of picture: 'Charlotte Brontë November 3$^{d}$–32. H Week–'. Watermark: 'J WHATMAN/ 1831' (final 'AN' cut off). For verso see **84a**.

The painting is pasted into a bound volume with Emily Brontë's drawing of the dog Grasper (**313**) and an initial page inscribed: 'For/ M$^{r}$ Shorter/ with kind regards/ from/ M. A. Nicholls/ [line ruled here]/ July 11$^{th}$/ 07'. The volume is titled on cover in gold lettering: 'DRAWING/ BY/ EMILY & CHARLOTTE BRONTË', quarter-calf binding, and has the bookplate of Clement K. Shorter inside front cover.

Gift of Cecelia N. Eareckson, Philadelphia, October 1986; purchased by her at Sotheby's sale of the effects of Clement K. Shorter, 18 June 1928, lot 60 (with **313**). As described above, the drawing was given to Shorter in 1907 by Mary Anne Nicholls, the widow of Arthur Bell Nicholls who had taken the drawing back to Ireland with him after Patrick Brontë's death.

*Brontë Parsonage Museum: C104*

Study of a single heartsease stem (*Viola tricolor*) with one purple flower, a half-opened bud at the top, and many leaves. The bottom petal of the central flower is pale mauve with black lines radiating out from a yellow centre; the remaining four petals are purple. Behind the pansy stem are several long sheaves of grass and one stem of tiny pink flowers (possibly also grass or bistort or knotweed).

## 84a

## Sketches of a leaf and tiny face

c. November 1832
Pencil on card
150 × 158 mm (whole sheet)

On verso of 'Study of a heartsease', which is signed and dated: 'Charlotte Brontë November 3$^{d}$–32'. See **84** for watermark and related details.

Gift of Cecelia N. Eareckson, Philadelphia, October 1986; see **84** for earlier provenance.

*Brontë Parsonage Museum: C104v*

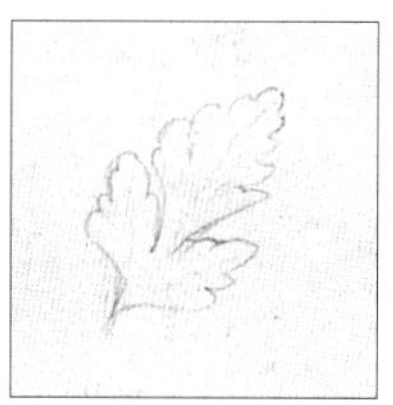

Detailed study of a leaf in pencil. This falls in the centre of an otherwise almost blank page, suggesting that this is a false start. The only other detail on the page is a small face with curly hair and hood, facing right, on the far right of the paper. These tiny sketches probably predate the watercolour on the other side.

## 85

## Bunch of wild flowers

c. November 1832
Watercolour on paper
174 × 149 mm

No inscription; but the verso has certain marks in ink that look like the reverse image of words that were written on another sheet and blotted by this one.

Given by Robert H. Taylor as part of his collection. Provenance immediately previous to this unknown, but a catalogue card at Princeton records: 'Flowers. Painted by Charlotte Brontë when she was about fourteen years of age and presented to Mary Wright Haworth [*sic*]. On Oct. 30, 1861 presented as a memorial by Mary Wright to Miss Eliza Watson'.

*Princeton University Libraries: Robert H. Taylor Collection*

Bunch of five stems of flowers and leaves, tied together at the base: two blue wild pansies; one white / lemon flower and bud, probably cowslips; three white / pink flowers with indented leaf (a type of cranesbill, such as herb Robert); and numerous white / pink buds and flowers of London Pride. The central cowslip has a bright yellow centre, but the colours have generally faded and the paint is worn.

The dating of this picture is based on a comparison with Charlotte's other flower studies at this time, in particular 'Study of a heartsease' (**84**) which is similar in conception and shows the same use of colour and paint.

## 86

## Pink begonia

28 December 1832
Watercolour on card
253 × 178 mm

Signed in pencil, in longhand, along bottom: 'C. Brontë December 28th 1832'; two illegible words follow (possibly the name of the plant) and are cut off at right-hand edge.

Provenance unknown; found in Bonnell safe, BPM, 7 February 1984.

*Brontë Parsonage Museum: C100*

Study of a single begonia stem with three large dark green heart-shaped leaves at the bottom and, after the stem divides in two, two tiny pink flowers at the top; several other small buds and two small leaves also at the top. The red veins of the leaves are clearly marked; the bottom right leaf is turned away from the viewer exposing the even more intricately veined underside.

## 87

## Blue convolvulus

c. December 1832
Watercolour on paper; gum arabic glaze
228 × 152 mm

Inscribed in pencil on verso in unknown hand: 'Painted by Charlotte Brontë'.

Purchased from Miss Brooksbank, Morecambe (formerly of Bradford), 1903, together with **88** and **319**.

*Brontë Parsonage Museum: C47*

Study of a single convolvulus stem, morning glory: one open blue flower facing right and two blue buds on either side; central large leaf below open flower and many small leaves on trailing tendrils.

The style and technique are similar to Charlotte's other flower studies of late 1832, which she is likely to have copied from contemporary engravings.

## 88

## Study of a blue flower

c. 1832
Watercolour on paper
161 × 139 mm

Papermark bottom right, only partly visible: 'BOARD'. Watermark, cut off on left: 'WHATMAN/1828'. Inscribed in pencil on verso, in unknown hand: 'Painted by Charlotte Brontë': see **88a**.

Purchased from Miss Brooksbank, Morecambe (formerly of Bradford), 1903, together with **87** and **319**.

*Brontë Parsonage Museum: C46*

Study of a single stem with two pale blue flowers, two small buds and two leaves; the flower at the top centre is open, revealing white markings and reddish stamens; the other is half-open and droops to the right; the nodes are marked by tiny star-like stipules.

The style and technique are similar to Charlotte's other flower studies of late 1832, which she is likely to have copied from contemporary engravings.

## 88a

### Tiny demure face

c. 1832
Pencil on paper
20 × 20 mm

Drawing occupies the centre of page (161 × 139 mm). Inscribed in pencil, in unknown hand: 'Painted by Charlotte Brontë', referring to the watercolour on the recto. See **88** for watermark and papermark.

Purchased from Miss Brooksbank, Morecambe (formerly of Bradford), 1903.
*Brontë Parsonage Museum: C46v*

Very small pencil drawing of a woman's head, below the inscription. The woman has short wavy hair, eyes downcast and a sweet smile. There is a faint outline of a tall hat on her head. This appears to be the beginning of a discarded drawing, and Charlotte has reused the paper for the watercolour now on the other side.

## 89

### Hartlepool Harbour

12 January 1833
Pencil on paper
131 × 161 mm (area visible inside mount)

Dated in pencil, immediately below illustration on left: 'Jan$^{y}$ 12$^{th}$ 1833'; signed on right: 'C Brontë'. Title in longhand, bottom centre: 'Hartlepool Harbour'. Inscribed in pencil on verso in Charlotte's hand: 'Miss Nussey'; in ink on verso by Ellen Nussey: 'A Drawing–By Charlotte Brontë when at School'; the date indicates that this is incorrect. Originally bound with Charlotte's last two letters to Ellen Nussey (BS 100: 'My dear Ellen / Thank you much [*sic*] for Mrs Hewitt's sensible clear letter'; and BS 101: 'My dear Ellen / I must write one line out of my weary bed').

Gift of Thomas James Wise, 1900; formerly owned by Ellen Nussey. Wise was an eminent, and often unscrupulous, bibliophile and collector of literary manuscripts. His Brontë collection formed part of his Ashley Library, which was later sold to the British Library. The story of his dealings in Brontë manuscripts is recorded in Christine Alexander, *A Bibliography of the Manuscripts of Charlotte Brontë* (Haworth and New York: The Brontë Society in association with Meckler Publishing, 1982), pp. xvi–xvii.
*Brontë Parsonage Museum: C20*

Busy harbour scene with boat traffic and fishermen in foreground; town surrounded by stone walls in left middle-distance; sailing boats and white cliffs in right distance.

This is a meticulously accurate copy of an engraving by William Le Petit of a drawing by Thomas Allom entitled 'Hartlepool, Durham'. It appears in a number of Allom's publications, including *Picturesque Rambles in Westmorland, Cumberland, Durham and Northumberland: Illustrated From Drawings on the Spot by Thomas Allom* (London: Peter Jackson, Late Fisher, Son & Co., 1837); and *Westmorland, Cumberland, Durham and Northumberland. Illustrated From Original Drawings by Thomas Allom*

(London: Fisher, 1832). As in all Allom's works, Thomas Rose provides the text, describing Hartlepool as 'a sea-port town of great antiquity' and ancient fortifications.

A gazetteer of the 1830s gives a picturesque description of Hartlepool in the time of the Brontës, recording much that Charlotte must have found of interest in the original engraving: the town

> stands on a promontory, nearly surrounded by the North Sea, which, on the south side of the town, forms a capacious bay, very commodious for the reception of vessels, and the landing of troops from the Continent; circumstances which rendered it a place of great importance to the Romans, and the family of Brus [from Robert de Brus, an attendant of William the Conqueror] were thence induced to secure it by fortifications... During the summer it is much resorted to by bathers; and additional buildings, and other accommodations, have lately been erected for the reception and convenience of those occasional visitants. The surrounding prospects are agreeable.... Hartlepool cannot boast of a very extensive trade, owing, perhaps, to the neglected state of the harbour, and to its distance from the places where the great staple commodities of this county, coal and lead, are abundant... The fishing business here is considerable and great variety of fine fish are caught, and sent into the inland parts of the country.... The persons employed in the fishery, who, except during the bathing season, are almost the only residents at Hartlepool, are a rude, but athletic and courageous race, very expert in their profession, and ever ready to brave the violence of the storm to rescue their fellow-creatures, in the numerous cases of shipwreck which occur upon this coast. A subscription life-boat was established here some years ago.
>
> (*Curiosities of Great Britain. England and Wales Delineated, Historical, Entertaining & Commercial. Alphabetically arranged By Thomas Dugdale, Antiquarian, assisted by William Burnett, Civil Engineer* (London: J. Tallis, c. late 1830s)).

## 90

## 'Cockermouth'

c. January 1833
Pencil on card
132 × 181 mm

Signed in pencil, in longhand, by Charlotte, on left: 'C Brontë'; titled in centre: 'Cockermouth'.

Purchased in 1904 from Edward Sunderland, son of Abraham Stansfield Sunderland to whom Charlotte Brontë gave the drawing in 1834 (see below).

*Brontë Parsonage Museum: C33*

Picturesque landscape with flowers in centre foreground in front of five grazing cows; trees and river in middle-distance; in far distance, a valley town surrounded by cultivated hills and lit by sunlight, with mountains beyond. Clouds above are parted to diffuse light over the typically Claudian scene.

This drawing is a meticulously detailed copy of an engraving by R. Sands of a drawing by T. Allom, entitled 'Cockermouth'. It appears in *The British Switzerland, Or, Picturesque Rambles in the English Lake District: Comprising a Series of Views of the Lake and Mountain Scenery in Westmorland, Cumberland, Lancashire, Durham, and Northumberland* (London and New York: The London Printing & Publishing Co., n.d.), p. 2. The plate also appears in a number of Allom's other publications in which he reused the same engravings, such as *Westmorland, Cumberland, Durham and Northumberland. Illustrated from Original Drawings by Thomas Allom* (London: Fisher, 1832).

In each of Allom's works the engravings are accompanied by descriptions of the place by Thomas Rose. In

*The British Switzerland*, Rose explains that Cockermouth is 'pleasantly situated in a narrow valley, at the mouth of the Cocker, by which river it is divided into two parts', the Cocker being a tributary of the Derwent. Rose focuses on the history of Cockermouth's castle and the church that contains a memorial window to Wordsworth, a native of the place and possibly the reason for Charlotte's choice of this engraving. He ends with a description of the accompanying view: 'taken from a beautiful woody eminence, bounding the rich corn-fields and meadows on the banks of the Derwent. The church and castle, though prominent objects in the distant mass of buildings, appear to occupy but little space in the extensive plain, stretching to the very foot of the mountains. The hills rise up like a fenced wall of colossal dimensions' (p. 3).

Charlotte made at least two other copies of drawings by Allom: 'Derwentwater' (**83**), dated October 1832, and 'Hartlepool Harbour' (**89**), dated 12 January 1833. It seems likely that 'Cockermouth' was also executed about this time when she had access to one of the above publications.

She gave her copy of this engraving to Abraham Stansfield Sunderland, who was organist at Keighley and employed by Patrick Brontë as music teacher for his children. He was the first to play the new organ at Haworth Parish Church in 1834 and offered his services *gratis* at the installation service on 23 March, at which John Greenwood, organist at Leeds, also played (see *Leeds Mercury*, 29 March 1834). Susan Jane Sunderland, daughter-in-law of Abraham, suggested (in a letter dated 15 August 1896, BPM) that it was on this occasion that he was entertained by the family 'with whom he was intimate' and that 'Miss Charlotte Brontë presented him with this drawing of Cockermouth'.

## 91

## 'Anne Brontë'

17 April 1833
Pencil on paper
300 × 233 mm (area visible inside mount)

Signed and dated in pencil, in longhand along bottom edge: 'April 17th 1833–Drawn by Charlotte Bron[të]'. Titled in Charlotte's hand immediately below centre of picture: 'Anne Brontë'; and inscribed below this: 'By my Daughter Charlotte / P. Brontë Minr'.

Purchased from Sotheby's, 16 December 1980, lot 272; this drawing had been the property of descendants of Sir William Robertson Nicoll, who acquired it from a sister of Martha Brown (probably Tabitha Ratcliffe) and reproduced it in *The British Weekly: a Journal of Social and Christian Progress*, founded by Hodder & Stoughton on 5 November 1886, with Robertson Nicoll as editor. T. H. Darlow records that 'the editor's charismatic interests showed themselves in a series of "New Literary Anecdotes" which … reproduced an unpublished pencil sketch of Anne Brontë by her sister Charlotte' (*William Robertson Nicoll: His Life and Letters* (London: Hodder & Stoughton, 1925), p. 72).

*Brontë Parsonage Museum: C17.5*

Delicate portrait of Anne in profile, sitting at a table with two books on it. Her shoulder-length hair is curled around the face and held on the right side by a comb.

A shawl, draped over the back of the head and shoulders in classical mode, is clasped on the right shoulder. Robertson Nicoll remarks in *The British Weekly*, 5 November 1886, that this drawing 'is identified as an excellent likeness of Anne Brontë by two of Martha Brown's sisters'.

Alongside this drawing is a detail study of the eye, forehead, nose and curl of the main portrait, at one time said to be the work of William Robinson, the Leeds artist who gave Branwell drawing lessons and may also have coached his sisters occasionally, although there is little evidence for this (see p. 26). However, Robinson did not begin the lessons until the following year. There are also several experiments in hatching by Charlotte along the right side of the drawing.

92

## Portrait of Anne Brontë

c. 1833
Watercolour on paper
74 × 55 mm (oval)

Originally owned by Ellen Nussey and possibly purchased from her by Alice Meynell (1847–92), the poet and essayist, then passed to her son, Everard; later acquired (together with a Brontë needle-case now lost) by the Rev. Henry Mitchell of Wayne, Pennsylvania (d. 1957), grandfather of the present owner.
Everard Meynell told Henry Mitchell that the portrait came 'direct to him' from Ellen Nussey. Since the Meynells were not married until 1877 and Everard would have been about eighteen at the time of Ellen Nussey's death in 1898, he may have acquired it on a visit to her with his mother. It is also possible that Ellen Nussey bequeathed it to Meynell in memory of his mother who was interested in Charlotte Brontë. There is no indication that the portrait was sold after Ellen's death. Meynell also told Mitchell that this portrait had at one time been displayed, with the needle-case, at a Brontë Exhibition at Haworth (letter in BPM); this is confirmed by a sepia photo of the portrait in an album formerly belonging to W. T. Field, secretary of the Brontë Society 1897–1920 (BPM).
*Private owner: on loan to Brontë Parsonage Museum (C107 LOAN)*

Half-length portrait of a young woman with reddish brown short curly hair parted in the centre; head turned to the right, shoulders and body facing the front. The face has small sharp features, clear blue eyes, tiny mouth with full red lips, teeth visible and a slightly receding chin. She wears an off-the-shoulder blue dress with white lace neckline, pleated bodice gathered at the waist in wide sash, full pleated skirt just visible, short puffed sleeves with an overlay of translucent organdie material. A narrow line of paint marks the oval shape of the portrait.

The body appears to be out of proportion and too small for the head and shoulders, a mistake commonly made by Charlotte in her drawing. There is the same delicate handling of the brush, not unlike her use of the pencil (see **91**), that we see in her other watercolours of late 1832–3.

93

## 'Portrait of A French Brunette'

14 May 1833
Watercolour and bodycolour on paper; gum arabic
162 × 129 mm

Signed and dated in pencil, in longhand by Charlotte, immediately below painting on left: 'C Brontë'; right:

'May $14^{th}$ 1833'; titled in pencil, in longhand by Charlotte, bottom centre: 'Portrait of / A French Brunette'. Watermark bottom right corner: embossed 'REYNOLD'S / ABRADED / SURFACE / DRAWING BOARDS'. On verso: rough pencil outline tracing of the figure on recto.

Bequest of Henry Houston Bonnell, 1927; acquired by him at Sotheby's sale of effects of Arthur Bell Nicholls, 26 July 1907.

*Brontë Parsonage Museum: Bonnell 23*

Young woman in peasant dress, holding a rose: rich auburn brown hair, parted in the middle, short ringlets on either side of her face, gathered together and fastened with two pink roses on the left, a braid of hair encircling the crown of the head; head inclining to the left, eyes looking towards left of picture, small pointed delicate features; bare neck and low neckline of plain white blouse, gathered at neck and cuffs, brown velvet bodice laced in the centre, with gold thread design; blue shawl draped behind and over right arm; hands held up delicately in front of right shoulder, a pink rose in the right hand.

The handling of the paint for the skin, flowers and clothes shows Charlotte's painstaking technique of using tiny daubs of grey paint as in stippling, painted over the basic colour to achieve the effect of light and shade and to highlight the texture of the skin and different materials. See also **26** for note on gum arabic, which Charlotte has used on the background.

A copy of an engraving, possibly from one of the Annuals. The portrait is suggestive of Charlotte Brontë's heroine Lily Hart, who features in her story of the same name, dated 7 November 1833, and who was probably inspired by 'Emily Hart', the early assumed name of Emma Lyon, later Lady Hamilton: see Christine Alexander, *The Early Writings of Charlotte Brontë* (Oxford: Basil Blackwell, 1983), pp. 108–9.

## 94

## Lake and castle

6 July 1833
Watercolour on paper; gum arabic glaze
133 × 168 mm

Signed and dated, in pencil, in longhand by Charlotte, bottom left: 'C. Brontë'; bottom right: 'July $6^{th}$ 1833'. Watermark, possibly cut off on left: 'WHATMAN / 1827'.

Purchased from sale at Hollis & Webbs, Leeds, 5 May 1922. This item, together with a letter by Charlotte, was at one time loaned to the BPM by J. Roebuck of Burley, near Leeds: see F. C. Galloway's *A Descriptive Catalogue of Objects in the Museum of the Brontë Society at Haworth* (Bradford, 1896), p. 20.

*Brontë Parsonage Museum: C34*

Oval-shaped landscape painting: in foreground, two fishermen (one in yellow and blue, the other in red and blue, both with black hats and rods), standing on brown embankment in front of a lake which extends into distance, sapling trees on left, fence post on right; in middle-distance, a castle (possibly ruined) on promontory stretching into lake from left; sailing ships and hills visible on right in distance; streaky pale blue and pink sky. The scene is lit from the right by sunrise or sunset, casting long shadows of the fishermen. Two brown oval lines of paint frame the picture.

## 95

### Landscape with figure of a lady

c. 1833–1835
Pencil on paper
96 × 145 mm (irregular shape)

Stamped: 'BRONTË/ MUSEUM/ HAWORTH', encircled. BPM number inscribed in ink, bottom left: '1014'; and above this in pencil: '22'.

Purchased at Hodgson & Co. sale, London, 31 March 1933, lot 449; formerly in the collection of Sir Alfred J. Law, Honresfeld (see **15**).

*Brontë Parsonage Museum: C74*

Landscape of a lake, trees and mountains in the distance; a veiled woman standing on a stone terrace in the central foreground and two small wooded islands in the middle distance to the left and right of the figure. The woman stands in profile, head raised to the sky, where light appears between parting clouds; her features are indistinct, veil draped over back of head, down her back and caught over her arm; arms crossed over her breast; one foot just visible. The heavy drapery worn by the woman suggests medieval or even classical dress. The elaborate fan-shape of the paper suggests that the drawing may be a copy from or an illustration for a needle-case: see **58** and **59**.

Fannie Ratchford (*The Brontës' Web of Childhood* (New York: Columbia University Press, 1941), p. 124) suggested that the figure was the Duchess of Zamorna in banishment at Alnwick, presumably because of her meditative pose and the suggestion of loneliness in the drawing. Compare, for example, these lines from an untitled poem written by Charlotte about January 1838:

> What does she dream of, lingering all alone
> On the vast terrace o'er the stream impending
> Through all the still dim night no life-like tone
> With the soft rush of wind and wave is blending

The dating of this drawing is inconclusive: the style suggests a much earlier date than 1838, possibly 1833–5 when Charlotte was at home absorbed in her tales of Glass Town and Angria, and painting portraits of her imaginary heroes and heroines.

## 96

### 'Santa Maura'

23 September 1833
Pencil on paper
92 × 144 mm (image only; the paper is considerably larger but is enclosed in a sealed mount)

Signed, titled and dated, immediately below drawing in faint pencil, on left: 'C. Brontë'; centre: 'Santa Maura'; right: 'Sept– 23$^{d}$ –33'. An affidavit by Arthur Bell Nicholls has been encapsulated in plastic and attached to the backing of the picture frame: 'This Drawing was executed by/ Charlotte Brontë & given by me–/ her husband – to Miss E. Taylor A: B: Nicholls/ [rule under signature]'. Miss E. Taylor is probably the person of the same name on Charlotte Brontë's list of wedding guests and a relative of Mary Taylor, Charlotte's school-friend who was in New Zealand at the time.

Gift of Robert H. Taylor of Princeton. Acquired by him from Ximenes Rare Books, Inc., 19 East 69th Street, New York, NY 10021, who bought the item at a Sotheby, Parke Bernet sale, New York, February 1983. The inscription by Nicholls describes the early provenance. The item then seems to have been in the hands of the Keighley dealer Alfred Gledhill as part of an exhibition in Keighley in January 1889: see newspaper article

'Keighley Conversaziones', the *Bradford Observer*, 8 January 1889, which says that 'A pencil drawing of a river, bridge, and mountain scene, with the title "Santa Maura" in Charlotte's handwriting, is very finely executed, almost resembling a steel engraving.' The drawing was then acquired, with the rest of Gledhill's collection, by Robinson and Francis Brown and may have been sold with their collection at Sotheby's, 2 July 1898 (possibly lot 38).

*Princeton University Libraries: Robert H. Taylor Collection*

Picturesque landscape with hazy view of sea and town. The view is seen from high rocks in the right foreground and four trees on the left. There are three peasant figures below in centre: one gesturing towards Santa Maura, one on horseback, the third a bystander admiring the view. The scene extends down from woodland towards a plain and settlement in middle-distance with a causeway structure extending into the sea (see below); sailing boats and rugged mountains beyond in far distance.

This is a copy of one of the plates illustrating the works of Byron. It was drawn by C. Stanfield from a sketch by W. Page, engraved by Edward Finden, and appeared in numerous editions of Byron published by John Murray. It appears, for example, in *Letters and Journals of Lord Byron: With Notices of His Life*, ed. Thomas Moore, 3rd edn., 3 vols. (London: John Murray, 1833), vol. 3, and in *The Poetical Works of Lord Byron*, 8 vols. (London: John Murray, 1839). In *Finden's Illustrations of the Life and Works of Lord Byron*, 3 vols. (London: John Murray, 1833–4), vol. 2, 'Santa Maura' is described by W. Brockedon, who quotes first from John Cam Hobhouse, *A Journey through Albania and other provinces of Turkey in Europe and Asia, to Constantinople, during the years 1809 and 1810* (London: J. Cawthorn, 1813) and ends with a verse from *Childe Harold's Pilgrimage*:

> On the 28th we sailed through the channel between Ithaca and the island of Santa Maura, and again saw Cefalonia stretching farther to the north. We doubled the promontory of Santa Maura, and saw the precipice which the fate of Sappho, the poetry of Ovid, and the rocks so formidable to the ancient mariners, have made for ever memorable.
>
> –*Hobhouse's Travels.*

Brockedon then says of Santa Maura:

> This island, forming at present one of the seven islands of the Ionian sea, known commonly by the name of the Septinsular republic, was in the time of Homer, and long after, attached to the continent, and formed the Leucadian peninsula.... The canal of Santa Maura, which separates it from the continent, is fordable in still weather; and the remains of a bridge built by the Turks, when they were in possession of the island, are seen, by which it was connected with the mainland.... The present town of Santa Maura is on the coast, below the ruins of the ancient city of Leucas, ... [Beyond] rises a grand range of snow-topped mountains (part of the chain of Pindos and Tomaros), terminating the horizon of Molossia. Below the spectator's eye are the town and fort of Santa Maura, and the rich Leucadian plain, covered with extensive groves of olive trees.... The descent towards Santa Maura is the subject of the annexed beautiful engraving, and the distant mountains on the continent are those observed from the sea by Byron on his way to Prevesa....
>
> Morn dawns: and with it stern Albania's hills,
> Dark Sule's rocks, and Pindus' inland peaks,
> Robed half in mist, bedew'd with snowy rills,
> Array'd in many a dun and purple streak,
> Arise; and as the clouds along them break,
> Disclose the dwelling of the mountaineer.
> Here roams the wolf, the eagle whets his beak;
> Birds, beasts of prey, and wilder men appear,
> And gathering storms around convulse the closing year.
>
> *Childe Harold*, canto 2, st. 42.

## 97

### 'Arthur Adrian Marquis of Douro', 1

c. 1833
Pencil on paper
195 × 112 mm

Titled beneath, in Charlotte's longhand, in faint pencil: 'Arthur Adrian Marquis of Douro'; further pencil inscription below has been erased except for the words 'FRONT 138' in pencil at the bottom. For verso see **98**.

Purchased from executors of Collingwood Pollard, 1924; acquired with Patrick Brontë's steel fob chain and watch key (J58), his two pairs of spectacles (J34 and J35), his surplice box (H118) and patchwork made by the Brontë sisters (D145). Pollard lived in Thornton, attended several early Brontë Society meetings and bought relics from Robinson Brown (though not those listed above).
*Brontë Parsonage Museum: C28*

Profile portrait of young delicate-looking officer in military costume (high collar, coat with frogging and braid, sash from right to left shoulder); fine features, long straight nose, profuse curly hair and long side whiskers. The carefully finished head and neck taper into a sketch from the shoulders to waist.

Described in BPM Stock Book as a drawing of 'Louis Phillippe of France. Drawn during Charlotte's stay in Brussels', but this seems unlikely. The title, although faint, can be clearly discerned. After January 1834, Charlotte's hero Arthur Adrian Augustus Wellesley became Duke of Zamorna and, a month later, King of Angria. It is unlikely that she would have used only her hero's early title, Marquis of Douro (as she does in this drawing), without the subsequent titles, so late as 1842–3, while in Brussels. By this time she had renounced her early writing and was considering a more realistic hero: see Christine Alexander, *The Early Writings of Charlotte Brontë* (Oxford: Basil Blackwell, 1983), pp. 245–6.

This drawing appears to be an early version of **101** completed on 15 October 1833.

## 98

### Two male portraits and buildings

c. 1833–1834
Pencil on paper
195 × 112 mm

Inscribed in pencil, upside down, top left corner: 'SB 450'. Titled on the other side in Charlotte's hand: see **97**.

Purchased from executors of Collingwood Pollard, 1924: see **97**.
*Brontë Parsonage Museum: C28v.*

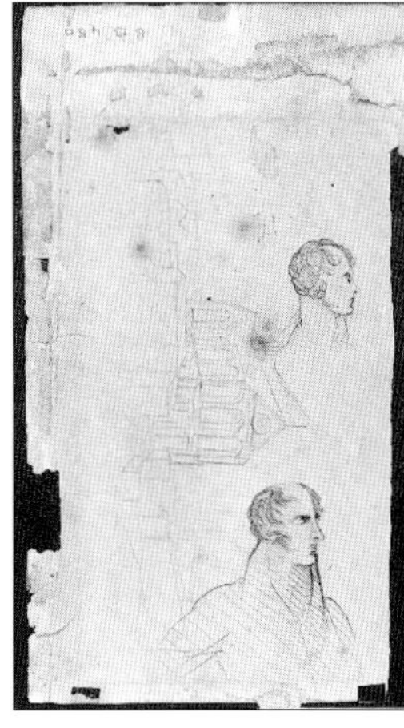

Two male portraits drawn one above the other down the right-hand side of the paper. The uppermost one depicts a young man's head seen in profile looking to picture right, with wavy hair brushed forward onto his face, receding at the top to show a high domed forehead and side whiskers. The man's neck is bare and the high collar of his jacket has been sketched in line. The drawing at the bottom of the page depicts the head and shoulders of a man with similar hair-style, large dark eyes, a long thin nose and down-turned mouth with a slightly sour expression. His high-collared jacket has been shaded in with rough diagonal lines.

These two male portraits are very similar to **104** and **105**, both drawn by Charlotte and probably depicting the Angrian anti-hero, Alexander Percy, Lord Ellrington and, later, Duke of Northangerland. Percy's rival, the Marquis of Douro, also drawn by Charlotte, is on the other side.

The drawing of the buildings is a townscape, made at right angles to the male portraits, and is most likely the work of Branwell. Branwell had a great interest in architecture and made many drawings of buildings from memory, from his imagination and sometimes from life. This one may be from life, since it resembles a typical chapel building in a northern town, possibly Bradford, or even Haworth itself, surrounded by the kind of closely built housing to be seen in such places. To the right, he has included a distant view of mill chimneys. The drawing is unfinished, sketched in line and unshaded.

This is an excellent example of the Brontës' reuse of paper, often worked over by several hands at different times.

## 99

### 'The Honble Miss Janet'

14 October 1833
Pencil on paper
82 × 52 mm

Dated in pencil, under left sleeve: 'October 14th –33'; and signed in pencil, under right sleeve: 'C Brontë'. Titled in pencil in Charlotte's hand, bottom centre: 'The Honble Miss Janet / [?Mobray-]'.

Purchased from Mrs G. M. Jones, 1971; apparently in the possession of the Jones family of Leeds for many years.

*Brontë Parsonage Museum: C18*

Three-quarter portrait of young lady with short curly hair dressed with two ostrich plumes, double-string necklace, off-the-shoulder dress with small belted waist and leg-of-mutton sleeves.

## 100

### 'Zenobia Marchioness Ellrington'

15 October 1833
Pencil on paper
90 × 79 mm

Signed in pencil, bottom left corner, just left of the scroll: 'C Brontë'; dated in pencil, bottom right corner, next to pillar: 'October 15th'; titled in pencil, in Charlotte's hand along the bottom of the page: 'Zenobia Marchioness Ellrington–'. Strips of gilt paper have been pasted along the outer edges of the drawing and across the corners by a previous owner, in keeping with a former fashion for framing pictures.

Bought by present owner from Dawsons of Pall Mall, in the 1960s. Given to the previous owner by Margaret Illingworth, who donated several items to the BPM in 1910: see **9**.
*Private owner*

Half-length portrait of a young woman, elaborately dressed in a plumed hat/ beret, long drop ear-rings and short thick necklace with central pendant, low necked (velvet?) dress with a high waistline. Her shoulders and upper arms are draped in a cloak with a high frilled lace collar (Elizabethan style) at the back. Only the lower left arm is visible, bent and resting on a pedestal. She wears a frilled bracelet and carries an open scroll in her hand. Her features are small and delicate, her hair short, dark and curly, like so many of Charlotte Brontë's female portraits at this time. There is a faint pile of books in the background to the right of the woman behind her left arm, suggesting that the subject is an author.

The portrait was identified in Dawson's sale catalogue as the Countess of Blessington (1789–1849), but this may have been based on a misreading of the faint final word of the title: 'Ellrington'. It is likely, however, that Charlotte modelled her heroine Zenobia, Countess of Ellrington and, later, Duchess of Northangerland, on a portrait similar to the one above. The face here (but not the hair or dress) bears some resemblance to the Countess of Blessington: see, for example, the portrait drawn by E. T. Parris, which appeared as the frontispiece to the second volume of Charles Heath's Annual, *Heath's Book of Beauty*, 1834, the year the Countess of Blessington took over the editorship; and a similar portrait of her appears in *The Keepsake*, 1844, which she also edited from 1841 until her death (though of course neither of these would have been Charlotte's original since they post-date her copy).

Lady Blessington's literary career and private life accord nicely with Zenobia's role in the early juvenilia, as the Glass Town blue-stocking, wife of Ellrington and platonic lover of the Marquis of Douro. Blessington's name was constantly before the public during the 1830s and 1840s, and the Brontës would have been aware of her role as a London hostess, of her ménage à trois with her husband and the Count d'Orsay, and of her friendship with Byron in Italy. They may perhaps have read her 'Journal of Conversations with Lord Byron' which appeared in 1832.

Zenobia, based originally on a combination of the historical Zenobia, Queen of Palmyra and the East (as recorded in Edward Gibbon's *The History of the Decline and Fall of the Roman Empire*), and Madame de Staël, features prominently throughout the Brontë juvenilia. She is noted for her scholarship and imposing stature; she is an accomplished author and always dresses elaborately in velvet gowns and plumed head-dresses, similar to those depicted above. This portrait of her belongs to the same private collection as **101** and **102** and was executed at the same date as these two drawings.

## 101

## 'Arthur Adrian Marquis of Douro', 2

15 October 1833
Pencil on paper
99 × 80 mm

Signed in pencil, in longhand, bottom left corner of portrait: 'C. Brontë'; dated bottom right corner of portrait: 'October 15'. Inscription in faint pencil, in

Charlotte's longhand, beneath portrait: 'Arthur Adrian / Marquis of / Douro'. Strips of gilt paper have been pasted along the outer edges of the drawing and a fancy shape cut out of gilt paper and stuck in each corner by a previous owner, in keeping with a former fashion for framing pictures.

Bought by owner from Dawsons of Pall Mall, in the 1960s. Given to the previous owner by Margaret Illingworth, who donated several items to the BPM in 1910: see **9**.

*Private owner*

Half-length profile protrait of a fine-featured young man, facing left and dressed as a military officer (high collar, coat with frogging and braid, sash from left shoulder diagonally across chest); delicate features, small mouth, long straight nose, profuse curly hair and long side whiskers.

The original of this portrait is most probably Arthur Wellesley, since it closely resembles other portraits of the historical Duke of Wellington in his youth. Charlotte's version is almost identical to another of her drawings of 'Arthur Adrian Marquis of Douro' (**97**), which may have been an early version of this more finished portrait of her hero in his youth. It is in the same private collection as **100** and **102** and was executed on the same date as these two drawings.

## 102

## 'Alexander Soult'

15 October 1833
Pencil on card
100 × 85 mm

Signed in pencil, in longhand, across bottom right corner below the portrait: 'C Brontë'; dated in pencil, in longhand, below left corner of portrait: 'October 15'. A very faint pencil inscription, in longhand beneath the centre of the portrait, appears to read: 'Alexander Soult / 1833'. There is a water stain down top left side of paper, to the left of the portrait.

Bought by present owner from Dawsons of Pall Mall, in the 1960s. Given to the previous owner by Margaret Illingworth, who donated several items to the BPM in 1910: see **9**.

*Private owner*

Half-length portrait of a fine-featured young man resembling several well-known studies of Byron (see p. 19). The closest original for Charlotte's drawing is an engraving by E. Portbury, based on a drawing by Westall entitled 'Childe Harold and Ianthe', published in *The Literary Souvenir* for 1830: see plate 3, for an illustration of the original.

The young man in Charlotte's portrait is facing towards the front but his head is in profile, facing right; the right arm is resting on a table, a book beneath the hand and an ink well and quill near the elbow, suggesting that the subject is a writer. The left arm is obscured by a cloak falling from the shoulder. The face has delicate small features and an intent gaze; curly dark hair, open-necked white shirt with stand-up collar and a pin at the centre of the throat (as in Westall's portrait of Byron); buttoned jacket with collar open at the top.

The portrait is in the same private collection as **100** and **101** and was executed at the same date as these two drawings. The inscription 'Alexander Soult' is in keeping with the titles of these two companion pieces: all appear to be based on historical figures but adapted to represent central characters in Charlotte's juvenilia.

Alexander Soult, Marquis of Marseilles and Duke of Dalmatia, was a close friend of Arthur Adrian Wellesley, Marquis of Douro. He became a noted Glass Town poet (and pseudonym of Branwell), and was later made Angrian Ambassador to Verdopolis: see Christine Alexander, *The Early Writings of Charlotte Brontë* (Oxford: Basil Blackwell, 1983).

## 103

## Young woman with 'Fairy Legend'

c. 1833–1834
Pencil on paper
113 × 84 mm

Inscribed in pencil, in Charlotte's minuscule hand, on the book in the drawing: 'Fairy Legend'. In pencil, in non-Brontë hand, bottom right: 'DRAWN BY/ CHARLOTTE BRONTË'.

Purchased at Hodgson & Co. sale, London, 31 March 1933, part of lot 447; formerly in the collection of Sir Alfred J. Law, Honresfeld (see **15**).
*Brontë Parsonage Museum: C94*

Half-length portrait of a petite young woman with short dark curly hair, delicate small features and large dark shining eyes gazing towards the top left corner of the picture; left elbow leaning on a table and her left hand supporting her head, leaning slightly to the left; a book, entitled 'Fairy Legend', in her right hand (the arm and sleeve are not sketched, only suggested); low-necked dress, tight-fitting over bust, tiny waist with a sash, full skirt, large leg-of-mutton sleeves, large white frilled collar; a long drop ear-ring visible from left ear, single-string necklace, brooch at centre neckline just above bust, jewelled bracelet around left sleeve.

Charlotte's technique of shading with heavy continuous pencil, back and forth in a zig-zag motion, creates the effect of velvet material for the dress; whereas the lighter shading of the collar gives the impression of finer translucent material, such as organdie.

The young woman is suggestive of Charlotte Brontë's descriptions of her early heroine Mary Percy; but she is also typical of the many female 'beauties' who adorned the pages of early nineteenth-century Annuals, such as *Heath's Book of Beauty* and its continuation *The Book of Beauty*, both edited by the Countess of Blessington (1834–49). She also bears a close resemblance to the figure of Ianthe in a plate from *The Literary Souvenir*, 1830, the source for the previous entry (see introductory essay 'The Influence of the Visual Arts on the Brontës' and plate 3, for an illustration and discussion of 'Childe Harold and Ianthe').

## 104

## 'Mr Ph Wood'

c. 1833–1834
Pencil on paper
154 × 122 mm

Original measurements given here; paper now inlaid into conservation paper. Inscribed in pencil, across the top, in Branwell Brontë's longhand: 'Mr Ph [?Wood]';

and under the drawing in Charlotte Brontë's longhand: 'Very good'. For verso, see **107**.

Purchased from Gladys Jane Brown of Ramsgill, 1950; previously owned by Robinson and Francis Brown but withdrawn from Sotheby's 1898 sale of Brown collection of Brontë relics (lot 27). For earlier provenance, see **42**.

*Brontë Parsonage Museum: C66*

Head and shoulders of scowling young man, wearing a high-collared coat and neck-cloth; receding hair, long side whiskers, prominent stubborn chin, suspicious ill-natured countenance suggestive of the Angrian character Alexander Percy, Lord Ellrington, whose name appears on the verso with an early draft of 'Mr Ph Wood': see **107**.

Although this drawing was previously attributed to Branwell, the style and subject of the portrait are similar to the two sketches by Charlotte in **98**. It should also be compared to **105**, 'Alexander Percy', which was probably executed at the same time.

The inscription 'Mr Ph Wood' may refer to Philip Wood, a relative of William Wood, the Haworth joiner, from whom the Brontës acquired frames for their pictures (see **331a** and p. 111). Wood was also given Branwell's paintings by Patrick Brontë as payment in kind: see **235**.

It is possible, then, that this sketch – initially suggested by an engraving – was influenced by a local personality, on whom the Brontës based their likeness of Alexander Percy. We may have further evidence here that Glass Town characters were sometimes based on local Haworth residents (see also **25**). There is little doubt that images of the Marquis of Douro were based on the historical Duke of Wellington and those of Zenobia Ellrington were based on Lady Blessington: see **100** and **101**.

## 105

## Alexander Percy

c. 1833–1834
Watercolour, bodycolour and pencil on paper
195 × 125 mm

Inscribed in pencil in non-Brontë hand, possibly that of Ellen Nussey, in bottom left corner: 'By P. Brontë'. Stamped: 'BRONTË / MUSEUM / HAWORTH', encircled. For verso see **106**.

Gift of William Edwin Briggs Priestley, Bradford, 1907; together with **156**, a letter from Charlotte to Martha Brown (BS69) and Patrick Brontë's spectacles (J17). Priestley was MP for Bradford, later knighted and a vice-president of the Brontë Society, 1909–20. He had previously lent this drawing to the Brontë Society in 1896 (F. C. Galloway's *A Descriptive Catalogue of Objects in the Museum of the Brontë Society at Haworth* (Bradford, 1896), p. 20).

*Brontë Parsonage Museum: B34*

Unfinished half-length portrait of a young man, whose fine delicate features express a distinct sneer: the chin is raised, the upper-lip curled and the eyes and brow show disdain and coldness. The figure lounges back in a complacent attitude, his left elbow resting on a pillar and his right hand thrust into his jacket in a typical Napoleonic pose.

Only the head has been finished; the remainder of the figure shows the work at varying stages of completion, allowing us a clear view of Charlotte's technique. As in her flower paintings, she works in detail first on the head or central feature, then on the remainder of the composition. The basic bodycolour of the jacket can be seen on the right of the painting and the darker overlay of blue watercolour is clearly visible even in this photographic reproduction. The red line across the waistcoat was probably intended to become a sash, indicating the subject's rank. His lips are coloured red, his eyes are a dark blue and his curling hair and long side whiskers are an auburn colour.

The portrait has been previously attributed to Branwell because of the non-Brontë inscription below; but it is quite unlike his style or working method. Branwell's pencil drawings are more vigorous than this and most of his portraits are in oil. Moreover this is typical of Charlotte's technique, described above, and similar to the many portraits of her delicate-featured heroes and heroines. Here the subject suggests the contemptuous Alexander Percy, Lord Ellrington, and later Duke of Northangerland, in his youth: the auburn hair, the haughty pose, the sneer and the affiliation with Napoleon are all indicative of this Angrian hero.

## 106

## Sketch of emaciated woman

c. 1833–1834
Pencil on paper
125 × 195 mm

Pencil sketches, as described below, and various indecipherable pencil markings. For reverse of sheet, see **105**.

Gift of William Edwin Briggs Priestley, Bradford, 1907: see **105**.

*Brontë Parsonage Museum: B34v*

Pencil sketches and doodles, the most significant of which is on the left of the sheet and illustrated above: the upper half of an emaciated woman, with extended neck, rising from the ground or water. Other crude outlines represent the face of a devil, on the right, and a ruled ladder in the top centre of the sheet. It is impossible to say who actually drew these crude sketches, but Charlotte seems to be the most likely candidate on grounds of style.

## 107

## Portrait of a young woman

c. 1833–1834
Pencil and crayon on paper; edges of paper torn
154 × 122 mm

Inscribed in pencil along the top edge in Charlotte's longhand: 'formerly Lord Ellrington', possibly referring to a faint pencil sketch beneath this portrait, a draft of the picture of the man on the recto of this sheet: see **104**.

Purchased from Gladys Jane Brown of Ramsgill, 1950; previously owned by Robinson and Francis Brown but withdrawn from Sotheby's 1898 sale of Brown collection of Brontë relics (lot 27). For earlier provenance, see **42**.

*Brontë Parsonage Museum: C66v*

Half-length portrait of a young woman in evening dress, reminiscent of those in *Heath's Book of Beauty* (1833–1849). This portrait has all the characteristics of Charlotte's other similar 'beauties': delicate doll-like features (lips coloured red), hair profusely curled at the sides of the face; long drop ear-rings, a waist-length necklace (and smaller single strand around throat), off-the-shoulder evening dress with frilled lace neckline, large leg-of-mutton sleeves and tiny waist (emphasized by a wide sash edged with beads); left hand clasping the necklace is just visible at the bottom of the drawing.

The ear-rings, hair, features and dress are almost identical to those of **103**, probably drawn about the same time. The faint outline of a previous sketch (an early draft of 'Mr Ph Wood', **104**) beneath 'Portrait of a young woman' indicates that the woman was drawn at a later date than **104**.

## 108

## Learning to draw

c. 1833–1834
Pencil on paper
140 × 189 mm

No inscription; but the verso has ink offset, in upper left corner, as if the sheet has been used as blotting paper.

The drawing has been stuck onto an elaborate flower- and leaf-embossed mount, typical of the 'framed' paper used by female amateur painters in the nineteenth century.

Purchased at Sotheby's, 16 December 1963, lot 69, through Winifred A. Myers.
*Houghton Library, Harvard University: fMS Eng 35.6*

Portrait of a woman teaching a young child to draw. Both have the same features: curly dark short hair parted in the centre and waving around the face, straight nose, small eyes and mouth. The woman is seated on a velvet and gilt stool, leaning over the child, her right arm extended guiding the pencil or brush in the child's hand; she is dressed in an off-the-shoulder long white muslin dress with lace neckline, short puffed sleeves, ribbon sash and frills of lace around the hem; her right foot is visible. The child is standing with the right foot extended, leaning back against the woman's knee; dressed in short dark dress, bare legs, dark slippers; looking at the picture which is supported by the left arm and hand, pencil in right hand (see **138** for a note on Charlotte's poor treatment of hands). Paintings are stacked to the right of the figures, the scene on one clearly visible as a castle on a hill behind a lake with two figures in the foreground (similar to Charlotte's **94**). Two heavy drapes frame the scene on either side, a tassel hanging from the one on the left. The ornamental effect is that of a typical 'fancy piece', commonly drawn by young Victorian women (see **16**).

The attribution of this drawing is not conclusive: although the figures and technique suggest those of Charlotte, especially of the years 1833–4, the depiction of a full scene like this is unusual.

## 109

### '[?P]orath from the Harbour'

16 December 1833
Pencil on card
119 × 159 mm

Signed and dated in pencil, in longhand, left: 'C Brontë'; centre: '[?P]orath from/ the Harbour'; right: 'Dec[br] 16 1833'. Embossed on verso, top left corner: 'SUPERFINE / LONDON BOARD', encircled with a crest in the centre. The BPM card index compiled by Dr Mildred Christian (see **34**), records an autograph note by 'Charlotte Brontë Nicholl [*sic*] of Bath', identifying this sketch (and **57**) as 'Two pencil drawings of/ Charlotte Brontë's, which she put into these frames herself'; the drawings are no longer in the original frames.

Gift (together with **57**) of Charlotte Brontë Nicholl, daughter of Arthur Bell Nicholls's brother Alan, 1930; she acquired the drawing from her aunt, second wife of Nicholls. See also **116** and **117**, given earlier by Charlotte Brontë Nicholl with Charlotte Brontë's inlaid workbox (H88).
*Brontë Parsonage Museum: C32*

Crowded harbour scene with women in four rowing boats centre and right, a duck fleeing out of the way of rowing boat in centre foreground; behind centre rowing boat, three square sails of boats moored at wooden wharf which extends into harbour on right; town buildings and church tower extend along quayside from left to right behind boats.

Copy of an engraving, possibly from a similar source to Charlotte's other views of ports and harbours, but more likely to be copied from a separate plate which was lent or hired by a local book- and printseller, or by the local library (see p. 17).

## 110

### 'The Sisters of Scio'

1833
Watercolour on paper

Titled, signed and dated in pencil, in longhand along bottom margin: 'The Sisters of Scio – By Charlotte Brontë 1833'.

Present owner unknown. Formerly in the hands of Mrs Binns, Oakworth, who lent it, framed, to the Brontë Society in 1896: see F. C. Galloway's *A Descriptive Catalogue of Objects in the Museum of the Brontë Society at Haworth* (Bradford: 1896), p. 13. Galloway also mentions (p. 10) a photo of the same drawing, lent by Joseph Binns, Manningham (together with photos of **58** and **138**); this is the ambrotype which survives in the BPM (Ph18), and is the only visual record we have of the painting. There is confusion about the provenance of the ambrotype: the BPM Stock Book records it as the gift of Mrs Greenwood in November 1966, but Stock Book correspondence relating to acquisitions records Miss Green, Ingrow, Keighley, as the donor.
*Location unknown*

Watercolour of two women dressed as one imagines Haidée and her maid Zoe to be clothed on their Greek island, in Byron's *Don Juan*, Canto II; seated on a grassy bank, the figure on the left is comforting the other, who hides her face in her sister's lap.

With only the black and white photograph for visual evidence, it is difficult to tell if there is water in the right foreground at the feet of the sisters, but they appear to be perched on a river bank or beside a rock pool on a seacoast. Both women have bare feet, white under-garments with long sleeveless jackets on top. The sister on the left, who appears to be the taller and elder of the two, has her dark hair pulled back and tied with a long striped flowing scarf; the hair of the younger hangs over the skirt of her sister, as she buries her face in her sister's lap, resting her head on the older sister's left hand which she holds with her own left hand. A grassy bank rises to the right and behind the figures; a wide skyscape fills the remainder of the picture.

Charlotte's painting has been copied from an engraving by Henry Rolls in *The Literary Souvenir* for 1830, entitled 'The Sisters of Scio', from the painting by A. Phalopon. What appears to be a grassy bank in Charlotte's coloured version is clearly a rocky coastline in the engraving; other essential details are the same. The engraving appears opposite a poem of the same name by Felicia Hemans (pp. 181–2), written to accompany the illustration. It is a dialogue in which the younger sister expresses her distress and the elder attempts to comfort and fortify her:

> "Sister, sweet sister! let me weep awhile!
> Bear with me – give the sudden passion way!
> Thoughts of our own lost home – our suny isle –
> Come, as the wind that o'er a reed hath sway;
> Till my heart dies with yearnings and sick fears; –
> Oh! could my life melt from me in these tears!
> ....
> "Yes, weep, my sister! weep, till from thy heart
> The weight flow forth in tears – yet sink thou not!
> I bind my sorrow to a lofty part,
> For thee, my gentle one! our orphan lot,
> To meet in quenchless trust: – my soul is strong –
> Thou, too, wilt rise in holy might, ere long....
> (II. 1–6; 13–18)

Scio is the modern name of Chios, in the Aegean Sea, one of the 'seven cities' that claimed the honour of being the birthplace of Homer. Byron, among others, refers to Homer as 'The blind old man of Scio's rocky isle' (*The Bride of Abydos*, canto II, v.II), and the island has an ancient history of trade and independent government. The image depicted here and in the poem, however, tells of the more recent massacre in 1822 of the inhabitants by the Turks, following an attack by Greek insurgents against the will of the natives. Many survivors fled to Syria, and Scio remained under Turkish rule until it passed peacefully to Greece during the Balkan War of 1912.

**111**

## Portrait of a young lady

January 1834
Conté crayon on paper
346 × 268 mm

Signed and dated in pencil, bottom left: 'Charlotte / Bronte / Jan$^{y}$ 183[?4]', date badly faded.
Inscribed in ink, bottom centre: 'By my Daughter Charlotte; / P. Brontë, Min$^{r}$'.
Provenance unknown.
*Brontë Parsonage Museum: C35*

Portrait of young woman in Regency dress with lattice design on bodice; long scarf draped around neck and tied in a knot at the bust; chain with flower clasp around neck, ear-ring on left ear visible, dark hair tightly curled in ringlets around face and piled in a knot on top with a wreath of leaves and berries around it. The face has a small neat mouth with lips tightly pressed in an 'over-sweet' smile, marked arched eyebrows and long straight nose; the eyes are gazing towards the left in a slightly sleepy manner.

112

## Young military man

c. 1833–1834
Pencil on thin card
102 × 66 mm

Stamped: 'BRONTË / MUSEUM / HAWORTH', encircled. The edges of the paper are unevenly cut where the image has been cropped from a larger sheet previously used for pencil sketches and doodles. Inscribed on verso in non-Brontë hand: 'Miss E Widdop / 26 Main Street/ Haworth'; and very faint pencil sketches, possibly by Branwell, of a church, a two-storey building with arched windows, sloping roof and decorative stonework; and a tree bending over a low fence and gate.

Acquired in 1897, together with **114**, from Elizabeth Widdop, whose mother Martha Redman worked at the Brontë Parsonage as an additional servant in 1850 (*The Brontës: Their Lives, Friendships and Correspondence*, ed. Thomas James Wise and John Alexander Symington, 4 vols. (Oxford: Basil Blackwell for the Shakespeare Head Press, 1932), vol. 3, p. 119). Elizabeth Widdop had previously lent these two items to the Brontë Society for display in 1896: see F. C. Galloway, *A Descriptive Catalogue of Objects in the Museum of the Brontë Society at Haworth* (Bradford, 1896), where they are listed as 'Two Pencil Sketches by Branwell Brontë, not signed; both portraits' (p. 25). Elizabeth Widdop's sister-in-law also owned a Brontë painting: see **30**.

*Brontë Parsonage Museum: B15*

Head-and-shoulders portrait of a young man in military evening dress: frilled shirt, epaulettes, high collar with a cape draped behind and held in the front by a jewelled clasp. A scarf, reaching to the chin beneath the collar, accentuates the long neck and patrician appearance. The subject has dark curly hair, fine features, straight nose, small mouth and large clear eyes looking directly to the right with an open, confident expression.

Faint cross-hatching in pencil, the remains of a previous sketch, can be discerned across the lower face and centre of the paper.

Although previously attributed to Branwell (see above), the portrait is quite unlike his style. It is difficult not to surmise that this is yet another portrait of Arthur, Marquis of Douro, or another Verdopolitan nobleman, so similar is it to Charlotte's other drawings of her early imaginary heroes drawn late 1833–4.

113

## 'King of Angria, Duke of Zamorna'

c. 1834
Watercolour and sepia, with pencil sketches
105 × 89 mm

Inscribed in background, in pencil, in a variety of Charlotte's scripts: 'King of Angria, Duke of Zamorna & Marquis of Douro' (along top right corner and down right edge); 'Field Marshal the most noble' (along bottom left edge); and some French phrases: 'conquèrant [*sic*] des cœurs et des couronnes' (written around the right shoulder), 'Vainque[u]r des fils et des femmes' (along the right side between portrait and first inscription).

Inscribed on a small label, on back of the wooden frame: 'Duke of Wellington, painted by/ Charlotte Brontë, and given to/ Mrs D. Howell, by Mrs Gaskell,/ at Haworth, Yorkshire, July 1865.'

Given to Eleanore Lang, Canada, by her aunt, Marie Howell of Dunnville, granddaughter-in-law of Mrs Daniel Howell of Galt, Ontario, to whom the painting was originally given by Elizabeth Gaskell at Haworth, July 1865, as noted above. The painting was brought to the BPM for inspection 1978.

*Mrs Eleanore Lang, Dundas, Ontario, Canada*

Half-length portrait of Charlotte Brontë's imaginary hero Arthur Wellesley, Duke of Zamorna and King of Angria, in full military dress: plumed hat with feathers falling to the right side of face and behind head; high-collared black velvet uniform with frogging and braid, cloak draped from left shoulder across the chest to waist; delicate features, aquiline nose and arched eyebrows, profuse curly hair and long curly side whiskers, twinkling eyes looking straight at the viewer and small red mouth with full lips curled at the corners.

The portrait is painted in monochrome, black watercolour and sepia (see **122**), with delicate colour tones used only for the face. This is the only portrait by Charlotte that is executed in this manner; it is highly successful in emphasizing the face and the dramatic, imposing character of the subject.

In the background there are tiny pencil sketches, which appear to be symbols of Zamorna's power: a crown and sceptre, sword hilt, ink pot and quill, artist's easel (all on right of portrait); lyre, sea serpent, stone tower behind a palm tree beneath which a woman is seated, and a blazing sun above.

The portrait is similar to **97**, which was probably executed by Charlotte at a slightly earlier date. Since her hero became 'King of Angria' in February 1834, it is likely that this painting was made at about the same time to celebrate his coronation. Later manuscripts describe him as an older man than the one depicted here.

## 114

## Arthur Wellesley

c. 1834
Pencil on paper
100 × 66 mm

Stamped: 'BRONTË/ MUSEUM/ HAWORTH', encircled. Inscribed on verso in non-Brontë hand: 'Miss E Widdop/ 26 Main Street /Haworth.' Also on verso: very faint pencil sketches possibly by Branwell, of two-storey house, temple with pillars and trees in leaf.

Acquired in 1897, together with **112**, from Elizabeth Widdop, daughter of Martha Redman (see **112**). Elizabeth Widdop had previously lent these two items to the Brontë Society for display in 1896: see F. C. Galloway, *A Descriptive Catalogue of Objects in the Museum of the Brontë Society at Haworth* (Bradford, 1896), where they are listed as 'Two Pencil Sketches by Branwell Brontë, not signed; both portraits' (p. 25).

*Brontë Parsonage Museum: B16*

Head-and-shoulders portrait of a young man with fine features and noble bearing. Although unsigned, this portrait has all the hallmarks of Charlotte's delicate handling of the pencil and is typical of her more effeminate male portraits. The figure is in three-quarter view, facing left, with a high brow, large clear eyes, a slightly aquiline nose, small firmly set mouth, small side whiskers and dimpled chin. The high collar, possibly of a military cloak, reaches to his chin and his hair is arranged in large wispy curls around his face.

Although previously attributed to Branwell (see above), the portrait is similar to early images of the historical Arthur Wellesley, the young Duke of Wellington; and it is probably an adaptation of one of these, made by Charlotte about 1834, when she was concerned to depict her own Arthur Wellesley, Marquis of Douro and Duke of Zamorna.

## 115

## Sketch of a 'beautiful lady'

c. January 1834
Pencil on paper
135 × 122 mm

The sketch is drawn across two pages (pp. 2–3) of a single sheet (154 × 122 mm) folded to form four pages. Pages 1, 4 and part of 3 are occupied by an early manuscript draft of the poem 'The moon dawned slow in the dusky gloaming', written in Charlotte's minuscule script and dated elsewhere 17 January 1834 (see *An Edition of the Early Writings of Charlotte Brontë*, ed. Christine Alexander, vol. 2, part 1 (Oxford: Basil Blackwell for the Shakespeare Head Press, 1991), pp. 348–50). Part of verse 6 is written over the sleeves and waist of the drawing; several Angrian names are written in minuscule script in the top right-hand corner of the page.

Bequest of Henry Houston Bonnell, 1927. Previously owned by Arthur Bell Nicholls and acquired by Bonnell at Sotheby's sale of the effects of Mary Anne Nicholls, 19 June 1914, lot 202.

*Brontë Parsonage Museum: Bonnell 89*

Half-length portrait of a young woman in evening dress, similar in pose and costume to the many engravings of fashionable young women in *Heath's Book of Beauty* (1833–49). Charlotte's beauty has delicate doll-like features, hair profusely curled at the sides of the face and held in a pile on top by a large elaborate comb; long drop ear-rings, single-strand necklace, off-the-shoulder evening dress with scalloped neckline, large leg-of-mutton sleeves and tiny waist. The figure is leaning forward to the right with the head resting on the left hand, the elbow supported on a table; the angle of the arm is disproportionately drawn in relation to the figure.

Three more smaller rough sketches, illustrating the front and back of a ball gown, full-length, and a head and shoulders, fill the top left corner of the picture; one of these sketches overlaps the left shoulder of the main portrait. Verses 6, 7 and 8 of the poem fill the bottom third of the picture and overlap the drawing as described above.

## 116

# Bolton Abbey

c. May 1834
Pencil on card
99 × 141 mm

Inscribed along the bottom edge margin, in pencil, in Charlotte's minuscule hand: 'Re-opening the Haworth Organ'; top left margin, lengthwise in minuscule longhand, in pencil: 'Grasper is [?1 word]/ Branwell', and lower left margin in same hand: 'The organ will be Re-opened'; top margin in large cursive hand, in pencil: 'morning' repeated several times. The sheet is irregularly cut and some of the writing appears to have been cut away.

Exhibited in the summer exhibition of the Royal Northern Society for the Encouragement of the Fine Arts, in Leeds, 1834.

Gift of Charlotte Brontë Nicholl [*sic*], 1928; daughter of Arthur Bell Nicholls's brother Alan. She acquired the drawing from her aunt, second wife of Nicholls. See also **117**, given by Charlotte Brontë Nicholl at the same time, with Charlotte Brontë's inlaid workbox (H88); and also **57** and **109**, given by her in 1930.

A detail of this drawing was reproduced 'by kind permission of Mr. Clement K. Shorter' with details of five other Brontë drawings (**117**, **137**, **343**, **344** and **346**), in *The Bookman*, October 1904, while the originals were still in the possession of Arthur Bell Nicholls.

*Brontë Parsonage Museum: C73*

Picturesque view of the ruins of Bolton Abbey (it was actually a priory, never an abbey), situated in North Yorkshire. The priory is seen in the middle-distance centre right, surrounded by low bushes and trees, with a bridge on the left beyond the priory; high hills behind the priory and in the distance; two trees dominate the right foreground throwing the priory into perspective and a river flows across the picture in the foreground, winding amidst trees to the left of the priory and receding under the bridge into the distance. The dramatic lighting suggests an evening or moonlit scene.

Charlotte Brontë would have been well aware that the painter J. M. W. Turner frequently sketched the ruins of Bolton Abbey and that William Wordsworth wrote his poem 'The White Doe of Rylstone' after a visit to the priory with his sister Dorothy. Charlotte visited the priory herself in mid 1833, with her family and school-friend Ellen Nussey, who records the event in her *Reminiscences*: see Barbara Whitehead, *Charlotte Brontë and her 'dearest Nell': The story of a friendship* (Otley: Smith Settle, 1993), pp. 56–7.

The drawing, however, was not made 'from nature'; it is a copy of Edward Finden's crisp view of 'Bolton Abbey, Wharfdale' which appeared in *The Literary Souvenir*, 1826 (facing p. 313). This engraving on steel is based on Turner's well-known drawing of 1809, now in the British Museum. The poem written to accompany the plate in the Annual includes the following lines:

This is the loveliest scene in all the land;—
Around me far a green enchantment lies,
Fed by the weeping of these April skies,
And touched by Fancy's fine, 'all-charming wand.'
Almost I expect to see a lightsome band
Come stealing through the hazel boughs, that cross
My path, or half-asleep on bank of moss,
Some Satyr, with stretched arm and clenched hand.
It is a place *all* beauty. There, half-hid
By yellowing ash and drooping aspens, run
The river waters swift to meet the sun;
And in the distance, in its boiling might,
The fatal fall is seen, the thundering STRID;
And over all the morning blue and bright.

Charlotte may have copied a separate plate of Finden's engraving, however, rather than the one in *The Literary Souvenir*, since no other plates were copied from this 1826 edition by the Brontës. The Bill of Sale of household effects, on the death of Patrick Brontë, 1861, listed two framed oil paintings, viz. 'Bolton Abbey' and 'Kirkstall Abbey'. It is possible that the word 'oil' was an error and that these were the originals of Charlotte's drawings of the same names, since they were listed in the handwritten record of the sale of contents at Haworth Parsonage (BPM) as simply '2 Prints & frame'.

Charlotte's own copies of these two views would have been framed for exhibition in Leeds in 1834 (see pp. 25–6, 52). 'Bolton Abbey' and 'Kirkstall Abbey' remained in the family and were later treasured by her widower; they were not given to servants and friends as mementoes, as were so many of her other works.

The inscription on Charlotte's copy, referring to the reopening of the Haworth organ, allows us to date the drawing about the time of the installation service of the new organ at Haworth Parish Church, on 23 March 1834 (*Leeds Mercury*, 29 March 1834). Charlotte presented a similar landscape to the Keighley organist, Abraham Stansfield Sunderland, for his services on the occasion: see **90**.

117

## Kirkstall Abbey

c. May 1834
Pencil on card
99 × 141 mm

Stamped embossed watermark: 'SUPERFINE / LONDON / BOARD', encircled.

Exhibited in the summer exhibition of the Royal Northern Society for the Encouragement of the Fine Arts, in Leeds, 1834.

Gift of Charlotte Brontë Nicholl [*sic*], 1928; daughter of Arthur Bell Nicholls's brother Alan. She acquired the drawing from her aunt, second wife of Nicholls. See also **116**, given by Charlotte Brontë Nicholl at the same time, with Charlotte Brontë's inlaid workbox (H88); and also **57** and **109**, given by her in 1930.

A detail of this drawing was reproduced 'by kind permission of Mr. Clement K. Shorter' with details of five other Brontë drawings (**116**, **137**, **343**, **344** and **346**), in *The Bookman*, October 1904, while the originals were still in the possession of Arthur Bell Nicholls.

*Brontë Parsonage Museum: C72*

Picturesque view of the ruins of Kirkstall Abbey, situated on the outskirts of Leeds, in West Yorkshire. The abbey is seen in the middle-distance centre and right, with a river visible on the left; hills in the distance; two trees frame the scene in the left foreground and low vegetation in the right foreground. Dense bright cumulus clouds above the abbey throw its ruined square tower into silhouette and the low lighting suggests that it is an evening scene; the building is surrounded by trees and overgrown with vegetation.

Despite the likelihood that Charlotte would have visited Kirkstall Abbey herself, the drawing is probably a copy of an engraving which had special significance for her: see **82**. Her copy appears to have been executed about the same time as 'Bolton Abbey' (**116**), since both are on the same size and type of paper card, both show the use of the same variety of lead pencils, and the similar subjects suggest a similar source. See **82** and **118** for other versions of Kirkstall Abbey by Charlotte.

The Bill of Sale of household effects, on the death of Patrick Brontë, 1861, announced the sale of two framed oil paintings, viz. 'Bolton Abbey' and 'Kirkstall

Abbey'. Perhaps the word 'oil' was an error and these were the originals of Charlotte's drawings of the same names? They are listed in the handwritten record of the sale of contents at Haworth parsonage (BPM) as simply 'Prints & frame'. Or perhaps these two oil paintings were Branwell's versions of the same popular originals.

## 118

## Kirkstall Abbey

1834
Pen and ink on paper

Signed by Charlotte Brontë and dated 1834 (recorded in letter of owner 1909). Given by either Charlotte Brontë or Patrick Brontë, after her death, to John Greenwood, bookseller, stationer and relieving officer at Haworth; then inherited by his eldest son, Richard M. Greenwood, who still possessed the picture in 1909 and had had it in his possession 'for nearly forty years'. John Lock and Canon W. T. Dixon quote a testimonial written by Patrick Brontë on 13 July 1859 for Richard Greenwood when he began to pursue his profession of dentist (*A Man of Sorrow: The Life, Letters and Times of the Rev. Patrick Brontë 1777–1861* (London: Thomas Nelson & Sons Ltd, 1965), p. 342).

The drawing has not been heard of or seen since 7 January, 1909, when R. M. Greenwood wrote to 'J. Brigg Esq. M. P.' (later Sir John), President of the Brontë Society, offering to sell the picture for £100 (see letter in BPM).

*Location unknown*

Picturesque view of the ruins of Kirkstall Abbey, situated on the outskirts of Leeds, in West Yorkshire. The pen-and-ink sketch is probably a copy of an engraving, similar to Charlotte's other versions of the same scene (**82** and **117**). It is not surprising that there should have been several different engravings of Kirkstall in the Brontë Parsonage: apart from its special significance for the Brontë family (see **82**), it was a famous local landmark.

The different provenance and the confident reporting of a signature and date on this picture, in the above letter of a previous owner, rule out the possibility of a confusion with the previous entry.

## 119

## 'Portrait of Anne Brontë'

17 June 1834
Watercolour on paper, cut into an oval shape
68 × 55 mm

Inscribed in pencil in Charlotte's longhand, on verso: 'Portrait of / Anne Brontë / By her Sister, Char / lotte Brontë, June 17$^{th}$ /–1834'.

Purchased from J. Horsfall Turner, 1907. He previously acquired this watercolour with a batch of items from Mary Anne Nicholls (see BPM letter, 6 April 1907).

*Brontë Parsonage Museum: C21*

Head-and-shoulders profile of Anne Brontë facing left; blue eyes, bright red lips, clearly defined eyebrow, dark brown ringlets around face and reaching down neck, black velvet ribbon around throat and fastened at the front with a gold and blue stone clasp; low-necked vibrant blue dress with large sleeves.

120

## Profile of a woman, possibly Elizabeth Branwell

c. 1833–1834
Watercolour on paper
139 × 118 mm

The painting is confined within an oval line, measuring 92 × 71 mm.

Formerly in the Law Collection at Honresfeld; possibly part of lot 450, sold at Hodgson & Co. sale, London, 31 March 1933, to Maggs Bros. for 70 guineas (see catalogue of sale in BPM). Item 4 of lot 450 describes 'a cardboard Box in five sections, with two Water-Colour Drawings and silk edgings'; the other watercolour may be **8**, 'Glass Town peasant woman' (see **15**).

*Private owner*

Profile portrait of a woman with brown hair piled up on her head and short wispy curls around the face. High white collar with frill under the chin and high waistline on the dress which is a cream colour. Red beads hang low around the neck (although this may be the neckline of an outer garment) and buttons are just visible down the front of the bodice.

The portrait bears a strong resemblance to the oval miniature of Charlotte's aunt Elizabeth Branwell in her youth, painted by J. Tonkin in 1799 and on display in the BPM (Bonnell 62). It is possible that Charlotte either copied an earlier portrait (as she did in the case of her mother, **36**), or made a study of her aunt from life. The dress and hair-style of this portrait would have been considered 'out-of-date' in the Brontës' day and Elizabeth Branwell was known for her old-fashioned appearance.

In the years 1832–5, Charlotte made every effort to prepare herself for a career in art, possibly as a miniaturist. This oval study was probably executed at this time. Charlotte's oval portrait of Anne (**92**) dates from this period, as do the majority of her miniature portraits.

121

## Profile heads

c. 1834
Pencil on paper
148 × 240 mm

Inscribed in pencil, in non-Brontë hand, next to drawing of profile head top right: 'Charlotte'; on left side at right angles to drawing of male profile bust: 'Branwell'; next to two drawings of female heads drawn at right angles to male portrait: 'Annie' and 'Emily'. Inscribed in ink, in another non-Brontë hand, bottom centre: 'Drawn by./ Bramwell [*sic*] Brontë / of Haworth'; in pencil, bottom right corner: 'over'. For verso see **122**.

Gift of Joseph Binns, 1902, a retired tailor of Manningham, Bradford, who had lived in Haworth as a young man. It is not known whether he was connected to the Binns family of Saltaire, or from where he acquired this item. F. C. Galloway (*A Descriptive Catalogue of Objects in the Museum of the Brontë Society at Haworth* (Bradford, 1896), p. 10) lists this item as on loan from Joseph Binns.

*Brontë Parsonage Museum: B33*

Sheet of paper bearing a collection of drawings of a male bust seen in profile looking to left and four female heads, three of them identified in a non-Brontë hand, as described above. None of the portraits are drawn in Branwell's style and are probably by Charlotte, with the names added speculatively later. The fourth female head, which is unfinished, is drawn at right angles to the male head. The supposed portrait of Branwell bears little resemblance to his known self-portraits (see plate 11, **267**, for example) and is more like one of Charlotte's rather feminine-looking male portraits (see **97** for example). The supposed 'Emily' and 'Annie' heads are two drawings of the same head. The supposed 'Charlotte' head has the same profile as the male portrait and is probably a first attempt.

122

## Moonlit scene with rocks and water

c. 1834
Ink wash and watercolour on paper
148 × 240 mm

Inscribed in pencil, in non-Brontë hand (different from that on **121**), at top: 'This by Bromwell [*sic*] Brontë'. Stamped: 'BRONTË / MUSEUM / HAWORTH', encircled.

Gift of Joseph Binns, 1902: see **121**.
*Brontë Parsonage Museum: B33v*

Monochrome ink and watercolour wash enclosed in an elliptical shape; depicting a channel of moonlit water seen between two rocky promontories. The image is similar to an engraving of a moonlit scene in [E. T. Bennett], *The Gardens and Menagerie of the Zoological Society Delineated*, vol. 1: *Quadrupeds* (London: John Sharpe, 1830), p. 272; purchased by Patrick Brontë in 1831 (see Appendix A).

There is another similar work by Charlotte in the BPM collection (see **123**), which is more successful, although the attempt to convey gradients of light in 'Moonlit scene with rocks and water' is an interesting experiment with bodycolour, ink and scraping out (see **81**). The previous attribution to Branwell probably depended on the attribution of the pencil drawings on the other side, which is erroneous (see **121**).

The ink used here is probably sepia, a popular medium in the early nineteenth century. It was only at the end of the previous century that a suitable chemical extraction method had been found to produce a concentrated ink from the natural sepia, taken from the ink-bag of the cuttlefish. Its colour ranged from the black seen here to the brownish tone of **124** and **135**.

## 123

### Bridge of Egripo

c. 1834
Ink wash and watercolour on paper
160 × 263 mm

Signed in pencil, in longhand, bottom right corner: 'C. Brontë'. Inscribed in pencil, in non-Brontë hand, top right corner: 'S. B1940'.

Purchased from William F. Hide, London, 1965. Previously part of the Brown collection of Brontë relics, sold by Sotheby's, 2 July 1898, lot 38, to an unknown buyer; seen and described by W. W. Yates as part of the Brown collection in 1894 ('Some Relics of the Brontës', *The New Review*, no. 59, April 1894, pp. 484–5).
*Brontë Parsonage Museum: C93*

Monochrome ink wash (probably sepia) of a keep on the edge of the water defending two bridges: the keep, rising in the centre of the picture, comprises three round towers (two in front with battlements and a round tower rising behind, with four windows and a tiled round sloping roof); a flag rises from the left round tower, which appears to extend into a rectangular structure but which may simply be a cliff rising from the water behind the keep; a narrow high wooden bridge spans the water from this left tower to another cliff rising vertically from the water on the left; a low stone bridge with three arches leads from the right side of the left tower to the right of the picture with mountain peaks rising in the distance behind. The keep, cliff and bridge are reflected in the water in the foreground.

W. W. Yates described this as 'a gloomy and sombre work ... which not even the aërial bridge shown on the left of the picture is able to relieve' (p. 484). When one realizes, however, that this experiment in ink wash is based on William Finden's engraving of 'Bridge of Egripo', it can be seen as an imaginative adaptation of the original. This is one of several works in which we can see Charlotte Brontë trying to come to terms with a new medium: her efforts here and in **124** have been more successful than in **122**.

The original engraving of 'Bridge of Egripo, Negropont' by W. Finden, after a drawing by C. Stanfield from a sketch by J. R. C. Helpman, first appears in *The Works of Lord Byron: With His Letters and Journals and His Life*, ed. Thomas Moore, 14 vols. (London: John Murray, 1832) and then in *The Poetical Works of Lord Byron*, 8 vols. (London: John Murray, 1839), vol. 2, either of which editions Charlotte may have used.

Charlotte's interest in Byron and his escapades reached a climax in late 1833 to 1834, with the writing of her early story 'High Life In Verdopolis' (20 February–20 March, 1834); several of her illustrations from the above editions of Byron (**96**, **125**, **128**) were executed at this time, and it seems likely that other copies from these sources, including the above picture, were made about the same time.

## 124

### Revenue cutter

c. 1834
Ink wash on paper, with possibly watercolour and pencil; gum arabic glaze
175 × 190 mm

Signed in pencil across bottom right corner: 'C. Brontë'. Inscribed on bottom edge: 'By M[rs] Cole'. Inscribed on verso (unidentified hand): 'Revenue Cutter / in a Calm'. Purchased from the Brown collection of Brontë relics, sold by Sotheby's, 2 July 1898 (lot 37, '"Revenue Cutter becalmed at Sea," by C. Brontë'). Previously acquired by Robinson and Francis Brown from Alfred Gledhill of Keighley. While in the possession of Gledhill it was exhibited at the 'Keighley Conversaziones' in January 1889 (*The Yorkshire Post*, 8 January 1889).

*Brontë Parsonage Museum: C15*

View from grassy shore of single-masted yacht towing a rowing boat and reflected in a calm sea; full moon, five distant figures on yacht and another yacht on the horizon.

See **122** and **123** for a discussion of Charlotte's use of ink (sepia) wash. *The Yorkshire Post* (see above) remarks on 'the considerable merit in a sepia drawing of a revenue cutter becalmed at sea in the soft moonlight'.

The inscription 'By M[rs] Cole' may indicate an owner of the painting, although it may equally well suggest that the attribution ascribed here should be treated with scepticism.

## 125

## 'Geneva'

23 August 1834
Pencil on thin card
126 × 171 mm

Signed and dated in pencil, in longhand, immediately below drawing, on left: 'C Brontë'; centre: 'Geneva'; right: 'Nov[br] 23[d] 1834'; the second 'e' of 'Geneva' is written over an 'a'; 'Nov[br]' is written over 'Aug[s]'.

Bequest of Henry Houston Bonnell, 1927; acquired by him at Sotheby's sale of effects of Arthur Bell Nicholls, 26 July 1907.

*Brontë Parsonage Museum: Bonnell 14*

Geneva viewed in the centre distance, with nine towers visible on the outskirts; rolling countryside in the foreground with a wide river from left bottom of the picture winding out of sight on the right behind a hill; a white mansion surrounded by trees on the far left above the river where a smaller tributary joins it; two women and a child seated in the centre foreground, high above the right bank of the river, viewing the city; two women walking in the distance on the right, with eight trees silhouetted on the hill behind them; in the far distance beyond the city, hills and high mountains, flock of birds top right.

Copy of an engraving by Edward Finden entitled 'Geneva', after a drawing by J. D. Harding from a sketch by W. Page. This engraving appears in a number of publications relating to Byron, such as the third edition of Thomas Moore's *Letters and Journals of Lord Byron: With Notices of his Life* (London: John Murray, 1833), vol. 2, opposite p. 217. The Brontës may have owned or had access for some time to this volume, since Charlotte had read the book and also copied another engraving from this source (see **127**); however, it is just as likely that she saw only the engraving since the plates were marketed separately (see **128**). The Finden brothers' engravings of Byron's beauties and landscapes also appeared in separate volumes without Byron's poems, such as

*Finden's Illustrations of the Life and Works of Lord Byron*, 3 vols. (London: John Murray, 1833–4) and *Finden's Landscape and Portrait Illustrations to the Life and Works of Lord Byron* (London: John Murray, 1834). 'Geneva' can also be found in volume 1 of both these works.

The author of the former work says (in volume 1) that Byron, having passed through the scenes which inspired the third canto of *Childe Harold*, reached Geneva in June 1816; and he then quotes from the text of Moore's *Life of Byron*:

> The spot whence the view is taken is not half an hour's drive from the city and few travellers fail to visit it. Geneva, with a little of its lake, is seen in the distance, backed by the mountains of the Voirons; and immediately below lies the junction of the Arve and the Rhône, where the white turbid waters of the former, descending on the right from the glaciers of Mont Blanc, unite slowly with the 'Blue waters of the arrowy Rhône,' and a long line of separation below their confluence in a common bed, marks the reluctant mingling of their streams.

## 126

## Landscape with bridge and cross

c. 1834–1835
Watercolour on paper
130 × 156 mm

Inscribed in ink, in margin below painting: 'By my Daughter Charlotte, / P. Bronte, Min[r].'

Previously owned by the Rev. Henry Mitchell of Wayne, Pennsylvania (d. 1957), grandfather of the present owner, who also owned **92**. His collection came from a variety of sources, but chiefly through Wright Howes, Old and Rare Books, 1144 South Michigan Avenue, Chicago, USA.

*Private owner: on loan to Brontë Parsonage Museum (C108 LOAN)*

Landscape with a bridge in the centre, spanning a wide river, and a view of a distant city on the top of a hill, in the top right of the picture. The left bank of the river in the foreground is unfinished but the shapes of two figures have been marked out against the dark bushes behind. A tall spindly tree leans from the left beside the figures and frames the bridge behind; behind the tree is a tall wooden cross, presumably on the side of the road leading to the bridge. The twin-arched stone bridge is extended on the right bank by wooden railings. A tree (partly obscuring the city in the distance behind) and dense shrubbery cover the right bank and immediately behind the bridge; two large bare hills rise behind, the top of the right one being occupied by the city.

The exotic appearance of the distant city with its minarets and cupolas suggests that this might be a view of Jerusalem, copied from one of the many books of engravings of Middle Eastern cities, popular during the Brontës' time. The trees and cross in the foreground, however, suggest an Italian or Spanish city: compare the engravings of 'Florence' and 'Madrid' by Edward Finden, in *The Poetical Works of Lord Byron*, 8 vols. (London: John Murray, 1839), vols. 2 and 8 respectively.

The style and subject of this watercolour suggest the period 1834–5 as a possible composition date; but because of the unfinished nature of the work and lack of other evidence it is impossible to be sure. Yet the unfinished nature of the work is also a bonus: it provides us with another revealing example of Charlotte's working method: see pp. 46–7 for a detailed discussion of her technique.

## 127

# The Maid of Saragoza

c. 1834
Watercolour and gum arabic on thin card
211 × 162 mm

Bequest of Henry Houston Bonnell, 1927; acquired by him at Sotheby's sale of effects of Arthur Bell Nicholls, 26 July 1907 (either lot 41 or lot 42).
*Brontë Parsonage Museum: Bonnell 25*

Half-length portrait of a young woman in peasant costume: dark brown hair covered with a net of pink laced ribbon with a flower of the same ribbon on the left; the hair braided in a plait hanging over her left shoulder and two ringlets covering her right ear. Her body faces towards the left front and the head is turned sharply to the right in three-quarter view, the face looking over her left shoulder. She has fine features, large brown eyes, highly coloured cheeks, a sallow complexion and bright red lips, dark shadows around the eyes. She wears a dark brown velvet bodice, white blouse with a blue lattice design on the collar and plain white full sleeves; and a pearl necklace to which a pendant gold and pearl cross is attached just above her breast. The lines of a stone wall are suggested behind the figure on the right.

See **26** for Charlotte Brontë's use of gum arabic with watercolour.

This drawing is a copy of an engraving by William Finden entitled 'The Maid of Saragoza', after a drawing by F. Stone. The engraving appears in a number of publications relating to Byron, such as the third edition of *Letters and Journals of Lord Byron: With Notices of his Life*, ed. Thomas Moore, (London: John Murray, 1833), vol. 2, opposite p. 139, which the Brontës may have owned or had access to for some time. Charlotte also made a copy of another engraving from this volume, probably at the same time: see **125**, dated 23 August 1834. This particular engraving of 'The Maid of Saragoza' (there were others by different artists) also appears in the following books of Finden illustrations: *Finden's Illustrations of the Life and Works of Lord Byron*, 3 vols. (London: John Murray, 1833–4) and *Finden's Landscape and Portrait Illustrations to the Life and Works of Lord Byron* (London: John Murray, 1834). See also **123**, for Charlotte's interest in Byron at this time.

Charlotte has deliberately altered significant details of the original (such as the replacing of an earring by two fashionable ringlets over the ear) in an effort to transform Byron's Italian peasant girl into an Angrian beauty, closer to the English beauties of the Annuals. This particular copy by Charlotte illustrates her description of Mina Laury, the Angrian peasant girl who became Zamorna's first and most faithful mistress: see Christine Alexander, *The Early Writings of Charlotte Brontë* (Oxford: Basil Blackwell, 1983), pp. 167–8. Byron's original and Finden's engraving had a strong influence on the conception of this heroine, who was 'strong-minded beyond her sex' yet, in the presence of her lover, 'weak as a child'. Compare the verse beneath Finden's engraving:

> Ye who shall marvel when you hear her tale,
> Oh! had you known her in her softer hour!

The tale of the Maid of Saragoza is told in Byron's *Childe Harold's Pilgrimage*, canto I, LIV–LVI.

## 128

# 'English Lady'

15 October 1834
Pencil on thin card
227 × 169 mm

Signed and dated in pencil, in longhand, immediately below drawing, on left: 'October 15th'; centre: '1834'; right: 'C Brontë'; and titled in pencil, in longhand, bottom centre: 'English Lady'. Stamped: 'BRONTË/ MUSEUM/ HAWORTH', encircled.

Bequest of Henry Houston Bonnell, 1927; acquired by him at Sotheby's sale of effects of Arthur Bell Nicholls, 26 July 1907.
*Brontë Parsonage Museum: Bonnell 2*

Highly finished head-and-shoulders portrait of a young woman in evening dress: dark glossy hair parted in the middle, with curls around the side of the face and ringlets gathered back in a pearl circlet and reaching down the back of her long neck; widely spaced oval-shaped dark eyes, long straight nose and small full lips, as in so many of Charlotte's portraits of young women; off-the-shoulder neckline of dark velvet dress with full lace sleeve visible on the right; shawl over right shoulder and arm; a single pearl brooch in the centre of her chest and a long string of pearls draped around the top of the sleeves and fastened with a clasp below the bust.

Copy of William Finden's engraving of the portrait of Lady Jersey, after the painting by E. T. Parris, which appeared in a number of contemporary publications, including *Finden's Illustrations of the Life and Works of Lord Byron*, 3 vols. (London: John Murray, 1833–4); *Finden's Landscape and Portrait Illustrations to the Life and Works of Lord Byron* (London: John Murray, 1834); and *The Poetical Works of Lord Byron*, 8 vols. (London: John Murray, 1839). Volume 3 of the first of these works includes the following passage on Byron's relationship with the Countess:

> there were few parties that he visited with more pleasure ... When his Lordship was about to leave his native land, because of scandal, and misrepresentation had assailed him, and made it as fashionable to shrink from his society as it had before been to seek it, Lady Jersey, at one of whose assemblies he made his last public appearance in England, received him with her wonted courtesy; and the kindness of his noble hostess upon that occasion was never forgotten by him ... Byron often praised the beauty of women abroad, by comparing them to Lady Jersey.

Since the plates for the books were marketed separately, however, Charlotte may never have seen these actual volumes, which were expensive. She may simply have copied one of the loose plates on hire or for sale at booksellers and art-dealers, such as Ackermanns.

Charlotte's version follows the original with meticulous accuracy except in the case of the jewellery and lace border around the neckline, changes that have been made intentionally and that recall more faithfully her verbal descriptions of early Angrian heroines (see p. 58). The features of her 'English Lady' are slightly younger and more doll-like than those of the original.

## 129

## 'Lycidas'

4 March 1835
Watercolour on paper
112 × 139 mm

Signed, titled and dated in pencil, in longhand, immediately below vignette, left corner: 'C Brontë'; centre: 'Lycidas'; right corner: 'March 4 '3[?5]'. The corners of the paper are inked across, suggesting large photo hinges: cf. **39**.

Purchased from Rose Emma Longbottom, 1906, together with **13**, **74**, **200**, **201**, **202** and **207**. Rose Longbottom was the great-granddaughter of Rose Bower, sister of Tabitha Aykroyd: see **13**.

*Brontë Parsonage Museum: C13*

Vignette of a seated figure in blue with curly light brown hair, bent double and leaning head and left arm on a rock; shepherd's crook lies beside the figure, emphasizing the horizontal position of the right leg. The background is a pale blue wash, shaped like a cloud, and beneath the figure there is bare ground to the left and grass centre and right.

A copy of Fuseli's 'Solitude at Dawn', which was inspired by Milton's poem 'Lycidas', dedicated to the memory of his childhood friend, Edward King, who died by drowning. The sleeping figure of the shepherd alludes to the budding personality of the youth as it is mourned in the elegy and to the dream-world or higher existence into which he is to be transported by his sudden death.

Fuseli painted three versions of this theme between May 1794 and August 1796, the final one being engraved by Moses Haughton and published in the *Milton Gallery*, September 1803 (see Gert Schiff, *Johann Heinrich Füseli 1741–1825*, 2 vols. (Zurich: Verlag Berichthaus, 1973), pp. 255 and 519–20). Another version (now missing) was exhibited in the Royal Academy Exhibition (Somerset House) in 1823 and was discussed in *Blackwood's Edinburgh Magazine* in July of that year. The review reports that the subject is suggested specifically by the following lines from 'Lycidas':

> Under the opening eye-lids of the morn,
> We drove a-field, and both together heard
> What time the gray fly winds her sultry horn

and that the 'general expression of the picture is touching and true' (p. 10). (The central line of verse here is erroneously omitted in the *Blackwood's* review.)

*Blackwood's Magazine* is not illustrated, so although Charlotte Brontë would have read the review, she must have copied the engraving from another source, possibly from a detached engraving hired locally or borrowed from a friend. This is an ambitious task and she succeeds in creating a delightful vignette closely resembling the original, apart from the moth which she omits, but which Fuseli was keen to include after he happened to find a beautiful specimen in a friend's garden at Fulham. The chief difference in Charlotte's version is that her shepherd is decidedly more feminine than Fuseli's original, in both body and face; and she has used her imagination in adding colour to the black and white engraving.

The final figure of the date is difficult to discern: it could be '30' or '35'. The black markings across the corners suggest a comparison with **39**, dated 15 December 1830, but the handling of the paint is too sophisticated for Charlotte at this date. The delicate brush strokes of the hair and the gradual merging of bodycolour and blue watercolour to suggest the sheen on the clothes, are much closer to her use of watercolour from 1832 to 1835, when she was painting at home after leaving school.

## 130

## 'Scene on the Rhine'

3 September 1835
Pencil on thin card
172 × 144 mm

Signed below right corner of drawing; 'C Brontë'. Dated below left corner: '[? September] 3d 1835'. Titled by Charlotte in longhand, below centre of drawing: 'Scene on the / Rhine'.

Purchased from Frances E. Bell, 1919, together with Charlotte's workbasket (H176); probably given to her by her aunt, Mary Anne Nicholls. The BPM also acquired other items from Frances Bell, in previous and subsequent years: see **66**.

*Brontë Parsonage Museum: C19*

Landscape of the bank of the Rhine with windmill in centre, a couple strolling in foreground, windmill and bridge in left distance and a church spire and city walls in the right middle-distance.

Copy of an engraving, taken either from a separate plate or from the same source as Charlotte's copy of a windmill scene at 'Aldborough, Suffolk' (**135**).

## 131

## Roman head

14 December 1835
Pencil on card
324 × 236 mm

Signed and dated in pencil, in longhand, immediately below drawing, on left: 'C Brontë'; centre: '1835'; right: 'Decbr 14th'.

Bequest of Henry Houston Bonnell, 1927; acquired by him at Sotheby's sale of effects of Arthur Bell Nicholls, 26 July 1907.

*Brontë Parsonage Museum: Bonnell 3*

Three-quarter head-and-shoulders portrait of a young woman in classical dress, looking towards the bottom right: short curled fair hair tied up with a headband from which a light veil falls down the back of the head and over the left shoulder; a plait of hair is also wound around the head next to the headband; face has plump cheeks, Roman nose, half-closed eyelids (eyes looking down towards right corner), small full mouth and chin, wide neck; top of Roman dress visible, with drapery caught in four buttons on the right shoulder.

The school term at Roe Head usually ended about 15 December, so this drawing must have been completed just before Charlotte's first Christmas holidays in her new position as teacher at Miss Wooler's school.

## 132

## Classical head

c. 1835
Pencil on paper, oval shape
435 × 320 mm

Inscribed in ink below: 'By my Daughter Charlotte, P. Brontë Min[r].'
Gift of Miss Wright, Mayfield, Keighley, 1911.
*Brontë Parsonage Museum: C31*

Classical female head and shoulders in style of Raphael; a copy of an engraving from a single plate or possibly from the same source as **131**. Both illustrations are executed with the same high degree of finish and in the same large format, suggesting a similar date of composition.

The woman has sculptured features, hair dressed in Roman style with diaphanous veil over head and shoulders, loose drapery around shoulders. She is looking down towards the left over her right shoulder.

There is a sophistication about this portrait that is lacking from Charlotte's other female classical-style heads, which she tended to 'prettify' in the style of Heath's female beauties (see *Heath's Book of Beauty* (1833–49)).

## 133

## Madonna and child

c. 1835
Pencil on paper
502 × 440 mm (area visible inside mount)

Inscribed on the board originally on back of drawing, in capitals: 'Drawn by Charlotte Brontë. Given to Reginald J. Smith Aug 1 1914 by Mrs Arthur B. Nicholls.' The inscription no longer exists, but it was noted by Dr Donald Hopewell in 1978 when he took delivery of the drawing in Oxford, for the Brontë Society.

Bequest of J. N. Bryson, Oxford, 1978 (not recorded in BPM Stock Book until 1980); purchased by Bryson at Sotheby's 'more than twenty years ago' according to the note by Dr D. Hopewell (BPM; record in Sotheby's catalogue not located). As recorded above, the drawing passed from Mary Anne Nicholls (second wife of Charlotte Brontë's husband), in 1914, to Reginald J. Smith, son-in-law of George Smith and also his successor as Chairman of Smith, Elder & Co., Charlotte's publishers.
*Brontë Parsonage Museum: C99*

Unusually large head-and-shoulders portrait of Madonna and child: both figures looking down towards bottom left corner of drawing. The child is held up by the Virgin Mary against her left shoulder, her right hand visible on his chest; the child has short curly hair, chubby cheeks, large eyes and nose, small mouth and chin, plump neck and arms, naked chest with swaddling cloth just visible, wrapped around chest; child's right arm reaching out towards left bottom corner. Mary has large classical features, oval face, high forehead, long straight nose, high cheek bones, widely set eyes, the lids half-closed because she is looking down, small full lips, long thick neck; dark hair parted in the middle, swept down and behind the head, and partly covered by a white veil draped over the head and shoulders; dress of fluted embroidered material just visible across the chest.

The drawing is copied from an engraving by Louis Schalz of Raphael's 'Madonna of the Fish'; the original, which Charlotte Brontë would never have seen, hangs in the Prado Museum, Madrid. Charlotte has chosen to duplicate only a detail of the central Madonna and child. In the original, St Jerome stands on the picture right of the Madonna, holding a book, a lion at his feet. On the left of the original, an angel presents to Mary a young boy carrying a fish.

As a teacher, Charlotte had little time for her own pursuits: she records in her Roe Head Journal her inability to write while supervising a class (see Christine Alexander, 'Charlotte Brontë at Roe Head', in *Jane Eyre*, ed. Richard J. Dunn, 2nd edn (New York: W. W. Norton & Co., 1987), p. 413), yet she was able to complete at least one detailed copy of an engraving (**131**), a relatively mechanical task compared with writing. 'Madonna and child' may have been begun at school, although it is more likely that she worked on it in her December vacation, having borrowed the original plate from Roe Head. The style and format of this Madonna and child are similar to her two heads of classical women (**131** and **132**), one clearly dated in December 1835. This is an unusually large copy in Charlotte's œuvre, evidence that she had now learnt to scale up her copy from a detail in a smaller engraving.

## 134

## Anne Brontë

c. 1835
Pencil on paper

Inscribed in ink below: 'By my Daughter Charlotte / P Bronte, Min[r]'

Provenance unknown: the drawing is known only through its reproduction in the Thornton Edition of *The Novels of the Brontës*, ed. Temple Scott (Edinburgh: John Grant, 1907). It appears as an illustration of Anne Brontë (though this is suspect), as the frontispiece to vol. 1 of her novel *The Tenant of Wildfell Hall*. It may also be 'the pencil drawing of the head and bust of her sister Anne' exhibited by Alfred Gledhill of Keighley at the 'Keighley Conversaziones', held by the Keighley Mechanics' Institute, in January 1889 (*The Yorkshire Post*, 8 January 1889), although this could also refer to **55**.

*Location unknown*

Head-and-shoulders portrait of a young woman facing right: more rounded features than those usually attributed to Anne Brontë. The portrait has the appearance of solidity: large strong eyes and eyebrows, straight nose and small mouth; thick neck and rounded shoulders. The hair is dark, parted in the middle and swept down at the sides and behind the ear, then gathered in ringlets behind the ear which is clearly prominent. There is the suggestion of a curl in front of the ear but not the usual ringlet associated with this hair-style, so common in portraits by Charlotte taken from life. The low neckline of the dress with a central bow is suggested in outline only.

It is impossible to date this drawing with any accuracy. Charlotte renewed her interest in studies of the head in late 1835, after the portrait painter William Robinson had been employed to teach Branwell (see p. 26), and this portrait has the same sculptural features as her three 'classical' copies of heads made at this time.

## 135

## 'Aldborough, Suffolk'

c. 29 December 1835
Ink and grey wash on paper
133 × 100 mm

Signed in ink, in longhand, bottom left corner below illustration: 'C. Brontë'; dated bottom right corner below illustration: 'Dec$^{br}$ 29$^{th}$' (no year); and titled in larger longhand in the centre, below the illustration: 'Aldborough / Suffolk'. Part of the Henry Houston Bonnell Brontë Collection, given by Helen Safford Bonnell in 1963, in memory of her husband, who died in 1926. The item was previously purchased from Tabitha Ratcliffe, sister of Martha Brown (Brontë servant), 1882, by Dr Dobie, who lent this item to the Brontë Society in 1896. The original Haworth Exhibition card accompanies the drawing, describing this provenance, which is confirmed in part by F. C. Galloway's *A Descriptive Catalogue of Objects in the Museum of the Brontë Society at Haworth* (Bradford, 1896), p. 14.
*Pierpont Morgan Library: Bonnell Collection MA 2696*

Harbour scene at Aldborough on the Suffolk coast: foreground comprises (in receding order) a craypot on right, a family playing on the sand on left, large fishing vessel in dry dock with windmill behind it centre right and another group of figures on the sand on left; harbour and town visible on left receding into the distance and on right in distance.

Charlotte's view is a copy of an engraving, taken either from a separate plate or from the same source as her 'Scene on the Rhine' (**130**), dated 3 September 1835, suggesting a similar year for the dating of this picture.

The following contemporary account gives a picturesque description of the scene Charlotte chose to copy:

> Aldeborough is pleasantly situated in the valley of Slaughton, and bounded on the eastern side by the sea, which has made considerable encroachments, and nearly washed a street away. The river Ald runs on the south side, and forms a convenient quay. The town is mean in construction, and chiefly inhabited by fishermen and seafaring people. Soles, lobsters, and other fish are abundant. It is remarkable as the birth-place of the late Rev. George Crabbe (1754–1832), emphatically styled the Poet of the Poor.
> (*Curiosities of Great Britain. England and Wales Delineated, Historical, Entertaining & Commercial. Alphabetically arranged By Thomas Dugdale, Antiquarian, assisted by William Burnett, Civil Engineer* (London: J. Tallis, c. late 1830s))

The ink used in this drawing, as in most of Charlotte's works, is sepia which was a fairly new and popular introduction in the early nineteenth century: see **122**.

## 136

# The Atheist viewing the dead body of his Wife

c. 1835–1836
Watercolour and gum arabic
85 × 130 mm

Bequest of Henry Houston Bonnell, 1927; acquired by him at Sotheby's sale of effects of Arthur Bell Nicholls, 26 July 1907.
*Brontë Parsonage Museum: Bonnell 27*

Interior scene of a young man contemplating a woman lying on a bier. The man, with dark hair and long side whiskers, stands with his head resting on his left hand, his right arm akimbo. He is richly dressed in period costume (Renaissance?), a white blouse beneath a black velvet doublet with gold collar, black hose, wide black belt with sword hilt visible, gold chain and long blue velvet cloak draped over his right shoulder and arm. A plumed black hat with gold trim lies behind him on the floor. On the elaborately carved bier (Napoleonic Empire style) lies a white-faced young woman with auburn hair flowing over the white pillows; she is covered by white drapery. A tall silver stand with marble base, and green sprays from an aromatic bush laid on top, is seen at the head of the bed on the far right of the picture. Purple velvet drapery hangs festooned behind the bier; the right side of the coffered arch reaches from the foot of the bed behind the man to the top left of the picture; the marble balustrade of a staircase leading down from the arch is visible, terminating in a marble statue of two figures, silhouetted against the blue sky beyond.

Charlotte's use of stippling with a darker tone of the basic watercolour is clearly seen here, as is her use of watercolour and gum arabic (see **26**). The gum glaze has been thickly applied to the surface of this painting, especially the purple curtain, and cracking is obvious.

Charlotte's painting is a copy of A. B. Clayton's hand-coloured lithograph, 'The Atheist viewing the dead body of his Wife', from the fourth edition of *The Sacred Annual: Being the Messiah, A Poem, In Six Books*, by Robert Montgomery (London: John Turrill, 1834), p. 40; a source first identified by Michael Campbell (*The Times*, **11** August 1984). The copy is particularly faithful to the original, although Charlotte's male is considerably slimmer and has more delicate facial features than the burly original. The stars in the sky of the original are not visible in Charlotte's painting, and there are variations in her rendering of the hat, the pavemented floor and the drapery of the bed. In the original the man has a purple cloak and brown belt.

The painting was probably executed sometime in 1835 or 1836, since both Charlotte's version and the original helped to inspire Branwell Brontë's description of Mary Percy, Queen of Angria, on her deathbed, her attitude to death and her tirade to her atheistic father, Lord Northangerland, who was causing her death:

> This chamber of death was opened now in all its dreary magnificence, lofty and airy, but hung and fashioned with velvet so dark as to seem shadowy in despite of the softly shining silver lamps that glistened from their white marble pedestals and centred their radiance on the bed where lay the shadow rather than the substance of the forsaken wife and crownless Queen. Over her the vast festoons of drapery hung from the coronetted tester as if even they were mourning ... and right opposite Mary's eyes, a wide and lofty arch opened sublimely to the sky; its curtains were drawn aside to display the full extent of waste midnight heaven and sad struggling moon .... What was she like? For such things as I have hitherto mentioned were only auxiliaries in the picture. Here was the principal figure, cold, white, and wasted, supported by a pile of pillows, with attenuated hands clasped, and glassy eyes fixed in unutterable anguish. All the once

> rich auburn curls were fallen back, and parted in long locks from her brow which, with her cheeks and lips, was stricken with the glistening light of death. This was not like the death-bed of her mother; there was no mingling of heaven with earth, nothing of that angelic hope of glory, that real triumph over death. This was the end of a child of earth, all whose soul and spirit were rooted in earth and perishing on being torn away from it....
> Into this room, then, came Lord Northangerland ...
> (*The Miscellaneous and Unpublished Writings of Charlotte and Patrick Branwell Brontë*, ed. Thomas James Wise and John Alexander Symington, 2 vols. (Oxford: Basil Blackwell for the Shakespeare Head Press, 1936–8), vol. 2, pp. 218–9).

The similarity between this description by Branwell and Charlotte's visual rendering of the same scene demonstrates the close co-operation between brother and sister in the development of the Angrian saga at this time: see Christine Alexander, *The Early Writings of Charlotte Brontë* (Oxford: Basil Blackwell, 1983), pp. 153–5, for further discussion on the Angrian situation related to this painting.

## 137

## 'The Cross of Rivaulx'

23 June 1836
Pencil on thin card
224 × 312 mm

Titled in pencil, in capital letters, centre bottom, below drawing: 'THE CROSS OF RIVAULX'. Signed and dated, in pencil, in minuscule script, immediately below bottom left corner: 'June 23$^{d}$'; below bottom right corner: 'C B 1836'. Embossed watermark, half only visible bottom right corner: 'HULL/ [SUPE]RFINE/ BOARD', crest in centre. The BPM card catalogue records an inscription in ink on the back of the original gold frame: 'Drawing by Charlotte Brontë which hung in the drawing room at Banagher given to R S by Mrs Nicholls. 1912'. 'R S' is probably Reginald J. Smith, who was given several illustrations by Mary Anne Nicholls, second wife of Charlotte's husband. Reginald Smith was the son-in-law of George Smith and also his successor as Chairman of Smith, Elder & Co., Charlotte's publishers.

Gift of Elizabeth Maud Gordon, Northants, 1986, as part of the Seton-Gordon bequest; Mrs Gordon was the granddaughter of George Smith.

A detail of this drawing was reproduced 'by kind permission of Mr. Clement K. Shorter' with details of five other Brontë drawings (**116**, **117**, **343**, **344** and **346**), in *The Bookman*, October 1904, while the originals were still in the possession of Arthur Bell Nicholls.

*Brontë Parsonage Museum: C102*

Picturesque view of a small church seen through an opening between trees, centre left; a glade in the foreground: on the right, a round low ruined monument with inscription (illegible) and ivy, surrounded by low plants; view behind of arched gateway and wall surmounted by three crosses, two on wall and one on gateway; all set beneath a variety of trees which cover the right side of the drawing; a plumed helmet and dagger lie amongst the plants, centre foreground; on the left, two tall trees framing the picture, with large rocks at their base and several trees behind. The church is a square stone structure, with small crosses on each corner and a short central square tower surmounted by a cross.

Copy of an engraving entitled 'Cross of Rivaulx', after a drawing by Rev. John Gilpin. This illustration inspired Charlotte Brontë's verbal picture of the surroundings of the hunting lodge of the same name in her early story, 'Passing Events', concluded on 29 April 1836, not long before she copied this engraving.

Gilpin's illustration is from a view taken from the grounds of Rievaulx Abbey, founded in 1131 by the Cistercians but now in ruins. It is in North Yorkshire, in Ryedale, at the foot of the Hambleton Hills.

## 137a

## 'Geneva' vignette

June 1837
Pencil on thin card?
c. 224 × 312 mm

Titled in pencil, centre bottom, below drawing, in capital letters similar to Charlotte's title 'THE CROSS OF RIVAULX' (**137**): 'GENEVA'. Dated in pencil, in minuscule script around bottom right corner of drawing: 'June [?18] 1837'. The signature on the left, visible in the photo (reproduced below), is illegible. It seems likely that the drawing was originally in the possession of Arthur Bell Nicholls, since the photo of this drawing, the only evidence we have of its existence, is accompanied by four other photos (**116**, **137**, **343** and **346**), which were all reproduced 'by kind permission of Mr. Clement K. Shorter' in *The Bookman*, October 1904 (opposite p. 31), while the originals were still in the possession of Arthur Bell Nicholls. Subsequent provenance may be associated with J. A. Symington, who owned five pencil drawings sold with these photos by Christie's, 18 December 1964 (see **162**).

*Location unknown: photo in private collection*

An elliptical-shaped view of Geneva, seen across the lake from the surrounding hills. The hilly foreground is wooded, but five small figures (four women and one man) can be seen in a clearing in the immediate foreground, near a partly obscured cottage. Behind the trees lies the lake with several boats, and beyond this is the city, with mountains rising in the distance.

The drawing, like Charlotte's earlier illustration of 'Geneva' (**125**), is undoubtedly a copy of an engraving, possibly by one of the Finden brothers from their many plates made for various editions of Byron's works. See **125** for Byron's association with Geneva.

Although this drawing is not unlike many of Anne Brontë's copies of engravings at this time, attribution to Charlotte is based on the similarity between her copying style and the lettering of the title of her drawing 'The Cross of Rivaulx' (**137**), produced the previous year. Further, the surviving photo of this drawing, as mentioned above, is accompanied by a photo of **137**, suggesting that the originals of both drawings were previously preserved together. The provenance and dimensions given above are conjectural, again based on **137**. Several Brontë art works and manuscripts, formerly in the possession of Nicholls and given away by his second wife, have emerged from obscurity during the course of this study (see for example **41a**). It would not be surprising if the original of this view of 'Geneva' came to light in the next few years.

## 138

## Welsh peasants

c. 1834–1837
?Ink and watercolour on paper

The catalogue for the Binns sale, Saltaire, 27 January 1886, records 'Welsh Peasants' (lot 372). William Scruton's scrapbook, which records the sale, notes that this item went to 'J. W. Binns' (Keighley Library); and in 1896, Joseph Binns of Manningham lent a 'Photo of

Charlotte Brontë's drawing of Welsh Peasants (Quarto)' (together with a photo of **58** and **110**) to the Brontë Society (F. C. Galloway, *A Descriptive Catalogue of Objects in the Museum of the Brontë Society at Haworth* (Bradford, 1896), p. 10).

However, in 1897 'Welsh Peasants' was published (together with **58**) in Marion Leslie, 'Mrs Gaskell's House and Its Memories', *The Woman at Home*, no. 45, June 1897; while it was in the possession of Elizabeth Gaskell's daughters, Margaret Emily ('Meta') and Julia, at Plymouth Grove, Manchester. It is reproduced above from this source.

It seems likely that the drawing was purchased by Meta Gaskell from J. W. Binns or from 'Mr Cornish, Dealer' at the same time as **58**, possibly on a visit to Saltaire. It was sold as part of Meta Gaskell's effects at 84 Plymouth Grove, Manchester, 13 February 1914, lot 1663, described as 'Copy of "The Welsh Ballad Seller", by Charlotte Brontë' (sale catalogue, Manchester Central Library).

*Location unknown*

Group of three figures, two women in Welsh national costume and a young boy. The woman on the left (three-quarter length and facing the viewer), in a Welsh hat, with typical white frill beneath the hat and around the face, carries a basket with ballads visible inside, on her left arm, and has a ballad in her left hand. Her right arm is around a young boy (head and shoulders visible only). The young woman on the right (half-length and facing towards picture left with head turned to the viewer), in a wide brimmed hat, short curls visible beneath and a ribbon tied around her neck, carries a ballad in her left hand.

This drawing is a copy of a print, a 'fancy piece' rather like **16**, **19** and **108**. This is not the type of print that usually attracted Charlotte, and without the original to examine it is difficult to say conclusively that it is by her. However, the provenance argues strongly for a Charlotte Brontë attribution, and the faces (especially the mouths, eyes and nose of the older Welsh woman) and the poor treatment of the hands are typical of those by Charlotte: see, for example, **108** for hands and **147** for similar facial features. Where possible Charlotte avoided drawing hands and never seems to have copied the usual exercises in hands and feet from contemporary drawing manuals, as she did in the case of eyes, mouths, ears, etc.

In the article in *The Woman at Home* (see above), the medium is described as 'Pen-and-ink', but the illustration suggests watercolour. It is possible that Charlotte used monochrome watercolour as in other drawings (see **123**), but there are no other examples of her use of ink wash for portraits like this. The tones suggesting the texture and shadow of the faces are especially close to those in which she used watercolour.

## 138a

## Sketches of two women

c. July 1837
Pencil on paper
90 × 113 mm

The sketches occupy almost the bottom half of a manuscript page (186 × 113 mm); the top half contains the final lines (p. 4) of a draft in Charlotte's longhand of her poem 'Mementos' (see below), first published in *Poems by Currer, Ellis, and Acton Bell* (London: Aylott & Jones, 1846). The draft of 81 lines, written on a single sheet folded over to make 4 pages, is unsigned and undated, but

has been conjecturally dated June–July 1837 by Victor A. Neufeldt (*The Poems of Charlotte Brontë: A New Text and Commentary* (New York and London: Garland Publishing, Inc., 1985), p. 465). Manuscript stamped 'BRONTË/ MUSEUM/ HAWORTH', encircled.
Bequest of Henry Houston Bonnell, 1927.
*Brontë Parsonage Museum: Bonnell 110*

Two unfinished sketches: a pencil outline of a woman's head, facing left, on the left-hand side of the page, immediately below the text; and a half-length sketch of an elegant young woman in the centre of the page, face looking down to the left, long wavy hair with a band of flowers at the top of her head, tight-fitting dress gathered at neckline, with large full sleeves and a wide skirt suggested in rough outline. To the right of the sketches there are several sums, which appear to be the addition of lines of poetry by Charlotte.

The sketches seem to be directly related to the accompanying text which begins on the facing page with the line 'Arranging long-locked drawers and shelves'. The speaker appears to have been a governess, and, as she sifts through 'cabinets, shut up for years', she recalls the house and its family as it was thirty years ago. The description immediately above the two sketches describes the two sisters, Frances and Clara:

> Clara and Frances were my care
> To teach in childhood and in youth
> To tend – each whim with mildness bear
> When gay to guard – when sad to soothe
>
> Clara had beauty from her birth
> Always fine eyes and flowing hair
> Her mother knew that beauty's worth
> And cultured it with constant care
> It prospered – she became each day
> More perfect in her symetry
> Her eyes acquired a brighter ray
> Her face a sweeter harmony
> She was at length her parents' pride
> And seldom left their fostering side

Lady Frances, who is now an heiress but prefers to live away from home, may be the subject of the head on the left; and beautiful Clara is probably shown in the central sketch.

## 139

## Horseman and gamekeeper

c. 1835–1838
Pencil on card with a decorative border of lace
93 × 113 mm

Inscribed on verso in ink: 'Drawing of Charlotte Brontë's/ given me by Miss Walker, Torquay,/ who was once a pupil of/ Charlottes. Aug 29. 1877'. Also on verso, in pencil, in Charlotte Brontë's longhand: '[Amelia] Walker [?1 word]'. Stamped: 'BRONTË/ MUSEUM/ HAWORTH', encircled.

Bequest of Henry Houston Bonnell, 1927; acquired by him from Maggs Bros. sale, London, n.d. (lot 671), at the same time as **62**, **308** and **324**. Previously owned by Sidney Biddell, who is probably the author of the inscription above; he acquired the drawing from Amelia Walker (see below), who, as a pupil, had been given it by Charlotte Brontë. An accompanying envelope confirms this provenance: 'Drawing of Charlotte Brontë/ given me by Miss Walker,/ Meadfoot Rock, Torquay, who/ was formerly a pupil of/ Charlotte – Aug 29. 1877.–/ Obtained for me by Rev[d] W. W. Self.' There were also three accompanying letters, one from the Reverend William Self and two from Amelia Walker, explaining the acquisition by Biddell via Self.
*Brontë Parsonage Museum: Bonnell 31*

Landscape with a horseman and two dogs, asking directions from a young man, possibly a gamekeeper, in the foreground. The horseman is respectably dressed with a top hat, frock coat, long trousers and cane; he sits astride his horse facing left downhill in front of a distant landscape of mountains and valley; his right hand is pointing ahead and his head is turned back as if in conversation with the gamekeeper standing behind the horse. The gamekeeper, with gun, hip bag, hat and high boots, has just emerged from the trees behind (on the right); his right hand is raised to his hat as if in greeting. Two greyhound dogs stand with heads raised, as if sniffing him curiously, in the right foreground beside two rocks. The roots of one of the trees on the right cover the rock immediately beside the game-keeper and dogs; lush grass covers the ground around.

A ready-made paper lace border has been superimposed on the drawing which has been cut to fit it, giving the work a finished decorative appearance for display. This is the only example of Charlotte's use of such frames, and it may have been fixed to the drawing by Amelia Walker after she received it from Charlotte.

This drawing, a copy of an engraving, was made some time between July 1835 and December 1838, while Charlotte Brontë was a teacher at Miss Wooler's school, first at Roe Head and then at Dewsbury. It was a common practice for her and other teachers to present their pupils with paintings or drawings they had made themselves, as prizes or mementoes. The recipient of this drawing was Amelia Walker, the younger daughter of Joseph Walker of Lascelles Hall, Huddersfield, and of Broadlands, Torquay. (Her sister, Jane, also attended school while Charlotte was at Roe Head.) It appears that Charlotte (now twenty years old) taught the fourteen-year-old Amelia Walker drawing, among other subjects. She had known Amelia earlier at Roe Head and drawn the younger girl's portrait when they were pupils together: see **51**.

## 140

## Landscape with cottage

c. 1837–1841
Pencil on card
90 × 126 mm

Unsigned and undated. Embossed mark, bottom corners of border, on left: 'DE LA RUE'; on right: 'LONDON'.

Provenance unknown: no entry in BPM Stock Book, which records acquisitions.

*Brontë Parsonage Museum: C90*

Landscape of cottage, two trees and a stone wall on the left; four saplings on a low hill on the right; a lake in the centre extending to hills in the distance. The stone cottage is seen from the side: it has a high sloping roof, tall chimney, a lean-to extension at the back, with a door and three windows visible. A small sailing boat is seen in the distance.

This drawing was probably made 'from life', since the lines are more fluid and definite than in Charlotte's copies of engravings. It is made on decorative card, which has an embossed border, possibly for a needle-case or similar container, intended as a gift (see pp. 50–1 for a discussion of 'accomplishments' practised by Charlotte Brontë).

141

## Sketches of heads

c. 1838
Pencil on paper
181 × 230 mm

Inscribed in pencil, beneath head of Elizabethan man: 'Shakspere [*sic*]'; this is in the same hand as the inscription 'Extraordinary' on **142**. Inscribed in pencil, by Ellen Nussey, next to a woman's head at the bottom of the sheet: 'By C B'. The sheet has been folded in the centre and is torn up the crease at the bottom. Watermark: 'Ruse & Turners / 1837'.

Purchased from M. Lee, 1986. Formerly owned by Ellen Nussey and bought by Alice Jane Needham from the sale of Ellen Nussey's effects, 18–19 May 1898.
*Brontë Parsonage Museum: C106*

Nine different heads sketched across the page: four character sketches of male faces (top left) including one of a Roman emperor with laurel leaves and one bearded man; in centre from left to right: profile of woman with hooked nose and deep-set eyes, shoulder-length dark curls; unfinished front view of woman with hair parted in the middle and curled back; man with dark curly hair and Elizabethan beard, moustache and ruffled collar, beneath which is written 'Shakspere'; a larger head in profile at the bottom ('By C B') with the same hair-style as the unfinished front view of the woman above, viz. hair pulled down at the sides of the face and curled back in front of the ear, and the back half of hair pulled back into a bun. A very faint sketch of a woman's face is visible to the right of this profile, in the bottom right corner: only the eyes, nostrils, mouth and strokes of hair are visible. There is another faint outline of a woman's head, top right. Various squiggles, rough sketches of reeds, grass and branches, fill the empty spaces on the sheet.

The last two portraits, the woman in profile and Shakespeare, are almost identical to the sketches in **142**, so helping to establish a similar provenance for the latter illustration. See **142** for a discussion of the attribution of these two drawings.

142

## Young woman at a table

c. 1838
Pencil on paper
272 × 219 mm

Inscribed in pencil, along top left, in non-Brontë hand: 'Extraordinary'; and in faint pencil longhand, possibly that of Charlotte, along the bottom: 'gaist/ghaist/ Ghost Ghaist/ Ghaist'. The paper has been tightly folded, once in half and then four times lengthwise, to fit into a pocket or purse; small tears had developed along the fold marks at the edges, but these have now been conserved and are less visible. For other side see **143**.

Provenance unrecorded, but probably owned by Ellen Nussey: see **141** and discussion below.
*Brontë Parsonage Museum: C97v*

Profile of a young woman sitting on a chair at a table: figure upright and stiff, looking straight ahead to the left, with a serious expression; fashionable hair-style as in other Brontë portraits 'from life' (e.g. **37** and **141**), with back half of hair pulled into a bun behind and the front parted in the middle and drawn straight down on each side into a short curl in front of the exposed ear; simple dress with an open neck and collar, elbow-length sleeves and shawl fastened just above the waist with a brooch, a bracelet on the left hand, which is holding the left cover of a book open on the table; right arm and hand unfinished and out of proportion; carved back of Pembroke-style chair visible behind the woman; a tall vase of flowers and leaves on the table immediately in front of the woman, on the far left of the picture; a small portfolio or book with the clasp open lies on the table in front of the vase. It is difficult to discern-whether the woman is reading or sketching the vase of flowers, since the object in front of her is faint and has been drawn over several times. It appears that a rounded object like a mixing well or water jar for painting has been superseded by a sketch of a book. There is no sign of a pen or paint-brush. A sprig of holly on the table, in the foreground, to the left of the woman, suggests that it was to be sketched next or pressed in the book.

A small faint half-length sketch of a bearded man in Elizabethan dress occupies the top left corner of the page; he is lying horizontally along the top, the paper having been turned around and the sketch made from a different angle. Next to this is the word 'Extraordinary', which is in the same hand as the inscription 'Shakspere', beneath a similar sketch: see **141**, which also includes a similar portrait of the woman.

A case for Brontë attribution can be supported by a comparison with **141**: the two portraits in this drawing are almost identical to two portraits sketched in **141**, which was originally in the possession of Charlotte's friend Ellen Nussey. Beside the portrait of the woman in **141**, Ellen Nussey has written 'By C B'.

The subject is unlikely to be one of the Brontës but it may be one of their school-friends, possibly Ellen Nussey (see above). It is also the kind of quick sketch one might make while superintending pupils in a classroom. The style, however is not especially typical of Charlotte. Since **141** belonged to Ellen Nussey, this item probably did too. Both may even have been drawn by her or by Charlotte on one of her many visits to Ellen's home, The Rydings, Birstall, possibly in 1838 (the watermark of **141** is 1837). It is also quite possible that the sketches in both drawings were made by several hands.

## 143

## Sketch of a house

c. 1838
Pencil on paper
219 × 272 mm

Stamped: 'BRONTË/ MUSEUM/ HAWORTH', encircled. The paper has been tightly folded, once in half and then four times lengthwise, to fit into a pocket or purse; small tears had developed along the fold marks at the edges, but these have now been conserved and are less visible. Further illustrations on the other side: see **142**.

Provenance unrecorded, but probably owned by Ellen Nussey: see **142**.

*Brontë Parsonage Museum: C97*

Unfinished sketch of a large square Victorian house with symmetrical design: central door with balcony, window and small canopy above on second storey; two windows on either side, top and bottom storey, the top windows with balconies and pediments reaching into roof line, the bottom windows at each side shaded by large canopies supported by (wrought iron?) pillars; three chimneys, tiled roof. Sketch of a small shed or glass house on left and stone wall on right.

This illustration is not especially typical of drawings by Charlotte, although it may have been made while she was staying with her school-friend, Ellen Nussey: see **142** for a discussion of attribution. It may also be part of an exercise in drawing, since it is very similar to an engraving of a Georgian house used as an exercise in geometrical drawing and scale, in *The Draughtman's Assistant; Or, Drawing made Easy: Wherein the Principles of that Art are rendered Familiar: In Ten Instructive Lessons ... By the Author of The Artist's Assistant* (London: R. Sayer & J. Bennett, 1777).

## 144

## 'The Remains of The Temple of Venus at Rome'

24 May 1839
Pencil on paper
235 × 278 mm

Dated in very faint pencil, bottom right corner just below drawing: 'May 24th 39'; title in very faint longhand beneath picture: 'The Remains of The Temple of Venus at Rome'. The title has been repeated in clear pencil in the hand of Miss M. Wood, secretary to John Alexander Symington (curator of the BPM in 1928 when the drawing was donated; see also 'Warwick Castle', Dubious attribution), beneath the original, with a question-mark inserted after 'Venus' and the date 'May 24–39' repeated, in the same hand, to the right of the original date. A possible signature can be discerned beneath the bottom left corner of the drawing. Also marked top left corner, in ink: '662'; in pencil: '662'. Watermark: 'J WHATMAN / 1833'.

Gift of Leslie H. Openshaw, 1928; together with a silhouette portrait of Elizabeth Branwell (SB663). Originally owned by Martha Brown, then inherited by her sister, Ann Binns, and sold in the Binns sale, Saltaire, 27 January 1886 (either lot 369 or lot 383). Abraham Riley (see **49**), acquired it at the sale and sold it in 1898 to Openshaw's father.
*Brontë Parsonage Museum: C22*

Landscape of Roman houses and antique ruins: a single column on the left and a ruinated entrance to a temple on the centre right (seven pillars with inscription on pediment). Italian houses in the background and four small figures in the foreground.

Copy of an engraving; typical of eighteenth- and nineteenth-century illustrations of Roman ruins after Piranesi.

The faint pencil inscription appears to be in Charlotte's hand, and the watermark and provenance indicate a positive attribution. Yet it is not difficult to notice how distinctly different the style of this drawing is to any of Charlotte's other works, especially in the treatment of the clouds and the trees.

## 145

## Easton House

September 1839
Watercolour on paper

Given by Charlotte Brontë to the Hudsons of Easton Farm; inherited by their niece Fanny Whipp, later Mrs North, and passed by her to her younger son, Edward Roundell Whipp North, who owned it in 1895 (see below). Winifred Gérin attributes this painting to the Bayle Gate Museum, Bridlington (*Charlotte Brontë: The Evolution of Genius* (Oxford: Clarendon Press, 1967),

p. 156), but they have no record of the original, apart from a photographic reproduction (70 × 100 mm) that itself seems to have been reproduced from a book or newspaper article, although it may be the photo made by P. F. Lee from the original painting for his article mentioned below. The photograph is inscribed in an unknown hand: 'Farmhouse at Easton from a water-colour drawing by Charlotte Brontë.'

*Location unknown*

View of a substantial two-storey white Georgian house, seen from the back with its large pleasant garden. It has a tiled roof and two large chimneys, each surmounted by four chimney-pots. The four pane-glass windows of the top storey appear to be mullioned; the ground floor has a door with portico and a large bay window on either side. The walls are covered with trellises, ivy and flowering vines. A high white wall runs behind the house on the far right, with a door presumably leading to the road outside; a flock of birds (probably crows as described below) fly overhead. A white path runs parallel with the house between it and the greensward in front.

In the foreground a couple sit casually chatting on a garden bench, the woman in a white cap with a dog on her lap, the man in top hat and frock coat. They are surrounded by flowering shrubs, carefully distinguished on the right, less delineated on the left and apparently forming a bower referred to as the 'summer house'. Winifred Gérin had no trouble identifying the garden and building in this watercolour as Easton House, which was still standing when she saw it in 1961 (p. 155).

Easton House lay two miles inland from Bridlington (then known as Burlington), but within sound of the sea. It was built in about 1810, red-brick but whitewashed and with a red tiled roof; one of two farmhouses on a 720-acre estate belonging to Sir George Strickland. The house was owned by Sophia and John Hudson, who were hosts to Charlotte Brontë and her friend Ellen Nussey for four weeks in September 1839. The Hudsons' niece Fanny Whipp was also staying at that time and Charlotte was apparently enchanted by the seven-year-old 'little Hancheon', as she called her. Charlotte would have executed this painting during this happy time. Ten years later, in June 1849, she was to return with Ellen to Easton Farm in depressing circumstances, for a week just after the death of Anne.

P. F. Lee saw the original of this watercolour when he visited Edward Roundell Whipp North, of Bridlington Quay, in 1895. Lee describes the house in the painting as 'looking so cosy', and the ivy-grown 'summer house' behind the group in the foreground, Mr and Mrs Hudson sitting on a rustic seat with their dog. The owner of the painting apparently informed him that Mr Hudson's only remark during the progress of the drawing was, 'Now don't forget to put in the crows, Miss Brontë' (P. F. Lee, 'Charlotte Brontë and the East Riding', *Brontë Society Transactions* (1896) vol. 1, part 4, p. 22).

Lee's informant also told him that much of Charlotte's time at Easton was spent in writing and sketching. She painted a small portrait of Mrs Hudson, which was inherited by Fanny North and passed to her elder son in London, who reported in 1895 that he had unfortunately mislaid it, together with a pair of slippers, worked by Charlotte at the same time, that he had also inherited.

## 146

## Miniature of a lady

c. 1837–1839

Watercolour on card, irregular shape

61 × 38 mm

Purchased from M. Lee, 1986. Formerly owned by Ellen Nussey and bought by Alice Jane Needham from the sale of Ellen Nussey's effects, 18–19 May 1898.

*Brontë Parsonage Museum: C105*

Portrait of a young woman looking over her right shoulder towards the viewer: head held high; broad, open features, large almond-shaped brown eyes, high arched eyebrows, long nose, full highly coloured pink cheeks and lips; glossy brown shoulder-length ringlets cover her head, part of a bow visible at back right; bare shoulders with a ribbon around neck.

The illustration is cut out around the head and shoulders, and two distinct needle-holes are visible just above the forehead where the portrait has been sewn, possibly to the leather case in which it was found. After purchase, Mrs Needham's daughter discovered it face downwards in this case which also contained a silver watch and chain and some needles.

It is said to be a portrait of Ellen Nussey by Charlotte, although there is little apart from the provenance to substantiate this. A letter from C. Mabel Edgerley (26 April 1940; Needham Collection, BPM) states that she can discern 'C. Brontë' on the right shoulder of the portrait but if this was so, there is no evidence of it now on the original painting. The dating, too, is uncertain. There are instances of Charlotte's interest in making needle-case illustrations and taking likenesses of friends during the years 1837 to 1839.

## 147

## Woman in leopard fur

October 1839

Watercolour and gum arabic on paper

183 × 147 mm

Dated in pencil, in minuscule script, bottom left: 'Oct$^{br}$'; bottom right: '1839'. Watermark along right edge: 'WHATMAN/ TURKEY MILL/ 1833 [only top half of this date visible]'. On verso: rough pencil outline tracing of the figure on recto.

Bequest of Henry Houston Bonnell, 1927; acquired by him at Sotheby's sale of effects of Arthur Bell Nicholls, 26 July 1907.

*Brontë Parsonage Museum: Bonnell 24*

Portrait of a young woman with long brown wavy hair, white dress and brown fur cloak, resembling leopard skin: facial features similar to other Brontë beauties, namely the large widely spaced clear eyes, wide arch of the line of the eyebrow and straight nose, small delicate mouth and chin. The woman has pale skin, blue eyes, pink lips, long curling hair flowing down her back and over her left shoulder. The brown hair colour matches the colour of the brown fur cloak draped over the right shoulder, behind and under the left arm. Her low-necked, plain white dress is of a satin material, leg-of-mutton sleeves and purple belt. Background of a sunset sky (pale yellow, reddish brown and blue), with green bush and trees silhouetted against the pale yellow in the distance.

This work is unusual since very few of Charlotte's portraits have a background, especially an outdoor scene. She has also experimented with her paint here, mixing the gum arabic (see **26**) with the darker watercolours and also applying the transparent film to the surface of the painting. The superficial cracking of the gum is obvious, especially on the hair and cloak.

Winifred Gérin points out that the date of this watercolour is contemporary with the writing of 'Caroline Vernon', suggesting that it might represent Charlotte's heroine of the same name (*Five Novelettes* (London: The Folio Press, 1971), opp. p. 321).

## 148

## Woman in a blue dress with red shawl

c.1839
Watercolour and pencil on card
231 × 182 mm

Unsigned and undated. Stamped on verso: 'BRONTË/ MUSEUM/ HAWORTH', encircled.

Bequest of Henry Houston Bonnell, 1927; acquired by him at Sotheby's sale of effects of Arthur Bell Nicholls, 26 July 1907.

*Brontë Parsonage Museum: Bonnell 26*

Three-quarter-length portrait of a woman sitting in a thoughtful pose, with her right elbow resting on her left hand and her right hand under her chin: dark brown hair in fashionable Victorian style, parted in the middle and swept down each side in short ringlets, the back section of hair gathered up behind, probably in a bun; large blue / grey eyes (left eye appears larger than the right), wide brown eyebrows, straight nose, small mouth with red lips; blue dress with long sleeves, large white collar and cuffs, a flower (pansy?) brooch fastened at the neckline where the collar meets, with a long gold chain reaching from this to the waist and up around the neck on the left; a fob watch attached to the dress beneath the bust; a red shawl with black markings (plaid?) is draped around the figure and spread over the chair on each side; left hand unfinished.

Although the face resembles several of Charlotte Brontë's portraits of young women, in particular **147**, the everyday dress and fashionable hair-style of this portrait, together with its more relaxed style, suggest that she was attempting to paint one of her friends or possibly one of her sisters.

See **26** for Charlotte Brontë's use of watercolour and gum arabic. Surface cracking of the gum arabic is clearly visible on the blue dress. The background of the painting has a pale brownish yellow wash.

## 149

## William Weightman

February 1840
Pencil on paper
154 × 115 mm

Unsigned and undated. Inscribed on the spines of books in drawing: 'Hall', 'Euseb', 'Hook'; in top left corner, BPM number: 'SB. 1011'. Stamped: 'BRONTË/ MUSEUM/ HAWORTH', encircled.

Purchased from Hodgson & Co., London, 31 March 1933 (part of lot 447). Formerly in the collection of Sir Alfred J. Law, Honresfeld (see **15**).

*Brontë Parsonage Museum: B35*

Head-and-shoulder profile portrait of a young man wearing a clerical collar and university gown. The man, facing right, has fine, almost delicate features, with long side whiskers reaching round his chin and wavy hair swept towards his face. The authors of the books stacked to the right of the subject are carefully labelled on their spines: Hall, Euseb(ius) and Hook, all church historians and writers, suggesting the interest or profession of the young man.

Dr Juliet Barker discusses the attribution and identity of this portrait in 'A Possible Portrait of William Weight-man', *Brontë Society Transactions* (1987), vol. 19, part 4, pp. 175–6. She points out that, although a genuine Brontë drawing, it was not attributed specifically to any one Brontë. After the Hodgson sale of 1933 it was thought to be by Branwell, though (as Dr Mildred Christian notes in a card index at the BPM: see **34**) the style is closer to that of Charlotte.

Barker also convincingly suggests that the portrait is of the Reverend William Weightman, curate of Haworth Parish Church from August 1839 until his premature death in 1842. She argues that, although Charlotte referred to 'the painting' of Weightman's portrait in a letter to Ellen Nussey on 17 March 1840 (*The Brontës: Their Lives, Friendships and Correspondence*, ed. Thomas James Wise and John Alexander Symington, 4 vols. (Oxford: Basil Blackwell for the Shakespeare Head Press, 1932), vol. 1, p. 201), Charlotte may have taken the opportunity to make this pencil sketch as well, since there was every reason to prolong the visits of the likeable young man.

It is possible, however, that this was the only portrait Charlotte made of Weightman. She seldom used watercolour and never oils for a portrait; pencil was her forte. Her reference to 'the painting of Miss Celia Amelia Weightman's portrait and that young lady's frequent and agreeable visits' was made in jest to Ellen Nussey on 17 March 1840: 'painting' might simply mean 'depicting' or 'drawing' here. Moreover, Ellen Nussey's later addition to this letter recalls 'the *taking* of Mr Weightman's portrait by Charlotte' (my italics). She continues her comment: 'The sittings became alarming for length of time required, and the guest [Ellen] had to adopt the gown, which the owner was very proud to exhibit, amusing the party with his critical remarks on the materials used, and pointing out the adornments, silk, velvet, etc.'

Charlotte's letter to Ellen refers to the painting of Weightman's portrait as a past event and implies Ellen's intimate knowledge of the numerous sittings; the work can therefore be dated to a three-week visit Ellen paid to Haworth during February 1840.

## 150

## Profile of a woman

c. 1840–1841
Pencil on thin card
141 × 131 mm

Inscribed in pencil on verso at top: '2 given to F. E. Bell by Mrs Arthur Bell Nicholls/ at the Hill House Banagher, as a/ Drawing by Charlotte Brontë.'; in pencil bottom right corner: '70'. There is also some shading on the left of the verso, possibly part of another drawing that was destroyed when the paper was cut.

Purchased from Frances E. Bell of Dublin, 1918, together with **66**, **350**, Charlotte's pocket book (BS22), a photo of Martha Brown (Ph71) and Harriet Martineau's visiting card; formerly given by Arthur Bell Nicholls to his second wife, aunt of Frances Bell, in Banagher, Ireland. In subsequent years other items were acquired by the BPM from Frances Bell: see **66**.

*Brontë Parsonage Museum: C64*

Half-length profile of a young woman, probably drawn from life. The figure stands erect, facing towards the left; small mouth and eyes, straight nose; dark hair parted half-way back on head and back section gathered in a bun behind, front section swept straight down at side of face and tucked under and around the ear in order to expose it; high-necked dress with pointed collar and long sleeves; a book (or sash?) projecting at the back from under the arm; heavy pencil shading behind the figure.

The provenance and style tend to suggest that this uncharacteristic Brontë portrait is by Charlotte, executed perhaps in the years just before she went to Brussels.

## 151

## Unfinished portrait of a boy

c. 1840–1841
Pencil and watercolour on card
196 × 157 mm

Found in Charlotte Brontë portable writing desk, together with a plait of Anne's hair and other drawings (**164–173**), a bequest of Alexander Murray Smith, 1943; formerly owned by Reginald J. Smith (see **133**), who acquired the desk at the Sotheby's sale of the effects of Arthur Bell Nicholls, 26 July 1907 (lot 31).
*Brontë Parsonage Museum: C89*

Unfinished three-quarter portrait of a boy in uniform, possibly a fancy dress: tall cap with braid and tassel hanging down on right side; chubby face, short hair just visible above left ear; large fancy collar and sleeves sketched in on frock-like tunic; right hand possibly holding a toy top; left arm leaning against a table or desk (no legs visible).

Charlotte's working method is clearly displayed here. She was obviously intending to make this a water-colour portrait and here we see the early stages of her technique. The brim of the hat and the shadows below lower left cheek and on right side of face are blocked in with watercolour, to serve as a base; the remainder of the illustration is a faint pencil outline of the engraving she has copied.

This is an unusual choice of subject compared with her early works, and, being unfinished, the picture has no date; but since it was found in Charlotte's desk after her death, it is likely to be one of the last illustrations she worked on. Although her final extant landscape is dated August 1845 (**163**), no other portraits by her exist after the year 1840, so it is possible that this drawing lay in her desk for some time, having been begun before she went to Brussels. She drew little after her return to Haworth.

## 152

### Tomb with ornamental urn

c. 1840–1841
Pencil on paper
185 × 186 mm

Inscribed in ink beneath the tomb: 'By my Dr Daughter Charlotte / P. Brontë, Minr of Haworth.' On verso: a slight watercolour sketch of a purple flower, and an inscription by Martha Brown: 'Given by Martha Brown to Mrs Greenwood/ on the 23rd February 1865. / Signed Martha Brown'.

Just before his death, Patrick Brontë gave Martha Brown this drawing, together with a letter from Charlotte to Martha (probably written about 29 October 1849). In 1865, Martha Brown gave both drawing and letter, together with a note authenticating them, to Sarah Greenwood. Her descendant, the late Colonel Bernard Greenwood of Swarcliffe, lent the drawing in about 1977 to the owner of Norton Conyers, where it was on display. It is reproduced here by kind permission of Colonel Greenwood's executors.

*Private owner*

Illustration of a tomb surmounted by a large urn. Nine lines of inscription are visible on the end of the tomb facing the viewer but the actual words are indecipherable. A sapling tree, with a few tufts of grass around, bends over the tomb in the left foreground, dense shrubs and trees in the background. The style suggests a later date, sometime before Charlotte went to Brussels.

It is an interesting twist of fate that this drawing by Charlotte should have been on display in a historic English house that she once visited as a humble governess. While she was employed by the Sidgwick family in 1839, Charlotte Brontë visited Norton Conyers which was being rented by the Greenwoods, Mrs Sidgwick's parents. There she heard the legend of a mad woman who had been confined in the Jacobean attic, and there she explored the house that is said to have contributed much to the image of Thornfield Hall in *Jane Eyre*.

## 153

### Doodle: face

c. March 1841
Ink on paper
5 × 10 mm

A slight sketch at the bottom of the last manuscript page (187 × 115 mm) of the main fragment (ch. 1 and part of ch. 2) of the unfinished story 'Ashworth', which is written in Charlotte Brontë's minuscule script.

Probably purchased by Eleanor Elkins Widener between April 1912 and July 1915, and added by her to the Harry Elkins Widener Collection; gift to the Harvard College Library, July 1915.

*Harvard College Library: Widener Collection*

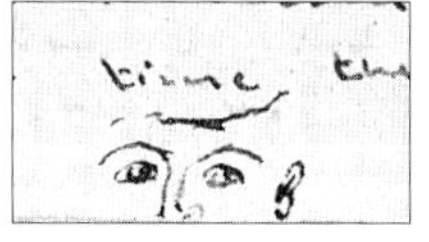

'Ashworth' is an unnamed, fragmentary manuscript written by Charlotte Brontë between December 1840 and March 1841, although earlier drafts of the story were begun as early as 1839 (see Christine Alexander, *The Early Writings of Charlotte Brontë* (Oxford: Basil Blackwell, 1983), p. 204). The story is known as 'Ashworth', after the principal character, a Yorkshire landowner, based on the Angrian character Alexander Percy. Only three chapters and an early draft of chapter 4 exist, in several fragments; and a reconstruction of the story can be found in 'Ashworth: An Unfinished Novel by Charlotte

Brontë', ed. Melodie Monahan, *Studies in Philology*, vol. 80, no. 4, Fall 1983.

The tiny sketch of part of a face (eyes, eyebrows, nose and ear) occupies the space at the bottom of the final page of chapter 2, which describes Ashworth's daughter's experience at a private boarding school in London. Since it appears just below the words: 'the last part of the sentence was said not sadly – but rather in a cheerful matter of fact way & with a glance upwards at Miss Ashworth accompanied by a half-smile', it is tempting to suggest that the expression on the drawing might relate to the text.

154

## River scene with trees

4 August 1842
Pencil on paper
363 × 464 mm

Signed and dated in pencil, in minuscule script, at bottom left corner: 'Bruxelles'; bottom centre: 'Ch. Brontë'; bottom right corner: 'Le 4 Août 1842'.

Gift of A. H. Green and Emily Green, 1947 (together with **282** and **283**); previously owned by the father of the donors, H. S. Green of Moss Side, Manchester, formerly of Dewsbury and a founder member of the Brontë Society, who lent this drawing and **282** and **283** to the BPM in 1896: see F. C. Galloway's *A Descriptive Catalogue of Objects in the Museum of the Brontë Society at Haworth* (Bradford, 1896), p. 15.
*Brontë Parsonage Museum: C23*

River scene probably drawn from nature, on one of the sketching expeditions into the countryside undertaken by Charlotte and Emily while at the Pensionnat Heger in Brussels. Possibly sketched from a bridge: river in central foreground meanders towards the right and disappears amongst trees in the middle-distance; wooden embankment and fisherman sitting on lock on left; wood and stone embankment on right; tree-covered hills in distance. The drawing, however, shows evidence of having been finished in the classroom; it has the same careful attention to detail in the stonework and trees that is found in Charlotte's many copies of engravings.

155

## Study of a tree and cottage

6 August 1842
Pencil on thin card
362 × 294 mm

Dated in pencil in Charlotte's minuscule script, bottom left corner: 'Bruxelles / 1842'; bottom right corner: 'le 6 Août'. An inscription in ink, bottom centre, reads: 'By my Daughter Charlotte / P Brontë Min$^{str}$ / [rule]'.
Gift of Margaret Illingworth, 1910, together with **9**, **10**, **11**, **12**, **19**, **80**, **81**, **184**, **185**, **188**, **189**, **197** and **334**. There are no records of Margaret Illingworth's acquisition, though she may have obtained these items from one of Martha Brown's relatives: see **9**.
*Brontë Parsonage Museum: C37*

Study of a tree with four intertwined trunks, standing before a simple L-shaped stone cottage with thatched roof; grass and shrubs in foreground around the tree. The unfinished appearance, uncertainty of the lines and smudging of the pencil – probably caused by Charlotte's sleeve as she drew – suggest that this is one of her few drawings 'from nature'.

The drawing was executed at Brussels just before the end of the school term. The Pensionnat Heger closed for the holidays on 15 August 1842, but Charlotte and Emily (together with the other English pupils, the Wheelwright sisters) were obliged to remain at school. During this time it was possible for them to make drawing expeditions into the surrounding countryside: see Emily's 'Study of a fir tree' (**326**), Charlotte's 'River scene with trees' (**154**) and 'Landscape with fallen trees' (**156**).

## 156

## Landscape with fallen trees

c. August 1842
Pencil on paper
362 × 456 mm

Inscribed in ink, bottom centre: 'By my Daughter Charlotte / P. Brontë Min[r]'.

Stamped: 'BRONTË / MUSEUM / HAWORTH', encircled. Gift of William Edwin Briggs Priestley, Bradford, 1907; together with **105**, a letter from Charlotte to Martha Brown (BS69) and Patrick Brontë's spectacles (J17). Priestley was MP for Bradford, later knighted and a vice-president of the Brontë Society, 1909–20. He had previously lent this drawing to the Brontë Society in 1896 (F. C. Galloway's *A Descriptive Catalogue of Objects in the Museum of the Brontë Society at Haworth* (Bradford, 1896), p. 20); and probably acquired it through James Miles, the Leeds bookseller, who bought it at the Binns sale, Saltaire, 27 January 1886 (see William Scruton's catalogue of the sale, Keighley Public Library). An article in the *Leeds Mercury* (29 January 1886) describing the sale lists 'A good landscape drawing, called "A Fallen Tree, etc."'

*Brontë Parsonage Museum: C92*

Landscape with two bare tree trunks lying across a stream in the foreground, a topless straggly fir tree behind them on the right and in the distance on the left a high cliff with bushes, trees and a castle or church faintly suggested on the top. Large stones lie on the far side of the stream beneath the tree trunks; grasses and low vegetation grow around the base of the fir tree and behind the trunks. The illustration may be unfinished: only the foreground (stream, trunks and fir) is drawn in detail.

This is one of Charlotte's few landscapes made 'from nature'. It is less detailed than her copies and there is evidence of smudging caused by her sleeve rubbing across the drawing as she worked with a board on her lap.

The same topless fir tree is the subject of one of Emily's drawings (**326**), seen from the opposite angle with the fallen trunks behind. It is significant that Emily chose to emphasize the romantic gothic qualities of the scene while Charlotte portrayed its more conventional picturesque aspects. Their styles, too, are distinctly different, with Charlotte's pencil strokes suggesting a light, rather hesitant touch, compared to Emily's firmer, confident style.

The two illustrations were probably made during one of the girls' rambles into the countryside from Brussels, most likely during the August holidays which they were obliged to spend at school (see **155**).

## 157

### Watermill

c. August 1842
Pencil on paper
212 × 290 mm

Signed in pencil in minuscule script, bottom left: 'C Brontë'; and inscribed in Charlotte's minuscule hand, bottom right corner: 'A token of affection and respect to / Madame Heger from one of her pupils'. Original inscription appears to have been 'Madame Heger from one of her pupils', but Charlotte has added 'A token of affection and respect to' crosswise above this. Also inscribed in another hand, bottom right corner: '405'. Purchased 1926, from Margaret (Meta) Mossman, a niece of Marian Douglas, who was a pupil of Madame Heger in Brussels at the school Charlotte and Emily Brontë attended. See provenance of Emily's 'The North Wind' (**325**) for further information on Brontë relics owned by the Hegers and mention of 'Watermill' in a letter from Genevieve Wigfall to Ellen Nussey, 10 December 1889.
*Brontë Parsonage Museum: C24*

Picturesque, gothic-style watermill with gables, towers, colonnades, mullioned windows; mill-pond surrounded by flowers and shrubs in centre foreground; trees on either side of the mill; possibly a naked figure standing on the water-wheel beneath a window, ready to dive into the pond.

Probably copied from an engraving and executed in Brussels during the August school holidays (see **155**). The inscription indicates that the drawing was given to Madame Heger as a gift, possibly for her birthday or as a memento when Charlotte left Brussels in November 1842.

## 158

### Picturesque landscape with tower and cottage

c. August 1842
Pencil on paper
334 × 402 mm

Inscribed in pencil below the drawing, in margin: 'By my Daughter Charlotte / P. Brontë Min$^{str}$'. Bookplate on verso reads: 'Richard Haworth, Dealer in Works of Art, Printseller, etc. 25 Preston Road, Blackburn.' The drawing is mounted on a low-quality board. The Paper Conservator at the Harry Ransom Humanities Research Center concludes that this mounting took place after the drawing had been stored rolled up for some time, indicated by tears on the left and right lower margins, with no corresponding tears in the backing. Furthermore, the drawing has surface grime not present on the backing.

Purchased in 1970 from Bertram Rota Ltd, Booksellers of London, who used this drawing on the cover of their catalogue, no. 158, Fall 1968. Bertram Rota apparently acquired the drawing from an art-dealer in the north of England.
*Harry Ransom Humanities Research Center, University of Texas at Austin: Art Collection, Item No. 70.6*

Picturesque mountain valley scene: river in foreground receding to left beneath steep wooded embankment; a tree bends over the right bank of the river in centre foreground and beside it a stone and timber cottage built around a medieval round tower; in distance,poplar trees and steep slopes on right, the ruins of a castle high on a rock overlooking the river behind the cottage in centre. A figure is walking down the wooden steps of the cottage. Three logs lie beside the river in front of the tree. The bottom right corner of the drawing is unfinished: large rocks or shrubs are blocked in and the outline of three figures is visible behind one of the rocks.

The subject, style and format of this work suggest that it was executed during the school holidays in Brussels, 1842 (though formerly attributed to 1831), at the same time as 'Watermill' (**157**). Its unfinished state allows us to glimpse Charlotte's typical working methods: her initial blocking in of the scene, then her concentration on the central object before working on the background or foreground.

Engravings of Italianate scenes were popular in Victorian England, partly as a result of the success of Byron's *Childe Harold* and an increasing interest in exotic places. Many drawing manuals also included such landscapes, as in the case of William Austin's *A Specimen of Sketching Landscapes, In a Free and Masterly Manner, with a Pen and Pencil* (London: by the author, n.d.). This work includes thirty etchings, made – as the title page declares – ' from Original Drawings of Lucatelli, after the life, in and about ROME'.

## 159

## 'Good-bye': a comic sketch

6 March 1843
Ink on paper
c.90 × 136 mm

The sketch fills the final half page of an autograph letter to Ellen Nussey, each page measuring 214 × 136 mm. The letter, in Charlotte Brontë's longhand, is signed above the drawing: 'Go-o-d-b-y-e / CB'; and dated 'Bruxelles March 6$^{\text{th}}$ / 43'. The figures in the drawing have been labelled by Charlotte as described below.

Formerly owned by J. Horsfall Turner; purchased from Bernard Quaritch Ltd, London, 1974, with the majority of J. Horsfall Turner's Brontë collection.
*Brontë Parsonage Museum: BS50.4*

Comic sketch showing a grotesque stunted little female figure on the left, waving 'Good bye' (written on a flag from the mouth, in comic-strip style) and labelled beneath 'C Brontë'. A beautiful young woman in a long fashionable gown and ringlets stands holding hands with a bespectacled man in tophat and tails on the right. The woman is labelled below, '~~Ellen Nussey~~', and above, 'Mrs O P ~~Vincent~~'; the man labelled above, 'The Chosen'. (Above this an earlier sketch of the woman's head has been scribbled out.) The two figures on the right are looking back at the stunted figure on the left; water with a steam-boat on the horizon represents the English Channel separating them.

Ellen Nussey heavily censored her letters from Charlotte Brontë, when Elizabeth Gaskell asked for material for her *Life of Charlotte Brontë*, 2 vols. (London: Smith, Elder & Co., 1857). She appears to have done the same before the abortive edition prepared by J. Horsfall Turner between 1885 and 1889, which had to be withdrawn because Arthur Bell Nicholls refused permission for publication. Since this letter formed part of the Turner collection, it may have been one of the original letters Ellen Nussey accused Turner of stealing, after she had lent him her letters for the edition (see Tom Winnifrith, *The Brontës and Their Background: Romance and Reality* (London: Macmillan, 1973), pp. 8–11).

Ellen Nussey's censorship is clearly seen here in the sketch: not only have names been crossed out (the word 'Vincent' has been heavily deleted and Ellen's name cancelled), but the sketch has been cut so that only the figure of 'The Chosen' remained attached to the letter. The separated fragment of the sketch, however, was restored at a later date and the drawing is now complete again.

The sketch was made after Charlotte's return to Brussels alone in January 1843, to continue her lessons and to assist with English tuition. The subject of the sketch is superficially humorous, referring to a shared joke about Ellen Nussey's latest suitor, but it reflects Charlotte's growing feeling of isolation at the time and her increasingly low self-esteem.

## 159a

## Hands in the margins of a text

April 1843
Ink on paper
5 × 8 mm

The sketches appear halfway down the left margins of two contiguous pages of text, entitled 'The Glove' and written in Charlotte's longhand. The text is in an exercise book labelled by Charlotte: 'German Translations'; and dated: 'Ch. Brontë April 25th 1843'. Only these two pages of translation (pp. 5–6) remain in the book, the remainder of which has subsequently been used by Charlotte for writing poetry and notes for novels.

Bequest of Henry Houston Bonnell, 1927.

*Brontë Parsonage Museum: Bonnell 117(2)*

Two small identical drawings of a hand, seen from the back, with a cuff round the wrist. The forefinger of each hand is pointing at the text from the left margin. The hand on the first page points to a large star-like asterisk which indicates where the missing passage should be inserted. The hand on the opposite page (not illustrated above) indicates the omitted text.

Distinctions between visual and written media become blurred in these two little sketches which are obviously an integral part of the text. Such graphic pointers are not uncommon in handwritten texts but they may have been suggested here by the subject of the exercise itself, namely a glove, used in a senseless display of chivalry.

## 160

## Abercrombie

c. 1843
Pencil on paper
142 × 140 mm; paper torn irregularly on a slope at the top.

Sketch inscribed above, in Charlotte Brontë's hand: 'Abercrombie'. Enclosed with an autograph letter in French, beginning 'Ma chère Jane ...', written by Charlotte Brontë about 1843, while at Brussels.

Bequest of Henry Houston Bonnell, 1927; acquired by him at Sotheby's sale of the effects of Mary Anne Nicholls, 19 June 1914, lot 175.

*Brontë Parsonage Museum: Bonnell 122*

Drawing of a young man in Highland dress facing towards the left: a plumed beret with tartan trim, high-necked jacket and tartan cloak draped diagonally across his chest. He has fine, sharp features; a stern proud look with a slight frown; the arms at the bottom of the page are not properly sketched in. There is a suggestion of high hills outlined in the background across the page.

There is no obvious connection between the letter, which is probably a school exercise in French composition, and the drawing: the latter may have been made at the same time as the letter, during hours of boredom or loneliness at school. The page appears to have been torn from an exercise book, possibly one of the books Charlotte used at the Pensionnat Heger, such as J. C. Russell, *Russell's General Atlas, of Modern Geography* (London: Baldwin & Craddock, [c. 1831]) or M. Noel and M. Chapsal, *Nouveau Dictionnaire de la Langue Française* (Bruxelles: J-B Tircher, 1841): see Appendix A.

## 161

## Stone cross on moorland

c. 14 October 1843
Watercolour over pencil on paper
143 × 220 mm

Illegible script (and possibly sketches) in pencil across the sky and at the bottom of the painting.

Part of the Henry Houston Bonnell Brontë Collection, given by Helen Safford Bonnell in 1963, in memory of her husband, who died in 1926. The painting was originally inserted inside the back cover of J. C. Russell, *Russell's General Atlas, of Modern Geography* (London: Baldwin & Craddock, [c. 1831]), owned by Charlotte Brontë and used in Brussels (see Appendix A). Bonnell acquired it, via Spencer (a dealer?), from Sotheby's sale of the effects of Mary Anne Nicholls, 19 June 1914, lot 644.

*Pierpont Morgan Library: Bonnell Collection MA 2696*

Watercolour wash of large stone cross, dominating the foreground of a barren moorland scene. Indecipherable pencil sketches and markings as described above, possibly indicating that the sheet has been recycled.

The Brontë attribution for this item is uncertain, although the similarity in tone and subject between the painting and an autograph note by Charlotte on the rear pastedown of *Russell's General Atlas, of Modern Geography* suggests a common ownership. The note begins as follows: 'Brussels – Saturday Morning / Oct$^{br}$ 14$^{th}$ 1843, – First Class – / I am very cold – there is no / fire – I wish I were at home / with Papa – Branwell. Emily / Anne & Tabby – I am tired of / being amongst foreigners it is / a dreary life –' (see Appendix A for continuation).

Although *Russell's General Atlas, of Modern Geography* gives no publication date, there is an advertisement in the back for the twelfth edition of *Guy's School Geography* which was published about 1831. This, together with the fact that the date '1833' is written in red crayon on p. 14 of the Index, suggests that Charlotte used this book at Roe Head and took it with her to Brussels.

## 162

## 'The Summer House on the lawn of Bolwell House'

23 April 1844
Pencil on paper
128 × 112 mm

Titled and dated in longhand, beneath illustration: 'The Summer House on the lawn of Bolwell House / April 23$^{rd}$ / 44'. There is no signature on this drawing, but the hand is identical to other examples of Charlotte's writing at this date, especially that of a Harvard manuscript letter dated 'April 7th [1844]'. The drawing was previously stuck into an album or onto a mount as there are the remains of dabs of glue on the back.

One of five small pencil drawings (the other four are listed under 'Dubious attributions') formerly in the possession of John Alexander Symington and sold by Christie's, 18 December 1964, lot 59. They are described in Christie's sale catalogue as 'Five small pencil drawings of houses (3), a rustic summer house and a rustic bridge over a stream with trees .... There are pencil captions on the drawings and one of these "Cottages near Wallasley" [*sic*] appears to be in Charlotte's hand. Included are 5 photographic reproductions of drawings by the Brontës' (p. 16). Earlier provenance may be associated with Arthur Bell Nicholls, since the five photos (**116**, **137**, **137a**, **343** and **346**), were reproduced (except **137a**) 'by kind permission of Mr. Clement K. Shorter' in *The Bookman*, October 1904 (opposite p. 31), while the originals were still in the possession of Nicholls.

*Private collection*

Sketch of a summer-house and surrounding garden scene. The summer-house is built to resemble a grotto, the entrance shaped like a gothic arch and the top of the structure covered with rough rocks and natural materials. A seat is visible inside and the entrance is framed by large bushes. A path appears to run to and from the summer-house on either side, and a large tree overhangs the whole structure from behind.

The sketch appears to have been made from nature. The situation is intriguing, since it probably indicates a garden Charlotte visited, possibly with the Taylor family; but unfortunately no record has been found so far of Bolwell House. Although all five drawings mentioned above may have been made by Charlotte Brontë (see Dubious list below), they have slight differences in style and inscription that make them distinguishable from **162**.

## 163

## 'Ashburnham Church On the Valley-Land'

August 1845
Pencil on paper
160 × 192 mm

Dated in pencil in minuscule script, bottom left corner: 'August 45'; signed bottom right corner: 'C. Brontë'; titled centre bottom: 'Ashburnham Church/ On the Valley-Land'. Watermark: 'J WHATMAN / 1833' (top of date partly cut off).

Purchased from the collection of le Docteur B. Dujardin, together with four other items: two devoirs ('Le Palais de la Mort', by Emily, and 'La Mort de Napoléon' by Charlotte) and two letters from Charlotte to Ellen Nussey. Originally sent by Charlotte Brontë to Constantin Heger, it then passed from him to Lucien Tamar, Brussels, and then to Louise Heger (see below).

*Brontë Parsonage Museum: C25*

Landscape of dense trees and shrubs with a group of stones in the centre foreground and church in the centre middle-distance; church has tiled roof, square tower surmounted by steeple. It bears little resemblance to the parish church of Ashburnham in East Sussex and the term 'Valley-Land' is unfamiliar there; the drawing is obviously a copy of an engraving but the source is unknown.

According to Frederika Macdonald (*The Secret of Charlotte Brontë, followed by some reminiscences of the real Monsieur and Madame Heger* (London: T. C. & E. C. Jack, 1914), facing p. 118), this drawing was sent by Charlotte to Constantin Heger; Frederika Macdonald acquired it for publication from Louise Heger. In an earlier article by Frederika Macdonald, 'The Brontës at Brussels', *The Woman at Home*, vol. 2, no. 10, July 1894, p. 290, this drawing is said to be in the possession of Lucien Tamar, Brussels, and is reproduced on p. 290. The fact that Charlotte chose to send this drawing to her revered 'master', suggests that she considered it to be one of her more accomplished copies of a contemporary engraving.

There is nothing original or new in this final extant illustration by Charlotte. It was probably enclosed with her last bleak letter to Constantin Heger, dated 18 November 1845. Her distress at his continued silence would have been soothed by the careful mechanical copying she had performed so well for so many years. In it she might express a more constant devotion than she dared to express in words.

## 164

### Pattern for a collar 1

n.d.
Ink and pencil on paper
212 × 273 mm

Pattern measurements: neck edge, 205 mm; outer edge of collar, 287 mm; width of collar, 103 mm. Stamped embossed watermark, top left corner: oval with 'ANGOULEME' stamped across centre.

Found in Charlotte Brontë's portable writing desk, together with a plait of Anne's hair and other drawings (**151** and **165–173**), a bequest of Alexander Murray Smith, 1943; formerly owned by Reginald J. Smith (see **133**), who acquired the desk at Sotheby's sale of the effects of Arthur Bell Nicholls, 26 July 1907 (lot 31).
*Brontë Parsonage Museum: C80*

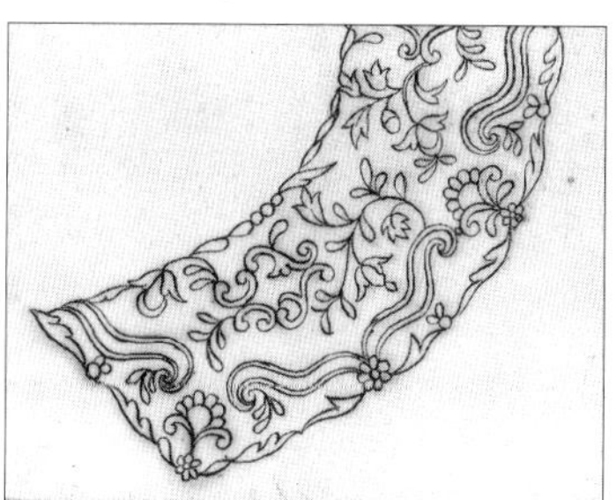

Drawing of half a collar: elaborate pattern for embroidery.

## 165

### Pattern for a collar 2

n.d.
Ink and pencil on paper
273 × 213 mm

Pattern measurements: neck edge, 160 mm; outer edge of collar, 202 mm; width of collar, 107 mm. Stamped embossed watermark, top left corner: oval with 'ANGOULEME' stamped across centre.

Found in Charlotte Brontë's portable writing desk, together with a plait of Anne's hair and other drawings (**151**, **164** and **166–173**), a bequest of Alexander Murray Smith, 1943; formerly owned by Reginald J. Smith (see **133**), who acquired the desk at Sotheby's sale of the effects of Arthur Bell Nicholls, 26 July 1907 (lot 31).
*Brontë Parsonage Museum: C81*

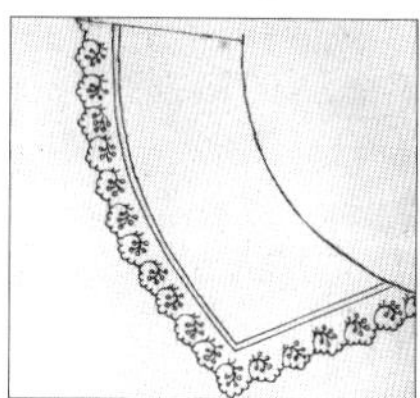

Drawing of half a collar: pattern for lace edging.

## 166

### Pattern for a collar 3

n.d.
Pencil and ink on paper
225 × 369 mm

Pattern measurements: neck edge, 338 mm; outer edge of collar, 470 mm; width of collar, 103 mm.

Found in Charlotte Brontë's portable writing desk, together with a plait of Anne's hair and other drawings (**151**, **164**, **165** and **167–173**), a bequest of Alexander Murray Smith, 1943; formerly owned by Reginald J. Smith (see **133**), who acquired the desk at Sotheby's sale of the effects of Arthur Bell Nicholls, 26 July 1907 (lot 31).

*Brontë Parsonage Museum: C82*

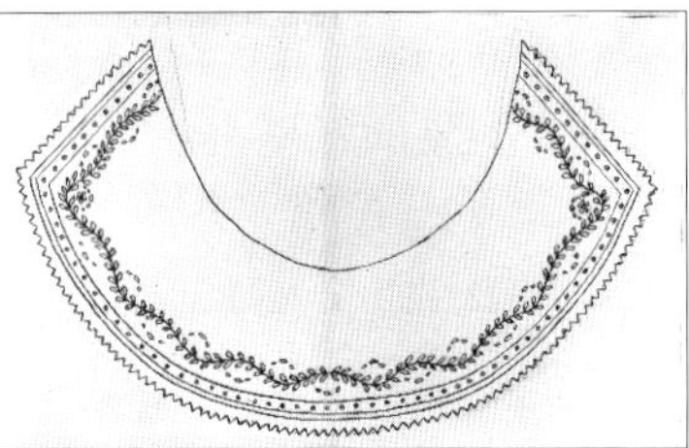

Drawing of a complete collar on the back of a piece of black-edged mourning paper: pattern and lace edging.

## 167

## Pattern for a collar 4

n.d.
Pencil on paper
214 × 275 mm

Pattern measurements: neck edge, 207 mm; outer edge of collar, 325 mm; width of collar, 104 mm.

Found in Charlotte Brontë's portable writing desk, together with a plait of Anne's hair and other drawings (**151**, **164–166** and **168–173**), a bequest of Alexander Murray Smith, 1943; formerly owned by Reginald J. Smith (see **133**), who acquired the desk at Sotheby's sale of the effects of Arthur Bell Nicholls, 26 July 1907 (lot 31).

*Brontë Parsonage Museum: C83*

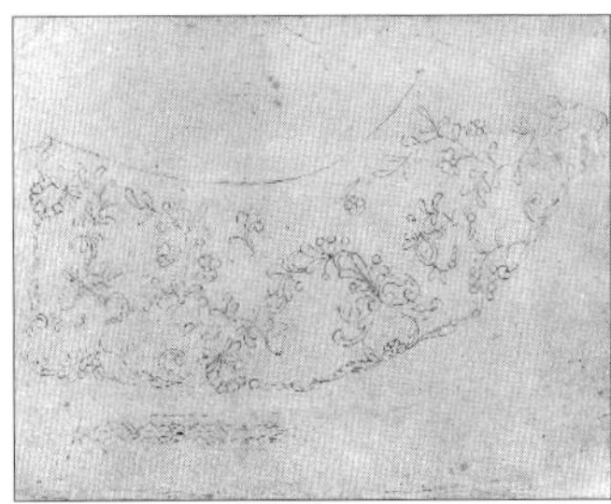

Drawing of half a collar: pattern for elaborate floral embroidery. At the bottom left of the page there is a detail for an alternative edging.

## 168

## Pattern for a cuff

n.d.
Ink and pencil on paper
105 × 324 mm

A line of German in Charlotte's longhand written along the top of the left half of a folded sheet; the cuff pattern occupies the right half of the sheet and extends onto the left half beneath the German. On verso, ten lines of German in the same hand, written on the right side of the sheet; the ink of the cuff pattern shows through from the recto, partly obliterating the German.

Found in Charlotte Brontë's portable writing desk, together with a plait of Anne's hair and other drawings (**151**, **164–167** and **169–173**), a bequest of Alexander Murray Smith, 1943; formerly owned by Reginald J. Smith (see **133**), who acquired the desk at Sotheby's sale of the effects of Arthur Bell Nicholls, 26 July 1907 (lot 31).

*Brontë Parsonage Museum: C88*

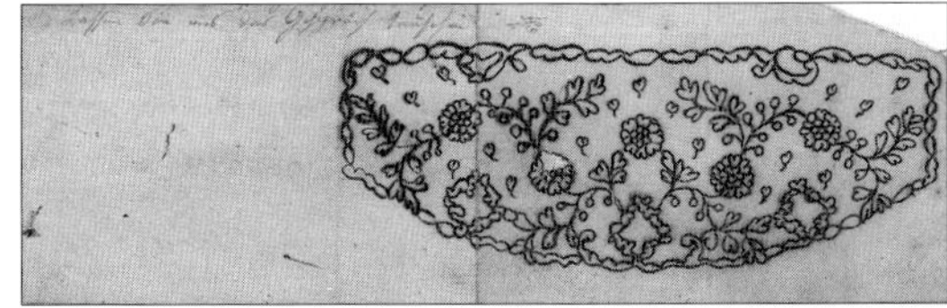

Elaborate floral design for an embroidered cuff, drawn on the bottom of a draft of a German exercise or letter, of which one line is still visible, top left. The pencil tracing for the design is visible beneath the ink. It appears that the cuff design was drawn after the sheet was cut, a thrifty habit practised by all the Brontës of making use of every scrap of paper. The German lines on the verso constitute part of the first side of the mutilated exercise and the line of German on the recto appears to be the final line.

## 169

## Two patterns for cuffs

n.d.
Pencil and ink on paper
273 × 213 mm

Cuff measurements for left pattern: length 198 mm, width 53 mm; right pattern: length 229 mm, width 59 mm. Stamped watermark, bottom right corner: 'ANGOULEME'.

Found in Charlotte Brontë's portable writing desk, together with a plait of Anne's hair and other drawings (**151**, **164**–**168** and **170**–**173**), a bequest of Alexander Murray Smith, 1943; formerly owned by Reginald J. Smith (see **133**), who acquired the desk at Sotheby's sale of the effects of Arthur Bell Nicholls, 26 July 1907 (lot 31).

*Brontë Parsonage Museum: C84*

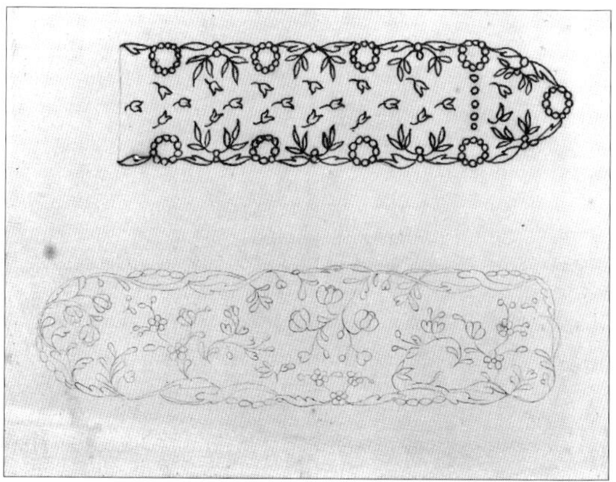

Two different patterns for elaborately embroidered cuffs with a floral design.

## 170

## Pattern for a coin purse

n.d.
Ink on paper, folded
230 × 186 mm

On the pattern back (inside) is pasted a pink paper rectangle carrying an autograph poem in Charlotte's tiny longhand (not her minuscule script). The poem is entitled 'I never can forget' (6 lines).

Found in Charlotte Brontë's portable writing desk, together with a plait of Anne's hair and other drawings (**151**, **164**–**169** and **171**–**173**), a bequest of Alexander Murray Smith, 1943; formerly owned by Reginald J. Smith (see **133**), who acquired the desk at Sotheby's sale of the effects of Arthur Bell Nicholls, 26 July 1907 (lot 31).

*Brontë Parsonage Museum: C36*

Pattern for a rectangular purse: a single strip of paper folded in three, in the shape of a cross. The top section forms the flap which folds down and is fastened to the top of the bottom section which folds up; the central section forms the back of the purse; the sides would be sewn together. There are triple rules around all edges and an edging pattern around the edge of the flap.

171

## Wallpaper pattern of flowers

n.d.
Watercolour on paper
106 × 101 mm, irregular shape

Found in Charlotte Brontë's portable writing desk, together with a plait of Anne's hair and other drawings (**151**, **164–170** and **172**, **173**), a bequest of Alexander Murray Smith, 1943; formerly owned by Reginald J. Smith (see **133**), who acquired the desk at Sotheby's sale of the effects of Arthur Bell Nicholls, 26 July 1907 (lot 31).
*Brontë Parsonage Museum: C85*

Watercolour design of repeated bunches of a single blue and white flower with brown and green leaves against a 'fish-scale' patterned background of faint large blue and grey squares. Two of the edges have been roughly cut, suggesting that part of the pattern was sent elsewhere. There is no evidence, apart from its location, to suggest that this fragment was painted by Charlotte.

172

## Wallpaper pattern of leaves and cherries

n.d.
Watercolour print on paper
113 × 113 mm

Found in Charlotte Brontë's portable writing desk, together with a plait of Anne's hair and other drawings (**151**, **164–171** and **173**), a bequest of Alexander Murray Smith, 1943; formerly owned by Reginald J. Smith (see **133**), who acquired the desk at Sotheby's sale of the effects of Arthur Bell Nicholls, 26 July 1907 (lot 31).
*Brontë Parsonage Museum: C86*

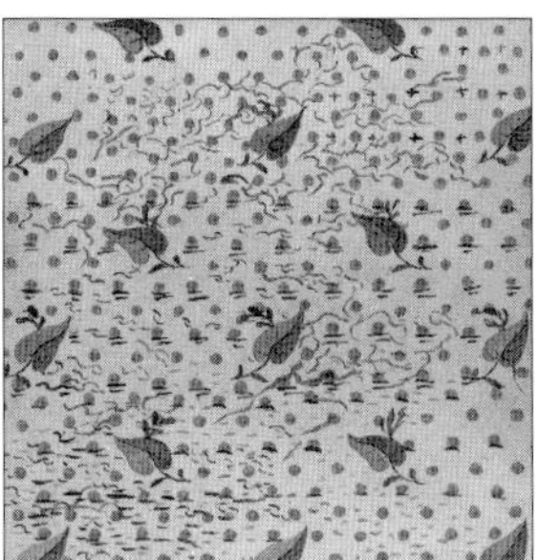

Watercolour design of repeated pointed grey/green leaves, red cherries and small grey/black markings against a buff-coloured background. There is no evidence, apart from its location, to suggest that this sample was the work of Charlotte. In fact, the sample is not hand-painted; it is printed by an early woodblock method for making wallpaper, which often looks very like watercolour painting. This may also be the case with the other two wallpaper samples (**171** and **173**), though so far this has proved impossible to verify.

173

## Wallpaper pattern of green sprigs with red flowers

n.d.
Watercolour on paper
113 × 113 mm

Found in Charlotte Brontë's portable writing desk, together with a plait of Anne's hair and other drawings (**151**, **164–172**), a bequest of Alexander Murray Smith, 1943; formerly owned by Reginald J. Smith (see **133**), who acquired the desk at Sotheby's sale of the effects of Arthur Bell Nicholls, 26 July 1907 (lot 31).
*Brontë Parsonage Museum: C87*

Watercolour design of repeated green sprig with a single red flower set against a background of vertical brown brush strokes. A rectangular sample has been cut from the bottom left corner, suggesting that part of the pattern was sent elsewhere. There is no evidence, apart from its location, to suggest that this sample was painted by Charlotte.

## Charlotte Brontë: Reattributions

**327** 'Flossy', now under Emily
**355** 'Unfinished Flossy 1', now under Anne
**356** 'Unfinished Flossy 2', now under Anne
**357** 'Portrait of a young woman in blue', now under Anne

# Charlotte Brontë: Dubious attributions

## Children with kitten and puppy

n.d.
Pencil on paper
254 × 203 mm

Inscribed bottom right corner, in non-Brontë hand: 'C.B.'.

Gift of William Firth, 1910; previously sold by Benjamin and Ann Binns (brother-in-law and sister of Martha Brown) at Binn sale, Saltaire, 27 January 1886, possibly lot 383, although the Binns family owned a variety of non-Brontë paintings and drawings. A letter (at back of BPM Stock Book), from William Firth to W. T. Field, secretary of the Bronte Society 1897–1920, records: 'I also send you by this post the ~~two~~ one sketches which I mentioned to you at the picnic. A M$^{r}$ Schutte gave them to me who said they were vouched for as genuine Brontë relics by the auctioneer at Saltaire who you will very likely know & who has signed them at the back of each; at any rate I send them to you to use your own judgement as to their worth & to do with them whatever you may think proper. They are not much value as works of art.' Field has added: 'N.B. 1 of these sketches was of no use so I put it amongst some loose papers in one of the showcases, unframed.'
*Brontë Parsonage Museum: C8*

The scene shows a boy lowering a kitten in a clog down a wall to a younger girl, who kneels with outstretched apron to catch the kitten; three children and a dog watching. This drawing is typical of the many crude outlines of children playing that appear in elementary drawing manuals of the period. They were intended to be copied as practice in perfecting outline but there is evidence that this particular one has been traced.

Although this drawing came from the Binns family who owned many genuine Brontë illustrations, the attribution of this item to Charlotte is dubious. The signature is not that of Charlotte, and the style, especially the shading and execution of the faces, is unlike her other work. Furthermore, the provenance as recorded above is shaky, to say the least; perhaps this item is the sketch that Field found 'of no use'.

## Landscape with trees, waterfall and figures

n.d.
Pencil on card, with surrounding embossed frame
165 × 126 mm

Inscribed in pencil, in non-Brontë hand, in margin below picture and outside embossed frame: 'Tabitha Tea-tray'.

Said to have been given to Sidney Biddell by Amelia Walker of Torquay (although this may be a confusion with another drawing: see **139**), and kept by him in his annotated edition of Elizabeth Gaskell's *The Life of Charlotte Brontë* (London: Smith, Elder & Co., 1876), now in the BPM: see Ivy Holgate, 'A Pilgrim at Haworth – 1879', *Brontë Society Transactions* (1961), vol. 14, part 71, pp. 33–4. The two items were probably acquired by the museum at the same time, as the gift of Thomas Talbot, 1961, who had been given the book by Sidney Biddell's widow.
*Brontë Parsonage Museum: C96*

View of wide river, centre distance, narrowing over a small waterfall into a stream in the foreground; two figures sitting on the right bank in the foreground: a male holding a staff with the left hand and pointing to the opposite bank with the right arm, a female seated behind; beyond the figures, in the distance, are three pillars of a classical ruin and faintly depicted hills; tall trees overhang the river on the left bank beyond the waterfall. Probably based on a copy of an engraving of an Italian peasant scene.

Although this drawing has been preserved in the Brontë canon for many years, there is nothing to indicate that it is a genuine Brontë work. The inscription appears to be irrelevant, although it could refer to Tabitha Aykroyd, the Brontë servant, and may be a design for a tea-tray, since prints were sometimes sold for this purpose. Alternatively, 'Tabitha Tea-tray' may have been an endearing nick-name for the faithful 'Tabby'. The figures, however, especially the faces, are different from those in other Brontë illustrations, and the technique (in particular the handling of the trees and foliage) is crude compared with the Brontës' detailed pencil work.

## Woman in a turban

n.d.
Pencil on paper
231 × 200 mm

Said to be one of eighteen drawings in a sketchbook of twenty sheets, interleaved with blue tissue and backed in mottled cardboard with leather corners.

Phyllis Bentley records, in 'A Charlotte Brontë Sketch Book' (*Brontë Society Transactions* (1948), vol. 11, part 58, pp. 164–5), that this drawing is in a sketchbook in the possession of Dora Farrar of Halifax, whose father, Joseph Farrar, bought it at the sale of Ellen Nussey's effects, 18–19 May 1898: see below. Family tradition attributed the sketchbook to Charlotte Brontë. There is no other record of Joseph Farrar's purchase, but a 'Mr Farrar, of Halifax' is recorded as having paid the highest price at the Nussey sale (£30) for a pearl necklace, earrings and brooch which apparently cost Ellen Nussey £100 (*The Bradford Observer*, 19 May 1898). Winifred Gérin credits the Brontë Parsonage Museum for permission to publish the illustration in *Five Novelettes* (London: The Folio Press, 1971), but she probably only acquired copies of photographs, since the sketchbook was never at the museum.

*Location unknown*

Half-length portrait of a young woman, dressed in a low-necked velvet evening gown and elaborate turban. The figure faces right, while the head is turned to the left, looking over the right shoulder. Her face, neck and body are plump, without the usual delicate features of Charlotte Brontë's other portraits; but she is evocative of Charlotte's heroine Julia Wellesley, as Winifred Gérin suggests in *Five Novelettes*, opp. p. 97. Julia is frequently described in rich velvet robes, jewels and a white ostrich feather. Zenobia Ellrington, too, dresses in velvet robes, plumes and a 'crown-like turban': see 'A Peep Into A Picture Book', 30 May 1834 (*An Edition of the Early Writings of Charlotte Brontë*, ed. Christine Alexander, vol. 2, part 2 (Oxford: Basil Blackwell for the Shakespeare Head Press, 1991), p. 88).

The turban in this portrait has a large pearl aigrette in the centre surmounted by an equally large white ostrich feather. A veil is draped over the turban and falls behind the figure, partly obscuring the dark shoulder-length curly hair. The dress has a beaded neckline, belt (with buckle) and edge of sleeves which are gathered up at the shoulder showing the top of the right arm.

The drawing is undoubtedly a copy of an engraving from one of the fashionable magazines or Annuals of the day. Francis Wall, a West Riding artist and specialist on the Brontë paintings, apparently told Phyllis Bentley that some of the illustrations in this sketchbook were adaptations of well-known pictures or portraits: 'For example, there is a vigorous rendering of Hayter's drawing of Leigh Hunt' (p. 165).

The attribution, however, must remain questionable. The catalogue for the Nussey sale (1898), referred to above, lists 'Album of choice Sketches' (lots 186 and 187), but there is no mention that the contents are by the Brontës. Phyllis Bentley, who knew Charlotte's hand well, says that the words 'Lord Byron' and 'the first End', which appear on two of the empty pages of the sketchbook, are very like Charlotte's angular writing; and she says that Francis Wall 'considered the attribution of the drawings to the hand of Charlotte legitimate, from internal evidence as well as external probability' (p. 165).

If the drawing is by Charlotte, then the style is very different from her other pencil portraits of women, such as 'English Lady' (**128**). There is a solidity about the turbaned lady and her counterparts in this sketchbook that is absent elsewhere. Moreover, the heavy pencil outline so obvious here (note the sleeve on the left of the picture) is only seen in sketches where she is hastily creating an impression and not a finished portrait, such as in **97**.

## Woman with a rose

n.d.
Pencil on paper
231 × 200 mm

Recorded by Phyllis Bentley in 'A Charlotte Brontë Sketch Book' (*Brontë Society Transactions* (1948), vol. 11, part 58, pp. 164–5): see previous entry.
*Location unknown*

Three-quarter-length portrait of a young woman, dressed in an elaborate evening gown, with a rose at the base of a low neckline, and wearing a head-dress with roses and ribbons. The figure faces the front but the head is turned towards the right. She has the same plump face, neck and arms as the other portrait known to have come from this sketchbook: see 'Woman in a turban'. She wears a long glove on her left hand (which may actually be holding the rose at her neckline, it is difficult to tell). The hand is awkwardly drawn and the body seems too large for the head, mistakes not uncommon in Charlotte's drawing.

It is difficult to agree with Winifred Gérin's suggestion (in *Five Novelettes* (London: The Folio Press, 1971) opp. p. 160) that this drawing is evocative of Charlotte Brontë's heroine Zenobia Ellrington (see **100**). Zenobia is invariably described as having an imposing stature, dark velvet robes and raven hair dressed with plumes or turban: see 'A Peep Into A Picture Book', 30 May 1834 (*An Edition of the Early Writings of Charlotte Brontë*, ed. Christine Alexander, vol. 2, part 2 (Oxford: Basil Blackwell for the Shakespeare Head Press, 1991), p. 88); whereas the subject of this portrait appears to be fair, has a shy, retiring look, and is dressed in a light material with fussy decorations, and the head-dress of a very young woman. The curls and ringlets around her face are not those of 'the prima donna of the Angrian Court'.

The drawing is probably a copy of an engraving from one of the fashionable magazines or Annuals of the day; but whether it is a genuine Brontë production is debatable. Francis Wall apparently told Phyllis Bentley that this drawing of the girl with a rose in her hair was 'almost certainly done by Charlotte – the handling of the neck particularly seemed to him decisive on this point' (p. 165). It is true that her portraits of 1835 tend to support this judgement, but other factors militate strongly against it: see the argument at the end of the previous entry, which applies to all three portraits in this sketchbook, executed by the same hand.

## Woman with a scarf

n.d

Pencil on paper

231 × 200 mm

Recorded by Phyllis Bentley in 'A Charlotte Brontë Sketch Book' (*Brontë Society Transactions* (1948), vol. 11, part 58, pp. 164–5): see above entries.

*Location unknown*

Three-quarter-length portrait of a young woman, dressed in a simple high-waisted gown, her dark hair piled up on top and secured with a long thin scarf which is then tied around the throat and hangs down over the right shoulder. The head is bent down to the left and the shoulders are slightly stooped; finely chiselled features, straight nose, pointed chin; the eyes look down and the mouth has a faint smile. The gown has a plunging neckline and small lace collar; a shawl is draped over the shoulders, its folds blending with the length of the scarf.

The drawing, like 'Woman in a turban' and 'Woman with a rose', is probably a copy of an engraving from one of the fashionable magazines or Annuals. All three have been executed by the same hand and are equally dubious in their attribution to Charlotte: see previous two entries.

## Leigh Hunt

n.d.

Pencil on paper

231 × 200 mm

In a sketchbook, as described in 'Woman in a turban' above.

Recorded in Phyllis Bently, 'A Charlotte Brontë Sketch Book' (*Brontë Society Transactions* (1948), vol. 11, part 58, pp. 164–5): see notes for above entries.

*Location unknown*

Said to be a copy of Hayter's drawing of Leigh Hunt, engraved by H. Meyer for Leigh Hunt, *Lord Byron and Some of His Contemporaries: With Recollections of the Author's life and of His Visit to Italy* (London: H. Colburn, 1828). Knowledge of this item is based on the judgement of Francis Wall, a West Riding artist, who took an interest in the Brontë paintings and who apparently told Phyllis Bentley that some of the illustrations in this sketchbook were adaptations of well-known pictures or portraits: 'For example, there is a vigorous rendering of Hayter's drawing of Leigh Hunt' (p. 165).

It would not be surprising to find such a copy made by Charlotte; she would have read of Hunt, followed his relationship with Byron and seen his portrait in such periodicals as *Fraser's Magazine*. Branwell, too, thought highly of Leigh Hunt and apparently sent him a poem entitled 'Brontë', illustrating the life of Nelson, for critical judgement (F. H. Grundy, *Pictures of the Past: Memories of Men I have met, and Places I have seen* (London: Griffith & Farran, 1879), p. 79).

However, since we have no copy of Charlotte's drawing to examine and since Wall's judgement on the other items in the same sketchbook has been called into question (see 'Woman in a turban' above), we must remain sceptical about whether Charlotte copied Meyer's engraving (seen above).

## 'Warwick Castle'

n.d.
Pencil on card
152 × 202 mm

Titled in pencil, in copperplate hand, in centre below drawing: 'Warwick Castle'. On verso: inscribed in pencil in unknown hand, along the top: 'Bought at Miss Ellen Nusseys sale at Moor lane / House Gomersal May 1898 amongst a bundle of / manuscripts & sketches – This drawing is probably by / Charlotte Brontë'; bottom left corner: 'C'; bottom right corner: illegible scribble. Previously owned by Ellen Nussey and sold at the sale of her effects, 18–19 May 1898. The drawing was subsequently owned by John Alexander Symington, who was the librarian of Lord Brotherton's collection of rare books and manuscripts, including Brontëana. He seems to have acquired some Brontë items himself while working for Lord Brotherton possibly through Thomas James Wise, who numbered Brotherton among his clients. Symington also worked with Wise as editor of the Shakespeare Head Brontë, which would have provided ample opportunity for the acquisition of Brontë manuscripts.

*Private owner*

Picturesque scene of the famous view of Warwick Castle seen from the bridge: six figures promenading on the bridge in the foreground (from left to right: young woman with dog, a man and woman chatting, an officer leaning on the balustrade admiring the view, and a woman and boy in bottom right corner); tall trees frame the picture on the left behind the bridge; the river is glimpsed in the centre with the castle rising impressively behind and extending to the right of the picture above some more trees on the right river bank. There are two large towers on the right of the castle rising above the trees (the right one with a flag flying). The format is in the shape of a vignette, similar to many of Charlotte's drawings such as **81**.

The scene is typical of Charlotte's many copies of engravings of famous sites in Britain, such as 'Conway Castle' (**65**) and 'Greta Bridge' (**63**). The style, too, especially the handling of the trees and foreground, is similar to her early landscape copies made as a pupil at Roe Head; but the heavy monochromatic sky suggests that the work may not be that of Charlotte. The copperplate writing is also unusual, although there are similar examples in Charlotte's hand (such as **61**); most young women learnt to produce this hand at school.

A number of items bought at the sale of Ellen Nussey's effects have been erroneously attributed to the Brontës in the past. It seems much more likely that this particular sketch was by Ellen Nussey herself, or by one of Charlotte Brontë's other contemporaries at Roe Head.

## Street scene with two women

n.d.
Sepia on paper
159 × 236 mm

Signed bottom right, 'C. Brontë' (dubious signature). Gift of Frances Watson Sunderland, 1928. Mrs Sunderland was a well-known Keighley artist who ran her own art school for fifty years. She knew Dr John Jeremy Brigg, son of Sir John Brigg, MP and like his father a founder member of the Brontë Society, who donated one of her watercolours of Top Withins to the BPM in 1935.

*Brontë Parsonage Museum: C4*

The scene shows two young women walking along a road towards the viewer; gabled and half-timbered houses on right, gardens on left, hills in distance. Brush strokes in the margin show experimentation with the range of ink tone available for the work.

The style is unusual for Charlotte, but this alone is no reason for rejection from the Brontë canon. The uncertain signature, however, means that this work must remain 'dubious'. It is a fairly mature work and suggests a later date, possibly when Charlotte was experimenting with different media. Here a brush, rather than a nib, has been used to apply the brown-toned sepia, which had become a popular drawing medium in the early nineteenth century. Charlotte had used this method before (see **122–124**), but with less success than is evident in this picture, which again makes attribution doubtful.

## 'Marianne'

n.d.
Pencil on paper
405 × 255 mm

It was not possible to trace the original. The title 'Marianne' is clearly visible below the portrait on the photograph available to the authors, but the signature and date immediately beneath the shoulder on the left are indistinct: '[?1834]'. None of the writing resembles Charlotte Brontë's hand.

Said to have been given by Charlotte Brontë to a cousin of Edward Sunderland, who presented it to him when he left England. Family tradition attributed the drawing to Branwell (letter from Edward Sunderland to Butler Wood, Librarian, Bradford, 26 August 1907; letter in BPM). In a further letter (dated 16 September 1907), Sunderland states: 'The picture undoubtedly came straight from Charlotte Brontë's hands into the possession of my relative and on that account is valued accordingly by me.' The BPM do not appear to have received their copy of the drawing until 1940, since a note with the copy records 'from Mrs Wroot. June 15. 1940–/ "Rec. 22 April 1933 – / Copy of a drawing in the possession of/ Edward Sunderland of 1353 Pandora / Avenue, Victoria – B. Columbia – / It was given by Charlotte Bronte to a / woman named Hey of Scartops, who/ said it was the work of Branwell / her brother."' The photo is in an album of postcards formerly belonging to Mrs Wroot.

*Location unknown*

Head-and-shoulders portrait of a young woman in a straw hat with a spray of flowers in her hair over her right ear. Her features are large, widely spaced almond eyes, large straight nose, small full mouth, and wide neck. The large collar of a coat or jacket with a draped scarf surrounds her neck.

The drawing bears no resemblance to any of Branwell's work, but may possibly be by Charlotte. The handling of the eyes and mouth with its small full lips is similar to those in several of her portraits, but the fine cross-hatching and the non-Brontë hand make any attribution to Charlotte dubious.

## Church and trees

n.d.
Watercolour on paper; gum arabic glaze
118 × 187 mm

Inscribed in pencil on verso: 'M$^{rs}$ Popplewell' (probably Eliza Popplewell, sister of Martha Brown). The BPM card index by Dr Mildred Christian (see **34**) records an inscription on upper right corner of original cardboard backing: 'From the Brontë collection of Martha Brown / W L' (possibly William Law, the original owner of the Law Collection).
Purchased at Hodgson & Co. sale, London, 31 March 1933 (part of lot 449); formerly in the collection of Sir Alfred J. Law, Honresfeld (see **15**). The inscription suggests that the painting passed from the Brontë servant Martha Brown, after her death, to her sister Eliza, who at one time also worked at the Brontë Parsonage.
*Brontë Parsonage Museum: C71*

Unfinished scene of a gate in the centre foreground, a hedge and two trees on either side, a path leading up to a church in the centre middle-distance, scattered gravestones on the grass in front of the church, and blocked-in trees behind and at the sides of the painting. The stone church has buttresses, sloping grey slate roof, arched windows and central door above which rises a square buttressed tower surmounted by a flagpole.

The two large trees are unfinished but show clearly the technique of blocking in a shape in light watercolour, then highlighting branches and trunk with a fine brush and darker shade. The foliage is suggested by diagonal lines and blocks of varying shades of brown and green. The whole painting shows a freer use of line than that usually exhibited by Charlotte, so much so that one must question its attribution. However, its unfinished state, the fact that it may have been painted 'from nature', and the usual reliability of items originating from Martha Brown make it impossible to say conclusively that it is not by Charlotte.

## 'Cottages opposite the Bank of Bolwell House'

30 April 1844
Pencil on paper
118 × 140 mm

Titled and dated in longhand, beneath illustration: 'Cottages opposite the Bank of Bolwell House / April 30$^{th}$'; the date is above the word 'House', on the right of the picture. There is no signature on this drawing, but the hand is almost identical to that of Charlotte, except for the unusual 'tt', the clumsy 'H' and the joining of words. It also appears to be the same hand as 'Cottage in Wallasley' and 'Cottage in lane near Mr Armstrong's' below (again except for the 'tt' of 'cottage'). The remains of glue are evident on the back, suggesting that the drawing was previously mounted or stuck into an album.

One of five small pencil drawings (three are listed immediately below and the other is **162**) formerly in the possession of John Alexander Symington and sold by Christie's, 18 December 1964, lot 59. They are described in Christie's sale catalogue as 'Five small pencil drawings of houses (3), a rustic summer house and a rustic bridge over a stream with trees .... There are pencil captions on the drawings and one of these "Cottages near Wallasley" [*sic*] appears to be in Charlotte's hand. Included are 5 photographic reproductions of drawings by the Brontës' (p. 16). Earlier provenance may be associated with Arthur Bell Nicholls, since four of the five photos (**116**, **137**, **343** and **346**, not **137a**) were reproduced 'by kind permission of Mr. Clement K. Shorter' in *The Bookman*, October 1904 (opposite p. 31), while the originals were still in the possession of Arthur Bell Nicholls.

*Private collection*

View of a house and two small adjoining cottages nearby, situated on a grassy incline with trees behind. A path leads from the foreground to the door of the house.

The sketch appears to have been made from life, but no record has been found so far of Bolwell House. Charlotte's drawing 'The Summer House on the lawn of Bolwell House' (**162**) was executed at the same place seven days before, on 23 April 1844. It is possible that both these drawings (and the following three entries) were made by her; however 'Cottages opposite the Bank of Bolwell House' (and the following three entries) seem bolder in style and more crude than Charlotte's other productions for this date. There are also minor variations in the script of the title compared to other examples of her hand at this time, which make attribution uncertain.

All five drawings (including **162**) were produced about the same time, possibly while Charlotte was staying at Hunsworth with Mary Taylor and her brothers in late April / early May 1844. It is possible that Charlotte may have made one sketch herself (**162**) and been given the others by the Taylors, which she may have inscribed, so accounting for the heavier style of the drawing and the close resemblance of the script to her own.

## 'Cottage in Wallasley'

c. 30 April 1844
Pencil on paper
100 × 144 mm

Titled in longhand, beneath illustration: 'Cottage in Wallasley'. There is no signature on this drawing, but the hand is almost identical to that of Charlotte (except for the 'tt'). The date is based on 'Cottages opposite the Bank of Bolwell House / April 30$^{th}$' above, which appears to be titled by the same hand. Part of the watermark 'J. WHATMAN' shows clearly through the right side of the paper. Charlotte was still using paper with this mark until August 1845 (**163**); and Margaret Smith has pointed out that Charlotte also used it for the joint letter with Mary and Martha Taylor of March / April 1842, from Brussels, suggesting that the drawings might have a Taylor connection. The remains of glue are evident on the back, indicating that the drawing was previously mounted or stuck into an album.

For further provenance see 'Cottages opposite the Bank of Bolwell House' above.

*Private collection*

Cottage, or possibly two cottages adjoining, with another one visible behind on the right. The cottage has a double high-pitched roof, surmounted by two chimneys. There is an entrance on the left through a side porch, and another door on the right, with a tree close by in front; a stone wall on the left and a picket fence on the right.

According to James Alexander Symington (see 'Cottages opposite the Bank of Bolwell House' above), this drawing is in Charlotte's hand, but the differences detailed in 'Cottages opposite the Bank of Bolwell House' make this uncertain.

## 'Cottage in lane near Mr Armstrong's'

c. 30 April 1844
Pencil on paper
83 × 121 mm

Titled in longhand, beneath illustration: 'Cottage in lane near M^r Armstrong's'. There is no signature on this drawing, but the hand is almost identical to that of Charlotte, except for the unusual 'tt' and the flattened appearance of the writing. The date is based on 'Cottages opposite the Bank of Bolwell House / April 30th' above, which appears to be titled by the same hand. Part of the watermark is visible: '[WHA]TMAN / MILL / 5'. The remains of glue are evident on the back, suggesting that the drawing was previously mounted or stuck into an album.

For provenance see 'Cottages opposite the Bank of Bolwell House' above.

*Private collection*

A cottage sketched from life, with a tiled roof, a lattice fence and hedge in front, creepers around the walls and windows and a small tree on the left. The style is rather heavy and crude, and the artist has had obvious difficulties with perspective. For a discussion of attribution see 'Cottages opposite the Bank of Bolwell House' above.

## 'Bridge near Wrottle'

c. 30 April 1844
Pencil on paper
116 × 122 mm

Inscribed beneath illustration: 'Bridge near Wrottle'. There is no signature on this drawing, but the hand is almost identical to that of Charlotte, especially the 'B', 'd' and 'g' of 'Bridge'; but the 'tt' and 'W' of 'Wrottle' are unlike her normal style. The date is based on 'Cottages opposite the Bank of Bolwell House / April 30th' above, which appears to be drawn and titled by the same hand. The remains of glue are evident on the back, suggesting that the drawing was previously mounted or stuck into an album.

For provenance see 'Cottages opposite the Bank of Bolwell House' above.

*Private collection*

This is a particularly crude landscape, unusual for someone with Charlotte Brontë's experience for this date. The artist has evidently had difficulties with the perspective of the bridge and it is not clear whether there is only one small stream or whether this is a tributary of a larger river in the background, beyond which there are trees on the far bank. There are two trees in the foreground, and hasty pencil strokes suggesting tufts of grass. Further discussion of attribution can be found in the three entries above.

## Portrait of a man (Mr Brocklehurst?)

n.d.
Pencil on paper
228 × 187 mm

Stamped embossed watermark, bottom right corner: (illegible oval pictorial mark). Drawing appears to have been folded at some time, the folds making nine sections.

Purchased from Gladys Jane Brown of Ramsgill, 1950; withdrawn from Sotheby's 1898 sale of Brown collection of Brontë relics, lot 6. For possible earlier provenance see **29**.

*Brontë Parsonage Museum: C65*

Head-and-shoulders portrait of a middle-aged man: receding hair, high forehead, forthright solemn expression, crease between eyebrows, large dark eyes, wide jaw; dressed in white cravat, dark waistcoat and embroidered smoking jacket (only the high collar is clearly outlined).

In 1894, W. W. Yates commented that some people profess to discover not only the likeness of Mr Brocklehurst (from *Jane Eyre*) in this portrait but also that of the conquerer of Waterloo; he himself admits that it is not typical of Charlotte's amateur productions and, like the best of her drawings, it may show the hand of the teacher upon it ('Some Relics of the Brontës', *The New Review*, no. 59, April 1894, p. 483).

The drawing was acquired with many other items originally collected by Robinson and Francis Brown. Apart from this attribution, however, there is no evidence to suggest that it is by Charlotte or any other member of the Brontë family. Nor is the style of this drawing similar to other authenticated Brontë illustrations from this same source.

## Sketch of Mr Nicholls

n.d.
Pencil on ordinary writing paper
115 × 105 mm

The drawing is enclosed in an envelope inscribed: '~~Three~~ one pencil sketches / by Charlotte Brontë, Signed. / & / 1 sketch of Mr Nicholls, / when he first went to Haworth'. The first sketch refers to Charlotte's portrait of 'Lady Jephia Bud': see **25**.

Part of the Henry Houston Bonnell Brontë Collection, given by Helen Safford Bonnell in 1963, in memory of her husband, who died in 1926. Aquired by Bonnell from Violet M. Bolster, née Bell, niece and executrix of Arthur Bell Nicholls.

*Pierpont Morgan Library: Bonnell Collection MA 2696*

Half-length sketch of a man facing left: three-quarter view of face, eyes looking slightly down, rounded features, bushy side whiskers and slightly receding hair, bow-tie at neck, high-collared coat with wide lapels (probably a frock-coat).

The portrait bears some resemblance to other images of Charlotte's husband, Arthur Bell Nicholls, and the provenance suggests a possible Brontë attribution; but the style is not typical of Charlotte.

# Branwell Brontë

174

## 'Battell of W[a]shington'

12 March 1827
Pencil and watercolour on paper
55 × 65 mm

The drawing occupies the whole of p. 2 of a hand-sewn 'little book' of eight pages in a blue paper cover, inscribed in pencil in Branwell's longhand on the inside front cover: 'Battell / Book / P B Bronte / March 12 / 1827–'. The drawing itself is titled in pencil in Branwell's minuscule hand, along the top: 'Battell of Wshington'. Stamped: 'BRONTË / MUSEUM / HAWORTH', encircled.

Purchased in London, 1899, from H. E. Gorfin, an agent of Thomas James Wise (see **89**).
*Brontë Parsonage Museum: BS 110*

Three soldiers in red with blue peaked hats, carrying muskets, stand on left and a faintly sketched flagbearer stands behind them. In the centre there is a soldier on horseback. Four soldiers, two of them in yellow, one with a musket, one a flagbearer, the other preparing to fire a cannon in the bottom right-hand corner. In the foreground a soldier in blue and the body of a dead soldier.

One of the earliest little books by the Brontë children to survive, this one has a blue paper cover cut from a sugar bag and four leaves (eight pages), hand-sewn together. It contains five drawings of battle scenes, castles and a map of America.

175

## Map of North and South America

12 March 1827
Pencil and watercolour on paper
55 × 65 mm

The drawing occupies the whole of p. 3 of a hand-sewn 'little book' of eight pages in a blue paper cover, inscribed in pencil, in Branwell's longhand on the inside front cover: 'Battell / Book / P B Bronte / March 12 / 1827–'.

Purchased in London, 1899, from H. E. Gorfin, an agent of Thomas James Wise (see **89**).
*Brontë Parsonage Museum: BS 110*

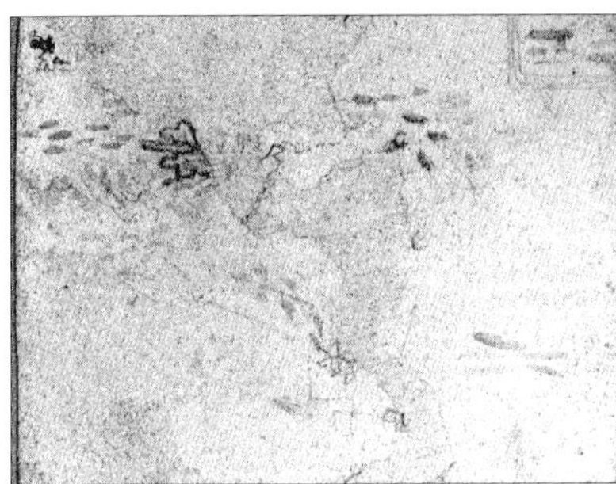

This drawing of a map of North and South America faces the drawing of the Battle of Washington. See **174**.

176

## Battle scene

12 March 1827
Pencil and watercolour on paper
55 × 65 mm

The drawing occupies the whole of p. 4 of a hand-sewn 'little book' of eight pages in a blue paper cover, inscribed in pencil, in Branwell's longhand on the inside front cover: 'Battell / Book / P B Bronte / March 12 / 1827–'. Stamped: 'BRONTË / MUSEUM / HAWORTH', encircled.

Purchased in London, 1899, from H. E. Gorfin, an agent of Thomas James Wise (see **89**).
*Brontë Parsonage Museum: BS110*

Soldiers in red with blue hats to the left, one on horseback bearing a flag, charge towards soldiers in blue on the right, one of whom is operating a cannon. Flagbearers and other soldiers with muskets follow behind the soldiers on the left, the leading flagbearer playing a trumpet. In the middle of the picture a soldier in blue, having been shot, falls to the ground which is strewn with corpses. See **174**.

## 177

## 'Bandy Castle'

12 March 1827
Pencil and watercolour on paper
55 × 65 mm

The drawing occupies the whole of p. 5 of a handsewn 'little book' of eight pages in a blue paper cover, inscribed in pencil, in Branwell's longhand on the inside front cover: 'Battell / Book / P B Bronte / March 12 / 1827–'. The drawing itself is titled in pencil in Branwell's longhand, below: 'Bandy Castle'.
Purchased in London, 1899, from H. E. Gorfin, an agent of Thomas James Wise (see **89**).
*Brontë Parsonage Museum: BS110*

Castle with arched door and two windows, a blue flag flying from the turret. On the left a larger building with two smaller buildings on the right, also with windows. The whole is surrounded by water. See **174**.

## 178

## Castle

12 March 1827
Pencil and watercolour on paper
55 × 65 mm

The drawing occupies the whole of p. 7 of a handsewn 'little book' of eight pages in a blue paper cover, inscribed in pencil, in Branwell's longhand on the inside front cover: 'Battell / Book / P B Bronte / March 12 / 1827–'.

Purchased in London, 1899, from H. E. Gorfin, an agent of Thomas James Wise (see **89**).
*Brontë Parsonage Museum: BS110*

Castle with blue arched door, a large blue flag flying from the turret, with a bridge joined to its left side which straddles a river or moat flowing past the castle. To the right, another castle-type building. See **174**.

## 179

### Pencil sketches of figures

12 March 1827
Pencil on paper
65 × 55 mm

The sketches occupy p. 8 of a hand-sewn 'little book' of eight pages in a blue paper cover, inscribed in pencil, in Branwell's longhand on the inside front cover: 'Battell / Book / P B Bronte / March 12 / 1827–'. The page is inscribed in pencil in Branwell's longhand, top left: 'Sneaky'; bottom, upside down: '~~Sn~~ Sneaky / was after-wards / Sneaky was / was afterw– / ward'. Stamped: 'BRONTË / MUSEUM / HAWORTH', encircled.

Purchased in London, 1899, from H. E. Gorfin, an agent of Thomas James Wise (see **89**).

*Brontë Parsonage Museum: BS110*

Faint doodles of figures. See **174**.

## 180

### A sleeping cat

January 1828
Pencil on paper
192 × 243 mm

Signed and dated in pencil, below drawing, right: 'P–B–Jan$^{y}$ 1828–'.

Bequest of J. Roy Coventry, Guernsey, 1955; together with **312**, **317**, **318**, **323**, **332** and **333**. Acquired by the donor from Tabitha Ratcliffe, younger sister of Martha Brown, 5 August 1907.

*Brontë Parsonage Museum: B1*

Profile view of a sleeping cat, facing right, with its front paws tucked into its chest and its tail curled neatly round the visible side of its body. Details such as its short stripy fur, its tightly shut eyes, its whiskers and the collar around its neck are clearly visible. The cat appears to doze either on a mat or on a stone-flagged floor.

A very similar image of a striped cat, with a dead bird, appears in Bewick (*A History of British Birds*, vol. 1: *Containing the History and Description of Land Birds* (Newcastle: T. Bewick; London: Longman & Co., 1816), p. 200) as a tail-piece to the entry on 'The Woodlark'. It is not, however, an identical copy, but the Bewick wood engraving may have given Branwell the idea to make this drawing of a cat from life. Branwell's drawing is unusually large in scale when compared to other drawings made at this early date.

## 181

### Farmyard scene with dog and chickens

28 July 1828
Pencil on paper
107 × 124 mm

Signed and dated in pencil, in minuscule hand, at top: '– ~~B~~ Patrick Branwell Brontë Aged 11 years – / [double rule]'; immediately below drawing, left corner: 'T Bewick'; right corner: 'P B Bronte'; centre: 'P B Bronté/–July–/28/[rule]/1828'.

Purchased from Sotheby's, London, 16 December 1980, lot 273; previously owned by Mrs N. W. Mallinson, a descendant of the Heaton family of Haworth; also acquired from Sotheby's in the same lot, a photograph of another Branwell copy from a Bewick engraving (see **192**).
*Brontë Parsonage Museum: B2.5*

In the left foreground a group of chickens peck at their food from a round dish beside a stone water trough. In the centre the furious mother hen, her tail feathers lifted, darts at the dog on the right, which snarls and cowers at the same time. In the background are two farm buildings and two haystacks enclosed by a wicket fence. An upturned cart is propped against the fence and beyond the farm a group of trees can be seen.

The wood engravings of Thomas Bewick were much admired by the Brontës and all four of them made copies from his illustrated book, *A History of British Birds*; this scene is found in vol. 1: *Containing the History and Description of Land Birds* (Newcastle: T. Bewick; London: Longman & Co., 1816), p. 284. The Brontëana collector William Law describes in a letter of 1894 to J. Horsfall Turner, Honorary Corresponding Secretary of the Brontë Society, how 'Some years ago I bought the two vols of Bewick's Birds from him [A. B. Nicholls] –The Brontë copy with Mr Brontë's notes'.

## 182

### Tiny sketch of a fort 1

September 1828
Ink on paper
20 × 50 mm

The sketch appears at the foot of the first page (120 × 111 mm) of a hand-sewn manuscript volume of twelve pages, inscribed in ink by Branwell, on grey paper cover: 'HISTORY OF THE/ REBELLION/ IN = =/ MY FELLOWS/ 1828'. The text of the manuscript begins: 'Chap 1 – Beginning from Sept. 1 to 5/ A number of Goodmans Forces ...'.

Purchased in London, 1899, from H. E. Gorfin, an agent of Thomas James Wise.
*Brontë Parsonage Museum: BS 112*

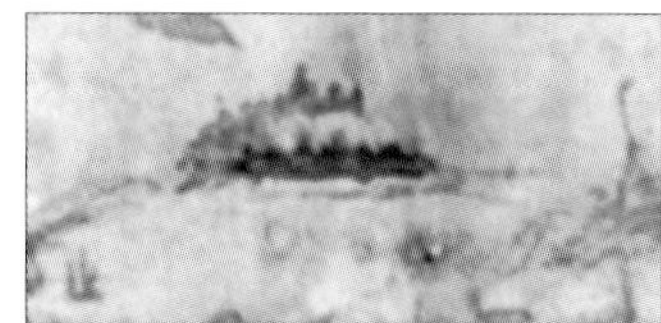

Tiny ink sketch of a fortified building standing on a mound, with smaller buildings in the foreground.

## 183

### Tiny sketch of a fort 2

September 1828
Ink on paper
15 × 30 mm

The sketch appears at the foot of the last page (120 × 111 mm) of a hand-sewn manuscript volume of twelve pages, inscribed in ink by Branwell, on grey paper cover: 'HISTORY OF THE/ REBELLION/ IN = =/ MY FELLOWS/ 1828'. The text of the manuscript begins: 'Chap 1 – Beginning from Sept. 1 to 5/ A number of Goodmans Forces ...'.

Purchased in London, 1899, from H. E. Gorfin, an agent of Thomas James Wise.

*Brontë Parsonage Museum: BS 112*

Tiny ink sketch of a fortified building standing on a hill, with smaller buildings arranged in ragged lines in the foreground. The word 'FINES' is inscribed in Branwell's hand beside the sketch.

## 184

## Ruined tower

17 November 1828

Pencil on paper

68 × 100 mm

Signed and dated in pencil, in minuscule hand, bottom centre: 'For Anne Brontë / PBB – Nov 17 – 1828 / [rule]'. Gift of Margaret Illingworth, 1910, together with **9**, **10**, **11**, **12**, **19**, **80**, **81**, **155**, **185**, **188**, **189**, **197** and **334**. A note written in Patrick Brontë's hand and acquired from the Brown sale by the Brontë Society may have originally accompanied this group of drawings: see **9**.

*Brontë Parsonage Museum: B3*

Ruined stone tower with an arched doorway and three slit windows stands on a grassy mound. Vegetation grows out of the broken stonework around its top. An isolated tree grows to the right of the tower and a group of trees behind. In the distance the top of a square tower, possibly a church, can be seen.

Buildings generally, and ruined buildings in particular, had an especial fascination for Branwell, an interest which derived from the accessibility of the prints based on picturesque landscapes of the eighteenth century found in the popular illustrated Annuals and other books devoured by the young Brontës. This particular drawing is generically similar to the numerous ruins to be found in the tail-pieces in Bewick's *A History of British Birds* (Newscastle: T. Bewick; London: Longman & Co., 1816).

Many of the marginal and inter-textual sketches found in Branwell's manuscripts are of ruins such as this one, made for his sister Anne (see p. 37). A very early example of this can be found in the drawing of Bandy Castle in Branwell's 'little book' of 12 March 1827 (**177**).

## 185

## Ruined tower, faces and female figure

c. 17 November 1828

Pencil on paper

68 × 100 mm

Gift of Margaret Illingworth, 1910: see **184**.

*Brontë Parsonage Museum: B3v*

Line drawing of a round ruined tower with three windows and an arched doorway; beside it a similar, smaller, square building with a door and one window. In the foreground there are lines depicting the tops of further towers. To the left of the round tower a swan and to the right two faces. On the far right, a full-length figure of a lady holding a small purse and dressed in a high-waisted gown with short puffed sleeves and a frilled neckline. The top of her head is cropped by the edge of the paper. The female figure may be Charlotte's handiwork. It would appear from the cropping of these sketches that the drawing on the recto was cut out of a larger piece of paper that was already covered with drawings on both sides.

## 186

### Tiny sketch of kairail fish

January 1829
Pencil on paper
10 × 25 mm

The sketch occupies only about a quarter of the first manuscript page (54 × 35 mm) of Branwell's tiny hand-sewn booklet of eight pages, titled 'Magazine / January 1829 / [rule]'. The cover of this volume, Branwell's first magazine for 1829, is made from an advertisement for books by John Wesley.

Formerly in the possession of Amy Lowell and given with the remainder of her collection to the Houghton Library c. 1925.
*Houghton Library, Harvard University: MS Lowell 1 (8)*

This faint drawing of a long thin fish with pointed snout like a swordfish and sharp scales illustrates the first article in Branwell's little magazine. The article is titled 'Natural History / O Deay / – Kairail – / – Fish –' and the drawing appears after the following lines: 'This Fish is generaly / found from 80 to 100 feet / Long. it [h]as large scales / The back blue belly & / sides white spoted with / Red Fines yellow – /'. He then continues with a description of its 'skin and horn', the latter being a gold transparent colour and used for ornament and in chemistry. When caught, the fish is never killed – only skinned and dehorned! This article is typical of Branwell's early contributions to the 'Young Men's Magazine': see Christine Alexander, *The Early Writings of Charlotte Brontë* (Oxford: Basil Blackwell, 1983), pp. 36–9.

## 187

### 'Mon and Wamon'

January 1829
Pencil and watercolour on paper
54 × 35 mm

The sketch occupies most of the space of the final page in the eight-page manuscript volume, titled on the cover in Branwell's minuscule hand 'Magazine / January 1829 / [rule]'.
For provenance see **186**.
*Houghton Library, Harvard University MS Lowell 1 (8)*

The figures in the sketch appear to be dressed as in a description written by Charlotte in 'The Foundling', 31 May–27 June, 1833 (Christine Alexander, *The Early Writings of Charlotte Brontë* (Oxford: Basil Blackwell, 1983), p. 95): 'black three cornered hats, blue coats, red waistcoats, ornamented with large white buttons, black breeches, white stockings, and one great round wooden shoe on which they shuffled about with great rapidity. The women wore blue gowns, red jackets, white aprons and little white caps without border or any other decoration other than a narrow red ribbon. Their shoes were similar in construction to the men's.' There are some slight differences in the actual sketch: the figures do not have large white buttons on their jackets and they have white rather than black breeches. They stand on an island and the man holds a staff. Between the man and woman is a dog. To the left of the woman is an oversized man, with the word 'KLUKE' printed on his hat or head, stepping towards the couple.

In the final article of 'Magazine January 1829', titled 'Travels N° 1 / Preparations set out for – / ~~Stumps island~~ Mons & W–s / Island maners – / Laws –', Branwell writes 'Some Dim Mountains were/ seen it was KLUKS -/ Moantin - in Mons and -/ Wamons wich they think/ the highst mountain in -/ the world and which is the/ highst in thier I islands -.' He then describes the dress of the inhabitants of Mons and Wamon's Island which he illustrates at the foot of the page. Presumably 'kluke' is the inhabitant of the area near the KLUKS mountain.

## 188

### Ruined building

23 February 1829
Pencil on paper
96 × 111 mm

Signed and dated in pencil, in minuscule hand, at top: 'COPY/ - For. Ann. Bronté by. b B Bronté Feb. 23. 1829'.

Gift of Margaret Illingworth, 1910, together with **9**, **10**, **11**, **12**, **19**, **80**, **81**, **155**, **184**, **185**, **189**, **197** and **334**. A note written in Patrick Brontë's hand and acquired at the Brown sale by the Brontë Society may have originally accompanied this group of drawings: see **9**.

*Brontë Parsonage Museum: B4*

View of a ruined building, possibly a church, with half of tower surviving, standing beside a river or moat. The tower has an arched doorway, two windows and foliage growing out of its top. To the left a wicket fence; to the right a solitary tree.

## 189

### Seascape

c. 23 February 1829
Pencil on paper
96 × 111 mm

Gift of Margaret Illingworth, 1910; see **188**.

*Brontë Parsonage Museum: B4v*

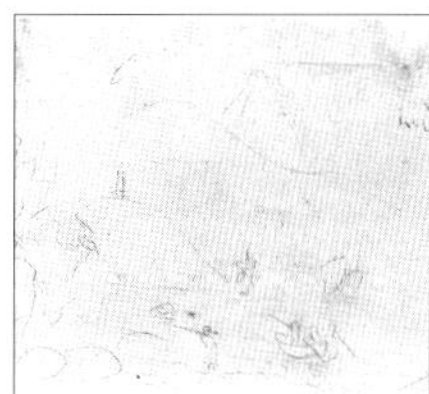

Pencil sketches of the outlines of a seascape view with large rocks in foreground and up the left side of the paper, an expanse of sea in the middle-ground with boats, beyond a series of three very steep hills, the nearest one with a tower on top. The sketch is similar to a print of a view of Holy Island, Northumberland, found in John Varley's *A Treatise on the Principles of Landscape Design* (1823). The rocks on the left of the view are reminiscent of those to be found in Anne Brontë's drawing 'Woman gazing at a sunrise over a seascape' (**350**).

## 190

### 'After Bewick'

31 March 1829
Pencil on paper

*Location unknown*

Listed by Henry Houston Bonnell as part of his collection in 1922 (Bonnell catalogue given to C. W. Hatfield, BPM). The drawing is not in the Bonnell Collection either at the Brontë Parsonage Museum or at the Pierpont Morgan Library, New York.

## 191

### Copy of William Hogarth's 'Idle Apprentices'

27 April 1829
Pencil on paper

Signed by Branwell, exact signature unknown.
*Location unknown*

Emma H. Cortazzo, a friend of Ellen Nussey, recorded a visit to Martha Brown's brother-in-law Benjamin Binns at Saltaire, Bradford; he showed her a number of Brontë relics, including 'many early drawings of the sisters', drawings of feet and ears and arms and hands, such as from drawing books young people used to be given as models to copy. Then came more elaborate efforts – a copy of Hogarth's *Idle Apprentices* by Branwell ...' (Helen H. Arnold, 'Reminiscences of Emma Huidekoper Cortazzo', *Brontë Society Transactions* (1958), vol. 13, part 68, p. 226). The drawing was sold at the Binns sale, Saltaire, 1886, lot 385, described in the catalogue as 'One [pencil drawing] (after Hogarth, by P. B. Bronte)'. It was acquired by Alfred Gledhill of Keighley for £2.12s. Gledhill's collection was acquired by Robinson and Francis Brown, cousins of Martha Brown, and later sold at the Brown sale, Sotheby's, 2 July 1898, lot 39, 'Pencil Copy from one of Hogarth's pictures by P. Branwell Brontë, April 27, 1829, signed'. The price was given as 13s but no buyer has been identified. According to newspaper reports, very few bidders appeared at this sale: 'It was rather surprising ... to find that very few prospective buyers assembled at the sale. In fact, the bidding was confined to some half dozen persons' (*Bradford Observer*, 4 July 1898). The article mentioned the bidders Messrs Wooller Jennings (for the Brontë Society), Sotherland (the well-known bookseller), Pollard, Law, Shorter, Goodwyn, Branwell, Crisp, Seymour, Armitage and Usher.

## 192

### Rural scene with two figures, cottage and castle

2 June 1829
Pencil on paper

Signed and dated in pencil, in minuscule hand, below drawing, left: 'T Bewick'; right: 'P B Brontë'; centre: 'P B Bronté. June. 2 / 1829 – / [rule]'.

According to the catalogue of the sale at Sotheby's, London, 16 December 1980, at which a photograph of this drawing (reproduced below) was acquired with **181**, lot 273, the drawing was purchased from Martha Brown by Sir William Robertson Nicoll, an early president of the Brontë Society (see also **91** and **317**), possibly when he visited her in 1879 when he is known to have bought a number of Brontë relics (see Ingeborg Nixon, 'The Brontë Portraits: Some old problems and a new discovery', *Brontë Society Transactions* (1958) vol. 13, part 68, p. 235).
*Location unknown*

In the foreground two men greet each other in front of a tumbledown cottage, its thatched roof overgrown. The figure nearest the hovel supports himself with a staff; the other carries a loaded sack on his back. A winding path leads into the background to a ruined castle with a round tower and a small cottage and a tree beside it.

The Bewick original can be found in Thomas Bewick, *A History of British Birds*, vol. 1: *Containing the History and Description of Water Birds* (Newcastle: T. Bewick; London: Longman & Co., 1816), p. 60.

## 193

### Decorative colophon and figure of 'Justice'

30 September 1829
Ink on paper
34 × 27 mm

The sketch occupies half the final page (67 × 53 mm) of a 24-page manuscript, inscribed in ink in Branwell's hand, on brown paper cover: 'YOUNG:/ SOULTS/ POEMS WITH/ NOTES: :/ IN II VOLS QUARTO/ VOL I.' On inside of front cover: rough sketch of a man fleeing. Stamped: 'BRONTË/ MUSEUM/ HAWORTH', encircled.

Purchased in London, 1899, from H. E. Gorfin, an agent of Thomas James Wise.

*Brontë Parsonage Museum: BS114*

Branwell's signature at the end of the poem is followed by a colophon in the form of a seal with a drawing in the centre of a tall building, mountain range in background, wagon wheel or shield on left-hand side, blank heraldic shields to either side. Below this, a tiny figure titled 'Justice', with heraldic shields at either side.

## 194

### Sketch of a dog

30 September 1829
Pencil on paper
65 × 50 mm

The sketch covers the whole of the inside cover of a hand-sewn manuscript volume of ten pages, inscribed in ink in Branwell's hand, on brown paper cover: 'YOUNG:/ SOULTS/ POEMS WITH/ NOTES: :/ IN II VOLS QUARTO/ VOL II'. White circular sticker, handwritten in ink, bottom left-hand corner: '115/ 210/ (a)'.

Purchased in London, 1899, from H. E. Gorfin, an agent of Thomas James Wise.

*Brontë Parsonage Museum: BS115*

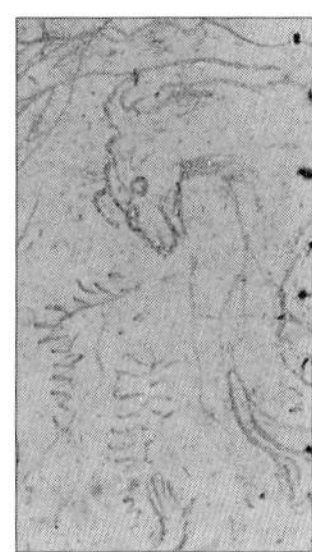

Rough pencil sketch of a dog-like creature, with trees in the background. The arm and leg of a person can be seen fleeing the picture left. The cropped images suggest that the cover of this little book has been cut from a larger sheet of paper which has previously been used for a number of sketches.

## 195

### Sketch of a warrior with a sword

30 September 1829
Pencil on paper
33 × 25 mm

The sketch covers the left side of the inside back cover (65 × 50 mm) of Branwell's hand-sewn manuscript volume of ten pages, entitled 'Young Soults Poems': see **194** for inscription.

Purchased in London, 1899, from H. E. Gorfin, an agent of Thomas James Wise.
*Brontë Parsonage Museum: BS 115*

Rough pencil sketch of a warrior in short tunic with a sword at his left side, head cropped and arms reaching up also cropped. The cropped images suggest that the cover of this little book has been cut from a larger sheet of paper which has previously been used for a number of sketches.

196

## Figure of 'Justice'

December 1829
Ink on paper
15 × 20 mm

Titled below: 'Justice'. The sketch appears on the title page (95 × 67 mm) of a hand-sewn manuscript volume of 20 pages, titled in ink in Branwell's hand, on brown paper cover: 'LAUSSANE / A TRAJEDY [*sic*] / BY / YOUNG SOULT / In I VOL Octavo / PBB : : '. Stamped: 'BRONTË / MUSEUM / HAWORTH', encircled. The manuscript is dated on the final page: 18–23 December 1829.

Bequest of Henry Houston Bonnell, 1927; acquired by Bonnell from Sotheby's sale of the effects of Arthur Bell Nicholls, London, 26 July 1907, possibly part of lot 44.
*Brontë Parsonage Museum: Bonnell 138*

Ink sketch of a figure of 'Justice', seated with arms outstretched, a sword in her right hand and an olive branch in her left. A lion-like creature sits at her feet on the left and a dog-like creature on the right.

197

## Grotesque figures and buildings

c. 1829
Pencil on paper
137 × 212 mm

Gift of Margaret Illingworth, 1910. See **9**.
*Brontë Parsonage Museum: C6v*

The page is dominated by the grotesque central figure which looks like the product of a game of 'pictorial consequences', which is what it may well be: one hand has drawn the balloon-shaped head with pipe looking to the left; a second hand has drawn the arms and torso and a third hand has added the hairy legs with drooping stockings. To the left of this composite creature is a series of distinctly separate drawings, mainly buildings. At the top, a terrace of artisans' cottages with smoking chimneys; below, a rectangular house with windows and an imposing front door, not dissimilar to Haworth Parsonage, with a wicket fence in the garden and several figures including a soldier in a plumed hat; to the left of this, a winged devil figure with claw-like hands and feet, below it two tiny cottages, and below these a tiny desert island with palm-trees and a sailing ship in the sea, the whole overlaid with a second devil-like figure. To the right of this, a drawing of Haworth Parsonage, with its symmetrical windows, tall chimney behind the house and wicket fence around the garden in which a man and woman walk hand in hand. A bare upper arm with long talons and a wide bracelet is drawn to the right of this scene. The bottom drawing of the series is a tiny view of a grand mansion in palatial grounds. The right-hand side of the paper contains various scribbles, including a soldier holding a long flag standing on top of a hill and drawings of legs.

This page of drawings probably contains the work of more than one hand but it is predominantly by Branwell.

## 198

## Grotesque figures and soldiers

c. 1829
Pencil on paper
122 × 176 mm

Inscribed in pencil, in Branwell's minuscule script, top right: 'Broms' you Ha Brou'; top right side, curving down the page: 'Marshall Milton Fygo'.

Gift of Mrs M. Barbara Smith, West Sussex, 1981. See **14**.
*Brontë Parsonage Museum: C3.5v*

The top half of the paper is completely covered by Branwell's juvenile drawings of numerous fighting stick men. On the far left, a full-length figure of a soldier in a uniform of tricorne hat, tunic, sash, epaulettes, breeches and long boots. To the right of this figure, two smaller ones of soldiers in uniform stand amidst the battling stick men; beside them two curious tall figures with long robes and large hats or haloes. In the centre of the drawing four large grotesque figures parade over a hill accompanied by two running dogs. All wear loose robes, like lunatics in an asylum. The group is dominated by the strange figure of a fat man dancing with uplifted arms. He may also be fleeing from the dogs that appear to be biting his leg; his mouth wide open as if screaming. In the lower part of the paper are two unfinished heads and several stick men, one of them sitting with his back to a mound, drawing and smoking a pipe.

## 199

## 'The Angel and Joshua at the Siege of Jericho'

17 February 1830

*Location unknown*

Listed by Henry Houston Bonnell as part of his collection in 1922 (Bonnell catalogue given to C. W. Hatfield, BPM). The drawing is not in the Bonnell Collection either at the Brontë Parsonage Museum or at the Pierpont Morgan Library, New York.

## 200

### 'Hermit'

30 April 1830
Watercolour, bodycolour and pencil on paper
188 × 222 mm

Signed and dated in pencil, in minuscule hand, below painting left corner: 'P B Bronté'; right corner: 'P B Bronté'; titled in large hand below centre: 'HERMIT R~~3333~~ ORIGINAL ~~322~~'; inscribed, bottom centre edge of paper in longhand: '(?) April = Patrick Branwell Bronte/ 000 April 30 1830'. On verso: pencil sketches of birds; watercolour sketches of plants scattered over the page. Inscribed on verso, in pencil, centre: 'Fs/ 1928'.

Purchased from Rose Emma Longbottom, 1906; together with **13**, **74**, **129**, **200**, **201**, **202** and **208**. See **13** for further provenance.

*Brontë Parsonage Museum: B5*

To the right of the scene, the hermit, an old man with a long grey beard wearing a monk's habit, sits on a stone bench reading. He turns to his left, resting his chin in his left hand and holding the book in his right. The hermitage is a stone-walled and paved room with pillars, two arches to the right and a high window on the back wall through which shafts of light fall to illuminate the scene. To the left foreground there lies a tangle of red drapery which can be discerned as a red cloak and cardinal's hat. On the floor to the hermit's left stands a tall pitcher, and to his right a heap of scrolls. Above and below the picture, the frame has been extended in pencil, with curls at each corner, to give the appearance of a painting on a scroll.

Although Branwell's painting is probably at least partially copied from a print, despite his claims that it is 'Original', it is possible that his choice of subject was inspired by the character of the hermit in his play in verse, 'Laussane A Trajedy By Young Soult' (see **196**), written four months prior in December 1829.

The iconography of this painting suggests that it is based on a representation of St Jerome, a popular subject in Western art from the 1300s until about 1700. Jerome's greatest achievement was to produce the Vulgate Bible used for centuries by the Catholic Church; he was the first to translate the Bible from the original Greek and Hebrew into Latin. As a child the Saint was a voracious reader of classical literature, which he renounced on his calling to Christianity and went to live as a hermit in the Holy Land where he spent long hours in devout study.

Although no specific source has been identified it seems very likely that the Brontës would have had access to prints of pictures depicting saints. St Jerome would surely have had a special appeal to them for his literary associations.

## 201

### 'Study'

6 May 1830
Watercolour, bodycolour and pencil on paper
178 × 125 mm

Signed and dated in ink, in minuscule script and capitals, below painting, centre: 'STUDY. P B Bronté/ MAY 6 1830/ ~~original~~ ["inal" repeated above deletion] Original' (final word added in pencil). Inscribed on verso, in non-Brontë hand, in ink: '~~Amelia Bower Picture~~' (deletion in pencil). Also on verso: indistinct pencil sketches, including one of a female head and shoulders. Purchased from Rose Emma Longbottom, 1906; together with **13**, **74**, **129**, **200**, **202** and **207**.

*Brontë Parsonage Museum: B6*

The picture is largely occupied with the figure of a man with a dark beard and moustache, a frown between his brows, wearing a dark red turban and a dark green robe. He sits at a small desk, leaning on his right hand and writing with his left on a scroll with three columns of script. An ink-pot and two large bound volumes are placed at his right elbow. Above him and to the right a heavy red curtain is draped diagonally across the corner of the room. To the left there is an arched window in the stone wall with a view to mountainous scenery outside.

The detail of the view through the window in the room of this solitary scholar suggests that it may be copied from a print derived from a sixteenth-century Northern European painting. Victor Neufeldt has suggested to the present author that the scribe may be an astrologer. An astrologer appears in Branwell's play 'The Revenge' of 16 March 1831.

## 202

## 'Terror'

11 May 1830
Watercolour, bodycolour and pencil on paper
188 × 125 mm

Signed and dated in pencil, in minuscule script and capitals below picture, centre: 'TERROR oFFF/ Original PBB/ P B Bronté/ May 11 1830'. ('oFFF' could read '. PBB'.) On verso: ruled lines along outer edge of drawing. On recto: sketches of two male heads, one of which is very similar to the face on the recto.

Purchased from Rose Emma Longbottom, 1906: together with **13**, **74**, **129**, **200**, **201** and **207**.
*Brontë Parsonage Museum: B7*

The picture is dominated by the half-length figure of a frowning, bearded man with short dark hair who looks fiercely to his right, gesturing vehemently with his muscular left arm held aloft and right arm across his body. He is clad in shining armour with an orange cloth draped around his torso and he carries a round shield on his back. Behind this figure a long column of spear-carrying soldiers can be seen approaching between two hills. To the right, two swordsmen fight; in front of them, a leafy bush occupies the bottom right corner of the painting. In the far distance, a glimpse of the sea and a yellowish horizon.

Battle scenes are numerous in Branwell's writings, and a recurrent theme in his drawings. This watercolour was probably copied from a print, as yet unidentified. See Appendix A for images of soldiers similar to those in the background detail of this painting.

## 203

## Sailing ship

26 June 1830
Ink on paper
20 × 20 mm

The sketch appears in the bottom left corner of p. 4 (127 × 100 mm) of a hand-sewn manuscript volume of 18 pages, with a coarse brown paper cover titled in ink, in Branwell's hand on the front: 'CARACTACUS/

A DRAMATIC/ =POEM BY/ YOUNG/ =SOULT/ IN/ II/ VOLUMN=/ QUARTO'; dated at the bottom of page 1: 'June 26. AD 1830'.

Formerly owned by Lord Brotherton, who began collecting in earnest *c.* 1922–5 (see **206**, **211–15**, **226**, **228–9**, **240**, **280–1**, **285**, **288–9**, **291–5**, **301–3**). Previously by John Drinkwater, whose bookplate appears in the slip-case signed and dated 1921, and a note inscribed by Drinkwater, in pencil, which reads: 'Patrick Branwell Bronte MS., written at the age of 13. See my introduction to his translation of Horace.'

*The Brotherton Collection, Leeds University Library*

Tiny sketch in ink of a ship in full sail on stormy waters.

204

## Sketch of a dog's head

c. June 1830
Pencil on paper
64 × 52 mm

The sketch appears on the inside front cover of a hand-sewn manuscript volume of 14 pages with a blue-grey card cover inscribed on the front, in ink, by Branwell: 'THE:/ LIAR DETECTED/ BY:/ CAPTAN JOHN BUD/ 1 VOL QUAR$^{TO}$/ [short rule]'. Inscribed on the inside front cover, top left corner: '139'. The first page of the manuscript written in ink, in Branwell's minuscule script begins: 'The Liar unmasked: by Cap$^{t}$ Bud/ June 19 1830'. Bequest of Henry Houston Bonnell, 1927; acquired by Bonnell from Sotheby's, London, 31 May 1912.

*Brontë Parsonage Museum: Bonnell 139*

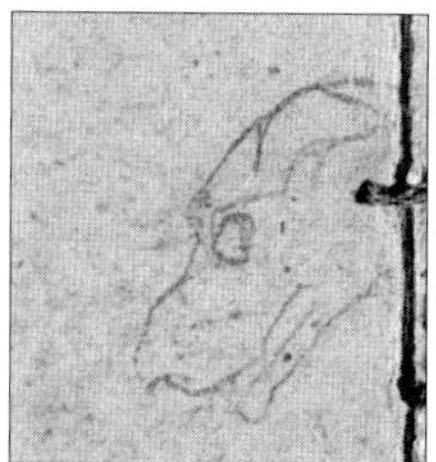

Sketch of a dog's head and other random lines, suggesting that the cover of the little book was cut from a larger piece of card already used for sketching.

205

## Sketch of a man with a distorted face

c. June 1830
Pencil on paper
64 × 52 mm

The sketch appears on the inside back cover of a hand-sewn manuscript volume of 14 pages with a blue-grey card cover inscribed on the front, in ink, by Branwell: 'THE:/ LIAR DETECTED/ BY:/ CAPTAN JOHN BUD/ I VOL QUAR$^{TO}$/ [short rule]'. The first page of the manuscript written in ink, in Branwell's minuscule script begins: 'The Liar unmasked: by Cap$^{t}$ Bud/ June 19 1830'. Bequest of Henry Houston Bonnell, 1927; acquired by Bonnell from Sotheby's, London, 31 May 1912.

*Brontë Parsonage Museum: Bonnell 139*

Sketch of a man with a curiously distorted face and other random lines, suggesting that the cover of the little book on which this appears was cut from a larger piece of card already used for sketching.

## 206

## Figure of 'Justice'

6 September 1830
Ink on paper
17 × 27 mm

Titled below: 'Justice'. The sketch appears on the title page (89 × 58 mm) of a manuscript volume of 18 pages. Above the sketch, inscribed in ink, by Branwell: 'LETTERS : : : / FROM / An Englishman To his Relative / IN : : / LONDON : : :'; signed at bottom of page: 'Patrick Branwell Bronté'; dated in longhand: 'September / 6th / Anno Dominii / 1830 ? ~~fecit~~'.

Formerly owned by Lord Brotherton: see **203**.
*The Brotherton Collection, Leeds University Library*

Sketch in centre of page of seated female figure of 'Justice', with her head inclined slightly to the right, arms outstretched, olive branch in her right hand, sword in her left. A dog sits at her right, looking up at her, and another creature, possibly a lion, at her left.

## 207

## 'Queen Esther'

December 1830
Watercolour, bodycolour and pencil on paper
140 × 179 mm

Signed and dated in ink in longhand along bottom of the image: 'Qeen [*sic*] Esther – Painted by Martin – / and copied by P. B – Bronté – Dec[r] 1830 –'. On verso: drawing of a many-windowed gothic-style building; pencil drawing of one male and three female heads; red watercolour palm tree; inscribed, in ornate script in pencil, top right: 'F / feathear [*sic*]'.

Purchased from Rose Emma Longbottom, 1906: together with **13**, **74**, **129**, **200**, **201** and **202**.
*Brontë Parsonage Museum: B8*

This watercolour was copied from the print of the subject by John Martin which was reproduced in the *Forget Me Not* Annual for 1831. The story is told in the Book of Esther 7–8. The scene depicted is the feast to which Queen Esther invited her husband King Ahasuerus in order to plead with him to spare the Jews from the massacre ordered by Haman, the king's chief minister. The event takes place in the impressive setting of the palace, with a lofty ceiling, massive pillars and a view of a biblical town in the distance. Queen Esther sits to the right beneath an elaborate crimson and purple draped canopy. In the centre guests sit at the banqueting table, in front of which stands a robed courtier with his arm outstretched, indicating the arrival of the King who approaches from the left with his arms upraised.

This picture was originally backed by a wash drawing by Charlotte (**13**) which was removed during conservation work in 1983 to reveal Branwell's drawing of a building and the watercolour sketches on the verso of this painting.

## 208

### 'Mentor'

15 December 1830–7 May 1831
Ink on paper
25 × 36 mm

Titled below: 'MENTOR'. The sketch appears at the bottom of the title page (123 × 100 mm) of a manuscript volume of 16 pages. The title page is inscribed in ink, by Branwell, in varying sizes of script: 'THE/ HISTORY OF/ THE –/ YOUNG MEN :=:/ FROM/ Their First Settlement/ TO/ The present time –/ COMPREHENDING AN ACCOUNT OF ASHANTEE/ FROM THE EARLIEST PERIOD TO THEIR ARRIVAL/ ~~B~~–¥. : BY :/ JOHN BUD ESQ'R/ CAPTAIN IN THE:/ 10 REGT OF HUSSARS/ VICE PRESIDENT OF THE ANTIQUARIAN society/ FELLOW OF THE LITERARY SOCIETY :./ FELLOW OF THE ASSOCIATION FOR:–/ THE REWARD OF LEARNING –/ CHEIF [*sic*] LIBRARIAN TO.–/ THE ROYAL GLASS.–/ TOWN LIBRARY–/ &c &c &c &c/ IN VOLUMNS:/ VOL I./ "It is my TASK/ "To Explore The Dark recesses of the past/ "And Bring to light the deeds of Former ages"/ Marquis Douro's/ School of Learning v. 139/ [sketch 'MENTOR' appears at this point] 1831/ – Great Glass Town printed and sold by. Seargent [*sic*] Tree'. Stamped: 'BRONTË/ MUSEUM/ HAWORTH', encircled.

Formerly owned by Thomas James Wise, who probably acquired the manuscript from Arthur Bell Nicholls.
*British Library: Ashley 2468*

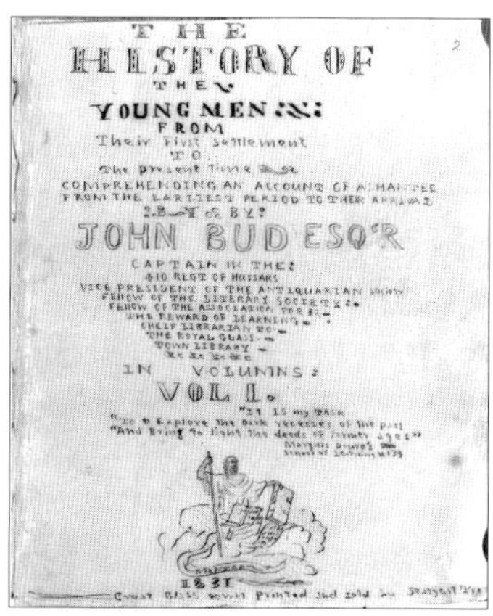


Pen-and-ink sketch of a man titled 'Mentor'. A bearded man seated among clouds, wearing loose robes and holding a long teacher's rod in his right hand whilst his left hand rests on a large, upright tome. There is another open book on his lap. 'Mentor' appears as a character in Homer's *Odyssey* as a trusted friend and adviser to Odysseus and his son, Telemachus. The name is usually taken to mean 'trusted counsellor'. In the Glass Town saga, Captain John Bud is an eminent political writer and historian, the 'greatest prose writer' among the Young Men of the early Glass Town.

## 209

### Map of Glass Town Federation

15 December 1830–7 May 1831
Coloured pencil on paper
195 × 320 mm

The sketch is on a fold-out sheet attached to the inside front cover, facing the title page, of Branwell's 16-page manuscript volume 'The History Of The Young Men': see **208**.

Formerly owned by Thomas James Wise, who probably acquired the manuscript from Arthur Bell Nicholls.
*British Library: Ashley 2468*

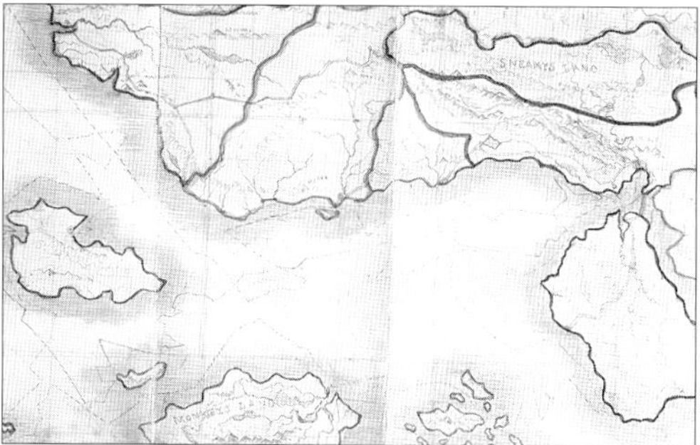

Map showing the division of the Glass Town kingdoms invented by the Brontë children and imagined by them to be situated on the East African coast. On the mainland are, from left to right, Wellington's Land, Parry's

Land, Ross's Land, Sneaky's Land and the Great Glass Town. The islands, from left to right, are Stumps's Land, outlined in deep red, Monkey's Land, outlined in orange, and Frenchy Land outlined in blue. Winifred Gérin (*Five Novelettes* (London: The Folio Press, 1971), p. 10) and Christine Alexander (*The Early Writings of Charlotte Brontë* (Oxford: Basil Blackwell, 1983), p. 262, n. 13) suggest a resemblance to a map of Northern Africa, including the Gulf of Guinea, which appeared in *Blackwood's Magazine*, June 1826 (printed as frontispiece to *An Edition of the Early Writings of Charlotte Brontë*, ed. Christine Alexander, 2 vols. (Oxford: Basil Blackwell for the Shakespeare Head Press, 1987; 1991), vol. 2, part 2.)

In his introduction to the History, Branwell explains how the stories invented by the Brontë children had their origins in a box of toy soldiers which their father brought back from Leeds in June 1826. The soldiers came to be known as the 'Young Men'. In her 'History of the Year' for 1829 (BPM: Bonnell 80(11)), Charlotte describes how the four Brontës chose a soldier each: Charlotte's was named 'Wellington'; Emily's was called 'Gravey', later 'Parry'; Anne's 'Waiting Boy', later 'Ross'; and Branwell's, 'Bonaparte'. The 'History of the Young Men' (there were twelve adventurers in total) recounts their journey from England to East Africa, and their settlement of the Glass Town.

## 210

## Figure of 'Justice'

7 May 1831
Ink on paper
17 × 50 mm

Titled below: 'Justice'. The colophon-like sketch appears at the bottom of the final page of Branwell's 16-page manuscript volume 'The History Of The Young Men': see **208**. The words immediately above the sketch, inscribed in ink by Branwell read: 'Here ends/ The I, VOLUMN [*sic*] of,/ The/ History of the Young Men/ Begun December 15th AD 1830/ Ended May 7.th AD 1831 =/ John Bud'. Formerly owned by Thomas James Wise, who probably acquired the manuscript from Arthur Bell Nicholls.

*British Library: Ashley 2468*

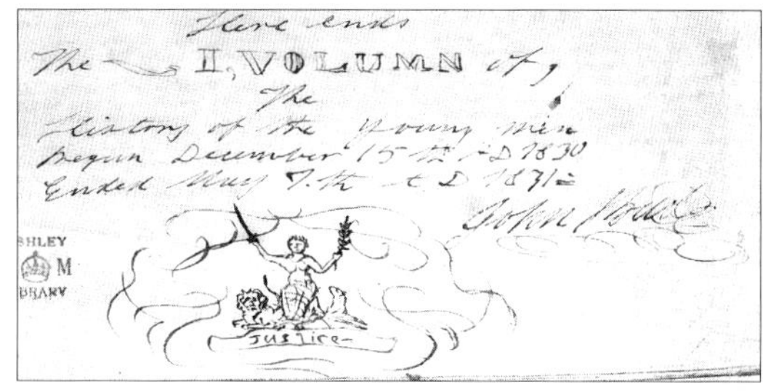


Pen-and-ink sketch of a seated figure of 'Justice'. A lion sits to the left of the figure, with a shield in the centre and a dog to the right looking up at the figure which holds aloft a sword in her outstretched right hand and an olive branch in her left.

## 211

## Figure of 'Justice'

8 June 1831
Ink on paper
20 × 23 mm

Titled below: 'Justice'. The sketch appears on the title page (90 × 57 mm) of a manuscript volume of 18 pages inscribed in ink by Branwell above the sketch: 'LETTERS/ FROM AN/ <<ENGLISHMAN>>/ TO/ HIS FREIND IN –/ LONDON/ BY/ =CAPTAIN JOHN FLOWER/ VOL IId'. Signed at foot of page: 'PATRICK BRANWELL/ BRONTE/ June 8.th. AD 1831.'

Formerly owned by Lord Brotherton (see **203**); possibly acquired from Thomas James Wise.

*The Brotherton Collection, Leeds University Library*

Pen-and-ink sketch of a female figure of 'Justice'. The figure stands amidst clouds; she wears a long robe and holds the scales of justice in her outstretched left hand. Shafts of light flow from her towards picture right.

212

## Figure of 'Justice'

11 June 1831
Ink on paper
23 × 25 mm

Titled below: 'Justice'. The sketch appears on the title page (93 × 58 mm) of Branwell's 20-page manuscript volume 'Letters from An Englishman'. Title page inscribed in ink above sketch: 'LETTERS:/ FROM AN/ :ENGLISHMAN. TO/ HIS/ FREIND IN./ LONDON:/ BY:/ CAPTAIN JOHN FLOWER:/ VOL III.'; below sketch: 'CT ROSS'S GLASS TOWN/ Printed and sold by/ SEARGT WINDIASS/ [double rule]/ BY PATRICK BRANWELL/ BRONTE/ June 11th AD 1831'.
Formerly owned by Lord Brotherton: see **203**.
*The Brotherton Collection, Leeds University Library*

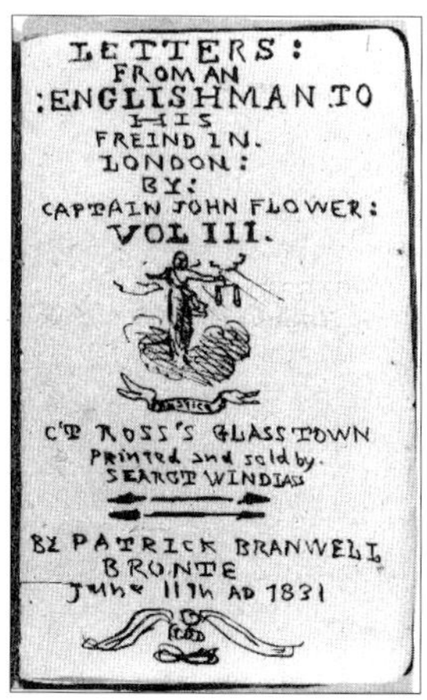


Pen-and-ink sketch of a male or female figure of 'Justice'. The figure stands amidst clouds wearing a long robe and holding the scales of justice in her outstretched left hand.

213

## Figure of 'Justice'

2 August 1832
Ink on paper
32 × 46 mm

Titled below: 'Justice'. The sketch appears on the title page (104 × 64 mm) of a manuscript volume of 20 pages. Inscribed in ink in Branwell's hand, above sketch: 'LETTERS FROM/ AN.:./ ENGLISHMAN./ To his Friend./ .IN LONDON./ BY/ CAPTAIN JOHN FLOWER/ .VOL: VI.'; below sketch: 'Capt Ross's Glass Town. Printed and sold/ By Seargt Winlass/ By Patric Branwell Brontë/ .August, 2d. 1832.'

Formerly owned by Lord Brotherton: see **203**.
*The Brotherton Collection, Leeds University Library*

Pen-and-ink sketch of a female figure of 'Justice'. The figure is leaping in the air above a cloud, rays of light fanning out behind her. She holds the scales of justice in her outstretched left hand and an olive branch in her right. A sword lies at her feet. It would appear that as Branwell progresses throughout the volumes of 'Letters From An Englishman', the little sketches of 'Justice' become more and more animated.

## 214

### Figure of 'Justice'

3 August 1832
Ink on paper
24 × 27 mm

Titled below: 'Justice'. The sketch appears on the title page (103 × 61 mm) of a manuscript volume of 20 pages, inscribed in ink in Branwell's hand, above sketch: 'LETTERS. From./ : AN./ ENGLISHMAN TO./ His Friend in/ LONDON./ BY/ CAPTAIN JOHN FLOWER./ .VOL. IV.'; below sketch: 'CT ROSS'S GLASS TOWN./ Printed and sold/ By Seargt Winlass./ [double rule]/ BY PATRICK BRANWELL/ : BRONTE/ August. 3. 1832:.'

Formerly owned by Lord Brotherton: see **203**.
*The Brotherton Collection, Leeds University Library*

Pen-and-ink sketch of a female figure, titled below 'Justice'. The figure stands on a feathery cloud, arms outstretched, holding an olive branch in her right hand and the scales of justice in her left hand. A sword lies at her feet. The figure has more sense of movement than earlier sketches of the same subject.

## 215

### Figure of 'Justice'

3 August 1832
Ink on paper
25 × 27 mm

Titled below: 'Justice'. The sketch appears on the title page (104 × 62 mm) of a manuscript volume of 18 pages, inscribed in ink in Branwell's hand, above sketch: 'LETTERS FROM./ AN./ ENGLISH MAN./ To His Freind./ In/ LONDON:/ BY/ CAPTAIN JOHN FLOWER/ VOL. V.'; below sketch: 'C$^{n}$ ROSS'S GLASS TOWN/ Printed and sold/ By Seag$^{t}$ Winlass./ [double rule]/ BY PATRICK BRANWELL/ BRONTE/ August 3. 1832'.

Formerly owned by Lord Brotherton: see **203**.
*The Brotherton Collection, Leeds University Library*

Pen-and-ink sketch of a female figure of 'Justice'. The figure stands on a feathery cloud, holding the scales of justice in outstretched left hand and an olive branch in her right. A sword lies at her feet.

## 216

### Sketches of buildings

c. 1832–1834
?Ink on paper
192 × 317 mm

The entry is based on a photocopy in the BPM; the British Library cannot locate the item at present.

Formerly owned by Thomas James Wise, who probably acquired the manuscript from Arthur Bell Nicholls.
*British Library: Ashley MS*

Page covered with drawings, mainly of buildings. Top right, a ruined classical building with three arches, the central arch inscribed 'ROMAN AD 539', in the style of Piranesi, with vegetation growing out of the stonework and figures in the foreground, one on a donkey. Beneath this drawing Branwell has written in his minuscule script: 'Fidena triumphal arch Roma'. 'Fidena' appears as a fictional city in the juvenilia, situated on the river Fidneaz in Sneachiesland (formerly 'Sneaky's Land'), three hundred miles from Verdopolis. John Sneaky was 1st Duke of Fidena. Fidena is also the name of an actual place, an inland town of Latium, north of Rome, conquered by the Romans in 435 BC.

Bottom right, a gothic-style church with a tall steeple, seen from the front. Centre, outline sketches of hills and mountains with tiny figures leaping and running on the slopes. Centre of page, bottom, outline sketch of a nine-arched pavilion-style structure. To the left of this, a serpent with two coils and forked tongue. Far left, a church with a steeple on top of a steep hill. Above the serpent, a sketch of a small classical pavilion with pillars, above which the word 'E-Q-U-A-T-O-R' is inscribed in Branwell's minuscule script. To the right of this, a tiny sketch of a ruin with arches set in a landscape. A large sketch of a gothic-style church occupies the whole of the top left quarter of the page, incorporating a detail of an equestrian sculpture with a rider holding aloft a pennant.

## 217

## Figure of 'Justice'

27 March–26 April 1833
Ink on paper
15 × 30 mm

Titled below in longhand: 'Justice'. The sketch appears at the top of the first page (226 × 175 mm) of a four-page manuscript 'newspaper', titled in ink, in Branwell's longhand: 'N° I.st. The Monthly Intelligencer'. Below masthead, in Branwell's minuscule script in ink: 'From March 27. AD 1833. To. April. 26th'; title of sketch follows; 'Great. Glass Town P Bronte. March 27'. The manuscript is dated at the end in Branwell's minuscule hand: 'P B Bronte. April. 26. 183[3]'. Stamped: 'BRONTË/ MUSEUM/ HAWORTH', encircled.

Purchased in London, 1899, from H. E. Gorfin, an agent of Thomas James Wise (see **89**).

*Brontë Parsonage Museum: BS117*

Pen-and-ink sketch of a female figure of 'Justice', positioned between 'The Monthly' and 'Intelligencer' of the newspaper title. The figure is seated amongst clouds, wearing a long robe and a star-shaped crown, holding a sword in her outstretched left hand and an olive branch in her right. A dog sits at her feet on her right, looking up at her. Another creature, probably a lion, sits on her left. Rays of light fan out from behind her towards picture right.

## 218

## 'Gos Hawk'

1833
Watercolour, bodycolour and pencil on paper
150 × 209 mm

Signed and dated in pencil, bottom left: 'P. B. Brontë/ 1833'; bottom centre: 'Gos Hawk'. Stamped: 'BRONTË/ MUSEUM/ HAWORTH', encircled.

Gift of Annie Keeling, 1932; formerly owned by Mrs Murgatroyd of Bradford, who claimed that her son was a godchild of Charlotte who taught him as a child at Haworth Sunday School.

*Brontë Parsonage Museum: B9*

Goshawk copied from Thomas Bewick, *A History of British Birds*, vol. 1: *Containing the History and Description of Land Birds* (Newcastle: T. Bewick; London: Longman & Co., 1816), p. 65. Branwell meticulously follows both Bewick's written description of the colours of the bird and the black and white lines of the engraving in order to produce this painting. The goshawk is seen from the side, looking to the left, standing with legs apart on a tree branch. The head and upper parts of its body are dark brown, its neck, breast and belly, white marked with bars of black. The legs are yellow, the claws black, the tail an 'ash grey' and its beady eyes are yellow.

## 219

## View of a building

1 July 1833
Pencil on paper
117 × 196 mm

Signed and dated in pencil, in minuscule hand, bottom left: 'P B Bronté'; bottom right: 'July 1 1833'. Stamped: 'BRONTË/ MUSEUM/ HAWORTH', encircled. On verso: faint pencil study of head and shoulders of curly-headed young man; below: four tiny drawings of heads, partially erased. The marks of four vertical fold lines are also visible.

Gift of Miss K. Lumb, 1928.
*Brontë Parsonage Museum: B10*

View of the gable end of a stone building two storeys high with a single-storey extension or outbuilding. There are two windows in the outhouse divided into panes, a similar one on the left of the main building and a further window on the upper storey. Two chimneys are seen in the centre and at the front of the main building. The main building is on raised ground, with a low stone wall in the middle-ground and a wicket fence beyond. An outcrop of rock appears in the foreground.

This view of a bleak, isolated building bears some resemblance to the south elevation of Haworth Parsonage as it may have looked in the 1830s. The parsonage, a Georgian building, is unusually tall for the area, as is this one. The unorthodox viewpoint and the rubbing of the paper would suggest that this drawing of a building was made from life.

See **220**, a similar drawing of a building executed only three weeks later.

## 220

## Moorland buildings

21 July 1833
Pencil on paper
102 × 164 mm

Signed and dated in pencil, in minuscule hand, bottom left: 'P. B. Bronte'; bottom right: 'July 21 1833'. Stamped: 'BRONTË/ MUSEUM/ HAWORTH', encircled. On verso: faint drawing of what appears to be a road map.

Gift of Mr or Mrs G. H. Pickles, 1934; by descent through donor's family, known by the donor to have been in their possession in early 1880s.

*Brontë Parsonage Museum: B11*

Two apparently separate stone buildings with Yorkshire stone tiled roofs. The larger of the two has a long sloping roof and a mullioned window; the smaller has two sets of mullions and a chimney on the left gable end. A hillock rises in the foreground with a solitary tree on top which towers over the roofs.

The buildings in this drawing are typical in all their detail of the vernacular architecture of the Haworth area. Like **219**, they were probably drawn from life, a possibility which is also suggested by the rubbing of the paper.

## 221

### Detailed sketch of tall building and bridge over river

15 November 1833
Ink on paper
76 × 94 mm

The sketch appears at the foot of p. 4 (181 × 114 mm) of a hand-sewn manuscript volume of 18 pages with a coarse brown paper cover, titled on p. 1 in ink, in Branwell's minuscule script: 'THE POLITICS. OF. = ./ VERDOPOLIS./ A Tale By. Captain John Flower MP. = ./ In. I. Vol::'. The text is written in Branwell's minuscule script throughout and p. 4 begins: 'glow with instant anger. never more might that person hope to regain her favour ...'. The manuscript is dated at the foot of p. 18 'P B Bronte Nov. 15th AD 1833'.

Bequest of Henry Houston Bonnell, 1927; acquired by Bonnell from H. Buxton Forman Collection, Anderson sale, 15–17 March 1920, item 82.

*Brontë Parsonage Museum: Bonnell 141*

Detailed ink sketch of a tall, rectangular, many-windowed building with a tower and cross at its pinnacle. To the left of the building is a distant view of a bridge with three arches across a river and two further buildings apparently on the far bank of the river. The view is not unlike that of the River Arno in Florence, although the architecture is a curious hybrid of styles and has probably emerged chiefly from Branwell's imagination. The text of the manuscript is written closely around the drawing in a manner which is characteristic of Branwell.

## 222

### Three figures seated beside rocks and foliage

c. 1833–1834
Pencil on paper
206 × 185 mm

Stamped: 'BRONTË/ MUSEUM/ HAWORTH', encircled. Purchased from Hodgson & Co. sale, London, 31 March 1933, part of lot 447. In the sale catalogue lots 437–50 are described as 'The Property of a Collector' and were formerly owned by Sir Alfred J. Law: see **15**.

*Brontë Parsonage Museum: B29*

Group of three figures, two of them wrapped in long cloaks, huddled together in front of a dark, cave-like opening in rocks. They are surrounded by dense foliage. The central figure of the group, a man, sits upright and his face is seen in clear profile against the dark hole. He looks up to picture right where a fiendish face with two hands holding drapery around its head looks down. The right-hand figure, perhaps a woman, crouches close to the main figure and looks forward with an intent gaze. The third figure hides behind the man, holding the folds of his cloak to his or her face.

The subject of the drawing is unidentified but the style is similar to that of the graphic work of Henry Fuseli, whose work the Brontës knew through prints. Charlotte made a watercolour derived from Fuseli's painting 'Solitude at Dawn', (see **129**). The figures in the drawing are characteristic of Branwell but the handling of the background is unusual for him.

## 223

## Studies of heads and faces with two kneeling figures

c. 1833–1834
Pencil on paper
185 × 206 mm

Inscribed in ink, bottom left corner at right angles to drawing: 'SB 1009'. The studies are on the verso of **222**. Purchased from Hodgson & Co. sale, London, 31 March 1933, part of lot 447. In the sale catalogue lots 437–50 are described as 'The Property of a Collector' and were formerly owned by Sir Alfred J. Law: see **15**.

*Brontë Parsonage Museum: B29v*

A number of studies in pencil are dispersed across the page. The main group, top centre, is composed of the heads and shoulders of three male figures seen from right profile, full face and left profile respectively, all of which are similar to the central figure in **222**. On the top right there is a second and similar group of four heads, the faces of which look more feminine, particularly the left head which has long ringlets of hair. Below this is a study of the head of the central figure in **222**; below it a small bald head looking left. Continuing to work clockwise: a tiny rough outline sketch of three seated figures, perhaps related to **222**; a pointed animal head; an outline profile looking left; two kneeling male figures in long robes in attitudes of prayer overlaid with outline dog's head, similar to a greyhound; a sword; profile of face looking left; profiles of two upper faces looking right. These drawings are interspersed with areas of heavy pencil shading.

All of these studies could be related to the finished drawing on the recto. It is interesting to note, however, that Branwell is here seen to experiment with the compositional problems posed by the representation of both three and four figures as a group portrait. This is a challenge he faced when painting his best-known portrait of his three sisters, in which, as we know, he originally included himself (see **225**). Artists through the ages have struggled to find pleasing pictorial solutions to the difficulties involved in representing more than two figures in a portrait. Branwell must have made some preparatory sketches for his portrait of Charlotte, Emily and Anne and it is tempting to speculate here that in these slight drawings we may be looking at a preliminary assault on this problem. At the same time, these studies could be straightforward exercises in drawing the human head.

## 224

## Emily Jane Brontë and the 'Gun Group'

c. 1833–1834
Oil on canvas
514 × 324 mm

Purchased through Reginald J. Smith from Mary Anne Nicholls, Arthur Bell Nicholls's second wife, 1914. This portrait fragment was inherited (as part of the 'Gun Group' portrait from which it was cut at an unspecified date after 1861) by Nicholls on the death of Patrick Brontë in 1861. It was found by Mary Anne Nicholls on the top of a wardrobe at their home, Hill House, Banagher in Ireland, together with 'The Brontë sisters' portrait (**225**), after Nicholls's death, in 1914.
*National Portrait Gallery, London: 1724*

Emily is seen in profile, half-length and seated, looking to picture left in an irregularly shaped fragment cut, with an arched top, from a larger oil painting. The dark shape just visible to her left is the right shoulder of Branwell, who appears second from the right in the group portrait known as the 'Gun Group' (see above), now indisputably established to be the painting from which this fragment was cut. Emily has a small thin face with dark eyes and a pale complexion. Her hair is dark brown, wavy and worn loose, curling over her ear and cheek and just touching the top of her shoulders. She is dressed in a simply styled greenish-grey gown with a wide low-cut neckline which slips off her left shoulder. The top of a table is just visible in front of her with a pile of three books, the uppermost one of which has an orange cover. The background is greyish-brown.

The condition of the picture is poor, with paint loss in various places and large cracks, especially over the shoulders and the dress, due to Branwell's use of bitumen, a rich brown pigment made from asphaltum, which was widely used during the eighteenth and nineteenth centuries. Bitumen never dries completely and it has been the cause of severe damage in many paintings of this period. In addition, as its documentation suggests (see below), this work was subjected to especially rough treatment from 1861 when it was inherited by Nicholls until 1914 when it was acquired by the National Portrait Gallery, having been cut out, transported between Yorkshire and Ireland on two occasions and then stored folded for many years on the top of a wardrobe.

In 1895 Clement K. Shorter, who visited Nicholls in Ireland that year, related: 'After Mr Brontë's death Mr Nicholls removed it [the 'Gun Group'] to Ireland. Being

of the opinion that the only accurate portrait was that of Emily, he cut this out and destroyed the remainder. The portrait of Emily was given to Martha Brown, the servant, on one of her visits to Mr Nicholls, and I have not been able to trace it' (Shorter, quoted in Ingeborg Nixon, 'The Brontë Portraits: Some old problems and a new discovery', *Brontë Society Transactions* (1958), vol. 13, part 68, p. 235). Nixon also records that, in 1879, Sir William Robertson Nicoll visited Martha Brown in Haworth and saw the fragment: 'I shall never cease to regret that I did not buy the portrait she had of Emily Brontë, though I got a few other things. I did not buy it because I could not very well afford it, and it has been irrevocably lost. I have made many efforts since, and have been helped by many of Martha Brown's relatives. But that really fine and expressive painting has hopelessly disappeared, and now we have nothing that deserves to be called a likeness of that rarely endowed girl.' The portrait of Emily Jane Brontë, then, was given by Nicholls to Martha Brown and at some later date returned by her to Mr Nicholls's home in Ireland where, in 1914, after his death, Nicholls's second wife Mary discovered it with 'The Brontë sisters' group portrait (**225**) on the top of a wardrobe and sold it to the National Portrait Gallery.

In 1961 the BPM purchased a set of three individual pencil tracings on waxed paper of the figures of Anne (P69:3), Charlotte (P69:1) and Emily Brontë (P69:2), taken from the 'Gun Group' portrait some time before 1861 by John Greenwood, the Haworth stationer in the Brontës' time. The tracings (see above) were acquired from Mary Preston, the great-granddaughter of John Greenwood: they each measure approximately 452 × 327 mm, and each is inscribed in pencil in the bottom left corner in Greenwood's hand: 'Charlotte Bronte,/ 18$^{th}$ year of her age', 'Emily Jane Bronte, 16$^{th}$ [the '6' was formerly written as a '5' and then corrected by the same hand] year of her age' and 'Anne Bronte, 14$^{th}$ year of her age', respectively.

The tracing of Charlotte is in soft pencil and depicts her half-length, viewed from the front with her head facing slightly to picture right. Her hair is parted in the centre, piled into a topknot with looped curls just covering her ears. Her dress is high waisted with full sleeves and long cuffs, the bodice pleated into a yoked neckline with a ruff collar. The left hand rests in front of her, slightly raised as if covering some object on a table.

The tracing in soft pencil of Emily Brontë has been proved by Mabel Edgerley to match exactly the outline of the fragment of the painting depicting Emily in the National Portrait Gallery, London, described in detail above. Mabel Edgerley, a former Honorary Secretary of the Brontë Society, took the tracings to the National Portrait Gallery in 1932 and closely compared them

('Emily Brontë: A National Portrait Vindicated', *Brontë Society Transactions* (1932), vol. 8, part 42, p. 27).

The tracing in soft pencil of the portrait of Anne Brontë made by John Greenwood from the now lost 'Gun Group' portrait depicts her half-length facing picture right. Her hair is loose and curly, worn in the same style as Emily, and the style of her dress is the same, with its full sleeves and yoked neckline. The fabric of the dress is very loose around her bosom and the gown is tied around tightly at her waist.

There is no known tracing of Branwell from the 'Gun Group' portrait. Whether or not Greenwood made one, it is impossible to say. Discrepancies in the details of the fragment oil portrait of Emily, an 1879 engraving of the 'Gun Group' portrait, seen below (J. Horsfall Turner, *Haworth – Past and Present: A History of Haworth, Stanbury and Oxenhope* (Brighouse: J. S. Jowett, 1879), facing p. 137) and the Greenwood tracings made it, until recently, impossible to say whether or not these were all related to one Brontë group portrait, or more than one.

In 1989, Dr Juliet Barker, former Curator/ Librarian at the BPM, made an important discovery in one of the many boxes of Dr Mildred Christian's papers left to the Brontë Society in that year (see **34**), which has thrown new light on the previously confused history of the 'Gun Group' portrait (Juliet Barker, 'The Brontë Portraits: A Mystery Solved', *Brontë Society Transactions* (1990), vol. 20, part 1, pp. 3–11). It is a photograph (57 × 93 mm) copied c. 1879 from a daguerreotype or ambrotype of 1858–61 of the intact portrait (BPM: Ph118). It was included in a collection of 38 photographs previously owned by J. Horsfall Turner which were intended for use in the production of drawn illustrations for his book, *Haworth – Past and Present: A History of Haworth, Stanbury and Oxenhope*. The photograph, seen at the head of this entry, is mounted on a card on which is printed 'J. Bottomley, photographer. 72, Market St. Shop, 51 Tyrrel Street, and 980, Leeds Rd. (3 minutes walk from Laisterdyke Station.) Bradford.' Barker has shown that the original photograph must have belonged to Martha Brown, since Martha says in a letter in the BPM dated 22 October 1879 to Sidney Biddell of South Kensington who had visited her in September that year: 'as you expressed a wish to have my photo when in Haworth I now enclose you one. & also a group from the Photograph taken from a painting by P. B. Bronte it was in Bradford at the time you were at Haworth you will remember me speaking about it.'

In the photograph of the painting Anne, Charlotte, Branwell and Emily are seen sitting from left to right behind a table on which there lies a collection of objects including game, books and papers. The figures of the sisters correspond in all details to the images in the Greenwood tracings. Anne Brontë is depicted half-length facing picture right. Charlotte is viewed from the front with her head also facing slightly to picture right. Her oval face is whited out by the tones of the photograph. Emily is seen half-length on the far right of the group, seated, in profile looking to picture left, and her body is largely obscured by the poor quality of the photograph.

Branwell occupies a position just right of centre of the picture, facing the viewer. His hair is short and bushy above his ears and his only visible facial features are his wide staring eyes. He wears a tight-fitting jacket with high collar and high-necked stock and cravat pin. A shot-gun is held upright in the crook of his left elbow.

The image contained in this photograph is indistinct but the information it conveys is very important for determining the source of the National Portrait Gallery fragment portrait of Emily, and for ascertaining that the known number of Brontë family group portraits by Branwell is limited to two (the lost 'Gun Group' and the National Portrait Gallery 'The Brontë sisters') rather than three or even four portraits as has been surmised over the years. Before this photograph was discovered the 'Gun Group' portrait was known only from the drawing produced, as we now know, from this photograph, for Horsfall Turner's book.

The artist commissioned to make the drawing, unable to make out the details of the photograph because of its poor quality, was therefore compelled to invent or embellish them. This led to the confusion described above, a mystery which Barker's research has now unravelled and solved.

## 225

## The Brontë sisters

c. 1834
Oil on canvas
902 × 746 mm

Purchased through Reginald J. Smith from Mary Anne Nicholls, 1914. This portrait was inherited by Arthur Bell Nicholls on the death of Patrick Brontë, in 1861. It was found by Mary Anne Nicholls on the top of a wardrobe at their home, Hill House, Banagher in Ireland, together with the 'Gun Group' portrait fragment of Emily (**224**), after Nicholls's death, in 1914.
*National Portrait Gallery, London: 1725*

The dating of this picture to c. 1834 is dependent on the words of Charlotte's biographer Elizabeth Gaskell in a letter of September 1853 describing her first visit to Haworth: 'One day, Miss Brontë brought down a rough, common-looking oil-painting, done by her brother, of herself, – a little, rather prim-looking girl of eighteen,– and the two other sisters, girls of 16 and 14, with cropped hair, and sad, dreamy-looking eyes.' (*The Letters of Mrs Gaskell*, ed. J. A.V. Chapple and Arthur Pollard (Manchester: Manchester University Press, 1966), p. 249). The three Brontë sisters are depicted against a very dark background three-quarter length, standing, with Anne, aged fourteen, at picture left, sixteen-year-old Emily in the centre and Charlotte, eighteen years old, on the right. Anne and Emily are seen three-quarter face, with Anne looking up to the right, displaying a very slight squint, and Emily looking at the viewer. A yellowish-brown pillar separates the figures of Emily and Charlotte, who gazes to picture left. The different colours of the girls' eyes are clearly distinguishable: Anne's are blue, Emily's a greenish blue and Charlotte's are brown. All three wear similar plain dresses with large square white voile collars; Anne is in dark blue, Emily in green and Charlotte in brown, as if to correspond with the colour of their eyes. All three girls have reddish-brown hair parted in the centre with curls or ringlets covering their ears. Charlotte's hair is clearly piled into a topknot whereas the other two girls appear to have short loose hair. Charlotte's complexion is noticeably paler than her sisters', but all three have touches of pink on their cheeks. All three appear to rest a hand on the back of a chair or table top in front of them.

Like the fragment portrait of Emily, this group portrait also has a strange history which evidences Nicholls's dislike of the painting and his determination to conceal its existence. When Clement Shorter visited Nicholls at Hill House in 1895, Nicholls revealed nothing of the whereabouts of either portrait to him, even though at the time both must have been languishing on top of the wardrobe upstairs. Perhaps he was respecting the wishes of his late wife, who, on 29 September 1850 at the time when *Agnes Grey* and *Wuthering Heights* were being republished, had written to W. S. Williams: 'I grieve to say that I possess no portrait of either of my sisters' (*The Brontës: Their Lives, Friendships and Correspondence*, ed. Thomas James Wise and John Alexander Symington, 4 vols. (Oxford: Basil Blackwell for the Shakespeare Head Press, 1932), vol. 3, p. 165). In a letter in the National Portrait Gallery archives dated 12 February 1914 Mary Anne Nicholls describes how the paintings were discovered: 'I daresay you may wonder how I never said anything of the Portraits before but till about six months ago I did not know they were in the House – They must have been put in a wardrobe (Top) years ago & servants took down the panel, dusted it & put them back again but about six months ago, I was sitting in the room & my nurse [who] was settling some things for me took down the panel & asked if I knew what was in it I did not, so was much surprised' (Richard Ormond, *National Portrait Gallery: Early Victorian Portraits*, 2 vols. (London: Her Majesty's Stationery Office, 1973), vol. 1, p. 58). It is indeed extraordinary that this painting has survived in view of the antipathy harboured towards it by both Charlotte and her husband.

Underneath the yellowish-brown pillar which separates the figures of Emily and Charlotte (the portrait has often been called 'The Pillar Portrait') the painted-out figure of Branwell can now be discerned. Oil paint tends to become slightly transparent with age which means that the artist's pentimenti, or alterations, are often revealed with time. In 1957 Jean Nixon was the first to notice the outlines of a figure beneath the pillar and infra-red photography revealed it to be that of a man in a black coat and cravat with a white shirt, his bushy hair sticking out at the sides, clearly identifiable as the artist (Ingeborg Nixon, 'The Brontë Portraits: Some old problems and a new discovery', *Brontë Society Transactions* (1958), vol. 13, part 68, p. 233). Examination of the picture revealed that the figure of Branwell had been originally included in this composition, and did not belong to an earlier canvas reworked, and also that Branwell had painted himself out during the picture's execution and not at some later date as the self-portrait is unfinished. It has been suggested that this act of self-erasure was motivated by self-loathing, but it is more likely that Branwell was dissatisfied with the cramped composition. In any case, at the age of seventeen, when this picture was painted, Branwell was years away from the self-inflicted degradation that was to be his downfall. The classical pillar, although rather crude and incongruous in the context of this picture, is a conventional background prop of the portrait painter which would have been familiar to Branwell.

There is a further dimension to this painting that gives visible clues to its history, and that is its condition. For over fifty years this rare portrait of three of the greatest English writers of the nineteenth century lay folded and hidden on top of a wardrobe in an Irish farmhouse. The marks of this interment add uniquely to the picture's mysterious quality. Two main folds run across the middle of the canvas from top to bottom and from side to side with extensive loss of paint, particularly in the centre. The second set of folds run through the eyes of Emily and Charlotte and also through their waists and Anne's bust. Colin Wiggins, National Gallery Lecturer, has pointed out in an unpublished lecture at the National Portrait Gallery in April 1990, that in any other portrait these disfiguring folds and resultant paint losses would have been painstakingly restored in an effort to recreate the original intentions of the artist. But here their very existence signifies an important aspect of the poignant Brontë story, namely Nicholls's simultaneous act of preservation and censorship which speaks of his sensitivity to the preying biographers.

The portrait does not look now as it did to Charlotte's first biographer, Elizabeth Gaskell: 'I have seen an oil painting of his, done I know not when, but probably about this time. It was a group of his sisters, lifesize, three-quarters' length; not much better than sign-painting, as to manipulation; but the likenesses were, I should think, admirable. I could only judge of the fidelity with which the other two were depicted, from the striking resemblance which Charlotte, upholding the great frame of canvas, and consequently standing right behind it, bore to her own representation, though it must have been ten years and more since the portraits were taken. The picture was divided, almost in the middle, by a great pillar. On the side of the column which was lighted by the sun, stood Charlotte, in the womanly dress of that day of jigot sleeves and large collars. On the deeply shadowed side, was Emily, with Anne's gentle face resting on her shoulder. Emily's countenance struck me as full of power; Charlotte's of solicitude; Anne's of tenderness' (E. C. Gaskell, *The Life of Charlotte Brontë*, 2 vols. (London: Smith, Elder & Co., 1857), vol. 1, p. 155).

Mrs Ellis H. Chadwick, writing, ironically, in about 1914, the very year that 'The Brontë sisters' was rediscovered, referred to this portrait, although she confused it with the 'Gun Group' picture: 'The original has disappeared, though fortunately a photograph on glass was taken by a Haworth photographer.' (*In the Footsteps of the Brontës* (London: Sir Isaac Pitman & Sons Ltd, 1914), p. 116). This early, retouched photograph of 'The Brontë sisters' (seen below) gives us some idea of how it must have looked to its most famous documenter, Elizabeth Gaskell.

There are no known studies for this portrait, but closer inspection of the versos of Branwell's drawings has revealed a number of small sketches which may be related to this portrait. In **223** there are two drawings of groups of three and four head-and-shoulders figures respectively. The heads are similar to the head of the central figure on the recto, a cloaked man sitting with two companions at the entrance to a cave, but are not otherwise related to the image on the recto. The larger of the two drawings depicts a group of three male figures facing each other, two of them seen in profile. The smaller group contains four figures, more feminine in their appearance with finer features and longer hair, arranged in a similar manner. Whether these are direct studies for the portrait it is impossible to say for certain, but clearly Branwell was experimenting with compositional formats for the representation of a group consisting of the same number of figures as in this one.

Closer study of a pencil portrait of 'Grimshaw, H.' (**271**) reveals below the main drawing, drawn in reverse to it, a half-finished pencil study of the head of Emily Brontë as she appears in this portrait. The head is tilted at a slightly different angle, to the right with the eyes looking to the right, but it is unmistakably Emily in every detail of the face.

## 226

## Sunset over seashore

18 February 1834
Ink on paper
27 × 114 mm

The sketch appears at the foot of the second page (187 × 114 mm) of two pages of prose, describing events preceding the formation of the Angrian parliament: the Duke of Zamorna, lieutenant-general of the victorious Verdopolitan army, gives a speech to parliament in which he makes a case for being given the kingdom of Angria as a reward, and is supported in a speech by his father-in-law, the Earl of Northangerland. The manuscript has been dated half-way down the first page 'Feb. 18./ 1834./ PBB.'

Formerly owned by Lord Brotherton: see **203**.
*The Brotherton Collection, Leeds University Library*

Pen-and-ink sketch of sunrise over an area of land and water. Boats sail on the water and stick figures or trees are visible in the left foreground.

## 227

### Figure of 'Justice'

June 1834
Ink on paper
20 × 36 mm

Titled below: 'Justice'. The sketch appears on the title page (187 × 113 mm) of a manuscript volume of 24 pages. Inscribed in ink by Branwell, above the sketch: 'THE./ WOOL IS RISING./ OR::/ THE ANGRIAN ADVENTURER./ –A Narrative of the proceedings/ –Of the Foundation of the –/ –Kingdom of Angria/ BY/ THE RIGHT HONOURABLE/ JOHN/ Baron Flower and Viscount Richton/ Secretary of State for/ Foreign Affairs/ Ambassador to the Court/ of Angria FLS. &c &c.'; below the sketch: 'Verdopolis printed and/ published by/ Seargt Tree =/ And sold by all other Booksellers =/ P B Brontë/ = June 26. AD 1834.' This is followed by a colophon of a rising sun at the foot of the page.

Formerly owned by Thomas James Wise, who probably acquired the manuscript from Arthur Bell Nicholls.
*British Library: Ashley 2469*

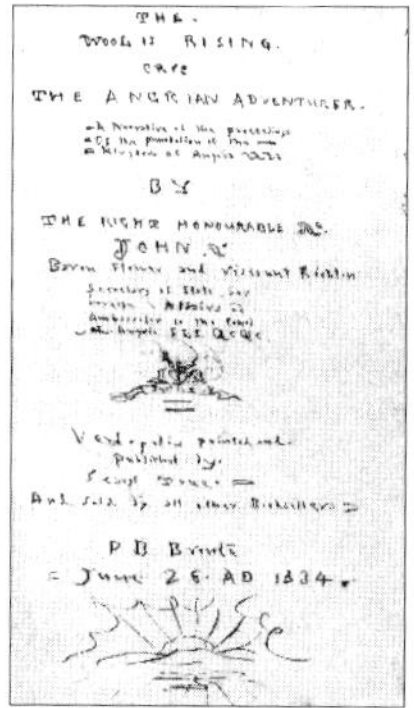

Small slightly smudged figure of 'Justice', with outstretched arms, a sword in her left hand, an olive branch in her right. A dog sits at her feet on her right, looking upwards, and on her left a lion.

## 228

### Profile of a man

September–October 1834
Ink on paper
15 × 15 mm

The sketch appears in the right-hand margin of p. 5 (186 × 113 mm) of a prose fragment of eight pages. The fragment describes the opening of the Angrian parliament, which is prefaced by Branwell's first draft of the poem 'The Angrian Welcome'.

Formerly owned by Lord Brotherton: see **203**.
*The Brotherton Collection, Leeds University Library*

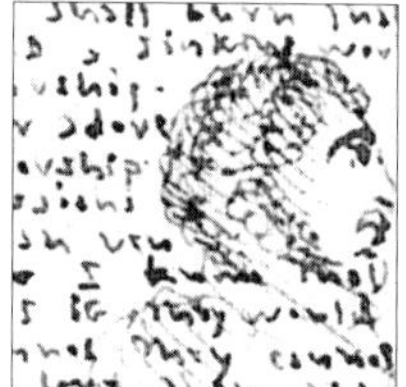

Ink sketch, merging into text, of a profile of a man with curly hair, moustache and beard.

## 229

### Map or architectural sketch

September–October 1834
Ink on paper
62 × 113 mm

The sketch appears in the centre of the text on p. 6 (186 × 113 mm) of a prose fragment of eight pages: see **228**.

Formerly owned by Lord Brotherton: see **203**.
*The Brotherton Collection, Leeds University Library*

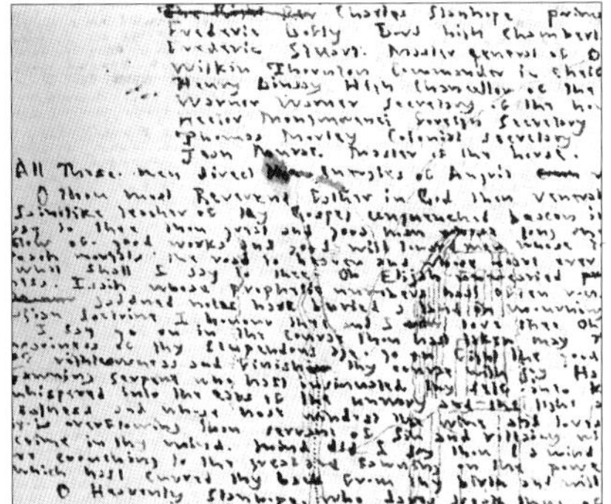

Outline map or sketch of part of a building, merging into the text of the manuscript.

## 230

## Sketches of buildings, mythical creature, trumpeter and fort

c. 1834–1836
Ink and pencil on paper
112 × 122 mm

The sketches appear on the second page (210 × 128 mm) of a two-page manuscript on which Branwell has inscribed drafts of three of his poems. The text at the top of the page begins: 'Sing for the power of thy foeman thats gone', an early draft of the last 27 lines of 'Sound the Loud Trumpet'. A further 14 lines appear upside down at the bottom of the page, beginning 'When on the thorny bed of death', trial lines for 'Misery'. Victor Neufeldt has dated these lines c. January 1835 (*The Poems of Patrick Branwell Brontë: A New Text and Commentary* (New York and London: Garland Publishing, Inc., 1990), p. 396). Stamped: 'BRONTË/ MUSEUM/ HAWORTH', encircled.

Purchased in London, 1899, from H. E. Gorfin, 1899; an agent of Thomas James Wise.
*Brontë Parsonage Museum; BS113*

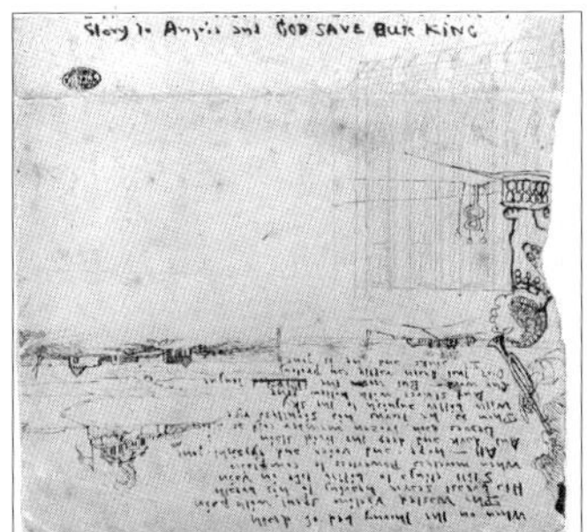

Detailed pencil sketch of an elevation of a gothic building with four high arches. Upside down and overlapping this sketch is a tiny sketch in ink of a mythical creature sitting on a podium. It has the paws of a lion, curly hair and a human face. Above this, in the margin, is an ink profile of a trumpeter. On the far right are ink sketches of further buildings, including a fort on a rocky outcrop.

Branwell had a great interest in architecture (see, for example, Darton's *Description of London*, Appendix A) and his facility for drawing buildings is recorded by Francis H. Grundy: 'Brontë drew a finished elevation of one portion of Westminster Abbey from memory, having been but once to London some years before' (*Pictures of the Past: Memories of Men I have met, and Places I have seen* (London: Griffith & Farran, 1879), p. 80). Whether or not Branwell actually went to London remains a matter for debate, but his ability to draw buildings, learnt by copying from engravings and by drawing from life (see, for example, **219**, **220**), is not in dispute.

## 231

## Horse with rider

c. 1834–1835
Oil on canvas
278 × 328 mm

Acquired in 1894 from Thomas Parker. A 'Mr Parker' bought '2 pictures' at the sale of Patrick Brontë's effects at Haworth Parsonage, 1–2 October 1861, lot 93. F. C. Galloway (*A Descriptive Catalogue of Objects in the Museum of the Brontë Society at Haworth* (Bradford, 1896), p. 19), lists an 'Oil Painting by Patrick Branwell Brontë' on loan from Mr Thomas Parker.

*Brontë Parsonage Museum: B30*

Small oil painting of a black horse and huntsman rider facing picture left. The rider is dressed in a short hunting-pink jacket, yellow breeches, black cap and boots and he is carrying a whip. Beneath the saddle there is a white blanket; the horse's reins and harness are clearly visible. In the foreground shrubs grow on the stony ground. In the background large buildings, including a stadium with many arches, are seen against a dramatically coloured sky with the yellow of the sun-tinged clouds contrasting vividly with the blue.

This small painting was probably copied from a sporting print as a practice work. It is very crudely painted by an artist who has clearly not mastered the technique of painting in oils and the cracking of the paint is clearly visible. It may well be one of the tasks set for Branwell by his painting teacher, William Robinson, c. 1834–5.

232

## John Barraclough (c. 1773–1835)

c. 1834–1838
Watercolour and pencil on paper
105 × 80 mm

Gift of Jill Kendrick, 1990; by descent through sitter's family to donor. John Barraclough was a member of the Haworth clockmakers' family and his son photographed Patrick Brontë in his old age. The donor's grandfather recorded that this portrait was made by Branwell.

*Brontë Parsonage Museum: P170*

Head-and-shoulders portrait of John Barraclough of Haworth seen looking to picture right. He appears to be in his early sixties and has short cropped grey hair and side whiskers, a long nose, prominent chin and pink lips and wears a high-collared black jacket. To his left there is a brown stone pillar. Behind the man's head there is a wash of brown shadow, shading to light in front of his face, painted in an elliptical shape as if the painting was originally intended to be framed beneath an oval mount. The edges of the paper have been cut unevenly and there are pinholes in the sides of the paper where it was originally sewn onto a piece of card with cotton thread.

The attribution to Branwell depends on oral tradition within the donor's family. Barraclough was a member of the Masonic Lodge at Haworth and it is possible that Branwell, who, despite his youthfulness, was admitted to the Lodge by 25 April 1836 and attended all its meetings that year and acted as Secretary at seven meetings in 1837, made portraits of fellow Masons, although John Barraclough's death in 1835 predates Branwell's membership. There are no other watercolour portraits by him extant and the style of the work is not typical of the artist. Branwell painted a design on a Masonic apron (**247**) formerly owned by Mr W. Thomas, Wine and Spirit merchant of Haworth, also a member of the Three Graces Lodge and the subject of a portrait by Branwell (see **260**).

233

## Shipwreck

c. 1834–1835
Oil painting
c. 762 × 895 mm

*Location unknown*

This painting was included in the sale of the property of J. H. Dixon of Harrogate at Sotheby's, 15 December 1916, lot 667. It was described in the catalogue as: 'A Shipwreck, much cracked and faded, 30 in. by 35 in., framed. Purchased by Mr Smith of Bingley, after the death of the Rev. P. Bronte, and subsequently in the possession of Charles Bainton; with a framed certificate of authenticity from Mrs Smith' and noted as 'Unsold'. According to the record of buyers at the sale of the contents of Haworth Parsonage, 1–2 October 1861, two lots including paintings were bought by a Rev. Mr Smith. They were lot 148 '2 Pictures' bought for 3s. and lot 150 'Large Oil Painting' bought for £1.5s. The Rev. Mr Smith was also the purchaser of lot 201, described only as 'Books'.

Dixon's collection also included the Brontës' cottage piano (withdrawn from the sale and given to the Brontë Museum), walking sticks, fluted bed posts from Charlotte's bedsteads, Charlotte and Emily's travelling trunk and a letter from Charlotte to Ellen Nussey. According to the catalogue of the sale many of the relics were obtained from Tabitha Ratcliffe (Martha Brown's sister), Mary Popplewell (niece of Martha), Sarah Wood (Martha's cousin) and various Haworth residents.

234

## Kitchen interior with figures

c. 1834–1838
Pencil on paper
132 × 199 mm

Unsigned and undated. Stamped: 'BRONTË/ MUSEUM/ HAWORTH', encircled. Watermark: 'Creswick'. On verso, drawn at right angles to this drawing: unfinished pencil sketch of a woman's head and shoulders; hair in ringlets, eyes downcast. This drawing resembles Charlotte's drawings of female heads, perhaps an unfinished portrait of Anne.

Purchased from Hodgson & Co., London, 31 March 1933; part of lot 449. Formerly part of the Law Collection (see **15**).

*Brontë Parsonage Museum: B14*

Line drawing of a scene set in a large room dominated by a huge fireplace with gargoyles at its top corners and a large cauldron suspended over the fire. There are altogether 18 figures, mostly male, dispersed around the room in various attitudes of repose; three men sit on the floor in front of the fire to warm themselves; others lounge against the walls or sit at a table. On the right there is a curtained recess or window. Various objects are slung from the ceiling beams, including a saddle and harness, and there are lamp holders on the wall. In the right foreground beside a tall basket lies a muzzled dog chained to the wall.

The room could be in a tavern, a subject in which Branwell displayed an early interest as a setting for the more disreputable low-life characters he wrote about. As early as August 1829 he vividly described such a place in his poem 'Interior of A Pothouse By Young Soult' (see *The*

*Poems of Patrick Branwell Brontë: A New Text and Commentary*, ed. Victor A. Neufeldt (New York and London: Garland Publishing, Inc., 1990), p. 7):

> the cheerful fire is blazing bright
> & cast[s] a ruddy glare
> on beams & rafters all in sight
> & on the sanded floor
>
> the scoured pewter on the shelf
> glitters like silver pure
> & all the ware of stony delf
> doth like to Gold allure
>
> and where this fire so magical
> doth spread its light around
> sure many scenes most magical
> are acted on that ground . . .

Mary Butterfield (*Brother in the Shadow: Stories & Sketches by Patrick Branwell Brontë*, ed. Mary Butterfield and R. J. Duckett (Bradford: Bradford Libraries and Information Service, 1988), p. 61) identifies this drawing as a shooting party, also comparing it with Emily Brontë's description of the kitchen at Wuthering Heights and suggesting that it might be a scene witnessed by Branwell at Ponden Hall, home of the Heatons at Stanbury near Haworth. The Heatons are believed to have been friends of the Brontë family as Robert Heaton, and later his son Robert, were Trustees of Haworth Church. The figures are very well observed, possibly drawn from life but more likely copied from a print.

## 235

## Jacob's dream

c. 1834–1838
Oil on canvas
460 × 600 mm

Gift of William Law, 1894 (see **15**). In a letter to J. Horsfall Turner, 11 September 1894 (BPM), Law wrote: 'I hear you are getting up a Museum of Brontë relics &c. I have an oil painting 24 × 34 [*sic*] by Branwell which I bought at Haworth some years ago from a man named Wood, a nephew I think of 'Old Tabby', he bought it at the sale after Mr Brontë's death. I should be glad to present this to the Museum if you would have it.'
*Brontë Parsonage Museum: B17*

The story of Jacob's dream is told in the Book of Genesis 28: 10–22: 'And Jacob went out from Beer-sheba, and went toward Haran. And he lighted upon a certain place, and tarried there all night, because the sun was set; and he took of the stones of that place, and put them for his pillows, and lay down in that place to sleep. And he dreamed, and behold a ladder set up on the earth, and the top of it reached to heaven: and behold the angels of God ascending and descending on it' (verses 10–12). This is the scene which Branwell depicts.

Overall, the picture is painted in dark, sombre colours. In the painting, Jacob, his lower body draped in a red cloth, lies asleep in the foreground. An angel in red robes stands at his head with one arm raised; at his feet three angels, in dark purple and green gowns, stand and look down on him. The nearest figure, seen from the back, points to Jacob with his right hand. Beyond, a grand stairway leads up to heaven. Two angels with their arms around each other, one painted in a muddy lilac, the other in yellow, stand on the bottom step and look down on the sleeping mortal. At the top of the steps an angel robed in a bluish lilac colour stands in the centre with outstretched wings and hands clasped. Other figures of angels approach from either side, draped in shades of green, lilac and cream, and in the distance can be seen massed ranks of angels painted in lighter tones of these colours. Above them the heavens open into an area of bright yellow ochre light shading into a greyish mauve. The picture is framed by purplish grey clouds, as if opening to reveal the scene. In the foreground rocks and plants can just be discerned.

The print titled 'Jacob's Dream' from which Branwell copied is preserved in the BPM collection (BPM: P108). It measures just 72 × 115 mm and has been cut from *The Literary Souvenir* for 1830 (see plate 10). It is inscribed in ink below the picture: 'Painted by Mr Allston A. R. A./ Engraved by E. Goodall / Jacob's Dream' and was presented by Eric Parkinson in 1932. According to the BPM records the frame previously bore a label, now lost, which read 'Bought at Mr Bronte's sale, Haworth, Oct. 1 & 2, 1861, John Milligan.'

The composition of the painting differs from the print only in the spacing of the foreground figures. Branwell would have practised the art of painting in oils by copying from the works of other artists, available to him only in the form of black and white engravings such as the one copied here. The generally muddy colours of the work show how difficult it was for Branwell to translate the image into colour. This was probably an exercise set for him by his teacher William Robinson of Leeds, which would therefore date the painting to 1834–5, before the presumed London trip, or 1837–8, predating the Bradford studio venture. Branwell's choice of this image, if it was his own choice and not his teacher's, probably had more to do with the dramatic light effects seen in the picture which are very similar to those employed by John Martin, the artist most admired by the Brontës.

Charles Hale, in 'An American Visitor at Haworth, 1861' (*Brontë Society Transactions* (1967), vol. 15, part 67, p. 131), relates a colourful story which he claims was told to him by William Wood, the Haworth joiner in the Brontës' time. The tale contradicts Law's version of how Wood came by the picture 'Jacob's dream' but it confirms the idea that this was one of the oils Branwell painted whilst in training to be an artist.

> One time Charlotte had set her heart on something in his shop which she desired for the better furnishing of the house ... After a while, Mr. Brontë consented to the purchase and the article was sent for and delivered. The price was five guineas.
>
> Now Branwell had been sent to study, ... with an artist of Leeds named Bradley [*sic*]; and under the eye & with the assistance of his master he had executed three oil paintings: one representing Jacob's Dream, & two others. These his father had purchased of the master for the price of ten guineas.
>
> Accordingly when the joiner went to the parsonage to get his money ... he found Mr. Brontë and Charlotte sitting by the new piece of furniture and the father told him he would give him these three pictures which had cost ten guineas, in payment of his bill for five.
>
> Our simple joiner of course was somewhat disconcerted at this proposition, which would pay him with something that he could not but regard as nearly worthless to him; and would have refused point blank; but Charlotte ... looked at him so pleadingly that he held his peace; until presently Mr. Brontë went out of the room saying, 'Well you may do just as you please; you may take away your Mirror ... or you may take away Branwell's three paintings. Suit yourself, I have nothing more to say.'
>
> Then Char-lotty said, 'Now William, please take the pictures and I will make it up to you some time.' So his heart softened and he went away with the pictures.

## 236

## The adoration of the shepherds

c. 1834–1838
Oil on metal
317 × 260 mm

Gift of Lucy Lund, 1919; the donor also presented Keeper's collar and pieces of crockery once owned by the Brontës. Lucy Lund may have been related to R. W. Lund of Ashfield, Malton, York, whose daughter donated

items to the Museum in 1950, including a plait of Emily's hair (J51) which once belonged to Martha Brown who sold or gave it to Lund's father. According to the BPM Stock Book this painting was originally in a gilt frame which had a label on the back stating that the picture had been acquired at the 1861 sale of Patrick Brontë's effects at Haworth Parsonage; frame and label no longer extant.
*Brontë Parsonage Museum: B18*

Nativity scene with the figures of the Virgin Mary and three shepherds kneeling in attitudes of prayer around the crib, in which sleeps the naked Christ child. A sheep lies in front of the crib. In the background is the figure of Joseph, with hands raised, and behind him the stable with an ox and an ass. Three cherubs, their heads cropped by the edge of the picture, hover above the scene. In the far distance the night sky can be seen. The whole image is very dark, the forms indistinct, as the picture itself is in such poor condition with a thick yellow varnish overall. Three areas have, however, been spot-cleaned: half of the figure of the baby in the cradle, the Virgin's face and neck and the group of cherubs. This does not enhance the general appearance of the picture but it does reveal the original bright quality of the oil colours: the gold and blue of the Madonna's robes and the red worn by the two shepherds on either side of her.

Like **235**, this picture is probably a copy, this time from a print of a seventeenth-century Italian painting, which Branwell was encouraged to make by William Robinson, his teacher, in order to practise the craft of oil painting and to learn from the Old Masters.

## 237

## The Lincolnshire link boy

c. 1834–1838
Oil on wood panel
235 × 200 mm

Gift of Gladys Shackleton, 1990; for many years this painting hung in Ponden Hall, Stanbury, near Haworth, home of the Heaton family, and is believed to have been presented to the Heatons by the Brontës as a token of friendship. After the demise of the Heaton family, George Helliwell (d. 1914) of Ponden purchased the painting from the estate as a memento of his friends. Helliwell was a local grocer and a trustee of Scar Top Chapel where John Heaton was choirmaster and organist. The picture was inherited by Clara Pickles, née Rushworth (d. 1951), who stored it carefully but burnt the original frame, which bore its title, for firewood during the fuel shortage in the Second World War. It was inherited by the donor c. 1951.
*Brontë Parsonage Museum: B45*

Link boys ran ahead of horse-drawn carriages carrying a lantern or a flaming torch to light the way ahead. This predominantly dark-toned painting depicts the half-length figure of the boy, wearing a peaked cap and tunic buttoned up to the neck, holding aloft a lantern in his right hand. The front of the boy's body is rather crudely painted in shades of orange, pink and yellow to suggest the effect of the lantern's rays falling on him from picture left. His face is given a devilish aspect by the effects of the yellowish light cast across his grinning features.

The choice of subject, probably derived from a print, would have appealed to Branwell less for its history and more for the opportunity it provided for exploring the technique of painting its powerful chiaroscuro effects. This interest in dramatic lighting comes from the artist's lifelong admiration for the work of John Martin. The attribution to Branwell is made primarily on stylistic grounds, given the rather tenuous provenance: the extent of the friendship between the Brontës and the Heatons is by no means certain. Notice, also, the way in which the line of the boy's brow-bone and nose has been painted, with an arched curve which seems to be peculiar to Branwell's manner of painting the face.

The painting is possibly one of a series of copies Branwell produced when he was studying with William Robinson.

## 238

## Landscape with cottage, river and bridge

c. 1834–1838
Oil on wood panel
437 × 603 mm

Provenance unknown
*Brontë Parsonage Museum: B37*

Painted on a wood panel which has at some time been split into two parts and repaired, the whole object is in poor condition. The subject can be distinguished as a moonlit landscape view of a cottage beside a tall tree to the left. The cottage appears to be approached via a foot-bridge across a stream. To the right of the picture is a river which flows beneath a bridge in the middle-ground. In the distance mountains can be seen.

This is a very crudely executed work; from the untutored style it would seem to be one of the oil paintings Branwell produced when he was a student.

## 239

## 'Zamorna. 35.'

1835
Ink on paper
242 × 183 mm

Inscribed in Branwell's longhand in ink, bottom centre: 'Zamorna. 35.'; in pencil, top right: 'Grassmere [*sic*]'. Watermark, top left: 'J WHATMAN / 1831'. On verso: pencil sketch of lines of hills, similar to faint sketch top right recto. Inscribed faintly in pencil across sketch: 'snow / fell / fell / feilds [*sic*]'.

Bequest of Henry Houston Bonnell, 1927; acquired by Bonnell from Sotheby's sale of the effects of Arthur Bell Nicholls, London, 26 July 1907, lot 41 or 42.
*Brontë Parsonage Museum: Bonnell 13*

Forceful drawing of a half-length portrait of a man seen in profile looking to picture right. The man has thick dark curly hair which is swept up on the top of his head and curls over his collar and onto his cheek. The face has a long straight nose, heavy brows, down-turned mouth and side whiskers. It is heavily shaded to suggest a dark complexion. He wears a high neckerchief and a caped coat, possibly intended to resemble military dress. Along the right side of the picture the remnants of a pencil sketch of a lake and trees are discernible. The pencil lines and notes on the verso would seem to refer to a plan for a landscape drawing or even a painting.

The inscription 'Grassmere' suggests that Branwell has reused a piece of paper on which a Lake District subject had been started. It may also refer to the Angrian Grassmere, modelled on the English equivalent and always spelt with a double 's': see Charlotte's 'High Life In Verdopolis', where Zamorna's faithful mistress, Mina Laury, lives in seclusion at Grassmere Manor (*An Edition of the Early Writings of Charlotte Brontë*, ed. Christine Alexander, 2 vols. (Oxford: Basil Blackwell for the Shakespeare Head Press, 1987; 1991), vol. 2, part 2, pp. 54–61).

The portrait's title describes the man as 'Zamorna'. In the Brontës' Angrian mythology the Duke of Zamorna was first known as Arthur Wellesley, eldest son of Wellington; Marquis of Douro and Alderwood; Earl of Evesham and Baron Leyden. Later he became King of Angria and eventually Emperor Adrian. Charlotte was in the habit of copying portraits of female beauties from engravings and adapting them (sometimes with changes of title) into images of heroines of the Brontës' shared imaginary world. In this drawing Branwell seems to be drawing straight from his imagination. Although the drawing copies the format of engraved portraits of contemporary heroes, as seen in the illustrated books and Annuals which were their most frequent source of inspiration, the strong lines suggest an original work.

See also 'Northangerland / Alexander Percy' (**240**), a similar drawing in ink which may have been produced around the same time.

## 240

## 'Northangerland./ Alexander Percy Esq.'

c. 1835
Ink on paper
225 × 180 mm

Titled in Branwell's longhand, in ink, centre top: 'Northangerland'; centre bottom: 'Alexander Percy Esq.'; up left side: 'John Brown'; up right side beneath heavy ink scrawl: 'Joseph Leyland'.

Formerly owned by Joseph Bentley Leyland and possibly kept in the Leyland family with the collection known as 'The Leyland Manuscripts' until it was acquired by Lord Brotherton: see **203**.

*The Brotherton Collection, Leeds University Library*

Half-length male portrait seen in profile and looking to picture right. The man has a high domed forehead with a high hairline. His longish dark hair clears his collar but is swept onto his face to meet his side whiskers. The face has dark eyebrows, a long thin pointed nose and a small mouth and chin. He wears a high collar and a plain tight-fitting jacket. The portrait somewhat resembles Branwell himself.

Alexander Percy, also known as Rogue, Percy, Ellrington and Northangerland, is Branwell's main hero and alter ego. He has three wives, four sons, two daughters and a number of mistresses, leads a life of dissipation, is killed, reincarnated, fights in numerous battles, sails around the world as Percy the Pirate, helps Zamorna become King of Angria, leads a rebellion against him, is exiled then pardoned and lives on into an abrasive and irritable old age.

John Brown, whose name appears on the drawing, was Branwell's friend and the Haworth sexton; Joseph Leyland was his friend the sculptor.

This ink drawing is very similar in style and format to **239** and was possibly drawn around the same time, although it belongs to the group of Branwell's illustrated letters commonly called 'The Leyland Manuscripts' which are in the Brotherton Collection, University of Leeds Library, the rest of which date from 1842 to Branwell's death in 1848.

241

## The pirate

c. 1835
Ink on paper
235 × 197 mm

Inscribed on verso in ink, in Branwell's longhand in mirror writing, apparently transferred from another sheet when ink was wet: 'In [2 words indecipherable] not [1 word indecipherable] lover, I am [1 word indecipherable]'.

Bequest of Henry Houston Bonnell, 1927; acquired by Bonnell from Sotheby's sale of the effects of Arthur Bell Nicholls, London, 26 July 1907, lot 41 or 42.
*Brontë Parsonage Museum: Bonnell 12*

Full-length portrait in ink of a man wearing the sixteenth-century costume of a large square white collar, doublet, hose and calf-length boots. His head is seen in profile looking to picture left, with long hair parted in the centre and a pointed beard. He adopts a heroic pose, seeming to look out to sea from the shore, his hands clasped to his chest and his mighty sword hanging on his right side. In the background two three-masted sailing ships at sea are drawn in outline. There are ink blots around his face. The style of the drawing is very similar to the portrait of Zamorna in **239**.

This is almost certainly a portrait of Alexander Percy as a pirate, one of the many roles he adopted in his long and colourful history, viz 'The Pirate' written by Branwell in February 1830 (BPM: Bonnell 140). Charlotte also described Percy the Pirate in 'The Green Dwarf' written 2 September 1833:

> Having thus wound up the dénouement of my brief and jejune narrative, I will conclude by a glance at the future fortunes of Colonel Percy and his accomplice.
>
> The sentence of death which had been passed on the former was afterwards commuted to exile for sixteen years. During this period he wandered through the world, sometimes a pirate, sometimes a leader of banditti, and ever the companion of the most dissolute and profligate of mankind.
>
> (*An Edition of the Early Writings of Charlotte Brontë*, ed. Christine Alexander, 2 vols. (Oxford: Basil Blackwell for the Shakespeare Head Press, 1987; 1991), vol. 2, part 1, p. 205).

242

## Sketches of human limbs

c. 1835
Ink on paper
113 × 45 mm

The sketches appear at either side of a fragment of verse on p. 2 (113 × 116 mm) of a single-leaf fragmentary manuscript. The page bears 13 trial lines with many deletions from the poem which describes Percy's seduction of Harriet O'Connor, written in ink in Branwell's minuscule hand, beginning: 'There is something in this Glorious hour' (see *The Poems of Patrick Branwell Brontë: A New Text and Commentary*, ed. Victor A. Neufeldt (New York and London: Garland Publishing, Inc., 1990), p. 441). Inscribed top left: 'B'. Reverse view of an embossed mark 'LONDON/ SUPERFINE' with a decorative colophon of a shield in the bottom right corner.

Bequest of Henry Houston Bonnell, 1927; acquired by Bonnell from Maggs Bros., London, 1916; previously owned by Thomas James Wise or Walter Slater. See **248**.
*Brontë Parsonage Museum: Bonnell 147.3*

On the left, three studies of the musculature of the human leg; on the right, two human legs in the action of walking, the right leg with a trouser pulled up above the knee; below this, a tiny decorative device.

These small sketches would appear to constitute a rare example of an attempt by Branwell at anatomical study (see also Appendix A, sketches on a page of William Darton's *Description of London*). Intriguingly, the verso of this scrap of paper bears a fragment of the draft letter to the Royal Academy of Arts in London, believed to have been written by Branwell, consisting of the words: 'Sir/ Having an ea/ to enter as probatio/ in the Royal Acade/ being possessed of'.

This manuscript was reproduced in facsimile as the work of Emily Brontë by Clement K. Shorter in 1911 (*The Complete Works of Emily Brontë*, 2 vols. (London: Hodder & Stoughton, 1911), vol. 2, p. 447).

243

## John Brown (1804–1855)

c. 1835–1839
Oil on canvas
770 × 620 mm

Purchased from J. Brown Binns, 1911. F. C. Galloway (*A Descriptive Catalogue of Objects in the Museum of the Brontë Society at Haworth* (Bradford, 1896), p. 9) lists an oil portrait of John Brown by Branwell on loan from Mr Armitage of Saltaire. Mrs Ellis H. Chadwick (*In the Footsteps of the Brontës* (London: Sir Isaac Pitman & Sons Ltd, 1914), p. 103) relates that in 1914 when the book was published 'Martha Brown's niece [perhaps Ellen Binns] also has an oil painting of John Brown, the sexton.'
*Brontë Parsonage Museum: B20*

Half-length portrait of John Brown set against a background of a stormy sky. The sitter looks up towards picture left, turning his head slightly. His complexion is fresh and pink, his hair thick and bushy, greying a little at the temples. He wears a high-collared, deep blue jacket, buttoned to one side, a white shirt and black neckerchief.

John Brown, Branwell's friend and senior by thirteen years, was a stonemason and for twenty years the sexton at Haworth Church during the Brontës' time. In this portrait he would appear to be in his early to mid thirties, which would date the painting to 1835–9 which encompasses the period when Branwell was both a student of art and a portraitist in Bradford.

The canvas is almost the same size as that of the William Brown portrait (**251**) but Branwell's attempt at 'the grand manner' is altogether more successful in this work, particularly in the painting of the stormy sky in the background.

244

## Sketches of male profiles

7 January 1836
Ink on paper

The sketches appear in the left margin of the top third of the last page (185 × 115 mm) of a 38-page manuscript volume, usually known as 'A New Year Story'. The story ends on p. 37 and the volume is inscribed in ink in Branwell's minuscule script on the first page: 'P B Bronte/ January 7th/ 1836'. Page 38 is inscribed with a line of poetry and several words in Greek, plus six lines of poetry in English. Stamped: 'ASHLEY/ BM/ LIBRARY'. Formerly owned by Thomas James Wise, who probably acquired the manuscript from Arthur Bell Nicholls.
*British Library: Ashley 187*

Several profiles in ink: in the top left-hand corner is a heavily drawn profile of a man with a bulbous nose. Below this is a heavily shaded profile head and shoulders of another bulbous-nosed man, wearing a cravat or high collar, the whole closely resembling the profile above. Below this is a face in ink, with a large nose and heavily drawn down-turned mouth, like that of a Greek tragic mask, and below this a further heavily shaded ink profile of a man's head with a heavy brow line and wavy hair.

There would seem to be some relationship between the sketches and the verse, because, as Everard Flintoff has pointed out, the first line of poetry on the manuscript page is from Homer's *Iliad*, Book One, and the poem itself is based on the form and style of the Greek funerary epigram ('Some Unpublished Poems of Branwell Brontë', *Durham University Journal*, vol. 81, June 1989, p. 242).

245

## Sketches of three heads

10 February 1836
Ink on paper
40 × 25 mm

The sketches appear on p. 3 (185 × 113 mm) of a manuscript fragment of four pages, made by folding one sheet of paper in half, containing prose and verse in ink in Branwell's minuscule script. The verse at the top of p. 3 begins: 'The moon in glory mounts above'. Stamped: 'BRONTË/ MUSEUM/ HAWORTH', encircled.

Bequest of Henry Houston Bonnell, 1927; acquired by Bonnell from Sotheby's sale of the effects of Arthur Bell Nicholls, London, 26 July 1907, lot 58.
*Brontë Parsonage Museum: Bonnell 152 (2) 3*

Grotesque profile heads of three men looking to picture right, all three heavily hatched in line.

## 246

### Head of a man

c. 1836
Ink on paper
53 × 42 mm

The sketch appears on p. 4 (186 × 114 mm) of a manuscript fragment of four pages, made by folding one sheet of paper in half, containing prose and verse in ink in Branwell's minuscule script and longhand. The verse on p. 4 begins: 'So spends its hours in thinking on'. Stamped: 'BRONTË/ MUSEUM/ HAWORTH', encircled.

Bequest of Henry Houston Bonnell, 1927; acquired by Bonnell from an unknown source but it is likely that it came from Arthur Bell Nicholls via Thomas James Wise as the three folded sheets preceding this fragment all originated from Wise: 1 and 3 are in the Ashley Library (British Library) and 2 is in the BPM (BS120C), purchased from Wise's agent H. E. Gorfin in 1899.

*Brontë Parsonage Museum: Bonnell 150 (2) 4*

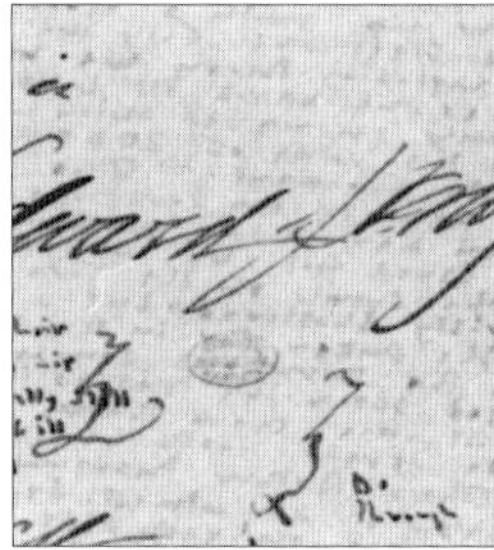

Profile head and shoulders of a man looking to picture right, with wavy hair swept onto his face and forehead and side whiskers, drawn with pen and ink over a circular area of brushed-on ink wash. Possibly a self-portrait. A number of scribbles outside the area of the ink wash could be read as the outline of a hand and arm.

## 247

### Masonic apron

c. 1836–1837
Watercolour on canvas
610 × 460 mm

*Don Thomas*

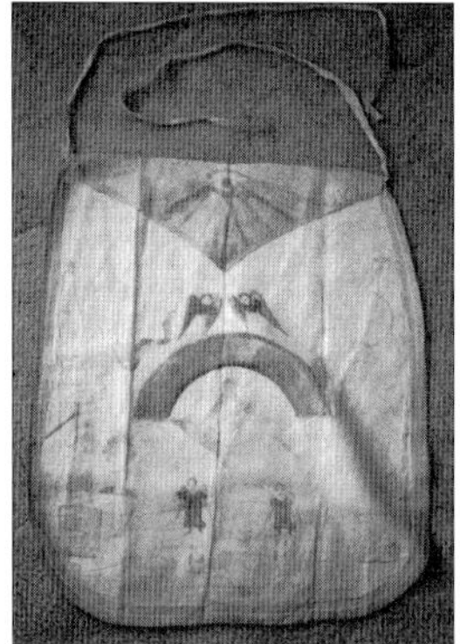

The canvas apron formed some part of ceremonial Masonic garb. It is rather crudely decorated with painted Masonic symbols. On the triangular flap at the top of the apron a single eye is painted in blue, with diagonal lines radiating out from its centre. The centre of the apron is dominated by a blue arch with gold ends, resembling a magnet, over the major Masonic symbol of the compass and right angle, painted in yellow edged with red. Above the arch are two heads with black wings, with to the left a serpent and to the right a ladder. Below the central symbol there are two squat little winged figures in long blue robes, standing either side of a table. To the left there are further indecipherable symbols, and a recognizable sun and moon. To the right, more symbols and marks, including a red bird. The background is the white of the canvas. The colours used throughout are red, blue and yellow.

This item is recorded as exhibit 193, 'Apron Painted by Branwell Bronte for Bro. R. Thomas' in the catalogue of an 'Exhibition of Masonic Treasures from King Edwin to the present day, at the Masonic Hall, Duncombe Place, York', Monday 16 July–Sunday 26 August, 1979. The Masonic apron was lent to the exhibition by its owner, Don Thomas, a descendant of W. Thomas of Haworth, who in a letter to the BPM dated 19 October 1985 writes: 'I have no idea who painted the apron which was handed down to me by my late father. It evidently was originally the property of one of my ancestors Mr W. Thomas of the firm of W. & R. Thomas, Wine and Spirit Merchants of Haworth. His portrait, which was painted by Branwell Brontë [**260**], hung in one of the upstairs rooms of the Parsonage on my last visit there. My father did disclose to me that the Thomas family was very friendly with the Brontës and according to letters from the Brontës which are now no longer in our family possession Mrs Thomas often nursed the Brontë children when they were ill. I also understand that Mr W. Thomas held high office in the Three Graces Masonic Lodge at Haworth when Branwell was secretary.'

## 248

## Sketch of a map

c. 19 January 1837
Pencil on paper
50 × 93 mm

The sketch appears at the foot of p. 2 (156 × 93 mm) of a manuscript of two pages, containing a poem of 18 verses written in ink in Branwell's minuscule script: 'Sleep Mourner sleep! – I cannot sleep'. The poem is an early draft of 'Poor mourner – sleep.' (see *The Poems of Patrick Branwell Brontë: A New Text and Commentary*, ed. Victor A. Neufeldt (London and New York: Garland Publishing, Inc., 1990), pp. 264–5, and pp. 496–7). The page on which the sketch appears, bears eight verses of the poem, beginning: 'All all is over freind or lover'. Stamped: 'BRONTË/ MUSEUM/ HAWORTH', encircled.
Bequest of Henry Houston Bonnell, 1927; acquired by Bonnell from Clark, a dealer in Cleveland, Ohio, in 1912; previously owned by Walter Slater or Thomas James Wise (see below).
*Brontë Parsonage Museum: Bonnell 146:5v*

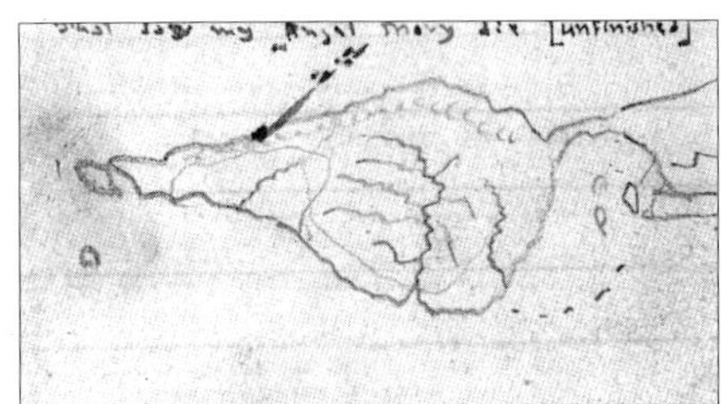

Rough pencil sketch of a map of an unspecified land in a leg-of-mutton shape with rivers, mountains and offshore islands marked. This manuscript was reproduced in facsimile as the work of Emily Brontë by Clement K. Shorter in 1911 (*The Complete Works of Emily Brontë*, 2 vols. (London: Hodder & Stoughton, 1911), vol. 2, pp. 450–1). The facsimile was reproduced from 'The Original Manuscripts in the possession of Mr THOMAS J. WISE and Mr. WALTER SLATER', according to Shorter (p. 417).

This sketch is very similar to one which appears in the Brontës' own copy of Reverend J. Goldsmith's *A Grammar of General Geography, For the Use of Schools and Young Persons* (London: Longman, Hurst, Rees, Orme & Brown, 1823): see Appendix A. This was first noted by C. W. Hatfield in Shorter's *The Complete Works of Emily Brontë*, where he reproduced both sketches on p. 451 in vol. 2. Both maps, when turned vertically, appear to be rough copies of the map of the continent of South America in Goldsmith's *Grammar*.

## 249

## Caricature of a lawyer or clergyman facing a goose

c. 1837–1838
Pencil on paper
80 × 120 mm

Sketch appears on p. 2 (245 × 195 mm) of a hard-backed notebook of 82 pages containing Branwell's transcripts of his poems written between 1833 and 1836, transcribed 1837–8. The sketch occupies the centre of the second page of the list of poems included in the notebook, written in ink in Branwell's longhand, beginning: '27 Lines on ~~his~~ leaving Africa. 1818 ... A Percy ... Dec$^{r}$ 1835 ... 20'; written above '1835 ... 20' are the words 'carried over 886', referring to the number of lines of verse.

Purchased at Sotheby's sale of the effects of Arthur Bell Nicholls, London, 26 July 1907, lot 57.
*Brontë Parsonage Museum: BS125*

Outline pencil sketch drawn in the manner of a cartoon of the head and shoulders of a lawyer or cleric, seen in profile looking to picture right and facing a sketch of a goose which is partially shaded in. The man has an aged, lined face with furrowed brow, beaked nose and an open mouth with protruding teeth. He appears to be shouting (or preaching) at the goose. He wears a wig of an exaggerated style, a collar with two ties and a cape or gown. The sketch of the goose has been created around an oval-shaped ink blot which represents the bird's head. Branwell may be making some satirical comment about the clergy or the legal profession here, comparing the old man to a honking or hissing goose. Alternatively, the two sketches may be unconnected doodles.

Branwell originally intended the notebook for quite another purpose: that of recording the minutes of the Haworth Operative Conservative Society, for which he briefly took on the role of secretary, as at the other end of the book there are several pages of minutes written in ink in Branwell's longhand.

## 250

## 'Thomas Parker'

22 December 1838
Oil on canvas
735 × 614 mm

Titled on back of canvas, in paint, in Branwell's hand: 'THOMAS PARKER. DECR 22ND 1838'.
Gift of J. T. Parker, 1928; the donor was the grandson of the sitter.
*Brontë Parsonage Museum: B21*

Half-length portrait of Thomas Parker, singer, of Haworth. The figure of the sitter takes up most of the picture space. The head is well modelled with a light source to picture left throwing the left side of the subject's face into shadow. He has thick brown wavy hair and his skin has warm pink tones; the eyes look downward giving the face a rather melancholy aspect. He wears a brown jacket with wide lapels, a black velvet collar and gilt buttons. Underneath it he sports a white shirt, yellow waistcoat and blue necktie. In the background on the right there is a violin and in the top left corner a triangle of brown drapery trimmed with a silk fringe and tassels.

Thomas Parker was a local celebrity who later won considerable fame as a tenor when he sang before Queen Victoria. The violin included in the background indicates the instrument which accompanied his voice. The glimpse of fringed curtain, a conventional portrait background prop, may perhaps also suggest the concert stage. Branwell did not usually sign, date or title his oil paintings, so his inscription on the back of this canvas is uncommon. This is certainly one of his better paintings in which he handles the light effects with some skill.

## 251

## William Brown (1807–1876)

c. 1838–1839
Oil on canvas
765 × 640 mm

Purchased from Gladys Jane Brown, 1950; probably inherited by Gladys Jane Brown from her father Francis Brown, son of the sitter William Brown. The picture was among 34 items acquired from Gladys Brown including many Brontë drawings: see **29** for provenance of Brown collection.

*Brontë Parsonage Musuem: B19*

Half-length portrait of a man, thought to be William Brown, brother of John Brown the Haworth sexton who was Branwell's friend. The man appears to be in his thirties which would date the portrait to the late 1830s when Branwell was practising as a portrait painter. He holds his arms away from his body and looks to picture right so that he is seen three-quarter face. His face is rather thin and haggard-looking with deep lines around his eyes and mouth. He has a ruddy complexion and smooth brown hair brushed to the right. The sitter wears a dark brown Regency-style jacket, cut short at the front with tails at the back, wide lapels and a high collar. His trousers are fawn, waistcoat gold satin, shirt white and neckerchief black. The background is dark brown with a faint bright glow in the bottom left corner. The portrait is painted on a large scale for Branwell, in 'the grand manner' which he would have learnt from his teacher William Robinson and which he uses less successfully here than in his portrait of John Brown, William's brother, (**243**).

## 252

## Portrait of John Feather

c. 1838–1839
Oil on canvas or panel

*Location unknown*

F. C. Galloway records an 'Oil Portrait of John Feather, by Branwell Brontë' on loan from Edwin Feather of Haworth (*A Descriptive Catalogue of Objects in the Museum of the Brontë Society at Haworth* (Bradford, 1896), p. 14).

## 253

## James Fletcher

c. 1838–1839
Oil on wood panel
305 × 250 mm

Presented by John Cubbon, 1950; by descent through the family of the sitter; the donor was the executor of the estate of Fanny Edith Cubbon, née Fletcher, daughter of James Fletcher.

*Brontë Parsonage Museum: B26*

Half-length portrait of James Fletcher who looks to picture right so that his face is almost in profile. His facial features are quite delicate and refined, with a sharp nose, high cheekbones, arched brows and full lips. He has dark brown wavy hair, brushed forward onto his temples, and wears a dark jacket, blue waist-coat, white shirt and black necktie. The background is brown, in shadow at either side of the figure and light around his head.

Little is known about James Fletcher, other than that he lived in Skipton which is close to Keighley and not far from Bradford. The style of this painting is very similar to that of the Kirby portraits (**257**, **258**) and it was probably one of the portraits Branwell painted during his time at Fountain Street.

## 254

## Miss Margaret Hartley

1838–1839
Oil on wood panel
330 × 273 mm

Gift of the Ingram family, 1952, together with **257** and **258**; by descent from Mrs Margaret Ingram, née Hartley, niece of the Kirbys and the subject of this painting.
*Brontë Parsonage Museum: B25*

Margaret Hartley is seen half-length and seated with her arms resting in her lap and her head turned sharply to picture right but with her gaze fixed on the viewer. Her glossy dark hair is coiled on the top of her head and hangs beside her face in ringlets, beneath which her pearl drop ear-rings can be glimpsed. She has a round, broad, not unattractive face, with big eyes and nicely arched brows. The left nostril is painted in a rather curious elongated manner. Branwell has here handled the flesh tones rather well and these are enlivened by the introduction of dark red and maroon shadows beneath the girl's chin. Her expression is almost impassive, perhaps a little shy. She wears a dark green silk dress with an off-the-shoulder neckline, elbow-length sleeves and a pleated bodice tied tightly into a satin sash positioned above her waistline. Conservation work on this painting in 1992 revealed that the sitter was apparently wearing a different dress when the portrait was begun. When the picture is viewed in raking light a painted-out frill around the neckline can be seen. The poor proportions of the figure, particularly the overlong arms, betray Branwell's lack of training in the study of the human figure. The background is dark and one can just make out the top of her chair back.

Branwell's portrait of Margaret is far more sympathetic than that of her aunt (**258**), and his kindly feelings towards her were reciprocated, as the sitter recollected in 1893:

> At a time when Patrick Branwell Bronté was 22 or 23 years of age he came to lodge with us, and had one

room as his studio, and there painted many portraits. He was low in stature, about 5 foot 3 inches high, and slight in build, though well proportioned. Very few people, except sitters, came to visit him, but I remember one, a Mr Thompson, a painter also. I recollect his sister Charlotte coming, and remember her sisterly ways. She stayed a day, and I believe that was her only visit. They left the house together, and he saw her off by the Keighley coach. I am not aware that his other sisters or that his father, the Rev. Patrick Brontë, ever came to Mr Kirby's. It was young Mr Brontë's practice to go home at each weekend, and I remember that while sometimes he took the coach for Keighley, he on other occasions walked to Haworth across the moors. He was a very steady young gentleman, his conduct was exemplary, and we liked him very much. He stayed with us about two years, and left, he said, to go to a situation, as a book-keeper. Whilst lodging with us he painted my portrait and those of my uncle and aunt, and all three were accounted good likenesses.

(W. W. Yates, 'The Bronte Family: A Suggestion. Two Years in the Life of Branwell Bronte', *Dewsbury Reporter*, 25 November 1893)

255

## Portrait of Rev. Henry Heap

c. 1838–1839
Oil on canvas or panel

*Location unknown*

Francis A. Leyland recorded that when Branwell worked as a portrait painter in Bradford 'Among others he painted portraits of [Rev. William Morgan], and of the Rev. Henry Heap, the vicar' (*The Brontë Family With Special Reference to Patrick Branwell Brontë*, 2 vols. (London: Hurst & Blackett, 1886), vol. 1, p. 175).

256

## Maria Ingham

c. 1838–1839
Oil on canvas
c. 589 × 498 mm; the painting was cut down about sixty years ago from its original size of approximately 1839 × 1220 mm.

The present owner is the great-grandson of the subject, Maria Ingham, née Taylor (1808–75). The painting passed from Maria Ingham to her daughter, Margaret Anne Ingham, who married Richard Richardson. Their daughter Mabel Richardson then inherited the work and passed it to her son, the present owner. The portrait is accompanied by a letter from Charlotte to 'Miss Taylor' of Stanbury, beginning 'I find I shall ... Wednesday Evening ...' [?4 September 1839].
*Private owner*

This head-and-shoulders fragment of a portrait of Maria Ingham depicts a woman of about thirty years of age with an oval face, round eyes, a long nose, thin lips and a dimpled chin. She wears her dark chestnut hair pinned to the top of her head in a tight bun with loose ringlets hanging in front of her ears in the fashion of the day. Her neck and shoulders are bare, painted with bluish shadows which contrast with the overall pinkness of the tones used to paint the flesh of her face. The proportions and lines of the neck and shoulders are distorted, betraying Branwell's lack of understanding of figure painting. The neckline of Maria's turquoise blue gown is just visible, with a tiny gold brooch pinned to its edge in the centre. Brownish-red draperies can be seen in the background.

If the estimated original size of the painting is accurate, this must have been an unusually large, and lucrative, commission for Branwell, certainly a full-length portrait. All Branwell's other known works are either head and shoulders, half or three-quarter length.

Maria Ingham was the daughter of Stephen and Mary Taylor of the Manor House, Stanbury. Stephen Taylor, a trustee of Haworth Church, appointed Mr Brontë to the living. Maria's sister Susannah married Thomas Ramsden, a brewer who lived at Jumples, a fine house near Halifax.

The Taylors were country gentry and the Brontës were on good terms with them. George Taylor was present at Charlotte's wedding and there were apparently many letters from Charlotte to Maria Ingham that have since been destroyed. From the evidence of this portrait commission it is obvious that Branwell used his local contacts in order to obtain work. No doubt his father put in a good word for his artist son in the time-honoured Yorkshire way. This information underlines the fact that Branwell was well-connected with a host of potential clients via family and friends, which makes it all the more likely that his studio in Bradford was abandoned not because of a lack of custom, but because of his own failure to pursue the business available to him.

A curious fact about the Ingham family is that a relative went to Papua New Guinea as an emissary but unfortunately was eaten in 1878. The town of Ingham in Queensland, Australia, is named after him.

## 257

## Isaac Kirby

1838–1839
Oil on wood panel
355 × 305 mm

Gift of the Ingram family, 1952, together with **254** and **258**; by descent from Mrs Margaret Ingram, née Hartley, niece of the Kirbys and sitter in **254**.
*Brontë Parsonage Museum: B23*

Isaac Kirby sits with his back to a wall or pillar, his body turned slightly away from the viewer but with his head turned towards us so that we can see him full face. The picture is painted in well-handled dark tones overall with the light coming from the left and illuminating the well-observed face and the white slash of the shirt front. His dark jacket is highlighted with a greenish blue which is picked up in the background colours. Kirby has a long face with heavy dark eyebrows, rather mournful brown eyes, long nose, thin upper lip and a jutting chin. His complexion is swarthy and his hair a rich dark brown. In the bottom left-hand corner Branwell has included a tantalizing glimpse of sea beneath a lowering sky.

When Branwell Brontë went to Bradford to work as a portrait painter his father's long-time friend William Morgan found accomodation for him in his own respectable street of residence. Branwell lodged and had a studio with Mr Kirby, an ale and porter merchant, his wife, children and their niece Margaret Hartley at 3 Fountain Street, where he painted their portraits (**254** and **258**). Winifred Gérin (*Branwell Brontë:*

*A Biography* (London: Hutchinson, 1961), p. 142) has suggested that he painted the portraits for his landlord in lieu of rent, because after he left Mrs Kirby made a number of demands on him concerning the pictures. This group of paintings constitute the artist's best work in oils. In this portrait of Isaac Kirby, Branwell manages to convey something of the character of the man, who appears to be a rather dreamy, melancholy type, an impression emphasized by the dark background.

## 258

## Mrs Isaac Kirby

1838–1839
Oil on wood panel
350 × 300 mm

Gift of the Ingram family, 1952, together with **254** and **257**; by descent from Mrs Margaret Ingram, née Hartley, niece of the Kirbys and sitter in **254**.
*Brontë Parsonage Museum: B24*

Mrs Kirby is portrayed half-length looking to picture right. The overall tones of the painting are dark, making a strong contrast to her pale face, white bonnet and diaphanous fichu. Her face is narrow and pinched looking with heavily hooded eyes which are puffy beneath. Her nose is long and pointed, her mouth small and mean. On her head she wears an incongruously frilly white bonnet, tied under her chin, around which crimped waves of hair protrude. Her gown is dark and plain and over her shoulders she wears a fine voile fichu with similar material tucked into the neck of her bodice. The background is dark, shading to a patch of light in the bottom right corner.

This is an extremely unflattering portrait and one suspects when looking at it that Branwell considered his landlady to be a rather vinegary character. In a letter dated 24 August 1839 written to his artist friend John Hunter Thompson after he had left Bradford (*The Brontës: Their Lives, Friendships and Correspondence*, ed. Thomas James Wise and John Alexander Symington, 4 vols. (Oxford: Basil Blackwell for the Shakespeare Head Press, 1932), vol. 1, p. 187) he gives vent to his unkind feelings towards her: 'Mrs Kirby's name is an eyesore to me – what does the Woman mean? – How can I come paddling to Bradford with my wallet on my Back in order to varnish her portraits – for I know of no other finishing she stipulated for?' We also learn that Thompson helped Branwell out with this particular commission: 'I dare not trespass farther on your extreme kindness toward me but I would give the amount contained in this letter or twice it to silence her chattering – The sentence comes ill off my pen point for it is neither pleasant or profitable to finish another mans daubs but I would gladly stand by what I have said.'

## 259

## Portrait of Rev. William Morgan

c. 1838–1839
Oil on canvas or panel

*Location unknown*

Francis A. Leyland recorded that Branwell painted a portrait of Morgan, husband of his mother's cousin (Jane, née Fenwell) and long-time family friend, when he set up in business as a painter in Bradford (*The Brontë Family With Special Reference to Patrick Branwell Brontë*, 2 vols. (London: Hurst & Blackett, 1886), vol. 1, p. 175).

## 260

### William Thomas

c. 1838–1839
Oil on canvas
740 × 590 mm

Gift of J. W. Wright, 1928; Wright says in an accompanying letter: 'My memory goes back to the time when Charlotte Bronte was buried. I was a scholar at the National School about 70 years ago, and I remember paying my respects to Mr Nicholls the then curate. I was also chorister in the church.' The donor was probably a descendant of Sarah Wright, née Thomas (b. 1816), sister of the sitter.
*Brontë Parsonage Museum: B22*

Half-length portrait of William Thomas (b. 1814) sitting in a red velvet armchair. He has a large, broad face with wide-set eyes gazing past the viewer and a thin mouth. His hair is brushed onto his forehead in a much affected fashion of the day. He wears a dark grey double-breasted jacket with a black collar and a white shirt.

William Thomas was the son of William Thomas senior, partner in the firm of W. & R. Thomas, wine and spirit merchants of Haworth. Branwell is known to have painted a number of local people and Mr Thomas, a prosperous Haworth tradesman, would seem to have been typical of the kind of patronage Branwell received during his brief career as a painter.

William Thomas senior was a member of the Three Graces Masonic Lodge at Haworth and he owned a Masonic apron decorated with a painting by Branwell, which is still in the possession of his descendants (**247**). The apron was displayed in an exhibition of 'Masonic Treasures' at the Masonic Hall, Duncombe Place, York, Monday 16 July–Sunday 26 August, 1979. Don Thomas, a descendant, wrote in a letter to the BPM dated 19 October 1985: 'My father did disclose to me that the Thomas family was very friendly with the Brontës and according to letters from the Brontës which are now no longer in our family possession Mrs Thomas often nursed the Brontë children when they were ill. I also understand that Mr W. Thomas held high office in the Three Graces Masonic Lodge at Haworth when Branwell was secretary.' Don Thomas also offered the information that according to oral tradition in his family, this portrait was painted by Branwell in lieu of debts to W. & R. Thomas for wine and spirits.

There is in the BPM collection an album which belonged to Sarah Thomas, sister of the sitter, contemporaneous to the Brontës and containing Charlotte's and the Rev. Patrick Brontë's autographs (BPM: BS13).

## 261

### Portrait of Mr M—

1839
Oil on canvas

*Location unknown*

Francis A. Leyland recorded that after Branwell had given up his studio at Bradford in 1839, he visited Liverpool with one or two friends. One of these, a 'Mr M—', bought some sheet music at Branwell's behest; in return Branwell painted his portrait during weekly sittings in his room at the parsonage (*The Brontë Family With Special Reference to Patrick Branwell Brontë*, 2 vols. (London: Hurst & Blackett, 1886), vol. 1, p. 239). Leyland describes the sitter as 'an accomplished musician' and relates (p. 240) that Branwell 'had painted the names of Johann Sebastian Bach, Mozart, Haydn, and Handel at each corner of the canvas respectively'.

## 262

### 'Henry Foster of Denholme'

c. 1838–1839
Oil on wood panel
380 × 295 mm

Inscribed on frame: 'HENRY FOSTER OF DENHOLME/ ATTRIBUTED TO BRANWELL BRONTË.'

Gift of Vera Morgan, 1975; by descent from Henry Foster through the family of the donor.
*Brontë Parsonage Museum: B44*

Half-length portrait of a man with a long face with large features, short reddish-brown hair and side whiskers. He wears a black jacket with a white frilled front shirt with a wing collar and a high black cravat. The background is dark.

Foster's father started the Mills at Denholme, a village near Haworth, and built White Shaw, the family home where the Foster family lived until the early 1970s, the last owner being Garnett Foster. The portrait of Henry Foster (1804–54) remained there until the house was sold. Oral tradition in the sitter's family had it that Henry Foster was a drinking friend of Branwell, and that the picture was painted in the Black Bull. Although it is possible that Foster was Branwell's friend it seems unlikely that the portrait was made in the Black Bull. The artist could perhaps have made a preliminary sketch there, but the painting would have been done in the studio.

In its general appearance this portrait is unlike Branwell's other authenticated portraits; in the handling of the paint, the tonal values, the way in which the figure occupies the picture space and in the scale of the work. The portrait measures 380 × 295 mm as compared to his more usual c. 770 × 640 mm or the smaller c. 350 × 300 mm. Uncharacteristically, it is also heavily varnished. Family tradition, however, persuades us that the painting is by Branwell.

## 263

### Head and shoulders of a young man

c. 1838–1839
Conté crayon on brown tinted paper
312 × 266 mm

Stamped: 'BRONTË/ MUSEUM/ HAWORTH', encircled. Recto bears a sticker with the number '271' which corresponds with the number in the 1908 catalogue of the Brontë Museum, Haworth. Verso stamped: 'BRONTË/ MUSEUM/ HAWORTH', encircled.
Purchased from James Hartley, husband of Martha Brown's sister Hannah, 1896, together with a number of other Brontë relics including two other drawings (**37** and **60**), a handkerchief (D46) and a coffee urn (H37).
*Brontë Parsonage Museum: B27*

Unfinished sketch of the head and shoulders of a young man with a heart-shaped face and very youthful features. He has his wavy hair parted on the right side and wears a high collar with a necktie tied in a bow and a wide-collared jacket. The paper has been cut at top and bottom.

The roughness of the sketch and the large scale of the drawing suggest that this could have been one of Branwell's working drawings: a preparatory study for a portrait in oils.

## 264

### Landscape with figures

c. 1838–1839
Oil on canvas
407 × 559 mm

Gift of the executors of Mr Hodgson, 1928. A small framed engraving of York Minster (BPM: P150) and a mortar and pestle (H39) also came from the estate of Mr Hodgson; both of these items had come originally from the 1861 sale of Patrick Brontë's effects at Haworth Parsonage, therefore it is likely that this painting came from the same source. When it was originally acquired by the BPM it was framed with the attribution to Branwell written on the frame; frame no longer extant.
*Brontë Parsonage Museum: B31*

The subject of this oil painting is much obscured by the poor condition of the picture itself. It appears to be a classical landscape, framed by groups of trees which occupy the full height of the picture on either side. A path winds its way from the foreground to the background into a hilly countryside with a glimpse of a lake and possibly a town on a distant hill. Two figures, one with a red coat, sit by the roadside in the foreground. The turquoise blue of the sky above sun-tinged clouds is still vivid, despite the poor state of the painting. At some time, squares of archival paper have been stuck to the surface of the picture at various points in the centre and over the right-hand group of trees, in an attempt to repair it. The paint surface is badly crazed and cracked overall.

This painting is probably one of Branwell's practice works; his teacher William Robinson encouraged him to copy from prints of the Old Masters as part of his training. See also **231**, **234** and **235**. The picture is not as crudely painted as **231**, for example, and was probably painted nearer the time of the Bradford studio venture.

## 265

### 'The Lonely Shepherd'

c. 1838–1839
Oil on wood panel
268 × 330 mm

Gift of Anna Harris, 1901. A letter relating to this acquisition from Oxton Hall, Tadcaster (now in North Yorkshire), 11 September 1901 in the BPM reads: 'Miss Harris has a small oil painting by Branwell Brontë which was bought from him by her father 50 or 60 years ago. As she is leaving Oxton Hall this autumn she would be glad to present it to the Brontë Museum if it would be liked and appreciated there.' The donor, Anna Harris (b. c. 1835), was the eldest daughter of Alfred Harris (1801–80), a member of the Bradford Quaker family who controlled the Bradford Old Bank for many years (David Verey, *The Diary of a Victorian Squire – Extracts from the Diaries and Letters of Dearman and Emily Birchall* (London: Alan Sutton, 1989)). Harris was a wealthy patron and collector of art who lived and worked in the Bradford area (Spring Lodge, Manningham Lane, Bradford from before 1841 until 1854; Rysworth Hall, Bingley 1854–72: Bradford and Bingley census returns 1841, 1861, Bradford City Library) until the move to Oxton Hall in 1872, therefore it is quite possible that he had frequent contact with local artists such as Branwell (Malcolm Hardman, *Ruskin and Bradford* (Manchester: Manchester University Press, 1986)).
*Brontë Parsonage Museum: B32*

The poor condition of this oil painting, with its cracked and crazed paint surface, was improved by conservation work in 1993. The overall dark tones, however, make the image indistinct. To the left foreground the shepherd, holding a crook and wearing a wide-brimmed hat, stands with his dog beneath a tree. In the middle-ground a group of sheep can just be made out. The sky is dark with a ray of moonlight appearing in the centre of the picture, a dramatic light effect which would have had a special appeal for Branwell, recalling as it does his interest in the work of John Martin. The subject may relate to Branwell's knowledge of Edwin Landseer's paintings such as 'The Old Shepherd's Chief Mourner', known widely through prints.

## 266

## 'Broughton Church'

2 March 1840
Pencil on paper
135 × 220 mm

Signed and dated in pencil, in Branwell's hand, bottom centre: 'BROUGHTON CHURCH./ March 2$^{d}$, 1840.'; lower right corner, in pencil in minuscule hand, on milestone in drawing: 'PBB'. For verso, see **267**.

Bequest of Henry Houston Bonnell, 1927; acquired by Bonnell from Sotheby's sale of the effects of Arthur Bell Nicholls, London, 26 July 1907, lot 41 or 42.
*Brontë Parsonage Museum: Bonnell 18*

View of the east end of a church at Broughton-in-Furness, Cumbria, where Branwell worked as a tutor to the sons of Mr Postlethwaite from January to June 1840. The church has a square battlemented tower with a finial at each corner with two windows visible. There is a low extension with a sloping roof, five windows and a door. In the churchyard there are six table tombstones and five uprights. A track leads from the foreground around the left side of the building with two trees in leaf to the left of it. In the bottom right corner there is a milestone with the artist's initials 'PBB' written on it. In the far distance mountains can be seen.

The small town of Broughton-in-Furness is perched up on a hill whereas the Parish Church of St Mary Magdalene is set on the floor of the valley immediately below the main street with a magnificent view from the churchyard of distant Black Comb. It is a picturesque and mysterious site, probably chosen when the church was first established there, in the twelfth century, because it then stood on the shores of the Duddon estuary. The church itself has been greatly altered since Branwell made his drawing of it; in 1874 a new nave was built, added on to the old, the original south wall of the Norman church replaced and a new tower erected.

There are three other drawings of buildings in the BPM which Branwell probably made from life: the two 1833 drawings of Haworth buildings (**219** and **220**) and an ink drawing of 1844 (**282**).

## 267

## Self-portrait

c. 1840
Pencil on paper
220 × 135 mm

Stamped: 'BRONTË/ MUSEUM/ HAWORTH', encircled.

Bequest of Henry Houston Bonnell, 1927; acquired by Bonnell from Sotheby's sale of the effects of Arthur Bell Nicholls, London, 26 July 1907, lot 41 or 42.
*Brontë Parsonage Museum: Bonnell 18v*

This drawing on the verso of **266** is a self-portrait of Branwell's head. He draws himself in profile, looking to the right, delineating his bumpy forehead, long sweeping nose and pronounced chin. His hair is swept forward from his high hairline, and onto his face to meet his side whiskers. A high collar or neckerchief comes right up to his chin. We cannot say to what extent this is a caricature of himself but he has probably exaggerated his own facial features. The face is very similar to that of 'Northangerland./ Alexander Percy' (**240**), Branwell's alter ego.

## 268

## 'T. Purser'

1840
Pencil on paper
215 × 129 mm

Inscribed in pencil, in non-Brontë hand below the picture: 'T Purser./ Sketched by Patrick/ Bramwell [*sic*] Brontë/ in Manchester/ Anno Domini 1840'.

Acquired by the present owner from the auction of the contents of a house in Bulawayo, Zimbabwe; earlier provenance unknown. This drawing was on loan to the BPM 1981–6 and was given the number B43.

*Private collection: B43*

Half-length portrait of a young man seen three-quarter face. He has thick wavy hair, curling above his ears and parted on the left, and a fullish, oval face with a pointed chin. His expression is serious and slightly anxious. The sitter wears a high-collared tight-fitting jacket, a waistcoat with wide lapels, a shirt and a cravat.

It is not known who T. Purser was, but there is some evidence to suggest that Branwell could have made this drawing on a visit to Manchester in 1840. Applications for a post with the Manchester–Leeds Railway Company were being received from 6 July 1840 and Branwell's appointment as Assistant Clerk in Charge at Sowerby Bridge, Halifax, was confirmed at the Board Meeting held at Hunt's Bank, Manchester, on 31 August 1840. Presumably Branwell attended for interview in Manchester between those two dates, so he could have made the drawing then. The paper shows the marks of folds, which might suggest that the portrait was drawn casually for an acquaintance made en route, and treated just as casually by the recipient. Branwell was dismissed from the company on 31 March 1842, when he was 'Summoned to appear before the audit of the company', so he may have been in Manchester a second time then. Francis A. Leyland (*The Brontë Family With Special Reference to Patrick Branwell Brontë*, 2 vols. (London: Hurst & Blackett, 1886), vol. 1, p. 290) relates how Branwell 'also visited Manchester on one occasion; and, on his return, he gave an account to a young clergyman [Sutcliffe Sowden], then living in the neighbourhood of Mytholmroyd, who sometimes went to his wooden shanty at Luddendenfoot to hear his conversation, of how he had been impressed with the architecture of the parish church at Manchester as he stood under the arched portal'.

This portrait is similar in style and format to **271**, **272**, **273** and **279**.

## 269

## 'Duncan'

c. 1840–1841
Pencil on paper
228 × 174 mm

Titled in pencil, in Branwell's longhand, bottom centre: 'Duncan'.

Bequest of Henry Houston Bonnell, 1927; acquired by Bonnell from Sotheby's sale of the effects of Arthur Bell Nicholls, London, 26 July 1907, lot 41 or 42.

*Brontë Parsonage Museum: Bonnell 11*

Head-and-shoulders portrait of a young man, heavily shaded around, seen three-quarter face looking to picture right. He has a plump face with a retroussé nose and short unkempt curly hair parted on the right, curling over his forehead and collar at the back, with long side whiskers. His clothes are dark, a heavy overcoat with a wide collar, an unbuttoned shirt and a cravat. He wears a mild, complacent expression.

Winifred Gérin (*Branwell Brontë: A Biography* (London: Hutchinson, 1961), p. 180) mentions that the Clerk in Charge at Sowerby Bridge Station was a man named George Duncan. Branwell was Duncan's assistant from the autumn of 1840 until 1 April 1841 when he was transferred to Luddenden Foot, and this is a portrait of the Clerk. The rather rough clothes worn by Duncan tell us that this was a portrait of an ordinary working man, rather than one of Branwell's more sophisticated and better-off friends.

See **268**, **271**, **272**, **273** and **279** for similar male portraits.

## 270

## 'Alexander Percy Esq-re M. P. Ætat 21.'

c. 1840–1842
Pencil on paper
225 × 162 mm

Titled in pencil, in Branwell's hand, bottom centre: 'Alexander Percy Esq-re M. P./ Ætat 21.'

Bequest of Henry Houston Bonnell, 1927; acquired by Bonnell from Sotheby's sale of the effects of Arthur Bell Nicholls, London, 26 July 1907, lot 41 or 42.

*Brontë Parsonage Museum: Bonnell 9*

Slightly less than half-length portrait of a man described by the artist as Alexander Percy, the hero of Branwell's juvenile writings. The man faces front but his head is turned towards picture right, with his eyes looking up to the right. The face has fat cheeks, small eyes and a thin mouth with a rather petulant expression. The hair is thin on top of the man's head with wings of limp curls brushed onto both sides of his high, domed forehead. Bushy side whiskers grow round his face and meet under his chin. Percy wears a pleated-front shirt with a high wing collar and a dark necktie wound several times around his neck and tied in a bow. His open jacket and buttoned waistcoat are very tight-fitting. There is some shading around the figure in the background.

The portrait of Percy is drawn with great assurance, as if the artist knew his subject very well, which, of course, he did. It is hard to say whether or not the figure was drawn from life or from the imagination; the details of the dress, which Branwell tends to skimp in his obviously imaginary drawings, would suggest the former, but with his hero in mind at the outset.

See **268**, **269**, **271**, **272**, **273** and **279** for similar male portraits.

## 271

## 'Grimshaw, H.'

c. 1840–1842
Pencil on paper
225 × 162 mm

Titled in pencil, in Branwell's decorative script, below: 'Grimshaw, H.' Stamped: 'BRONTË/ MUSEUM/ HAWORTH', encircled.

Bequest of Henry Houston Bonnell, 1927; acquired by Bonnell from Sotheby's sale of the effects of Arthur Bell Nicholls, London, 26 July 1907, lot 41 or 42.

*Brontë Parsonage Museum: Bonnell 9v*

In the upper half of the paper there is an almost half-length portrait of a heavily built man facing front. He has a broad face with a large nose, heavy brows and a dignified, rather sad expression. The details of his clothing are well-observed, including a side-fastening collared waistcoat with many small buttons, a neatly fitting coat with high collar and wide lapels and a white cravat. His shiny dark hair is parted on the right side, brushed low over the left forehead and with curls around his ears.

On the bottom half of the paper, reversed, there is an unfinished drawing of a woman's head looking to picture right, with short, loose hair parted in the centre and bare shoulders. This head is like that of Emily in 'The Brontë sisters' (**225**), c. 1834, and, given Branwell's habit of recycling drawing paper, this could be a preparatory sketch. The portrait of Grimshaw appears to belong to a group which includes **268**, **269**, **272**, **273** and **279**. All would appear to be portraits drawn, or derived, from life. At this time Branwell, despite his woes, was enjoying a very sociable time with a host of male friends, many of them fellow artists and writers, meeting up with them in public houses around Halifax and Haworth. The drawings could well be portraits of some of these cronies.

272

## 'Henry Scott'

c. 1840–1842
Pencil on paper
232 × 169 mm

Titled in pencil, in Branwell's decorative hand, bottom centre: 'Henry Scott'. Watermark: 'J WHATMAN/ 1831'. Stamped: 'BRONTË/ MUSEUM/ HAWORTH', encircled. Bequest of Henry Houston Bonnell, 1927; acquired by Bonnell from Sotheby's sale of the effects of Arthur Bell Nicholls, London, 26 July 1907, lot 41 or 42.
*Brontë Parsonage Museum: Bonnell 10*

Head and shoulders of a young man seen three-quarter face, looking to picture left. He has a long face with a large chin and his expression is pleasant and relaxed. His hair is straight, parted in the centre and flattened down to his head, becoming straggly around his ears. His side whiskers are long and meet under his chin. He wears a buttoned, collared waistcoat, the neckline filled with a dark cravat, and a jacket with wide lapels. The sleeves and jacket collar are left largely unshaded.

We do not know who Henry Scott was, but from his unkempt appearance, rough working clothes and the familiar use of his Christian name in the inscribed title, he would appear, like 'Duncan' (**269**), to have been one of Branwell's workmates on the Leeds–Manchester railway.

See **268**, **269**, **271**, **273** and **279** for similar male portraits.

273

## Portrait of a man holding aloft a wineglass

c. 1840–1842
Pencil on paper
232 × 169 mm

Bequest of Henry Houston Bonnell, 1927; acquired by Bonnell from Sotheby's sale of the effects of Arthur Bell Nicholls, London, 26 July 1907, lot 41 or 42.
*Brontë Parsonage Museum: Bonnell 10v*

Unfinished half-length portrait of a man leaning back in an armchair holding aloft a wineglass in his right hand, with his left arm resting on the arm of the chair. He turns his head to look towards picture right with a slightly leering expression. The man's features are coarse, with a large nose and curving mouth, and his general mien is degenerate; his hair is straggly and unkempt, his clothes unbuttoned and in disarray. The outlines of an underdrawing of another face with curly hair can just be made out beneath the lower part of this drawing, drawn in reverse to it, possibly the beginnings of a self-portrait.

Branwell has endowed this figure with a strong sense of character, which may suggest that he had in mind one of his imaginary heroes, or anti-heroes, when he made this portrait.

See **268**–**272** and **279** for similar male portraits.

## 274

### Portrait of a man

c. 1840–1842
Pencil on paper
228 × 174 mm

Stamped: 'BRONTË/ MUSEUM/ HAWORTH', encircled. Bequest of Henry Houston Bonnell, 1927; acquired by Bonnell from Sotheby's sale of the effects of Arthur Bell Nicholls, London, 26 July 1907, lot 41 or 42.
*Brontë Parsonage Museum: Bonnell 11v*

Unfinished half-length portrait of a stout man looking to picture right. The head is drawn in some detail, with a profusion of dark curly hair, long side whiskers, a prominent forehead and chin, large nose and round eyes with dark brows. He wears a high stock and wing collar which are shaded in, with the pleated shirt, buttoned waistcoat and open high-collared jacket drawn only in outline.

This is clearly a portrait drawn forcefully and directly from the artist's imagination, closely resembling the Duke of Zamorna as depicted in **239**.

## 275

### Two male profiles

c. 1841–1842
Pencil on paper
112 × 56 mm

The sketch is on p. 1 (158 × 100 mm) of a manuscript notebook consisting of 52 pages and a maroon leather-backed card cover, containing sketches, lines of verse and other writings in both Branwell's longhand and minuscule script throughout, commonly called the 'Luddenden Foot Notebook', kept during Branwell's time there working for the Manchester–Leeds Railway from April 1841 until his dismissal on 31 March 1842. Inscribed in pencil at top of page: 'HOLV/ HOLY IESV/ Wakefield Miscellany/ to be established shortly/ published Messr[s] Nicholls/ and Sons.'; up left side of page, at right angles to text a top: '3 waggons and 3 covers/ for Sowerby'. A line is drawn vertically in pencil down the centre of the page with these letters written at intervals along it: 'V E D O V E B L E'.

Purchased in London, 1899, from H. E. Gorfin, an agent of Thomas James Wise.
*Brontë Parsonage Museum: BS127*

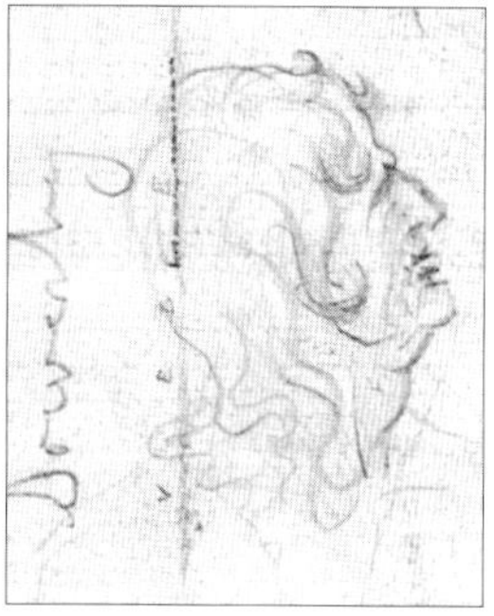

Two pencil profiles of male heads: one, on right-hand side, of a man with a high forehead, long flowing hair and beard; the other, below (seen here), a more detailed sketch of a man with flowing shoulder-length hair, craggy nose and chin, looking towards picture right, his head inclined slightly upwards. The man's undraped shoulders and torso are roughly outlined.

Branwell was dismissed from his post as Clerk in Charge at Luddenden Foot for a discrepancy in the accounts of £11.1s.7d, an amount which was probably embezzled by the Assistant Clerk but for which Branwell was ultimately responsible. The notebook exists as a document of his carelessness about his employment – intended for the records of trains and cargoes passing through the station, it is primarily devoted to drafts of poems, sketches, doodles and caricatures – and also of Branwell's prolific creative activity at the time.

## 276

# Sketch of two boxers

c. 1841–1842
Pencil on paper
42 × 36 mm

The sketch is at the top of p. 2 (158 × 100 mm) of a manuscript notebook consisting of 52 pages and a maroon leather-backed card cover, containing sketches, lines of verse and other writings in both Branwell's longhand and minuscule script throughout, commonly called the 'Luddenden Foot Notebook' kept during Branwell's time there working for the Manchester–Leeds Railway from April 1841 until his dismissal on 31 March 1842. The sketch appears above the lines of a poem written in ink in minuscule script beginning: 'Man thinks too often that his earthl~~y life~~ above cares'. Stamped: 'BRONTË/ MUSEUM/ HAWORTH', encircled.

Purchased in London, 1899, from H. E. Gorfin, an agent of Thomas James Wise.

*Brontë Parsonage Museum: BS127*

Pencil sketch of two pugilists, both stripped to the waist and fighting bare-fisted. The boxer on the left, seen three-quarter profile, is dark-haired, wears loose trousers and is considerably smaller than his similarly attired but fair-haired opponent, seen in profile on the right. Inscribed above the men's heads are the figures '$5^{ft}$–9' (left) and '$7^{ft}$–$3^{in}$' (right), presumably meant to indicate their respective and unequally matched heights. These numbers are inscribed again at the foot of the page.

Branwell, a boxer himself, had a lifelong interest in the sport of boxing and there are other references in his art to boxing (see for example **304**). This sketch may well have been copied from a contemporary engraving.

See **275** for details of Branwell's dismissal from his post, and the significance of the notebook.

## 277

# Tiny sketch of a church and profile

c. 1841–1842
Pencil and ink on paper
15 × 18 mm

The sketch of the church (15 × 18 mm) occupies a space at the top of p. 11 (158 × 100 mm) and the sketch of the profile (18 × 12 mm) is on the left side of p. 11 in a manuscript notebook consisting of 52 pages and a maroon leather-backed card cover, containing sketches, lines of verse and other writings in both Branwell's longhand and minuscule script throughout, commonly called the 'Luddenden Foot Notebook' kept during Branwell's time there working for the Manchester–Leeds Railway from April 1841 until his dismissal on 31 March 1842. Inscribed in longhand, in ink at the top of the page: 'He far away by Tempests born 6/° clock'; sketch of church inset within inscribed title: 'ROBERT BURNS'. The lines of Branwell's poem of this name are written in ink in longhand below, beginning: 'He little knows–when life has smoothly passed'. Stamped: 'BRONTË/ MUSEUM/ HAWORTH', encircled.

Purchased in London, 1899, from H. E. Gorfin, an agent of Thomas James Wise.

*Brontë Parsonage Museum: BS127*

Tiny sketch of a church with cross and steeple, outlined in pencil and hatched in ink, set within the title 'ROBERT BURNS', referring to the poem below. In the left margin, alongside the verse, a heavily hatched profile in ink of a man with a bulbous nose.

See **275** for details of Branwell's dismissal from his post, and the significance of the notebook.

## 278

## Two male portraits and self-portrait

c. 1841–1842
Pencil on paper
130 × 89 mm

The sketches occupy most of p. 17 (158 × 100 mm) of a manuscript notebook consisting of 52 pages and a maroon leather-backed card cover, containing sketches, lines of verse and other writings in both Branwell's longhand and minuscule script throughout, commonly called the 'Luddenden Foot Notebook' kept during Branwell's time there working for the Manchester–Leeds Railway from April 1841 until his dismissal on 31 March 1842. Inscribed in pencil in Branwell's longhand, top of page: 'Applications for shares to be made to/ White & Barrett 35 Lincolns Inn Fields/ Rackham & Cooke Norwich &c/ of whom may be had prospectuses.' Inscribed in ink, left centre: 'Guido ~~Burns~~/ Tasso/ Galileo/ Milton Otway/ Johnson/ Cowper/ Burns/ ~~John~~'. Stamped: 'BRONTË/ MUSEUM/ HAWORTH', encircled. Purchased in London, 1899, from H. E. Gorfin, an agent of Thomas James Wise.
*Brontë Parsonage Museum: BS127*

These three pencil portraits appear on a page which is typical of the Luddenden Foot Notebook: at the top of the page there is a note about an application for shares, relating to Branwell's everyday world of work on the railway, and down the left-hand side a list of great authors and poets. The head of a man at top left appears to be a caricature, with distorted, flattened features, rather like a boxer's face, with deep-set eyes, jutting brow and down-turned mouth, a high forehead and receding wavy hair. The portrait to the right is more finished, depicting the head and shoulders of a man with short dark curly hair with side whiskers and heavy but pleasant, slightly smiling features. He has a long nose, wide mouth and pronounced cheekbones and his head is tilted shyly downwards as he looks up at the artist. He wears a wide-lapelled jacket, waistcoat and white shirt. This would appear to be one of Branwell's impromptu portraits of a nameless social acquaintance. The profile self-portrait at the foot of the page is easily recognizable, with its long sharp nose, receding locks and side whiskers and round spectacles. It is not worked up in any detail and tends towards a ruthless self-caricature, typical of Branwell.

See **275** for details of Branwell's dismissal from his post, and the significance of the notebook.

## 279

## 'Johannes Murgatroides'

c. 1841–1842
Pencil on paper
115 × 53 mm

The sketch is on p. 18 (158 × 100 mm) of a manuscript notebook consisting of 52 pages and a maroon leather-backed card cover, containing sketches, lines of verse and other writings in both Branwell's longhand and minuscule script throughout, commonly called the

'Luddenden Foot Notebook' kept during Branwell's time there working for the Manchester–Leeds Railway from April 1841 until his dismissal on 31 March 1842. Titled in pencil in capitals in Greek lettering, above drawing: 'Johannes Murgatroides'; inscribed in pencil in Branwell's hand, in Greek lettering, below drawing: 'George Richardson'.

Purchased in London, 1899, from H. E. Gorfin, an agent of Thomas James Wise.
*Brontë Parsonage Museum: BS127*

Full-length pencil sketch of John Murgatroyd, owner of a woollen mill at Oats Royd, Luddenden, seated cross-legged in a high-backed chair of the type found in public houses. He wears a top hat, a dark, wide-lapelled jacket with a buttoned waistcoat, a cravat just visible underneath and white trousers. His left arm rests on the arm of the chair and his right hand is either tucked into his trouser pocket or resting in his lap. The man's facial expression is impassive.

Branwell has written Murgatroyd's name in Greek lettering, perhaps to show off his classical education. Similarly, the name of 'George Richardson', then controller of the wharves and warehouses at nearby Sowerby Bridge, is written in Greek script at the foot of the page. Daphne du Maurier has suggested that the sketch is a composite portrait of the two men and speculates on whether Branwell saw them in the local inns: 'symbolizing – to the young draughtsman sketching in the opposite corner – a single man of substance, great in power, to whom boaties roared and weavers touched their forelocks?' (*The Infernal World of Branwell Brontë* (London: Gollancz, 1960), pp. 128–9). The mode of the portrait, however, would not seem to be intended to inspire great respect, appearing rather to be an impromptu sketch made on one of Branwell's customary evenings in a public house.

See **275** for details of Branwell's dismissal from his post, and the significance of the notebook.

## 280

## Sketches of a boxer and male heads

c. 1841–1842
Pencil on paper
58 × 32 mm

The sketches are written over by text (see below). They are on p. 8 (158 × 100 mm) of 14 loose pages of manuscript that formerly belonged to a notebook now consisting of 52 pages and a maroon leather-backed card cover, containing sketches, lines of verse and other writings in both Branwell's longhand and minuscule script throughout, commonly called the 'Luddenden Foot Notebook' kept during Branwell's time there working for the Manchester–Leeds Railway from April 1841 until his dismissal on 31 March 1842 (**275–279**).

Formerly owned by Lord Brotherton: see **203**. Possibly acquired by him from Thomas James Wise.
*The Brotherton Collection, Leeds University Library*

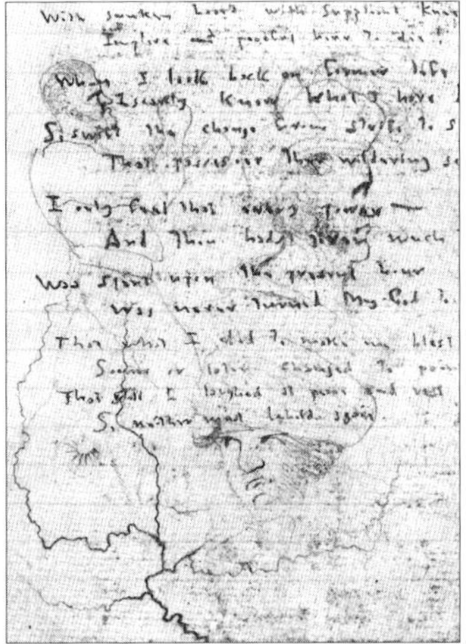

Halfway down the page on the left-hand side is a three-quarter length pencil sketch (58 × 32 mm) of a bearded pugilist, stripped to the waist, with his bare fists raised in fighting challenge (a sketch of boxers also appears on p. 2 of the Luddenden Foot Notebook: **276**). To the right of this figure is a pencil profile (50 × 30 mm) of the head and shoulders of a man facing picture right, with a prominent brow-line and down-turned mouth. Over his curly hair he wears a soft beret with a plume in the style of a Scottish tam-o'-shanter. Midway between these two figures, at the foot of the page, is a pencil sketch (40 × 33 mm) of the head of a man wearing a turban, looking to picture left.

Five stanzas of poetry, beginning 'My body is oppressed with pain, my mind is prostrate with despair', have been written in pencil over the sketches. C. W. Hatfield has marked these stanzas as a continuation of the poem on the previous page, which begins 'Oh Thou whose beams were most withdrawn', dated by Branwell 8 August 1841, an early draft of the poem 'The Triumph of mind over body'.

A further sketch (40 × 30 mm) has been drawn upside down at the top of p. 4 of this batch of loose pages taken from the Luddenden Foot Notebook: it consists of a pencil profile of the head and shoulders of a man or woman with hair pulled up in a topknot, loose curls falling beside a face with strong features and a thick masculine neck, wearing a loose robe. An unfinished pencil outline of the same profile appears on the left of the same page. At the foot of the page, other faint sketches of profile heads.

## 281

## 'Resurgam'

1842
Ink on paper
70 × 120 mm

Signed in sepia ink in printed capitals, below drawing, right corner: 'P.B.B.'; inscribed on tombstone: 'RESURGAM'.

Formerly owned by Joseph Bentley Leyland and possibly kept in the Leyland family with the collection known as 'The Leyland Manuscripts' until it was acquired by Lord Brotherton: see **203**.

*The Brotherton Collection, Leeds University Library*

Minutely detailed drawing in pen and black ink of a desolate graveyard. In the foreground a gravestone with an arched top is set at a backwards-leaning angle in stony ground surrounded by weeds. It is decorated with a skull and crossbones at the top and the word 'RESURGAM' below, the same inscription described by Charlotte on Helen Burns's grave in *Jane Eyre*, chapter 9, and before this on the grave of Lady Rosamund Wellesley in 'Henry Hastings' (see Christine Alexander, *The Early Writings of Charlotte Brontë* (Oxford: Basil Blackwell, 1983), p. 186). Behind it is a toppled table-top tombstone, and in the distance to picture right two gravestones on a small mound. A large hill can be seen on the horizon with a darkening sky above.

The folds in the paper of the drawing apparently coincide with those in a letter of 15 May 1842 written to the sculptor Joseph Bentley Leyland, beginning 'My Dear Sir, I have received great pleasure from the examination of the three drawings which you put in the hands of Mr J. Brown …' (*Patrick Branwell Brontë: A Complete Transcript of the Leyland Manuscripts*, ed. J. Alex Symington and C. W. Hatfield (Leeds: privately printed, 1925), p. 11). The graveyard motif recurs in the little vignettes which form the many 'tail-pieces' engraved by Thomas Bewick in his *A History of British Birds* (see for example vol. 2: *Containing the History and Description of Water Birds* (Newcastle: T. Bewick; London: Longman & Co., 1816), p. 235, from which Branwell may have taken his inspiration for this drawing).

## 282

# The Old Hall, Thorp Green

25 August 1844
Ink on paper
203 × 265 mm

Signed and dated in ink, in longhand, below drawing, bottom left corner: 'P B Bronté.'; bottom centre: '1844.'; bottom right corner: 'Aug 25.th'. Inscribed at the foot of the page in longhand, in ink: 'This is only a rough pen and ink sketch of the back of my lodgings – the "old Hall." built about 1680 – or 85.'
Gift of A. H. Green and Emily Green, 1947; together with **154** and **283**, formerly owned by their father Henry S. Green of Moss Side, Manchester, formerly of Dewsbury and a founder member of the Brontë Society, who lent them to the Brontë Society in 1896. (See F. C. Galloway, *A Descriptive Catalogue of Objects in the Museum of the Brontë Society at Haworth* (Bradford, 1896), p. 15.) Galloway describes the drawing as 'one of the best specimens of Branwell's artistic work. It is reproduced in the "Life of Charlotte Brontë", by Mrs Gaskell.'
*Brontë Parsonage Museum: B13*

Detailed drawing in ink of the rear view of the seventeenth-century country house (correct name 'Monk's House') in the grounds of Thorp Green Hall, near York, where Branwell lodged when he worked as a tutor there to Edmund Robinson from January 1843 until his dismissal in July 1845.

The central part of the house is viewed from the gable end; there are four windows, one on each floor. A tall chimney stack sticks out of its roof. To the left, three extension buildings, becoming progressively lower; to the right a further part of the house set at right angles with a doorway, three windows and a chimney. A low stone wall and a tall tree close off the view of its gable end. A long gutter pipe leads diagonally down the wall into a large rain butt. A path leads from the near foreground to the doorway, to the left of which is a patch of scrubby land with three stunted old trees.

It is curious that Branwell has chosen to draw the building from what was probably its most unattractive angle, with all the debris of its backyard. He chooses similarly undistinguished viewpoints in his two 1833 drawings of buildings from life (see **219** and **220**). It is as if he wanted to tuck himself away from public view when he worked. At the same time, there is a sense here that Branwell was showing off to the recipient of the drawing, probably his family, about his relatively grand lodgings. This is the only known drawing by Branwell dating from his period at Thorp Green Hall.

The paper of this drawing is torn on three sides. Victor Neufeldt has pointed out that during this period Branwell had a tendency to use drawing paper for his writings as well as his drawings, tearing it up into different sizes.

## 283

# Figure studies

c. 1844
Pencil on paper
203 × 265 mm

Inscribed in pencil in Branwell's hand (top right) 12
8
96
12
216

This numerical calculation has been identified by Victor Neufeldt as one of Branwell's calculations of the number of lines in a poem. There is a second numerical calculation in ink beside this one which has been heavily deleted and is illegible.

Gift of A. H. Green and Emily Green, 1947; together with **154** and **282**, both formerly owned by their father Henry S. Green of Moss Side, Manchester, formerly of Dewsbury and a founder member of the Brontë Society, who lent them to the Brontë Society in 1896. (See F. C. Galloway, *A Descriptive Catalogue of Objects in the Museum of the Brontë Society at Haworth* (Bradford, 1896), p. 15.)

*Brontë Parsonage Museum: B13v*

Although these pencil sketches on the verso of **282** are tiny they are worth noting as they contain images of decadent behaviour, which, bearing in mind the speculation about Branwell's own conduct at this period, may have some significance. To the left is an embracing couple and to the right a group of three men lounging on the ground, all of them with their legs crossed loosely above the ankle. Two of them, facing in opposite directions, smoke pipes and the third man appears to be masturbating. Long-barrelled guns lie on the ground. It is possible that the men are smoking opium and that all of them are indulging in masturbation. The guns could be intended as phallic symbols, as they are sometimes depicted in risqué late eighteenth-century prints. It is quite likely, given the obsessions of his last years, that Branwell was in the habit of making indecent drawings and that these were usually quickly destroyed by himself, or later by Charlotte.

## 284

### 'Penmaenmawr'

c. July–August 1845
Pencil on paper

The sketch occupies the top third of a page of manuscript of a draft of the poem 'Lydia Gisborne', written in pencil in Branwell's longhand, beginning: 'Cannot my soul depart – ~~H~~ [illegible]'. The verse is written over the sketch which is inscribed on the right side: 'PENMAENMAWR'.

Sold as part of lot 183 at the sale of the effects of Mary Anne Nicholls, 19 June 1914; last known in possession of Mrs C. B. Branwell. A photograph of the manuscript was presented to the BPM by Agnes Hatfield, daughter of C. W. Hatfield, 1991.

*Location unknown*

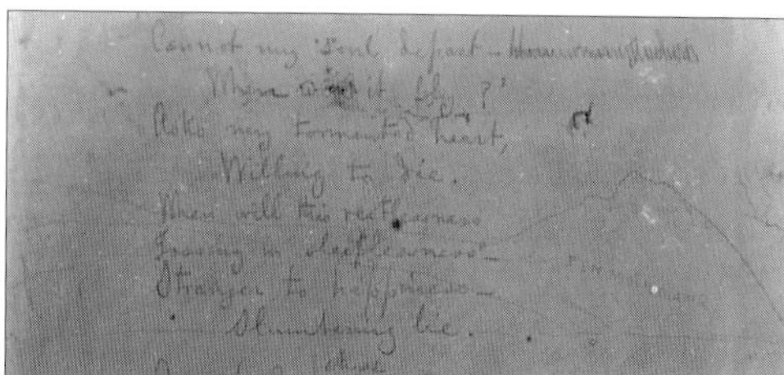

Simple outline sketch of some hills, possibly inspired by Branwell's trip from Liverpool to North Wales which took place between 29 July and 3 August 1845.

## 285

### 'Bendigo "taking a sight"./ "Alas! poor Caunt!"'

10 September 1845
Ink on paper
15 × 80 mm

Titled in ink, in longhand, below: 'Bendigo "taking a sight"./ "Alas! Poor Caunt!"' This drawing is found at the end of a letter of three pages (180 × 230 mm) from Branwell to Joseph Bentley Leyland, dated 10 September 1845, beginning: 'MY DEAR SIR, I was certainly sadly disappointed at not having seen you on the Friday you named for your visit, but the cause you alledge [*sic*] for not arriving was justifiable with a vengeance ...' (*Patrick Branwell Brontë: A Complete Transcript of the Leyland Manuscripts*, ed. J. Alex Symington and C. W. Hatfield (Leeds: privately printed, 1925), pp. 18–20). The bottom section of p. 3 has been torn away: see **286**.

Formerly owned by the Leyland family and possibly kept in the Leyland family in the collection known as 'The Leyland Manuscripts' until it was acquired by Lord Brotherton: see **203**.

*The Brotherton Collection, Leeds University Library*

Drawing depicting two male figures seen in profile kneeling on a mound of earth. The man on the left, crouching in the attitude of a slave with chains dangling from his wrists, faces the other man who lifts himself up on his knees and raises his enormous hands above the other's head. Both figures are drawn in solid black as though they were silhouettes, although the knee-length breeches of the man on the right are white. The sketch is condensed between Branwell's signature at the end of the letter and its title below. Taking a sight is a shooting term, meaning to get a good view of the target.

In *Patrick Branwell Brontë: A Complete Transcript of the Leyland Manuscripts* (ed. J. Alex Symington and C. W. Hatfield (Leeds: privately printed, 1925)), p. 20, Symington and Hatfield identify the two figures as the boxers 'Bendigo', or William Thompson, and Benjamin Caunt who, in April 1838, defeated Bendigo after 75 rounds to become champion of England. In a return bout held on 9 September 1845, the day before this drawing was made, Bendigo won in 93 rounds, after a controversial foul. Neither boxer was black, as the drawing appears to suggest.

It is uncertain precisely what Branwell intended this drawing to mean, other than, perhaps, a symbol of his own inner conflict or possibly just a topical subject. The choice of imagery is unsurprising as Branwell was himself a boxer, a sport which at the time was fashionable with the upper classes, including the Brontë hero Lord Byron. Francis A. Leyland (*The Brontë Family With Special Reference to Patrick Branwell Brontë*, 2 vols. (London: Hurst & Blackett, 1886), vol. 1, p. 117) writes of how Branwell 'read with eagerness the columns of "Bell's Life in London" and other sporting papers of the day. The names and personal appearances of the celebrated pugilists who, at that time, to the delight of the elite of society, pounded each other till they were unlike anything human – for the applause of the multitude, and the honour of wearing the "Champion's Belt", –were familiar to him.' Further drawings of sparring boxers appear in the Luddenden Foot Notebook (**276**).

Below this sketch on the bottom half of the page there was a second drawing which was torn away and is now lost (see **286**).

## 286

## 'A Cast – cast down but not castaway'

10 September 1845
Ink on paper
c. 165 × 180 mm

Inscribed in ink, in Branwell's longhand, below: 'A Cast – cast down ~~east~~ but not / castaway –'. The drawing was torn from the third page of a letter from Branwell to Joseph Bentley Leyland dated 10 September 1845: see **285**.

The reproduction of this drawing was taken from a newspaper cutting in the BPM Library: an article from

the *Daily Mail*, Friday 27 December 1929, about the collection of Lady Charnwood, the then owner, who inaccurately attributes the drawing to Charlotte. Lady Charnwood purchased the drawing, along with two Charlotte Brontë letters and a signature, at a sale some years previously.
*Location unknown*

On the left of the picture the silhouetted figure of a woman stands facing picture right in profile with her hair in a topknot and wearing a dark gown, white collar, apron and possibly long white cuffs. Her arms are outstretched and she may be holding sculptor's tools in her hands. On the ground before her lie the head and shoulders of a large stone bust with jagged edges, clearly recognizable as a Branwell self-portrait because of his familiar facial profile, hair-style and spectacles. The drawing and its inscription would seem to refer to the imagined state of the artist's relationship with Lydia Robinson, the wife of his recent employer, and to imply that although she wields the power, and has cast him down like a sculptor frustrated with her work, there is still hope for him that he is not yet 'castaway'. In the opening paragraph of the letter to which this drawing was formerly attached, Branwell apparently refers to the drawing –' I should have been as cracked as my cast' – in his commiserations with Leyland about a piece of the sculptor's work which has apparently been damaged.

## 287

### Two views of Morley Hall

c. 1846
Ink on paper

Inscribed in ink in Branwell's longhand, below uppermost of two drawings: 'View of Morley Hall while in course of erection – A.D. 1847./ with a portrait of the Architect.'; below lower of the two drawings: 'View of Morley Hall as it WILL appear – A.D. 1947./ With the monument of the Architect.' A reproduction of these two drawings, together on one page, was found in the papers of J. Alex Symington in the BPM. It is possible that the drawing formerly belonged to the Leyland family as it is similar to other drawings in 'The Leyland Manuscripts', the Brotherton Collection, Leeds University Library.
*Location unknown*

Two drawings, one above the other, on one sheet of paper. The drawing at the top of the page depicts the figure of a man asleep on his front amidst building materials and a semi-built wall. To his right a spade stands upright in a pile of sand with beside it a rectangular piece of stone with the inscription 'I LAZY.' apparently carved on it. To the man's left, beside his elbow, there is a jug and a tankard, which suggests that he is unconscious due to drink rather than hard work. Beyond the wall a few lines are drawn to suggest a rising sun.

The lower drawing portrays the finished building, an impressive gothic mansion with a hexagonal tower to the left and five two-storeyed window bays with tall chimneys above, ranging across the building from left to right. Trees are roughly sketched in on either side of the building and a circular drive in front. To the right is the blacked-in figure of a Phoenix on top of a tall column, the 'monument' symbolizing the architect risen from the ashes of his despair.

'Morley Hall' is the title of one of Branwell's poems from the period 1846–7. He intended it to be an epic 'in several cantos, dealing with a succession of romantic episodes, of which an elopement which actually took place … was the chief feature' (Francis A. Leyland, *The Brontë Family With Special Reference to Patrick Branwell Brontë*, 2 vols. (London: Hurst & Blackett, 1886), vol. 2. p. 242). The elopement, of Edward Tyldesly and Anne Leyland, was something of a legend in the Leyland family, whose ancestral home was Morley Hall, Leigh, Lancashire. Branwell mentions 'Morley Hall' several times in the letters to Joseph Bentley Leyland preserved in the Brotherton Collection, Leeds University Library. His letter to Leyland of 28 April 1846 begins:

> MY DEAR SIR,
> As I am anxious – though my return for your kindness will be like giving a sixpence back for a sovereign lent – to do my best in my intended lines on 'Morley' I want answers to the following questions.
>
> 1st (As I cannot find it in the map or Gazzeteer) In what district of Lancashire is Morley situated?
> 2nd Has the Hall a particular name?
> 3rd. Do you know the family name of its owners when the occurrences happened which I ought to dwell on?
> 4th Can you tell in what century they happened?
> 5th What, told in the fewest words, was the nature of the leading occurrence?
>
> (*Patrick Branwell Brontë: A Complete Transcript of the Leyland Manuscripts*, ed. J. Alex Symington and C. W. Hatfield (Leeds: privately printed, 1925), p. 25).

In June 1846 Branwell opened a letter to Leyland with the words: 'MY DEAR SIR, I should have sent you "Morley Hall" ere now, but I am unable to finish it at present from agony to which the grave would be far preferable' (ibid., p. 29). With this letter Branwell enclosed an ink drawing of himself as a martyr tied to the stake (**289**), illustrating a phrase in the letter; therefore it is possible that this drawing, referring to his inability to finish the poem, was also enclosed. A few months later, in October 1846, 'Morley Hall' receives another mention in a letter containing a number of drawings interspersed within the text (**291**): '"Morley Hall" is in the eighth month of her pregnancy and expects ere long to be delivered of a fine thumping boy whom its father means to christen Homer at the least, though the mother suggests that "Poetaster" would be more suitable, but that sounds too aristocratic' (ibid., p. 36).

## 288

### 'Our Lady of greif.'

28 April 1846
Ink and wash on paper
230 × 175 mm

Inscribed in ink, in Branwell's longhand, at top: '"Our Lady of greif."/ "Nuestra Senóra de la pena."' and printed in capitals in ink on the tombstone, bottom right: 'NUESTRA/ SENORA/ DE LA/ PENA'. Branwell enclosed this drawing with a four-page letter written to Joseph Bentley Leyland, 28 April 1846, quoted above in **287**.

Formerly owned by Joseph Bentley Leyland and possibly kept in the Leyland family with the collection known as 'The Leyland Manuscripts' until it was acquired by Lord Brotherton: see **203**.

*The Brotherton Collection, Leeds University Library*

In the text of the letter which accompanies this drawing Branwell includes a draft of his poem 'I implore for rest' (see **297**) and records his intention to write an epic poem about a succession of romantic episodes associated with Morley Hall, Leigh, Lancashire, ancestral home of the Leyland family. He goes on to describe how miserable he is at Haworth, how unsympathetic his family is to his plight and how he is considering looking for a situation abroad. After a comment on the hopelessness of sending any of his writings to a London publisher he writes: 'I enclose an ill-drawn daub done to wile away the time this morning. I meant it to represent a very rough figure in stone.'

The 'ill-drawn daub' depicts a full-length figure of a statue of a woman, standing on a plinth, in a pose of penitence and despair with head bent and long limp hair falling forward to cover her face. Her shoulders and most of her chest are bare and she holds her hands clasped in front of her. A lopsided gravestone stands to the right of the plinth bearing the inscription of the title. The image has first been drawn in pen and ink then wash has been added with a brush to form the shadows on the figure and to suggest a distant view of a castle on a hill in the bottom left.

The figure is no doubt intended to refer to Lydia Robinson, the wife of Branwell's employer at Thorp Green, with whom he is alleged to have had a love affair, on account of which he was dismissed from his post as tutor to the Robinsons' son in July 1845. Indeed, as Francis A. Leyland notes, 'We need not entertain a doubt as to whom it is intended to represent' (*Patrick Branwell Brontë: A Complete Transcript of the Leyland Manuscripts*, ed. J. Alex Symington and C. W. Hatfield (Leeds: privately printed, 1925), p. 27).

A number of the drawings added to Branwell's letters to his sculptor friend Leyland contain allusions to the art of sculpture.

## 289

## 'Myself.'

June 1846
Ink on paper
230 × 180 mm

Inscribed in ink, in Branwell's longhand, below: 'Myself.' This drawing was enclosed on a separate sheet of paper with a letter from Branwell to Joseph Bentley Leyland sent in June 1846, which begins: 'MY DEAR SIR, I should have sent you "Morley Hall" ere now, but I am unable to finish it at present from agony to which the grave would be far preferable' (*Patrick Branwell Brontë: A Complete Transcript of the Leyland Manuscripts*, ed. J. Alex Symington and C. W. Hatfield (Leeds: privately printed, 1925), pp. 29–30).
Formerly owned by Joseph Bentley Leyland and possibly kept in the Leyland family with the collection known as 'The Leyland Manuscripts' until it was acquired by Lord Brotherton: see **203**.
*The Brotherton Collection, Leeds University Library*

Both the contents of the letter accompanying the sketch and the state of its presentation – scrawled writing, heavy lines, blots of ink and furious deletions – demonstrate Branwell's distressed frame of mind. Branwell opens with the news that Mr Robinson of Thorp Green is dead and that his coachman has brought him word that Lydia Robinson is ill with grief and despair over the loss and the harsh terms of the will which leaves her 'powerless'. He writes melodramatically and at length of his own suffering, his inability to eat or sleep and how he visualises 'a dreary future which I as little wish to enter on as could a martyr to be bound to the stake'.

The rough outline ink drawing depicts Branwell seen half-length, in profile facing picture right. He is naked from the waist up, displaying a muscular torso, tied around the waist to a stake, his hands chained together in front of him. The head has long flowing hair, is tipped back with closed eyes and is disproportionately small in relation to the body. The figure is engulfed in smoke and flame, suggested by roughly drawn lines. The image is clearly a literal translation of Branwell's fear of the future as described in the letter.

## 290

## 'Lydia Gisborne.'

1 June 1846
Ink on paper
106 × 185 mm

The sketch occupies the lower half of a manuscript page (232 × 185 mm). The page is titled at the top in Branwell's hand, in decorative Greek lettering: 'LYDIA Gisborne.', followed by his poem which begins: 'On Ouses grassy banks, last Whitsuntide'.

Purchased at Sotheby's, London, 13 December 1993, lot 37. Last known to be in the possession of Mrs C. B. Branwell; and previously sold at Sotheby's sale of the effects of Mary Anne Nicholls, 19 June 1914 (part of lot 178). A photograph of the manuscript was presented to the BPM by Agnes Hatfield, daughter of C. W. Hatfield, 1991.

*Brontë Parsonage Museum: BS128.5*

View of a landscape with three or four poplar trees right foreground on the near bank of a river, with a view across to a grassy plain. The tiny silhouetted figure of a man in a top hat holding a walking stick stands in the foreground slightly right of centre, gazing at the sunset discernible in the distance. In the bottom right corner (which is partially torn away), a gravestone bears the inscription 'EHEV' (Alas!). In the bottom left corner is a stone bearing the word 'MEMORIA' (in memory).

The sketch depicts the image described in the poem above it, which is Branwell's lament, written after his dismissal from Thorp Green Hall, at the loss of his happiness in his love for Lydia Robinson, whose maiden name appears in his private code of Greek lettering at the top of the page. The artist's sense of grief and loss is symbolized by the dying sun sinking below the distant horizon. Everard Flintoff has suggested that the addition of the sketch to this particular manuscript is a reference to Branwell's memory of art-sessions with Lydia, although it is not certain that he was Lydia's art tutor ('Some Unpublished Poems of Branwell Brontë', *Durham University Journal*, vol. 81, June 1989).

## 291

## 'Paradise/ Purgatory'

October 1846
Ink on paper
55 × 180 mm

Two scenes titled 'PARADISE.', and 'PURGATORY.', at the top of the first page (230 × 180 mm) of a two-and-a-half-page letter from Branwell to Joseph Bentley Leyland, written early October 1846 and beginning: 'MY DEAR SIR, Mr. John Brown wishes me to tell you that if, by return of post, you can tell him the nature of his intended work' (*Patrick Branwell Brontë: A Complete Transcript of the Leyland Manuscripts*, ed. J. Alex Symington and C. W. Hatfield (Leeds: privately printed, 1925), pp. 35–6).

Formerly owned by Joseph Bentley Leyland and possibly kept in the Leyland family with the collection known as

'The Leyland Manuscripts' until it was acquired by Lord Brotherton: see **203**.

*The Brotherton Collection, Leeds University Library*

Two scenes alongside each other, divided by a skull on a post. In the left scene, 'PARADISE.', a figure of a man drawn in silhouette leans drunkenly back in an armless chair with a full glass raised in his right hand, his left hand extended and his feet lifting off the floor. Behind him a stool overturns and in front of him a smaller stool and a round table fall over, upsetting a pitcher, a wine-glass and a bottle. In the background there is an outline drawing of an inn with a sign hanging from the gable wall. In a speech balloon issuing from the man's mouth the words 'DAMN YOU! I'M KING AND A HAUF!' are inscribed.

In the second scene, 'PURGATORY.', the same man stands in a graveyard with a view of Haworth Church to his left. He faces picture right looking down and holding a hammer or chisel in his hands. A speech balloon issues from his mouth inscribed inside with the words 'WHAT IVVER MUN I DO? [!]'. On top of a low table-top tombstone in front of him the tools of the stonemason's trade are laid out. Behind him is a lopsided arched-top gravestone decorated with a skull and crossbones at the top and the words 'HERE/ LIETH/ THE/ BODY' below, another sign of Branwell's self-centred doomladen thoughts, perhaps.

The first paragraph of the letter which starts below the drawing refers to John Brown, Branwell's Haworth stonemason friend, who is going to do some work for Leyland, the sculptor. The second paragraph contains a string of classical and Biblical allusions: 'He [John Brown] has only delayed answering your communication from his unavoidable absence in a pilgramage from "Rochdale on the Rhine" to "the land of Ham" and from thence to Gehenna, Tophet, Golgotha, Erebus, the Styx and to the place he now occupies called Tartarus where he along with Sisyphus, Tantalus, Theseus, and Ixion lodge and board together.' The implication of this passage, in tandem with the drawing, is that John Brown has been on an expedition away from Haworth which has involved excessive indulgence in drink, resulting in a journey through various hellish places and on to Tartarus where the most sinful of all were forced to undergo eternal punishment. Branwell was intimately acquainted with the family's copy of J. Lemprière's *Bibliotheca Classica; Or, A Classical Dictionary* (3rd edn., London: T. Cadell & W. Davies, 1797) and he knew from its description that the entrance to the region of Tartarus 'was by a large and lofty tower', perhaps wickedly symbolized here by the tower of Haworth Church.

The two cartoon-like drawings probably depict John Brown in the two opposing modes of pleasure and work, or drunkenness and sobriety, equivalent to Paradise and Purgatory; on the left, drunk in a public house and on the right lettering a gravestone in the churchyard. There is some evidence to suggest that John Brown had a fondness for drink. Mrs Ellis H. Chadwick (*In the Footsteps of the Brontës* (London: Sir Isaac Pitman & Sons Ltd, 1914), p. 158) recounts that one of John Brown's daughters told her that he 'liked his glass' and was much to blame for 'leading young Branwell on'.

This drawing appears in the same letter as **292**, **293**, **294** and **295**.

## 292

## 'Augustus Caesar'

October 1846
Ink on paper
40 × 60 mm

Enclosed in a roundel and titled below, following the circular curve: 'AUGUSTUS CAESAR'. This drawing appears in the middle of the second page (230 × 180 mm) of a two-and-a-half-page letter from Branwell to Joseph Bentley Leyland written early October 1846: see **291**.

For provenance see **291**.

*The Brotherton Collection, Leeds University Library*

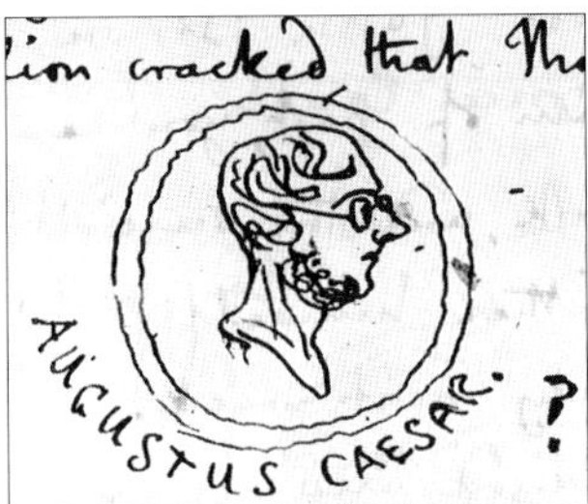


Self-portrait head seen in profile within a double circle. The paragraph in the letter which precedes this drawing reads: 'Is the medallion cracked that Thorwaldsen executed of [Augustus Caesar]?'. Thorwaldsen was a neo-classical sculptor of the early nineteenth century, but the medallion to which Branwell refers is Leyland's plaster relief portrait of Branwell, which now hangs in the dining room of the Brontë Parsonage Museum.

This drawing appears in the same letter as **291**, **293**, **294** and **295**.

## 293

## 'Fallen'

October 1846
Ink on paper
30 × 40 mm

This drawing appears below **292** on the second page (230 × 180 mm) of a two-and-a-half-page letter from Branwell to Joseph Bentley Leyland written early October 1846: see **291**.

For provenance see **291**.

*The Brotherton Collection, Leeds University Library*

The text of the manuscript letter immediately preceding the drawing reads: 'I wish I could see you, and, as Haworth fair is held/ on Monday after the ensuing one, your presence there would/ gratify one of the [sketch] FALLEN.'. The written line veers cleverly into a sketch of a tiny figure plunging into an abyss, with the word 'FALLEN' below.

This drawing appears in the same letter as **291**, **292**, **294** and **295**.

## 294

## 'an old Maid's Squeamish Cat'

October 1846
Ink on paper
30 × 80 mm

This drawing appears on the third page (230 × 180 mm) of a two-and-a-half-page letter to Joseph Bentley Leyland written early October 1846: see **291**.

For provenance see **291**.

*The Brotherton Collection, Leeds University Library*

The penultimate paragraph of the letter, which precedes this drawing, reads: 'constant and unavoidable depression of mind and/ body sadly shackle me in even trying to go on with/ any mental effort which might rescue me from the/ fate of a dry toast soaked six hours in a glass of/ cold water, and intended to be given to an old Maid's/ Squeamish Cat.' This amusing little sketch depicts a cat's face wearing a miserable expression between two extended hands holding glasses of water.

This drawing appears in the same letter as **291**, **292**, **293** and **295**.

## 295

### Man at the gallows

October 1846
Ink on paper
70 × 140 mm

This drawing forms the tail-piece of a two-and-a-half-page letter from Branwell to Joseph Bentley Leyland written early October 1846: see **291**.
For provenance see **291**.
*The Brotherton Collection, Leeds University Library*

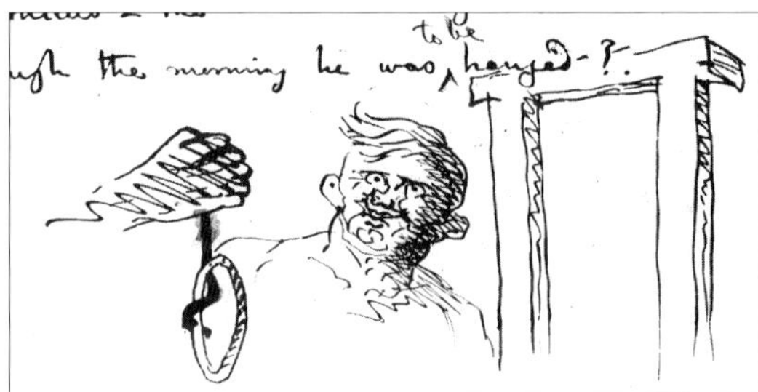


The last paragraph of the letter reads: 'Is there really such a thing as the "Risus Sar-/ -donicus" – the Sardonic laugh.? Did a man ever/ laugh the morning he was to be hanged?.' Below it is an ink sketch of a hand holding up a noose, a portrait of a coarse-looking, grinning man's head and a gallows. Francis A. Leyland (*Patrick Branwell Brontë: A Complete Transcript of the Leyland Manuscripts*, ed. J. Alex Symington and C. W. Hatfield (Leeds: privately printed, 1925), p. 36) identifies the man as 'John Brown, and an excellent portrait, grinning at the rope that is to terminate his existence!'.

This drawing appears in the same letter as **291**, **292**, **293** and **294**.

## 296

### 'The results of Sorrow.'

1846
Ink on blue paper
70 × 113 mm

Titled in ink, in Branwell's longhand, below drawing, at bottom of page: 'The results of Sorrow.' The drawing occupies approximately the lower half of a manuscript page (184 × 113 mm) in Mary Pearson's 'Commonplace Book', a personal album in which she collected written contributions and sketches from friends and relatives, and pasted in various memorabilia. The top of the page contains a poem, inscribed in ink in Branwell's longhand, titled: 'SONNET.' (see below). Pasted on verso: newspaper clipping from the *Halifax Guardian* of the poem 'Letter From A Father On Earth To His Child In Her Grave' by 'Northangerland'.

Purchased from Maggs Bros., New York, 1965; earlier provenance unknown.
*Harry Ransom Humanities Research Center, The University of Texas at Austin*

Head-and-shoulders portrait of a man which graphically illustrates the physical effects of the harrowing emotions described in the poem:

SONNET.
Why hold young eyes the fullest fount of tears,
    And why do happiest hearts most sadly sigh
When fancied friends forsake, or lovers ~~sigh~~ die,
Or other's heart-strings crack, oerstrained by cares?
Ah! Thou who askest me art young in years
    Or Time's rough voice had long since told
        thee why!

Increase of days increases misery,
And misery brings selfishness, which sears [?scars]
The soul's best feelings – Mid the battle's roar,
In Death's grim grasp the Soldiers eyes are blind
To others dying – So he whose hopes are oer
Smiles sternest at the sufferings of mankind.
A wounded spirit will delight in gore –
A tortured heart will make a tyrant mind.
Northangerland.

The figure is seen in profile looking to picture right, wearing the familiar garb of high collar, stock and wide-lapelled coat. The head has a high forehead with long white hair swept back and the ravaged face is heavily lined around the sunken eyes, the cheeks and the drooping mouth. The profile is similar to Branwell's own, with a prominent nose and chin, and it is not unreasonable to assume that this is intended as a form of self-portrait.

This drawing is one of six illustrations by Branwell entered in Mary Pearson's 'Commonplace Book'. Branwell stayed with Mary Pearson's family at Ovenden Cross near Halifax in 1846. See also **297**, **298** and **299**.

## 297

## 'I implore for rest'

1846
Ink on cream paper
50 × 113 mm

Titled in ink, in Branwell's hand on the gravestone within the drawing: 'I/ IMPLORE/ FOR/ REST.' The drawing occupies approximately the lower half of a manuscript page (184 × 113 mm) in Mary Pearson's 'Commonplace Book', a personal album in which she collected written contributions and sketches from friends and relatives, and pasted in various memorabilia. The top half of the page contains a poem, inscribed in ink in Branwell's longhand, titled: 'SONNET.' (see below). Pasted on verso: newspaper clipping from the *Halifax Guardian* of the poem 'Penmaenmawr' by 'Northangerland'.

Purchased from Maggs Bros., New York, 1965; earlier provenance unknown.

*Harry Ransom Humanities Research Center, The University of Texas at Austin*

Drawing in ink, depicting in the foreground a lopsided gravestone with an arched top set in stony ground. The stone bears the inscription 'I/ IMPLORE/ FOR/ REST.' above a skull and crossbones. In the background is a view of Haworth Church with a square battlemented tower, with mountains beyond.

The morbid subject matter reflects the doleful tone of the Sonnet, and Branwell's own distressed state of mind at the time of writing, which was some time in 1846 after the Thorp Green debacle:

SONNET.

When all our cheerful hours seem gone for ever –
All lost that caused the body and the mind
To nourish love or friendship for our kind
And Charons boat prepares, oer Lethe's river
Our souls to waft, and all our thoughts to sever
From what was once lifes light, still there may be
Some well loved bosom to whose pillow we
Could heartily our utter self deliver;
And if, toward her grave, Death's dreary road
Our Darling's feet should walk – each step by her
Would draw our own steps to the dark abode,
And make a festival of sepulture,
For what gave joy, and joy to us has owed
Should Death affright us from when he would her restore?
Northangerland.

Branwell enclosed an earlier version of the poem in a letter to Joseph Bentley Leyland of 28 April 1846 beginning: 'MY DEAR SIR, As I am anxious – though my return for your kindness will be like giving a sixpence back for a sovereign lent –' (*Patrick Branwell Brontë: A Complete Transcript of the Leyland Manuscripts*, ed. J. Alex Symington and C. W. Hatfield (Leeds: privately printed, 1925), pp. 25–6) and accompanied by the drawing 'Our Lady of greif' (see **287** and **288**).

This drawing is one of six illustrations by Branwell entered in Mary Pearson's 'Commonplace Book'. Branwell stayed with Mary Pearson's family at Ovenden Cross near Halifax in 1846. See also **296**, **298** and **299**.

## 298

### 'Alexander. Percy. Esq$^{R}$ M.P.'

1846
Ink on green paper
184 × 113 mm

Titled in ink, in Branwell's hand, below drawing, in centre of page: 'ALEXANDER. PERCY. ESQ$^{R}$ M.P.'. The drawing occupies the top half of a manuscript page (184 × 113 mm) in Mary Pearson's 'Commonplace Book', a personal album in which she collected written contributions and sketches from friends and relatives, and pasted in various memorabilia. Below the drawing, in ink, four lines of verse in Branwell's longhand: 'No more – no more – oh never more on me/ The freshness of the heart shall fall like dew,/ Which, out of all the lovely things we see/ Extracts emotions beautiful and new!/ Lord Byron.'; below this a further drawing. Pasted on verso: newspaper clipping from the *Halifax Guardian* of three poems: 'Speak Kindly', anonymous; 'The Death Bed' and 'Stanzas' by Thomas Hood, with a note that Hood's verses were written only days before his own death.

Purchased from Maggs Bros., New York, 1965; earlier provenance unknown.

*Harry Ransom Humanities Research Center, The University of Texas at Austin*

Vigorous ink drawing of a half-length portrait of 'Alexander Percy', seen three-quarter face and looking to picture right. Curiously, this portrait is quite youthful and optimistic looking compared to the other Branwell drawings in this book. The face is rounded and unlined and the expression, with the eyes looking upward, is an alert and hopeful one. The man's hair is thick, dark and curly, brushed onto his forehead in the usual fashionable style; his clothes too are smart and well ordered: white pleated shirt and stock, wing collar, buttoned waistcoat and tight-fitting jacket with a high collar. Perhaps Branwell also had in mind remembered images of the poet Lord Byron, whose lines appear below the drawing.

At the foot of the page, occupying about one sixth of the space, there is a second drawing in rough ink outline of a male corpse in a shroud lying on a bier, its head propped up on a block. This gloomy image reflects the theme of the lines of the poem and provides a stark contrast to the buoyant figure of the young man above. Branwell surely intended the two drawings to refer to his present and former self.

The drawings are two of six illustrations by Branwell entered in Mary Pearson's 'Commonplace Book'. Branwell stayed with Mary Pearson's family at Ovenden Cross near Halifax in 1846. See also **296**, **297** and **299**.

## 299

# Self-portrait and figure of a man looking out to sea

1846
Ink on cream paper
184 × 113 mm

The drawings occupy approximately the top and bottom thirds of a manuscript page (measurement above) in Mary Pearson's 'Commonplace Book', a personal album in which she collected written contributions and sketches from friends and relatives, and pasted in various memorabilia. Inscribed in ink, in Branwell's longhand, below the first drawing (65 × 65 mm) and above the second one (42 × 113 mm): 'Think not that life is happiness,/ But deem it duty joined with care./ Implore for Hope in your distress,/ And for your answer get Despair./ Yet travel on, for Life's rough road/ May end, at last, in rest with GOD./ Northangerland.' Inscribed in ink, in Mary Pearson's longhand, bottom right corner of page: 'Look over Edwin'. For verso see below.

Purchased from Maggs Bros., New York, 1965; earlier provenance unknown.
*Harry Ransom Humanities Research Center, The University of Texas at Austin*

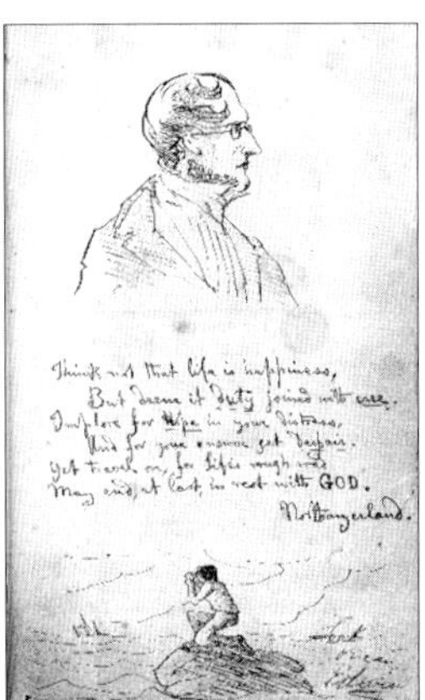

Head-and-shoulders self-portrait in ink, seen in profile and looking to picture right. If this first drawing is compared with an earlier self-portrait, **267** for example, it is clear that Branwell does not flinch from delineating the ravages wrought on his appearance by his emotional and self-inflicted sufferings, in the sagging look of his profile, the thinning hair and the lines beneath his eyes.

In the centre of the page are the lines of verse and below these a second drawing in ink which, as Mary Pearson has intuited in the passage she has written on the following pages, seems to symbolize Branwell's then physical and mental state. A weeping male figure crouches on his knees on a small rock, clutching a handkerchief to his face. The waves of the sea lap around him and in the distance a ship sinks below the water. The image very closely resembles a little scene engraved by Thomas Bewick in *A History of British Birds*, vol. 2: *Containing the History and Description of Water Birds* (Newcastle: T. Bewick; London: Longman & Co., 1816), p. 202.

Branwell stayed with Mary Pearson's family at Ovenden Cross near Halifax in 1846. The drawings are two of six illustrations (see also **296**, **297** and **298**) entered by him in her 'Commonplace Book'. On the verso of **299**, Mary Pearson has written in ink, in longhand, the following inscription:

> Who was Northangerland/ My Son may enquire into/ Whose hands this may fall/ after my departure from/ this changing life,/ his real name/ was Bronte He was Son of/ the Incumbent of Haworth/ of that name, & Brother to/ the gifted lady who wrote by/ the cognomen of Cora [*sic*] Bell,/ Jane Eyre was one of her/ productions,/ The little Sketch/ over the leaf and some others,/ you will meet with in this book/ were written by him when/ staying at my Father's House/ at Ovenden Cross in the Autumn/ of 1846, the Pen & Ink profile/ is an excellent one of himself/ the other little sketch is highly/ descriptive of the morbid state/ of mind under which he then/ laboured, the result as I was subsequently told of A disappointment/ in love, At the time we speak/ of he was an inveterate drunkard/ his whole energies and talents/ were shipwrecked,/ He was A lamentable/ instance of what man becomes/ who trusts for happiness in earthly/ things alone 'they are of the earth/ earthy' instead of relying upon that/ God, who sanctifys earthly/ afflictions

to our eternal welfare/ And commands us not to make/ Idols/ And bids us be of good cheer/ Poor Bronte however died at/ the early age of 28 A victim/ to intemperance; Alas My Son/ only one among many such/ may these ~~examples~~ shipwrecks be your/ Landmarks is your Mothers/ daily prayer/ Mary Pearson/ June 1st 1856.

## 300

### Gravestone in a hilly landscape

c. 1846–1847
Ink on paper
70 × 117 mm

The sketch appears in the top third of p. 6 (231 × 178 mm) of a six-page draft manuscript of the poem 'Juan Fernandez', written in ink in Branwell's longhand. The page begins: 'Tossed over board my perished crew'. The verse is written partially over the sketch. Inscribed in ink, in Branwell's hand in Greek-style lettering, top left: 'Lydia'.

Bequest of Henry Houston Bonnell, 1927; acquired by Bonnell from Sotheby's sale of the effects of Arthur Bell Nicholls, London, 26 July 1907, lot 182.

*Brontë Parsonage Museum: Bonnell 154*

Simple outline sketch of a perpendicular gravestone with an arched top inscribed with a cross; hills in the background.

## 301

### 'Pobre!'

c. 1847
Ink on paper
70 × 180 mm

The drawing is found at the foot of a single-page letter (160 × 180 mm), written and signed in ink: 'P. B. Bronté –'. The letter is addressed to Joseph Bentley Leyland, c. 1847, and begins: 'MY DEAR SIR, I only enclose the accompanying fragment, which is so soiled that I would have transcribed it if I had the heart to exert myself, …' (*Patrick Branwell Brontë: A Complete Transcript of the Leyland Manuscripts*, ed. J. Alex Symington and C. W. Hatfield (Leeds: privately printed, 1925), p. 42).

Formerly owned by Joseph Bentley Leyland and possibly kept in the Leyland family with the collection known as 'The Leyland Manuscripts' until it was acquired by Lord Brotherton: see **203**.

*The Brotherton Collection, Leeds University Library*

Drawing of a stone set in a bleak landscape with mountains beyond. The cross bears the single word 'POBRE!'. Across the foot of the page, below the drawing, Branwell has written: 'The best Epitaph ever written – It is ~~writt~~ carved on a rude cross, in Spain,/ over a murdered traveller – and simply means "Poor Fellow!"'.

The letter contains a plea for reassurance in Branwell's attempt to persuade his friend that his writings are worth reading. The drawing and its 'Epitaph' give a visual emphasis to his overwhelming state of self-pity.

## 302

# Three late drawings

c. January 1847
Ink on paper
230 × 180 mm

These three drawings each occupy a third of a single sheet of paper (measurements above), which was enclosed with a letter of c. January 1847 to Joseph Bentley Leyland, beginning: 'DEAR SIR, I had a letter written, and intended to have been forwarded to you a few days after I last left the ensnaring town of Halifax' (*Patrick Branwell Brontë: A Complete Transcript of the Leyland Manuscripts*, ed. J. Alex Symington and C. W. Hatfield (Leeds: privately printed, 1925), p. 37).

Formerly owned by Joseph Bentley Leyland and possibly kept in the Leyland family with the collection known as 'The Leyland Manuscripts' until it was acquired by Lord Brotherton: see **203**.

*The Brotherton Collection, Leeds University Library*

Cartoon-like drawing at the top of the page, executed in a similar manner to 'Paradise/ Purgatory': see **291**. In the centre of the drawing two men seen in silhouette face each other over a large carafe of wine. They are both teetering drunkenly on their stools and spilling wine out of their glasses. A speech balloon from the mouth of the one on the left contains the words 'J. B. L–D./ To speak plain truth. If I/ could not floor PHIDIAS/ Blast my eyes!'. The figure on the right replies 'Northangerland –"I would take/ Homer and Shakspeare – one down/ and the other come on – Sink/ my soul if I wouldn't".' To the far left a sculpture of a man without hands or feet is propped in a sitting position on a pile of blocks, with the words 'THESEUS./ "Damn you!"' coming out of its mouth. On the right a winged black devil gesticulates with its skinny arms over an open book with the words 'COWP/ -ERS/ ANAT-/ OMY.' inscribed on the left hand page and a figure drawing on the right. A line drawn across the page below the drawing separates it from the one below.

The drawing seems to depict a drinking session shared by Branwell and Leyland at which they discuss Phidias, Homer and Shakespeare as if they were opponents in a boxing match. Although Francis A. Leyland (*Patrick Branwell Brontë: A Complete Transcript of the Leyland Manuscripts*, ed. J. Alex Symington and C. W. Hatfield (Leeds: privately printed, 1925), p. 38) claims that this sheet of drawings was enclosed with Branwell's letter of c. January 1847, there is a reference in his letter of 25 November 1845 to Leyland, not containing any drawings, which seems to describe the depiction of the sculpture of Theseus in this drawing: 'I saw Murray's monument praised in the papers, and I trust you are getting on well with Beckworth's, as well as with your own personal statue of living flesh and blood. Mine, like your Theseus, has lost his hands and feet, and, I fear, its head also, for it can neither move, write or think as it once could' (Ibid., p. 23). This reference to a damaged cast or sculpture could also be connected to Branwell's mention in the opening paragraph of his letter of 10 September 1845 of some misfortune that has befallen one of Leyland's works: 'I should have been as cracked as my cast had I entered a room and seen the labours of weeks or months destroyed ... in a moment' (ibid., p. 18): see **286**.

The central drawing, occupying about the same space as the first, is a self-portrait of the artist recumbent, probably in death, depicted in the manner of a tomb sculpture. He is naked, his head to the left, his right arm by his side and his left resting across his body.

Draperies cover the lower half of his body and pillows support his head.

The third drawing depicts a tilted gravestone set in the foreground of a hilly landscape with two bent fir trees to the right and a half-moon with a human profile, smoking a pipe, in the sky. The gravestone has moss growing on it and is decorated with a skull and cross-bones and the inscription 'HIC/ JACET' (Here lies). It is similar to a Thomas Bewick vignette. The drawing is inscribed below: '"MARTINI LIUGI IMPLORA ETERNA QUIETE!":/ "Martin Luke implores for eternal rest!" (Italian Epitaph.)'. Above the drawing these lines are written:

> 'Thy soul is flown,
> And clay alone
> Has nought to do with joy or care;
> So, if the light of life be gone
> There come no sorrows crowding on,
> And powerless lies DESPAIR!'

Formerly owned by Joseph Bentley Leyland and possibly kept in the Leyland family with the collection known as 'The Leyland Manuscripts' until it was acquired by Lord Brotherton: see **203**.

*The Brotherton Collection, Leeds University Library*

## 303

### 'Patrick Reid "turned off", without his cap. 1848' and 'The rescue of the punchbowl. a scene in the Talbot.'

January 1848
Ink on paper
230 × 180 mm

Two drawings, the one immediately below the other, both titled (see below), on the front page of a folded sheet, on the third page of which is written a letter from Branwell to Joseph Bentley Leyland, January 1848, which begins: 'DEAR SIR, I send you herewith two scrawls on the beforehand page, which you had better burn the moment you see them' (*Patrick Branwell Brontë: A Complete Transcript of the Leyland Manuscripts*, ed. J. Alex Symington and C. W. Hatfield (Leeds: privately printed, 1925), p. 46).

Top half of the page is occupied by Branwell's grimmest self-portrait: a head-and-shoulders portrait with a rope noose around his neck. He is naked and his lined face looks downward and his glasses seem to have been blacked out like a blindfold. Below this harrowing image he has written across the page: 'Patrick Reid "turned off", without his cap. 1848'. The phrase 'turned off' means to be hanged on the gallows, originating from the expression 'to turn off the ladder'. Patrick Reid was a local murderer, whose crime was reported in the *John Bull* newspaper, 25 December 1847: 'Assizes: York, Dec. 20. – THE MURDER AT MIRFIELD. Patrick Reid was charged with the murder of Caroline Ellis, at Mirfield, on the 12th day of May 1847'.

Immediately below this is a drawing of a drunken scene with four men collapsing around a circular pedestal table set on a tiled floor. As they fall off their chairs a silhouetted figure rushes forward to steady the toppling punchbowl on the table. The four drunks are labelled left to right 'SUGDENIENSIS.', 'DRACO/ THE FIRE DRAKE.', 'PHIDIAS' and 'St Patrick alias/ Lord Peter.' The rescuer of the wine is labelled 'St John in the wilderness.' At the bottom of the page Branwell has titled the drawing: 'The rescue of the ~~Talb~~ punchbowl. a scene in the Talbot.' Most of the figures can be identified as Branwell and his drinking friends: 'Sugdeniensis', Dan Sugden; 'Phidias', J. B. Leyland; 'St John', John Brown and 'St Patrick', Branwell himself.

The greater part of the accompanying letter (see above) is devoted to Branwell's excuses for his (probably drunken) behaviour the previous week in Halifax public houses, including the Talbot. Presumably the scene of the spilt punchbowl was one of the incidents that evening, which Branwell, rather shamefacedly, has turned into a cartoon to entertain his friend. The overtones of both letter and drawings remain depressed and confused with even more explicit references to Branwell's own death.

## 304

## 'A Parody'

c. 22 July 1848
Ink on paper
189 × 237 mm

Inscribed above the drawing in ink in Branwell's longhand: 'Jack Shaw, the Guardsman, and/ Jack Painter of Norfolk.'; inscribed below the drawing: 'Question – "The half minute time is up, so/ Come to the ~~scrat~~ scratch; wont you?"/ Answer – "Blast your eyes, it's no use, for/ I cannot come!"/ A PARODY.'

Bequest of George S. Parkinson, 1916. The drawing probably belonged originally to Joseph Bentley Leyland to whom it may have been sent in a letter of 22 July 1848 which begins: 'MY DEAR SIR, Mr. Nicholson has sent to my father a demand for the settlement of my bill owed to him, immediately, under penalty of a Court Summons' (*Patrick Branwell Brontë: A Complete Transcript of the Leyland Manuscripts*, ed. J. Alex Symington and C. W. Hatfield (Leeds: privately printed, 1925), p. 47).
*Brontë Parsonage Museum: B28*

Drawing, made in the style of a cartoon, depicting Branwell huddled miserably in bed and being summoned by Death in the form of a tall skeleton. Branwell lies naked, half-covered with crumpled blankets, on a half-tester bed with ornately carved legs and side, the bed-curtains drawn back. He lies with his head to picture left, clutching the bedclothes to his chest and turning his face into the pillow with closed eyes to avoid the summons of the ghastly figure standing over him. The skeleton stands at the end of the bed leaning forward with its left arm outstretched and its right raised in the attitude of a boxer, challenging the supine form of the artist to a fight, exhorting him to 'come to the scratch' ('the scratch' being the line drawn across the boxing ring where the pugilists meet for the challenge). In the background picture right there is the familiar outline of Haworth Church tower. The drawing is made largely in line with heavy shading on the bedcovers and underneath the bed.

This drawing, in both style and subject matter, clearly belongs to the group of sketches sent in letters to Joseph Bentley Leyland in the last few years of Branwell's life, now in the Brotherton Collection, Leeds University Library. Mary Butterfield (*Brother in the Shadow: Stories & Sketches by Patrick Branwell Brontë*, ed. Mary Butterfield and R. J. Duckett (Bradford: Bradford Libraries and Information Service, 1988), p. 123) claims that this drawing was sent with the letter dated 22 July 1848, just two months before Branwell's death (see above). Certainly, it is possible to make connections between the drawing and the letter. Indeed, there are visible folds in the paper of the drawing and the paper size is approximately the same as that of other drawings contained in the Leyland papers. The two-page letter opens with a catalogue of Branwell's debt problems, including the bill he has run up with Mr Nicholson at the Old Cock public house in Halifax. He writes desperately: 'If he refuses my offer and presses me with law, I am RUINED. I have had five months of such utter sleeplessness, violent cough and frightful agony of mind that jail would destroy me for ever.' He goes on to plead with Leyland to help smooth the way for him with his creditors and ends 'Yours sincerely, but nearly worn out ...'

The drawing combines the metaphor of the boxing match, as seen in Branwell's letters to Leyland in the sketch 'Bendigo "taking a sight"', 10 September 1845 (**285**) and the recurrent image of Branwell either facing death or on his deathbed. The pose of the figure on the bed is reminiscent of the corpse-like figure included in the sheet of drawings sent to Leyland with Branwell's letter of January 1847 (**302**), both of which recall tomb sculptures. Mary Butterfield (*Brother in the Shadow: Stories & Sketches by Patrick Branwell Brontë*, p. 123) relates that 'Jack Shaw the Guardsman and Jack Painter of Norfolk' were boxers who met to fight on 18 April 1815. Shaw was very tall and heavy compared to the slight figure of Painter, so perhaps Branwell compares his struggle with death with this uneven bout.

This is the last known drawing made by Branwell and it could be read as a premonition of his closely impending death. Other references to death are the drawing of Haworth Church and the solitary gravestone pictured in front of it. The little sketch of Haworth Church is a leitmotiv of Branwell's last drawings, appearing below the title 'Purgatory' in the drawing heading his letter to Leyland of October 1846 (**291**) and in the graveyard drawing 'I implore for rest' entered in Mary Pearson's 'Commonplace Book' in 1846 (**297**). It was perhaps intended as a symbol of the home where he felt so little sympathy in his last dreadful months of life.

## Branwell Brontë: Reattributions

**104** Mr Ph Wood', now under Charlotte

**105** 'Alexander Percy', now under Charlotte

**112** 'Young military man', now under Charlotte

**114** 'Arthur Wellesley', now under Charlotte

**121** 'Profile heads', now under Charlotte

**122** 'Moonlit scene with rocks and water', now under Charlotte

**149** 'William Weightman', now under Charlotte

# Branwell Brontë: Dubious attributions

## A Staffordshire bull terrier dog

n.d.
Pencil on paper
223 × 330 mm

Signed with initials in pencil, in non-Brontë hand, bottom left: 'B. B.' On the verso: pencil drawing of series of spiralling lines; set of numerical calculations to right, illegible.

Gift of Ernest Wright, 1947; an article in the *Leeds Mercury* of Saturday 20 May 1944 headed 'A Gift to the Brontë Society' describes how in c. 1904 Wright acquired two sketches 'out of a portfolio belonging to the Brontes' from Abraham Riley of Bramley and Ilkley, an auctioneer, valuer and antique dealer. The other drawing had no Brontë connection. Wright is quoted: 'Riley told me he had obtained a lot of things from Miss Ellen Nussey and the sketches were ... among them. I am under the impression that he also got a Bronte cradle from her. The sketches are two out of a number that Mr Riley had. I suppose he would buy these things from Miss Nussey.' The drawing probably came from the Ellen Nussey sale held at Moor Lane, Gomersal, in May 1898.
*Brontë Parsonage Museum: B38*

Drawing in soft pencil of a Staffordshire bull terrier lying down with head outstretched between its front paws, eyes open, and its back legs curled beneath its body. The dog wears a collar and has left ear erect, the right drooping. The ground around the dog is shaded. One long edge of the paper is roughly torn, as if it had been ripped out of a sketchbook.

The attribution to Branwell is highly dubious as he does not sign any other work with the initials 'B.B.' The provenance is also suspect. It is possible that the drawing originally came from the Ellen Nussey sale at Gomersal in 1898 which included 'an album of drawings by an unknown artist' and two albums 'of choice sketches', but this in itself does not give the work credence: a number of dubious 'Brontë items' originated from the Nussey sale.

## Two figures, heron and rabbit

n.d.
Watercolour on card
128 × 178 mm

Inscribed in pencil in non-Brontë hand, top of page: 'Brandwell [*sic*] Bronte brother/ to Charlotte'. Verso: watercolour study of the head of a stag (see next entry).

Gift of Leslie H. Openshaw, 1928. Openshaw, of Bury, wrote to J. A. Symington on 2 August 1928: 'I have several authentic Bronte relics purchased by my father from one Abraham Riley, antique dealer of Ilkley in October 1898. I have Mr Riley's signed certificate that the articles are part of the Bronte relics from a sale of Martha Brown's effects at Saltaire in January 1886.' The items in Openshaw's possession included a silhouette portrait of Miss Branwell, an inscribed 1858 edition of *Shirley*, a small unsigned pencil drawing (**144**) and a card painted on both sides with small watercolour sketches ('Two figures, heron and rabbit', and 'Stag's head'). Dubious entries 'Two figures, heron and rabbit' and 'Stag's head' cannot be identified in the catalogue of the Binns sale at Saltaire. The only watercolour sold then was the watercolour of 'Flossy' (**327**). Nor was the silhouette of Miss Branwell listed. An edition of *Shirley* was sold to James Miles, bookseller of Leeds. Lots 396 and 383 were described as containing 'pencil drawings by Charlotte Bronte'. Abraham Riley is associated with other dubious items in the BPM collection, for example dubious entry, 'A Staffordshire bull terrier dog'.
*Brontë Parsonage Museum: B39*

Four unrelated sketches in watercolour spread across the page. From left to right: figure of a boy in a brown hat and coat carrying a bundle of firewood; side view of a brown rabbit looking right, sitting in a clump of green grass; a greenish-grey heron with a yellow beak looking to picture left standing in a bed of grey reeds; a peasant girl in blue and red bundled up in ragged clothes, including an apron and bonnet, carrying a yellow basket over her right arm and a bundle of kindling in her left hand.

## Stag's head

n.d.
Watercolour on card
128 × 178 mm

Gift of Leslie H. Openshaw; see dubious entry, 'Two figures, heron and rabbit'.
*Brontë Parsonage Museum: B39v*

Stag's head with large antlers seen facing the viewer, its body cut off just below the neck by the edge of the paper. Its coat is of thick brown fur.

The watercolour figures on both sides of this piece of paper bear no resemblance to any other authentic works by Branwell. The provenance is also obscure, which makes it impossible to verify these drawings. They would appear to be pages taken from a sketchbook, not necessarily Brontë.

# Emily Brontë

## 305

# Mullioned window

19 January 1829
Pencil on paper
120 × 105 mm

Inscribed in pencil, in large longhand, at top of verso: 'Emily Jane Bronte aged 10/ Jan the 19 1829–'; numbers inscribed at bottom: '1008', 'EJB1'.

Inscribed bottom right corner in pencil: '23'; top left: '1005'. Stamped: 'BRONTË/ MUSEUM/ HAWORTH', encircled. Purchased at Hodgson & Co. sale, London, 31 March 1933, as part of lot 447. Formerly in the collection of Sir Alfred J. Law, Honresfeld (see **15**).

*Brontë Parsonage Museum: E1*

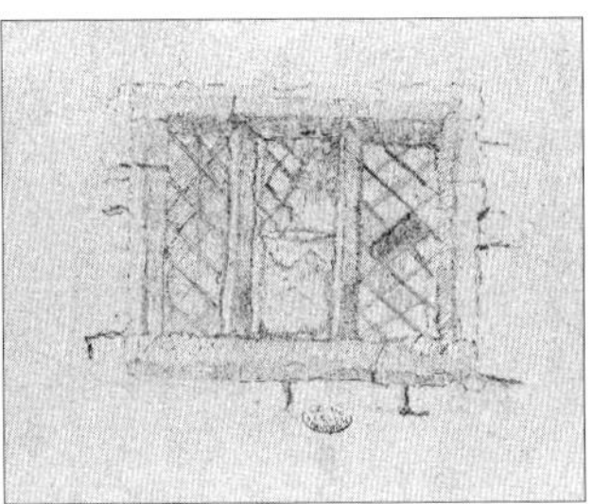

Window in three sections divided by two stone mullions and paned with lead lights; the glass and lead of the central section are broken and the gap has been covered at the bottom with paper or slate. Those who have read *Wuthering Heights* might fancy the suggestion of a hand protruding through the broken glass in the top right of the central panel.

It has also been suggested that if the picture is inverted, a second, feminine hand can be seen beneath the first and two drops of blood on the stone casement beneath (Mary Butterfield, '*Wuthering Heights*: A Brontë Illustration?', *Brontë Society Transactions* (1988), vol. 19, part 5, p. 220). Mary Butterfield assumes that it is 'highly unlikely that Emily Brontë could have produced such a detailed line drawing at the age of ten!' and therefore it must be by Branwell and the inscription on the verso must be in an unknown hand (*Brother in the Shadow: Stories & Sketches by Patrick Branwell Brontë*, ed. Mary Butterfield and R. J. Duckett (Bradford: Bradford Libraries and Information Service, 1988), pp. 67–8). Anyone who has made a study of Emily's script, however, cannot help but conclude that the inscription is genuine and comparison with other early illustrations by her quickly reveals that she was indeed capable of producing this study of a mullioned window, possibly a local Yorkshire one. Mary Butterfield suggests an exact source: the small bedroom window of the 'Old House' built in 1634 opposite Ponden Hall, and now in ruins. The young Brontës often passed Ponden Hall on their rambles across the moors. They are known to have visited the Heaton family there and to have borrowed books from their substantial library.

The suggestion of a second hand is also dependent on inverting the drawing and therefore putting the bottom window sill into shadow, which is very unlikely. However, this is an early drawing and inaccuracies in perspective and lighting make it difficult to confirm or deny various theories. It is also possible that this mullioned window is based on patterns for ruined elements of landscape, common in the drawing manuals of the day (see p. 108).

## 306

# 'The Whinchat'

1 April 1829
Pencil on paper
75 × 126 mm

Signed, dated and titled in pencil, below centre of drawing: 'Emily Jane Bronte April the First 1829/ THE WHINCHAT'. On verso: several incomplete sketches, including a bird's head.

From the Cora Kennedy Aitken Sada Autograph Collection presented to the Houghton Library by Dr Harris Kennedy, Wellesley, Massachusetts, 26 January 1943.

*Houghton Library, Harvard University: Autograph File*

Small long-bodied bird perched on a rock, facing left with beak pointing towards the top left corner; dark markings over head, back, wings and tail, breast faintly speckled, underbody white; grasses and flowers surrounding the rock.

Copied from Thomas Bewick, *A History of British Birds*, vol. 1: *Containing the History and Description of Land Birds* (Newcastle: T. Bewick; London: Longman & Co., 1816), p. 240. The original is considerably larger than Emily's little bird, but she has faithfully recorded all the details of Bewick's illustration. The whinchat is a bird Emily would have seen often on her moorland walks: as Bewick points out, it is 'a solitary bird, frequenting heaths and moors: it has no song, but only a simple unvaried note' (p. 241).

## 307

## The farmer's wife

25 April 1829
Pencil on paper
134 × 179 mm

Signed and dated in pencil, in minuscule script, beneath drawing: 'Emily Jane Bronte April the 25 1829'. Inscribed in pencil, in non-Brontë hand, bottom right: 'a[t] 10 years'; in ink, top left: '1012'. Watermark: '[J WHATM]AN', end only visible. Stamped: 'BRONTË/ MUSEUM/ HAWORTH', encircled. On verso there is a pencil sketch of the figure on recto, including stick and one farm building, probably a false start.

Purchased at Hodgson & Co. sale, London, 31 March 1933, as part of lot 449. Formerly in the collection of Sir Alfred J. Law, Honresfeld (see **15**), and loaned by his uncle William Law (original owner of the collection) to the Brontë Society in 1896: see F. C. Galloway's *A Descriptive Catalogue of Objects in the Museum of the Brontë Society at Haworth* (Bradford, 1896), p. 19.
*Brontë Parsonage Museum: E2*

Miniature landscape of farm buildings, trees and haystacks in the background; a duck pond in the left middle-distance; and a woman fending off an attack by a goose in the centre foreground. She is standing on a grassy mound, her right arm raised and holding a stick ready to strike a white goose that is pulling at her skirt. She is dressed like a farmer's wife with plain clothes, apron and hat. She has a basket on her left arm that suggests she is gathering eggs, a possible reason for the attack. A mother duck and five ducklings are grouped in the bottom right corner.

Copied from one of Thomas Bewick's amusing little tail-pieces in *A History of British Birds*, vol. 2: *Containing the History and Description of Water Birds* (Newcastle: T. Bewick; London: Longman & Co., 1816), p. 253.

## 308

## Ring ouzel

22 May 1829
Pencil on paper
132 × 201 mm

Signed and dated, in pencil, below picture: 'Emily Jane Bronte May the 22 1829'; BPM number in ink top right: '33'. Stamped: 'BRONTË/ MUSEUM/ HAWORTH', encircled.

The top corners of the paper have been cut to produce rounded edges. The picture was originally stuck to poor-quality cardboard inscribed: 'Emily Brontës "Starling" (?)/ Purchased by me of M^rs Hartley (Martha Brown's Sister)/ Feb^y 4^th 1881. In the division of Martha Brown's effects / M^rs Hartley received this drawing and others –/ Sidney Biddell / 32 The grove – Bolton. S. W./ December 8^th 1884./ Miss Ellen Nussey tells me there is only one letter of Emily Brontë's/ in existence, which Lord Houghton has.'

Bequest of Henry Houston Bonnell, 1927. Previously owned by Sidney Biddell, Bolton Gardens, South Kensington, London, who purchased the drawing in February 1881 from Hannah Hartley, sister of Martha Brown, former Brontë servant. Sidney Biddell sold the drawing, together with **62**, **139** and **324**, to Maggs Bros., London, from whom they were purchased by Henry Houston Bonnell, n.d. (lot 673), with an authenticating inscription attached to the verso of 'Roe Head', similar to the one above: see **62**.

*Brontë Parsonage Museum: Bonnell 33*

Dark speckled bird with a pointed beak and distinctive white band under the throat, facing right; wings and square tail feathers of a different texture and colour; perched on a rough piece of ground. Also known as Emily Brontë's 'Starling', as it was referred to thus by previous owners.

Copied from Thomas Bewick, *A History of British Birds*, vol. 1: *Containing the History and Description of Land Birds* (Newcastle: T. Bewick; London: Longman & Co., 1816), p. 122. Bewick notes that the ring ouzel is 'found chiefly in the wilder and more mountainous districts'; there is little doubt that Emily's choice of subject here has been dictated by her familiarity with the bird on the Yorkshire moors.

## 309

## 'Forget me not'

c. 1830
Watercolour on paper
239 × 193 mm

Inscribed in ink, in margin at the bottom, in Emily's early longhand: 'Emily Bronte.'; titled in ink at the top: 'Forget me not'.

Acquired in 1941; part of the library of W. T. H. Howe. Previously purchased by Maggs Bros. at Hodgson & Co. sale, London, 31 March 1933, part of lot 446. Formerly in the Law Collection (see **15**), and probably acquired by William Law from the Haworth joiner, William Wood, at the same time as **38**.

*New York Public Library: Berg Collection*

Young woman seated in an arched cloister, leaning her right arm and head against the side of the arch in a pose of distress; a dog (whippet?) sits at her feet, bottom right corner, looking earnestly up at her, and a letter has fallen to the ground beside her right foot, bottom left. The arch, dramatically lit and covered on the bottom left by red climbing roses, frames the top and left side of the picture. The woman has brown hair, fastened behind in a bun, and curling around her face, which seems lined with anxiety; long white neck, chest and shoulders; triple-strand chain with pearl pendant; off-the-shoulder long white gown, long sleeves and blue cloak draped behind and over the raised right arm; orange/ red sash and black slippers. Through the arch in the distance can be seen, in receding order, a fence, a group of deer, a lake with a sailing boat and castle amongst trees. Above and below the picture, the frame has been extended in pencil, with curls at each corner, to give the appearance of a painting on a scroll.

This scene is a copy of a drawing entitled 'The Disconsolate', by H. Corbould, engraved by C. Rolls, for the *Forget Me Not* Annual of 1831; also copied by Charlotte Brontë (**40**). The Annuals usually appeared on the market late in the previous year, in time for Christmas; the Brontës appear to have purchased this Annual as soon as it was published. The illustration is accompanied by a poem of the same name, by 'L. E. L.' (Letitia Elizabeth Landon), expressing the grief of a young woman deserted by her childhood sweetheart.

It has been suggested that this painting may have been by Branwell, despite the inscription by Emily (Jane Sellars, 'The Art of Emily Brontë', Emily Brontë Conference paper, 1992). Certainly the style of the figure is close to that of Branwell: it is looser, bolder and more schematic than that of Charlotte, especially in the handling of the face and drapery, and the corner scroll markings are similar to those on several of Branwell's paintings (eg. **200**); but the natural surroundings are handled with care and interest. Furthermore, there are few copies of engravings by Emily to compare this with. One would suspect that Emily, who was content to devote time and patience to a portrait of a favourite dog that held special significance for her, would be less painstaking about an inanimate image that she decided to copy at the same time as her sister. Perhaps the sympathetic dog in this engraving appealed to her? She was, of course, younger than Charlotte, which may also help to account for her more schematic, cruder style. Nevertheless, Emily shows considerable skill in her handling of light and shade here, and in her use of colour, which she has added to the black and white original.

The attribution to Emily, however, must remain inconclusive: as Jane Sellars points out, Branwell did dedicate a couple of early drawings to Anne and may have made this picture for Emily (hence her name). She further suggests that it is even more likely to be a sly comment by him on Emily's mood at the time, implying that Emily resembles the disconsolate maid of the original engraving. Yet it still remains difficult to explain away the inscription and signature; Emily used a bewildering variety of signatures over a period of time and even within the same year. The inscription is not unlike other examples of her early longhand, such as her signature on the verso of **305**.

## 310

## Roe Head

December 1832
Pencil on paper

Signed Emily Brontë; and dated December 1832 (see below).

Owned by Miss A. Roberts, Hillside, Nightingale Road, Rickmansworth, in 1930.
*Location unknown*

Drawing of Roe Head by Emily Brontë, possibly the same as those by Charlotte and Anne, and by Susan Carter: see **62**, **339** and plate 7. The date suggests that it was copied by Emily from Charlotte's drawing of the same title (**62**), after Charlotte had returned from Roe Head in 1832 and was eager to teach her sisters all she had learnt there.

This drawing existed in 1930 when the Brontë Society declined an offer to purchase it. The drawing was owned by Miss A. Roberts who says in a letter dated 13 November 1930 (BPM) that her drawing is in pencil, signed by Emily Brontë, and dated December 1832. 'The subject is Roe Head', she adds.

Miss Roberts's drawing was left to her by her great-aunt, Miss Caris, who was a pupil of 'Miss Bronte' at school: 'I think Miss Bronte taught drawing in the school where my Aunt was educated' (Miss A. Roberts to BPM, 10 November 1930). Miss Caris was apparently given the drawing 'either by Miss Charlotte or Miss Emily Bronte, as a small prize. My great Aunt was quite intimate with the Bronte family, on some occasions Miss C Bronte spent her vacation with my Aunts family at the sea.'

It is also possible that this drawing may be Emily Brontë's 'Guwald Tower': see **311** for a discussion of this theory.

## 311

## Guwald Tower, Haddington

8 December 1832
Pencil on paper
164 × 149 mm

Signed in Emily's minuscule script in pencil, sideways along right side of drawing: 'E J Brontë'. Inscribed in ink, in Ellen Nussey's longhand, around bottom left corner of drawing: 'Miss Brontë'; bottom right corner of drawing: 'Roe Head'; and dated by her in ink below these inscriptions, in bottom corners of paper: '1832' (left), 'December 8' (right). Inscription in unknown hand on verso: '14 Kent [?Way]/ Mr Roberts/ 1/2 [?Guin]/ 1/3 [?Fm Bn]'.

Provenance unknown; the inscription suggests ownership by Ellen Nussey.

*Princeton University Libraries: Robert H. Taylor Collection*

Picturesque landscape divided by a river flowing from the bottom left to centre, then obscured; trees on left and tall ruined tower in centre, both on left bank; two cottages and a mound in foreground on right. The tower, smoking chimney of the left-hand cottage and two saplings on the mound constitute the central features.

This drawing is identical (except for very minor stylistic differences) to one by Charlotte Brontë, entitled 'Guwald Tower Haddington' (**57**) and made as an art exercise while she was a pupil at Roe Head in June 1831.

Emily's signature on this second drawing is genuine; yet it is curious that it has been inscribed 'Miss Brontë', a nineteenth-century formality usually reserved for the eldest daughter of a family, the younger ones signing only with their Christian names. It appears that Ellen Nussey failed to see Emily's minuscule signature, written in faint pencil and tucked away in an unusual place close to the actual drawing. Ellen would have remembered Charlotte doing the same drawing at school and, at a later date, attributed it to her, also recording the date and place of execution from memory. It is possible the dating is based on a similar drawing by Ellen herself, made as a school exercise from the same original print, at the same time as Charlotte's copy: see **57**.

Emily probably copied Charlotte's drawing at home, some time after Charlotte left Roe Head in May 1832. Emily herself did not attend the school until 29 July 1835, staying there for less than three months.

Tracey Messenger (BPM Research Assistant) has suggested that this might be **310**, the Emily Brontë drawing that the Brontë Society declined to purchase from Miss A. Roberts, Hillside, Nightingale Road, Rickmansworth, in 1930. Miss Roberts says (letter dated 13 November 1930) that her drawing is in pencil, signed by Emily Brontë, dated December 1832, and 'the subject is Roe Head'. She may have mistaken the 'Roe Head' inscription for a title. The anonymous author of a letter (of 14 November 1930, BPM) to Dr J. Hambley Rowe, Chairman of the Brontë Society, suggests that Miss Roberts's drawing is similar to others of the school itself: he says the Museum has a drawing of Roe Head by Charlotte and also one by Anne and another in the Bonnell Collection (by Susan Carter): 'It would be interesting to have one by Emily.' It is possible that once the Council saw Miss Roberts's drawing and realized it was not of Roe Head itself, they decided not to purchase it. Furthermore, the 'Roberts' inscribed on the verso might also be related to Miss A. Roberts. It is difficult, however, to reconcile Ellen Nussey's inscription with this attractive theory.

## 312

## St Simeon Stylites

4 March 1833
Pencil on paper
217 × 145 mm

Signed in pencil, at the base of pillar: 'E J Bronte'; dated, bottom left: '[?F] March 4th –33'. The initials and capital 'B' have been partially erased through rubbing of the paper, making identification of the signature difficult. Inscribed on verso, later erased but still visible: 'Mrs Popplewell / £4'.
Bequest of J. Roy Coventry, Guernsey, 1955; together with **180**, **317**, **318**, **323**, **332** and **333**. Originally owned by Martha Brown, the Brontës' servant, from whom it passed first to her sister Eliza Popplewell, and then to her niece, Miss Popplewell of Ilkley, from whom Coventry purchased it on 27 September 1907.
*Brontë Parsonage Museum: E3*

Unfinished sketch of an old man with bald head, long hair and a beard, dressed in skins and kneeling on a stone pillar, his left arm raised holding a cross. Clouds are lightly blocked in behind the figure and mountains can be discerned, in faint outline, in the distance to left of pillar; also four faint figures waving in the distance, bottom right.

In the catalogue to his collection, J. Roy Coventry lists this drawing as signed by 'C. Bronte', but it has always been catalogued at the BPM as the work of Emily. The signature is indistinct but the hand is that of Emily and not Charlotte. Furthermore, the subject and pencil shading are unlike that of other drawings made by Charlotte in 1833.

The drawing is copied from an engraving of 'St. Simeon Stylites, Hermit of the Pillar', by S. Williams, in *The Every-Day Book; Or, Everlasting Calendar of Popular Amusements*, ed. William Hone (London: for William Hone, 1826), vol. 1, p. 35. A text of several pages accompanies the engraving describing the saint and numerous legends associated with him.

St Simeon Stylites of Syria (390–459) spent some thirty years on a pillar which was gradually increased to the height of 40 cubits. He appears to have founded a cult or class of ascetics located especially in Syria, Mesopotamia, Egypt and Greece between the fifth and tenth centuries. They lived at the tops of pillars (or stylites) from which they never descended. It is not difficult to understand that this subject of asceticism might have had a particular appeal to the self-reliant Emily Brontë.

## 313

## 'Grasper – from life'

January 1834
Pencil on paper
102 × 98 mm

Titled, dated and signed in ink, in minuscule script, along the top edge, after an ink scribble: 'Grasper – from life – January 1834 – Emily Jane Brontë –'. (An early misreading of this title led biographers to refer to Grasper as 'Ginger' for many years.) The drawing is pasted into a bound volume with Charlotte's 'Study of a heartsease' (**84**) and an initial page inscribed: 'For/ M^r^ Shorter/ with kind regards/ from/ M. A. Nicholls/ [line ruled here]/ July 11^th^/ 07'. The volume is titled on cover in gold lettering: 'DRAWING/ BY/ EMILY & CHARLOTTE BRONTE', quarter-calf binding, and has the bookplate of Clement K. Shorter inside front cover.

Gift of Cecelia N. Eareckson, Philadelphia, October 1986; purchased by her at Sotheby's sale of the effects of Clement K. Shorter, 18 June 1928, lot 60 (with **84**). As described above, the drawing was given to Shorter in 1907 by Mary Anne Nicholls, the widow of Arthur Bell Nicholls who had taken the drawing back to Ireland with him after Patrick Brontë's death.
*Brontë Parsonage Museum: E10*

Study of an Irish terrier, a Brontë pet that had lived at the Haworth Parsonage for at least four years before Emily drew this sensitive record. She has used a soft lead pencil for solid areas of shading and to achieve the effect of coarse hair. The head and shoulders are in profile, facing right, with a rough area of cross-hatching filling the blank sheet to the bottom right of the dog. The corners have been closely cropped to produce rounded edges, but this may have been done before the drawing or just after, since the inscription follows the curve of the cropping at the top.

Grasper appears to be wearing a leather collar, with brass label recording his owner and address, unlike the solid brass collars worn by the Brontës' two later dogs, Keeper and Flossy: see **319** and **327**. The collar was part of the legal obligation of the dog tax and records exist of Patrick Brontë paying '8s tax under Schedule G' for Grasper in 1831 (John Lock and Canon W. T. Dixon, *A Man of Sorrow: The Life, Letters and Times of the Rev. Patrick Brontë 1777–1861* (London: Thomas Nelson & Sons Ltd, 1965), pp. 272–3). Grasper, like Keeper, belonged officially to Patrick Brontë, but Emily made both dogs her own.

Apart from this study, there is little known about Grasper, although he is probably the dog referred to by Ellen Nussey in her 'Reminiscences of Charlotte Brontë' (*Scribner's Monthly*, May 1871, p. 29). Ellen describes how during Miss Branwell's reign at the parsonage, the love of animals had to be kept in moderation. She mentions one dog, probably Grasper, which was admitted to the parlour at stated times and to which Emily and Anne always gave a portion of their breakfast of oatmeal porridge. Grasper probably survived until about late 1837 or early 1838, when his successor Keeper is first mentioned (see **319**).

## 314

## Sketch of two cows 1

23 October 1835
Pencil on paper
96 × 162 mm

Measurements indicate area visible through sealed mount. Dated and signed in pencil, top left: 'October 23 1835 E J B'. Inscribed in another hand, in pencil, top right corner: '1608(a)'. Stamped: 'BRONTË/ MUSEUM/ HAWORTH', encircled. Waterstain along lower edge of paper. On verso another rough pencil sketch of two cows (**315**).
Purchased from Sotheby's sale, 24 November 1952, as part of lot 178, which was owned by Mrs L. C. G. Hayne, and possibly Emma Cortazzo before her. Lot 178 also included a letter from Emily to Ellen Nussey (15 July, n.y.), which suggests that she may also have owned this sketch.
*Brontë Parsonage Museum: E4*

Outline of two cows facing each other; the face of the cow on the right is turned towards the front, and both have horns; also rough grass sketched around their feet.

This is probably a sketch 'from nature', although many contemporary drawing manuals include studies of cattle and horses, to be copied after the human faces, hands and feet have been perfected. This sketch, however, seems to have been made quickly, maybe in nearby fields during the two and a half months Emily spent at Roe Head, from 29 July to late October 1835. The paper is torn at the top: it appears to have been removed from the same octavo-size notebooks in which Emily wrote so many of her poems.

It is interesting to compare Emily's realistic outlines with Charlotte's description of Jane Eyre's ideal drawings of 'Cuyp-like groups of cattle' (*Jane Eyre*, ed. Jane Jack and Margaret Smith (London: Clarendon Press, 1969), p. 87), a contrast that clearly distinguishes the early artistic conceptions of the two sisters.

## 315

### Sketch of two cows 2

23 October 1835
Pencil on paper
95 × 161 mm

Measurements indicate area visible through sealed mount. Two vertical fold marks clearly indicate the sheet has previously been folded in three. Inscribed in pencil, top left corner: '1608'. On other side, dated and signed in pencil, top left: 'October 23 1835 E J B', above another sketch of two cows: see **314**.

Purchased from Sotheby's sale, 24 November 1952, as part of lot 178, which was owned by Mrs L. C. G. Hayne, and possibly Emma Cortazzo before her. Lot 178 also included a letter from Emily to Ellen Nussey (15 July, n.y.), which suggests that she may also have owned this sketch.

*Brontë Parsonage Museum: E4v*

Rough pencil sketch of two cows, one from the side, the other from the rear. The foreshortening of the latter is well handled.

As with the sketch on the other side, this is probably from nature and made during the short time Emily was at Roe Head: see notes to **314**.

## 316

### Diary paper sketch of Anne and Emily

26 June 1837
Pen and ink on paper
c. 58 × 78 mm

The sketch fills approximately a third of the sheet (112 × 91 mm), the remainder being occupied by the text of the diary paper, which appears above, below and to the right of the sketch as described below. It is written in ink, in Emily's minuscule script, dated 'June 26 1837' and signed 'Emily Jane Brontë – Anne Brontë'. Heavy fold marks indicate where the sheet has been folded three times, first in half, then in quarters and again diagonally.

Gift of the family of Shem Paget, Keighley, 1950.

*Brontë Parsonage Museum: E9*

The sketch complements the accompanying text, showing Emily and Anne composing their diary paper. Anne is seated at the top left of the table (the inscription 'Anne' appears above her chair), leaning over it, her elbows on the table, her head supported by her hands. Emily is sitting in the foreground, at the end closest to the viewer ('Emily' inscribed to the right of her chair); she has her back to us and is facing Anne. The figures are in outline only, with no facial features visible, but Anne is wearing a dress with large leg-of-mutton sleeves. Books, papers and a box are visible on the table, several labelled as follows (from left to right): 'The Tin Box', 'The papers', 'The papers'.

The diary papers were part of a conspiracy between Emily and Anne, written at irregular intervals of about four years, carefully folded as described above and then preserved in 'The Tin Box', which still survives in the BPM (H109). The old papers were reopened and read when a new one was written, the hopes and events of earlier years reassessed in the light of present circumstances.

The papers and their accompanying sketches are valuable for the biographical evidence they offer. In particular, their amalgam of fact and fiction gives vivid evidence of the way the imaginative world of the Brontës impinged on their reality. This particular diary paper begins:

> Monday evening June 26 1837
> A bit past 4 o'clock Charlotte working in Aunts room Branwell read-/ ing Eugene Aram to her Anne and I writing in the drawing room – Anne/ a poem beginning "fair was the evening and brightly the sun – I Agustus –/ Almedas life

Emily notes that while Tabby (the servant) is in the kitchen, 'the Emprerors and Empresses of/ Gondal and Gaalddine [are] preparing to depart from Gaaldine to Gondal to/ prepare for the coranation which will be on the 12th of July', corresponding to Queen Victoria's forthcoming ascent to the throne on 20 July 1837. Emily ends with a postscript that 'this day 4 years we shall/ all be in this drawing room comfortable/ I hope it may be so/ Anne guesses we shall all be gone some-/ where together comfortable We hope it/ may be either.'

## 317

## Geometric figures

9 September 1837
Pen and iron-gall ink on paper
182 × 223 mm

Signed and dated in ink, bottom right corner: 'E. J. Brontë/ September the/ 9th 1837–'. Each diagram is inscribed in detail by Emily, as recorded below. Inscribed in pencil, in another hand, bottom left: '25'. The corners of the paper have been cut to produce rounded edges. On verso: various doodles and scribbles, overdrawing of lines on recto and rough sketches of four buildings (**138**).

Bequest of J. Roy Coventry, Guernsey, 1955, together with **180**, **312**, **318**, **323**, **332** and **333**. Formerly in the collection of Sir Alfred J. Law, Honresfeld (see **15**), having been purchased in 1907 by his uncle, William Law, from Tabitha Ratcliffe, younger sister of Martha Brown. Subsequently bought by J. Roy Coventry at the Hodgson & Co. sale, London, 31 March 1933, part of lot 448. This is one of the drawings which Sir William Robertson Nicoll saw when he visited 'a sister of Martha Brown', and purchased Charlotte's pencil sketch of Anne (**91**).

*Brontë Parsonage Museum: E5*

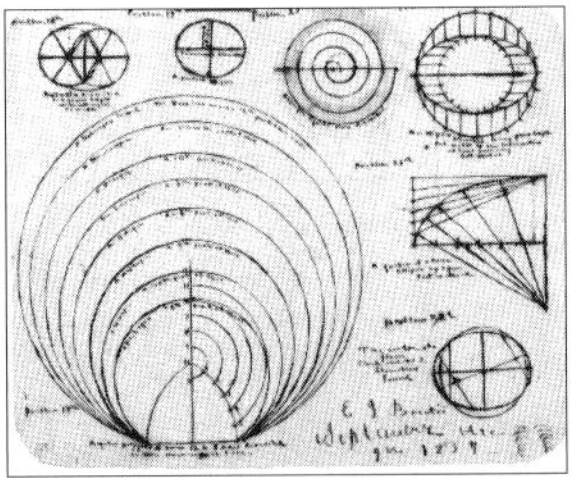

Seven diagrams, copied from a geometry book or drawing manual, and labelled in detail by Emily in ink, in minuscule script. The first large diagram on the left ('problem $17^{th}$') illustrates 'Regular polygons of from 12 to 5 sides described/ to the given length of one side', each polygon inscribed by Emily, for example 'A pentagon 5th part of this', etc. The six smaller diagrams along the top and down the right side are all numbered top left and labelled, from left to right, as follows:

(1) 'problem $18^{th}$'; 'An oval – described/ in a given length/ without regard/ to width'.
(2) 'Problem $19^{th}$'; 'A perfect Ellipsis', 'Transverse diameter' and 'Consup[?] diameter' (marking lines on diagram).
(3) 'problem $23^{d}$'; 'A simple spiral line discribed [*sic*]'. This diagram seems to have been drawn on another piece of paper, stuck onto this sheet and scored around.
(4) 'problem $20^{th}$'; 'An Ellipsis discribed [*sic*] to any given length/ And width by the intersection/ of lines producing/ Ordinates'.
(5) 'problem $21^{st}$'; 'A quarter of a true/ Ellipsis by a per-/ fect method'.
(6) 'problem $22^{d}$'; 'The centre of a/ given/ Circle and its 2/ diameters/ Found'.

An article by 'N' (probably William Robertson Nicoll), entitled 'Literature: The New Literary Anecdotes. 1. The Brontë Sisters', in *The British Weekly: A Journal of Social and Christian Progress*, 5 November 1886, suggests that these figures are from the eleventh book of Euclid. The author of the article notes: 'I may add that in the course of my search for Emily Brontë's portraits I had in my hands some of her manuscripts, which show her to have been an accomplished mathematician; some of the figures being from the eleventh book of Euclid.' *The British Weekly: A Journal of Social and Christian Progress*, was founded by Hodder & Stoughton on 5 November 1886, with Robertson Nicoll as editor (see also **91**).

It is possible that these figures are from an early drawing manual rather than a geometry book. Proficiency in drawing was viewed as a necessary skill for the navy, army and various trades from the time of Samuel Pepys when, in 1672, he persuaded King Charles II to endow a Royal Mathematical School at Christ's Hospital. The curriculum included perspective, chart-making, and taking prospects, and this was soon extended for all trade and naval apprentices. The artist Bernard Lens became the first drawing-master there and developed a set of drawings for the pupils of Christ's Hospital, which were published by his son Edward in 1750 and became the basis of most drawing manuals of the later eighteenth century (E. Lens, *For the Curious Young Gentlemen and Ladies … A New and Compleat Drawing Book*, London, 1750). Many of these books included figures from Euclid. For example, a chapter on 'The Elements of Euclid' appears in *First Volume of the Instructions Given in the Drawing School established by the Dublin Society, … To enable Youth to become Proficient in the different branches of that Art, and to pursue with success, Geographical, Nautical, Mechanical, Commercial, and Military Studies* (Dublin, 1769).

## 318

## Sketches of buildings

9 September 1837
Pencil on paper
182 × 223 mm

On the verso of **317**, which is signed and dated in ink, bottom right corner: 'E J Brontë/ September the/ $9^{th}$ 1837–'.
Bequest of J. Roy Conventry, Guernsey, 1955, together with **180**, **312**, **317**, **323**, **332** and **333**. For earlier provenance see **317**.
*Brontë Parsonage Museum: E5v*

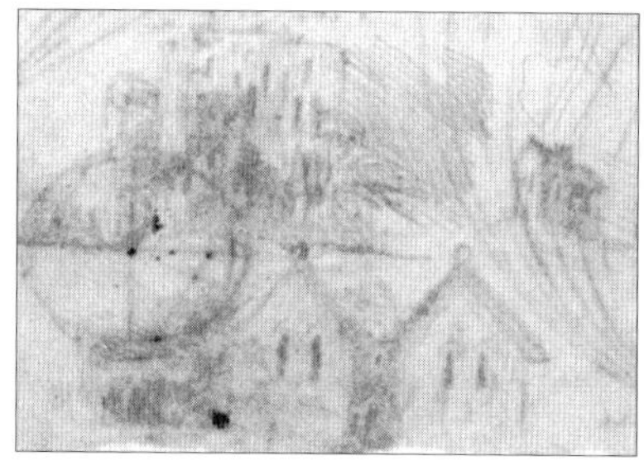

Four tiny sketches of houses in the bottom left quarter of sheet. The remainder of the sheet is covered with cross-hatching and scribbles that look like foliage. The ink geometry figures of **317** show clearly through on this side.

## 319

## 'Keeper–from life'

24 April 1838
Watercolour on paper
132 × 157 mm

Titled, dated and signed in ink, in minuscule script, along top edge: 'Keeper–from life – April 24th 1838– Emily Jane Brontë –'; signed again, bottom left: 'Brontë', the initials and part of 'B' cut away to form curved corners on the sheet. On verso formless pencil sketches and inscription in non-Brontë hand: 'Spon / oak / 2° margr / Cream', probably referring to coloured cakes of paint or possibly a recipe!

Purchased from Miss Brooksbank, Morecambe (formerly of Bradford), 1903, together with **87** and **88**.
*Brontë Parsonage Museum: E6*

Head, neck, left shoulder and paw of a sandy-coloured labrador and mastiff cross-breed, in left profile: large forehead and cheeks, narrow black eyes, crumpled ears, black nose and mouth. The dog is resting, lying with his head on his paw, on some brown shaded, rough grass. The dog's coat is delicately handled, the tiny brush strokes creating the impression of a silky short fur.

Keeper's reputation for ferocity was apparently legendary in Haworth and his large brass collar, worn as part of the legal obligation of the dog tax (see **313**), still survives in the BPM (H 110) and gives some indication of his size and power. Keeper probably joined the Brontë household in late 1837 or early 1838, since he is mentioned for the first time in Emily and Anne's diary paper of 30 July 1841, but doesn't appear in the previous one of 26 June 1837. This painting of Keeper was therefore made soon after his arrival at the parsonage.

Despite his ferocity, Keeper was utterly devoted to his mistress. Elizabeth Gaskell tells a now famous story about Emily's savage punishment of this beloved dog, for his habit of lying on the beds upstairs, and her later loving care for the wounds she had made to the dog's head. She tells too how Keeper followed Emily's coffin to the grave and moaned for many nights outside her bedroom door (*The Life of Charlotte Brontë*, 2 vols. (London: Smith, Elder & Co., 1857), vol. 1, pp. 309–10).

Ellen Nussey described Emily as habitually kneeling on the hearth reading a book, with her arm round Keeper; and Charlotte recalls this same habit in *Shirley*: 'The tawny and lion-like bulk of Tartar is ever stretched beside her; his negro muzzle laid on his fore paws, straight, strong, and shapely as the limbs of an Alpine wolf. One hand of the mistress generally reposes on the loving serf's rude head, because if she takes it away he groans and is discontented' (ed. Herbert Rosengarten and Margaret Smith (Oxford and New York: Clarendon Press, 1979), p. 436). Keeper died in December 1851, three years after Emily, and was buried in the garden of Haworth Parsonage.

## 320

## Images of cruelty

c. 1838
Pen and ink on paper
17 × 115 mm

The sketch occupies the centre of a manuscript page (190 × 115 mm), written in ink, in Emily Brontë's hand.

It has been conjecturally dated 1838, since the page is accompanied by another manuscript (a translation of the *Aeneid*, Book 1) signed: 'E J Brontë March the/ 13 1838'.

Formerly owned by Hugh Walpole and purchased by him from Maggs Bros., who acquired it from the Hodgson & Co. sale, London, 31 March 1933, lot 443. It is listed in the Hodgson's sale catalogue (*A Catalogue of Fine and Rare Books*, p. 33) as 'The Property of a Collector', but was formerly in the collection of Sir Alfred J. Law, Honresfeld (see **15**). The description reads: 'Bronte (Emily J.) Three Fragments of Original Manuscripts, one signed, "*E. J. Bronte, March the 13, 1838*", and another having a crude pen-and-ink sketch'; the item is marked as sold to Maggs Bros. for £26. The manuscripts are also listed in Rupert Hart-Davis, *Hugh Walpole: A Biography* (London: Macmillan & Co. Ltd, 1952), Appendix C: 'Catalogue of the Hugh Walpole Collection at the King's School Canterbury', p. 470.

*The King's School, Canterbury: Walpole Collection*

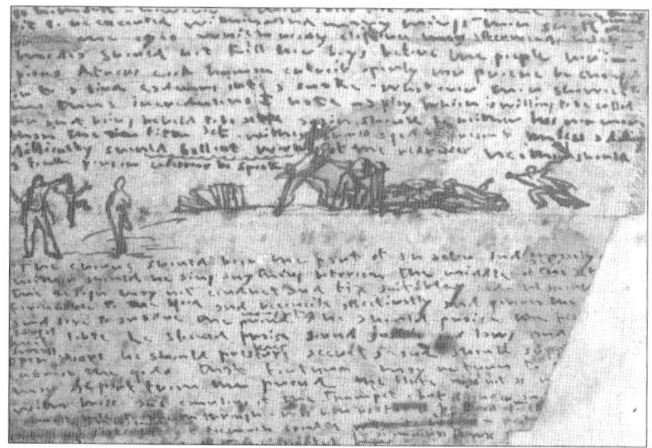

Small sketch illustrating the fifth page of a drama fragment, the only surviving prose manuscript (apart from the diary papers) in Emily Brontë's hand. It depicts a scene of two brutal images: the first shows a man with a whip holding a child aloft by the hair, while another man stands complacently watching; the second illustrates a man being flogged, with what appear to be a pile of bodies nearby, one with a sword in it. A third figure on the right, again carrying a whip or stick, is rushing to the scene. Between the two sketches there appears to be a row of books, stacked together, with some lying on their side, although their identification is uncertain.

The boldly drawn, vigorous pen-and-ink outlines are similar to sketches by Branwell and the subject of male brutality is a feature of his early manuscripts, although it is not absent from those of Charlotte. However, the surrounding text is clearly written in Emily's hand, making her authorship of the sketches conclusive, and giving us a graphic foretaste of the cruelty encountered in *Wuthering Heights*.

## 320a

## Dancing stick figure

c. July 1839
Pen and ink on paper
25 × 25 mm

The sketch occupies the bottom right corner of the poetry manuscript 'I'm standing in the forest now', written in ink, in Emily Brontë's hand. The manuscript page (84 × 100 mm) is unsigned and undated, but the verso includes the poem 'Come hither child – who gifted thee', which is dated 19 July 1839. The page is part of fifteen leaves of various sizes bound together in morocco by Rivière, all containing manuscript poems by Emily Brontë.

Bequest of Henry Houston Bonnell, 1927.

*Brontë Parsonage Musuem: Bonnell 127 (1)*

Ink 'doodle' of a bizarre dancing stick creature with fuzzy hair, hands and feet, not unlike eucalyptus tree blossoms or the needles of a pine tree. The figure is full of movement and fun, rather like the later fantasy characters of May Gibbs, 'Little Ragged Blossom' or the 'Wicked Banksia Men' in the Australian children's classic, *The Complete Adventures of Snugglepot and Cuddlepie* (London and Sydney: Angus & Robertson, 1984; originally published 1919).

The poetry fragment, 'I'm standing in the forest now', is an early variant draft of the undated poem 'To A.G.A.', beginning 'Thou standest in the greenwood now', from Emily Brontë's 'Gondal Poems' Notebook. The dancing figure expresses the same joy in nature found in the poem:

The breeze sings like a summer breeze
 Should sing in summer skies
And towerlike rocks and tentlike trees
 In mingled glory rise

The murmur of their boughs and streams
 Speaks pride as well as bliss
And that blue heaven expanding seems
 The circling hills to kiss.

In this tiny illustration, the kind of 'doodle' we all indulge in while thinking, listening or day-dreaming, we see a distinct relationship between the visual and verbal in the creative process.

## 321

## Winged serpent sketches

12 August 1839
Pen and ink on paper
129 × 100 mm

The sketches occupy the margins of the poetry manuscript 'How long will you remain? The midnight hour', written in ink, in Emily Brontë's hand, and dated by her: 'August 12th/ 1839'. The page is part of fifteen leaves of various sizes bound together in morocco by Rivière, all containing manuscript poems by Emily Brontë.

Bequest of Henry Houston Bonnell, 1927.
*Brontë Parsonage Museum: Bonnell 127 (15)*

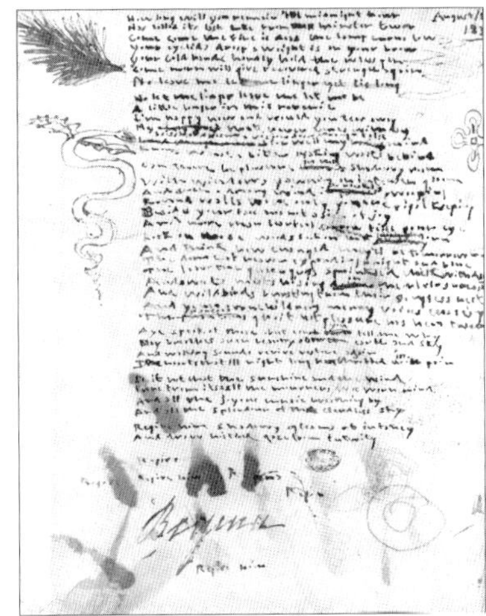

Sketches of a feather and a winged serpent in the left-hand margin, swirling lines and a decorated cross (possibly a Celtic clasp) in the right-hand margin, and two concentric circles at the bottom right corner of the page. They all appear to be 'doodles', embellishing an already messy, ink-blotched page. The sketches, the frequent deletions in the text of the poem and the repeated word 'Regive' at the bottom of the page, all indicate Emily's thoughtful and hesitant state of mind as she ponders her composition.

Edward Chitham (*A Life of Emily Brontë* (Oxford and New York: Basil Blackwell, 1987), p. 123) has described the 36-line poem as 'a splendid example of Emily's poetic struggle and processes'. The sketches undoubtedly add to our understanding of this process, but one can only guess at the real significance of the winged serpent which is drawn in swirls down the page and occurs opposite Emily's description of her vision:

I'm happy now and would you tear away
My blissful dream that never comes with day
A vision dear though false for well my mind
Knows what a bitter waking waits behind

The poem is a dialogue between two speakers. Chitham suggests that the interlocutor must be Charlotte, although (as Janet Gezari notes, *Emily Jane Brontë: The Complete Poems* (London: Penguin, 1992), p. 259) the reference to 'your own children's merry voices' works against this reading.

Chitham also notes (p. 125) that the sketches 'bear a remarkable similarity to the drawings Shelley drew in his notebooks, which of course Emily had certainly not seen or heard of', and may relate to the 'worm Ouroboros', symbolic of eternity. It seems a little fanciful, however, to interpret two concentric circles as Ouroboros, the serpent that devours its own tail.

## 322

## Diary paper thumb-nail sketches

30 July 1841
Pen and ink on paper
c. 12 × 15 mm

The tiny sketches, each about the same size (above), are placed either side of the heading: 'A Paper to be opened/ when Anne is/ 25 years old/ or my next birthday after –/ if/ – all be well –/ [short rule]/ Emily Jane Brontë July the 30$^{th}$ 1841'. The remainder of the sheet (c. 115 × 95 mm) is occupied by the text of the diary paper, which – like the sketches – is written in ink. Approximate measurements are based on other extant diary papers and on the facsimile of the manuscript in Clement K. Shorter, *Charlotte Brontë and Her Circle* (London: Hodder & Stoughton, 1896), opp. p. 146.

Formerly in the collection of Sir Alfred J. Law, Honresfeld (see **15**).
*Location unknown*

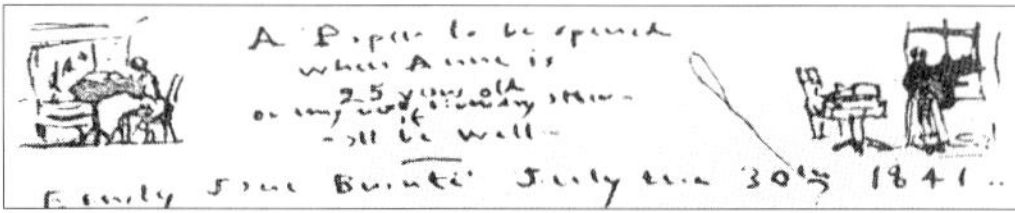

Two thumb-nail sketches on either side of the heading to this diary paper, both drawn to complement the text: on the left, the author is seated, working at a small table, her portable writing desk placed on top of the table; on the right, the same tiny figure has left her desk (still visible on the left) and is gazing out of the parsonage window, surveying the 'bleak look-out' described in the text. The window has the same recognizable panes repeated in the larger sketch four years later, which accompanies the diary paper of 30 [31] July 1845 (see **331**).

See **316** for information on the diary papers. The text of this diary paper begins: 'It is Friday evening– near 9 o'clock–wild rainy weather'; and ends: 'and now I close sending from far an ex-/ hortation etc Courage ~~&~~ [?~~word~~] courage! to exiled and harassed Anne/ wishing she was here.' Anne was at Scarborough with the Robinsons of Thorp Green, having just returned to her post as governess after a holiday at home the previous month. Emily records that Charlotte is a governess at Upperwood House, Branwell is at Luddenden Foot, and 'A Scheme is at present in agitation for setting us up in/ A School of our own as yet nothing is determined but I hope/ and trust it may go on and prosper and answer our highest/ expectations –'. She continues to paint a happy picture of the sisters flourishing in their own seminary and then describes the present state of her more violent imaginative world: 'The Gondalians ~~are~~ are at present in a threatening state but/ there is no open rupture as yet –'.

## 323

## Woman's head with tiara

6 October 1841
Pencil on paper
186 × 162 mm

Signed and dated in pencil, in minuscule script, bottom left corner: 'E J B'; bottom right corner, 'October 6th 1841'.

Bequest of J. Roy Coventry, Guernsey, 1955, together with **180**, **312**, **317**, **318**, **332** and **333**. Formerly in the collection of Sir Alfred J. Law, Honresfeld (see **15**), having been purchased by his uncle, William Law, from Tabitha Ratcliffe, younger sister of Martha Brown. Subsequently bought by Coventry at the Hodgson & Co. sale, London, 31 March 1933, part of lot 448.
*Brontë Parsonage Museum: E7*

Head-and-shoulders portrait in profile of a young woman, with long, curling hair loosely arranged and pulled back from the face by a metal or leather tiara, which gives the figure a Greek or Roman appearance. The face has strong, sharp features, a pointed chin and nose and a slightly worried, earnest look; the neck and throat are bare and a simple garment is draped around the shoulders. It is tempting to suggest that this intense, strong-featured and handsome woman is not unlike Emily's similar heroines of the Gondal saga. Its direct original, however, is probably a copy from an engraved plate.

Unlike Emily's painting technique, which is delicate and painstaking (see **319**, **324**), the pencil touch here is firm and sure, giving the impression of solidity, especially in the handling of the hair, tiara and throat. This same firmness of touch is noticeable in Emily's pencil drawing of 'Grasper' (**313**) and her 'Study of a fir tree' (**326**).

## 324

## Nero

27 October 1841
Watercolour on card
245 × 209 mm

Signed and dated along top edge: 'By E. J. B. të – Octr 27th 1841./ [line ruled underneath]'; the two dots of 'të' are run together rather like a grave accent. Stamped: 'BRONTË/ MUSEUM/ HAWORTH', encircled. Inscribed on verso: 'H. S. Green/ Dewsbury.'; also inscribed in another hand: 'Given to me by Martha Brown/ on her death bed – To whom it was given by Mr Brontë –/ S. B. –' Another note, dated 8 December 1884 and signed by Sidney Biddell, attached to the back confirms that Biddell was given this painting via Robert Ratcliffe, brother-in-law and executor of Martha Brown: 'she expressed a wish before her death that you should/ have the Hawk which was Emily (Brontës) drawing'. Biddell also states: 'Martha Brown assured me/ that her Master, the Revd P Brontë,/ gave her this drawing after the/ death of his daughter Charlotte,/ with many other things./ I had two long interviews with her (Martha Brown)/ in September 1879, at Haworth'.

Bequest of Henry Houston Bonnell, 1927; acquired by him at Maggs Bros, sale, n.d. (lot 672). Previously owned by Sidney Biddell, Bolton Gardens, South Kensington, London, who acquired it from Martha Brown as described above. Possibly owned then by H. S. Green of Moss Side, Manchester, formerly of Dewsbury and a founder member of the Brontë Society (see inscription above); although Sidney Biddell sold three other drawings (**62**, **139** and **308**) to Maggs Bros., London, that were purchased by Bonnell, and this appears to have accompanied them.
*Brontë Parsonage Museum: Bonnell 34*

Study of a merlin, a bird of prey, facing right and perched on one claw, on a broken tree stump protruding from the right of the picture. The other claw is withdrawn into its speckled breast. The hawk has a white chin and underbody, large black eye, hooked beak, dark brown head and folded wing tapering to grey under the tail feathers; the feather markings of wing, tail and breast are clearly visible and the claws are executed with care and delicacy. The background has a cream wash, with darker brown and blue tones behind the branch and tail, suggesting the foliage of nearby tree tops.

It is possible that Emily adapted Thomas Bewick's black and white illustration of 'The Merlin'; certainly she would have read about the bird in the Brontë copy of *A History of British Birds*, vol. 1: *Containing the History and Description of Land Birds* (Newcastle: T. Bewick; London: Longman & Co., 1816), pp. 80–1. However, her other copies from Bewick were all made twelve years earlier. If she did use the old volume, it is likely to have been only for reference. Her merlin is much closer in execution to her late animal illustrations, all drawn 'from nature'.

Although she does not title the painting, her pet merlin 'Nero', which she had rescued from an abandoned nest on the moors, would have provided ample opportunity for the close observation of plumage and colouring evident in her work. This hawk has been referred to as 'Hero' in many publications, but – as Margaret Smith has pointed out – this is a mistranscription of the name in Emily's diary papers.

Emily mentions Nero 'in his cage' in her diary paper of 30 July 1841 (**322**). He was probably acquired early in 1841, since she speaks of a bird pining for the liberty of 'Earth's breezy hills and heaven's blue sea' in a poem dated 27 February 1841, known as 'The Caged Bird'. The bird of the poem, however, is not in a cage but on a chain; yet Emily identifies wholly with its 'cold captivity':

> Ah could my hand unlock its chain
> How gladly would I watch it soar
> And ne'er regret and ne'er complain
> To see its shining eyes no more

On her return from Brussels in November 1842, Nero had gone: 'lost the hawk Nero, which, with the geese, was given away, and is doubtless dead, for when I came back from Brussels, I inquired on all hands and could hear nothing of him': Emily's diary paper, 30 [31] July 1845 (**331**).

## 325

## 'The North Wind'

1842
Watercolour on paper

Signature not visible in black and white published version; but the illustration was probably signed and titled in pencil, since it is traditionally known as 'The North Wind'.

Previously owned by the Heger family in Brussels and probably given to them by Emily while she was at school there. Passed by Louise Heger (together with a lock of Charlotte's hair, a Brontë seal, a photograph of Patrick Brontë and a sampler worked by Martha Trotman, the Hegers' English nurse at the time of the Brontës) to one of two English sisters, pupils at the Pensionnat Heger soon after the Brontës. This sister (referred to as 'D') apparently passed the relics to her niece ('L'), also a pupil at the Pensionnat in the 1880s; and Walter R. Cunliffe, of Charlwood, Surrey, inherited the relics in 1949 (see Edith Weir, 'New Brontë Material Comes To Light', *Brontë Society Transactions* (1949), vol. 11, part 59, p. 249; the above illustration has been reproduced from the frontispiece to this volume).

The recipient of the Hegers' gift was probably Marian Douglas, mentioned in a letter from Genevieve Wigfall to Ellen Nussey, 10 December 1889: 'Yesterday I spent the day at Ilkley with Miss Douglas & saw all of her Brontë relics, & <u>how</u> interesting they are! She has an exquisite drawing of C. B.'s with an inscription by her to Madame Heger, & a watercolour of Emily Brontë's (signed) that is most spirited and beautiful –' (BPM: Cadman collection, XIV P6). This watercolour seems to be 'The North Wind', since Wigfall also notes: 'I think Monsieur Heger has given Miss Douglas all of her things'. Charlotte's 'Watermill' (**157**), also referred to here by Wigfall, was purchased by the Brontë Society in 1926 from Margaret (Meta) Mossman ('L' above), the niece of Marian Douglas who (like her aunt) was a pupil of Madame Heger.

This argument is further supported by another statement in Genevieve Wigfall's letter which is corroborated by Edith Weir's article in *Brontë Society Transactions*. Wigfall states that 'Miss Douglas has recently been to Haworth with her dear friend Mrs Walford, who has written an essay on the visit to be published I think she said by Longmans'. Weir describes an article on 'The Home of Charlotte Brontë', in *Longman's Magazine* (vol. 15, no. 87, January 1890), 'written by a Mrs Walford, a minor novelist of the eighties. Her companion on her visit to Haworth was "D"' (p. 250).

Confirmation can also be found in a more recent note which states that after Margaret Mossman's death her sister Mary (May) 'gave the Heger letters to Mr Cunliffe along with the remaining Brontë relics' (Edith Weir,'The Hegers and a Yorkshire Family', *Brontë Society Transactions* (1963) vol. 14, part 73, p. 32). The painting then appears to have passed to Felicity Craven in the 1960s, when Winifred Gérin was working on her biography of Emily Brontë (see acknowledgements in 'List of Plates', *Emily Brontë: A Biography* (Oxford: Clarendon Press, 1971)).
*Location unknown*

Half-length portrait of a young woman who appears to have been caught in flight: her dark curly hair is blown back towards the left side and the neck of her blue cloak billows back to the left behind her. She wears a white Roman-style dress beneath the cloak, caught on the right shoulder with a clasp. Her throat and chest are bare; nor is there any ornament on her right wrist or hand which loosely clasps the cloak around her, bottom left. Her left arm (only partly visible) is extended beneath the cloak in the direction she is travelling. She appears to be rushing to the right, but her head is turned back to the left as if her attention has been suddenly arrested. The portrait is full of symbolic suggestion (discussed on pp. 116–17) and movement, which Emily has expertly caught in her watercolour adaptation of the original.

Emily probably made this painting during her year in Brussels (see provenance above), where it is quite possible that she had access to one of the many Continental editions of Byron from which it is copied.

The exact plate she copied from is William Finden's engraving of Richard Westall's 'Ianthe' (Lady Charlotte Mary Harley), published as the frontispiece to Thomas Moore's *Life of Byron* (London: John Murray, 1839), vol. 2. Emily's version, which she apparently named 'The North Wind', has a more mature, challenging expression than the original. Her eyes are piercing and have none of the wide-eyed innocence of Westall's original. She has all the features of the first Catherine in *Wuthering Heights*, though she could equally well have suggested one of the heroines of the Gondal saga.

This particular engraving of 'Ianthe' (there were several others by different artists) can also be found in volume 2 of *Finden's Illustrations of the Life and Works of Lord Byron*, 3 vols. (London: John Murray, 1833–4); and in the first volume of *The Poetical Works of Lord Byron*, 8 vols. (London: John Murray, 1839). If Emily made the painting before she went to Brussels then she probably used the latter source, since three other plates were copied from this same volume by Charlotte (see **96**, **123**, **128**). However, it seems more likely that she had access to a foreign edition or to a separate engraving of 'Ianthe' (see pp. 16–17) while she was in Brussels.

The poem 'To Ianthe' formed the dedication to Byron's *Childe Harold*. It was addressed to Lady Charlotte Mary Harley (1801–80), who was only eleven years old at the time. In Shelley's poem 'Queen Mab', Ianthe is the maiden to whom the fairy grants a vision of the world.

## 326

## Study of a fir tree

c. 1842
Pencil on paper
279 × 203 mm

Signed in pencil, bottom right corner: 'Emily Bronté'; the lower part of 'Emily Bro' has been trimmed off, suggesting that the whole drawing has been cropped at some stage. Stamped: 'BRONTË/ MUSEUM/ HAWORTH', encircled.

Acquired from Albert de Bassompierre, Belgium, in 1929. The donor inherited it from his aunt, Louise de Bassompierre, who was given the drawing by Emily Brontë while the two girls were both studying at the Pensionnat Heger, Brussels, from February to November 1842 (see Butler Wood, 'Two Brussels Schoolfellows of Charlotte Brontë', *Brontë Society Transactions* (1913), vol. 5, part 23, pp. 25–7, for Louise de Bassompierre's account of how she acquired the drawing). In 1963, the drawing was stolen from the Bonnell Room in the BPM but later returned.
*Brontë Parsonage Museum: E8*

Pine/fir tree with a double trunk: the right side a broken stump, with the broken part lying on the ground behind; the live trunk has also lost its top, but the lower branches are covered with needles and extend to the edges of the picture like arms reaching out; moss and grass cover the rocks at the base of the tree in the foreground. A steep rocky slope is suggested on the left behind the tree and, beyond that, faint mountains.

Several of Emily's illustrations have been cropped (for example **319**) and it appears that this is no exception: the signature has been partially cut (see above) and the tips of several branches on the left appear to have been trimmed.

This drawing (discussed in detail on pp. 118–21) shows every sign of having been made 'from nature'. Jane Sellars has pointed out the rubbed surface of the picture, where Emily has leant across the paper as she worked with a board on her lap ('The Art of Emily Brontë', Emily Brontë Conference paper, 1992). Moreover, this appears to be the same tree, seen from a different angle, as that of Charlotte's study 'Landscape with fallen trees' (**156**); both drawings were probably executed at the same date 'en plein air', during their school holidays together in Brussels (see **156**). Charlotte's work exhibits a light, hesitant touch, whereas Emily's drawing of the same subject shows the confidence and strong style of pencil studies such as 'Grasper' (**313**) and 'Woman's head with tiara' (**323**). The association of the drawings with the Brontës' schooling in Brussels is further strengthened by the provenance: Louise de Bassompierre's name was used by Charlotte Brontë for one of her characters in *Villette*.

The romantic subject of a blasted tree, the movement suggested in the impressionistic handling of the rocks in the foreground and the firm yet almost feathery quality of the foliage on the branches, suggests that Emily was able to match in visual terms the imaginative qualities so powerfully displayed both in her poetry and in *Wuthering Heights*.

## 327

# Flossy

c. 1843

Watercolour on paper

242 × 345 mm

Various sketches on the verso, probably by several hands including some by Emily: see **330**.

Purchased from the Brown collection of Brontë relics, sold by Sotheby's, 2 July 1898, lot 18: 'Water-colour Drawing of Charlotte Brontë's [*sic*] favourite dog "Floss" by C. Brontë'. Originally a gift from either Patrick Brontë or Arthur Bell Nicholls to Martha Brown, who left it to her sister Ann Binns; acquired by Alfred Gledhill of Keighley at the Binns sale, Saltaire, 27 January 1886 (lot 370 'Water Colour Drawing, their favourite Dog "Floss," By Charlotte Brontë [*sic*]'); and then sold to Robinson and Francis Brown (see **29**). While in the possession of Gledhill it was exhibited at the 'Keighley Conversaziones' in January 1889; *The Yorkshire Post*, 8 January 1889, erroneously referred to it as a watercolour of 'Charlotte's favourite dog Floss'.

*Brontë Parsonage Museum: C30*

Landscape of rolling moorland with black and white spaniel racing after a bird; dog has curly black coat on head and back, white underneath, tan markings on face, mouth open, eyes intent on bird, tail outstretched and brass collar.

Although the sale catalogue for the auction of the effects of Benjamin Binns lists this painting as 'By Charlotte Brontë' and the painting has been attributed to Charlotte ever since, Binns himself told Emma Huidekoper Cortazzo that this 'spirited watercolour was by Emily, of Flossy, Anne's dog, a brown and white spaniel, chasing a bird over the moor' (Helen H. Arnold, 'The Reminiscences of Emma Huidekoper Cortazzo: A Friend of Ellen Nussey', *Brontë Society Transactions* (1958), vol. 13, part 68, pp. 226–7). After Charlotte's death it was both fashionable and profitable to attribute unsigned Brontë relics to the famous author. This practice was followed by several local dealers in particular, such as Alfred Gledhill (mentioned above) who assigned not only the painting but also the dog to Charlotte.

The style of the painting, especially the handling of the dog and the misty background, is closer to Emily Brontë's other animal illustrations, in particular 'Keeper, Flossy and Tiger' (**329**), 'Nero' (**324**) and 'Keeper – from life' (**319**), than to any of Charlotte's extant watercolours or drawings. Moreover, the paper used has the same texture and is roughly the same size as that used by Emily for her animal paintings. The sheets give the appearance of having been removed from a single extant sketchbook used by her after her return from Brussels: see **328**. There is no evidence that this painting was by Charlotte, apart from the early misattribution in the Binns sale catalogue.

There is little doubt, however, that this is an illustration of Anne's dog, Flossy; although the composition was probably adapted from one of the many engravings available in drawing manuals of spaniels in pursuit of a bird. The scene is a common motif of catchpenny prints of the eighteenth century and even features as a tailpiece in Thomas Bewick's *A History of British Birds*, vol. 2: *Containing the History and Description of Water Birds* (Newcastle: T. Bewick; London: Longman & Co., 1816), p. 41.

Flossy is said to have been given to Anne by her pupils, the Robinsons of Thorp Green, and brought to Haworth about 1843. The painting was probably made soon after Flossy's arrival: see the notes for Emily's watercolour 'Keeper, Flossy and Tiger' (**329**). Flossy wore the brass collar (H111) illustrated here as part of the legal obligation of the dog tax of 8 shillings, paid for all house dogs at the time: see **313** and **319**.

The summer following Flossy's acquisition, she had a puppy, also named Flossy, that was apparently given to Ellen Nussey. Anne's dog, which features regularly in letters and diary papers over a period of eleven years, was referred to by Ellen Nussey as 'long, silky-haired, black and white Flossy'. On 26 January 1848, Anne wrote to Ellen that 'Flossy is fatter than ever, but still active enough to relish a sheep hunt'. She outlived her mistress, dying sometime in 1854, as Charlotte records in a letter to Ellen Nussey (7 December 1854).

## 328

## Unfinished sketches of Flossy

c. 1843
Pencil on paper
On three pages (each 225 × 290 mm) of a 25-page sketchbook

Sketchbook (BS27.5) inscribed in ink on front brown card cover: 'Drawing Book/ Bot/ At M[r] Bronte's Sale/ Oct 1[st] 1861/ C. Brontes Book', and in top right corner: '[?J]. I. REDDIH[OUGH]'. (A 'Joseph Reddyough' is listed as one of the buyers at the 'Sale by Auction at Haworth Parsonage', 1 and 2 October 1861, after the death of Mr Brontë.) Binder's ticket inside front cover: 'ACKERMANN & C[o]/ Repository of Arts/ –96. Strand. –' Price on back inside cover in pencil: '5/6'. Originally accompanied by an autograph signed letter of Francis Brown.

Purchased in 1950 from Gladys Jane Brown of Ramsgill, who inherited the book from her father, Francis Brown. A number of illustrations belonging to Robinson and Francis Brown had previously been sold at Sotheby's sale of the Brown collection of Brontë relics, 2 July 1898; but a number of items were also withdrawn from sale and remained in the possession of Gladys Brown. For the provenance of the Brown collection see **29**.

*Brontë Parsonage Museum: C38*

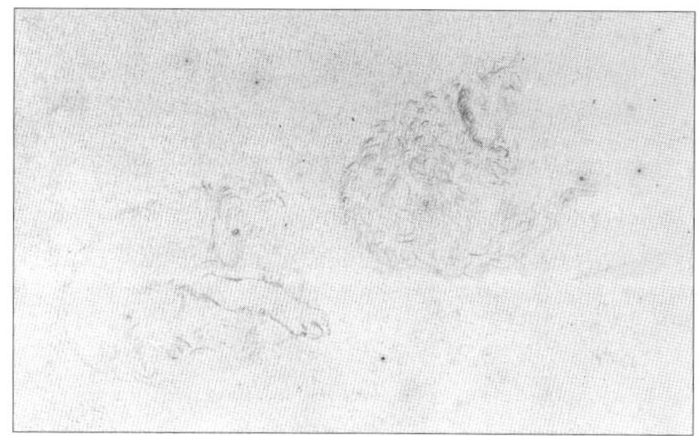

The first illustration (p. 2 of the sketchbook) has a curled-up dog on the left and the hind quarters and ear of the same dog on the right; the second (p. 4) has the barest outline of the back of an animal, probably the beginning of a sketch of another dog; the third (p. 6) has the outline of a couchant dog with large ears. All are incomplete, the remnants of a sketchbook used and probably owned by Emily Brontë. The book is made up of heavy 'wove' paper (the wire mesh of the paper-making tray is tightly woven so that a smooth finish is produced), more suitable for art work than the cheaper 'laid' paper of the period.

Despite the inscription on the cover by a later owner, the paper is similar in texture and roughly the same size as that used by Emily in her series of animal paintings, namely 'Flossy' (**327**), 'Nero' (**324**) and 'Keeper – from life' (**319**), which may have been cut from one of the sketchbook sheets. The sketchbook has obviously had pages removed and the remaining sketches of a couchant dog described here appear to be Emily's preliminary studies of Flossy for her painting of 'Keeper, Flossy and Tiger': see **329**. Emily's paintings of the family animals all date from this time, about 1843, the period after her time in Brussels, when she was at home on her own, with only her father, the two servants and the animals.

## 329

## Keeper, Flossy and Tiger

1843
Watercolour
225 × 326 mm

Signed and dated: 'E J Brontë 1843'. According to Sotheby's sale catalogue, 17 March 1937, a label on the painting read: 'This water-colour ... was hanging for nearly fifty years in the drawing room of A. B. Nicholls at Banagher, Ireland.'

Purchased by Bernard Quaritch Ltd, London, from Sotheby's, 17 March 1937, lot 646. This sale included the final portion of the library of the late Clement K. Shorter, who had probably acquired this item, together with other Brontë works, from Arthur Bell Nicholls when he visited him in Banagher, sometime after his first visit of 1895. In a letter to Shorter (5 September 1895), Nicholls writes 'my wife does not wish to part with the drawing of the two dogs by Emily'; and the following 11 September, repeats to a persistent Shorter that his wife 'will not relent as to the picture, as it has been hanging in our room ever since our marriage' (letters in the Brotherton Collection, Leeds University Library). In 1897, Shorter (presumably having finally purchased the painting) published a photo of it in 'Relics of Emily Brontë', *The Woman at Home*, no. 47, August 1897, p. 908. The painting also appears in 'Charlotte Brontë', *The Queen, The Lady's Newspaper*, 15 November 1913, p. 888, by Priscilla Countess Annesley, who acknowledges illustrations 'from the collection of Mr Clement Shorter'. When Winifred Gérin printed a copy of the picture in *Emily Brontë: A Biography* in 1971 (Oxford: Clarendon Press), she acknowledged the Brontë Society; but she was probably supplied simply with a photo taken from one of the two previous publications. *Location unknown*

Study of three animals lying together on a grassy hillside, with a barren moorland landscape in the distance and the end of a moss-covered drystone wall on the right. The two dogs bear a close resemblance to other illustrations of Emily's dog Keeper (centre left) and Anne's dog Flossy (on right). The cat, Tiger, sits between Keeper's left front and hind legs. Flossy is curled up into a ball at the back of Keeper, her distinctive curly black and white coat clearly visible in the poor-quality black and white photo that is all that survives of this painting. Tiger's striped markings can just be discerned on the cat's back and tail.

This is the only known watercolour of the Brontë cat Tiger, mentioned by Emily in her diary paper of 30 [31] July 1845 (see **331**). She records: 'We have got/ Flossy, got and lost Tiger–lost the hawk Nero/ ... Tiger died/ early last year.' (The Brontës were seldom without a cat and Tiger was succeeded by a black tabby, Tom.)

The close similarity of this painting in subject, style and background to Emily's watercolour 'Flossy' (**327**, previously attributed to Charlotte) strongly suggests that they were executed by the same hand at about the same date, in 1843. Moreover, the sleeping

Flossy in Emily's animal group here bears a remarkable resemblance to studies of a similar dog in a Drawing Book previously attributed to Charlotte (see **328**); these studies appear to be preliminary sketches, taken from life, for the illustration of Flossy in this animal group, which is more an amalgam of separate studies than a realistic composition.

The presence of Tiger in this dated painting supports the similar dating for Emily's illustration of 'Flossy', since there is a sketch of a cat on the verso of 'Flossy' which may also be of Tiger (see **330**). A date of 1843 for both paintings also ties in with a date between Emily's diary paper of July 1841, in which there is no mention of Tiger, and early 1844, when the cat seems to have died.

This painting was obviously treasured by the Brontë family. It hung on the parsonage walls and John Elliot Cairnes remembered seeing it there in September 1858, when he visited the Reverend Patrick Brontë after Charlotte's death (T. P. Foley, 'John Elliot Cairnes' Visit to Haworth Parsonage', *Brontë Society Transactions* (1984), vol. 18, part 94, p. 293). Nicholls must have taken it with him to Banagher, Ireland, after Patrick Brontë's death, as suggested above.

## 330

## Sketches of heads, animals and buildings

c. 1843
Pencil on paper
242 × 345 mm

Watercolour painting on verso of **327**, attributed to Emily.

Purchased from the Brown collection of Brontë relics, sold by Sotheby's, 2 July 1898, lot 18: see provenance of **29** for sources of the Brown collection.

*Brontë Parsonage Museum: C30v*

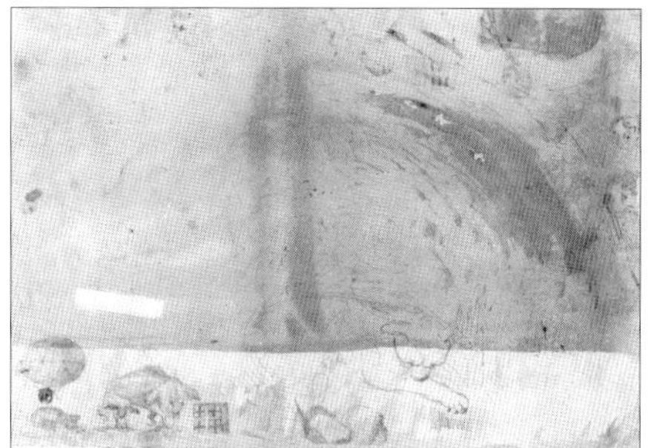

Rough sketches on verso of **327**: bottom from left to right, sleeping cat (possibly Tiger) with study of the end of a log above, a grotesque dog/ boar, decorated box, study of two rocks (these all appear to be by the same hand, possibly Emily); above the rocks is a study of a dog lying with its head turned to clean its right paw (similar to Emily's dog Keeper); around the top and right edges are less mature sketches of a dog's head made into a lion, two dog heads (same shape as Flossy, Anne's dog), buildings (like others in Branwell's doodles), back three-quarter view of a figure, and two tiny male heads.

It is impossible to give an exact attribution to these sketches: they appear to be drawn over a period of time, possibly by different hands. The initial sketches described above, however, are most likely to have been done by Emily: they are neatly placed along the bottom of the sheet suggesting a composition date after the illustration of 'Flossy' on the other side. The other sketches are lighter, more hasty, and partially obscured by the cutting of the sheet for 'Flossy'.

## 331

## Diary paper sketch of Emily with her animals

30 [31] July 1845
Pen and ink on paper
c. 45 × 75 mm

The sketch fills the bottom third of p. 3 (c. 118 × 75 mm) of Emily's diary paper. Since no original is available, approximate measurements of the sketch are based on other extant diary papers and on the facsimile of pp. 2 and 3 of this paper in Clement K. Shorter, *Charlotte Brontë and Her Circle* (London: Hodder & Stoughton, 1896), opp. p. 154. It is written in ink, in Emily's minuscule script; signed at the end: 'E J Brontë'; and dated at the beginning (on verso, p. 1): 'Haworth, Thursday, July 30th, 1845.' Emily is actually writing on the following day since she was mistaken about the date (see below).

Sold at Sotheby's, 17 March 1937, lot 892; together with **329** and Anne Brontë's 1845 diary paper; both previously part of the collection of Clement K. Shorter: see **329** for possible earlier provenance. Bought by Bernard Quaritch Ltd, London; believed to be in private hands in the USA.

*Location unknown*

The sketch illustrates Emily writing and sketching her diary paper in her small bedroom, that was once the Brontë children's nursery. She sits on the far right, facing left into the room, with only the back of her head visible. She wears a dress with long flowing sleeves; her hair is gathered behind in a bun, with curls at the side; and on her lap is the portable writing desk (seen also in **322**) at which she is working. Keeper, her dog, lies on the floor to her left, in the centre foreground. Anne's dog Flossy and a cat lie on the bed, illustrated at the far end of the room. Behind this is the window with its large panes: the bed is obviously pushed hard against the window allowing maximum use to be made of the relatively narrow room. To the left of the bed is a tall chest of drawers, which can still be seen in the BPM; and along the right wall, behind Emily, there appears to be some more low indistinguishable furniture. The 'E' of Emily's signature has been partly obscured by the ink lines of the top of the chest of drawers.

Anne's companion diary paper is dated 31 July 1845. Emily also wrote her paper on the 31st but dated it the day before, when she had intended to reopen her previous paper and write this new one. She explains: 'By mistake I find we have opened the paper/ on the 31st instead of the 30th. Yesterday/ was much such a day as this but the morn/ing was divine –'.

See **316** for information on the diary papers and their distinctive mix of reality and imagination. This particular diary paper begins with the words: 'My birthday – showery, breezy, cool. I am twenty-seven years old today.' Emily records important biographical facts: Charlotte's and Emily's return from Brussels as a result of their aunt's death, Charlotte's further period there and her final return on New Year's Day 1844, the termination of Branwell's job with the railway at Luddenden Foot and his tutorship at Thorp Green (which he had recently left), Anne's return home from her situation as governess at Thorp Green 'of her own accord' in June 1845, and Anne's and Emily's 'first long journey by ourselves' to York. She explains that during their excursion they pretended to be Gondal characters 'escaping from the palaces of instruction to join the Royalists who are hard driven at present by the victorious Republicans'. She describes the recent history of her pets and the household chores she should be attending to, as well as the latest news about her imaginative world: 'The Gondals/ still flourish bright as ever I am at present/ writing a work on the First Wars – Anne has/ been writing some articles on this and a book/ by Henry Sophona – We intend sticking firm by/ the rascals as long as they delight us which/I am glad to say they do at present.'

## 331a

## Girl and dog

n.d.
Pencil on paper

Signed in minuscule script; exact notation unknown.

Given by Emily Brontë to William Wood, the Haworth joiner (see below).
*Location unknown*

The only record we have of this drawing is the brief description of William Wood's relics made by Charles Hale in 1861 ('An American Visitor at Haworth, 1861', *Brontë Society Transactions* (1967), vol. 15, part 77, pp. 126–38): 'He has also a pencil sketch by Emily Brontë of early date, of a girl and dog, with her name in juvenile letters'. It is just possible that this illustration might refer to **309** (a girl and dog drawing also owned by William Wood); but **309** is a watercolour and the signature is not in 'juvenile letters'.

Mrs Chadwick gives an endearing description of the relationship between William Wood and the Brontë children: see p. 111. This illustration of 'a girl and dog' seen by Charles Hale appears to be one of the few relics William Wood still retained in 1861 and 'would not part with these for any consideration' (p. 137). However he appears to have later sold several items to William Law (see **38** and **309**), although these may have been acquired from William Wood's nephew (as in the case of **235**). An illustration by Charlotte of 'Mr Ph Wood' (**104**) is probably of a son or relative of the Haworth joiner.

## Emily Brontë: Reattributions

**40** 'The Disconsolate', now under Charlotte
**242** 'Sketches of human limbs', now under Branwell
**248** 'Sketch of a map', now under Branwell

# Anne Brontë

## 332

### Church surrounded by trees

29 August 1828
Pencil on paper
93 × 125 mm

Signed and dated in pencil below the drawing: 'Anne Bronte, August the 29 1828'. On verso: part of a pencil drawing of a tree, the remainder cut away.

Bequest of J. Roy Coventry, 1955; together with **180**, **312**, **317**, **318**, **323**, and **333**. Acquired by the donor from Mary E. Popplewell, daughter of Eliza Popplewell, younger sister of Martha Brown, on 15 August 1907, with **312** and **333**.

*Brontë Parsonage Museum: A1*

Tiny drawing of a view of the upper part of a church tower with a steeple, surrounded by trees in a churchyard enclosed by a low stone wall with a wooden gate on left. Beneath the pencil is a light ink wash. The drawing has been cut out unevenly from a larger sheet of paper.

## 333

### Cottage with trees

7 April 1829
Pencil on paper
103 × 118 mm

Signed in pencil, in longhand, below the drawing, centre: 'Anne Bronte'; dated in pencil below the signature: 'April 7th 1829/ [rule beneath]'.

Bequest of J. Roy Coventry, 1955; together with **180**, **312**, **317**, **318**, **323**, and **332**. Acquired by the donor from Mary E. Popplewell, daughter of Eliza Popplewell, younger sister of Martha Brown, on 5 August 1907, with **312** and **332**.

*Brontë Parsonage Museum: A2*

Tiny drawing of a view of a cottage with a gabled wing and chimney, half-hidden by the foliage of surrounding hedge and trees behind; roughly sketched lines to suggest water in front of the building. The little scene is copied from one of Thomas Bewick's 'tail-piece' engravings (Thomas Bewick, *A History of British Birds*, vol. 2: *Containing the History and Description of Water Birds* (Newcastle: T. Bewick; London: Longman & Co., 1816), p. 273).

## 334

### Magpie standing on a rock

23 April 1829
Pencil on paper
81 × 99 mm

Signed and dated in pencil, in minuscule script, bottom left: 'Anne Bronte April the 23 1829'. On verso: pencil outline of the bird drawing. On recto: pencil drawing of a house with two windows, door and chimney.

Gift of Margaret Illingworth, 1910, together with **9**, **10**, **11**, **12**, **19**, **80**, **81**, **155**, **184**, **185**, **188**, **189** and **197**. An autograph note by Patrick Brontë (BS179) sold at

Sotheby's as part of the Robinson and Francis Brown collection, 2 July 1898, may have originally accompanied this group of drawings: see **9**.

*Brontë Parsonage Museum: A3*

Tiny drawing of a stream with a magpie standing on a rock, its tail aloft, bending towards a bottle floating in the water. To the left, a twig sticks out of the water. The scene is copied from one of Thomas Bewick's 'tail-piece' engravings in his *A History of British Birds*, vol. 1: *Containing the History and Description of Land Birds* (Newcastle: T. Bewick; London: Longman & Co., 1816), p. 225.

## 335

## Three juvenile sketches

c. 1829

Pencil and watercolour on brown tinted paper

146 × 123 mm, bottom left corner missing

Inscribed in pencil, in unknown hand, top right corner: '(a'. These sketches are part of a collection of ten loose drawings contained within a sketch block, signed and dated in pencil at the top of the inside front cover: 'Anne Brontë August 29th/ AD 1843', kept within a green leather folder (for more details of the sketch block see **360**). The sheet used for these three sketches does not appear to have been torn from the sketch block.

Formerly owned by John Greenwood, the Haworth stationer in the Brontës' time; given by him to his daughter Jane Helen Widdop, and then to her daughter Judith Moore, who gave them to the present owner.

*Private owner*

Three juvenile sketches, one beneath the other. At the top, a sketch of a broken-down wooden fence on a grassy mound; in the centre, a group of rocks, highlighted with yellow watercolour, with clumps of grass; at the bottom a still smaller detail of a couple of rocks with grass growing around them. Although the three sketches do not appear to be copied exactly from the vignettes found throughout Thomas Bewick's *A History of British Birds*, 2 vols. (Newcastle: T. Bewick; London: Longman & Co., 1816), the book does contain numerous little studies of rocks, foliage and fences, so it is possible that these details derive from Bewick.

These sketches are very similar to **332**, **333** and **334**.

## 336

## 'A bit of Lady Julet's hair done by Anne'

24 November 1834

Ink on paper

c. 30 × 12 mm

The tiny sketch is in the left margin of p. 1 (99 × 60 mm) of a single-leaf autograph manuscript diary paper, written all over on both sides in ink, in a combination of longhand and minuscule script, by Emily Brontë. Page 1 is signed and dated in longhand at the top: 'November the 24/ 1834 Monday/ Emily Jane Bronte/ Anne Brontë'. Stamped: 'BRONTË/ MUSEUM/ HAWORTH', encircled, between the two names. This ink sketch of a ringlet of hair is drawn at right angles to the text and beside it, on the left, is written in ink in minuscule script: 'A bit/ of Lady/ Julet's hair/ done by/ Anne'.

Bequest of Henry Houston Bonnell, 1927; acquired by Bonnell at Sotheby's sale of the effects of Arthur Bell Nicholls, London, 26 July 1907, lot 196.

*Brontë Parsonage Museum: Bonnell 131*

This tiny drawing, made when Anne was fourteen years old, appears in the first of a series of diary papers written by Emily and Anne beginning with the words 'I fed Rainbow, Diamond/ Snowflake Jasper pheasent (alias[)]/ this morning'. The later diary papers tended to be written every four years or so on Emily's birthday and most of them include some form of illustration. The scrawled handwriting and poor spelling are no credit to Emily, an intelligent girl of sixteen, but the informal style and dialogue contained in the text paint a vivid picture of everyday life at the parsonage and give some indication of how the Brontës' real and imaginary worlds dovetailed together: 'The Gondals are ~~dise~~/ discovering the interior of Gaaldine/ Sally Mosley is washing in the back–/ Kitchin'. It would appear that the sisters were reusing a fragment of paper which already bore Anne's drawing, because the handwriting has been adapted to fit around it. There is also a deleted upside-down date at the foot of the page ('November the 24 1834') which would confirm this theory.

## 337

## 'Oak Tree'

27 October 1835
Pencil on card
200 × 184 mm

Signed and dated in pencil, in minuscule hand, immediately below drawing, left corner: 'Anne Brontë'; right corner: 'Oct 27 1835'; titled in pencil, in longhand, below drawing, centre: 'Oak Tree'. Stamped on verso: 'BRONTË/ MUSEUM/ HAWORTH', encircled.

Bequest of Henry Houston Bonnell, 1927; acquired by Bonnell at Sotheby's sale of the effects of Arthur Bell Nicholls, London, 26 July 1907, lot 42.

*Brontë Parsonage Museum: Bonnell 15*

Single large, leafy oak tree standing on a small grassy mound with flat, open land behind. In the near distance there is a large Palladian-style mansion, behind which a mountain can be seen in the far distance. A similar Palladian building appears in Anne's unfinished drawing of a girl with a dog (**354**).

Possibly copied from William De la Motte's *Characters of Trees* (Sandhurst: privately published by De la Motte, Professor of Drawing at the Royal Military College, 1822), which the Brontës are known to have owned and from which a number of plates survive in the BPM collection with pencil drawings by Branwell on the backs of them (see Appendix A). There are two other drawings of single trees by Anne in the BPM (**338** and **367**) and a woodland scene containing detailed drawings of different species of trees (**368**).

## 338

### 'An Elm Tree'

13 November 1835
Pencil on paper
213 × 170 mm

Signed and dated in pencil, in minuscule script, immediately below drawing, left: 'Anne Bronte'; centre: '1835'; right: 'Nov 13'. Titled bottom centre, below date: 'An Elm Tree'. Stamped: 'BRONTË/ MUSEUM/ HAWORTH', encircled. Watermark: 'Ruse and Furners 1833'. Acquired originally in a card mount, now removed, which bore the inscription in pencil, in non-Brontë hand: 'Miss Wooler/ 3 Albion Crescent/ Scarborough'.

Gift of Ernest O. Wooler, 1932; previously owned in succession by donor's sister Harriet Ann Wooler (1843–1938) and by donor's aunt Margaret Wooler, Charlotte's teacher and friend at Roe Head, Mirfield.
*Brontë Parsonage Museum: A4*

Large elm tree in full leaf standing on a grassy hillock with large-leaved plants in the foreground and a view of distant mountains seen faintly in the background. A flight of nine birds is seen to the upper left of the tree.

The 'Elm Tree' is possibly copied from William De la Motte's *Characters of Trees* (Sandhurst: privately published by De la Motte, Professor of Drawing at the Royal Military College, 1822) which the Brontës are known to have owned and from which a number of plates survive in the BPM collection with pencil drawings by Branwell on the backs of them (see Appendix A). There are two other drawings of single trees by Anne in the BPM: an oak (**337**) and an untitled tree, which is either an ash or a lime, with a man sitting at its foot (**367**). There is also a woodland scene containing detailed drawings of different species of trees (**368**).

## 339

### 'Roe Head, Mirfield'

c. 1835–1837
Pencil on paper
191 × 155 mm

Titled in pencil, in longhand, bottom centre of drawing: 'Roe Head, Mirfield'.

Gift of J. A. Erskine Stuart, 1907. The drawing originally belonged to Margaret Wooler (1792–1885), principal of Roe Head in the Brontës' time. She passed the drawing on to her nephew Frederic Sykes Wooler (1849–1929), who presented the drawing to J. A. Erskine Stuart in 1896.
*Brontë Parsonage Museum: A9*

View from the front gate of Roe Head, named after the hamlet on the northern edge of Mirfield, overlooking Dewsbury and the Calder valley, twenty miles away from Haworth. In the immediate foreground there is a row of stylized plants bending exaggeratedly in different directions. To the right there is a small tree in leaf; to the left a smaller one. Beyond, occupying the middle-ground, is a large expanse of lawn across which the large, square, many-windowed school house is seen, with white driveways arranged in a T-shape in front of it. To the left of the house is a row of three tall trees and to the right the kitchen extensions and smoking chimney. The paper has been trimmed right up to the edge of the image.

The drawing is an exercise, probably made while Anne Brontë was a pupil at Roe Head. Apart from the medium and details of foliage in the foreground, it is similar to drawings of 'Roe Head' by both Charlotte Brontë and Susan Carter (plate 7): see **62** for further discussion on Roe Head. Like Susan Carter's drawing, Anne's building appears to be at a greater distance than that of Charlotte, and Anne has paid more attention to the cloud formation and sky.

## 340

## Head and shoulders of a young woman

c. 1835–1837
Pencil on card
223 × 182 mm

Bequest of Henry Houston Bonnell, 1927; acquired by Bonnell at Sotheby's sale of the effects of Arthur Bell Nicholls, London, 26 July 1907, lot 42.

*Brontë Parsonage Museum: Bonnell 7*

Portrait of a woman's head and naked shoulders, with the face seen three-quarters, looking to her right. The face is full and rounded with well-proportioned features: large eyes, a straight nose, small mouth with full lips and a dimple in the chin. The woman's hair-style, coiled back at the sides into a headband, has a classical look to it, which, combined with the naked shoulders and regular features, would suggest that this portrait was studied from an engraving of a classical head and was intended as an educational exercise.

The portrait is identical to the one made by Charlotte in April 1831 at Roe Head (**52**), one of a number of similar drawings of classical heads (**51**, **55** and **56**). Presumably Anne copied from the same plate when she was a pupil at Roe Head from late October 1835 until December 1837. Although this drawing is not signed it can be accurately attributed to Anne on stylistic grounds; note the characteristically enlarged orbs of the eyes, as seen, for example, in her 'Portrait of a young woman' (**359**).

## 341

## Landscape with trees and lake

c. 1835
Pencil on paper
68 × 60 mm

Acquired originally in a card mount, now removed, on which was inscribed in non-Brontë hand: 'Done by Ann [*sic*] Bronte/ at Roe Head/ Mirfield:/ about 1835'.

Gift of Lucy Ethel Fraser, 1941. The donor inherited this drawing from her mother Caroline Fraser, née Atkinson (b. 31 December 1822), who was the daughter of Rev. Christopher Atkinson, incumbent of St Paul's Church, Leeds, and later at Elland, Halifax, and the wife of Rev. A. C. Fraser, a curate at Elland; a letter from the donor which accompanied this item reads: 'My sister who died in 1934 sent you a few years ago an etching [*sic*] of Roe Head where our mother was at school with Miss Wooler. At this time Charlotte Bronte was a mistress and her two sisters were pupils'. The 'etching' mentioned in the letter is the Conté crayon drawing of Roe Head, signed 'S. Carter' and illustrated in plate 7 (see p. 42 and **62**); the BPM Stock Book (SB630) records that 'Caroline Atkinson afterwards Mrs Fraser was her (Charlotte Bronte's) pupil'.

The donor's inscription on the back of the envelope which originally contained Anne's drawing, reading 'Anne Bronte's/ drawing, given to/ Mother by her –/ at School –', authenticates the attribution to Anne. The donor's great-uncle and great-aunt, Rev. and Mrs Thomas Atkinson, were Charlotte's godparents who paid her school fees at Roe Head.

*Brontë Parsonage Museum: A7*

Small drawing of a lakeland scene with trees in leaf on left and right banks of a stream in the foreground which leads to a lake in the middle-ground. A mountain can be seen in the distance and a castle on a promontory on the right shore of the lake. Probably a copy of an engraving. The paper has been trimmed right up to the edge of the image.

342

## A ruined church

10 February 1836
Pencil on card
180 × 274 mm

Signed and dated in pencil, in minuscule script, immediately below drawing, left corner: 'Feb 10'; centre: 'Anne Bronte'; right corner: '1836'. Stamped on verso: 'BRONTË/ MUSEUM/ HAWORTH', encircled. Bequest of Henry Houston Bonnell, 1927; acquired by Bonnell at Sotheby's sale of the effects of Arthur Bell Nicholls, London, 26 July 1907, lot 42.

*Brontë Parsonage Museum: Bonnell 16*

Close-up view of a ruined church without its roof, with trees growing in and around the ruin. One gable end and adjoining chantry with three stone buttresses remain, as do three gothic arched windows with the remains of stone tracery. The ruin is enclosed by an intact low stone wall. The figure of a girl wearing a bonnet and apron and carrying a basket is seen walking across the bare middle-ground, her back to the viewer. In the foreground plants and flowers grow, drawn in some detail, and to the right the top of a truncated stone pillar, or wall end, beside a tall tree trunk, its upper part broken off and one leafy branch growing to the left. The damaged tree echoes the ruinous state of the building in the manner of picturesque landscape.

There are three other drawings signed and dated by Anne to the year 1836 (**343**, **345** and **346**). **344** is undated, but also belongs stylistically to this group. All five drawings were probably made whilst Anne was at Roe Head.

## 343

## Landscape with castles

22 March 1836
Pencil on paper
271 × 353 mm

Signed and dated in pencil, in minuscule script, below the bottom edge of the image, left corner: 'March 22'; centre: 'Anne Bronte'; right corner: '1836'. Embossed, bottom right of paper: 'TURNBULLS / SUPERFINE / LONDON BOARD'. Watermark: 'Ruse and Furners 1834'. Purchased from Sotheby's, London, 17 December 1973 (lot 261), together with **344** (lot 262); formerly the property of J. R. W. West. The Sotheby's sale catalogue entry reads: 'The present sketch and that in the following lot are understood to have come, earlier in this century, from Hill House, Banagher, Offaly, where Charlotte Bronte stayed on her honeymoon.' A detail of this drawing was reproduced in *The Bookman*, October 1904, 'by kind permission of Mr. Clement K. Shorter' with details of five other Brontë drawings (**116**, **117**, **137**, **344** and **346**), which at the time were all in the possession of Arthur Bell Nicholls.

*Brontë Parsonage Museum: A4:5*

Landscape view from a high grassy knoll in foreground which is dominated by three trees in leaf with exaggeratedly curved trunks. Two men in top hats appear centre foreground, one of them sitting on the ground drawing the view, the other standing with his back to the viewer. In the middle-ground, a wide river leading from the left into a lake on the right, its right bank lined with a castellated wall, towers, houses and churches beyond a heavily wooded area in the foreground below the knoll. In the far distance mountains can be seen, one of them with a castle on top.

The stylized nature of the landscape suggests that Anne Brontë copied this drawing from an engraving of an idealized picturesque view. It was quite possibly executed at Roe Head where Anne was a pupil from late October 1835 until December 1837. This was typical of the kind of drawing exercise undertaken by girls in such an establishment.

There are three other drawings signed and dated by Anne to the year 1836 (**342**, **345** and **346**). **344** is undated, but also belongs stylistically to this group. All five drawings were probably made whilst Anne was at Roe Head.

## 344

## Landscape with castle, bridge and female figure

c. 1836
Pencil on paper
234 × 355 mm

Purchased from Sotheby's, London, 17 December 1973 (lot 262), together with **343** (lot 261); formerly the property of J. R. W. West, and thought to have originally come from Hill House, Banagher, Offaly, where Charlotte Brontë stayed on her honeymoon: see **343**. A detail of this drawing was reproduced in *The Bookman*, October 1904, 'by kind permission of Mr. Clement K. Shorter' with details of five other Brontë drawings (**116**, **117**, **137**, **343** and **346**), which at the time were all in the possession of Arthur Bell Nicholls.

*Brontë Parsonage Museum: A4.6*

View of a double-arched stone bridge over a river flowing across the page horizontally, with the figure of a girl dressed in a long hooded cloak, apron and wide-brimmed bonnet, carrying a covered basket over her arm, seen approaching over the bridge in the foreground. To the right, the end of a high stone wall and a low stile. In the middle-ground, tall trees in leaf grow on either side of the bridge, their differing shapes and textures carefully detailed by the artist, who frequently demonstrates a particular love of trees in her choice and depiction of the subject. In the centre distance the roofs of a line of houses and an elevated ruined castle tower can be seen.

The bridge in the drawing could be the same as the one in **63**, which is possibly a view of Greta Bridge, County Durham, a well-known North of England beauty spot which was much drawn and painted by artists of the period. Views of Greta Bridge appear in many of the illustrated books from which the Brontës were known to copy.

The drawing is very similar in style, scale and general appearance to **342**, **343**, **345** and **346**, which suggests that it may also have been executed c. 1836–7, when Anne was a pupil at Roe Head. The former four drawings by Anne are all signed and dated by her to the year 1836, and were probably made whilst Anne was at school there.

## 345

## Man with a dog before a villa

30 May 1836
Pencil on paper
166 × 270 mm

Signed and dated in pencil, in minuscule script, immediately below drawing, left corner: 'May 30 1836'; right corner: 'Anne Bronte'. There are some odd marks just below the drawing, centre left, which are not letters. They stand out from the rest of the underbrush to which they seem to belong.

Gift of Robert H. Taylor, as part of his collection; acquired by him at Sotheby's, 25 May 1954. This drawing clearly belongs to the group of Anne's schoolgirl drawings which includes **342**, **343**, **344** and **346** and was probably also formerly owned by Arthur Bell Nicholls.
*Princeton University Libraries: Robert H. Taylor Collection: USA OA1*

In the centre of the drawing a stony road is seen, with on the left a promontory of rock on top of which grows a leafy tree and overhanging foliage. A profusion of plants and flowers grows at the foot of the rock. To the right is a villa with a pantiled roof and an imposing porch with tall arched doorway and two side windows, set into a high stone wall which closes the building off from the road. The top of the wall is overhung with wisteria and large rocks are placed at intervals along its base. The main part of the villa is taller than its porch and has three windows, one half-covered by a blind. The figure of a man wearing a long coat, wide-brimmed hat and holding a walking stick stands with his back to the viewer in the middle of the road while a skinny black and white dog bounds towards him from picture right. Beyond the villa is a mass of trees in leaf which meet the edge of the rock on the left and close off the view further down the road. Taking into account the architectural style of the building, the scene would appear to be set in Italy. Illustrated Annuals of picturesque Italian views were common in the 1820s and 1830s; Anne probably copied from one of these.

There are three other drawings signed and dated by Anne to the year 1836 (**342**, **343** and **346**). **344** is undated, but also belongs stylistically to this group. All five drawings were probably made whilst Anne was at Roe Head.

## 346

### Landscape with cattle and haycart

15 December 1836
Pencil on paper
213 × 296 mm

Signed and dated in pencil, in minuscule script, immediately below left corner of drawing: 'Anne Brontë'; right corner: 'December 15 1836', (the 'D' of December is reversed). Stamped: 'BRONTË/ MUSEUM/ HAWORTH', encircled. Gift of Miss C. White, 1938; acquired with **79**, which was inscribed on original backing: 'Drawing by Charlotte Bronte/ given me/ by Mrs Nicholls/ July 1914', together with a photograph of Arthur Bell Nicholls in Banagher 1890, a photograph of his home in Ireland and various correspondence with Rosse Butterfield. The items probably belonged to Nicholls's second wife, as suggested here: see **79** for further information. A detail of this drawing was reproduced in *The Bookman*, October 1904, 'by kind permission of Mr. Clement K. Shorter' with details of five other Brontë drawings (**116**, **117**, **137**, **343** and **344**), which at the time were all in the possession of Nicholls.
*Brontë Parsonage Museum: A5*

Landscape view with a river to left, spanned by a single-arched stone bridge, and road to right with rear view of a loaded haycart accompanied by a figure on horseback. In the centre foreground a group of four cattle, two couchant, two standing on the grass between road and riverbank: a copse and wicket fence behind them in the centre of the scene. The whole is framed by a tall tree to the right of the scene which curves over the road to the left.

There are three other drawings signed and dated by Anne to the year 1836 (**342**, **343** and **345**). **344** is undated, but also belongs stylistically to this group. All five drawings were probably made whilst Anne was at Roe Head.

## 347

### Portrait of a child's head, looking upwards

31 August 1837
Pencil on thin card
222 × 158 mm

Stamped: 'BRONTË/ MUSEUM/ HAWORTH', encircled. Inscribed on verso, in non-Brontë longhand: 'Annie Bronte./ August 31 1837'.

Bequest of Henry Houston Bonnell, 1927; acquired by Bonnell at Sotheby's sale of the effects of Arthur Bell Nicholls, London, 26 July 1907, lot 42.
*Brontë Parsonage Museum: Bonnell 4*

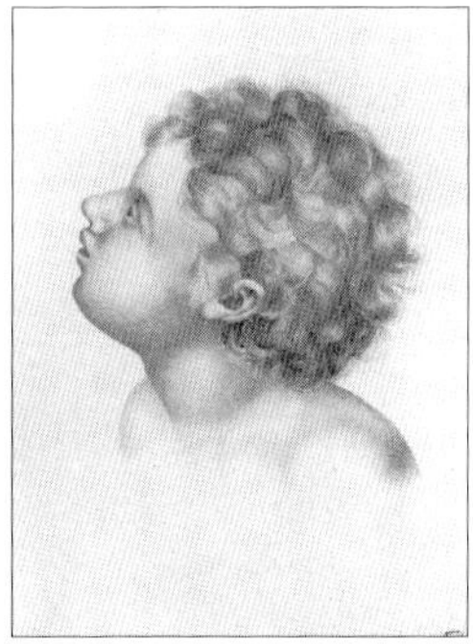

Portrait of a child's curly-haired, chubby-featured head seen in profile and looking upwards to the left. The eyes are wide open with the long fair lashes clearly visible and the lips are slightly parted. The look on the child's face could be said to be one of surprise, which suggests that it was intended as a study of a specific facial expression. It is clearly one of a series of drawings copied from prints by both Anne (see **348** and **349**) and Charlotte (**53** and **54**) whilst at Roe Head. Other drawings of the same subject show the child laughing, crying and sleeping.

348

## Portrait of a child's head

15 November 1837
Pencil on card
289 × 232 mm

Signed and dated in pencil, in minuscule script, below, left corner: 'November 15. 1837'; right corner: 'Anne Brontë'. Stamped on verso in two places: 'BRONTË/ MUSEUM/ HAWORTH', encircled.

Bequest of Henry Houston Bonnell, 1927; acquired by Bonnell at Sotheby's sale of the effects of Arthur Bell Nicholls, London, 26 July 1907, lot 42.

*Brontë Parsonage Museum: Bonnell 5*

Portrait of a child's head seen almost full-face and tilted down to the right, with eyes looking to the right. The child is chubby featured with short curly hair brushed back to reveal the right ear. The eyes are portrayed as extraordinarily large, with pupils, irises, lashes and brows drawn in clear detail, in a manner that is characteristic of Anne Brontë. The look on the child's face is alert and interested, as though its attention has momentarily been caught. It is clearly one of a series copied from prints by both Anne (see **347** and **349**) and Charlotte (**53** and **54**) whilst at Roe Head. Other drawings of the same subject show the child laughing, crying and sleeping.

349

## Head of a sleeping child

c. 1837
Pencil on sepia card, with embossed decorative border
215 × 240 mm

Inscribed in pencil, bottom right corner: 'M. A. B'. Embossed to mid-right of decorative border: 'DOBBS LONDON'. Inscribed on verso in non-Brontë hand, bottom right corner: 'M. A. B. 1828'.

Gift of Rosamund Wheatley, 1984; formerly owned by the donor's mother Marion Saville, who had previously presented Brontë relics belonging to her grandmother (Florence Armitage) to the BPM in 1964: viz., a plait of Anne's hair (J24:1), a small rosewood box containing Anne's signature (H81:1) and a shell and bead necklace (H81:2/J22).

*Brontë Parsonage Museum: A10*

Head and shoulders of a curly-haired child, tilted to the left with eyes closed in sleep; shadow hatched in to the left. The drawing has been made on a manufactured piece of card with the central area enclosed by a decorative embossed border of classical palmettes. This type of card was purchased specifically for framing drawings during the period and a number of the Brontës' drawings are framed in this way.

This drawing is accepted as being by Anne, in spite of the date on the verso, 1828, and the inscribed initials 'M. A. B.' J. A. Erskine Stuart, with whom the donor was connected, did have a collection of genuine Brontë relics. Furthermore, a drawing of a 'Sleeping Child' does appear in the catalogue of the Brown collection of Brontë relics.

There are two other drawings of heads of children by Anne (**347** and **348**) and two by Charlotte (**53** and **54**) which were probably copied from prints at Roe Head. Girls at the time were in the habit of exchanging such drawings to paste into albums as memorials of their friends. Indeed, there is in existence an album put together by one of the Brontës' schoolfellows which includes a drawing by Charlotte of 'St Martin's Parsonage, Birmingham' (**77**).

## 350

## Woman gazing at a sunrise over a seascape

13 November 1839
Pencil on paper
182 × 226 mm

Signed and dated in pencil, in minuscule script, below drawing, left corner: 'Anne Brontë'; right corner: 'November 13th 1839'.

Purchased from Frances E. Bell of Dublin, the niece of Mary Anne Bell, Arthur Bell Nicholls's second wife, 1918; formerly owned by Nicholls. This drawing was part of a group of six Brontë relics purchased from Frances Bell in 1918 which also included **66**, **150**, a carte de visite photograph of Martha Brown (Ph 71), a small pocket book containing entries in Charlotte Brontë's writing (BS22) and Harriet Martineau's visiting card. In 1919 the Brontë Society acquired a further two items from Frances Bell: Charlotte's drawing of a 'Scene on the Rhine' (**130**) and her workbasket (H176). The Society refused the offer of 'A book containing ferns gathered and pressed by Charlotte Bronte during her stay at Killarney' (Letter from Frances Bell of 3 March 1919).

*Brontë Parsonage Museum: A6*

Seascape with the rear view of a figure of a young woman in the foreground, left of centre; her right hand raised to shade her eyes, in her left hand a white handkerchief. She wears a dark dress with short sleeves, the neckline slipping off her left shoulder, and her hair is in loose ringlets cascading around her bare neck. Rocks frame the picture, on the left running up to the top in a curious stylized formation. Two isolated rocks poke out of the sea on the right. The sea is calm, with a rowing boat, over which flies a group of seagulls, and a distant view of two sailing boats on the left; on the right, a sailing ship; coastal land in the far distance. On the horizon the sun is seen to rise in five pronounced beams into a cloudy sky.

There are certain aspects of the drawing's handling which suggest that it is drawn partly from the artist's imagination rather than being a straightforward copy of a print, for example the softness and slight uncertainty of its lines and shading. The rock formation which runs up the left side of the picture is curious. It could derive partially from a print with added imaginative touches. The Roe Head album which contains Charlotte's drawing of 'St Martin's Parsonage, Birmingham' (**77**) includes (p. 21) a landscape with a similar rock formation as the one seen here. Also, on the verso of **188** there is a faint outline drawing which could be a copy of a view of Holy Island, Northumberland, which contains a similar detail of rocks on the left of the picture.

The image of the girl is reminiscent of the melancholy figures often found in nineteeth-century northern European romantic landscapes, notably in the work of Caspar David Friedrich.

351

## Profile of a female head

c. 1839
Pencil on paper
178 × 227 mm

Inscribed in pencil, below sketch, left: 'B'. Stamped in two places: 'BRONTË/ MUSEUM/ HAWORTH', encircled. For provenance see **350**.
*Brontë Parsonage Museum: A6v*

Outline drawing of a female head seen in profile looking to picture right. The face has large eyes, arched brows and full lips and the girl's long hair is coiled up on top of her head. This sketch was revealed in 1983 during conservation work on 'Woman gazing at a sunrise over a seascape' (**350**), when it was discovered beneath two blank backing sheets of paper.

352

## Woodland with deer

c. 1839–1843
Pencil on card
162 × 196 mm

Watermark on verso: 'J WHATMAN/ 1839'. Stamped: 'BRONTË/ MUSEUM/ HAWORTH', encircled.

Bequest of Henry Houston Bonnell, 1927; acquired by Bonnell at Sotheby's sale of the effects of Arthur Bell Nicholls, London, 26 July 1907, lot 42.
*Brontë Parsonage Museum: Bonnell 22*

Unfinished pencil drawing of a landscape which is largely drawn in outline with only the central part shaded in. The view is framed by trees in leaf through which a river can be seen flowing from the front to the back of the picture. On the distant left bank in the shaded area is the figure of a man armed with a bow, pursuing five fleeing deer with his two hunting dogs. A stag drinks from the riverbank in the middle-distance. The scene on the opposite bank is watched by a seated figure with his back to the viewer positioned right foreground.

The drawing is attributed to Anne Brontë. Its unfinished state provides us with valuable information as to the artist's working methods when copying from a print.

353

## 'What you please'

25 July 1840
Pencil on card
182 × 214 mm

Signed, titled and dated in pencil, in minuscule script, immediately below drawing, left: 'Anne Brontë'; centre: 'What you please.'; right corner: 'July 25th 1840'. Stamped on verso: 'BRONTË/ MUSEUM/ HAWORTH', encircled.

Bequest of Henry Houston Bonnell, 1927; acquired by Bonnell at Sotheby's sale of the effects of Arthur Bell Nicholls, London, 26 July 1907, lot 42.
*Brontë Parsonage Museum: Bonnell 17*

Young girl with a heart-shaped face and loose shoulder-length wavy hair standing beside a gnarled tree trunk at the edge of a clearing in a wood. She wears a long pale dress with a low, frilled neckline, a V-shaped waistline and full elbow-length sleeves, a dark cloak draped over her shoulders. Her pose is one of arrested movement, with her left hand raised towards her face and her right resting on the trunk of the sapling by her side, as if to steady herself. To the left the hefty trunk of a tree with plants and flowers, including tall foxgloves, growing around its roots, closes off the composition. In the background is seen the clearing surrounded by shrubs and trees.

Anne apparently drew this picture when she was staying at Scarborough during her first summer with the Robinson family of Thorp Green, where she was governess. She may well have had more leisure time to give to her own enjoyment of drawing when the family were on holiday. Although the detail of the work suggests that it was probably copied from a print, the choice of subject may well have been a symbolic one, the girl at the edge of the wood representing Anne herself, poised nervously on the edge of a new life, as Edward Chitham has suggested (*A Life of Anne Brontë* (Oxford and Cambridge, Massachusetts: Basil Blackwell, 1991), p. 79). The title is enigmatic but, as Chitham remarks, it may echo a phrase of Mrs Robinson's: 'You may do what you please, Miss Brontë.'

## 354

## Portrait of a girl with a dog

c. 1840–1845
Pencil on card
182 × 205 mm

Stamped on verso: 'BRONTË/ MUSEUM/ HAWORTH', encircled.

Bequest of Henry Houston Bonnell, 1927; acquired by Bonnell at Sotheby's sale of the effects of Arthur Bell Nicholls, London, 26 July 1907, lot 42.

*Brontë Parsonage Museum: Bonnell 8*

Unfinished drawing of a young girl stroking a dog. The scene is set out of doors, presumably in the grounds of the Palladian-style mansion seen in the far distance. The girl, seen in profile, kneels on the right side of the picture fondling the dog's neck with her right hand and in her left holding a book. Her hair is in ringlets and she wears a high-waisted, short-sleeved dress with a braid trim around the wide, off-the-shoulder neckline. The spaniel-type dog on the left, which is large in relation to the size of the girl, lies on its stomach and looks up at her. Only the girl's upper body, the left arm and book and the dog's head are finished in any detail; the rest of the drawing is just sketched in.

The depiction of the dog is very similar to that in two unfinished watercolours formerly attributed to Charlotte (**355** and **356**). These three works are most likely all by the same hand, probably Anne's on account of the style of the drawings. The dog resembles Flossy, the spaniel given to Anne by her employers the Robinsons in 1843, which was also painted by Emily (**327** and **329**).

There is a possibility that this drawing, and the watercolours, could have been begun by Anne at Thorp Green and that this is a portrait of a Robinson girl. The house in the background is similar to Kirby Hall, the neighbouring house to Thorp Green Hall (see Edward Chitham, *A Life of Anne Brontë* (Oxford and Cambridge, Massachusetts: Basil Blackwell, 1991), p. 104). This building is also very like the one in the background of Anne's drawing of 'Oak Tree' (**337**). However, Palladian mansions, such as this one, were a common feature of the picturesque landscape prints so often copied by the Brontës.

## 355

## Unfinished Flossy 1

c. 1840–1845
Watercolour and pencil on card
175 × 206 mm

Stamped: 'BRONTË/ MUSEUM/ HAWORTH', encircled.

Purchased at Hodgson & Co. sale, London, 31 March 1933, part of lot 449; formerly in the collection of Sir Alfred J. Law, Honresfeld (see **15**), and prior to that the drawing was probably owned by his uncle William Law who may have acquired it (with **356**) from Abraham Riley: an article by Alfrey Porter in the *Yorkshire Weekly Post*, 7 May 1898, entitled 'Relics of the Brontës', describes his visit to Riley's antique shop in Ilkley where he saw an unfinished sketch of a black and tan spaniel.

*Brontë Parsonage Museum: C78*

Unfinished study of a spaniel sitting in a window sill, facing left; window panes raised, deep casement; curtain on right pulled back and caught in top right corner; a house (or church) and shrubbery are suggested in the distance. Pencil lines are visible and the darker areas have been blocked in by an initial light wash; only the head has been finished in black, tan and white paint, showing a delicate light touch with a fine brush.

The dog is said to be Anne's spaniel Flossy, given to her at Thorp Green: see notes to **327**.

The attribution of this work is not easy to establish: it appears to have been executed by the same hand as **356**, which (like **355**) was previously attributed to Charlotte. Another unfinished drawing of similar content and style (**354**) is attributed to Anne: it depicts a spaniel with a young girl and has a tiny building in the distance reminiscent of Kirby Hall, the neighbouring property to Thorp Green Hall, where Anne was a governess. It seems most likely that all three works were by Anne, begun at Thorp Green and left unfinished on her return home.

## 356

## Unfinished Flossy 2

c. 1840–1845
Watercolour and pencil on card
176 × 203 mm

Stamped: 'BRONTË/ MUSEUM/ HAWORTH', encircled.

Purchased at Hodgson & Co. sale, London, 31 March 1933, part of lot 449; formerly in the collection of Sir Alfrey J. Law, Honresfeld (see **15**), and prior to that the drawing was probably owned by his uncle William Law who may have acquired it (with **355**) from Abraham Riley: an article by Alfrey Porter in the *Yorkshire Weekly Post*, 7 May 1898, entitled 'Relics of the Brontës', describes his visit to Riley's antique shop in Ilkley where he saw an unfinished sketch of a black and tan spaniel.

*Brontë Parsonage Museum: C79*

Unfinished study of a spaniel sitting in a window sill, facing right; window sash raised, deep casement; curtain on left pulled back and caught in top left corner; hills and shrubbery in the distance. The study is virtually a mirror image of **355** but in a more advanced stage of completion. Few pencil lines are visible and the dog's black, white and tan coat is painted in detail; only the head and front legs remain unfinished. The view through the window and the casement are also unfinished.

See notes for **355**, on attribution and on Anne's dog Flossy.

## 357

## Portrait of a young woman in blue

c. 1840–1845
Watercolour on paper
173 × 124 mm

Dr Mildred Christian's card index in the BPM (see **34**) records a note on the verso (possibly on an early backing no longer extant), in pencil, unsigned and undated but probably written by Mrs E. Foster, referring to her mother-in-law, the former owner: 'My husband's mother in her young days lived at Gt Ouseburn, near both Green Hammerton & Thorpe [*sic*] Green Hall when Anne Brontë was governess to the children who gave her the portrait. It has been in my husband's family for over 60 years. His mother's maiden name was Anderson.' Stamped: 'BRONTË/ MUSEUM/ HAWORTH', encircled.

Purchased from Mrs E. Foster, 1950; previously owned by her mother-in-law Mrs Foster née Anderson.
*Brontë Parsonage Museum: C 77*

Head-and-shoulders portrait of a young woman with thick, wavy chestnut hair which she wears parted in the middle and dressed in a loose coil over her right shoulder, with one small curl in front of her ear. She has a full round face with ruddy cheeks, the shadows of her face modelled in blue. The eyes are unusually large, a feature of Anne Brontë's drawings of faces (see **359**), and the mouth is small and red. The girl's head is turned away from the viewer, giving a three-quarter view of the face, with a demure, downward look of the eyes to picture right. She wears a vivid royal blue shawl draped around her shoulders.

When it was acquired in 1950 this drawing was identified by the BPM as a portrait of Anne by Charlotte. The image bears little resemblance to the known portraits of Anne (see **91**, **92** and **225**). Edward Chitham (*A Life of Anne Brontë* (Oxford and Cambridge, Massachusetts: Basil Blackwell, 1991), p. 93) has discovered from Slater's *Directory of Yorkshire*, 1848, that there was a William Anderson, a tailor and draper, living in Great Ouseburn during the relevant period, which helps to confirm the work's provenance, and has pointed out that although there is little reason for the local draper to have been given a portrait of Anne by Charlotte and then to have treasured it, once Charlotte's name had become famous 'the chances of the picture being kept would be far greater'. Chitham attributes the picture to Anne and also suggests that it may be a portrait of

Mary Robinson aged twelve or thirteen, which is possible, but the figure is more likely copied from a plate in an illustrated Annual such as *Heath's Book of Beauty*.

The style, colouring and application of paint in this portrait are very similar to the work of both Anne and Charlotte, but the depiction of the facial features, especially the eyes, and the Thorp Green provenance lead the authors to reattribute the painting to Anne.

The church is identifiably Little Ouseburn Church near Thorp Green, the one attended by Anne with the Robinsons and situated next door to Monk's House where Branwell lodged. Edward Chitham has established that Anne took her view from Townend Field, across what was once a lake and is now a beck which runs in front of the church (*A Life of Anne Brontë* (Oxford and Cambridge, Massachusetts: Basil Blackwell, 1991), p. 103).

## 358

### Little Ouseburn Church

c. 1840–1845
Pencil on thin card
164 × 220 mm

Stamped on verso: 'BRONTË / MUSEUM / HAWORTH', encircled.

Bequest of Henry Houston Bonnell, 1927; acquired by Bonnell at Sotheby's sale of the effects of Arthur Bell Nicholls, London, 26 July 1907, lot 42.

*Brontë Parsonage Museum: Bonnell 21*

View of the east end of a church seen from across a small lake. The east window is large, arched and has stone tracery work. At the west end of the building there is a square stone tower with double lancet windows on each side. The church is surrounded by leafy trees and stands on the grassy bank which leads down to the water, in which the church is seen to be reflected. Both banks are lined with water-reeds, seen in detail on the nearside bank in the foreground.

## 359

### Portrait of a young woman

24 June 1842
Pencil on paper
212 × 185 mm

Signed and dated in pencil, in minuscule script on the verso: 'A very bad picture drawn June 24th 1842 by Anne Brontë'. Stamped on verso: 'BRONTË / MUSEUM / HAWORTH', encircled.

Bequest of Henry Houston Bonnell, 1927; acquired by Bonnell at Sotheby's sale of the effects of Arthur Bell Nicholls, London, 26 July 1907, lot 42.

*Brontë Parsonage Museum: Bonnell 6*

Head-and-shoulders portrait of a young woman with a round face, straight nose, small mouth, huge eyes and clearly defined eyebrows. She has shoulder-length dark hair which is parted in the centre and hangs in long ringlets at the side. The girl wears a heavily draped robe or mantle, the folds of which she lifts towards her face with her left hand.

This portrait was drawn at Haworth as Anne was at this date known to be at home on holiday from Thorp Green. Edward Chitham suggests this is a portrait of a Robinson girl and when Anne describes the picture as 'bad' in her inscription, she means that it is a poor likeness (*A Life of Anne Brontë* (Oxford and Cambridge, Massachusetts: Basil Blackwell, 1991), pp. 93–4). However, the facial features, hand and arm are disproportionately drawn, which could also explain Anne's self-criticism. The drawing could also be an attempt at a self-portrait, drawn from Anne's reflection in a mirror.

## 360

## Unfinished landscape with river, trees and deer

c. 1843
Pencil on paper
166 × 255 mm

This drawing is part of a collection of ten loose drawings contained within a sketch block, signed and dated in pencil at the top of the inside front cover: 'Anne Brontë August 29th/ AD 1843', kept within a green leather folder. The sheet of paper has been torn from the sketch block, described below. Inscribed in unidentified longhand, in pencil on verso, along the top edge: 'This drawing was on the block when received from the Brontës'.

Formerly owned by John Greenwood, the Haworth stationer in the Brontës' time; given by him to his daughter Jane Helen Widdop, and then to her daughter Judith Moore, who gave it to the present owner.
*Private owner*

Faintly sketched beginnings of a landscape view with a river curving across the centre of the picture, with groups of fir trees on both banks. To the right, a group of three deer sit and graze beneath the trees. Very similar figures of deer appear in another unfinished landscape by Anne Brontë, **352**.

The size of the sketch block from which the paper for this drawing has been torn is 263 × 183 mm; its cover is a shot-silk-effect dark brown cloth with dark brown paper binding on the seams and the remains of a green thread tie. The front cover forms a pocket to store finished drawings; the inside centre spine has a slot to hold a pencil and the inside back cover bears an unused portion of the sketch block of paper (each sheet measures 255 × 166 mm), 25 mm thick, still stuck to the backboard.

A printed label pasted in the centre of the inside cover explains the purpose of the sketch block: '"TABLETTES A DESSIN,"/ OR/ FRENCH SKETCHING BLOCKS./ Persons accustomed to make Sketches from Nature, have experienced much trouble in securing/ their Drawing Paper in the open air. This simple contrivance is offered to the public in the/ expectation that its usefulness, economy, and portability, will procure for it extensive patronage,/ and general adoption./ When a Drawing is required to be made on these Blocks, nothing more is necessary than to slip/ off with a penknife the outer sheet of Tinted Paper; a firm and flat surface is then presented to the/ Artist, as solid as a board; and having completed his Sketch, a similar application of his knife will/ produce another surface, and so on till all the leaves have been used./ The French Blocks are also prepared in a still more convenient form, with

Pockets for the finished/ Drawings, Loops for pencils, &c.; thus arranged, they are entitled "IMPROVED SKETCH BOOKS."/ SOLD BY/ Dobbs and Company,/ 134, FLEET STREET; AND 13, SOHO SQUARE, LONDON;/ AND BY ALL RESPECTABLE STATIONERS IN THE UNITED KINGDOM.'

361

## Unfinished study of roses

c. 1843
Watercolour and pencil on paper
255 × 166 mm

This drawing is part of a collection of ten loose drawings contained within a sketch block, signed and dated in pencil at the top of the inside front cover: 'Anne Brontë August 29th/ AD 1843', kept within a green leather folder. The sheet of paper has been torn from the sketch block, described in **360**. Watermark, bottom right: 'J WH'.

Formerly owned by John Greenwood, the Haworth stationer in the Brontës' time; given by him to his daughter Jane Helen Widdop, and then to her daughter Judith Moore, who gave them to the present owner.
*Private owner*

Largely unfinished watercolour study of a spray of roses; pencil outline of blooms, thorny stems and leaves sketched in. A pale green watercolour wash has been applied quite roughly over most of the paper. A round of paper has been left exposed in the centre of the wash, presumably for painting the flower head in a different colour.

362

## Unfinished view of a building

c. 1843
Pencil on paper
166 × 255 mm

This drawing is part of a collection of ten loose drawings contained within a sketch block, signed and dated in pencil at the top of the inside front cover: 'Anne Brontë August 29th/ AD 1843', kept within a green leather folder. The sheet of paper has been torn from the sketch block, described in **360**. Watermark, bottom left, at right angles to the edge of the paper: 'W'.

Formerly owned by John Greenwood, the Haworth stationer in the Brontës' time; given by him to his daughter Jane Helen Widdop, and then to her daughter Judith Moore, who gave them to the present owner.
*Private owner*

Unfinished drawing of a large two-storey building, a manor house or farmhouse, with mullioned windows, extended into a series of outbuildings. The view appears to be of the rear of a building, drawn in more detail on the left-hand side. The faint outline of three trees can be seen behind the house. The line at the foot of the drawing suggests that this could be a view drawn from a window, possibly a building in the vicinity of Thorp Green Hall, near York, where Anne was a governess from 1840 until 1845.

## 363

### Ruined building in a wooded landscape

c. 1843
Pencil on paper
166 × 255 mm

This drawing is part of a collection of ten loose drawings contained within a sketch block, signed and dated in pencil at the top of the inside front cover: 'Anne Brontë August 29th/ AD 1843', kept within a green leather folder. The sheet of paper has been torn from the sketch block, described in **360**. Inscribed in pencil, bottom left: 'stu'.

Formerly owned by John Greenwood, the Haworth stationer in the Brontës' time; given by him to his daughter Jane Helen Widdop, and then to her daughter Judith Moore, who gave them to the present owner.
*Private owner.*

Almost finished drawing of a semi-ruined roofless Georgian house in a hilly wooded landscape. The symmetrical design of the house is not dissimilar to Haworth Parsonage, with five windows on the upper floor and four on the ground floor. Trees surround the house, drawn in some detail. The perspective of the hills is rather confusing; it is difficult to say whether they are intended to appear steep or gently rolling. The gable ends of two other houses can be seen in the hills and trees behind the ruined building. A long stone wall runs from the left of the house to a large gate-post at its end.

## 364

### Hen in a basket

c. 1843
Pencil on paper
135 × 210 mm

This drawing is part of a collection of ten loose drawings contained within a sketch block, signed and dated in pencil at the top of the inside front cover: 'Anne Brontë August 29th/ AD 1843', kept within a green leather folder (for more details of the sketch block see **360**). The sheet used for this drawing does not appear to have been torn from the sketch block.

Formerly owned by John Greenwood, the Haworth stationer in the Brontës' time; given by him to his daughter Jane Helen Widdop, and then to her daughter Judith Moore, who gave them to the present owner.
*Private owner*

Detailed drawing of a speckled hen sitting in an oval basket lined with straw, pieces of which hang over the edge of the basket. The hen looks to the left and is seen in profile. The tight weave of the basket is very clearly portrayed. The drawing is placed within a carefully drawn circle. The image is reminiscent of Thomas Bewick's engravings of birds.

## 365

### Unfinished sketch of a house

c. 1843
Pencil on paper
140 × 195 mm

This drawing is part of a collection of ten loose drawings contained within a sketch block, signed and dated in pencil at the top of the inside front cover: 'Anne Brontë August 29th/ AD 1843', kept within a green leather folder (for more details of the sketch block see **360**). The sheet used for this drawing does not appear to have been torn from the sketch block.

Formerly owned by John Greenwood, the Haworth stationer in the Brontës' time; given by him to his daughter Jane Helen Widdop, and then to her daughter Judith Moore, who gave them to the present owner.
*Private owner*

A large building, possibly a church, has been sketched in outline on the right-hand half of the page. A gothic-style arched doorway and window with stone tracery appear at one end of the building. To the right, a shuttered window in the roof and a tall chimney; below it a half-drawn arched window.

## 366

### Portrait of a little girl with a posy

12 September 1843
Watercolour and pencil on card
205 × 175 mm

Signed and dated in pencil, in longhand on the verso at bottom of paper: 'Anne Bronte September 12th 1843'. Originally owned by Ann Marshall, confidential maid to Mrs Lydia Robinson at Thorp Green when Anne was a governess there. Ann Marshall died unmarried at the age of 38 on 16 April 1847, but the painting has remained in her family and the present owner is a descendant.
*Private owner*

A little girl, four or five years old, is seen three-quarter length, seated and looking to picture left. She has a happy, chubby face with dark blue eyes, pink cheeks and red lips. Her hair is blonde and wavy, parted in the centre, shorter around her face and longer at the back, falling onto her shoulders. The child wears a wide-necked white dress with the shadows of its folds in bodice, skirt and short puffed sleeves painted in a pale grey-blue. The same blue shading is used in the painting of the flesh. A green satin sash creates a stronger splash of colour in a picture painted mainly in delicate tones. The little girl's right arm is partially hidden by her skirt and her left hand rests in her lap holding a little bunch of purple and mauve heartsease, or violets, and yellow flowers which could be celandines. The violet is the Christian symbol of humility and is often found in paintings of the infant Christ. In this picture of a little girl the flowers are intended as symbols of her innocence and also of the transience of life, youth and beauty.

This delicately handled watercolour was almost certainly painted at Thorp Green because it was presented by Anne to Ann Marshall, her employer's confidential maid, and inscribed with a date in September when she would have been at Thorp Green. There are very few watercolours by Anne in existence and this is the most pleasing. Anne's 'Portrait of a young woman in blue' (**357**), originally attributed to Charlotte, shows a heavier and cruder use of colour than here. The unfinished watercolours of the dog Flossy sitting in a window sill are hard to judge because of their incompleteness (**355** and **356**). It is unlikely that this is a portrait of a child known to the artist; it is far more likely to have been copied from one of the numerous prints of pictures of little girls, popular throughout the nineteenth century.

## 367

## Study of a tree with figure of a man

19 October 1843
Pencil on paper
232 × 159 mm

Signed and dated in pencil, in minuscule script, immediately below drawing, left corner: 'Anne Brontë'; right corner: 'Oct 19th 1843'.

Bequest of Henry Houston Bonnell, 1927; acquired by Bonnell at Sotheby's sale of the effects of Arthur Bell Nicholls, London, 26 July 1907, lot 42.

*Brontë Parsonage Museum: Bonnell 19*

Single large tree in leaf, possibly an ash or lime, standing on a grassy mound with a view of a lake and rolling hills in the distance. A man in a top hat, dark jacket and light-coloured trousers sits reading at the foot of the tree, with a dog lying at his feet.

It is possible that this was drawn at Thorp Green, where Anne would have been in October 1843. The composition and general appearance of the drawing relate it to her studies of 'Oak Tree' (**337**) and 'An Elm Tree' (**338**), both of which may have been copied from plates in William De la Motte's *Characters of Trees* (Sandhurst: privately published by De la Motte, Professor of Drawing at the Royal Military College, 1822). There is also a drawing of a woodland scene by Anne which details a number of different species of trees (**368**), drawn two months later.

## 368

## Landscape with trees

16 December 1843
Pencil on card
252 × 327 mm

Signed and dated in pencil, in minuscule script, immediately below drawing, left: 'Anne Brontë'; right corner: 'Dec 16th 1843'. Stamped on verso: 'BRONTË/ MUSEUM/ HAWORTH', encircled.

Bequest of Henry Houston Bonnell, 1927; acquired by Bonnell at Sotheby's sale of the effects of Arthur Bell Nicholls, London, 26 July 1907, lot 42.

*Brontë Parsonage Museum: Bonnell 20*

Densely detailed woodland scene with a river leading from the left foreground to the middle-distance. All the trees are in full leaf and the varieties are made distinct, for example on the right a massive beech with its foliage occupying half of the picture. In the centre, by contrast, is a stunted, bare-trunked tree with one branch in leaf, the others broken, leaning over the river. In the immediate foreground there are detailed flowers and foliage, and in the far distance a glimpse of a large building.

The surface of this drawing is marked by scattered water drops, as if rain had fallen on the paper. This may suggest that the drawing was made in the open air at Thorp Green. However, the amount of precise detail would suggest that this is a copy from an engraving. Alternatively, the work could have begun as a study from nature and been worked up into a more finished drawing when Anne was at home in Haworth, with more leisure time, in the Christmas holiday.

There are also three drawings by Anne of single trees (**337**, **338** and **367**).

# Anne Brontë: Dubious attributions

## Unfinished landscape with plants and flowers

c. 1843
Pencil on paper
166 × 255 mm

This drawing is part of a collection of ten loose drawings contained within a sketch block, signed and dated in pencil at the top of the inside front cover: 'Anne Brontë August 29th/ AD 1843', kept within a green leather folder. The sheet of paper has been torn from the sketch block, described in **360**. Traces of gum arabic (see **26**) around the outer edge of the paper. Stamped on verso, in gothic script: 'Brontë Greenwood'.

Formerly owned by John Greenwood, the Haworth stationer in the Brontës' time; given by him to his daughter Jane Helen Widdop, and then to her daughter Judith Moore, who gave them to the present owner.
*Private owner*

The beginnings of a study of a rocky landscape with plants and flowers. The poor quality of the drawing and the 'Brontë Greenwood' stamp on the verso of this item suggest that it is not the work of Anne Brontë, even though the paper came from a sketch block formerly owned by her. The unexplained traces of gum arabic also appear on the drawing 'Windmill and buildings in a rocky landscape', found with the same collection and not attributed to Anne Brontë for stylistic reasons.

## Windmill and buildings in a rocky landscape

c. 1843
Pencil on paper
166 × 255 mm

This drawing is part of a collection of ten loose drawings contained within a sketch block, signed and dated in pencil at the top of the inside front cover: 'Anne Brontë August 29th/ AD 1843', kept within a green leather folder. The sheet of paper has been torn from the sketch block, described in **360**. Traces of gum arabic (see **26**) around the outer edge of the paper.

Formerly owned by John Greenwood, the Haworth stationer in the Brontës' time; given by him to his daughter Jane Helen Widdop, and then to her daughter Judith Moore, who gave them to the present owner.
*Private owner*

Detailed drawing of a view of a quarry with a roofless or flat-roofed brick-built building in the centre foreground, behind which stands a wooden windmill with four sails. The windmill appears to be operating a pulley which lifts a load suspended on the left. A one-storey shack is built at either side of the main building. In the background, a view of large blocks of stone scattered across a hillside, which suggests that the scene is set within a stone quarry in the Haworth locality.

If this is a Haworth scene, it is possible that the buildings were at a coal-mine in the neighbouring village of Stanbury. From the early 1830s until about 1867, there were a number of coal-mines on Stanbury

Moor which supplied the mills with fuel for the steam-powered machinery.

The heavy handling of the pencil and the crude modelling of the forms are uncharacteristic of Anne Brontë, whose drawing at this date was far more accomplished. For these reasons, this drawing cannot be attributed to her.

## Unfinished sketch of a landscape with cottages and figures

c. 1843
Pencil on paper
181 × 115 mm

This drawing is part of a collection of ten loose drawings contained within a sketch block, signed and dated in pencil at the top of the inside front cover: 'Anne Brontë August 29$^{th}$/ AD 1843', kept within a green leather folder (for more details of the sketch block see **360**). The sketch is drawn on a fragment of writing paper with an embossed crown in the top left corner; it was not torn from the sketch block. Stamped on verso, in gothic script: 'Brontë Greenwood'. Watermark, top left, upside down and in reverse to the sketch: 'H/ FINE'.

Formerly owned by John Greenwood, the Haworth stationer in the Brontës' time; given by him to his daughter Jane Helen Widdop, and then to her daughter Judith Moore, who gave them to the present owner.

*Private owner*

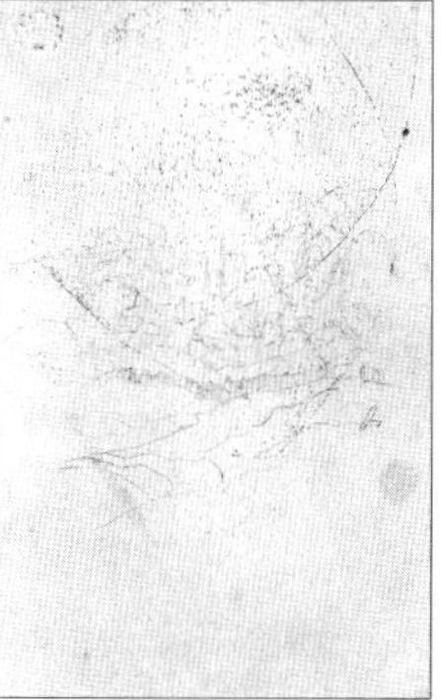

The lines of the sketch are very faintly drawn. In the foreground there is a curving path and possibly a stream. In the centre, a wicket fence with a stile or gate in the middle. Two female figures stand either side of this, a young girl and a woman, both wearing capes and bonnets. Beyond them, a cottage with tall chimneys. Possibly the beginnings of a drawing of a snow scene.

The 'Brontë Greenwood' stamp on the verso suggests that this sketch is not by the hand of Anne Brontë.

# Appendix A

## List of books owned by the Brontës, with sketches and scribbles

All drawings made by the Brontës in printed books belonging to them are recorded below; and other relevant inscriptions in the same works are also listed.

**[Bennett, E. T.],** ***The Gardens and Menagerie of the Zoological Society Delineated,*** **Vol. 1:** ***Quadrupeds.*** **London: John Sharpe, 1830 (BPM: bb69)**

PLATE 18 Pine marten, in *The Gardens and Menagerie of the Zoological Society Delineated*

Inside front cover, on pastedown at the bottom, in pencil: picture of a pine marten (see plate 18), similar to the marten illustrated on p. 225; a woman's head drawn immediately above the back of the marten. The head (in profile) was sketched first since the back of the animal is shaded over the shoulders of the woman.

Inscribed in ink on front fly-leaf: 'B–t in May, 1831 = price 1£=1=0=/ Secundum D-um Br-d-y,/ &c. The wooden cuts, in/ this Book, are excellent –/ Being done by the first/ of living engravers, on Wood –/ B.'

Page 50: engraving copied by Charlotte, 'Palm squirrel': see **74**.

Page 225, bottom right corner: pencil sketch of a foot.

Page 272: engraving similar to Charlotte's 'Moonlit scene with rocks and water': see **122**.

Rear pastedown: head-and-shoulders sketch of a woman, face in profile, similar to profile head inside front cover. Also a pencil profile line of a forehead, nose, mouth and chin; and another sketch of a face, with no hair or back of head, only three-quarter view of face. Sketches attributed to Anne whose signature 'Anne Brontë' appears in longhand above them (BPM: A8, A8v).

**[Darton, William],** ***A Description of London; Containing a Sketch of its History and Present State, and of all the most celebrated Public Buildings, &c.*****, London: William Darton [1824] (BPM: bb35)**

Inscribed on front fly-leaf, in ink, in Branwell's longhand: 'P B Brontë. aged. 10 years/ and 9 months. March. 21. –1828 –'.

Signed on title page, in non-Brontë hand: 'Hannah Brown./ Haworth.' A small sketch of Haworth Church drawn on left of title page and extending across seam of book to frontispiece margin. Frontispiece has colour engravings of St Paul's Cathedral and the Bank of England; below these Branwell has written 'capital' and 'very Bad' respectively.

Inside front cover on pastedown: pencil drawing of emaciated cattle, bones in foreground, mountains in distance; face of central cow has human features; hindquarters of fleeing beast on left, two animals fighting in distance (BPM: B2).

Between pp. 12 and 13, Branwell has inscribed comments beneath colour engravings, as follows: Somerset House 'Tolerable', Covent Garden Theatre 'capital', Westminster Abbey 'capital', Westminster Hall '~~good~~ Tolerable'. Outline pencil drawing of a building above the top left corner of the plate of Somerset House. Small pencil drawings below the last engraving: anatomical study of a leg showing muscles (on right); naked figure on all fours straddling a recumbent figure (bottom centre).

Facing p. 24, Branwell has commented below engravings as follows: The Royal Exchange 'good', Waterloo Bridge 'capital'.

Between pp. 30 and 31, Branwell has commented below engravings: Carlton Palace '~~Tolerable~~ ~~bad~~ Tolerable', Hay Market Theatre 'execrable', The Horse Guards 'Tolerable bad', White Hall 'capital'.

Back fly-leaf: pencil drawing of outline perspective view of building with two towers and onion domes.

PLATE 19 Emaciated cattle, in William Darton, *A Description of London*

Rear pastedown (see plate 19): scene of the Valley of Death with two emaciated cattle fleeing, bones and skull in foreground (B2v).

**De la Motte, William, *Characters of Trees*, London: 'Published by W^m^ De la Motte Professor of Drawing at the Royal Military College, Sandhurst', 1822 (BPM: B42)**

Title page inscribed in ink, possibly in Branwell's longhand, above publishing details at the bottom of page: 'No 2' (left), 'Price 5/-' (right). All the following sketches are by Branwell.

Verso of title page: vigorous drawing of a battle scene with warriors and hunting dogs, possibly relating to one of the many battles Branwell wrote about in his early manuscripts, such as the Battle of Thermopylae. Four bearded soldiers dominate the foreground, bare-legged and wearing plaid, or possibly armoured tunics, cloaks and helmets or berets. They may be related to classical mythology but also have a Scottish appearance. In the background, two columns of stick-like figures emerge from between the hills, holding spears and shields. Signed in ink, in Branwell's longhand, top right: 'Brawell [*sic*] Bronte/ Drawing', c. 1830–3 (BPM: B42.1).

Plate of 'Spruce Fir': tiny figure dancing, drawn in bottom right corner of engraving; tiny sketch of woman on left of engraving.

Verso of 'Spruce Fir': various sketches, including square biblical-style temple, several views of church ruins with various shaped arches, girl flying with large wings and arrows in her hand, another woman with wings and a spear, caricatures of tall thin bearded man bowing to another man, and other faint figures and sketches.

Verso of 'Scotch Fir': various sketches, including three cats on their hind legs drawing; a man with a pointed nose writing on a book labelled 'Novel'; several ducks; female profiles; half-length sketch of woman with sharp features, wispy hair and necklace; head-and-shoulders of a military man with cape, curly hair and large curled moustache.

Plate of 'Birch': small rough sketch of figure on a horse (bottom left) and female head (bottom right).

Verso of 'Birch': pencil sketches, including classical warrior figures (and parts of figures) with bow and arrows, swords and spears; round table with central leg; quivers with arrows and bows; three figures blowing curled horns, one only a head, one in full-length classical gown; tiny landscape with two figures talking.

Verso of 'Beech': sketches of four fantastic flying 'things'; tiny figure on hill silhouetted at sunrise; sprigs of flowers; two elderly figures, one reading; back view of a head in a top hat; three studies of male faces, one in profile.

Blank end-paper: another battle scene (see plate 20) similar to the one in the front of the book. In the foreground the foreshortened figure of a half-naked soldier bends down to operate some kind of war weapon. To his right a similar figure reaches up to load a tall contraption with a pulley which also appears to be a device for firing on the enemy. To the left of the foreground a body lies flat on the ground. In the centre five figures, wearing battledress, fight with swords and shields. In the background columns of soldiers carrying spears advance between hills to fight a battalion of men up on the top of the hill. The whole scene is packed with action, executed in a most inventive way, especially in the details of the imaginary machines of war and the well-observed poses of the central battling group.

PLATE 20 Branwell Brontë, Battle scene, in William De la Motte, *Characters of Trees*

**Dryden, John, trans., *The Works of Virgil, Translated into English Verse*, London: printed for C. & J. Rivington & the other Proprietors, 1824 (BPM: bb64)**

Inside front cover, on pastedown, in minuscule Brontë script, in pencil: Angrian names including Percy, Zamorna, Wellington, Fidena, Thornton, Lady Maria, Charles, Julia, Edward.

Front fly-leaf, in non-Brontë pencil longhand: 'John Binns Book'.

Inside back cover, on pastedown: seven faces probably by Branwell. They are most likely Angrian characters, possibly those listed inside the front cover, although one appears to be of Wellington and one is a classical-style bust of a woman.

Page 167, at bottom: three-quarter pencil profile of a man with long thin face, large ears, stubby beard and moustache.

Page 273, in margin: tiny ink figure, possibly a warrior with a spear.

**Fresnoy, Abbé Lenglet Du, *Geography for Youth*, Dublin: P. Wogan, 1795 (BPM: bb200)**

Front fly-leaf (which folds out for frontispiece of map of the world on reverse): childish ink and pencil sketches of heads and figures, including three heads of a bearded king, a crowned figure with a knife, a man in a top hat and two roosters. Also inscription in pencil: 'Walsh Bronte/ National/ School/ 1884'. Other names inscribed throughout, including 'The Revd P Bronte' (dubious signature), 'Walsh Bronte', 'Hugh Bronte His/ Book in the year 1803'.

Verso of a back fly-leaf: ink head in profile and a pencil head; also inscription, in unknown hand, from Deuteronomy; and the signature 'Walsh Bront'.

**Goldsmith, Rev. J., *A Grammar of General Geography, For the Use of Schools and Young Persons*, London: Longman, Hurst, Rees, Orme, & Brown, 1823 (BPM: bb217, Bonnell 45)**

Inside front cover, on pastedown which contains an advertisement for 'Dr. Butler's Classical Geography': sketches of female heads in pencil and ink.

PLATE 21 Sketches in Goldsmith's *Grammar of General Geography*

PLATE 22 Frowning man in John Hornsey, *The Pronouncing Expositor*

Front fly-leaf (see plate 21): inscribed in Charlotte's longhand, in ink: 'Bronté/ Fordly pig/ Charlotte/ Charlotte/ Fordly pig'; sketches in pencil and ink, including a pair of dancing legs, wearing Scottish dancing socks and kilt; small Bewick-style vignette of tall house amongst trees; four women in long dresses, one with leg-of-mutton sleeves and bonnet; a large face behind the women with an absurdly small top hat; other rough profiles.

On fold-out map of South America between pp. 70 and 71, top left corner: tiny pencil sketch of a map, which, when turned vertically, resembles the map of the continent.

Throughout the book there are tiny sketches and inscriptions in minuscule script of Gondal place names, the most significant being names written in Anne Brontë's hand into the 'Vocabulary of Names of Places' at the back.

Rear pastedown: scribbled writing and calculations drawn over with ink and pencil sketches of heads.

**Hornsey, John, *The Pronouncing Expositor; or, A New Spelling Book*, Eleventh edition, York, 1829 (The Houghton Library, Harvard University: Educ T 20758.29.456*)**

On bottom third of rear pastedown, inverted: head-and-shoulders pencil sketch of a man with a distinct frown (see plate 22). This appears to be a rough image taken 'from life'. It was previously attributed to

Charlotte because of an inscription on the remainder of the pastedown. The inscription, however, is partly erased and too faint to be legible, but the words 'Miss C Brontë/ Mirfield' appear below the inscription in Charlotte's hand, just above the sketch which is drawn upside down. The book would have been used by Charlotte while she was a teacher at Roe Head, but the sketch bears no relationship to her style. The strongly characterized face and firm outlines suggest that Branwell may have used this book and drawn 'Frowning man', possibly while he was a tutor.

**Mangnall, Richmal, *Historical and Miscellaneous Questions, for the Use of Young People*, London: Longman, Hurst, Rees, Orme, & Brown; Wakefield: John Hurst, 1813 (BPM: Bonnell 43)**

Inscribed inside front cover, on pastedown, in pencil in Charlotte's longhand: 'Charlotte [overwritten in ink] Jan$^{y}$ 17/ 1831/ C Brontë September/ Charlotte Brontë/ Susan Ledgard/ Mary Taylor/ [?1 word] Brooke/ Ellen Nussey/ Miss Taylor'.

Verso of title page, in pencil, in Charlotte's longhand: 'Charlotte Brontë/ November 16 1831'.

Page 141: tiny pencil sketches of flowers.

**Murray, Lindley, *English Grammar, Adapted to the Different Classes of Learners*, London: Longman, Hurst, Rees, Orme, & Brown, and Darton & Harvey; York: Wilson & sons, 1818 (BPM: Bonnell 44)**

Inscribed inside front cover, on pastedown, in Charlotte's longhand, in pencil: 'Charlotte Brontë Jan$^{y}$ 17 1832'; 'Charlotte Brontë/ July 29$^{th}$ 1832'; 'Aug$^{t}$ 29$^{th}$ 1832'.

Page 75, in left margin: tiny pencil sketch of a hand pointing to part of the grammar.

Page 111, in right margin: pencil sketch of a hand pointing to grammar.

**[New Testament in English] (BPM: bb5, title page missing)**

Inside front cover, on pastedown, in ink: juvenile sketches and scribbles, probably by Branwell; head of a man at the top.

Inscribed on first page of text, in margin, in Branwell's script: 'P. B. Brontë Began Matthew. Nov 13. 1829 in latin'. Throughout the text Branwell has made similar inscriptions recording the progress of his translation from English into Latin.

Page 11, bottom of page: tiny pencil sketch of a cottage, signed and dated '1829/ PBB'.

Rear pastedown and final page of text: childish ink sketches similar to those at the front of the book and unlike other Brontë sketches. The final sketch appears to be a plan of a classroom, possibly a Sunday School.

**[New Testament in Latin] (BPM: bb4, title page missing)**

Inside front cover, on pastedown: pencil sketches by Branwell of two men fighting with swords, and a man being savaged by a large dog.

Page 23: profile of a face at top of page.

Inscribed on rear fly-leaf, in Charlotte's longhand, in pencil: 'April 12th On the afternoon of the 12th of April 1833. the Sage Branwellius. had a vision in which he beheld Lord Althorpe ...'

Rear pastedown, in pencil: tiny outline sketch of a building and other scribbles.

**Noel, M. and Chapsal, M., *Nouveau Dictionnaire de la Langue Française*, Bruxelles: J-B Tircher, 1841 (BPM: bb43)**

Inscribed on half-title, in Charlotte's longhand, in ink: 'C. Brontë/ Bruxelles 1843'.

Page 76, at foot of page in pencil: sketch of a face, with large sinister eyes and bald head.

**Porny, Mr. *Grammatical Exercises, English and French*, London: printed for F. Wingrave, J. Walker, Wilkie & Robinson, Scratcherd & Letterman, J. Richardson, and Gale & Curtis, 1810 (BPM: bb47)**

Leather front cover, top left corner, in ink: tiny female head.

Inscribed inside front cover, on pastedown, in Charlotte's longhand, in pencil: 'Charlotte Brontë January 17/ 1831'; in Charlotte's miniature script: 34 lines of poetry.

Rear fly-leaf, in Charlotte's longhand, in ink: 13 lines of translation from French, two crossed through.

Verso of rear fly-leaf, in Charlotte's minuscule script, in pencil: four lines of poetry; in ink: a name, squiggles and several rough sketches, viz. a headless man in coat-tails, hands in pockets; tiny profile of a woman; man in left profile, in round-tailed coat and slouch hat; man in right profile with full three-quarter-length coat, large-brimmed hat, lead in right hand which runs into a female head with tiny monkey on left shoulder; head of old man with very long beard and prominent nose.

Rear pastedown, top left corner, in ink: tiny female head in profile.

**Russell, J. C., *Russell's General Atlas, of Modern Geography*, London: Baldwin & Cradock [c. 1831] (Pierpont Morgan Library: Bonnell: MA 2696)**

Inside front cover, on pastedown: pencil sketch of a face with bald head, written over by long numerical calculation on right; cancelled sentence on left, in Emily's script: 'What is is [*sic*] the word used to express the enlightenment of a room'; and various words in longhand down centre of page.

Contents page, turned upside down: full-length pencil sketch of a woman with ringlets piled up behind her head, lace shawl and full skirt.

Verso of contents page: sketch of woman's face (upside down), more numerical calculations.

Verso of map of France: half-length sketch of a woman in veil (see plate 23), three-quarter view of face, hair caught up behind head, high-necked dress with collar and brooch.

PLATE 23 Charlotte Brontë, Woman with veil, in *Russell's General Atlas; of Modern Geography*

Verso of map of Australia: head-and-shoulders sketch of a woman, hair parted in centre and pulled back behind the head, prominent eyebrows, high-necked collar; possibly a sketch of a fellow pupil in Brussels.

Rear fly-leaf, turned upside down: various names in ink in longhand, plus the inscription, 'All of Fleet-Ditch/ Arrested for swindling/ Crime of Arson proved/ against three of/ the Number. the/ fourth escaped by/

turning King's/ Evidence.' To the left of this inscription is an outline of a large man dancing, with five smaller outline men dancing behind him.

Rear pastedown: sketches of heads and buildings, a tiny dancing figure; names written upside down in Charlotte's longhand: 'Bromley Simpson Barlow'; inscription in Charlotte's minuscule script, also written upside down: 'Brussels – Saturday Morning/ Oct$^{br}$ 14$^{th}$ 1843, – First Class –/ I am very cold – there is no/ fire – I wish I were at home/ with Papa – Branwell. Emily/ Anne & Tabby – I am tired of/ being amongst foreigners it is/ a dreary life – especially as there/ is only one person in this house/ worthy of being liked – also another/ who seems a rosy sugarplum/ but I know her to be coloured/ chalk –'.

**Scott, Walter, *The Lay of the Last Minstrel, A Poem*, London: Longman, Hurst, Rees, & Orme; Edinburgh: A. Constable & Co., 1806 (BPM:bb54)**

Inscription in ink, facing introduction, in Patrick Brontë's longhand: 'P Brontë. B.A./ St. Johns. College,/ Cambridge –'

Page 270, left margin, in pencil: two faces in very childish style.

Rear pastedown, in Branwell's minuscule script, in pencil: four lines of poetry.

**Tocquot, Mr., *A New and Easy Guide to the Pronunciation and Spelling of the French Language*, London: printed for the author, 1806 (BPM:bb62).**

Leather front cover, upside down, in ink: two female heads and a half-length sketch of woman with right arm raised.

Inscribed inside front cover, on pastedown, in longhand: 'Charlotte Bronté Jan 17/ 1831'; in Charlotte's minuscule script: three lines of poetry.

Rear fly-leaf: names of Shakespearian characters.

Rear pastedown, in longhand, in pencil and ink: three pencil sketches of dancing figures; list of place names, some Latin, some fictitious such as 'Gondoline'.

CHRISTINE ALEXANDER

# *Appendix B*

## Note on the provenance of Brontë art works

A study of the provenance of the Brontë paintings and drawings reveals that the Brontës' commonplace productions have rarely been collected for their intrinsic artistic merit. Generally more accessible and less expensive than manuscripts, they have been acquired along with locks of hair and items of clothing as 'personal relics' of the enigmatic novelists.

It could be said that the collecting of 'Brontëana' began with the Reverend Patrick Brontë cutting the letters of his daughter Charlotte into strips in response to requests for samples of her handwriting. Visitors had begun to come to Haworth during Charlotte's own lifetime in the hope of catching a glimpse of the mysterious author 'Currer Bell'. Many more came to Haworth after Elizabeth Gaskell's bleak portrayal of the lives of the sisters, *The Life of Charlotte Brontë*, was published in 1857.

Photographs of the parsonage, Haworth Church and Patrick Brontë and other souvenirs were soon on sale in Haworth. But the collecting of Brontë manuscripts, drawings and personal effects did not begin in earnest until those who had a sentimental attachment to these items had died. A large collection of paintings and drawings was released by the death of the Brontës' servant Martha Brown in 1880. Haworth then began to prove a fruitful hunting ground for collectors in pursuit of original material. As those who had known the Brontë family passed away, villagers who had once jealously guarded their Brontë treasures were found willing to sell at the right price. There was no shortage of collectors willing to pay it.

The reason why so many Brontë paintings and drawings were available in Haworth at this time is not difficult to discern: the Brontës themselves had preserved the majority at their parsonage home. The paintings and drawings of Emily and Anne in particular had never been intended for a public audience; a few had been given as tokens 'of affection and respect'[1] to friends, acquaintances, teachers and family servants; the others they had kept. Though Charlotte was more serious than her sisters about a career as an artist, we do not know for certain that she ever sold a single painting. Like her sisters she gave away drawings as gifts but kept the majority.

The history of Branwell's work is rather different, as he had attempted a career as an artist and had a much wider social circle than his sisters; from their completion a large number of his works were in the hands of private clients, friends and acquaintances.

Charlotte Brontë outlived all of her siblings. Following the deaths, in rapid succession, of Branwell, Emily and Anne in 1848–9, she became their self-appointed executrix. (Technically, as Anne and Emily had died intestate, their estates would have passed to their father.) It is possible that she may have destroyed letters and manuscripts by Emily and Anne, as little of their early prose writing survives. Fortunately she seems not to have destroyed drawings as she even preserved unfinished sketches by Anne, for example 'Woodland with deer' (**352**).

On her death in 1855 at the age of 38 Charlotte's estate passed not to her father but to her husband of nine months, the Reverend Arthur Bell Nicholls. Nicholls stayed at Haworth Parsonage to help his ailing father-in-law. The former coolness between the two men gradually disappeared and by the terms of his will Patrick Brontë, who died in June 1861, left the bulk of his estate to his 'beloved and esteemed son in law'. Thus Nicholls found himself heir to an enormous collection of Brontëana, including a substantial number of paintings and drawings.

Nicholls gave away many of these with other items to the Brontës' faithful servant and housekeeper Martha Brown. Those items he chose not to keep for himself or to give away were offered to the public at the sale of the contents of the house on 1 and 2 October 1861.

Though the Brontës had by then achieved a degree of literary fame it seems that relic hunting had not yet begun on a large scale. One of the earliest American visitors to Haworth, Charles Hale, who made his pilgrimage three weeks after the sale had taken place, noted that it was 'considered a matter of no consequence, it was not widely advertised nor largely attended'.[2] Those who did attend were mainly locals more interested in getting a good bargain than in acquiring mementoes of the famous authors. As Nicholls had retained for himself or given to Martha Brown the bulk of the paintings and drawings by his wife and her sisters, none appear to have been included in the sale. However, as is evidenced elsewhere (see, for example, the history of the 'Gun Group' (**224**), Nicholls was less than fond of Branwell's work and it appears that some of Branwell's oil paintings and sketches may have been included in the sale (see **233** and **236**).

Shortly after the sale Nicholls left Haworth to return to his native Ireland, taking his substantial Brontë collection with him. Though he had expected to be offered the living of Haworth he had evidently made himself unpopular with the church trustees and the appointment was not offered to him. Nicholls settled at the home of his aunt, Harriet Bell (née Adamson), in King's County (now Offaly). He resigned his clerical orders and became a gentleman farmer. In 1864 he married again, taking as his second wife his cousin, Mary Anne Bell, who had met Charlotte Brontë when she visited Ireland on honeymoon.

Nicholls's collection of Brontë relics remained inaccessible to collectors for another thirty-five years. Apart from its location, the main factor which kept the collection beyond the reach of relic hunters was Nicholls's own dislike of them. Though his pride in his first wife's talents was evident from the decoration of his home, where the walls were adorned by pencil drawings and watercolours by Charlotte, Emily and Anne, Nicholls seemed to have had a deep-seated distaste for collectors of Brontëana.

This repugnance had been well known in Haworth. In the years after Charlotte's death Nicholls's reluctance to admit interested visitors to the parsonage had been legendary. Haworth villagers told how he had once turned away the daughters of Lord John Russell, with the retort that 'the house was not a picture gallery'.[3] According to some, he had even taken to Ireland the footstool, fixtures and furnishings used by his wife in the Brontë family pew in Haworth Church to prevent relic hunters appropriating them.[4]

As the Brontës' fame grew and the enthusiasm for collecting began to develop in the 1880s and 1890s, it was inevitable that Nicholls should eventually be tracked down by Brontëphiles and relic hunters. The Lancashire manufacturer and collector William Law (see **15**) was among those who applied to Nicholls in the hope of obtaining something: he managed to secure Patrick Brontë's copy of Bewick's *History of British Birds* but little more.[5]

In the 1890s Nicholls allowed journalists and Brontë scholars to visit him at his home and view the collection. J. Horsfall Turner visited in 1894[6] and in the following year the Brontë biographer Clement K. Shorter paid a call. He evidently came at the right time for he managed to obtain a packet of juvenilia, though he remarked that it was only 'with extreme unwillingness'[7] that Nicholls had consented to the publication of some of Charlotte's letters. Although it seems that Shorter was also given permission to take photographs of the Brontë paintings and drawings in Nicholls's collection, his wife insisted that they were not for sale – Nicholls obviously attached great sentimental value to them.[8]

Indeed it seems that most of the Brontë paintings and drawings Nicholls possessed remained in his collection until his own death in 1906, at the age of 88.

Shorter, who paid several visits to Nicholls, had evidently made a favourable impression. In 1907 Mary Anne Nicholls gave him Emily's drawing of the dog 'Grasper–from life' (**313**) and Charlotte's 'Study of a heartsease' (**84**). J. Horsfall Turner purchased a large collection of items from Mary Anne Nicholls, some of which he then sold to the Brontë Society, including a Charlotte Brontë watercolour of her sister Anne (**119**).[9] Other paintings and drawings from Nicholls's collection were given to his nieces, Frances E. Bell and Charlotte Brontë Nicholl [*sic*], to family friends such as Miss White (see **79**) and the Adamsons (see **61**). The executrix of the estate, Nicholls's cousin Violet Bolster (née Bell), kept some drawings for herself which she later sold to the Brontë Society and to American collectors including Henry Houston Bonnell from Philadelphia.

The remainder of the paintings and drawings were auctioned with other items from the collection by Sotheby, Wilkinson & Hodge on 26 July 1907. With the emergence of the Americans as serious buyers of literary artefacts, the collecting of Brontëana had become a competitive and lucrative business. The press noted that 'there was an interested crowd of buyers and onlookers' with the 'leading booksellers' all represented as well as 'many amateurs, British and American'.[10]

Most of the items acquired by booksellers at the sale were offered to collectors, including the two lots of drawings which were sold to Bonnell, who was quietly amassing the world's finest collection of Brontëana. Curiously, the drawings he acquired, catalogued at the sale as the work of Charlotte and Anne, included several pen-and-ink sketches by Branwell. Bonnell was no fan of Branwell's work[11] and it is interesting to speculate whether or not Nicholls, given his treatment of Branwell's oil paintings, knew the author of these unsigned portraits.

Among those described by the press as 'amateur' at the Nicholls sale were representatives of the fledgling Brontë Society. Sadly the Society was able to purchase very little. A report in the *Yorkshire Daily Observer*[12] noted that 'the limited funds at their disposal ruled them out of the later stages of a bidding which, in one instance, ran to three figures'. The Brontë Society had been founded in Bradford in 1893 by a group of Yorkshire Brontë enthusiasts who were alarmed at the rapid dispersal of so many Brontë items from Haworth to private collectors in Britain and America. Though at this time the Nicholls collection was shielded from collectors, an equally large proportion of drawings and other Brontëana was already being scattered following the death of the owner of the second largest collection of Brontëana, Martha Brown.

Martha Brown, second daughter of the Haworth sexton, John Brown, came to Haworth Parsonage in 1840, at the age of eleven. She remained the Brontë family's servant and later housekeeper until the death of Patrick Brontë in 1861. She had been given several drawings by the Brontës during their lifetimes as 'fond mementos',[13] and her collection was substantially augmented by the items given to her by Nicholls following the deaths of his first wife and father-in-law.

'Martha' had been identified as the Brontës' servant in Elizabeth Gaskell's *The Life of Charlotte Brontë* and she was pleased to talk to visitors to Haworth who were interested in her Brontë connection. The Bradford antiquarian and writer William Scruton called at her modest home in 1879 and was shown 'an old portfolio filled with the pencil drawings and water-colour sketches of Branwell and his three sisters'.[14] Scruton noted that Martha 'had had many opportunities of parting with her treasures'; but although she was happy to show her collection to visitors, she was reluctant to sell items which held such sentimental value, and few items left the collection during her lifetime.

Martha died in 1880 and left her effects, including the Brontë items, to be divided equally amongst her five sisters, Ann, Eliza, Tabitha, Mary and Hannah. This fact soon became common knowledge in Haworth and further afield. In a newspaper article on Martha, published after her death, Scruton divulged that the collection had 'been apportioned amongst her surviving relatives'.[15]

Thirty of the drawings and other items from Martha's collection were sold by her older sister, Ann Binns, when the contents of the Binns home were auctioned at Saltaire on 29 January 1886. There was a mixed reaction to the sale, and to the quality of the drawings, but 'there was no lack of bidders for these amateurish efforts among the large numbers of persons who attended the auction'.[16] Those who attended were mainly local people. Several of the wealthy industrialists of Bradford, proud of the Brontës' Yorkshire associations, were beginning to collect Brontë items. Interest in the Binns' collection led to an exhibition of items from the Saltaire sale at the Bradford Free Library Art Gallery in Darley Street in April 1886. Among those local people who owned one or more Brontë drawings were W. E. B. Priestley and Alfred Illingworth, both MPs, the bankers Alfred Harris and George Ackroyd, a Miss Brooksbank and the manufacturer R. H. Rudd, though it is not clear from which particular source they obtained their treasures. Many of these collectors lived in the city's wealthy Manningham district where Branwell had attempted to establish himself as a portrait painter.

Not all Yorkshire people, however, approved of the exhibitions and sales of Brontë relics: the most vehement reaction came from Charlotte's lifelong friend, Ellen Nussey. Miss Nussey wrote to her friend Emma Cortazzo in February 1886: 'I send the list cut from the paper of the Brontë relics [evidently the Binns sale] – it makes me feel sick.'[17] In March she wrote of the sale: 'My feelings are anything but pleasant on the subject – I can't bear the sight of the list [of relics] – How dreadfully shocked dear C. would be, could she see it – to me it is vulgar desecration and insult to everything that was precious in her –.'[18] Sadly Ann Binns, recently widowed, may have had no option but to sell her Brontë items. None of Martha Brown's sisters was particularly well off, a fact which accelerated the dispersal of her collection. Collectors who tracked down Martha's sisters found that they were prepared to part with items for a suitable price.

Among these collectors was the Lancashire leather manufacturer William Law, who had unsuccessfully petitioned Nicholls for relics. He bought several items from Martha's sister Tabitha Ratcliffe, and from the Haworth joiner William Wood, to add to an extensive collection of art and manuscripts at his home, Honresfeld, Littleborough, near Rochdale (see **15**, **38**, **235**, **309**, **317** and **323**).

J. Roy Coventry began collecting in the early 1900s and found that Martha Brown's sisters still had Brontë items to sell. He tracked down Martha's sister Tabitha Ratcliffe, still living in Haworth though then in her seventies, and Martha's niece, Mary Popplewell, then living in Ilkley, the daughter of Martha's sister Eliza. Coventry was a frequent visitor to Haworth and wrote regularly to Mrs Ratcliffe and Miss Popplewell in the hope of acquiring items for his collection: it seems that they were reluctant to sell off large batches of relics and Coventry bought drawings individually over a period of time (see, for example, **180**, **312**, **317**, **318**, **323**, **332** and **333**).

In 1889 Martha Brown's cousins Robinson and Francis Brown, the sons of John Brown's brother William, put on display a collection of Brontëana in a room above their refreshment rooms in Haworth's Main Street. During the 1880s they had been avidly collecting Brontë items. Though they later claimed that much of their collection had come to them first hand from their father William and their cousin Martha it would appear that they actually purchased most of it from other sources.

In May 1889 they had acquired a large number of Brontë paintings and drawings from a Keighley dealer, Alfred Gledhill, who had purchased many of the drawings at the Binns sale at Saltaire in 1886 (see **42**, **43**, **53** and **54** for example). A newspaper article on Gledhill's Brontë collection stated that he had 'formed the purpose of collecting all the relics on which he could possibly lay his hand'.[19] Gledhill had several generous offers for parts of his collection: it was reported in the *Yorkshire Weekly Post* that it was believed that 'a commissioner, acting for the Earl of Rosebery, endeavoured, but vainly, to secure ten of the choicest pictures';[20] but Gledhill hoped the Keighley Municipal Authorities would buy his collection intact. In January 1889, he exhibited the collection at one of the Keighley 'Conversaziones', held in association with the Mechanics' Institute, and soon after the collection went to the Brown brothers. The Browns had also bought a small collection of Brontëana from William Scruton and unspecified items from Ellen Nussey.

The Browns' Museum, though advertised as 'the largest that has ever been got together',[21] was not a commercial success and in 1892 the brothers removed to Blackpool, taking with them their collection of Brontëana, which included thirty Brontë paintings and drawings as well as shawls, samplers and household items used by the Brontës. The Brontë Society, founded in 1893, negotiated with the brothers Brown for the purchase of the collection, which they believed would be 'an admirable foundation for the proposed museum',[22] but felt the asking price of £500 was too high. However, the opening of the new Brontë Museum in a room above the Yorkshire Penny Bank at the top of Haworth Main Street in 1895 did encourage donations and loans from local people who were often keen that their Brontë items should stay in Yorkshire.

On 2 July 1898, the Browns' collection was sold at Sotheby's. The sale attracted some press derision and was poorly attended. The watercolour of Flossy (**327**) went for the relatively high price of £12, but some of the watercolours of flowers went for as little as 2 shillings each. Ten of the thirty drawings on offer were purchased by the Brontë Society; and Branwell's pencil copy of Hogarth's 'Idle Apprentices' (**191**) went to a private buyer. There were no bidders for the remaining paintings and drawings, and these, nineteen in total, were retained by the Brown family and remained hidden from public view for another half a century until they were purchased by the Brontë Society from Gladys Jane Brown, a daughter of Francis Brown, in 1950.

It may seem surprising that little mention has been made of Charlotte's lifelong friend Ellen Nussey, the recipient of so many of Charlotte's letters; but in comparison with Arthur Bell Nicholls and Martha Brown, Ellen had few Brontë drawings. However, Ellen did own one of Charlotte's watercolours of Anne, and a drawing that was donated to the Brontë Parsonage Museum in 1900 by the unscrupulous bookdealer Thomas James Wise.[23] Charlotte's pencil copy of 'The Italian Scene' (**41**), sold to the Brontë Society by Wise's associate, Herbert Gorfin, may also have originally been owned by Ellen Nussey.

We know that Ellen also had some unidentified 'pencil sketches' by Charlotte as these are mentioned in a letter from A. Wilkes, who had retained them for work on a book.[24] It is not known what happened to these. Several collectors, including William Law of Littleborough and James Miles, the Leeds bookseller, attended the sale of Ellen Nussey's effects, 18–19 May 1898, but they must have been disappointed to find few original Brontë items on offer. Several Brontë items of dubious authenticity can be traced back to this sale.

Given the story of their dispersal it may seem astonishing that so many paintings and drawings have returned to their original home at Haworth, where they are now preserved at the Brontë Parsonage Museum: there are comparatively few paintings and drawings in overseas collections or in private hands though the full total of the latter is unknown. The Society's acquisition of Haworth Parsonage in 1928 as a permanent home for its Brontë collection encouraged a wave of donations and bequests. The Brontë Society's collection was substantially augmented by the bequest, in 1927, of a large number of manuscripts and drawings formerly owned by Henry Houston Bonnell: Bonnell had died in 1926 and his wife sent in 1928 a large part of the collection in accordance with his wishes. It included thirty-two paintings and drawings, of which two were by Emily and twelve were by Anne: as examples of their work are so much scarcer than that of Charlotte or Branwell, these were especially welcome additions to the Museum. The remainder of Bonnell's collection was bequeathed to his wife and later became the Bonnell Collection of Brontë Manuscripts in the Pierpont Morgan Library, New York.

Over half of the Brontë Parsonage Museum's present collection of paintings and drawings had been acquired by the Brontë Society in its first twenty-five years, chiefly through purchases in the 1920s from Nicholls's nieces Frances E. Bell and Charlotte Brontë Nicholl and his executrix Violet Bolster. In the sixty-five years since the opening of the Brontë Parsonage Museum in the family's original home, paintings and drawings have continued to return, though in smaller numbers. The largest acquisition was in 1950 with the purchase of drawings and paintings from Gladys Jane Brown. Other items which had been kept in the families of those who had known the Brontës have also reappeared after over a hundred and fifty years, for example 'The Disconsolate' (**40**, see plate 1). Though this painting must have been given to Tabitha Aykroyd with a number of the Brontës' childhood watercolours, it was inherited by a different branch of the family and thus did not return with the other items, from Rose Emma Longbottom, great-granddaughter of Tabitha Aykroyd's sister Rose Bower, in 1906. Nothing was known of the existence of this watercolour, handed down through four generations of the same family, until its owner brought it to the Brontë Parsonage Museum for inspection, in 1991.

Though paintings and drawings which went to the United States in the early years of this century have tended to stay there, chiefly in the important collections of the New York Public Library, Princeton University Library and the Pierpont Morgan Library, some owners have preferred that their Brontë items return to their original home. This occurred recently when one of only four known portraits of Anne

Brontë, acquired by the owner's grandfather in the early years of this century, returned on loan to the Parsonage Museum. This tiny portrait of Anne hung on the walls of the family's home for three generations before it was brought to the attention of the Brontë Society. There is no doubt that there are other Brontë paintings and drawings in private ownership. Some are known from descriptions in old sale catalogues and other contemporary sources; still others wait to be rediscovered.

TRACEY MESSENGER

# *Notes*

1 See **157**, drawing given by Charlotte to the owner of the school she attended in Brussels, which is inscribed 'A token of affection and respect to/ Madame Heger from one of her pupils'.

2 Charles Hale, 'An American Visitor at Haworth, 1861', *Brontë Society Transactions* (1967), vol. 15, part 77, p. 132.

3 Thomas Ackroyd, 'A Day at Haworth: A Reminiscence', *Brontë Society Transactions* (1986), vol. 19, parts 1 & 2, p. 54.

4 Hale, 'An American Visitor at Haworth, 1861', p. 133.

5 William Law to J. Horsfall Turner, 11 September 1894 (BPM Stock Book no. 1, letter 1894).

6 'An Interview with Charlotte Brontë's husband', *The Yorkshire Post*, 12 September 1894.

7 Clement K. Shorter, preface to *Charlotte Brontë and Her Circle* (London: Hodder & Stoughton, 1896).

8 Kathleen Tillotson, 'Back to the Beginning of this Century', *Brontë Society Transactions* (1986), vol. 19, parts 1 & 2, p. 11.

9 J. Horsfall Turner to unnamed Brontë Society official, 6 April 1907 (BPM Stock Book no. 1, letter 6).

10 'The Brontë Sale', *Yorkshire Daily Observer*, 27 July 1907.

11 Henry Houston Bonnell to C. W. Hatfield, letter postmarked 25 April 1922, Bonnell–Hatfield correspondence, BPM: 'The one aggravating feature of Brontë collecting is the mass of worthless brass one is obliged to accumulate for the sake of association, under Branwell's name. I am one of the Americans referred to by Mr Birrell who "have no use" for that young man.'

12 'The Brontë Sale', *Yorkshire Daily Observer.*

13 See autograph note by Patrick Brontë in catalogue entry **9**, recording his gift of drawings to Martha Brown (BPM: BS179).

14 William Scruton, 'Martha Brown and the Brontës', *Yorkshireman Royal Summer Number*, 1882.

15 Ibid.

16 'The Sale of Brontë Relics at Saltaire', *Leeds Mercury*, 29 January 1886.

17 Ellen Nussey to Emma H. Cortazzo, 9 February 1886 (BPM: Cortazzo Collection).

18 Ibid., 4 March 1886 (BPM: Cortazzo Collection).

19 'The Brontë Relics', *Yorkshire Weekly Post* [1889].

20 Ibid.

21 Advertisement for Brown's [*sic*] Refreshment Rooms and Museum of Brontë Relics, Keighley Reference Library. Reproduced in W. R. Mitchell, *Hotfoot to Haworth: Pilgrims to the Brontë Shrine* (Seattle: Castleberg, 1992), facing p. 58.

22 Untitled newspaper cutting, *Bradford Daily Argus*, 15 January 1894.

23 See **89**, and Christine Alexander, *A Bibliography of the Manuscripts of Charlotte Brontë* (Haworth and New York: The Brontë Society in association with Meckler Publishing, 1982), p. xvi.

24 A. Wilkes to Ellen Nussey, 2 June 1882 (BPM Cadman Collection, XIV F5).

# *Bibliography*

A great many nineteenth-century newspapers, reviews, directories, catalogues and drawing manuals have been used in the course of this study; these are noted in full in the relevant essays and catalogue entries. The following list includes all other works consulted in this study.

## BOOKS

Abbey, J. R., *Life in England in Aquatint and Lithography, 1770–1860*, Folkestone and London: Dawsons of Pall Mall, 1972

Alexander, Christine, *A Bibliography of the Manuscripts of Charlotte Brontë*, Haworth and New York: The Brontë Society in association with Meckler Publishing, 1982

*The Early Writings of Charlotte Brontë*, Oxford: Basil Blackwell, 1983

(ed.), *An Edition of the Early Writings of Charlotte Brontë*, vol. 1: *The Glass Town Saga 1826–1832*, Oxford: Basil Blackwell for the Shakespeare Head Press, 1987; vol. 2: *The Rise of Angria 1833–1835: part 1 1833–1834, part 2 1834–1835*, Oxford: Basil Blackwell for the Shakespeare Head Press, 1991; vol. 3 forthcoming

Allom, Thomas, *The British Switzerland, Or, Picturesque Rambles in the English Lake District: Comprising a Series of Views of the Lake and Mountain Scenery in Westmorland, Cumberland, Lancashire, Durham, and Northumberland*, London and New York: The London Printing & Publishing Co., n.d.

*Westmorland, Cumberland, Durham and Northumberland. Illustrated From Original Drawings by Thomas Allom*, London: Fisher, 1832

*Picturesque Rambles in Westmorland, Cumberland, Durham and Northumberland: Illustrated From Drawings on the Spot by Thomas Allom*, London: Peter Jackson, Late Fisher, Son & Co, 1837

Allott, Miriam (ed.), *Charlotte Brontë: 'Jane Eyre' and 'Villette': a casebook*, London and Basingstoke: Macmillan, 1973

*The Artists' Colourmen's Story*, London: for Windsor & Newton, 1984

Balston, Thomas, *John Martin 1789–1854: His Life and Works*, London: Duckworth, 1947

Barrell, John (ed.), *Painting and the Politics of Culture: New Essays on British Art 1700–1850*, Oxford and New York: Oxford University Press, 1992

Beatie, W., *The Ports, Harbours, Watering Places and Coast Scenery of Great Britain*, London: G. Virtue, 1842

Beck, Hilary, *Victorian Engravings*, London: Victoria and Albert Museum, 1973

Bewick, Thomas, *A General History of Quadrupeds*, London: Longman, Hurst, Rees, Orme, & Brown, 1811

*A History of British Birds*, vol. 1: *Containing the History and Description of Land Birds*; vol. 2: *Containing the History and Description of Water Birds*, Newcastle: T. Bewick; London: Longman & Co., 1816

Boyle, Andrew, *An Index to the Annuals*, vol. 1: *The Authors (1820–1850)*, Worcester: Andrew Boyle Booksellers Ltd, 1967

Brontë, Anne, *Agnes Grey*, ed. Hilda Marsden and Robert Inglesfield, The Clarendon Edition, Oxford: Clarendon Press, 1988

*The Tenant of Wildfell Hall*, ed. Herbert Rosengarten, The Clarendon Edition, Oxford: Clarendon Press, 1992

Brontë, Charlotte, *Jane Eyre*, ed. Jane Jack and Margaret Smith, The Clarendon Edition, London: Clarendon Press, 1969

*Jane Eyre*, ed. Richard J. Dunn, Norton Critical Edition, 2nd edition, New York: W. W. Norton & Co., 1987

*Shirley*, ed. Herbert Rosengarten and Margaret Smith, The Clarendon Edition, Oxford and New York: Clarendon Press, 1979

*Villette*, ed. Herbert Rosengarten and Margaret Smith, The Clarendon Edition, Oxford and New York: Clarendon Press, 1984

*The Professor*, ed. Margaret Smith and Herbert Rosengarten, The Clarendon Edition, Oxford and New York: Clarendon Press, 1987

Brontë, Charlotte, Emily and Anne, *Poems by Currer, Ellis, and Acton Bell*, London: Aylott & Jones, 1846

Brontë, Emily, *Wuthering Heights*, ed. Hilda Marsden and Ian Jack, The Clarendon Edition, Oxford: Clarendon Press, 1976

Brontë, Patrick Branwell, transl., *The Odes of Quintus Horatius Flaccus*, Book I, ed. John Drinkwater, London: privately published, 1923

Brontë, The Rev. P., 'Kirkstall Abbey, A Fragment Of A Romantic Tale', *The Rural Minstrel: A Miscellany of Descriptive Poems*, Halifax: privately printed for the author, 1813

Butterfield, Mary and Duckett, R. J. (eds.), *Brother in the Shadow: Stories & Sketches by Patrick Branwell Brontë*, Bradford: Bradford Libraries and Information Service, 1988

Byron, George Gordon, Lord, *The Poetical Works of Lord Byron*, 8 vols., London: John Murray, 1839

Campbell, Colin, *Vitruvius Britannicus: or the British Architect, containing the plans, elevations, and sections of the regular buildings, both publick and private, in Great Britain, with variety of new designs*, London: The Author, 1745

Chadwick, Mrs Ellis H., *In the Footsteps of the Brontës*, London: Sir Isaac Pitman & Sons Ltd, 1914

Chapple, J.A.V. and Pollard, Arthur (eds.), *The Letters of Mrs Gaskell*, Manchester: Manchester University Press, 1966

Chitham, Edward (ed.), *The Poems of Anne Brontë: A New Text and Commentary*, London and Basingstoke: Macmillan, 1979

*A Life of Emily Brontë*, Oxford and New York: Basil Blackwell, 1987

*A Life of Anne Brontë*, Oxford and Cambridge, Massachusetts: Basil Blackwell, 1991

Chitham, Edward and Winnifrith, Tom, *Brontë Facts and Brontë Problems*, London and New Jersey: Macmillan, 1983

Darlow, T. H. (ed.), *William Robertson Nicoll: His Life and Letters*, London: Hodder & Stoughton, 1925

Denvir, Bernard, *The Early Nineteenth Century: Art, design and society, 1789–1852*, London and New York: Longman, 1984

Dugdale, Thomas and Burnett, William, *Curiosities of Great Britain. England and Wales Delineated, Historical, Entertaining & Commercial. Alphabetically arranged By Thomas Dugdale, Antiquarian, assisted by William Burnett, Civil Engineer*, London: J. Tallis, [c. late 1830s]

Du Maurier, Daphne, *The Infernal World of Branwell Brontë*, London: Gollancz, 1960

Dunthorne, Gordon, *Flower and Fruit Prints of the 18th and early 19th centuries*, London: The Holland Press, 1970

Ellis, Mrs, *The Daughters of England, Their Position In Society, Character and Responsibilities*, London: Fisher, 1845

Fawcett, Trevor, *The Rise of English Provincial Art: Artists, Patrons, and Institutions outside London 1800–1830*, Oxford: Clarendon Press, 1974

Faxon, Frederick W., *Literary Annuals and Gift Books: A Bibliography 1823–1903*, Middlesex: Private Libraries Association, 1973

Feaver, William, *The Art of John Martin*, Oxford: Clarendon Press, 1975

Finden, William and Edward, *Finden's Illustrations of the Life and Works of Lord Byron*, 3 vols., London: John Murray, 1833–4

*Finden's Landscape and Portrait Illustrations to the Life and Works of Lord Byron*, London: John Murray, 1834

*Finden's Byron Beauties: Or, The Principal Female Characters in Lord Byron's Poems. Engraved from Original Paintings under the superintendence of W. and E. Finden*, London: Charles Tilt, 1836

*Finden's Royal Gallery of British Art*, London: J. Hogarth, 1838–40

Finlay, Michael, *Western Writing Implements in the Age of the Quill Pen*, Wetheral, Carlisle: Plains Books, 1990.

Fraser, Rebecca, *Charlotte Brontë*, London: Methuen, 1988

Gaskell, E. C., *The Life of Charlotte Brontë*, 2 vols., London: Smith, Elder & Co., 1857; 3rd edition, 'revised and corrected', 1857

Gérin, Winifred, *Branwell Brontë: A Biography*, London: Hutchinson, 1961

*Charlotte Brontë: The Evolution of Genius*, Oxford: Clarendon Press, 1967

*Emily Brontë: A Biography*, Oxford: Clarendon Press, 1971

(ed.), *Five Novelettes*, London: The Folio Press, 1971

Gezari, Janet (ed.), *Emily Jane Brontë: The Complete Poems*, London: Penguin, 1992

Gilbert, W. S., *Catalogue of Engravings*, London: Frost & Reed, n.d. (becomes *The 'Homelovers' Book of Etchings, Engravings and Colour Prints*, 23rd edition, Bristol and London: Frost & Reed, [1938])

Gilpin, William, *An Essay Upon Prints*, London: J. Robson, 1768

*Remarks on Forest Scenery, and other Woodland Views, (Relative Chiefly to Picturesque Beauty)*, 2nd edition, 2 vols., London: R. Blamire, 1794

Grundy, F. H., *Pictures of the Past: Memories of Men I have met, and Places I have seen*, London: Griffith & Farran, 1879

Guillaud, Jacqueline and Maurice (eds.), *Caspar David Friedrich: Line and Transparency*, Paris: Centre Culturel du Marais, 1984

Hardie, Martin, *Water-colour Painting in Britain*, vol. 3: *The Victorian Period*, London: B. T. Batsford Ltd, 1968

Hardman, Malcolm, *Ruskin and Bradford*, Manchester: Manchester University Press, 1986

Hart-Davis, Rupert, *Hugh Walpole: A Biography*, London: Macmillan & Co. Ltd, 1952

Harvey, J. R., *Victorian Novelists and their Illustrators*, London: Sidgwick & Jackson, 1970

Hayter, Alethea, *Opium and the Romantic Imagination: Addiction and Creativity in De Quincey, Coleridge, Baudelaire and Others*, Wellingborough: Crucible, 1988

Herrmann, Luke, *Turner Prints: The Engraved Work of J. M. W. Turner*, Oxford: Phaidon, 1990

Hobhouse, John Cam, *A Journey through Albania and other provinces of Turkey in Europe and Asia, to Constantinople, during the years 1809 and 1810*, London: J. Cawthorn, 1813

Hone, William (ed.), *The Every-Day Book; Or, Everlasting Calendar of Popular Amusements*, London: for William Hone, 1826

Hugo, Thomas, *Bewick's Woodcuts: Impressions of Upwards of 2000 Wood-Blocks, Engraved, For the Most Part, by Thomas and John Bewick*, London: L. Reeve & Co., 1870

Hulme, F. Edward, *Art Instruction In England*, London: Longmans, Green & Co., 1882

Hunnisett, Basil, *An Illustrated Dictionary of British Steel Engravers*, London: Scolar Press, 1989

Hunt, Leigh, *Lord Byron and Some of His Contemporaries: With Recollections of the Author's life and of His Visit to Italy*, London: H. Colburn, 1828.

Jack, Ian, *English Literature 1815–1832*, Oxford: Clarendon Press, 1963

Krill, John, *English Artists Paper Renaissance to Regency*, London: Trefoil, 1987

Lemon, Charles, *A Centenary History of the Brontë Society 1893–1993*, Haworth: The Brontë Society, 1993

Leyland, Francis A., *The Brontë Family With Special Reference to Patrick Branwell Brontë*, 2 vols., London: Hurst & Blackett, 1886

Lock, John and Dixon, Canon W. T., *A Man of Sorrow: The Life, Letters and Times of the Rev. Patrick Brontë 1777–1861*, London: Thomas Nelson & Sons Ltd, 1965

Loudon, Mrs [Jane], *The Lady's Country Companion, Or How to Enjoy A Country Life Rationally*, London: Longman, Brown, Green & Longmans, 1845

Macdonald, Frederika, *The Secret of Charlotte Brontë, followed by some reminiscences of the real Monsieur and Madame Heger*, London: T. C. & E. C. Jack, 1914

Mangnall, Richmal, *Historical and Miscellaneous Questions, for the Use of Young People*, London: Longman, Hurst, Rees, Orme, & Brown; and Wakefield: John Hurst, 1813

Manwaring, Elizabeth Wheeler, *Italian Landscape in Eighteenth Century England*, London and New York: Oxford University Press, 1925

Martin, John, *The Paradise Lost Of Milton*, London: Septimus Prowett, 1827
*Illustrations Of The Bible*, London: published by John Martin, 1831–5

Mitchell, W. R., *Hotfoot to Haworth: Pilgrims to the Brontë Shrine*, Seattle: Castleberg, 1992

Montgomery, Robert, *The Sacred Annual: Being the Messiah, A Poem, In Six Books*, London: John Turrill, 1834

Moore, Thomas (ed.), *The Works of Lord Byron: With His Letters and Journals and His Life*, 14 vols., London: John Murray, 1832
*Letters and Journals of Lord Byron: With Notices of His Life*, 3rd edition, 3 vols., London: John Murray, 1833
*Life of Byron*, 2 vols., London: John Murray, 1839

More, Hannah, *Coelebs In Search of a Wife*, London: T. Cadell & W. Davies, 1808

*Strictures on the Modern System of Female Education, with a View of the Principles and Conduct Prevalent Among Women of Rank and Fortune*, New York: Evert Duyckinck, 1813

Neufeldt, Victor A. (ed.), *The Poems of Charlotte Brontë: A New Text and Commentary*, New York and London: Garland Publishing, Inc., 1985

(ed.), *The Poems of Patrick Branwell Brontë: A New Text and Commentary*, New York and London: Garland Publishing, Inc., 1990

Nunn, Pamela Gerrish, *Victorian Women Artists*, London: The Women's Press, 1987

Oliphant, Mrs [Margaret], *Annals of a Publishing House: William Blackwood and His Sons, Their Magazine and Friends*, 2 vols., Edinburgh and London: William Blackwood & Sons, 1897

Ormond, Richard, *National Portrait Gallery: Early Victorian Portraits*, 2 vols., London: Her Majesty's Stationary Office, 1973

Parker, Rozsika, *The Subversive Stitch: Embroidery and the Making of the Feminine*, London: The Women's Press, 1984

Ratchford, Fannie E., *The Brontës' Web of Childhood*, New York: Columbia University Press, 1941

(ed.), *Gondal's Queen: A Novel in Verse by Emily Jane Brontë*, Austin: University of Texas Press, 1955

Rawlinson, W. G., *Turner's Liber Studiorum: A Description and a Catalogue*, London and New York: Macmillan & Co., 1906

Ray, Gordon N., *The Illustrator and the Book in England from 1790–1914*, New York: Pierpont Morgan Library; London: Oxford University Press, 1976

Raymond, Ernest, *In the Steps of the Brontës*, London: Rich & Cowan, 1948

Roscoe, S., *Thomas Bewick*, Folkestone and London: Dawsons of Pall Mall, 1973

Rowse, A. L., *The English Past: Evocations of Persons and Places*, London: Macmillan & Co. Ltd, 1951

Ruskin, John, *Modern Painters*, Kent: George Allen, 1888

Schiff, Gert, *Johann Heinrich Füseli 1741–1825*, 2 vols., Zurich: Verlag Berichthaus, 1973

Scott, Walter, *The Lay of the Last Minstrel*, London: Longman, Hurst, Rees, & Orme; and Edinburgh: A. Constable & Co., 1806

Scott-James, Anne, Desmond, Ray and Wood, Frances, *The British Museum Book of Flowers*, London: British Museum Publications, 1989

Shanes, Eric, *Turner's Picturesque Views in England and Wales 1825–1838*, London: Chatto & Windus, 1979

Sherman, Clare Richter, with Holcombe, Adele M., *Women as Interpreters of the Visual Arts, 1820–1979*, Westport, Connecticut, and London: Greenwood Press, 1981

Shorter, Clement K., *Charlotte Brontë and Her Circle*, London: Hodder & Stoughton, 1896

(ed.), *The Complete Works of Emily Brontë*, 2 vols., London: Hodder & Stoughton, 1911

Stone, Reynolds, *Wood Engravings of Thomas Bewick*, London: Rupert Hart-Davis, 1953

Symington, J. Alex and Hatfield, C. W. (eds.), *Patrick Branwell Brontë: A Complete Transcript of the Leyland Manuscripts showing the Unpublished Portions from the Original Documents In the Collection of Col. Sir Edward Brotherton, Bart., LL.D.*, Leeds: privately printed, 1925

Thackeray, William Makepeace, *The Paris Sketch Book and Art Criticisms*, ed. George Saintsbury, London, New York and Toronto: Oxford University Press [1908]

Turner, J. Horsfall, *Haworth – Past and Present: A History of Haworth, Stanbury and Oxenhope*, Brighouse: J. S. Jowett, 1879

Verey, David, *The Diary of a Victorian Squire – Extracts from the Diaries and Letters of Dearman and Emily Birchall*, London: Alan Sutton, 1989

Warner, Marina, *Queen Victoria's Sketchbook*, London: Macmillan, 1979

Wees, Dustin J., and Campbell, Michael J., *Darkness Visible: The Prints of John Martin*, Williamtown, Massachusetts: Sterling and Francine Clark Art Institute, 1986

Westall, Richard and Martin, John, *Illustrations Of The Bible*, London: Edward Churton, 1835

*Illustrations Of The New Testament*, London: Edward Churton, 1836

Whitehead, Barbara, *Charlotte Brontë and her 'dearest Nell': The story of a friendship*, Otley: Smith Settle, 1993

Williams, Iolo, *Early English Watercolours*, Bath: Kingsmead Reprints, 1970

Winnifrith, Tom, *The Brontës and Their Background: Romance and Reality*, London: Macmillan, 1973

Wise, Thomas James and Symington, John Alexander (eds.), *The Brontës: Their Lives, Friendships and Correspondence*, The Shakespeare Head Brontë, 4 vols., Oxford: Basil Blackwell for the Shakespeare Head Press, 1932

(eds.), *The Miscellaneous and Unpublished Writings of Charlotte and Patrick Branwell Brontë*, The Shakespeare Head Brontë, 2 vols., Oxford: Basil Blackwell for the Shakespeare Head Press, 1936–8

Wood, Christopher, *Dictionary of Victorian Painters*, London: Antique Collectors' Club, 1971

Yeldham, Charlotte, *Women Artists in Nineteenth-Century France and England*, New York and London: Garland Publishing, 1984

## ANNUALS AND PERIODICALS

*Blackwood's Edinburgh Magazine*, Edinburgh: William Blackwood; London: T. Cadell, 1817–50

*Forget Me Not, a Christmas and New Year's Present*, London: R. Ackermann & Co., 1823–42

*Fraser's Magazine for Town and Country*, London: J. Fraser, 1830–1869

*Friendship's Offering, a Literary Album*, London: Lupton Relfe, 1824–6; Smith, Elder & Co., 1827–44

*Heath's Book of Beauty*, ed. L. E. L[andon] 1833; ed. The Countess of Blessington, London: Longman, Rees, Orme, Brown, Green, & Longman, 1834–49

*The Keepsake*, ed. Frederic Mansel Reynolds, London, 1828–44

*The Lady's Magazine; or Entertaining Companion for the Fair Sex, Appropriated Solely for their Use and Amusement*, London: G. Robinson, vol. 19, 1788

*The Literary Souvenir: or Cabinet of Poetry and Romance*, ed. Alaric Watts, London: Longman, Rees, Orme, Brown & Green, 1825–45

*Repository of Arts*, London: R. Ackermann & Co., 1809

## ARTICLES

Ackroyd, Thomas, 'A Day at Haworth: A Reminiscence', *Brontë Society Transactions* (1986), vol. 19, parts 1 & 2

Alexander, Christine, 'Art and Artists in Charlotte Brontë's Juvenilia', *Brontë Society Transactions* (1991), vol. 20, part 4

'"That Kingdom of Gloom": Charlotte Brontë, the Annuals, and the Gothic', *Nineteenth-Century Literature*, vol. 47, no. 4, March 1993

Annesley, Priscilla Countess, 'Charlotte Brontë', *The Queen, The Lady's Newspaper*, 15 November, 1913

Arnold, Helen H., 'The Reminiscences of Emma Huidekoper Cortazzo: A Friend of Ellen Nussey', *Brontë Society Transactions* (1958), vol. 13, part 68

Bacon, Alan, 'Jane Eyre's Paintings and Milton's *Paradise Lost*', *Notes and Queries*, vol. 31, March 1984

Barker, Juliet, 'A Possible Portrait of William Weightman', *Brontë Society Transactions* (1987), vol. 19, part 4

'The Brontë Portraits: A Mystery Solved', *Brontë Society Transactions* (1990), vol. 20, part 1

Bell, H. K., 'Charlotte Brontë's Husband: his later life and surroundings', *The Cornhill Magazine*, January 1927

Bentley, Phyllis, 'A Charlotte Brontë Sketch Book', *Brontë Society Transactions* (1948), vol. 11, part 58

Bermingham, Ann, 'The Origin of Painting and the Ends of Art: Wright of Derby's "Corinthian Maid"', in John Barrell (ed.), *Painting and the Politics of Culture: New Essays on British Art 1700–1850*, Oxford and New York: Oxford University Press, 1992

Butterfield, Mary, 'Wuthering Heights: A Brontë Illustration?', *Brontë Society Transactions* (1988), vol. 19, part 5

Charlier, Gustave, 'Brussels Life in *Villette*. A Visit to the Salon in 1842', *Brontë Society Transactions* (1978), vol. 12, part 65

Cook, Davidson, 'Brontë Manuscripts in The Law Collection', *The Bookman*, vol. 69, no. 410, November 1925

Cooper, Dorothy J., 'A French Thesis on Emily Brontë', *Brontë Society Transactions* (1954), vol. 12, part 64

Dewhirst, Ian, 'Drawing Master to the Brontës', *Yorkshire Ridings Magazine*, June 1968

Edgerley, C. Mabel, 'Emily Brontë: A National Portrait Vindicated', *Brontë Society Transactions* (1932), vol. 8, part 42

Flintoff, Everard (ed.), 'Some Unpublished Poems of Branwell Brontë', *Durham University Journal*, vol. 81, June 1989

Foister, Susan, 'The Brontë Portraits', *Brontë Society Transactions* (1985), vol. 18, part 95

Foley, T. P., 'John Elliot Cairnes' Visit to Haworth Parsonage', *Brontë Society Transactions* (1984), vol. 18, part 94

Friedman, Joan, 'Every Lady Her Own Drawing Master', *Apollo*, vol. 105, no. 182, new series, April 1977.

Hale, Charles, 'An American Visitor at Haworth, 1861', *Brontë Society Transactions* (1967), vol. 15, part 77

Hatfield, C. W., 'Catalogue of the Bonnell Collection in the Brontë Parsonage Museum', *Brontë Society Transactions* (1932), vol. 8, part 42; rpt. London: Wm Dawson & Sons, 1968

Higonnet, Anne, 'Secluded Vision: Images of Feminine Experience in Nineteenth-Century Europe', *Radical History Review*, vol. 38, 1987

Holgate, Ivy, 'A Pilgrim at Haworth – 1879', *Brontë Society Transactions* (1961), vol. 14, part 71

Irwin, Francina, 'Lady Amateurs and their Masters in Scott's Edinburgh', *The Connoisseur*, December 1974

Jack, Ian, 'Physiognomy, Phrenology and Characterisation in the Novels of Charlotte Brontë', *Brontë Society Transactions* (1970), vol. 15, part 80

Langford, Thomas, 'The Three Pictures in *Jane Eyre*', *The Victorian Newsletter*, no. 31, Spring 1967

Lee, P. F., 'Charlotte Brontë and the East Riding', *Brontë Society Transactions* (1896), vol. 1, part 4

Leslie, Marion, 'Mrs Gaskell's House and Its Memories', *The Woman at Home*, no. 45, June 1897

Longbottom, John, 'Bradford Literary Circle', *Yorkshire Notes and Queries*, vol. 1, no. 4, July 1904

Lonoff, Sue, 'Charlotte Brontë's Belgian Essays: The Discourse of Empowerment', *Victorian Studies*, vol. 32, no. 3, Spring 1989

Macdonald, Frederika, 'The Brontës at Brussels', *The Woman at Home*, vol. 2, no. 10, July 1894

Mackay, Angus M., 'The Brontës. Their Fascination and Genius', *The Bookman*, vol. 27, no. 157, October 1904

Monahan, Melodie (ed.), 'Ashworth: An Unfinished Novel by Charlotte Brontë', *Studies in Philology*, vol. 80, no. 4, Fall 1983

[Nicoll, William Robertson], 'Literature: The New Literary Anecdotes. 1. The Brontë Sisters', *The British Weekly: A Journal of Social and Christian Progress*, 5 November 1886

Nixon, Ingeborg, 'The Brontë Portraits: Some old problems and a new discovery', *Brontë Society Transactions* (1958), vol. 13, part 68

Nussey, Ellen, 'Reminiscences of Charlotte Brontë', *Scribner's Monthly*, New York: Scribner & Co., May 1871; rpt. *Brontë Society Transactions* (1899), vol. 2, part 10

Nussey, John, 'Blake Hall Gardens, Mirfield and John Hepworth – Last of "Six Clever Men"', *Old West Riding*, vol. 2, no. 2, Winter 1982

'Blake Hall, In Mirfield, and its Occupants During the 18th and 19th Centuries', *The Yorkshire Archaeological Journal*, vol. 55, 1983

'Recent Gifts and Other Additions to the Museum and Library', *Brontë Society Transactions* (1951) vol. 12, part 61

Senseman, Wilfred M., 'Charlotte Brontë's Use of Physiognomy and Phrenology', *Papers of the Michigan Academy of Science, Arts, and Letters*, vol. 38, 1953

Shorter, Clement K., 'Relics of Emily Brontë', *The Woman at Home*, no. 47, August 1897

Skirrow, Eunice, 'Upper Worth Valley Schools in the Nineteenth Century', *Brontë Society Transactions* (1991), vol. 20, part 3

Sloan, Kim, 'Drawing – A "Polite Recreation" in Eighteenth-Century England', in Harry C. Payne (ed.), *Studies in Eighteenth-Century Culture*, vol. 2, Madison: University of Wisconsin Press, 1982

Smith, George Charles Moore, 'The Brontës at Thornton', *The Bookman*, vol. 27, no. 157, October 1904

Smith, Margaret, 'The Letters of Charlotte Brontë: some new insights into her life and writing', *Conference Papers*, The Brontë Society and The Gaskell Society Joint Conference, 1990

Stedman, Jane W., 'Charlotte Brontë and Bewick's "British Birds"', *Brontë Society Transactions* (1966), vol. 15, part 76

Tillotson, Kathleen, 'Back to the Beginning of this Century', *Brontë Society Transactions* (1986), vol. 19, parts 1 & 2

Walford, L. B., 'The Home of Charlotte Brontë', *Longman's Magazine*, vol. 15, no. 87, January 1890

Weir, Edith, 'New Brontë Material Comes To Light', *Brontë Society Transactions* (1949), vol. 11, part 59

'The Hegers and a Yorkshire Family', *Brontë Society Transactions* (1963) vol. 14, part 73

[Whone, Clifford], 'Where the Brontës Borrowed Books: The Keighley Mechanics' Institute', *Brontë Society Transactions* (1950), vol. 11, part 60

Wilks, Brian, 'Schools and Schooling in the Life and Literature of the Brontë Family', *Brontë Society Transactions* (1985), vol. 18, part 95

Wood, Butler, 'Some Old Bradford Artists', *The Bradford Antiquary*, 1895

'Two Brussels Schoolfellows of Charlotte Brontë', *Brontë Society Transactions* (1913), vol. 5, part 23

Yates, W. W., 'Some Relics of the Brontës', *The New Review*, no. 59, April 1894

# *Acknowledgements of sources*

Thanks are due to the following organizations for permission to reproduce photographs accompanying catalogue entries as listed:

The British Library: **208**, **209**, **210**, **216**, **227**, **244**

The Brontë Parsonage Museum: all catalogue numbers not included in this list and not listed 'private owner'

Harry Ransom Humanities Research Center, The University of Texas at Austin: **158**, **296**, **297**, **298**, **299**

The Houghton Library, Harvard University: **108**, **186**, **187**, **306**, 'Frowning man' (Appendix A); Widener Collection, Harvard College Library: **153**

The Hugh Walpole Collection, The King's School, Canterbury: **320**

The Brotherton Collection, Leeds University Library: **203**, **206**, **211**, **212**, **213**, **214**, **215**, **226**, **228**, **229**, **240**, **280**, **281**, **285**, **288**, **289**, **291**, **292**, **293**, **294**, **295**, **301**, **302**, **303**

National Portrait Gallery, London: **224**, **225**

Henry W. and Albert A. Berg Collection, The New York Public Library Astor, Lenox and Tilden Foundations: **18**, **21**, **38**, **309**

Bonnell Collection, The Pierpont Morgan Library, New York: **25**, **27**, **135**, **161**, MA 2696, dubious 'Sketch of Mr Nicholls'

Robert H. Taylor Collection, Princeton University Libraries: **85**, **96**, **311**, **345**

*(Individual owners are listed in the relevant catalogue entries)*

Thanks are also due to the Bradford City Art Galleries and Museums for permission to reproduce their 'Self-Portrait' of John Bradley (plate 5), and to the Kirklees Cultural Services (Red House Museum) for permission to reproduce 'A night-eruption of Vesuvius' (plate 6).

# *Index of Drawings and Paintings*

In the index, titles in inverted commas represent those given by the Brontës. Titles not in inverted commas are descriptive titles given by the authors. Bold numbers in brackets indicate catalogue number, which is used for all cross-referencing in the text. Dubious items are listed but have no catalogue number.

Numbers in italics indicate pages with illustrations. As virtually all catalogue entries are illustrated, the illustrations within the catalogue section (pp. 153 to 421) are not separately indexed. Illustrations in books owned by the Brontës have not been indexed here (see Appendix A). Numbers in bold indicate page(s) of catalogue entry. Roman numerals refer to illustrations in the special plate section, which falls between pp. 151 and 152.

## Charlotte Brontë


Abercrombie (**160**), **262–3**

'Aldborough, Suffolk' (**135**), **242**

Alexander Percy (**105**), 46, 130, 216, **220–1**

'Alexander Soult' (**102**), 18, *19*, 130, **218–19**

'Amelia Walker' (**51**), 43, 180, **184**

'Anne Brontë' (**91**), 45, 137, 144, **210–11**

Anne Brontë (**134**), 5, 137, 186, **241–2**

'Annual Lavatera' (**61**), 43, **190**

'Arthur Adrian Marquis of Douro' 1 (**97**), 17, 130, **215**, 218, 226

'Arthur Adrian Marquis of Douro' 2 (**101**), 18, 19, 130, XXXVIII, 215, **217–18**

Arthur Wellesley (**114**), 130, 225, **226–7**
'Ashburnham Church On the Valley-Land' (**163**), 58, **264–5**
Atheist viewing the dead body of his Wife, The (**136**), 14, 21, 47, 130, XIII, **243–4**

'Bessy Bell and Mary Gray' (**39**), 15, IX, **176–7**, 178, 238
Bird's nest (**75**), *48*, 50, **199–200**
Blue convolvulus (**87**), 49, XIX, **207**
Bolton Abbey (**116**), 26, 52, **228–9**
'Boy and Dog' (**16**), 46, 111, **162**
Branch of a tree (**22a**), **166**
'Bridge near Wrottle', 58, **280–1**
Bridge of Egripo (**123**), 18, **233**
Bunch of wild flowers (**85**), 49, **206**

Castle on a hill (**59**), 50, **189**
Children with kitten and puppy, **272**
Church and trees, **278**
Classical head (**132**), 57, XLIV, **240**
'Cockermouth' (**90**), 45, XLVII, **209–10**
Conway Castle (**65**), 54, **194**
Copy of a portrait of Mrs Brontë (**36**), VII, **174–5**
Cormorant on rocky coast (**14**), **160–1**, 195, 203
'Cottage in lane near Mr Armstrong's', 58, **280**
'Cottage in Wallasley', 58, **279–80**
'Cottages opposite the Bank of Bolwell House', 58, **278–9**
'Cross of Rivaulx, The' (**137**), 16, **244–5**
Crying child (**54**), 28, 180, **186**

Derwentwater (**83**), 5, 54, **204–5**, 210
Diminutive sketches (**15**), **161–2**, 176
Disconsolate, The (**40**), 4, *15*, 15, 47, 112, **177–8**, 372–4, 441
Doodle: face (**153**), **257–8**
'Dulwich' (**13**), 40, **159–60**

Earliest map of Glass Town (**7**), 130, **156**
Easton House (**145**), 5, **251–2**
'English Lady' (**128**), 16, 56, 130, **237**

'Fancy Piece, A' (**19**), 46, 72, 157, **164**
Fisherman sheltering against a tree (**24**), **167**

'Geneva' (**125**), 16, 18, 54, **234–5**
'Geneva' vignette (**137a**), 5, **245**
Glass Town peasant woman (**8**), 6, 130, **157**, 161
'Good-bye': a comic sketch (**159**), 57, **261–2**
Greta Bridge (**63**), **192–3**
'Guwald Tower Haddington' (**57**), 43, **187–8**, 374

Hands in the margins of a text (**159a**), **262**
Hartlepool Harbour (**89**), 45, **208–9**, 210
Head and shoulders of a young woman (**52**), 138, 180, **184–5**
Head of Scottish soldier (**80**), 157, **202–3**
'Honble Miss Janet, The' (**99**), 130, **216**
Horseman and gamekeeper (**139**), 57, 191, **247–8**

'Italian Scene, The' (**41**), 4, 54, **178–9**, 440

Juvenile painting of a castle (**2**), **154**
Juvenile painting of a house (**1**), **154**
Juvenile painting of a lady walking (**5**), **155–6**
Juvenile painting of a rowing boat (**3**), **154–5**
Juvenile painting of a sailing ship (**4**), **155**
Juvenile painting of a sick-room (**6**), **156**

'Keep of the Bridge, The' (**21**), 130, **165**
'King of Angria, Duke of Zamorna' (**113**), 130, XXVIII, **225–6**
Kirkstall Abbey (**117**), 26, *52*, 52, 204, **229–30**
Kirkstall Abbey (**118**), 5, 204, **230**
Kirkstall Abbey amongst trees (**82**), 45, 47, XLVI, 160, 195, **203–4**

'Lady Jephia Bud' (**25**), 130, **167–8**
Lake and castle (**94**), 47, XXVI, **212**
Landscape of tower and river (**81**), 47, 157, **203**
Landscape with bridge and cross (**126**), 47, 178, **235**
Landscape with cottage (**140**), **248**
Landscape with fallen trees (**156**), 41, 117, 118–19, **259**, 387
Landscape with figure of a lady (**95**), 50, **213**
Landscape with trees, waterfall and figures, **272–3**
Laughing child (**53**), 28, 180, **185–6**
Learning to draw (**108**), **222**
Leigh Hunt, **275–6**
'Ludlow Castle Shropshire' (**64**), 44, **193–4**
'Lycidas' (**129**), XVI, 159, 199, **238**

Madonna and child (**133**), 57, XLV, **240–1**
Maid of Saragoza, The (**127**), 49, 56, 130, XXII, **236**

'Marianne', **277–8**
Mermaid fountain and urn (**58**), 50, **188–9**
Miniature of a lady (**146**), 50, **252–3**
Moonlit scene with rocks and water (**122**), **232**, 422
'Mountain Sparrow, The' (**26**), 23, I, **168–9**
'Mr Ph Wood' (**104**), 180, 216, **219–20**, 222
'Muccross Abbey, Lake of Kilarney' (**60**), **189–90**

Pale pink flowers (**32**), 3, 170, **172–3**
Palm squirrel (**74**), 22, 50, 159, **199**, 422
Pattern for a coin purse (**170**), 50, **267**
Pattern for a collar 1 (**164**), 50, **265**
Pattern for a collar 2 (**165**), 50, **265**
Pattern for a collar 3 (**166**), 50, **265–6**
Pattern for a collar 4 (**167**), 50, **266**
Pattern for a cuff (**168**), 50, **266–7**
Picturesque landscape with tower and cottage (**158**), **260–1**
Pink begonia (**86**), 49, XVIII, **206–7**
Pink roses (**30**), 131, 170, **171–2**
'[?P]orath from the Harbour' (**109**), **223**
Portrait of a child with hat and basket (**35**), XXVII, **174**
Portrait of a classical head (**55**), 180, **186**
'Portrait of A French Brunette' (**93**), 47, XXI, **211–12**
Portrait of a lady (**37**), 41, **175**
Portrait of a lady with wreath (**79**), **202**
Portrait of a man (Mr Brocklehurst?), **281**
Portrait of Anne Brontë (**92**), 49, 137, VIII, **211**, 231
'Portrait of Anne Brontë' (**119**), 49, 137, **230**
Portrait of a young lady (**111**), 45, XXXIX, **224–5**
Portrait of a young woman (**107**), 20, 180, **221–2**
Profile heads (**121**), **231–2**
Profile of a woman (**150**), 194, **255–6**
Profile of a woman, possibly Elizabeth Branwell (**120**), 6, 157, 161, **231**
Profile of face and nose (**48**), 180, **182–3**

Red grouse (**67**), 160, **195**, 203
'Remains of the Temple of Venus at Rome, The' (**144**), **251**
'Revenante Castle' (**20**), **164**
Revenue cutter (**124**), **233–4**
River scene with church and bridge (**66**), **194–5**
River scene with trees (**154**), 41, 117, **258**
Roc Head (**62**), 45, 113, 137, **191–2**
Roman head (**131**), 57, XLIII, **239**
Rough sketches of heads, dogs and Roman (**11**), 157, **158**, 166
Ruined tower (**9**), 37, 136, XXXV, 154, **157–8**
'ruins of [?Caractacus] Palace, The' (**18**), **163**

'Santa Maura' (**96**), 3, 16, 18, 54, **213–14**
'Scene on the Rhine' (**130**), 195, **239**, 242
'Sisters of Scio, The' (**110**), 5, 19, **223–4**
Sketch of a 'beautiful lady' (**115**), **227**
Sketch of a house (**143**), **250–1**
Sketch of emaciated woman (**106**), **221**
Sketch of Mr Nicholls, **281**
Sketches of a leaf and tiny face (**84a**), **205–6**
Sketches of boy's head, towers, figures and faces (**17**), 28, **162–3**
Sketches of Glass Town characters (**23**), 130, **166–7**
Sketches of heads (**141**), **249**, 250
Sketches of two women (**138a**), **246–7**
Sketches of woman in long gown (**12**), 157, **159**, 166
'St Martin's Parsonage, Birmingham' (**77**), 44, **200–1**
Stone cross on moorland (**161**), 57, **263**
Street scene with two women, **277**
Study of a blue flower (**88**), 49, **207**
Study of a head (**56**), 180, **187**
Study of a heartsease (**84**), 49, XVII, **205**
Study of a primrose (**33**), 48, XV, 170, **173**
Study of a primula (**34**), 24, 170, **173–4**
Study of a tree and cottage (**155**), 41, 117, XLVIII, 157, **258–9**
Study of a white rose (**29**), **170–1**
Study of bearded profiles (**50**), 180, **183**
Study of ears (**43**), **180–1**
Study of eyes (**42**), 43, XLI, **180**
Study of flowers 1 (**70**), **197**
Study of flowers 2 (**71**), **197**
Study of flowers 3 (**72**), 46, **198**
Study of fruit 1 (**68**), 180, **196**
Study of fruit 2 (**69**), 180, **196**
Study of lower face (**45**), 180, **181**
Study of mouth and nose (**47**), 180, **182**

Study of mouths (**46**), 180, **182**
Study of noses (**44**), XL, 180, **181**
Study of two profiles (**49**), XLII, 180, **183**
Stylized flowers and bird on silk (**73**), *48*, **198**
'Summer House on the lawn of Bolwell House, The' (**162**), 58, **263–4**, 279

'Temple of Shamrocks, The' (**22**), **165**
Thatched cottage (**10**), 37, 136, XXXVI, 154, 157, **158**, 159
Tiger lilies (**31**), 3, 170, **172**
Tiny demure face (**88a**), 207, **208**
Tiny dog (**76**), 50, 199, **200**
Tomb with ornamental urn (**152**), **257**
Two male portraits and buildings (**98**), 130, LVII, **215–16**, 220
Two patterns for cuffs (**169**), 50, **267**
Two tiny sketches of heads (**27**), **169–70**

Unfinished portrait of a boy (**151**), 46, **256**

Wallpaper pattern of flowers (**171**), 50, **268**
Wallpaper pattern of green sprigs with red flowers (**173**), 50, **268–9**
Wallpaper pattern of leaves and cherries (**172**), 50, **268**
'Warwick Castle', **276**
Watermill (**157**), **260**, 261
Wellington monument (**41a**), 6, 130, **179–80**
Welsh peasants (**138**), 5, **245–6**
'Wild Roses From Nature' (**28**), 49, XIV, **170**, 171, 176
William Weightman (**149**), 44, XLIX, **254–5**
Woman in a blue dress with red shawl (**148**), **254**
Woman in a turban, **273–4**
Woman in leopard fur (**147**), 47, XXV, 169, **253–4**
Woman with a rose, **274–5**
Woman with a scarf, **275**
Woman with a veil (**78**), **201–2**
Woman with lyre (**38**), 161, **175–6**

Young military man (**112**), **225**
Young woman at a table (**142**), **249–50**
Young woman with 'Fairy Legend' (**103**), 20, **219**, 222

'Zenobia Marchioness Ellrington' (**100**), 18, 130, XXXVII, **216–17**

## Branwell Brontë

adoration of the shepherds, The (**236**), **318–19**
'After Bewick' (**190**), 5, **290**
'Alexander Percy Esq-re M.P. Ætat 21.' (**270**), 88, 130, **338–9**
'Alexander. Percy. Esq[R] M.P.' (**298**), 18, 93, 130, **357**
'Angel and Joshua at the Siege of Jericho, The' (**199**), 5, **294**
'Augustus Caesar' (**292**), 92, 95, **353–4**

'Bandy Castle' (**177**), 60, 68, 130, **285**
'Battell of W[a]shington' (**174**), 13, 60, 68, 130, **284**
Battle scene (**176**), 60, 68, 130, **284–5**
'Bendigo "taking a sight"./ "Alas! poor Caunt!"' (**285**), 92, 94, **347–8**
Brontë sisters, The (**225**), 65, 67, 73–6, 137, XXIV, 306, 308, **310–12**, 339
'Broughton Church' (**266**), 85, **336**

Caricature of a lawyer or clergyman facing a goose (**249**), **326–7**
'Cast – cast down but not castaway, A' (**286**), 5, 92, 94, **348–9**
Castle (**178**), 60, 68, 130, **285**
Copy of William Hogarth's 'Idle Apprentices' (**191**), 5, **291**, 440

Decorative colophon and figure of 'Justice' (**193**), **292**
Detailed sketch of tall building and bridge over river (**221**), **305**
'Duncan' (**269**), 88, **338**

Emily Jane Brontë and the 'Gun Group' (**224**), 65, 67, 73–6, 137, XXIII, **307–10**, 434

'Fallen' (**293**), 92, 95, **354**
Farmyard scene with dog and chickens (**181**), 69, **286–7**
Figure of 'Justice' (**196**), **293**
Figure of 'Justice' (**206**), **298**
Figure of 'Justice' (**210**), **300**
Figure of 'Justice' (**211**), **300–1**
Figure of 'Justice' (**212**), **301**
Figure of 'Justice' (**213**), **301**
Figure of 'Justice' (**214**), **302**
Figure of 'Justice' (**215**), **302**

Figure of 'Justice' (**217**), **303**
Figure of 'Justice' (**227**), **313**
Figure studies (**283**), 90, **346–7**

'Gos Hawk' (**218**), 69, II, **303–4**
Gravestone in a hilly landscape (**300**), **359**
'Grimshaw, H.' (**271**), 75, 88, **339**
Grotesque figures and buildings (**197**), 72, 157, **293–4**
Grotesque figures and soldiers (**198**), 160, 203, **294**

Head and shoulders of a young man (**263**), **334**
Head of a man (**246**), **325**
'Henry Foster of Denholme' (**262**), **334**
'Henry Scott' (**272**), 88, **340**
'Hermit' (**200**), 70, XI, 159, 199, **295**
Horse with rider (**231**), **314–15**

'I implore for rest' (**297**), 93, **356–7**
Isaac Kirby (**257**), 84, XXXI, **331–2**

Jacob's dream (**235**), 19, 21, 80, *81*, 81, LIX, **317–18**
James Fletcher (**253**), **328–9**
'Johannes Murgatroides' (**279**), 88, **343–4**
John Barraclough (c. 1773–1835) (**232**), **315–16**
John Brown (1804–1855) (**243**), XXIX, **323**

Kitchen interior with figures (**234**), **317–18**

Landscape with cottage, river and bridge (**238**), 86, **320**
Landscape with figures (**264**), 86, **335**
Lincolnshire link boy, The (**237**), **319–20**
'Lonely Shepherd, The' (**265**), 82, **335–6**
'Lydia Gisborne.' (**290**), **352**

Man at the gallows (**295**), 92, 95, **355**
Map of Glass Town Federation (**209**), 13, 130, **299–300**
Map of North and South America (**175**), 60, 68, 130, **284**
Map or architectural sketch (**229**), **313–14**
Maria Ingham (**256**), **330–1**
Masonic Apron (**247**), **325–6**, 333
'Mentor' (**208**), **299**
Miss Margaret Hartley (**254**), 84, XXX, **329–30**
'Mon and Wamon' (**187**), 130, **289–90**
Moorland buildings (**220**), 72, **304–5**
Mrs Isaac Kirby (**258**), 84, XXXII, **332**

'Myself.' (**289**), 92, 94, **351–2**
'Northangerland./ Alexander Percy Esq.' (**240**), 130, **321–2**

Old Hall, Thorp Green, The (**282**), 90, 147, LX, **346**
'old Maid's Squeamish Cat, an' (**294**), 92, 95, **354**
'Our Lady of greif.' (**288**), 92, 94, **350–1**

'Paradise/ Purgatory' (**291**), 92, 94, **352–3**
'Parody, A' (**304**), 92, 93, *95*, 95, **362–3**
'Patrick Reid "turned off", without his cap. 1848' and 'The rescue of the punchbowl. a scene in the Talbot.' (**303**), 92, 93, 94, **361–2**
Pencil sketches of figures (**179**), 60, 68, **286**
'Penmaenmawr' (**284**), 5, **347**
pirate, The (**241**), 18, 71, 130, LXII, **322**
'Pobre!' (**301**), 93, **359**
Portrait of a man (**274**), **341**
Portrait of a man holding aloft a wineglass (**273**), 89, LVII, **340**
Portrait of John Feather (**252**), 5, **328**
Portrait of Mr M– (**261**), 5, **333–4**
Portrait of Rev. Henry Heap (**255**), 5, 83, **330**
Portrait of Rev. William Morgan (**259**), 5, 83, **332**
Profile of a man (**228**), **313**

'Queen Esther' (**207**), 20, 70, XII, 159, 199, **298**

'results of Sorrow, The' (**296**), 92–3, **355–6**
'Resurgam' (**281**), 22, **345**
Ruined building (**188**), 37, 60, 136, 154, 157, **290**, 406
Ruined tower (**184**), 37, 136, XXXIV, 154, 157, **288**
Ruined tower, faces and female figure (**185**),157, **288–9**
Rural scene with two figures, cottage and castle (**192**), 5, 69, **291**

Sailing ship (**203**), **296–7**
Seascape (**189**), 157, **290**
Self-portrait (**267**), 27, *88*, 88, **336–7**
Self-portrait and figure of a man looking out to sea (**299**), 93, **358–9**
Shipwreck (**233**), 5, **316**
Sketch of a dog (**194**), **292**
Sketch of a dog's head (**204**), **297**
Sketch of a man with a distorted face (**205**), **297**

Sketch of a map (**248**), **326**
Sketch of a warrior with a sword (**195**), **292–3**
Sketch of two boxers (**276**), 88, **342**
Sketches of a boxer and male heads (**280**), **344–5**
Sketches of buildings (**216**), **302–3**
Sketches of buildings, mythical creature, trumpeter and fort (**230**), **314**
Sketches of human limbs (**242**), **322–3**
Sketches of male profiles (**244**), **324**
Sketches of three heads (**245**), **324**
sleeping cat, A (**180**), 69, 109, **286**
Staffordshire bull terrier dog, A, **366**
Stag's head, **367**
Studies of heads and faces with two kneeling figures (**223**), **306–7**, 312
'Study' (**201**), 70, 159, 199, **295–6**
Sunset over seashore (**226**), **312–13**

'T. Purser' (**268**), **337–8**
'Terror' (**202**), 28, 70, X, 159, 199, **296**
'Thomas Parker' (**250**), **327–8**
Three figures seated beside rocks and foliage (**222**), 75, **305–6**
Three late drawings (**302**), 80, 92, 93, 94, **360–1**
Tiny sketch of a church and profile (**277**), **342–3**
Tiny sketch of a fort 1 (**182**), **287**
Tiny sketch of a fort 2 (**183**), **287–8**
Tiny sketch of kairail fish (**186**), **289**
Two figures, heron and rabbit, **366–7**
Two male portraits and self-portrait (**278**), 88, **343**
Two male profiles (**275**), **341**
Two views of Morley Hall (**287**), 5, 92, **349–50**

View of a building (**219**), 72, **304**

William Brown (1807–1876) (**251**), **328**
William Thomas (**260**), 82, 326, **333**

'Zamorna. 35.' (**239**), 18, 71, 130, LXI, **320–1**, 322, 341

## Emily Brontë

Dancing stick figure (**320a**), 103, **381–2**
Diary paper sketch of Anne and Emily (**316**), 103, 106, 115, LIV, **377–8**
Diary paper sketch of Emily with her animals (**331**), 6, *104*, 104, 107, 110 n.25, 130, **391–2**
Diary paper thumb-nail sketches (**322**), 6, 104, 110 n.25, 115, **383**

farmer's wife, The (**307**), 108, 110, **371**
Flossy (**327**), 3, 121, 146, IV, **388–9**, 390, 440
'Forget me not' (**309**), 4, 15, 112, LV, **372–3**, 393

Geometric figures (**317**), 40, 102, 115, **378–9**
Girl and dog (**331a**), 6, 110 n.25, 111, **393**
'Grasper – from life' (**313**), 102, 113, 121–2, V, **375–6**
Guwald Tower, Haddington (**311**), 43, 113, LVI, 188, **374–5**

Images of cruelty (**320**), 103, 112, **380–1**

Keeper, Flossy and Tiger (**329**), 5, 102, 110 n.25, 121, 146, 388, **390–1**
'Keeper – from life' (**319**), 102, 115, 121–3, III, **380**, 388, 390

Mullioned window (**305**), 108, **370**

Nero (**324**), 115, 121, 127, VI, 191, **384–5**, 388, 390
'North Wind, The' (**325**), 6, 20, 29, 110 n.25, *114*, 114, 116–17, **385–7**

Ring ouzel (**308**), 102, 108, 110, **371–2**
Roe Head (**310**), 6, 110 n.25, 113, **373–4**

Sketch of two cows 1 (**314**), 114, **376–7**
Sketch of two cows 2 (**315**), 114, **377**
Sketches of buildings (**318**), 115, **379–80**
Sketches of heads, animals and buildings (**330**), **391**
St Simeon Stylites (**312**), 113, **375**
Study of a fir tree (**326**), 41, *116*, 116–21, 131, 259, **387**

Unfinished sketches of Flossy (**328**), 122, **389–90**

'Whinchat, The' (**306**), 108, 110, **370–1**
Winged serpent sketches (**321**) 7, 103, **382–3**
Woman's head with tiara (**323**), 29, 106, 114, 115, LIII, **384**

## Anne Brontë

'bit of Lady Julet's hair done by Anne, A' (**336**), 106, 137, **397–8**

Church surrounded by trees (**332**), 136, XXXIII, **396**
Cottage with trees (**333**), 136, **396**

'Elm Tree, An' (**338**), 16, 138–9, **399**

Head and shoulders of a young woman (**340**), 138, 141, 185, **400**
Head of a sleeping child (**349**), 141, **405–6**
Hen in a basket (**364**), 141, **414**

Landscape with castle, bridge and female figure (**344**), 140, **402–3**
Landscape with castles (**343**), 140, **402**
Landscape with cattle and haycart (**346**), 140, 202, **404**
Landscape with trees (**368**), *139* 139, 143, **416–17**
Landscape with trees and lake (**341**), 141, **400–1**
Little Ouseburn Church (**358**), 147, **411**

Magpie standing on a rock (**334**), 136, 157, **396–7**
Man with a dog before a villa (**345**), 140, LII, **403**

'Oak Tree' (**337**), 16, 138, **398**

Portrait of a child's head (**348**), 141, **405**
Portrait of a child's head, looking upwards (**347**), 141, **404**
Portrait of a girl with a dog (**354**), 146, 147, **408–9**, 398
Portrait of a little girl with a posy (**366**), 146, XX, **415–16**
Portrait of a young woman (**359**), 144, **411–12**
Portrait of a young woman in blue (**357**), 144, **410–11**, 416
Profile of a female head (**351**), **407**

'Roe Head, Mirfield' (**339**), 45, 137, **399–400**
Ruined building in a wooded landscape (**363**), 141, 145, **414**
ruined church, A (**342**), 140, **401**

Study of a tree with figure of a man (**367**), 16, 139, **416**

Three juvenile sketches (**335**), 136, **397**

Unfinished Flossy 1 (**355**), 147, **409**, 410
Unfinished Flossy 2 (**356**), 147, **409–10**
Unfinished landscape with plants and flowers, **420**
Unfinished landscape with river, trees and deer (**360**), 141, 145, **412–13**
Unfinished sketch of a house (**365**), 141, **415**
Unfinished sketch of a landscape with cottages and figures, **421**
Unfinished study of roses (**361**), 141, 145, **413**
Unfinished view of a building (**362**), 141, 145, **413**

'What you please' (**353**), 142, 146, LI, **407–8**
Windmill and buildings in a rocky landscape, **420–1**
Woman gazing at a sunrise over a seascape (**350**), 135, 141, L, 194, 290, **406**, 407
Woodland with deer (**352**), *141*, 141, **407**, 412, 433

# *Index of names and subjects*

Numbers in italics indicate pages with illustrations. As virtually all catalogue entries are illustrated, the illustrations within the catalogue section (pages 153–421) are not separately indexed, except for portraits.

accomplishments, 49–52, 59, 114, 189, 198
Ackermann & Co., 14, 43, 138, 169, 237
*Ackermann's New Drawing Book of Light and Shadow, in Imitation of Indian Ink*, 40, 45, 159
Ackroyd *see* Aykroyd
Adamson, Alan Joseph, 190
Adamson, Harriet Lucinda *see* Bell, Harriet
Adamson, Julia Turriff, 190
Adamson family, 179, 190, 435
'Adventure in Ireland, An' (CB), 161
Allbutt, Dr George, 200
Allbutt, Rev. Thomas, 193, 200
Allom, Thomas, 45, 55, 83, 204, 208, 209–10
Alston, J. W., 46
Allston, Washington, *81*, 318
Anderson, John Wilson, 83, 87
Anderson, William, 410
Andrews, James, 49
'Anecdotes of the Duke of Wellington' (CB), 166, 179
Angria *see* Glass Town and Angria
'Angrian Welcome, The' (BB), 313
Annesley, Priscilla Countess, 390

Annuals, 14–16, 43, 54, 78, 106, 108, 109, 119, 146–7, 373
*Forget Me Not*, 15, 20, 54, 70, 112, 176, 177, 178, 179, 298, 373
*Friendship's Offering*, 15, 54, 174
*Literary Souvenir, The*, 15, *19*, 54, *81*, 219, 224, 228, 318
*Sacred Annual, The*, 14–15, 21–2, *21*, 27, 243
works illustrated in, 20, 21–2, *21*, *81*, 174, 219, 228, 274, 288
Armitage, Joseph and Florence, 188, 323, 405
art
as accomplishment, 10–11, 41, 49, 50, 51–2, 402
attribution of works to Brontës, 2, 3–4
and copying, 11, 14, 38–41
Brontës' education in, 1
Brontës' knowledge of, 10–11
education in, 29, 38, 39–41, 42–6, 79, 80
influence on Brontës, 9–35
picturesque in, 15–16
*see also* Brontë, Anne; Brontë, Branwell; Brontë, Charlotte; Brontë, Emily; drawing manuals
artists
admired by Brontës, 11–12, 24
amateur female, 10, 36, 39, 41, 46, 141, 222
professional, 10, 41
professional in the provinces, 79–80
'Ashworth' (CB), 257–8
Atkinson, Rev. and Mrs Thomas, 401
Atkinson, Rev. Christopher, 400
Audubon, John James, 54
Austin, William, 261
Aykroyd, George, 160, 167, 437
Aykroyd, Rose, 177
Aykroyd, Tabitha, 159, 176, 177, 199, 273, 441

Bainton, Charles, 316
Barker, Juliet, 255, 309, 310
Barraclough, John, 315, *315*
Barrans, Mrs E. J., 170, 176
Bassompierre, Albert de, 387
Bassompierre, Louise de, 118, 387
Bartolommeo della Porta, Fra, 12, 24
'Battell Book' (BB), 68, 284–6
Bell, Frances E., 194–5, 239, 255, 406, 435, 441
Bell, Harriet, 434
Bell, Mary Anne *see* Nicholls, Mary Anne
*Bell's Life in London*, 348
Bennet, E. T., 199
Bentley, Joseph Clayton, 83
Bentley, Phyllis, 274, 275
Bewick, Thomas, 15, 22, 54, 199, 361, 414
copying of his works by Brontës, 20, 22, 23, 50, 69–70, 107, 108, 110, 125,136, 160–1, 167, 169, 195, 199, 286, 287, 288, 291, 304, 345, 358, 371, 372, 385, 388, 396, 397, 435
*General History of Quadrupeds, A* , 199
*History of British Birds, A*, 22, 38–9, 108, 110, 125, 136, 286, 287, 288, 291, 345, 358, 371, 372, 385, 388, 396, 397, 435
influence on Brontës, 20, 22, 95, 107, 110, 125, 199, 286, 287, 345, 427
Bewick, William, 26
Bible, illustrations of scenes from, 21–2
*Bibliotheca Classica; Or, A Classical Dictionary* (Lemprière), 353
Biddell, Sidney, 191, 247, 272, 309, 372, 384
Binns, Ann (née Brown), 168, 180, 183, 184, 185, 186, 187, 188, 251, 259, 272, 366, 388, 437, 438, 439
Binns, Benjamin, 121, 168, 180, 183, 184, 186, 272, 291, 388
Binns, Ellen, 173, 323
Binns, J. Brown, 323
Binns, John, 426
Binns, Joseph, 188, 223, 231, 232, 245–6
Binns, Mrs, 223
Blackman, George, 48
*Blackwood's Edinburgh Magazine*, 12, 13, 15, 54, 68, 103, 108, 117, 238
'Blackwood's Young Men's Magazine' *see* 'Young Men's Magazine'
Blake Hall (Mirfield), 135
Blessington, Countess of, 217, 219, 220
Bolster, Violet M. (née Bell), 164, 168, 281, 435–6, 441
Bonnell, Helen Safford, 168, 170, 242, 263, 281, 441
Bonnell, Henry Houston, 134, 168, 290, 294, 436, 441

Bonnell Collection, 154, 155, 156, 164, 165, 166, 168, 170, 191, 206, 212, 227, 234, 236, 237, 239, 242, 243, 247, 253, 254, 262, 263, 281, 290, 293, 294, 297, 305, 320, 322, 324, 325, 326, 336, 338, 339, 340, 341, 359, 372, 374, 381, 384, 398, 400, 401, 404, 405, 406, 407, 408, 411, 416, 436, 441

*Book of Beauty, The* (Heath), 219

books

availability of, 14–15, 54

Brontë sketches in, 2, 13, 16, 38, 67, 70, 71, 91, 103, 112, 422–31

owned by Brontës, 13, 16–17, 20, 77, 398, 399, 422–31

used by Brontës, 16–18

*see also* Annuals; drawing manuals

Boswell, James, 54

Bower, Jonas, 177

Bower, Rose, 159, 199, 441

Bower, Thomas, 177

Bradley, John, 22–4, *23*, 40, 108, 166, 168–9, 173

Bradley, John Thomas, 23–4, 25, 168–9

Bradley, T. W, 173

Branwell, Aunt Elizabeth, 89, 101, 136, 157, 174, 376, 392

portraits of, 231, *231*, 251

Branwell, Mrs C. B., 347, 352

Brigg, Dr John Jeremy, 277

Brigg, Sir John, 277

'Brontë', (BB), 275

Brontë, Anne, 134–50, 396–421

*Agnes Grey*, 51, 134, 144–5, 311

animals, drawings of, 397, 408, 409, 410, 414

art education, 3, 24, 26, 28, 108, 137–9, 144, 185, 399

art works by, 2, 290, 396–421

assessment of own work, 102, 137, 144

attitude to art, 11, 66, 134

at Blake Hall, Mirfield (Ingham family), 135

character, 65, 66, 135–6, 137, 148

copying art, 14, 22, 68, 70, 108, 135, 136, 137, 138, 141, 142, 143, 144, 147, 245, 396, 397, 402, 404, 405, 406, 407, 408, 411, 416, 417

death, 252, 433

destruction of works, 433

diary papers, 103–5, 136–7, 144, 377–8, 380, 389, 392, 398

drawing from nature, 10, 41, 135, 144, 145, 412, 417

dubious attributions, 420–1

early drawings, 10, 109, 134, 135, 136–7, 396–9

early writings, 1, 103, 105, 106, 128, 136, 398, 433

education, 135, 136

and Emily, 136, 378, 383, 398

figures and faces, drawings of, 141–3, 400, 404–6, 407, 408

gifts of drawings, 144, 146, 415, 416, 433

heads, studies of, 28–9

health, 37

illustrations and writing made for, 37–8, 154, 155, 156, 157, 158, 159, 288, 290

imagination, drawing from, 142–3, 406

influences on, 9, 14–24

intestacy, 433

landscapes, 16, 139, *139*, 140, 141, *141*, 143, 147, 401–4, 406, 407, 409, 412, 414, 415

media, style and technique, 135, 141, 400, 405, 407, 410, 420, 421

mementoes of, 265, 266, 267, 268, 405

pets, 50, 376, 388, 390, 392, 409, 410

portraits by, 141, 144, 146–7, 185, 408, 409, 410, 411, 412, 415

portraits of, 45, 73, 74, 101, 103, 137, 210–11, *210*, *211*, 230, *230*, 241, *241*, 307–12, *307*, *310*, 316, *316*, 378, *378*, 410, 442

at Roe Head, 17, 24, 28, 45, 109, 135, 137–9, 185, 192, 374, 399–400, 401, 402, 403, 404, 405, 406

at Scarborough, 104, 142, 383, 408

self-portraits, supposed, 142, 143, 144

and siblings, 136

sketches in books, 423, 427

symbolism, use of, 142, 143, 146

talent, 134,148

as a teacher, 11, 102, 104, 134, 135, 137, 142–3, 144, 148; *see also* at Thorp Green

*Tenant of Wildfell Hall, The*, 29, 49, 134, 135, 139–40, 142, 143–4, 145, 146, 148

at Thorp Green, 89, 104, 135, 139, 142–3, 144–7, 388, 392, 408, 409, 410, 411, 412, 413, 415, 416, 417
trees as favourite subject, 16, 138–9, *139*, 396, 398–9, 408, 416–17
visual/literary connections, 28–9, 134, 140
watercolours, 135, 416
Brontë, Branwell, 1, 37, 65–100, 275, 284–367, 428
anatomy not studied, 80, 83, 85, 329
animal pictures, 286–7, 289, 292, 297, 303–4
apron, painted, 316, 325–6, *325*
architectural pictures, 285, 287–8, 290, 291, 293–4, 298, 302–3, 304–5, 314, 349
architecture, interest in, 13, 23, 72, 77, 216, 288, 314, 423
art education, 3, 23–4, 26, 52, 69, 71–2, 73, 76–7, 78, 79, 80, 83, 84, 85, 108, 211, 315, 318, 319, 320, 335
art works by, 2, 67, 203, 216, 220, 221, 225, 226, 227, 284–367, 370
assessment of his art, 65, 66
battles, interest in, 13, 67, 68, 70, 284–6, 424, 425
battle scenes, 284–5, 294, 296
biblical scenes, 298, 317–19
biographies of, 37, 84, 87, 330, 332, 333, 337, 351, 355, 360
books owned by, 13, 20
boxing, interest in, 88, 94, 342, 344–5, 347–8, 360, 363
in Bradford, 26, 82–5, 318, 323, 329–30, 331–2, 333, 437–8
career in art, 1, 9, 24, 26, 66–7, 70, 71–2, 73, 78, 79–80, 82–5, 86, 95, 330, 331
caricatures, 326, 343, 349, 350, 352, 354, 360, 361, 362, 363
character and behaviour, 27, 78, 82, 83, 84, 85, 87–8, 89, 90, 92, 330, 346, 351, 352, 353, 354, 359, 361, 362
copying art, 13, 14, 15, 20, 21, 22, 69–70, 80–1, *81*, 108, 176, 287, 290, 295, 304, 314, 315, 317, 318, 319, 320, 335, 358
correspondence of, 78, 80, 91, 92–4, 348, 349, 350–1, 352, 353–4, 355, 357, 359, 360, 361, 362, 363
death, 91, 102, 359, 363
decadence and drunkenness, images of, 20, 92–5, 316–17, 334, 346–7, 353, 360, 361–2
deterioration, 91–4, 351–2, 353, 356, 358, 361, 362, 363
disposal of works, 434, 436
drawing from nature, 10, 68, 109, 286, 314, 317, 336
drawings, 88–9, 90, 92–6
drawings for sisters, 136, 373
drawing skills, 68–9, 83, 84
drug and alcohol addiction, 65, 66, 78, 87–8, 90, 91–4, 311, 339, 347, 358–9
dubious attributions, 366–7
early drawings, 10, 68, 70, 71, 108, 160
early writings, 1, 9–10, 12–13, 16, 18, 68, 71, 77, 86, 108, 128, 163, 168, 284, 285, 286, 287, 289–90, 292, 293, 297, 298, 299–300, 301, 302, 305, 312, 313, 314, 316, 322, 323, 324, 325, 326, 337, 339, 340, 341–5, 346, 359, 381
education, 72
employment, 72
engravings owned by, 12
exploration, interest in, 13
and family, 65, 88, 89, 92, 95, 327
figures and faces, 286, 292–3, 294, 295–6, 297, 298, 300–3, 306–12, 313, 314, 315, 319, 320–5, 329, 330, 334, 338–41, 343, 344–5, 346–9, 353–4, 355–6, 357, 358, 360, 361
and Freemasonry, 78, 82, 316, 325, 326, 333
friends, 83, 84, 87–8, 322, 323, 330, 333, 334, 337, 338, 339, 340, 345, 348, 349, 350, 351, 352–3, 354, 356, 359, 360, 361, 362
at Halifax, 75, 86–7, 337
Hastings, as Captain Henry, 13
history, knowledge of, 13
illustrations of Glass Town, 21, 299–300, *299*, 303, 314
illustrations of Glass Town characters, 289–90, 320, *320*, 321–2, *321*, *322*, 337, 338–9, *338*, 357, *357*
imagery, 20, 348, 349, 351–2
influences on, 9, 13, 14–24, 324, 336, 343
knowledge of art, 13, 24, 68
landscapes, 86, 91, 288, 320, 335–6, 347, 349, 352, 359

landscapes, picturesque, 288, 336
last drawings, 20, 92–5, *95*
in Leeds, 26
London, presumed visit to, 76–7, 314, 318
at Luddenden Foot, 87–9, 338, 341–5, 348, 383, 392
Manchester, visits to, 337–8
map drawing, 13, 284, 299–300, 314, 326
materials, technique and style, 69, 70–1, 84, 221, 307, 311, 315, 328, 332, 334, 346, 381
as Northangerland, 337, 355, 356–7, 358, 360
oil paintings by, 3, 5, 74, 80–1, 82, 86, 307–12, 314, 315, 318, 319, 320, 327–36
oils, use of, 23, 26–7, 70, 74, 221, 315, 318
pen and ink work, 70, 71, 90, 91
poetry, 67, 82, 84, 87, 90–1, 92, 93, 275, 292, 293, 323, 324, 325, 326, 327, 341, 342, 345, 350, 351, 352, 355, 356, 357, 358, 359, 361
portraits by, 26, 75, 79, 80, 82–5, 88–9, 91, 137, 221, 307–12, 315–16, 323, 326, 327–34, 338–41, 343–4, 433
portraits of sisters, 65, 66, 73, 74–6, 307–12
railways, working for, 86–9, 330, 337–8, 339, 340, 341–5
reading, 348, 353
reattributions, 256, 277, 278, 326, 363
and Royal Academy of Arts, 26, 76–8, 85, 323
sale of paintings, 82, 434, 436
seascapes, 290, 312
self-portraits, 73, 75–6, *88*, 92–3, 94, 307–10, *307*, 311, 325, *325*, 336–7, *337*, 343, *343*, 348, 349, *349*, 350, 351–2, *351*, 354, *354*, 355–6, *356*, 357, *357*, 358, *358*, 361, *361*
signed work, 70, 327, 328, 336, 346, 366
sketches in books, 2, 13, 67, 70, 71, 91, 112, 422–31 *passim*
soldiers, drawings of, 203
Soult, as Alexander, 18, 163, 167, 219, 292, 293–4, 295, 297, 316
subjects favoured, 13
talent in art, 2, 66, 68, 69, 78
talent in writing, 2, 66, 67
technique, 320, 328, 329, 331, 334, 351
at Thorp Green and after, 65, 89–91, 93, 94, 146, 147, 346, 350, 351, 352, 353, 354, 355, 356, 358, 392, 411
toy soldiers given to, 68, 105, 157, 300
translation of Horace, 67, 85
as tutor to Postlethwaite children, 84–5, 336
visits Hartley Coleridge, 85
visits Pearson family at Ovenden Cross, 92–3
visual/literary connections, 10, 29, 68, 71, 296, 299–300, 316–17, 337, 340, 341, 355, 356–7, 358, 360
watercolours by, 69
Wiggins, as Patrick Benjamin, 27
Brontë, Charlotte, 36–64, 134, 154–281, 318, 358, 402
and Anne, 134, 135–6
animal pictures, 160, 162, 168–9, 198–200
art, aspirations of career in, 11, 27, 37, 41, 49, 51–2, 58, 59, 66, 231, 433
art, knowledge of, 11–12
art critiques in early writings, 15–16
art education, 3, 23–4, 26, 28, 37, 39, 40, 42–4, 45–6, 49, 51–2, 57, 58–9, 108, 158, 165, 166, 170, 173, 174, 180–3, 184, 185, 187, 192, 193, 194, 195, 196, 197, 198, 246
artists admired by, 11–12, 24
art materials used, 44–9, 159, 166, 169
art modifies biography, 1, 37–8
artworks by, 2, 6, 154–281, 289, 298, 363, 373, 376, 400
assessment of own talent, 36, 37, 57, 58, 102
attitude to art, 11, 37–8
biography, 42, 65, 66, 75, 117, 135, 137, 261, 346, 380, 432
and Branwell, 65, 86–7
in Brussels, 57, 89, 256, 258–62, 263, 279, 392, 431
character, 37, 41, 114, 118, 262, 330, 346
copying art, 14–15, *15*, 16, 18, 22, 23, 37, 38–41, 43, 45, 46, 50, 54, 56, 57, 59, 68, 70, 106, 108, 112, 125, 158, 159–61, 163, 165, 174, 176–7, 178, 179, 180, 181, 182, 185, 186, 190, 193, 194, 197, 198, 199, 204–5,

207, 208–10, 212, 214, 219, 220, 223, 227, 228, 229, 230, 232, 233, 234, 235, 236, 237, 238, 239, 240, 241, 242, 243–4, 245, 246, 248, 251, 258, 265, 274, 321, 373, 386, 400, 404, 405, 406
correspondence, 259, 263, 264, 279, 330, 331, 349, 389, 432, 435, 440
at Cowan Bridge School, 50
as Currer Bell, 193, 194, 358, 432
drawing from nature, 10, 38, 41, 49, 57, 59, 109, 117, 118, 119, 165, 170, 171, 172, 173, 174, 184, 192, 241, 248, 258, 259, 264, 387
dubious attributions, 272–81
early illustrations, 10, 38, 108, 154–68
early writings, 1, 9–10, 12, 16, 24, 27, 38, 53, 68, 108, 128, 154, 155, 156, 157, 166, 167, 168, 169, 213, 215–18, 227, 233, 245, 254, 257, 262, 273, 274, 289, 322
exhibits drawings, 1, 25–6, 36, 52, *52*, 228–30
faces, features and figures, 158, 162, 166–7, 169–70, 174–7, 180–7, 201–3, 208, 213, 215–17, 230–2, 236–7, 239–42, 245–8, 249–50, 252–6, 262
'fancy pieces', 162, 164, 222, 246
flower and fruit illustrations, 44, 46, *48*, 49, 51, 109, 170–5, 190, 196–8, 205–7, 221
friends and pupils, 1, 43, 54, 55, 194, 213, 228, 247–8, 303, 373, 400; *see also* Nussey, Ellen; Taylor, Mary
genre scenes, 162, 164, 222, 242
gifts of pictures, 4, 193, 201, 209, 210, 230, 247–8, 250, 260, 277, 385, 433
gothic in her art, 179, 259, 260
as governess, 57, 257
illustration of Glass Town characters, 18, *19*, 166, 218, 219, 236, 243–4, 273
influences on, 9, 11–12, 14–24, 161, 217, 233
*Jane Eyre*, 22, 36, 38–9, 56, 58, 59, 106, 161, 257, 281, 345, 358, 377
knowledge of art, 11–12, 24, 74
landscapes, 46–7, *52*, 72, 154, 155, 158, 160, 163, 164, 165, 179, 191, 193–5, 201, 203–5, 208–10, 212–14, 223, 228–30, 232–5, 239, 242, 244–5, 248, 250–2, 256, 257, 258–61, 263–5
landscapes, picturesque, 15–16, 38, 54–5, 58, 118–19, 179, 187–8, 189–90, 192, 194, 209–10, 228, 229, 260–1
media and methods, 46–7, 48–9, 52–3, 169, 171, 193, 195, 196, 203, 204, 211, 212, 216, 226, 229, 232, 234, 236, 242, 243, 246, 253–4, 255, 256, 261, 266, 277
mementoes of, 173, 187, 194–5, 211, 223, 228, 229, 239, 255, 256, 265–6, 316, 333, 366, 385, 388, 406, 435
music education, 210
needlecase by, *48*, 50, 199–200, 253
needlework patterns and pieces, *48*, 50, 189, 199, 252, 253, 265–7
paintbox, 38, 47–8, *48*
painting on silk, 50, 198
portraits by, 18–20, *19*, 44, 45, 46, 47, 49, 50, 56, 137, 174–5, 184, 185, 210–12, 215–27, 230–1, 236–7, 239–42, 246, 248, 252–6
portraits of, 65, 66, 73, 74, 307–12, *307*, *310*
*Professor, The*, 58, 59
publisher, relations with, 36, 65
reading, 53–4, 234, 236
and 'reading' faces, 18, 27–8
reattributions, 269, 349, 375, 388, 391, 409, 410
Roe Head, pupil at, 17, 24, 26, 28, 40, 41–4, 45, 51, 109, 136, 173, 180–7, 190, 191–2, 193, 194, 195, 196, 197, 198, 200, 248, 263, 267, 276, 374, 404, 405, 406
Roe Head, return from, 51, 53, 113, 192, 213, 238
Roe Head, returns to teach at, 56, 137, 184, 192, 239, 241, 247–8, 250, 373, 400, 428
Roe Head Journal, 241
school, plans for, 115, 383
sewing by, *48*, 50, 53
*Shirley*, 16, 25, 41, 59, 123, 380
sketches in books, 38, 112, 422–32 *passim*
sources of drawings, 54
subjects favoured, 40, 43, 106
teaching sisters, 54, 72, 113, 192
technique, 169, 171, 173, 175, 177, 178, 211, 212, 219, 221, 222, 232, 235, 238, 241, 246, 248, 259, 276, 278, 377, 387
trees as a subject, 118, 120, 166, 167, 250–9, 264, 387

at Upperwood House, 383
*Villette*, 11, 39, 58–9, 387
visual/literary connections, 1–2, 10, 15–16, 18, 28–9, 55–6, 58–9, 66, 215–18, 236, 243–4, 245, 246–7, 262
wallpaper patterns, 268–9
watercolours, 44, 45–7, 49, 172, 173, 178
word-painting, 56
writing, aspirations of career in, 58
*see also Blackwood's Young Men's Magazine*; Gaskell, Elizabeth; Glass Town; Glass Town characters; Nussey, Ellen; Zamorna
Brontë, Elizabeth, 9, 101
Brontë, Emily, 100–33, 177, 370–93
animals, attitude to, 100, 124–8, 376, 380, 385, 388
animals, pictures of, 370–1, 372
and Anne, 136, 378, 383
architectural pictures, 370, 379–80
art education, 3, 23–4, 26, 57, 101, 108, 109, 110, 113, 114, 115–16, 117–18
art, knowledge of, 111
art works by, 2, 3, 100, 102, 106, 107, 109, 110–11, 114, 127–8, 161, 191, 192, 264, 370–93
assessment of own work, 102
attitude to art, 24
in Brussels, 24, 41, 57, 89, 101, 115–16, 123, 385, 386–7, 392
character, 78, 100, 101, 102, 105, 111, 114, 115–16, 117, 118, 120, 121, 122–3, 375, 380
collaboration with Anne, 377–8
copying, 11, 14, 15, 22, 43, 68, 70, 100, 107, 108, 109, 110, 112, 113, 114, *114*, 117, 125, 176, 178, 371, 372, 373, 374, 375, 379, 385, 386, 388
correspondence, 372, 376
at Cowan Bridge, 101
death, 102, 380
destruction of manuscripts of, 102, 433
diary papers, 53, 69, 100, 101, 103–5, 106, 115, 136–7, 377–8, 380, 383, 385, 389, 390, 391–2, 398
dubious attributions, 373
early drawings, 10, 108, 109, 110, 112–13, 370–2
early writings, 102, 103, 105–6, 108, 128, 378, 381, 433
education, 101, 117
figures, 372–3, 375
geometrical drawing by, 40, 100, 115, 378–9
gifts of drawings, 111, 116, 387, 393, 433
'Gondal Poems' Notebook, 382
imagery, 116–17, 119, 120
influences on, 9, 14–24
knowledge of art, 24, 74
landscapes, 371, 374, 387
materials and techniques, 122, 259, 373, 376, 377, 381, 384, 387, 388, 389
mementoes of, 316, 319
at Miss Patchett's school, Law Hill, 101, 102, 115, 122–3
musical ability, 116
nature, attitude to, 3, 66, 100, 122–8
nature, drawing from, 10, 41, 57, 109, 113, 114, 116, *116*, 117–18, 119, 373, 377, 380, 385, 387
pets, illustrations of, 5, 66, 100, 101, 102, 104, *104*, 113, 115, 121–4, 128, 146, 205, 373, 375–6, 380, 384–5, 387, 388–92, 408
poetry, 100, 103, 106–7, 109, 115, 116, 117, 124, 377, 381–2, 385, 387
portraits by, 20, 101, 103, 384, 386
portraits of, 65, 66, 73, 74, 75, 76, 307–12, *307*, *310*, 339
reading, 108, 116, 125, 128, 380
'reading' of faces, 28, 29, 107, 126–7
reattributions, 322, 326, 393
at Roe Head, 17, 26, 101, 109, 114–15, 137, 373, 374, 377
and romanticism, 116–17, 119–20
school, plans for, 115, 383
self-portraits, 101, 103, *104*, 378, *378*, 383, *383*, 392, *392*
signatures, 370, 373, 374, 376
sketches in books, 103, 112
subjects favoured, 100, 103, 105, 106, 113, 114, 115, 116
talent in art, 101, 107, 109, 112, 114, 118, 119, 121
trees as a subject, 116, *116*, 117, 118, 119, 120, 121, 127, 387
visual/literary connections, 1–2, 10, 29, 66, 103, 107, 112, 377, 382–3, 385, 386, 387
watercolours, 5, 100, 107

writing, 102, 105, 128
*Wuthering Heights*, 20, 29, 73, 103, 107, 108, 109–10, 111–12, 116, 119, 120, 123, 124–5, 126–7, 134, 311, 317, 370, 381, 386
Bronte, Hugh, 426
Brontë, Maria (Mrs), 9, 136, 174–5, *175*, 204
Brontë, Maria, 9, 101
Brontë, Rev. Patrick, 10, 66, 76, 82, 204, 230, 288, 290, 331, 376, 385, 396, 433
authentification of Brontëana, 191, 192, 224, 235, 240, 241, 257, 259, 260
books owned, 2, 16, 22, 171, 199, 236, 287, 422–31
and Brontëana, 102, 118, 157, 180, 184, 210, 220, 257, 307, 310, 314, 316, 376, 384, 388, 391, 433
and children, 2, 10, 66, 68, 72, 330
engravings owned, 11, 12, 21
interest in education, 82
mementoes of, 215, 220, 259, 333
poetry, 194, 204
portraits of, 23, 175, 315
sale of property of, 229–30, 314, 318, 319, 335, 389, 434
Bronte, Walsh, 426
Brontëana, collecting, 432–3, 434–6, 438, 439
Brontë Parsonage Museum, 134, 316, 317
Brontë Society, 277, 291, 346, 347, 435, 436, 439–42
Brooke, Anna Maria (later Allbutt), 200
Brooke, J., 44
Brooksbank, Miss, 207, 380, 437
Brotherton, Lord, 297, 298, 300, 301, 302, 312, 314, 321, 322, 345, 348, 349, 350, 351, 353, 359, 360, 361, 362
Brown, Eliza, 436, 438; *see also* Popplewell, Eliza
Brown, Francis, 185, 186, 328, 389; *see also* Brown, Robinson and Francis
Brown, Gladys Jane, 180, 181, 182, 184, 186, 196, 220, 221, 281, 328, 389, 440, 441
Brown, Hannah, 175, 189, 191, 334, 423, 437; *see also* Hartley, Hannah
Brown, John, 94, 95, 171, 321, 322, 323, *323*, 324, 352, 353, 354, *354*, 362, 438
Brown, Martha, 111, 121, 134, 157, 168, 171, 173, 175, 183, 188, 189, 190, 191, 194, 201, 220, 255, 259, 278, 291, 316, 323, 334, 372, 378, 384, 396, 406, 432, 436
and Brontëana, 173, 180, 184, 185, 186, 187, 188, 189, 191, 199, 201, 203, 251, 256, 259, 291, 308, 309, 319, 366, 372, 375, 384, 388, 433–4, 436–7
Brown, Mary, 201, 437
Brown, Tabitha *see* Ratcliffe, Tabitha
Brown, Robinson, 184, 215
Brown, Robinson and Francis, 171, 180, 214, 220, 221, 234, 281, 291, 388, 397, 438–40
Brown, William, 323, 328, *328*, 438, 439
Brown collection, 157, 158, 170, 172, 180, 182, 184, 185, 186, 187, 196, 197, 198, 210, 220, 221, 233, 278, 328, 372, 388, 389, 391, 432, 436–7, 438, 439–40
Brown family, 168, 272, 316
and Brontëana, 134, 164, 203, 210, 258, 316
Brussels *see* Brontë, Charlotte; Brontë, Emily; Heger, Constantin Romain; Pensionnat Heger
Bryson, J. N., 240
Bunyan, John, 16
Burgess, Eleanor, 173
Burns, Robert, 16
Butterfield, Mary, 362, 363, 370
Byron, George Gordon, Lord, 53
*Byron Gallery*, 17
*Childe Harold's Pilgrimage*, 18–20, *19*, 116, 214, 235, 236, 261, 387
*Don Juan*, 224
engravings of works of, 14, 16–17, 18–19, *19*, 214, 234–5, 236, 237, 245, 386
heroes in works by, 18, *19*
influence of, 14, 17, 261
influence on Brontës, 14, 16, 17–20, 108, 116, 214, 224, 233, 234, 275, 348, 357, 386
Moore's *Life of Byron*, 16, 20, 54, 114, 116, 214, 233, 234, 235, 236, 386
portraits of, 18–19, 218
women related to, 17, 18, 19–20, 55–6, 117, 386, 387

'Caged Bird, The' (EB), 385
Cairnes, John Elliot, 75, 391
Campbell, Michael, 243

Campbell, Thomas, 16, 53
'Caractacus. A Dramatic Poem' (BB), 297
Caris, Miss, 373
Carmichael, J. W., 26
'Caroline Vernon' (CB), 254
Carracci, Annibale, 12
Carter, Rev. Edward Nicholl, 192
Carter, Susan (née Wooler), *42*, 45, 57, 192, 194, 373, 400, 401
Caunt, Benjamin, 94, 347–8
Chadwick, Mrs Ellis H., 86, 312, 323, 353, 393
Chantry, Sir Francis Legatt, 78
*Characters of Trees* (William De la Motte), 70, 398, 399, 416, 424–5
Charnwood, Lady, 349
'Chat, Le' (EB), 126
*Childe Harold's Pilgrimage* (Byron), 18–20, *19*, 116, 214, 235, 236, 261, 387
Chitham, Edward, 142, 143, 144, 382, 408, 410, 412
Christian, Mildred, 173, 193
'Churchyard A Poemn, The' (CB), 169
Cignani, Carlo, 12
Clairmont, Claire, 17
Clayton, A. B., 243
Clennell, Luke, 161
Cole, Sir Henry, 39
Coleridge, Hartley, 85
Coleridge, Samuel Taylor, 108
'Collection of Poems by Young Soult the Ryhmer [*sic*], A' (BB), 163
'Come hither child – who gifted thee' (EB), 381
*Confessions of an English Opium Eater* (De Quincey), 91
*Connoisseur, The*, 19
Conté, Nicolas Jacques, 44, 193
Corbould, H., 112, 177, 373
Correggio, Antonio, 12
Cortazzo, Emma Huidekoper, 291, 376, 377, 388, 438
Cousen, Joseph, John and Charles, 83
Coventry, J. Roy, 375, 378, 379, 384, 396, 438
Cowan Bridge School, 50, 101
Cox, David, 44, 45, 108
Craven, Felicity, 386
Crosland, Betty, 201
Cubbon, Fanny Edith, 328
Cunliffe, Walter R., 385, 386
Cuvier, Baron Georges de, 28, 162–3
Cuyp, Aelbert, 377

D'anno, Olivio, 25, *25*
Darton, William, 13, 77, 80, 314, 423–4
*Daughters of England, Their Position in Society, Character and Responsibilities* (Mrs Ellis), 10, 11
Da Vinci, Leonardo, 12, 24
Deardon, William, 24, 87
'Death of a Christian' (CB), 194
De la Motte, William, 70
Delta (David Macbeth Moir), 177
De Quincey, Thomas, 91
*Description of London, A* (Darton), 13, 77, 80, 314, 423–4
Dewsbury, 248
Dixon, J. H., 316
Dobie, Dr, 242
Douglas, Marian, 260, 385, 386
drawing manuals, 16, 39, 40–1, 42–3, 44, 45–6, 49, 51, 57, 79, 108, 114, 138, 162, 173, 180, 181, 183, 261
  Brontë's use of, 158, 159, 165, 170, 194, 197, 246, 251, 379, 388
Drinkwater, John, 2, 67, 297
Dryden, John, 426
Dujardin, le Docteur B., 264
du Maurier, Daphne, 344
Duncan, George, 88, 338, *338*

Eareckson, Cecelia N., 205, 376
Easton House (near Bridlington), 251–2, *252*
Edgerley, C. Mabel, 253, 308–9
Eldridge, W., 138, 139
Ellis, Mrs, 10, 11
*English Grammar, Adapted to the Different Classes of Learners* (Murray), 428
engravings, 12, 13, 14
  in Annuals, 14, 20, 21–2, *21*, *81*, 174, 219, 228, 274, 288

attitudes to, 14,15
availability, 11, 12, 14, 138
copying, 9, 10, 11, 14, 38–41, 45, 46, 68, 81, *81*, 117, 138
influence on the Brontës, 9, 15, 109–10, 295
lending, 17, 43, 138, 223, 237
technology, 12, 14, 138
*see also* 'copying' under Brontë, Anne; Brontë, Branwell; Brontë, Charlotte; Brontë, Emily; Roe Head, art education
Etty, William, 24, 27
*Every-Day Book: Or, Everlasting Calender of Popular Amusements, The* (Hone), 113, 375
exhibitions
Brontës' visits to, 25–6
Charlotte exhibits at, 25–6

Farrar, Dora, 273
Farrar, Joseph, 273
Feather, Edwin, 328
Feather, John, 328
Fennell, John, 10
Field, W. T., 211
Fielding, Copley, 26
Finden, Edward, 18, 55–6, 214, 228, 235
Finden, William, 18, 55–6, 114, 177, 233, 234, 237, 387
*Finden's Byron Beauties*, 17, 18, 234
*Finden's Illustrations of the Life and Works of Lord Byron*, 55, 117, 214, 234, 236, 237, 245, 386
*Finden's Landscape and Portrait Illustrations to the Life and Works of Lord Byron*, 235, 236, 237, 245
*Finden's Royal Gallery of British Art*, 17
Firth, William, 272
Fletcher, James, 328–9, *329*
Flintoff, Everard, 90–1, 324, 352
Foister, Susan, 73
*Forget Me Not* Annual *see* Annuals
Foster, Henry, 334, *334*
Foster, Mrs E., 410
'Foundling, The' (CB), 289
Fradelle, H., 26
Franks, Elizabeth, 193
Fraser, Caroline, 400, 401
Fraser, Lucy Ethel, 400
*Fraser's Magazine*, 20, 54, 108, 117, 275
Friedrich, Caspar David, 121, 142, 406
*Friendship's Offering see* Annuals
Fuseli, Henry, 24, 25, 28, 75, 238

Gandee, B. F., 51
*Gardens and Menagerie of the Zoological Society Delineated, The* (Bennett), 22, 28, 50, 199, 232,422–3
Gaskell, Elizabeth, 188, 272
biography of Charlotte, 42, 65, 66, 75, 117, 135, 137, 261, 346, 380, 432
and Brontëana, 73, 188, 226, 310, 312
Gaskell, Julia, 188, 246
Gaskell, Meta (Margaret Emily), 188, 246
Gelder, James, 83
Geller, William Overend, 79, 83
*Geography for Youth* (Abbé Lenglet Du Fresnoy), 426
Gérin, Winifred, 85–6, 146, 251, 252, 254, 273, 274, 338
Gibson, John, 79
Gilpin, Rev. John, 244–5
Gilpin, William, 16, 54, 119–20
Glass Town and Angria, 1, 13, 127, 163, 244, 303, 312, 314
art in, 12–13
artists in, 15, 27
geography, 13, 21, 55, 156, 299–300, 321
heroines, 10, 56, 212, 213, 216–17, 219, 220, 237, 243–4, 273, 274, 321, 323, 345
history, 312, 313
inhabitants of, 157, 289–90
origins, 68, 105, 157, 300
society, 12, 15, 22
writers of, 18, 163, 167, 168, 219, 293, 295, 297, 299, 300–2, 316
Glass Town characters, 18, 105, 166, 168, 220, 426
Binn, Mrs, 168
Bud, Captain John, 168, 297, 299, 300
Bud, Lady Jephia, 167–8, *168*
Bud, Sergeant, 168

de Lisle, Frederick (also Dr or Sir Edward), 12, 15, 18, 27
Etty, Sir William, 27
Fidena, Duke of *see* Sneaky, John
Flower, Captain John (later Baron Flower and Viscount Richton), 300, 301, 302, 313
Grenville, Ellen, 10
Hart, Lily, 212
Hume, Marian, 10, 56
Laury, Mina, 236, 321
O'Connor, Harriet, 323
Parry, Captain (later Sir) William Edward, 13, 105, 300
Percy, Mary (Duchess of Zamorna, Queen of Angria), 219, 243–4
Ross, Captain John, 300, 301, 302
Sneaky, John (Duke of Fidena), 286, 303
Soult, Alexander, 18, *19*, 163, *166*, 167, 218–19, *218*
Sydney, Lady Julia, 2
Tree, Sergeant, 299, 313
Warner, Warner Howard, 55
Wellesley, Julia, 273
Wellesley, Lady Rosamund, 345
Wellesley, Lord Charles, 2, 17–18, 105–6, 167, 179
Wellington, Duke of, 18
Wentworth, Charles, 77
Wiggins, Patrick Benjamin, 27
Winlass, Sergeant, 301, 302
Zamorna, Duchess of, 213; *see also* Mary Percy, Queen of Angria
Zenobia, Marchioness Ellrington, 18, 216–17, *217*, 220, 273, 274
*see also* Northangerland, Duke of (Alexander Percy, Lord Ellrington); Zamorna, Duke of (Marquis of Douro, King of Angria)
Gledhill, Alfred, 171, 180, 184, 186, 187, 213, 234, 241, 291, 388, 439
'Glove, The' (CB), 262
Goldsmith, Oliver, 53
Goldsmith's *Grammar of General Geography*, 54, 68, 326, 426–7
Gondal, 1, 17, 103, 105, 106–7, 113, 115, 127, 136, 378, 382, 383, 392, 398, 433
characters, 17, 20, 105, 106, 384, 386, 392
geography 105, 106, 427
history, 398
origins, 105
'Gondal Poems' Notebook (EB), 382
Goodall, E., 81, *81*, 318
Gordon, Elizabeth Maud, 188, 244
Gorfin, H. E., 178, 284, 285, 286, 287, 288, 292, 293, 303, 314, 325, 341, 342, 343, 344, 440
*Grammar of General Geography, A* (Goldsmith), 54, 68, 326, 426–7
*Grammatical Exercises, English and French* (Porny), 429–30
Green, A. H. and Emily, 258, 346, 347
Green, Henry S., 258, 346, 347, 384
Green, Miss, 223
'Green Dwarf, The' (CB), 322
Greenwood, Colonel Bernard, 257
Greenwood, John, 73, 135, 171, 210, 230, 308, 309, 397, 412, 413, 414, 415, 420, 421
Greenwood, Mrs, 223
Greenwood, Richard M., 230
Greenwood, Sarah, 257
Grimshaw, H., 75, 88, 339, *339*
Grundy, Francis Henry, 87, 89, 314

Hale, Charles, 80, 111, 171, 176, 318, 393, 434
Hamilton, Lady (née Emma Lyon), 212
Harding, J. D., 234
Harley, Lady Charlotte Mary, 20, 386, 387
Harris, Alfred, 82, 385, 437
Harris, Anna, 82, 335
Harrison, W.H., 179
Hartley, Hannah (née Brown), 175, 189, 191, 372
Hartley, James, 175, 189
Hartley, Margaret, 84, 329–30, *329*, 331
Hartley, Mrs C, 160, 167
Harvey, William, 199
Hatfield, Agnes, 347, 352
Hatfield, C.W, 347, 352
Hatton, Rev. C, 203
Haughton, Moses, 238

Haworth Operative Conservative Society, 327
Haworth Parsonage *see* Parsonage, Haworth
Haydon, Benjamin Robert, 78
Hayne, Mrs L. C. G., 376, 377
Hayter, Sir George, 6, 266, 275
Heap, Rev. Henry, 79, 83, 330
*Heath's Book of Beauty*, 56, 217, 219, 222, 227, 240
Heaton, Robert (Jnr), 317
Heaton, Robert (Snr), 317
Heaton family (Haworth), 287
Heaton family (Ponden Hall), 316, 319, 370
Heger, Claire Zoë, 116, 260, 386
Heger, Constantin Romain, 115–16, 117, 123
  Charlotte's attachment to, 57, 265
  Charlotte's correspondence with, 264, 265
  and Brontëana, 260, 386
Heger, Louise, 264, 265, 385
Helliwell, George, 319
Helpman, J. R. C., 233
Hemans, Felicia, 224
'Henry Hastings' (CB), 345
Hickson, Jane, 193, 200
Hickson album, 193, 195, 200
'High Life In Verdopolis' (CB), 53, 54–5, 56, 233, 321
*Historical and Miscellaneous Questions, for the Use of Young People* (Mangnall), 428
'History of the Rebellion In My Fellows' (BB), 287
'History of the Year, The' (CB), 300
'History Of The Young Men, The' (BB), 68, 299, 300
Hodgson, Mr, 335
Hogarth, George, 87
Hogarth, William, 291
Hogg, James, 108
Holmes, James, 19
Holroyd, Abraham, 160, 167
Homer, 113, 324, 375
Hood, Thomas, 357
Horace *see Odes of Quintus Horatius Flaccus, The*
Houghton, Lord, 372
Howe, W. T. H.,163, 165, 176, 372
Howell, Mrs Daniel, 226
'How long will you remain? The midnight hour' (EB), 382–3
Hudson, Sophia and John, 251–2
Hulme, F. Edward, 39, 40, 46
Hume, David, 53
Hunt, Leigh, 6, 274, 275

'I never can forget' (CB), 267
Illingworth, Alfred, 437
Illingworth, Margaret (Mrs Alfred), 157, 158, 159, 164, 203, 217, 218, 258, 288, 290, 293, 396
'I'm standing in the forest now' (EB), 381–2
Ingham, Margaret, 330
Ingham, Maria, 330–1, *330*
Ingram, Margaret, 329, 331, 332
Ingram family, 331, 332
'Interior of A Pothouse By Young Soult' (BB), 316–17
'Islanders Play', 105

'Juan Fernandez' (BB), 359
Judson, Miss, 188
juvenilia *see* Glass Town and Angria; Glass Town characters; Gondal; individual entries for Brontës, early writings
Jersey, Lady, 237
Jopling, John and Mary (née Brown), 201
Jones, Mrs G. M., 216

Kay, Linda, 199
Kay, Sybil, 199, 200
Keighley Mechanics' Institute, 23, 439
Keighley Mechanics' Institute Library, 23, 54, 113
Keeling, Annie, 303
'Keep of the Bridge, The' (CB), 163, 165
Kendrick, Jill, 315
Kennedy, Harris, 370
Killick, Henry Fison, 160, 195, 203
Kirby, Isaac, 82, 84, 331–2, *331*
Kirby, Mrs Isaac, 84, 332, *332*
Kirby family, 84, 329, 331
Kitson, A. M., 44

Landon, Letitia ELizabeth, 15, 112, 178, 373
Landseer, Edwin, 24, 82, 138, 174, 336
Lang, Eleanor, 226
'Laussane A Trajedy By Young Soult' (BB), 293, 295
Lavater, Johann Kaspar, 28, 163
Law, Sir Alfred J., 161, 176, 213, 219, 378
Law, William, 161, 176, 287, 317, 371, 372, 384, 393, 409, 435, 438
Law collection, 6, 157, 161, 176, 189, 231, 254, 278, 305, 316, 370, 371, 372, 378, 381, 383, 384, 409
Lawrence, Sir Thomas, 24, 25, 26, 74
*Lay of the Last Minstrel, A Poem, The* (Scott), 431
Le Brun, 28
Lee, M., 249
Lee, P.F., 252
L. E. L. *see* Landon, Letitia Elizabeth
Lemprière, J., 353
Lens, Bernard, 379
Lens, Edward, 379
Le Petit, William, 208
'Letter From A Father On Earth To His Child In Her Grave' (BB), 355
'Letters From An Englishman To his Relative' (BB), 298
'Letters From An Englishman To His Friend In London' (BB), 300, 301, 302
Leyland, Anne, 350
Leyland, Francis A., 37, 83, 330, 332, 333, 337, 351, 355, 360
Leyland, Joseph Bentley, 26, 78, 80, 87, 88, 89, 93–5, 321, 322, 345, 348, 349, 350, 351, 352–3, 354, 356, 359, 360, 361, 362
'Liar Detected, The' (BB), 297
'Lily Hart', 212
Linnel, John, 26
*Literary Souvenir, The see* Annuals
Lockhart, John Gibson, 54
Longbottom, Rose Emma, 159, 176, 199, 238, 295, 296, 298, 441
Lorrain, Claude, 27, 58
Loudon, Mrs, 41
Lowell, Amy, 289
'Luddenden Foot Notebook' (BB), 341–5, 348
Lumb, Miss K., 304
Lund, Lucy, 318
Lund, R.W., 318
'Lydia Gisborne' (BB), 347

Macdonald, Frederika, 264, 265
Macreth, Robert, 26
magazines in Brontë household, 11, 12, 13, 15, 54, 68, 103, 108, 117, 238, 275
Mallinson, Mrs N. W., 287
'Man thinks too often that his earthly life above cares' (BB), 342
Marshall, Ann, 145–6, 415, 416
Martin, John, 12, 24, 70, 83
  engravings copied by Brontes, 298, 319
  engravings owned by Brontës, 21
  influence on Brontës, 20–2, *21*, 319, 320, 336
  works by, 20, 21, *21*, 25
Martineau, Harriet, 194, 255, 406
'Mementos' (CB), 246
Meynell, Alice, 211
Meynell, Everard, 211
Michelangelo, 12
Miles, James, 171, 184, 186, 187
Milligan, John, 318
Milton, John, 16, 53, 108, 161, 238
*Milton Gallery*, 238
'Misery' (BB), 314
Mitchell, Rev. Henry, 211, 235
Mitford, Mary Russell, 49
Montgomery, Robert, 14, 21
'Monthly Intelligencer, The' (BB), 12–13, 303
'moon dawned slow in the dusky gloaming, The' (CB), 227
'moon in glory mounts above, The' (BB), 324
Moore, Judith, 397, 412, 413, 414, 415, 420, 421
Moore, Thomas (*Life of Byron*), 16, 20, 54, 114, 116, 214, 233, 234, 235, 236, 386
More, Hannah, 50–1
Morgan, Rev. William, 82, 330, 331, 332
Morgan, Vera, 334
'Morley Hall' (BB), 350, 351

Mossman, Margaret, 260, 386
Mulready, William, 25
Murgatroyd, John, 88, 343–4, *344*
Murgatroyd, Mrs, 303
Murray, Lindley, 428
Myers, Winifred A., 222

Nasmyth, Alexander, 26, 78
Needham, Alice Jane, 249, 252, 253
Neufeldt, Victor A., 67, 296, 314, 346
*New and Easy Guide to the Pronunciation and Spelling of the French Language* (Tocquot), 431
Newman, John, 48
New Testament in English, 428–9
New Testament in Latin, 429
'New Year Story, A' (BB), 324
Nicholl, Charlotte Brontë, 187, 223, 228, 229, 436, 441
Nicholls, Alan Bell, 187, 223, 228, 229
Nicholls, Mary Anne (née Bell), 179, 406, 434
  and sale of Brontëana, 154, 155, 156, 163, 165, 187, 190, 202, 205, 223, 227, 228, 229, 230, 239, 240, 244, 245, 255, 262, 263, 307, 308, 310, 311, 347, 352, 376, 390, 404, 435–6
Nicholls, Rev. Arthur Bell, 159, 202, 228, 229, 281, 333, 404, 433
  attitude to Brontëana, 75, 76, 229, 307–8, 310, 311, 312, 434–6
  disposal of Brontëana, 5, 203, 213, 433–4, 438
  inherits Brontëana, 433–4
  ownership of Brontëana, 21, 47, 102, 134, 164, 168, 179, 180, 184, 190, 205, 212, 227, 228, 229, 244, 245, 255, 264, 279, 287, 299, 300, 302, 307, 310, 313, 320, 322, 324, 325, 376, 388, 390, 391, 402, 403, 404, 406, 433–6
  sale of effects, 134, 212, 234, 236, 237, 239, 243, 253, 256, 265, 266, 267, 268, 293, 324, 326, 336, 338, 339, 340, 341, 359, 398, 400, 401, 404, 407, 408, 411, 416, 436
Nicholson, John, 87
Nicoll, Sir William Robertson, 210, 291, 308, 378, 379
Nixon, Ingeborg, 308, 311
North, Edward Roundell Whipp, 251, 252
North, Fanny *see* Whipp, Fanny
Northangerland, Duke of (Alexander Percy, Lord Ellrington), 257, 312, 355
  character of, 18, 243, 321–2
  life of, 321–2, 323
  portraits of, 46, 71, 88–9, 93, *215*, 216, 220–1, *220*, 321–2, *321*, *322*, 337, 338–9, *338*, 357, *357*
*Nouveau Dictionnaire de la Langue Française* (Noel and Chapsal), 429
Nussey, Ellen, 41, 118, 125, 138, 193, 195, 203, 220, 228, 252, 255, 260, 291, 366, 376, 385, 388, 389, 428, 438
  Brontëana owned by, 4, 6, 171, 178, 208, 211, 249, 250, 251, 252–3, 261–2, 374, 375, 376, 439, 440
  Charlotte visits, 250, 251
  correspondence with Charlotte, 53, 76, 208, 255, 261–2, 264, 316
  purported portraits of, 50, *249*, 250, 252–3, *253*
  'Reminiscences of Charlotte Brontë', 376
  sale of possessions, 249, 252–3, 273, 274, 276, 366

*Odes of Quintus Horatius Flaccus, The*, Branwell's translation of, 67, 85
'Oh Thou whose beams were most withdrawn' (BB), 345
'On Landseer's painting – "The Shepherd's Chief Mourner" A dog keeping watch at twilight over its master's grave' (BB), 82
'On Ouses grassy banks, last Whitsuntide' (BB), 352
Openshaw, Leslie H., 251, 366, 367
*Outlines of the Physiognomical System of Drs Gall and Sputzheim*, 163

Page, W., 214, 234
Paget, Shem, 377
Painter, Jack, 95, 363
'Palais de la Mort, Le' (EB), 127
Palladio, Andrea, 13
'Papillon, Le' (EB), 125, 126
*Paradise Lost*, 21
Parker, Thomas, 314, 327–8, *327*
Parkinson, Eric, 318
Parkinson, George S., 362

Parris, E. T., 237
Parsonage, Haworth
images of, 72–3, 156, 294, 353, 356, 363
life in, 103, 111, 136–7, 156, 171, 225, 376, 378, 398
*see also* Aykroyd, Tabitha; individual entries for Brontës; Brown, Martha
'Passing Events' (CB), 245
Patchett's (Miss) school, Law Hill, 101
Pearson, Mary, 92–3, 355–9, 363
'Peep Into A Picture Book, A' (CB), 17–18, 273, 274
Pensionnat Heger (Brussels), 101, 115–16, 117–18, 259, 385–7
*see also* Brontë, Charlotte; Brontë, Emily; Heger, Constantin Romain
Percy, Alexander *see* Northangerland, Duke of
pets, Brontës', 50, 69, 100, 146, 376, 388, 390, 392, 409, 410
illustrations of, 66, 100, 101, 102, 104, 113, 115, 121–4, 128, 146, 205, 373, 375–6, 380, 384–5, 387, 388–92, 408
phrenology, 27–8
physiognomy, 27–8, 163
Phalopon, A., 224
Pickles, Clara, 319
Pickles, G. H., 305
Piranesi, Giovanni Battista, 303
'Pirate, The' (BB), 322
Plummer, Thomas, 24, 40, 69, 108
*Poems by Currer, Ellis, and Acton Bell*, 246–7
'Politics of Verdopolis, The' (BB), 305
Pollard, Collingwood, 215
Ponden Hall (Stanbury), 316, 319, 370
*see also* Heaton family
Pope, Alexander, 53
Popplewell, Eliza (née Brown), 203, 278, 316, 375, 396
Popplewell, Mary E., 396, 438
Popplewell, Miss, 375
Portbury, E., 19, 218
Porter, Alfrey, 409
Postlethwaite family, 84–5, 336
'Poor mourner-sleep' (BB), 326
Preston, John Emanuel, 160
Preston, Mary, 308
Pretty, Edward, 170
Priestley, William Edwin Briggs, 220, 221, 259, 437
*Pronouncing Expositor; or, A New Spelling Book* (Hornsey), 427–8
Prout, Samuel, 138
provenance, 432–44
Purser, T., 337–8, *337*

Radcliffe, Ann, 54
Ramenghi, Bartolommeo, 12
Ramsden, Thomas and Susannah, 331
Raphael, 11, 24, 44, 57, 240, 241
Ratchford, Fannie, 213
Ratcliffe, Ben, 160, 167
Ratcliffe, Mrs B., 160
Ratcliffe, Robert, 384
Ratcliffe, Tabitha (née Brown), 210, 242, 316, 378, 384, 437, 438
Reddyough, Joseph, 389
Red House (Gomersal), 25, 198
*see also* Taylor, Mary
Redman, Martha, 171, 225, 226
Reid, Patrick, 361
Reni, Guido, 11
'Revenge A Tragedy, The' (BB), 296
Riley, Abraham, 183, 251, 366, 409
'Robert Burns' (BB), 342–3
Roberts, Miss A., 373, 374, 375
Robinson, Lydia (at Thorp Green), 65, 90–1, 94, 145, 146, 349, 351
Robinson, William, 24, 25, 26–7, 73, 77, 78, 80, 83, 211, 242, 315, 318, 319, 320, 335, 351, 352
Roebuck, J., 212
Roe Head school, 41, *42*, 44, 45, 114, 135, 137–8, 191–2, *191*, 200, 239, 373, 399–400, *399*
album, 43–4, 406
art education, 42–4, 55, 57, 109, 137, 138, 141, 173, 184, 185, 187, 192, 193, 194, 196, 373, 374, 400, 402, 405, 406
*see also* Brontë, Anne; Brontë, Charlotte; Brontë, Emily

Rollin, Alexandre Auguste Ledru, 53
Rolls, C., 112, 178
Rolls, Henry, 224, 373
Romano, Giulio, 11
'Romantic Tale, A' (CB), 161
Rosa, Salvator, 120, 179
Rose, Thomas, 204, 209–10
Rowlandson, Thomas, 88
Royal Academy, 24, 73, 80
  Branwell plans to study at, 26, 76–7, 85
Royal Northern Society for the Encouragement of Fine Arts (Leeds), 25–6, 36, 73, 228–30
Rubens, Sir Peter Paul, 12
Rudd, Richard Henry, 161, 162, 437
*Russell's General Atlas, of Modern Geography*, 263, 430–1
Rydings, The (Birstall), 250
  *see also* Nussey, Ellen

*Sacred Annual, The, see* Annuals
Sada, Cora Kennedy Aitken, 370
Sands, R., 209–10
Saville, Marion, 405
Schalz, Louis, 241
'School Rebellion', 105
Schutte, Mr, 272
Schwanfelder, C. H., 26, 79
Scott, Henry, 88, 340, *340*
Scott, Sir Walter, 16, 53, 54, 108, 431
Scruton, William, 171, 245, 437, 439
Self, Rev. William, 247
Shackleton, Gladys, 319
Shakespeare, William, 16, 53, 108
Shaw, Jack, 95, 363
Shelley, Percy Bysshe, 20, 108, 116, 387
Shorter, Clement K., 6, 205, 244, 245, 264, 279, 307–8, 310, 323, 376, 390, 392, 402, 404, 435
Sidgwick family, 257
Slater, Walter, 323, 326
'Sleep Mourner sleep! – I cannot sleep' (BB), 326
Smith, Alexander Murray, 256, 265, 266, 267, 268
Smith, Elder & Co., 36, 240, 244
Smith, George, 188, 240, 244
Smith, George Charles Moore, 193
Smith, M. Barbara, 160, 195, 203, 294
Smith, Margaret, 279
Smith, Miss E. J. Moore, 193
Smith, Mr, 316
Smith, Reginald J., 240, 244, 256, 265, 266, 267, 268, 307
Smith, T. A., 168, 173
'Sonnet' ('When all our cheerful hours') (BB), 356
'Sonnet' ('Why hold young eyes') (BB), 355–6
'So spends its hours in thinking on' (BB), 325
'Sound the Loud Trumpet' (BB), 314
Southey, Robert, 54
souvenirs of Brontës *see* Brontëana
Sowden, Sutcliffe, 338
'Spell, The' (CB), 53
Staël, Anne Louise Germaine De, 217
Stanfield, C., 214, 233
Stevenson, Ian D., 177
Stevenson, Maria (née Bower), 177
Strickland, Sir George, 252
Stuart, J. A. Erskine, 399, 405–6
Stubbins, T. K., 195
Suffolk Street Galleries, 20
Sugden, Dan, 362
Sunderland, Abraham Stansfield, 209, 210, 229
Sunderland, Edward, 209, 277
Sunderland, Frances Watson, 277
Sunderland, Susan Jane, 210
Sutherland, 40, 159
Syme, Patrick, 49, 170
Symington, J. A., 245, 251, 263, 276, 279, 280, 349, 366

Talbot, Thomas, 272
Tamar, Lucien, 264, 265
Taylor, George, 331
Taylor, Martha, 44, 118, 279
Taylor, Mary, 11, 17, 25, 42, 44, 50, 54, 118, 138, 194, 198, 213, 279, 428
Taylor, Miss E., 213
Taylor, Robert H., 206, 213, 403

Taylor, Stephen and Mary, 330, 331
Taylor family, 118
Thackeray, William Makepeace, 14, 15
'There is something in this Glorious hour' (BB), 323
'There was once a little girl and her name was Ane' (CB), 37, 154–6
'Think not that life is happiness' (BB), 358
Thomas, Brother R., 325
Thomas, Don, 326, 333
Thomas, Mrs William, 326
Thomas, Sarah, 194
Thomas, William ('Bendigo'), 94, 347–8
Thomas, William (Jnr), 326, 333, *333*
Thomas, William (Snr), 316, 326, 333
Thomas family, 326
Thompson, John Hunter, 83, 85, 330, 332
Thompson, William, 94
Thomson, James, 53
Thorp Green Hall, 135, 346, *346*, 351
*see also* Brontë, Anne; Brontë, Branwell; Robinson, Lydia
Thorwaldsen, Bertel, 354
'Thy soul is flown' (BB), 361
Titian, 11, 24
'To A. G. A.' (EB), 382
Tonkin, J., 231
Top Withens, 73, 277
'Triumph of mind over body, The' (BB), 345
Trotman, Martha, 385
Turner, J. Horsfall, 73, 204, 230, 261, 287, 309, 317, 435
Turner, J. M. W., 24, 25, 47, 52, 83, 228, 309
'Two Romantic Tales' (CB), 161
Tyas, Robert, 49
Tyldosly, Edward, 350

Van Dyck (Vandyke), Sir Anthony, 12, 24
Varley, John, 28, 78, 194, 290
*Vitruvius Britannicus*, 13

Walford, Mrs, 386
Walker, Amelia, 43, 184, *184*, 185, 247–8, 272
Wall, Francis, 266, 275, 276
Walpole, Hugh, 381
Watson, Eliza, 206
Weightman, Rev. William, 142, 255
CB's portrait of, 44, 254–5, *255*
Wellington, Duke of, 218, 220, 227
West, Benjamin, 12, 70
West, J. R. W., 402
Westall, Richard, 19, *19*, 20, 25, 42, 114, 116, 218, 386
Westmacott, Sir Richard, 78
'What does she dream of, lingering all alone' (CB), 213
Whatman, J., 49
Wheatley, Rosamund, 405
Wheelwright sisters, 118, 259
Whipp, Fanny, 251, 252
White, Gilbert, 54
White, J. A., 174
White, Miss C., 202, 404, 435
Widdop, Elizabeth, 225, 226
Widdop, Jane Helen, 171, 397, 412, 413, 414, 415, 420, 421
Widdop, William, 171
Widener, Eleanor Elkins, 257
Widener, Harry Elkins, 257
Wigfall, Genevieve, 260, 385–6
Williams, S., 375
Williams, W. S., 36, 38, 311
Windsor & Newton, 47, 48
Winnifrith, Tom, 66
Wise, Thomas James, 178, 208, 284, 285, 286, 287, 288, 292, 293, 299, 300, 302, 303, 313, 314, 323, 324, 325, 326, 341, 342, 343, 344, 440
Wood, Philip, 220
Wood, Sarah, 111, 316
Wood, William, 111, 176, 220, 276, 317, 318, 372, 393, 438
Wooler, Ernest O., 399
Wooler, Frederic Sykes, 399
Wooler, Harriet Anne, 399
Wooler, Margaret, 41, 43, 135, 192, 193, 399, 400
*see also* Carter, Susan; Roe Head school
Wooler, Marianne (later Allbutt), 193, 200
'Wool Is Rising, The' (BB), 313
Woollett, William, 70

Wordsworth, William, 38, 53, 54, 85, 86, 228
*Works of Virgil, The* (Dryden), 426
Wright, Emma, 194
Wright, Ernest, 366
Wright, J. W., 333
Wright, Mary, 206
Wright, Miss, 240
Wright, Sarah, 333
Wroot, Mrs, 277
Yates, W. W., 281
'Young Men's Magazine' (CB/BB), 12, 167, 289
'Young Men's Play', 157
'Young Soults Poems' (BB), 292, 293

Zamorna, Duke of (Marquis of Douro, King of Angria), 167, 219, 220, 299
  drawings of, 18, 71, 215, *215*, 217–18, *218*, 225–7, *225*, *226*, 320, *320*, 341
  life, 56, 236, 312, 321, 322
  various names, 18, 127, 215, 321